UNDERSTAND YOURSELF, UNDERSTAND YOUR PARTNER

THE ESSENTIAL ENNEAGRAM GUIDE TO A BETTER RELATIONSHIP

Jennifer P Schneider M.D., Ph.D.
Ron Corn M.S.W.

FOR INFORMATION CONTACT:

Jennifer P. Schneider M.D., Ph.D.
3052 N. Palomino Park Loop
Tucson, AZ 85712
(520) 990-7886
email: jennifer@jenniferschneider.com

Ron Corn
10 N. Norton Avenue, Suite 140
Tucson, AZ 85719
(520) 577-5169
email: Roncorn@aol.com

Please visit Dr. Schneider's website at:
www.jenniferschneider.com

Copyright © 2013 Jennifer P. Schneider M.D. Ph.D. and Ron Corn M.S.W.
ISBN: 1484869389
ISBN 13: 9781484869383
Library of Congress Control Number: 2013909789
CreateSpace Independent Publishing Platform
North Charleston, South Carolina

This book is based on a survey filled out by many men and women who were willing to let us into their lives and to describe in detail the gifts and challenges of their primary relationship. This book is dedicated to all of them.

About the Authors

Jennifer Schneider, M.D., Ph.D. received her B.S. from Cornell University, her M.S. and Ph.D. in Human Genetics from the University of Michigan, and her M.D. from the University of Arizona College of Medicine. She is Board Certified in Internal Medicine, certified by the American Society of Addiction Medicine, and is a Diplomate of the American Academy of Pain Management. After practicing Internal Medicine for many years, she then specialized in medical management of patients who were living with chronic pain. In addition, for over 25 years she has been a researcher, speaker, and author in the field of compulsive sexual disorders, with a special interest in the effects of sex addiction on the couple relationship. She has written books and papers about couple issues. Dr. Schneider has been studying the enneagram for nearly 20 years.

Ron Corn, M.S.W. is a recovering Type Two (Giver) who admits to relapsing from time to time. He has a Masters Degree in counseling and is certified in the Helen Palmer Narrative Tradition. He coaches individuals and couples using the enneagram.

ADVANCE PRAISE FOR
Understand Yourself, Understand Your Partner

"What a delightful book! If you want to understand your mate's as well as your own strengths and character challenges, this book is for you. Jennifer Schneider and Ron Corn intrigue the reader with interesting descriptions of personality types and how each experiences the world and has specific assumptions about it. Not only do the authors offer insight but they also provide practical advice about how to manage differences in relationships. They also provide tips for how to actually enjoy each other. A fun and rewarding book!"
M. Deborah Corley, Ph.D. Co-owner, Co-founder, and Clinical Consultant of Santé Center for Healing, Argyle, Texas.

"I am excited to have such a thorough book on enneagram types and relationships. In my therapy practice most patients know their type and ask me which type they can best get along with. Jennifer and Ron let people know that there is no perfect type relationship and give guidance to how each combination of enneagram types can savor their assets and work on their downside. Kudos!"
Brenda Schaeffer, D.Min., author of Is it Love or is it Addiction?

"This book is a real eye-opener for couples. No matter who you are, you will find yourself and your partner in these pages and say "aha!" This engaging and deeply human book has the potential to bridge the gulf that separates people from one another. The authors present the enneagram framework in a way that allows the reader to easily identify and understand personality types, where they come from and how they shape the way couples relate. There is a wealth of well-researched detail on styles of relating and helpful exercises for couples of each personality combination. When we know how someone's basic temperament determines what they do, we can become less judgmental

and more accepting. In this book you will find an essential framework for building compassion and bonding."
Linda Hatch PhD, author of Relationships in Recovery: A Guide for Sex Addicts who are Starting Over; and Living with a Sex Addict: The Basics from Crisis to Recovery.

". . . a comprehensive, research-based, yet extremely engaging look at the enneagram types and how they influence individuals and coupleships. The authors' explanations and myriad examples bring the Types to life and offer practical insights and exercises to help couples better navigate their relationship. Once I determined my own Type and that of my husband, I was fascinated when I saw how closely we matched the examples about our pairing. This guide is fun, illuminating and very helpful!"
Marnie C. Ferree, M.A., author of No Stones - Women Redeemed From Sexual Addiction and editor of Making Advances - A Comprehensive Guide for Treating Female Sex and Love Addicts.

"The authors have fully and accurately described every personality type in an easily understandable way. They've covered all bases so that a person who's never heard of the enneagram can learn the background and the individual differences quickly. The seasoned enneagram expert can refresh memory or fine tune specifics thoroughly.
Readers of all backgrounds will find the information and the many examples interestingly presented and the exercises most helpful. In a word, Schneider and Corn have 'nailed it.'"
Lee Marie Schnebly, M.Ed., Marriage and Family Counselor, retired,

"*Understand Yourself, Understand Your Partner* is brilliant! I wish the book had been available ten years ago when my husband and I were newly married and custom- building our house. This book is especially helpful in identifying and understanding the qualities that we each individually and as a couple bring to the marriage and how to minimize their downside and maximize

opportunities for change and growth. Kudos to the authors for an enlightening and supremely helpful book."
Judy Kidder, Tucson AZ

"To see the world through a new lens can be life changing for you and others in your life. This book will help you do just that. It will be your "go to" book on the enneagram, with clear definitions and real life examples taken from interviews. It also includes exercises for couples, and practical suggestions for improving the relationship. As the authors suggest, you will have a better understanding of yourself and others after using this book.
Marilyn Schnur, Librarian

"*Understand Yourself, Understand Your Partner* provides any couple the equivalent of their own professional relationship counselor. It presents the tools for couples to discuss what personality traits they bring to the relationship – and then to work together to avoid the inevitable pitfalls that their pairing might create. This is an essential guide for understanding the human experience. You will find yourself relying on this resource to help navigate not only relationships with those closest to you but also those in your larger community of friends and co-workers."
Ken and Karen, Arizona

"Negotiating the tangled thickets that comprise most romantic relationships is simplified by the useful tools and strategies offered by the authors of this valuable reference book. This is a comprehensible and comprehensive explanation of the Enneagram personality system, which is a beneficial psychological interpretation of human behavior and motivation. The accompanying exercises are creative and valuable additions to the text."
Dolly Spalding, Editor and Writer, Tucson, AZ

"*Understand Yourself, Understand Your Partner* is a wonderful book which I am using to enhance and transform my life as well as to impact the life of

my Coaching clients. As an ongoing student and teacher of the enneagram, I have found the insights and tools in this book helpful in understanding myself and my partner better and in turn, in creating healthier choices for myself in or out of relationship. Reading this book will transform your relationships to their full potential starting with the most important relationship, the one with yourself , then flowing into the other relationships in your life."
Alan Maness, Life Coach, Tucson, Arizona

Table of Contents

SECTION TWO: UNDERSTANDING YOU AND YOUR PARTNER IN RELATIONSHIP

FOREWORD

Some 15 years ago, when I first learned about the enneagram, I was amazed. Like many of us, I began reviewing myself, my friends, and my relatives through the lens of the enneagram, and all of a sudden I had explanations for so much of what had happened to me both personally and professionally, my choices in life, the things that were important to me and those that weren't, my values and my priorities, and most of all, my relationships. As someone who has authored several books on couple relationships, I have found the chief fascination of the enneagram for me to be its value in understanding and helping the couple relationship. Coming from a research background (and also undoubtedly as a result of the insights I had gained into my own two marriages), I became more and more interested in the prospect of writing a research-based book on the strengths and challenges of the various pairings of enneagram types. My enneagram teacher beginning almost 20 years ago was Ron Corn, a psychotherapist whose enneagram knowledge has proven instrumental in his counseling of couples.

Fast forward several years. My enthusiasm for the enneagram was as strong as ever. Ron and I designed a relationship survey to be completed by members of the enneagram community who knew their type and that of their (current or former) spouse or partner. The heart of the survey comprised questions about the strengths and challenges of the respondent's marriage or committed relationship. We distributed this survey at enneagram conferences and, more recently, made it available on the Internet. Based on the actual experience of many people who completed the survey we began writing what we hope is an accessible and informative book that will be very useful to couples who seek to improve their relationship. We believe you will find this book both useful and enjoyable.

Finally, we are very aware that this book was written on the shoulders of giants. We would like to express our gratitude for the work of Helen Palmer,

David Daniels, Richard Rohr, Don Riso and Russ Hudson, and Tom Condon, as well as Renee Baron and Elizabeth Wagele. All of these authors have been a tremendous inspiration to us. We would also like to thank Dolly Spalding and Jim Totman for their meticulous copy-editing and proof reading of the material, and Debra Kaplan for her support and suggestions.

Jennifer Schneider
August 2013

Section One:

Understanding Yourself

CHAPTER ONE

Introduction: Seeing the World Through Different Lenses

You don't see things as they are. You see things as you are.
-- Talmud

Say not, "I have found the truth," but rather, "I have found a truth."
-- Khalil Gibran

Disagreements and misunderstandings between people are inevitable. Have you ever felt that if you could only explain your position clearly enough to your spouse or partner, he or she would surely see things your way? Have you ever felt frustrated when, despite lengthy explanations and multiple ways of trying to convince your partner, you were unable to make him or her abandon their position and agree with your point of view? You may have told your partner, "Gosh, it seems like we come from two totally different worlds!"

Psychologist John Gray was on the right track when he suggested, in his book of the same name, that "men are from Mars and women are from Venus." Dr. Gray limited himself to only two planets, whereas those who work with the enneagram believe that we choose our partners from *nine* different worlds. The mistake many of us make in relationships is that we assume that our partner sees the world the same way we do (or "should" see the world the same way we do). At the core of all conflicts is that each of us thinks we have cornered the market on the truth. We erroneously assume that if our partner sees things differently, he or she is confused or mistaken. In our effort to get our partner to see what we think is the truth, we hold on tightly and commit all attention to persuading him or her to live through our perspective. What becomes lost in the process is understanding each other's inner world.

We see this happening in all kinds of day-to-day interactions. For example, have you ever found yourself waiting patiently in a long line hoping you'll get to your goal in time? The person in front of you doesn't move forward. You don't understand why he's not moving. In this situation, many people would first get confused, then irritated. They might ask themselves, "Why isn't he paying attention?" or they might decide to go around him. A person who's easily angered might say, "Hey, buddy, what's the matter with you – are you blind? Can't you see the line is moving?" It seems that the person in front is deliberately holding back in order to annoy the rest of the line. Then it turns out that that person is, in fact, blind. Instantly, your anger will evaporate. You now have a whole new perspective on the situation. You realize that your assumptions about his motivation were not as you had imagined.

This is what happens in relationships. We tend to take our partners' actions personally, making assumptions about why they are behaving as they are without having all the information at our disposal.

The goal of this book is to give you information about yourself and your partner's worldview so that you will have a better appreciation for their perspective. Once you begin to understand the personality system taught in this book you are very likely to reflect on the various relationships in your life, trying to figure out the type of that partner or family member whom you love and/or with whom you struggle. When thinking about former relationships, once you recognize your previous partner's type, you may gasp and say, "Oh…now I see why we had the problems we did!" You might also ask, "Given my type, what is the best type for me to be with?" The correct answer is a healthy, mature person of any type, but it is true that some combinations of types are more or less challenging. In later chapters we will describe the typical strengths and challenges of each combination, but let's begin by describing the personality system called the enneagram.

What Are These Nine Different Worlds?

Understanding Yourself, Understanding Your Partner is based on a personality system called the enneagram (pronounced (ANY-a-gram), which assumes that there are actually nine very different points of view. It's as though at some point in our lives we put on eyeglasses with lenses that filter the world into one of nine different ways. The word *enneagram* comes from the Greek root *ennea-* which means nine. This system is believed to have originated generations ago, but it began to be disseminated in the Western world only in the mid-20th century, when Oscar Ichazo and also Claudio Naranjo correlated each of the nine types with a different psychological disorder. In the 1980's, the enneagram became increasingly known in the United States. Don Riso, in his 1987 book *Personality Types,* described each enneagram Type as encompassing a spectrum of behaviors, from very healthy to very unhealthy. Descriptions of the unhealthy end of each Type agreed with the earlier works of the Ichazo and Naranjo. In her very accessible 1988 book *The Enneagram,* Helen Palmer described the nine Types, making them more widely known. In recent years the enneagram system has been refined, expanded, subdivided, and further publicized. It is now used not only for improving one's psychological health, but also in the corporate world, in religious and spiritual settings for spiritual growth, and, as in the present book, to understand and improve relationships.

The nine Types are based not on people's outward behavior, but on their internal motivations and fears and the way they see the world. The same behavior (for example, repeatedly being late), may be found among several different Types, but in each for a different reason. Of course, people are complex and every person is unique. It may seem absurd to think we can categorize people into nine types, or even into sixteen, as does the highly respected Myers-Briggs Type Inventory. The enneagram system is actually complex, as each Type has variations and each Type also has connections to several other Types. The Appendix lists some recommended books in which you will find not only a description of the Types, but suggestions for becoming emotionally healthier and overcoming the challenges of each Type.

We like the enneagram system because it so focused on understanding people's motivations, and because the professionals who have written about it and who use it have stressed not just putting people into categories, but rather the direction of growth needed by each of the nine Types. No one Type is "better" than another. What matters is not which Type you are, but rather the level of health you are within that Type. You can't change your fundamental personality Type, but you can become healthier within that Type

Here is a summary of the nine Types, which are referred to by name and number (we will use both. Also, different authors have used various names for each type, which can be a little confusing):

Perfectionists (Type Ones) —also called Critics or Reformers -- see the world as **a place that is full of errors,** full of problems that need to be solved, full of imperfections that need to be fixed. They see themselves the same way – as imperfect people – and spend their lives striving for perfection in themselves and in others. They try to help others fix themselves, get involved in worthy causes, and may believe they're never perfect enough to earn others' love and respect.

Givers (Type Twos) – also called Helpers -- see the world as **a place where love must be earned by pleasing other people.** Their approach is *quid pro quo*, giving to get. They become very good at sensing others' needs, and are always there to fulfill them. They remember people's birthdays and anniversaries, are on the spot when others are ill and need help, and gravitate to the helping professions. Givers tend to understate their own needs – often failing to recognize them -- but hope or expect others to see them and respond to them.

Achievers (Type Threes) – also called Performers -- believe that **the way to earn love is by achieving**. They become productive, goal-oriented people whose work and accomplishments are the focus of their lives. They may be champion athletes, star salesmen, hard-working business executives, or workaholic professionals. Their self-esteem becomes inextricably linked with their achievements. They want to look like successful people. As soon as Achievers accomplish one goal, they are driven to strive to the next one.

In marked contrast are the **Romantics (Type Fours),** who see the world as a place where the **way to get the love is to be special or unique** and, above all else, never to be ordinary. They may have an active imagination that lends itself to a strong intuition and a heightened sense of aesthetics, but also usually contains an image of a past love relationship that they compare to their present relationships and to other people's relationships. When theirs doesn't match up, Romantics may feel that something is missing. They may also repeatedly attempt to assuage this seemingly perpetual sense of loss through strong feelings, intensity and even drama.

A different view lens for **Observers (Type Fives)** involves seeing **knowledge and competence as a way to get love and feel safe**. They may have a strong need for protection against feeling overwhelmed or smothered in life; on the other hand they may fear that life may not provide enough for them. Because of these feelings, conserving time and energy and the need for privacy rank high on Observers' priority list. In consequence they become great observers and analyzers of life and can be perceptive and insightful in assessing the big picture.

Detectives (Type Sixes) – also called Troopers, Questioners, or Devil's Advocates – believe that **the world is a dangerous place** and have a built-in hyper-awareness of others' motives and intentions as well as anything that could be harmful or dangerous to them. They may become skeptics who ask

. For example, Jennifer (one of the authors of this book) is
nneagram Type One), a personality that notices mistakes
d to fix them. The lens through which she views the world
that need to be made better, whether it's people or manu-
errors seem to jump out at her from the written page, which
proofreader. But the same skill can be a problem. A sign on
reads, "No trespassing. Violatators will be prosecuted." She
t that sign every day with her dog, and every day she would
itation as she found herself thinking, "If **I** were in charge, I'd
ake!" Obviously, the person in charge didn't feel the same!
t still pops into her head as she walks past that sign, but is
iately by laughing at herself as she realizes that, despite all
ment work, she still notices errors that are totally unimport-
ce is that she no longer feels that sense of irritation. What
at she has become more conscious of her ingrained patterns.
l all too easy for Jennifer to get caught up in automatic reac-
ess of her way of noticing the world gives her choices in how
t actions to take.

seek counseling usually come in with some specific prob-
n often turns out to be only the latest rendition of what we
classic fight," a recurrent disagreement based on differences
ers' personalities. The details of the current version may be
ern is an old one. Focusing on the details of the latest prob-
al solution. The key to resolving the problem is to identify
f systems that underlie the classic fight. Once each member
lerstands their own and their partner's underlying premises,
gin to resolve the current problem and lessen similar future
vork is not easy, as the patterns are usually entrenched and
o our own particular world view is quite strong; but by ac-
l possibly accepting each other's perspective we may be bet-
stand why we continue to get stuck and how we can co-exist
ifferent worlds.

may be saying, "But I *like* my partner to be different from
only to a point. We may like how our partner stimulates our
or how he comes up with interesting and fun things to do
have otherwise thought of, but when it comes down to what
as "our truth," we usually want our partner to think pretty
ay we do. "Our truth" usually consists of such things as: how
y should be spent and managed, how sex and commitment

hard questions about the reliability and trustworthiness of others. **To earn love, Detectives place the highest priority on being loyal, responsible and dutiful.**

Adventurers (Type Sevens) – also called Enthusiasts or Epicures – see **the world as a place full of opportunities and options**. They fill their active minds with plans for all the positive things so as to ward off any unpleasant or painful experiences. **Adventurers earn love by being able to uplift others' spirits and through creating stimulating and fun experiences.** In relationships they can be imaginative and delightful, yet sensitive to limitations, structure, and pain.

Leaders (Type Eights) – also called Bosses or Challengers -- have a bold and expansive outlook. Their hallmark is being in control and making sure they are not seen as weak. **Leaders believe that the way to earn love is to be strong, to protect, and to champion others**, especially the underdog. In relationships, their partners may feel protected and safe, yet Leaders may have difficulty allowing themselves to be vulnerable with their partners and letting go of control.

Finally, **Mediators (Type Nines)** – also called Peacemakers -- see a world in which the viewpoints of others all seem equal in their importance or validity. To Mediators, **the way to earn love is to bond deeply or even merge with others into a sense of oneness.** In relationships, they may express a non-threatening sweetness, yet most likely shy away from necessary conflict and have difficulty finding their own agenda.

Nature versus nurture – How do we acquire our personality type?

The above list is a summary of the personality Types of the enneagram system. You might wonder how these nine different worldviews are formed. We know that our "personality type" first appears in childhood. Ask anyone why they are the way they are, and you are likely to hear explanations relating to their childhood. Many people date their worldview back to a critical event in their childhood such as divorce. Let's take the first three points of view listed above and imagine that each perspective belongs to one of three siblings growing up in the same family. Mom and Dad have decided they are going to divorce, and each child sees the divorce through the perspective of their own unique lens. For example:

> **The Perfectionist (Type One):** Jennie's parents divorced
> when she was eight years old. She didn't see much of her
> father after that. Her mother was really stressed out, and if

Jennie did anything wrong, she felt that Mom criticized her. Jennie didn't want to make things harder for Mom, so she tried to be the perfect child, to earn her mother's love. As an adult, she is still trying to be perfect.

The Giver (Type Two): Ronnie's parents divorced when he was six years old. He didn't see much of his father after that. His mother seemed to fall apart, and he vowed to help her in any way he could. Mom would talk to Ronnie about her feelings and he would empathize with her and kiss her. She really needed him, and it felt good. As an adult, Ronnie still is focused on helping people.

The Achiever (Type Three): Mickey's parents divorced when he was four years old. He didn't see much of his father after that. Mickey's father loved baseball. Mickey joined the Little League and played softball, and when his team won, his father began attending the games and encouraging him to win. Mickey worked very hard on his athletic prowess. He learned early on that winning was a sure way to get his father's love.

Obviously, these three siblings are going to have some feelings in common no matter what personality Type they are, but as you can see, the same event will evoke different responses in children of different inherent personality Types.

If you are the parent of more than one child, you have surely discovered that babies have inborn temperaments. When Jennifer brought home her first baby, she found that from day one he hated to be bathed. His daily bath was an ordeal. Two years later, to her surprise, she found that his newborn sister considered her bath one of her favorite activities. Jennifer even began calling her daughter "my water baby." Another parent talks about how her child repeatedly nearly kicked out the end of her crib as if she wanted to be free from any barrier or limitation. And another parent of an eight-year old talks about what a helpful child he is, setting the dinner table and helping to clean the house.

The consensus among scientists who study the development of personality in children is that temperament is inborn, but that the child's personality is further defined and solidified by his experience. Together they function

as a personality style or coping stra and a role in the family that helps feel safe. This is why, as shown in th temperaments interpret the same ch ture (the inborn temperament) and bine to create a basic personality s world and interact with it.

If we see temperament and pe then most likely Type is with us fron our early childhood experiences in a ity style (nurture). If this is true, the sifies both our negative and positive enneagram report feeling as if their not as apparent until some significa at that point their personality seems book we will go into more detail ab now an interesting exercise for you event or memory and how you read tions in one of the nine worldview worry -- later in this section we w Type in detail.

Understand yourself, understand

As we grow older, the coping s comes outdated in some ways. Mar of viewing the world isn't necessaril doesn't get us the results we want friends may tell us, "You are much about lightening up? You are way to tain way", or else "You are too inte enneagram is a great tool for helpin in childhood but still adhere to, so w an adult. It is not easy to change our we succeed and learn to act in diffe very tempting. Remember, those r temperament and by the lens thro established in our childhood, and th

A reasonable goal, then, becor ferently on it. Most of us react aut

personality Ty a Perfectionst and feels the n highlights thin scripts. Spellin makes her a go Jennifer's stree used to walk p feel a sense of i correct that mi Now that thou followed imme her self-improv ant. The differe has changed is Although it is s tions, the aware to react and wl

Couples w lem. This prob have termed "tl in the two part new, but the pa lem is not the the couples' be of the couple u they then can l difficulties. The our attachmen knowledging a ter able to und in possibly two

Some of yo me!" That is tru thinking proce that we wouldn we've referred much the same we feel our mo hard questions about the reliability and trustworthiness of others. **To earn love, Detectives place the highest priority on being loyal, responsible and dutiful.**

Adventurers (Type Sevens) – also called Enthusiasts or Epicures – see **the world as a place full of opportunities and options**. They fill their active minds with plans for all the positive things so as to ward off any unpleasant or painful experiences. **Adventurers earn love by being able to uplift others' spirits and through creating stimulating and fun experiences.** In relationships they can be imaginative and delightful, yet sensitive to limitations, structure, and pain.

Leaders (Type Eights) – also called Bosses or Challengers -- have a bold and expansive outlook. Their hallmark is being in control and making sure they are not seen as weak. **Leaders believe that the way to earn love is to be strong, to protect, and to champion others**, especially the underdog. In relationships, their partners may feel protected and safe, yet Leaders may have difficulty allowing themselves to be vulnerable with their partners and letting go of control.

Finally, **Mediators (Type Nines)** – also called Peacemakers -- see a world in which the viewpoints of others all seem equal in their importance or validity. To Mediators, **the way to earn love is to bond deeply or even merge with others into a sense of oneness.** In relationships, they may express a non-threatening sweetness, yet most likely shy away from necessary conflict and have difficulty finding their own agenda.

Nature versus nurture – How do we acquire our personality type?

The above list is a summary of the personality Types of the enneagram system. You might wonder how these nine different worldviews are formed. We know that our "personality type" first appears in childhood. Ask anyone why they are the way they are, and you are likely to hear explanations relating to their childhood. Many people date their worldview back to a critical event in their childhood such as divorce. Let's take the first three points of view listed above and imagine that each perspective belongs to one of three siblings growing up in the same family. Mom and Dad have decided they are going to divorce, and each child sees the divorce through the perspective of their own unique lens. For example:

> **The Perfectionist (Type One):** Jennie's parents divorced when she was eight years old. She didn't see much of her father after that. Her mother was really stressed out, and if

Jennie did anything wrong, she felt that Mom criticized her. Jennie didn't want to make things harder for Mom, so she tried to be the perfect child, to earn her mother's love. As an adult, she is still trying to be perfect.

The Giver (Type Two): Ronnie' s parents divorced when he was six years old. He didn't see much of his father after that. His mother seemed to fall apart, and he vowed to help her in any way he could. Mom would talk to Ronnie about her feelings and he would empathize with her and kiss her. She really needed him, and it felt good. As an adult, Ronnie still is focused on helping people.

The Achiever (Type Three): Mickey's parents divorced when he was four years old. He didn't see much of his father after that. Mickey's father loved baseball. Mickey joined the Little League and played softball, and when his team won, his father began attending the games and encouraging him to win. Mickey worked very hard on his athletic prowess. He learned early on that winning was a sure way to get his father's love.

Obviously, these three siblings are going to have some feelings in common no matter what personality Type they are, but as you can see, the same event will evoke different responses in children of different inherent personality Types.

If you are the parent of more than one child, you have surely discovered that babies have inborn temperaments. When Jennifer brought home her first baby, she found that from day one he hated to be bathed. His daily bath was an ordeal. Two years later, to her surprise, she found that his newborn sister considered her bath one of her favorite activities. Jennifer even began calling her daughter "my water baby." Another parent talks about how her child repeatedly nearly kicked out the end of her crib as if she wanted to be free from any barrier or limitation. And another parent of an eight-year old talks about what a helpful child he is, setting the dinner table and helping to clean the house.

The consensus among scientists who study the development of personality in children is that temperament is inborn, but that the child's personality is further defined and solidified by his experience. Together they function as a personality style or coping strategy that helps the child gain an identity and a role in the family that helps him to get the "goodies" or to survive or feel safe. This is why, as shown in the examples above, children with different temperaments interpret the same childhood experience differently. Thus, nature (the inborn temperament) and nurture (the child's environment) combine to create a basic personality style that determines the way we see the world and interact with it.

If we see temperament and personality type as basically synonymous, then most likely Type is with us from birth (nature) and then is influenced by our early childhood experiences in a developmental way, creating a personality style (nurture). If this is true, then what happens to us in childhood intensifies both our negative and positive personality traits. Many students of the enneagram report feeling as if their personality Type lay dormant or was just not as apparent until some significant event(s) occurred in their childhood; at that point their personality seems to have made its appearance. Later in the book we will go into more detail about these nine personality Types, but for now an interesting exercise for you to do is to recall a significant childhood event or memory and how you reacted to it. See if you can place your reactions in one of the nine worldviews we described earlier. If you can't, don't worry -- later in this section we will describe each enneagram personality Type in detail.

Understand yourself, understand your partner

As we grow older, the coping strategy that we developed as a child becomes outdated in some ways. Many of us begin to recognize that our way of viewing the world isn't necessarily always the best way, that sometimes it doesn't get us the results we want as it did when we were younger. In fact, friends may tell us, "You are much too competitive in your work", or "How about lightening up? You are way too rigid about needing things to be a certain way", or else "You are too intense" when it comes to relationship. The enneagram is a great tool for helping us identify patterns that we developed in childhood but still adhere to, so we can learn to respond differently now as an adult. It is not easy to change our thinking and our behaviors. Even when we succeed and learn to act in different ways, the same initial responses are very tempting. Remember, those responses are determined by our inborn temperament and by the lens through which we view the world that was established in our childhood, and those have not changed.

A reasonable goal, then, becomes to notice our response but act differently on it. Most of us react automatically to situations that trigger our personality Type. For example, Jennifer (one of the authors of this book) is a Perfectionst (enneagram Type One), a personality that notices mistakes and feels the need to fix them. The lens through which she views the world highlights things that need to be made better, whether it's people or manuscripts. Spelling errors seem to jump out at her from the written page, which makes her a good proofreader. But the same skill can be a problem. A sign on Jennifer's street reads, "No trespassing. Violatators will be prosecuted." She used to walk past that sign every day with her dog, and every day she would feel a sense of irritation as she found herself thinking, "If **I** were in charge, I'd correct that mistake!" Obviously, the person in charge didn't feel the same! Now that thought still pops into her head as she walks past that sign, but is followed immediately by laughing at herself as she realizes that, despite all her self-improvement work, she still notices errors that are totally unimportant. The difference is that she no longer feels that sense of irritation. What has changed is that she has become more conscious of her ingrained patterns. Although it is still all too easy for Jennifer to get caught up in automatic reactions, the awareness of her way of noticing the world gives her choices in how to react and what actions to take.

Couples who seek counseling usually come in with some specific problem. This problem often turns out to be only the latest rendition of what we have termed "the classic fight," a recurrent disagreement based on differences in the two partners' personalities. The details of the current version may be new, but the pattern is an old one. Focusing on the details of the latest problem is not the real solution. The key to resolving the problem is to identify the couples' belief systems that underlie the classic fight. Once each member of the couple understands their own and their partner's underlying premises, they then can begin to resolve the current problem and lessen similar future difficulties. The work is not easy, as the patterns are usually entrenched and our attachment to our own particular world view is quite strong; but by acknowledging and possibly accepting each other's perspective we may be better able to understand why we continue to get stuck and how we can co-exist in possibly two different worlds.

Some of you may be saying, "But I *like* my partner to be different from me!" That is true only to a point. We may like how our partner stimulates our thinking process or how he comes up with interesting and fun things to do that we wouldn't have otherwise thought of, but when it comes down to what we've referred to as "our truth," we usually want our partner to think pretty much the same way we do. "Our truth" usually consists of such things as: how we feel our money should be spent and managed, how sex and commitment should be approached, how much time one should spend with a spouse or partner and how love and affection gets expressed, what our home environment needs to look like, or what our religious and political preferences are. EHarmony, one of the more popular online dating websites focuses on what it calls the "29 dimensions of compatibility." Most likely they have created a very lucrative business on the premise that people for the most part want to hook up with others who are similar to them.

Wanting or expecting people to be similar to us runs very deep. It is difficult for us to first recognize and then accept that our partner may have his or her own personality Type and worldview. The enneagram is a powerful tool in helping us bridge these differences and for us to be able to develop understanding and compassion for both ourselves and our partners. As enneagram teacher Helen Palmer likes to say, the enneagram is about "Understanding people as they are to themselves" and not as we want them to be or expect them to be. Once we reach this level of understanding and acceptance, we can make great strides in communicating with one another in a more intimate and authentic way.

The goals of this book

Understand Yourself, Understand Your Partner is designed to enhance your relationship with your spouse or partner. The premises of this book are that by understanding your enneagram personality Type and that of your significant other:

- You will recognize that your partner's behaviors are not intended to drive you crazy, nor is he or she "out to get you," but rather are based on their particular assumptions about the world.
- You will be able to understand yourself and your partner better
- You will have more compassion for yourself and your partner
- You will have some powerful insight and communication tools to understand the different points of view held by your partner and you, and how to resolve your differences
- And finally, you and your partner will have the opportunity to grow individually and to grow closer together as a couple

These are the goals for all of us, regardless of personality. In Section One, Chapter Two will introduce you to the nine points of the enneagram and help you to determine which Type you are; your spouse or partner will probably want to do the same. This chapter will be followed by separate chapters that describe how each of the personality types plays out in relationships. The remainder of the book, Section Two, is devoted to in-depth descriptions of the 45 possible pairings of the nine personality Types. We don't expect you to read every line of Section Two. Rather, you might choose to use this section as a resource or reference book. We encourage you and your partner to read the nine individual Type chapters, identify your Type and that of your partner, and then go to the chapter describing your pairing. You will be amazed at the insights that will immediately jump out at you about your relationship. In addition, each Type chapter and each Pair chapter ends with a series of exercises. We hope you and your partner will take the time to do the exercises, which we believe can be very valuable for you and your relationship.

task is to do it correctly. Their vocabulary is peppered with
...sts," "oughts," and "it's the right thing to do." A strong inner
...r judging them, telling them they could do a better job. Per-
...be drawn to "causes," and they tend to displace their anger
...indignation over injustices. Another name for this type is the
...ause of their attraction to solving social problems.

...ists are not wishy-washy. They are used to having a strong sense
...ght thing to do in a situation, and they are more comfortable
... is clear. They generally prefer black-and-white to shades of
...omes to making decisions. Uncertainty is uncomfortable.

...ists like to avoid losing self-control or violating social norms.
...perceived as inflexible, overly serious, and critical of others. It
...rfectionists to have fun just for the sake of fun. Perfectionists
...not touchy-feely people, and they can sometimes be perceived
...e cold.

...amonly report feeling harshly criticized or punished as chil-
...ental message perceived by the child was, "Unless you are 'good'
...en 'perfect,' you are not acceptable." They grew up trying their
...ect, and they were the "good little boys and girls" in the family.
...es are preoccupied with avoiding error and getting things right
...g good or perfect. They are often ready to correct those they
...hearted example of a One at work is Professor Higgins in the
...Lady." In the play and film, the rather uptight and emotionally
...fessor's mission is to turn the urchin Eliza Doolittle into a high-
...an upper crust British accent.

...ists save their strongest faultfinding for themselves. Their se-
...critic criticizes them for not being perfect, for not trying hard
...r being selfish. Their worldview, as stated by Helen Palmer, is
...e world is an imperfect place. I work toward perfection. Ones
...ht, strive higher, work to improve others, and they try to be be-
...n so as not to be condemned by anyone. Perfectionists compare
...ly there with what should be.

...y Ones are uptight and rigid. They moralize and criticize people
...ey should do or how things should be. A healthy One, with a
...ence and sense of moral obligation, knows right from wrong
...m bad.

...issue of the Perfectionist, also called the "passion" of the Type, is
...ionists see direct anger as not "nice" or as inappropriate, so they
...s it. It then can leak out as resentment or may suddenly explode

CHAPTER TWO

Introduction to the Nine Types

The enneagram personality system consists of nine Types. Each of the Types shows up in a certain way and brings a particular gift or truth based on the lens through which its owner sees the world. Specific behaviors reflect each point of view, behaviors that through our lifetime get practiced over and over so that we each acquire a particular skill set. At the same time, we need to learn certain lessons, especially in those areas connected to our particular enneagram style, in which our focus might be distorted and behaviors compulsive. Each enneagram Type is a filter that excludes various portions of reality.

The enneagram system uses a nine-pointed star or diagram (Figure 1) around which each of the nine Types is placed.

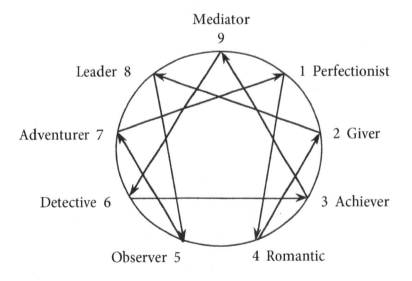

The enneagram is a map of sorts that identifies our basic personality and points out the direction for growth as well as unhealthy behaviors. The enneagram system uses numbers to identify the Types, because numbers are value-neutral. Enneagram teachers have attached names to the Types primarily for better identification and teaching purposes. In this book, we will mostly use the names given by Helen Palmer. It is common to find a little of yourself in each Type, as we are really comprised of all nine. The Types in total represent the whole human condition, but usually one or two personality styles will stand out as being the closest to you.

Using the enneagram enables a better understanding of yourself, which can hopefully lessen your own human suffering and enable you to grow. Through understanding others, you can have more compassion for why people act as they do. You will also be able to understand others as they are, rather than seeing them only from your point of view.

No one Type is "better" or "worse" than any other, and each has both a gift and a liability with an underlying theme or pattern that drives (or motivates). The negative pattern or "compulsion" is an overuse of the gift. For example, a person whose gift is to achieve and focus on getting results can become a workaholic who tramples on others to get to his or her goal and ignores their own family; a person whose strength is to lead can become a controlling bully; and someone whose gift is being able to see all sides of a situation and all people's points of view may find it so difficult to prioritize and assert himself that he gets easily distracted and loses track of his own wishes. If the Enneagram is to be useful, one must not only focus on one's gift, but also on one's negative pattern.

Each Type can take a valuable human quality and make it a compulsion by pushing it to extremes. The degree to which each person does this varies, so that psychological health can also vary. Once you recognize your own style, you are in a better position to change your narrow approach to the world and develop a broader perspective. As you become familiar with this approach, you will see the fundamental similarities among people of the same Type and you may also be able to identify your own.

In this chapter, you will be briefly introduced to the nine different enneagram personality Types. We have found that sometimes a particular style will just jump out, and you will just know that it describes you to a T. Some people will vacillate between two or three Types, not sure at first which one fits best. Some people relate to all nine in some fashion. Whatever your experience, reasons why this could happen might even have something to do with

---

the Type variations that you possess. W
of learning about the Types as you try t

If at first you do not clearly identif
clarity is to observe and listen to peopl
limelight. Although we don't know fo
have actually questioned them, their p
a caricature of a particular style throu
strongly expressed beliefs. This is why
cludes names of well-known people on
gram experts agree. For an excellent de
esting and enjoyable book, *The Enneag*
not only enneagram styles, but also pu
and summaries of characteristic films.

For each Type, the *core issue* (also c
element with which the Type struggles.
more the core issue interferes with his
each Type was born with is the *virtue*, t
and corrupted as our worldview or outl
of the lens through which we operate. E
expression of that gift, to be the best he

Type One: The F

Worldview: The world is an imperfe
Chief motivation: To do things the "
others. "I need to make myself and the w
Chief fear or avoidance: To be impe
Strongest positive traits: Ethical, re
cipled, self-disciplined, organized
Strongest negative traits: Judgmenta
overly serious, controlling, anxious
Core issue ("Passion"): anger
Virtue: serenity

Perfectionists are disciplined, conscie
to live up to their high ideals – and they
tionists have a strong inner sense of right
reality to an internal set of standards and
notice the errors and imperfections of th
rect them. They are detail- and goal-orien

---

completing th
"shoulds," "m
critic is forev
fectionists ca
into righteou
Reformer, be

Perfectio
of what's the
when the tas
gray when it

Perfectio
They may be
is hard for P
are generally
as being a lit

Ones co
dren. The pa
or possibly e
best to be pe
As adults, O
and with bei
love. A light
play "My Fai
repressed pr
class lady wi

Perfectio
vere interna
enough, or
as follows: I
want to be ri
yond criticis
what is actua

Unhealt
about what
strong cons
and good fre

The core
anger. Perfe
tend to repr

Introduction to the Nine Types

The enneagram personality system consists of nine Types. Each of the Types shows up in a certain way and brings a particular gift or truth based on the lens through which its owner sees the world. Specific behaviors reflect each point of view, behaviors that through our lifetime get practiced over and over so that we each acquire a particular skill set. At the same time, we need to learn certain lessons, especially in those areas connected to our particular enneagram style, in which our focus might be distorted and behaviors compulsive. Each enneagram Type is a filter that excludes various portions of reality.

The enneagram system uses a nine-pointed star or diagram (Figure 1) around which each of the nine Types is placed.

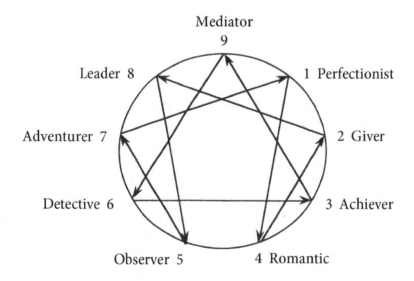

The enneagram is a map of sorts that identifies our basic personality and points out the direction for growth as well as unhealthy behaviors. The enneagram system uses numbers to identify the Types, because numbers are value-neutral. Enneagram teachers have attached names to the Types primarily for better identification and teaching purposes. In this book, we will mostly use the names given by Helen Palmer. It is common to find a little of yourself in each Type, as we are really comprised of all nine. The Types in total represent the whole human condition, but usually one or two personality styles will stand out as being the closest to you.

Using the enneagram enables a better understanding of yourself, which can hopefully lessen your own human suffering and enable you to grow. Through understanding others, you can have more compassion for why people act as they do. You will also be able to understand others as they are, rather than seeing them only from your point of view.

No one Type is "better" or "worse" than any other, and each has both a gift and a liability with an underlying theme or pattern that drives (or motivates). The negative pattern or "compulsion" is an overuse of the gift. For example, a person whose gift is to achieve and focus on getting results can become a workaholic who tramples on others to get to his or her goal and ignores their own family; a person whose strength is to lead can become a controlling bully; and someone whose gift is being able to see all sides of a situation and all people's points of view may find it so difficult to prioritize and assert himself that he gets easily distracted and loses track of his own wishes. If the Enneagram is to be useful, one must not only focus on one's gift, but also on one's negative pattern.

Each Type can take a valuable human quality and make it a compulsion by pushing it to extremes. The degree to which each person does this varies, so that psychological health can also vary. Once you recognize your own style, you are in a better position to change your narrow approach to the world and develop a broader perspective. As you become familiar with this approach, you will see the fundamental similarities among people of the same Type and you may also be able to identify your own.

In this chapter, you will be briefly introduced to the nine different enneagram personality Types. We have found that sometimes a particular style will just jump out, and you will just know that it describes you to a T. Some people will vacillate between two or three Types, not sure at first which one fits best. Some people relate to all nine in some fashion. Whatever your experience, reasons why this could happen might even have something to do with the Type variations that you possess. We encourage you to enjoy the process of learning about the Types as you try to discover your own.

If at first you do not clearly identify your own style, a good way to gain clarity is to observe and listen to people who are celebrities or in the public limelight. Although we don't know for sure what Type they are unless we have actually questioned them, their public persona may appear as almost a caricature of a particular style through Type-specific behaviors or very strongly expressed beliefs. This is why each description that we provide includes names of well-known people on whose personality styles most enneagram experts agree. For an excellent description, Tom Condon's very interesting and enjoyable book, *The Enneagram Movie & Video Guide,* describes not only enneagram styles, but also public figures and actors for each Type and summaries of characteristic films.

For each Type, the *core issue* (also called *passion*) is the chief personality element with which the Type struggles. The less healthy the individual, the more the core issue interferes with his interactions. The particular gift that each Type was born with is the *virtue,* the power that has become narrowed and corrupted as our worldview or outlook progressively constricts because of the lens through which we operate. Each personality Type strives for full expression of that gift, to be the best he or she can be.

Type One: The Perfectionist

Worldview: The world is an imperfect place. I work toward perfection.

Chief motivation: To do things the "right" way, to improve yourself and others. "I need to make myself and the world perfect."

Chief fear or avoidance: To be imperfect

Strongest positive traits: Ethical, responsible, fair, conscientious, principled, self-disciplined, organized

Strongest negative traits: Judgmental, righteous, rigid, critical of others, overly serious, controlling, anxious

Core issue ("Passion"): anger

Virtue: serenity

Perfectionists are disciplined, conscientious, and principled. They strive to live up to their high ideals – and they want others to do the same. Perfectionists have a strong inner sense of right or wrong. They constantly compare reality to an internal set of standards and value fairness and honesty. They notice the errors and imperfections of the world and try very hard to correct them. They are detail- and goal-oriented people, but just as important as completing the task is to do it correctly. Their vocabulary is peppered with "shoulds," "musts," "oughts," and "it's the right thing to do." A strong inner critic is forever judging them, telling them they could do a better job. Perfectionists can be drawn to "causes," and they tend to displace their anger into righteous indignation over injustices. Another name for this type is the Reformer, because of their attraction to solving social problems.

Perfectionists are not wishy-washy. They are used to having a strong sense of what's the right thing to do in a situation, and they are more comfortable when the task is clear. They generally prefer black-and-white to shades of gray when it comes to making decisions. Uncertainty is uncomfortable.

Perfectionists like to avoid losing self-control or violating social norms. They may be perceived as inflexible, overly serious, and critical of others. It is hard for Perfectionists to have fun just for the sake of fun. Perfectionists are generally not touchy-feely people, and they can sometimes be perceived as being a little cold.

Ones commonly report feeling harshly criticized or punished as children. The parental message perceived by the child was, "Unless you are 'good' or possibly even 'perfect,' you are not acceptable." They grew up trying their best to be perfect, and they were the "good little boys and girls" in the family. As adults, Ones are preoccupied with avoiding error and getting things right and with being good or perfect. They are often ready to correct those they love. A light-hearted example of a One at work is Professor Higgins in the play "My Fair Lady." In the play and film, the rather uptight and emotionally repressed professor's mission is to turn the urchin Eliza Doolittle into a high-class lady with an upper crust British accent.

Perfectionists save their strongest faultfinding for themselves. Their severe internal critic criticizes them for not being perfect, for not trying hard enough, or for being selfish. Their worldview, as stated by Helen Palmer, is as follows: The world is an imperfect place. I work toward perfection. Ones want to be right, strive higher, work to improve others, and they try to be beyond criticism so as not to be condemned by anyone. Perfectionists compare what is actually there with what should be.

Unhealthy Ones are uptight and rigid. They moralize and criticize people about what they should do or how things should be. A healthy One, with a strong conscience and sense of moral obligation, knows right from wrong and good from bad.

The core issue of the Perfectionist, also called the "passion" of the Type, is anger. Perfectionists see direct anger as not "nice" or as inappropriate, so they tend to repress it. It then can leak out as resentment or may suddenly explode as "righteous indignation" over some perceived injustice. Their challenge is to lighten up, have more fun, and be easier on themselves and others. Their "virtue," which is what very healthy Perfectionists seek, is serenity– that is, acceptance of what is. When the One is able to see the perfection in all things without the need to fix them, he or she gains a sense of serenity.

According to Tom Condon in his book *The Enneagram TV and Movie Guide,* well-known people who are Perfectionists are: U.S. President Harry S. Truman; U.S. Senator and Secretary of State Hillary Clinton, Senator and Secretary of State John Kerry, Vice President Al Gore, and Senator Barry Goldwater. Other Ones include General Colin Powell; crusader Ralph Nader; Dr. Jack Kevorkian; "etiquette mavens "Miss Manners" and Emily Post; Sir Thomas More; Martin Luther; Anderson Cooper, actors Jane Alexander, Julie Andrews Gregory Peck, Harrison Ford, Charlton Heston, Laura Linney, Emma Thompson and Meryl Streep; Martha Stewart; playwright Arthur Miller, and advice-giver Dr. Laura Schlesinger. Also, the culture of the Amish and the Puritans, plus the city of Singapore, and New Zealand.

Type Two: The Giver

"Alas, I know if I ever became truly humble,
I would be proud of it."
-- Ben Franklin

Worldview: People depend on my help. I am needed
Chief motivation: To be loved and appreciated. "The way to get love is to give love."
Chief fear or avoidance: To be seen as needy
Strongest positive traits: Warm, nurturing, sensitive to others' needs, loving, generous, enthusiastic, positive
Strongest negative traits: Possessive, prideful, hostile, martyr-like, manipulative, hysterical
Core issue ("Passion"): Pride (in being needed by others while having no needs yourself).
Virtue: Humility

Givers – called Helpers by some -- are warm, nurturing, and sensitive to other people's needs. They are generous, enthusiastic, and caring. Motivated by the need to give in order to receive love, they define themselves through service to others. It is easy for them to give, but they find it hard to receive; they pride themselves on having no needs, yet they crave apprecia-tion. Givers avoid being dependent on others, and they fear disappointing others or feeling rejected or not needed. Relationships are more important to them than anything else. Givers with a One (Perfectionist) wing are detail-oriented. Givers thrive on being "the power behind the throne" rather than the leader. When they get angry, it's usually in sudden emotional outbursts and accusations.

As children, Twos earned love and respect by meeting other people's needs. Because of this, they developed excellent radar. They come to feel pride in believing they are indispensable. Because Givers continually focus on others, their own needs may go unrecognized. The childhood message is, "I am loved and needed when I am helpful and pleasing." As adults, they avoid acknowledging their own needs. Their worldview, according to Palmer, is people depend on my help. I am needed.

Unhealthy Twos inevitably overextend themselves, helping too many people, sitting on too many committees, giving advice to too many friends. Intruding into others' lives, they believe that survival is not possible without their offered help. After a while, their charity work burdens and physically wears them out, and they become angry and resentful about not being ap-preciated. Healthy Givers are altruistically generous, caring, helpful, loving, and thoughtful, able to recognize the needs of others in a respectful manner, as well as being able to recognize their own needs and limitations.

The core issue (passion) of Givers is Pride. This is excessive pride, when the Two takes a "one-up, one-down" view: "Others have needs, but I don't." Twos' challenge is to become aware of their own needs and begin to get them met directly rather than by manipulating others. The virtue of this type is humility and freedom, seeing oneself as not having all the answers to others' problems and not being immune to the same ills to which others are sus-ceptible. From this humility comes a sense of freedom that releases the Two from believing he or she must shoulder everyone else's problems.

Well-known Givers include: Princess Diana, Nancy Reagan, Monica Le-winsky, Florence Nightingale, Mother Teresa, singers Whitney Houston, Ce-line Dion, and Dolly Parton, and actors John Travolta, Faye Dunaway, Alan Alda, Glenn Close, Bill Cosby, and Melanie Griffith.

Type Three: The Achiever

People have a universal compulsion to cover their face with some other face. Masks are used to hide or to become

someone else. Living a lie is what masks are about. The face on top and the one underneath need to become the same.
-- Anthropologist Meredith Small

Worldview: The world values a champion. I must avoid failure.
Chief motivation: To achieve, succeed. "The way to get love is to be successful."
Chief fear or avoidance: failure
Strongest positive traits: Energetic, goal-oriented, self-assured, optimistic, efficient, practical
Strongest negative traits: Competitive, conniving, superficial, narcissistic, deceptive, pretentious
Core issue ("Passion""): Deceit (They'll turn themselves into whatever projects the image of success).
Virtue: Honesty

Achievers, also called Performers, are motivated by the need to be productive, achieve success, and avoid failure. Measuring themselves by external achievements, they want to look good and project the image of someone who can successfully handle any situation. They are often described as workaholics; they tend to bring their laptops and Smartphones with them even on vacations. Achievers would rather talk about their work than their feelings. Their self-worth is dependent on their accomplishments, and they believe that others judge them the same way.

Threes were children who were prized for their achievements, and were valued for *doing* rather than *feeling*. They learned to perform well, to compete, to handle several jobs at once, and to promote themselves. The message was to avoid failure, because only winners were worthy of love. As adults, to avoid rejection, they want to improve themselves, get attention, be admired, impress others, and use or do whatever it takes to stay on top. Their worldview, writes Helen Palmer, is: The world values a champion. I must avoid failure. Threes say, "Be like me – I know how to succeed," and "if you work hard enough and put your mind to it, you can do it – and accomplish any goal."

Unhealthy Achievers are image conscious, extremely competitive workaholics who are detached from their feelings. Healthy Threes are self-assured and emotionally connected, enjoying high self-esteem, believing in themselves and their own value. They can accomplish lofty goals. The core issue (passion) of the Achiever is deceit—they even deceive themselves. In order to be successful, they keep changing into whatever they perceive the group wants them to be. In the process, they lose track of who they really are and what they are feeling. For unhealthy Achievers, what counts is the image rather than the reality. Because of their fear of failure, they tend to put a positive spin (to themselves and others) on anything negative that happens to them. The virtue for the Achiever is <u>honesty</u> and hope. Threes who are healthy have gained a sense of honesty and integrity in their lives. They discard the mask and discover and stay true to their authentic self. The result is that they comprehend that they are loved for who they are and not for what they do.

Famous Achievers, according to Condon, include: Rev. Jesse Jackson, O.J. Simpson, Arnold Schwartzenegger, athletes Lance Armstrong, Tiger Woods, and Michael Jordan; Oprah Winfrey; Prime Minister Benjamin Netanyahu of Israel; Dutchess of Windsor Wallis Simpson; John Edwards, NBC's Bryant Gumbel and Diane Sawyer, and actors Tom Cruise, Sylvester Stallone, Will Smith, Christopher Reeve, Wesley Snipes, Halle Berry, Demi Moore and Sharon Stone. Also, the overall culture of the U.S. (California, however, has more of a Seven culture).

Type Four: The Romantic

Worldview: Something is missing. I have been abandoned.

Chief motivation: To be truly understood, to be seen as special and unique

Chief fear or avoidance: To be ordinary, but also to be abandoned

Strongest positive traits: Warm, perceptive, artistic, inspiring, compassionate, intuitive, and introspective.

Strongest negative traits: Moody, withdrawn, guilt-ridden, stubborn, self-absorbed, self-conscious

Core issue ("Passion"): Envy

Virtue: Equanimity (balance)

Romantics are motivated by the need to experience their feelings, to be understood, to search for the meaning of life, and to avoid being ordinary. They like to be perceived as unique and take special care to make their appearance and surroundings special. They believe they feel more deeply than others, and often what they feel is melancholy and loss. Romantics seek peak experiences and see themselves as being sensitive and creative. Music, art, theater, writing, and other creative endeavors are favorite methods of expression. Romantics are compassionate, warm, intuitive, introspective people who are sometimes depressed or upbeat and dramatic. Some Fours slide from one extreme to the other, and if experiencing the depressed, withdrawn, and moody side, they may flirt with death and even commit suicide. The underlying theme in childhood for Fours is a feeling of loss, abandonment or being misunderstood. Because of this, they basically tell themselves, "I am not acceptable. I am defective. To become acceptable, I need to be unique and elite." Fours feel forced to create their own identities by looking inward to their imagination. They choose emotional intensity as the antidote to feelings of loss and separation, therefore avoiding the ordinary. Because of this, Romantics as adults have a tendency to focus on what is "missing" in their lives; they long for what others are enjoying, for what is being denied them. They blame their "defectiveness." Their worldview is: <u>Something is missing. Others have it. I have been abandoned.</u>

Unhealthy Romantics are moody and self-absorbed tormented souls, wallowing in their own melancholy, living their lives through their imaginations and fantasies. They envy others who get to live ordinary lives. In relationship, they long for the unavailable person, but when they actually have someone, they tend to push him or her away. Healthy Fours are intuitive and sensitive to others' suffering. Their truly inspiring creations can profoundly affect others. The core issue of the Romantic is envy, a yearning that usually involves the satisfying relationships and fulfilling lives they believe others are having and they aren't. Their virtue is equanimity or balance. Finding a sense of equanimity can be a wonderful relief for Fours whose lives are often filled with highs and lows, intensity and drama. Balance in the Four's life can include the realization that the connection so yearned for was always there inside.

Among famous Romantics are: poet Sylvia Plath; painter Vincent Van Gogh; singers Curt Cobain, Michael Jackson, Billie Holliday, and Judy Collins; Prince Charles; writers Jack Kerouac and Virginia Woolf; and actors Cate Blanchett, Johnny Depp, James Dean, Judy Garland, Nick Nolte, Laurence Olivier, Marlon Brando, Meryl Streep, Liv Ullman, Kate Winslett, John Malkovich, and Liam Neeson. And the culture of France.

Type Five: The Observer

Worldview: The world is invasive. I need privacy to think and to refuel my energy.

Chief motivation: To be self-sufficient and conserve time, energy, and space-related concepts

Chief fear or avoidance: To be smothered, to be incompetent, that there won't be enough to go around.

Strongest positive traits: Knowledgeable, insightful, analytical, curious, sensitive, objective, persevering

Strongest negative traits: Withholding, stubborn, critical of others, intellectually arrogant, negative

Core issue ("Passion"): Avarice

Virtue: Nonattachment

Observers are motivated by the need to know and understand everything, and the desire for self-sufficiency. They are analytical, perceptive, and objective people, but they can also be intellectually arrogant, critical of others, and unassertive. They perceive the world as invasive. They need privacy to think and refuel their energies. Observers believe that they will be safe in the world if only they can gather enough information. To Fives, knowledge is power. They tend to avoid strong feelings or demanding people, and they tend to experience their feelings more deeply when they are alone, keeping others at a distance. As a result, other people may see them as detached. It is more comfortable for them to observe than to participate.

The Five child's theme is that the world came in and took too much away—or perhaps didn't give enough. The unspoken bargain that the child struck with the primary caretakers was, "I won't ask much from you, so don't ask much from me." Because of this dynamic, Fives learned to detach from their needs and focus on an intense mental life. As adults, very private and independent people, their chief attachment is to knowledge instead of people and material objects. Observers find their place in the world and thereby obtain security and self-esteem by using the mind. They consider themselves thinkers and intellectuals, because more than in the world of action or practicality, their real life is within. Their worldview is: <u>The world is invasive. I need privacy to think and to refuel my energy.</u>

Unhealthy Observers are reclusive and isolated from others. They can appear eccentric and argumentative. Often they exude an air of superiority. They analyze everything and see no benefit from feelings. Healthy Fives are able to observe their environment with extraordinary perceptiveness and insight. They love learning and can possess an incredible amount of knowledge. As experts in their fields, they understand the abstract and might even accomplish brilliant discoveries.

The core issue (passion) for the Observer is avarice or greed. This Type tends to be minimalists, priding themselves on getting by with as little as possible. Observers believe that the resources of the world are limited, so they need to hold on to what they do have. This doesn't necessarily refer to money, as many Observers are very generous; but in the arenas of time and emotions, they jealously guard their solitude and privacy. They feel easily invaded by others, and when they find themselves among a group of people, they might need time afterwards to recover. They value their own space, whether that's their home, a room, or a desk. They don't want others touching those areas. Spouses complain that the Observer just doesn't give enough, likes to spend too much time alone, doesn't want to talk about feelings and prefers to withdraw whenever emotional problems arise. The virtue for the Five is nonattachment, which in this situation is somewhat paradoxical. When Fives are into their Type's passion, they withhold and detach so as to not become dependent or depleted, a "scarcity mindset" approach. In contrast, the nonattachment approach comes from a belief in abundance, knowing that it is unnecessary to hold on to things, that the universe will provide. The challenge for the Five is to become more generous in spirit, especially when it comes to giving their thoughts and feelings.

Some well-known Observers, according to Tom Condon, are: Jacqueline Kennedy Onassis; Bill Gates; Albert Einstein; J. Robert Oppenheimer; Amelia Earhart; chimpanzee expert Dr. Jane Goodall; Joe DiMaggio; chess player Bobby Fisher; Howard Hughes; writers Ken Wilber, Dr. Oliver Sacks, Jean-Paul Sartre, Philip Roth, and Michael Crichton; actors Montgomery Clift, Daniel Day-Lewis, Robert DeNiro, Ralph Fiennes, Anthony Hopkins, Jeremy Irons, Sam Neill, Keanu Reeves, and Al Pacino. And the culture of England.

Type Six: The Detective

Worldview: The world is a threatening place. I question authority.

Chief motivation: Safety, security. "The world is an unsafe place. If I make every effort to notice the dangers around me, I might be able to avoid harm." [phobic Six]. "The world is an unsafe place, and I have to make every effort to detect danger. If I then face the danger head on, I might be able to avoid harm." [counterphobic Six]

Chief fear or avoidance: Uncertainty

Strongest positive traits: Loyal, trustworthy, warm, practical, responsible, caring

Strongest negative traits: Defensive, mistrustful, second-guesses oneself, hyper-vigilant, testy, self-defeating, looks for potentially bad outcomes of any situations.

Core issue ("Passion"): Fear, doubt

Virtue: Courage and faith

Type Six people are called Detectives or Questioners, because their attention fixes on potential difficulties and dangers in their environment and other people. Their core belief is that the world is a dangerous place and that they need to be vigilant in order to feel safe. Fear and anxiety are their frequent companions. So-called phobic Sixes are outwardly fearful and seek approval, searching for reliable and trustworthy authority figures. They tend to seek protectors, defenders they can trust. Counterphobic Sixes (those who move against their fears), in contrast, directly challenge the source of their fear, question authority, and may deliberately participate in potentially dangerous activities in order to have a clear and realistic idea of the risks. They unconsciously recognize that what is in their imagination is often more frightening than reality; therefore surviving dangerous situations can be reassuring. Consciously, however, they do not consider themselves fearful people, whereas Phobic Sixes are very much in touch with their fears and need for security. Most Detectives have some combination of phobic and counterphobic behaviors, but are predominantly one or the other.

Detectives can be extremely loyal (they are also called Loyalists), devoted to their families and friends. They can be warm, witty, practical, helpful, and responsible, but they might also be defensive, hyper-vigilant, suspicious, sarcastic, and skeptical of others' motives. Attention is usually focused on the possible negative outcomes of every situation, and they need to be reassured that this has been addressed before they're ready to take action. They spend a lot of time preparing for possible disasters. They think they never have enough knowledge or equipment to be adequately prepared; therefore they are often labeled as procrastinators. Even after they take action, many Sixes tend to revisit their decision and wonder if it was right. Because of this, Detectives are sometimes said to have "a doubting mind."

Sixes lost faith in authorities when young. They remember being afraid of those who had power over them and of being unable to act on their own behalf. Their childhood script becomes: "The world will protect me if I am obedient and dutiful, although I must first find a good protector, someone who will really take care of me." As adults, they are apt to scan the environment for signs of anything harmful and to watch people for possible hidden intentions. Their worldview, according to Palmer, is: <u>The world is a threatening place. I question authority.</u>

Detectives approach a perceived threat in either a phobic or counterphobic style. The Phobic Six imagines danger and somewhat sensibly runs away. The counterphobic Six imagines danger and takes an aggressive approach to seek it out.

Unhealthy Sixes view the world as a place where people's motives can't be trusted, the worst-case outcome is forever expected, external success runs the risk of prompting resentment from others, and the need for vigilance makes it difficult to ever fully relax. Healthy Sixes develop faith in themselves, others and the universe. They can become truly courageous and may end up dealing with causes related to the ordinary or the oppressed. Cooperative, loyal, and responsible to friends, family, and community, they ask the "hard questions" that can ward off negative consequences. The core issue for the Detective is fear and doubt, and the virtue is courage and faith.

Some famous phobic Sixes are: President George H. W. Bush; President Richard Nixon; comedian Ellen De Generes; commentator Jon Stewart: actors Woody Allen, Kim Basinger, Warren Beatty, Sally Field, Ed Harris, Jack Lemmon, Marilyn Monroe, and Anthony Perkins.

Counterphobic Sixes include: President G.W. Bush, Charles Manson, J. Edgar Hoover, Attorney General Janet Reno, commentator David Letterman, filmmaker Michael Moore; Ted Turner; Elton John and Wynonna Judd; Director Spike Lee; and actors Carrie Fisher, Mel Gibson, Gene Hackman, Dustin Hoffman, Tommy Lee Jones, Paul Newman, Richard Pryor, Julia Roberts, Meg Ryan, Susan Sarandon, and Steven Segal.

Type Seven: The Adventurer/Enthusiast

Worldview: The world is full of opportunity and options. I look forward to the future.

Chief motivation: To have fun, to experience novelty and adventure

Chief fear or avoidance: Suffering and pain, being hemmed in

Strongest positive traits: Optimistic, energetic, lively, fun to be with, spontaneous, imaginative, charming, enthusiastic, productive

Strongest negative traits: Poor follow-through, impulsive, narcissistic, undisciplined, restless, manic

Core issue ("Passion"): Gluttony

Virtue: Sobriety

Adventurers or Enthusiasts– called Epicures by some because they see life as a smorgasbord - are motivated by the need to be happy and plan enjoyable activities in a world full of opportunities and options. They assiduously avoid pain and suffering and chafe at limitations, constraints and rules. They fill their lives with many activities. They prefer the start-up phase of hobbies or careers and crave variety. Sitting still or quieting their minds is hard for them, and they tend not to be introspective. They are often described as charming, spontaneous, quick-witted and with a great sense of humor. But they can also be impulsive, undisciplined, restless, rebellious, and unwilling to commit. Many gravitate to comedy or entertainment careers, and even if they don't do this professionally, their friends see them as fun to be around.

Adventurers are always ready for new adventures, moving quickly from one to another. Along the way, many leave unfinished projects, as they are much more enthusiastic about initiation than follow-through. They tend to have a broad superficial knowledge, which makes them interesting conversationalists; however, they could lack depth of experience. They are creative, imaginative people who leave the details and grunt work to others. Many Adventurers' lives include multiple jobs, relationships and residences – a lot of changes.

Sevens as children may have felt a lack of nurturing and therefore believed they must rely solely on themselves. As adults, this lack of childhood emotional support becomes a quest for self-nurturance, a quest to ensure satisfaction. Adventurers want unlimited enjoyment and amusement. Their every contact with the world invigorates them for more; every experience enlarges their capacity for additional experiences. Their worldview is: <u>The world is full of opportunity and options. I look forward to the future</u>. Fear of pain and deprivation are strong motivators.

Unhealthy Adventurers are narcissists who want instant gratification and immunity from all suffering. If they see something they want, they must have it. If something occurs to them to do, they must do it right away. If something gives them pleasure, they want more of it immediately. Healthy Sevens become more deeply involved, not avoiding pain or fearing deprivation. They internalize their experiences so as to create the necessary anchors for stability and security. Their focus of attention shifts away from themselves to the external world and they come to understand that the world exists for purposes other than their own gratification.

The core issue (passion) of the Adventurer is gluttony – which is an all-consuming appetite for novelty and enjoyable experiences. The virtue is sobriety and spiritual work, which involves staying in the present moment with a more singular focus and commitment.

Famous Adventurers, according to Tom Condon, include: U.S. President John F. Kennedy; Sarah Ferguson; Phillip, the Duke of Windsor; Newt Gingrich; Magic Johnson; comedians Steve Allen, Jack Benny, Victor Borge, Allan King; directors Francis Ford Coppola, and Steven Spielberg; commentators Larry King, Katie Couric, Jay Leno, and Stephen Colbert; singers Loretta Lynn, Linda Ronstadt and Luciano Pavarotti; and actors Antonio Banderas,

Kenneth Branagh, Michael Caine, Chevy Chase, George Clooney, Gerard Depardieu, Leonardo DeCaprio, Michael J. Fox, Clark Gable, Ava Gardner, Cary Grant, Tom Hanks, Goldie Hawn, Ron Howard, Michael Keaton, Greg Kinnear, Jack Nicholson, Leslie Nielsen, Peter O'Toole, Brad Pitt, Dennis Quaid, Susan Sarandon, Barbara Streisand, Lily Tomlin, and Robin Williams.

Type Eight: The Leader (the Boss)

Worldview: The world is an unjust place. I defend the innocent
Chief motivation: To be strong, powerful, self-reliant
Chief fear or avoidance: To show weakness
Strongest positive traits: Self-confident, energetic, self-reliant, protective, direct, authoritative
Strongest negative traits: Controlling, domineering, self-centered, aggressive, rebellious, insensitive, explosively angry
Core issue (passion): Lust
Virtue: Innocence and truth

Leaders (also called Champions, Bosses or Asserters) are motivated by the need to be self-reliant and strong and to make an impact on the world. They are very protective of themselves, family and friends, and may act aggressively, sometimes even combatively. Leaders are comfortable with overt anger and welcome confrontation – they like to get things out in the open whereas feeling weak or dependent is anathema to them. Often described as loyal, direct, energetic, blunt, and self-confident, gregarious Eights love to swap stories with others, but sometimes are insensitive, domineering, and controlling. They tend to overindulge in food, sex, or drugs, living by the principle that "if some is good, more is better." When Leaders show that they care for others, they are much better at acting than listening.

When Leaders are afraid or sad, it will emerge as anger. Any other emotions are perceived as signs of weakness. Whereas most of us (especially Perfectionists and Mediators) are uncomfortable with this, Leaders believe that confrontation is the way to get the measure of another person. Quick to anger, they as easily return to their positive, outgoing behavior. Having just blasted someone else with their over-the-top outburst, they have a hard time understanding why an hour later that person is still upset.

Many Eights say they felt as if they needed to play the protector in their family of origin. Some of them describe a combative childhood where strength was respected and weakness was not; therefore they learned to protect themselves. As adults, Eights continue to view themselves in this light, concerned with fairness and justice. Their worldview is: <u>The world is an unjust place. I defend the innocent.</u> The central issue is control. As Palmer relates, Eights seem to ask the question, "Who's in charge here?" and "Will that person be fair?" They also want the power to both set and ignore limits. They exercise their will like muscles, which results in enormous willpower and strong egos, an unquestioned belief in themselves, and a confidence in their ability to get their way.

Leaders have a low tolerance for frustration. It is hard for them to refrain from acting on impulses or returning for a third plateful. In friendships, fighting is felt to be fundamentally necessary so that people will blurt out their real feelings. Leaders believe truth comes out in a fight.

When healthy, no other personality Type has as great a capacity for exerting such a powerful, constructive influence in the lives of so many. But the reverse is that no other Type can so completely misuse power or become so totally destructive as an unhealthy Eight. Then, they turn everything into an adversarial relationship, proud of combativeness. If they feel they have been hurt unfairly, they resort to retaliation and revenge, and then rationalize their behavior by citing fairness and justice. Healthy Leaders identify with others, have empathy and compassion, and are nurturing, generous, helpful, and genuinely concerned about others' welfare. They learn the power of love rather than being obsessed with the love of power. The core issue or passion for the Eight is lust and vengeance. Lust manifests itself as lust for life. They truly believe that if some is good, more is better. Unlike Adventurers, who want variety and novelty, Leaders want quantity – more food, more sex, more money, and more power. Their virtue is innocence and truth. Healthy Eights not only champion the oppressed and abused, but they also can accept their own innocence and vulnerability without fear of being taken advantage of. They are also able to loosen their grasp on their specific version of the truth, especially when it comes to fairness and justice, and allow a more expansive, trusting, and absolute truth to emerge.

Leaders are sometimes initially confused with counterphobic Sixes. However, whereas Detectives are driven by fear, fret about the potential negative consequences of any action, and endlessly analyze potential decisions, Leaders tend to charge ahead, take control, and rarely second-guess their actions.

Tom Condon lists the following famous Leaders: Napoleon Bonaparte, Fidel Castro, Jimmy Hoffa, Saddam Hussein, Lyndon Johnson, Muammar Qaddafi, Nikita Khrushchev, Mao Tse-tung, Golda Meir, Theodore Roosevelt, Joseph Stalin, General George Patton, Governor and wrestler Jesse

Ventura, and Donald Trump; singers Johnny Cash and Frank Sinatra; TV host Mike Wallace; and actors Sean Connery, Russell Crowe, Matt Damon, Danny DeVito, Morgan Freeman, Sean Penn, Julianne Phillips, Queen Latifah, , George C Scott, Denzel Washington, and John Wayne. Other Eights include Dr. Phil McGraw and Rosie O'Donnell.

Type Nine: The Mediator

Worldview: The world won't value my efforts. Stay comfortable. Keep the peace.

Chief motivation: To keep the peace, to obtain consensus

Chief fear or avoidance: Conflict or separation

Strongest positive traits: Good-natured, supportive of others, generous, empathic, patient, open-minded, diplomatic

Strongest negative traits: Unassertive, stubborn, forgetful, procrastinates, easily distracted, passive-aggressive

Core Issue: Sloth

Virtue: Right action and love

Mediators are motivated by the need to keep the peace and to avoid conflict. Also called Peacemakers, they can easily see all points of view, which makes them skilled at helping others resolve conflicts. Mediators' friends generally see them as easygoing, peaceful, nonjudgmental, agreeable people. In a group, they'll usually go along with whatever others want to do, and they tend to be very well liked by their many friends. They are generous, giving people who (unlike the Giver [Two]) are not looking for reciprocity. Mediators are very uncomfortable with anger. When upset, they are likely to keep quiet or react indirectly.

The ability to see all sides of every issue often makes it difficult for Mediators to make decisions or take action. They are easily distracted, and sometimes have difficulty setting priorities. It's hard for them to say no, so they may find themselves overcommitted. When faced with a problem, Mediators tend to ignore it or put it off, hoping that somehow it will go away or solve itself.

Mediators tend to defer action until the last minute. They are so used to focusing on others that sometimes rather than knowing what they really want, they only know what they <u>don't</u> want. When unhappy with a situation, Mediators are stubborn or passive–aggressive instead of overtly angry. They sometimes seem to "forget" themselves, and their friendly, unassuming, undemanding demeanor can make it easy for others to assume that they'll agree to anything.

Many Nines report feeling overlooked as children, that their point of view was seldom heard, and that other people's needs were more important than their own. They also strongly identified with the whole system and felt a responsibility to maintain internal harmony. Thus, a peacekeeping role was familiar. As adults, they desire union with others. They want to avoid conflict and tension, ignore whatever would upset them, and maintain peace at almost any price. Their worldview is: The world won't value my efforts. Stay comfortable. Keep the peace. The overt message is, "It's not important"; the covert message is, "I'm angry about being overlooked." Nines attempt to resolve the dilemma of whether to comply or rebel by not choosing either option — there is always time, there is always tomorrow, problems will work themselves out.

Unhealthy Nines are obstinate and stubborn when feeling the slightest pressure, yet can also lose themselves in others. They deny that any problems or conflicts exist and numb their feelings with addictive behaviors and substances and are therefore neglectful and irresponsible. Healthy Mediators are serene, accepting, and trusting of self and others. They are easygoing and at ease with life. They are good comforters, having a calming, healing influence on others by being nonjudgmental and giving unconditional acceptance.

The Nine's dominant issue is slothfulness and self-effacement. Slothful is not the same as lazy. They, in fact, may be involved in many activities, but because they are easily distracted from the important things they themselves have decided to do, it's almost impossible for them to work on themselves.

The virtue of the Nine is right action and love. Healthy Nines are able to not only know what is appropriate action, but they can show up and assert themselves in the world. They take a position and act on it. This more assertive, confident self comes from the antidote to self-forgetting, which is self-love.

Some well-known Mediators, says Tom Condon, are: Queen Elizabeth II, U.S Presidents Dwight Eisenhower, Gerald Ford, Ronald Reagan, and Bill Clinton; the Dalai Lama; Nelson Mandela of South Africa; King Hussein of Jordan; Patricia Hearst; and actors Jennifer Aniston, Antonio Banderas, Annette Bening, Ingrid Bergman, Gary Cooper, Kevin Costner, Matt Damon, Clint Eastwood, Anjelica Huston, Grace Kelly, Andie MacDowell, Eva Marie Saint, Martin Sheen, Kevin Spacey, Mary Steenburgen, James Stewart, and Billy Bob Thornton.

More about the Enneagram

By now you probably have recognized your Type – and perhaps that of your spouse or partner – from the descriptions above. The nine points of view are not, however, a random collection of different personality types. The system is actually very orderly, with connections among various Types and with subtypes as well. If you wish to go into greater depth about these aspects of each Type we recommend you read the books *Personality Types* by Don Riso and Russ Hudson; *The Essential Enneagram* by David Daniels and Virginia Price; and Helen Palmer's books *The Enneagram* and *The Enneagram in Love and Work*. The next chapter further breaks down the nine Types into additional categories.

CHAPTER THREE

More about the Enneagram

The enneagram personality system is actually more complex than simply describing nine specific types. If by now you recognize your and your partner's point of view, you will definitely be able to benefit from this book. However, you're likely to understand yourself and your partner better and to find this book even more useful if you are willing to learn a little more about this approach to personality typing. Here is an overview of three additional features: the *centers* (also referred to as *triads*), the *wings*, and the *subtypes*. Together, they explain the uniqueness of each individual and contribute to easing relationship difficulties.

The Centers (or Triads)

Look again at the nine-pointed star of the Enneagram (p. 11). The arrangement of personality Types is not random. To begin, notice that the nine Types are placed roughly in a circle. The circle can be divided into three triads or *centers*, each consisting of three adjacent Types. Types Two, Three and Four constitute the <u>heart</u> or <u>feeling</u> center, Types Five, Six and Seven, the <u>head</u> or <u>thinking</u> center, and Types Eight, Nine and One, the <u>gut</u>, <u>belly</u>, or <u>instinctive</u> center. People who share the same center also share a similar focus of attention on one of the following: image (the heart center), fear (the head center), and anger (the gut center). Within each center, people of different Types have individual strategies for dealing with the same focus of attention.

The Heart (Feeling) Center (Types Two, Three, and Four)

Heart center personalities are concerned with the way they appear to the world. It's important to them to present the right image and they live their lives playing a role. Their identity and self-esteem are derived from what others think and feel about them. Because they are so dependent on others, they are very good at sensing other people's needs and wants. Rather than asserting themselves directly, they get what they want indirectly through manipulation, self-pity and guilt. Givers (Twos) present a loving image. They are chameleon-like, making themselves over to please others. Achievers (Threes) present the image of success and want to be perceived as winners. Romantics (Fours) strive to appear unique. In order to be seen as original, young Romantics might dress all in black and sport blue hair or wear unusual clothes. They definitely do not want to be perceived as ordinary. In their quest for the right image, members of the heart center may lose their own sense of identity.

- Twos are so busy pleasing others that they neglect their own needs.
- Threes are so busy achieving that they become human "doers" rather than human "beings." They never have the time to stop and figure out who they are and what they really want.
- Fours spend so much time focused on being unique and having deep feelings that they too are often actually out of touch with their true self. .

Using different strategies, all three types seek attention and love, and in the process, lose track of their own identity.

The Head (Thinking) Center (Types Five, Six, and Seven)

Head center personalities all have issues around fear, and each of the three types deal with their fear and try to find security differently.

- Observers (Fives) believe that if they have enough information, they will feel safer.
- Detectives (Sixes) fall into two categories: Phobic Sixes seek safety in authority figures; Counterphobic Sixes, believing that directly facing a danger is less frightening than imagining what might happen, will pursue potentially risky situations or dangerous people and assertively approach them. They are also more likely to rebel against authority. Some Counterphobic Sixes are out of touch with their fear, whereas Phobic sixes are always aware of it.
- Adventurers (Sevens) fill their minds and lives with so many endless activities, plans for the future, and new adventures, that nothing but fun and positive thoughts can manifest — they bury their fears beneath their activities, avoiding unpleasant emotions. They reframe anything negative into an opportunity for something new.

The Gut (Belly) Center (Types Eight, Nine, and One)

Gut center personalities have anger issues. Each might express anger in different ways, but all have it.

- Leaders (Eights) feel comfortable expressing their anger directly. When they feel sad or afraid, it appears as anger.
- Mediators (Nines) avoid anger and are often detached from their own emotions. When they feel angry, it is often expressed as passive-aggressive behavior.
- Perfectionists (Ones) might say that they rarely get angry, and that what they feel instead is resentment or righteous indignation.

All three Types seek autonomy: Eights strongly resist being controlled (often, by controlling others); Nines tune out when conflict or unpleasantness appears; and Ones are convinced of the rightness of their position and have a tendency to impose it on others.

The Wings

On the enneagram diagram, each personality type is bordered by two others. Although each type has the features described in Chapter Two, your personality is likely to be influenced by one or the other adjacent types, called that type's *wing*. If you have a sense of your own basic Type, then the list below may help you understand other aspects of your worldview. The characteristics of each Type are enhanced by certain attributes of their wing.

- Ones (Perfectionists) with a Nine (Mediator) wing add coolness, objectivity, and devotion to principles (rather than people). They are more practical and devoted to rules.
- Ones with a Two (Giver) wing are warmer to other people and quite helpful, but also can be critical and controlling.
- Twos with a One wing add concern about ethical issues and respect for others' boundaries. They are more critical, judgmental and introspective.
- Twos with a Three (Achiever) wing are competitive, ambitious, and outgoing and might be manipulative.
- Threes with a Two wing are gregarious and popular; therefore, excellent mentors. They focus on appearing ideal to others and also on being on top.
- Threes with a Four (Romantic) wing are cooler, more introverted and introspective. They can also be both artistic and pretentious.

- Fours with a Three wing tend to be extroverted, outgoing and ambitious. Flamboyant and image-conscious, they often conceal their feelings in public and appear otherwise in private. But, sometimes they want their emotions to be visible and, when unhealthy, they go for dramatic gestures – a hand smashed through a window, lots of drama.
- Fours with a Five (Observer) wing are likely to be introverted and lonely. They are intellectual, possibly depressed, ashamed and familiar with pain and loss.
  Fours with a Five wing who are unhealthy are more likely to withdraw from the world to sort out their overwhelmingly negative feelings rather than expressing them.
- Fives with a Four wing are often artistically talented. They are creative, empathic, and imaginative, self-absorbed, arrogant and critical.
- Fives with a Six (Detective) wing are likely to be interested in science and technology, analytic and sometimes patient teachers. They appear less threatening and more endearing. Although loyal, they can also be anxious, suspicious, and skeptical.
- Sixes with a Five wing are introverted and intellectual, idiosyncratic, and sometimes cynical, plus standoffish and remote.
- Sixes with a Seven (Adventurer) wing are extroverted and social, impulsive and warm. They can be funny and cheerful. Counterphobic Sixes with a Seven wing are often aggressive and accusatory.
- Sevens with a Six wing tend to be responsible, lovable, loyal, anxious, and sweet, but also suspicious and irresponsible. Some fall in and out of love easily.
- Sevens with an Eight (Leader) wing add self confidence, aggression, materialism and competition. Some can be impatient and narcissistic and might have difficulty with sexual monogamy.
- Eights with a Seven (Adventurer) wing are extroverted, expansive, powerful, and generous. They can also be egocentric, have addiction problems, anger more easily, and overreact.
- Eights with a Nine (Mediator) wing are introverted, nurturing, calmer and slower to erupt.
- Nines with an Eight (Leader) wing are extroverted and assertive. They can get things done and make good leaders. They can also switch from being amiable to exploding with anger.

- Nines with a One (Perfectionist) wing tend to be modest, orderly, and endearing. They also tend to be critical, and are more likely to neglect themselves and their own needs.

The Subtypes

Each of the nine Types describes a different set of distorted beliefs about reality that the person has (also termed "cognitive distortions") -- a mindset, a way of looking at the world and of noticing particular things and ignoring others. The nine Types are nine ways of thinking about the world. In addition to Type, however, we tend to focus our energy on one of three drives that influence our actions. As we go through life, each of us concerns ourselves with three areas – (1) basic survival needs such as food, money, home, health; (2) relationships and interaction with groups; and (3) intimacy and bonding with significant others. Although all are a necessary part of our lives, once basic needs are taken care of, many put too much emotional energy into one of these three areas:

- The *self-preservation subtype* focuses on home, family, possessions, and his or her health and comfort. More concerned with their own well being than with what others are doing, they are more likely to be introverts than the other subtypes.
- The *social subtype* pays attention to what other people are doing and enjoy being with other people. They tend to be the most judgmental of the three subtypes, with definite opinions about how other people should behave and are also the most concerned among the three subtypes with social issues.
- The *sexual* or *one-to-one* subtype is most concerned with intimate relationships and attracting and holding onto a significant other. Of the three subtypes, they are most likely to be extroverted, but also most likely to be interested in appearance.

These three subtypes (also called *instinctual drive*) strongly influence the way each of us expresses the characteristics of our specific personality Type. We focus on our subtype issues through the filter of our enneagram Type. That is, we use our basic viewpoint most pointedly in the area of our subtype.

Below is a summary of how the subtypes influence the expression of each Type. The names of the 27 subtypes come from Helen Palmer's work, *The Enneagram*. Mario Sikora, in an article in *The Enneagram Monthly* (October 2005, p. 11) suggested particular associations between subtypes and wings, which are listed below as well.

The Perfectionist (Type One)

Self-Preservation (Worry or Anxiety) Ones: They are anxious about basic survival needs – food, health, money, and security. They worry about having a secure future. Self-Preservation Ones more often have a Nine (Mediator) than a Two (Giver) wing.

Social (Inadaptable) Ones: They tend to have rigid opinions of "right and wrong" in social groups. For example, anger might be expressed through religious fervor, political outrage, or environmental advocacy. Social Ones more often have a Two (Giver) than a Nine (Mediator) wing.

Sexual or One-to-One (Jealousy) Ones: Their anger is directed at those who take what isn't deserved. They feel intensive possessiveness and red-hot anger when their relationship desires are thwarted.

The Giver (Type Two)

Self-preservation (Privilege/Me First) Twos: They get a sense of pride in feeling they are more important to others than to themselves. They get to know people who can place them in positions where they feel privileged and do not have to obey the usual rules. Self-preservation Twos more often have a One (Perfectionist) than a Three (Achiever) wing. They are more focused on their own needs than are the other subtypes and may resemble Fours.

Social (Ambition) Twos: They like to be "the power behind the throne," getting involved with people who have influence and status. These Twos get their needs met through knowing the right people. Social Twos more often have a Three (Achiever) than a One Perfectionist) wing.

Sexual or One-to-One (Seduction/Aggression) Twos: Pride for these Twos comes from being desirable and having others seek them out. They seduce others in various ways or aggressively seek attention from others.

The Achiever (Type Three)

Self-preservation (Security) Threes: They use their achievement skills to maximize their income and climb professional ladders. They are particularly concerned with productivity and independence.

Social (Prestige) Threes: They are particularly concerned with their status, position, titles, image, and with being recognized for their accomplishments.

They seek leadership roles in groups. Social Threes more often have a Two (Giver) than a Four (Romantic) wing.

Sexual or One-to-One (Masculine/Feminine Image) Threes: They tend to reinvent themselves to be attractive to a partner. Their image is tailored to be sexually appealing to a partner, whether in personal life or business. Sexual Threes more often have a Four than a Two wing.

The Romantic (Type Four)
Self-preservation (Reckless/Dauntless) Fours: They are so focused on obtaining a certain lifestyle that they will take chances that actually threaten their basic needs. Once the dream is obtained, they tend to discount and destroy it so that it will again seem desirable. Self-Preservation Fours more often have a Three (Achiever) than a Five (Observer) wing.

Social (Shame) Fours: Constantly comparing themselves to others, they are sure to come up short. They feel a lot of shame about being defective and therefore believe they are sure to be rejected.

Sexual or One-to-One (Competition) Fours: Focusing on what is missing in life, these Fours try to reduce their envy by exposing the faults of the other person. They are very competitive. In their personal relationships, they work hard to attract and seduce the other, only to reject him/her first, before the other rejects them. Sexual Fours more often have a Five (Observer) than a Three (Achiever) wing.

The Observer (Type Five)
Self-preservation (Castle) Fives: Their focus is on being independent by acquiring all the resources they need and by needing as little as possible. They are extremely protective of their personal space and private time.

Social (Totem) Fives: These Fives gravitate toward groups that have a serious purpose, such as math or computer departments, music groups and concerts, global warming study groups, and chess clubs. They like to expand their learning in group contexts. Social Fives more often have a Six (Detective) than a Four (Romantic) wing.

Sexual or One-to-One (Confidence) Fives: Like other Sexual subtypes, Fives focus on their intimate relationships, but they may experience the emotions most when they are alone. They will preserve a love through distance and death, without it fading away. Sexual Fives more often have a Four than a Six wing.

The Detective (Type Six)

Self-preservation (Warmth or Affection) Sixes: These Detectives achieve their sense of safety and security with others by being warm and affectionate. Self-preservation Sixes more often have a Five (Observer) than a Seven (Adventurer) wing.

Social (Duty) Sixes: To achieve security these Sixes faithfully and loyally participate in groups, drawing strength from the group's authority. They are highly motivated by sense of duty to a group or a cause rather than for personal gain. They more often have a Seven than a Five wing.

Sexual or One-to-One (Strength and Beauty) Sixes: These Sixes, more likely to be Counterphobic than Phobic, attain safety through their own strength, although they may be more bark than bite. They may combine charm and aggressiveness to attain their goals. According to Dr. David Daniels, Sexual Sixes can look like Type Four (Romantic) or Eight (Leader).

The Adventurer (Type Seven)

Self-preservation (Like-minded) Sevens: These Sevens surround themselves with a family group, whether traditional or chosen, with whom they share enjoyable activities. Self-Preservation Sevens more often have a Six (Detective) than an Eight (Leader) wing.

Social (Sacrifice) Sevens: Social Sevens enjoy pursuing their many activities in the company of other like-minded people. They prefer equality and a minimum of rules in groups rather than hierarchy and rigidity. Social Sevens are willing to sacrifice immediate pleasure in order to achieve some future goal.

Sexual or One-to-One (Fascination) Sevens: Focusing their desire for variety on intimate relationships, they are genuinely interested in other people (for a while) and are very likable and charming. Initially idealizing a romantic partner, they may soon lose interest and find someone else. They are limited by only one relationship and have a great deal of difficulty with commitment. Sexual Sevens more often have an Eight than a Six wing.

The Leader (Type Eight)

Self-preservation (Satisfactory survival) Eights: Self-preservation Eights try to make sure they have more than enough of their creature comforts, including food and beverages. Their motto is "Be prepared." They want to feel in control of their environment and those in it. They are more likely than not to have a Nine (Mediator) wing than a Seven (Adventurer) wing.

Social (Friendship) Eights: Social Eights are very protective out of solidarity and friendship against apparent injustice. They become intensely involved in their friendships as well as in worthy projects. They have an "us against them" mentality and are willing to become violent in the defense of their group.

Sexual or One-to-One (Possession/Surrender) Eights: Sexual Eights want to take charge of their intimate partner, protecting him or her, making decisions, and being in control. More often they have a Seven (Adventurer) wing than a Nine (Mediator) wing

The Mediator (Type Nine)

Self-preservation (appetite) Nines: Self-preservation Nines focus on food, TV, travel, collecting – and similar sources of gratification that substitute for getting their real needs met. They settle for appeasing these appetites and not having to act. These Nines more often have a One (Perfectionist) wing than an Eight (Leader) wing.

Social (Participation) Nines: Social Nines like to participate in organized groups, where they can benefit from the group's momentum and join in group activities without having to expend a lot of energy.

Sexual or One-to-One (Union) Nines: Sexual Nines desire to merge completely with another person and take on that person's life. The other person's needs become much more important than the Nine's. These Nines more often have an Eight wing than a One wing.

As you have seen, the enneagram personality system is much more complex than just having nine types. Two persons of the same basic Type (such as Giver or Observer) may have elements of one or the two Types that are adjacent to them on the enneagram diagram (i.e., their wing), and additionally will focus their energy primarily either on their basic needs, their social grouping, or on a primary relationship (i.e. their subtype). There is yet another way in which people may differ. Take another look at the enneagram diagram (on page 11) and you'll see that there is a pattern of lines that connect specific points. Each Type or point is connected to two others; these are called that type's "connecting points".

Research has shown that when people are stressed out, they tend to take on some aspects of another Type – called that person's "stress point," whereas when they are relaxed and doing very well, they will take on some aspects of a different connecting point, called that personality Type's "security point." For example, the Perfectionist (One) has connecting points at Seven and Four, as you can see on the enneagram diagram. When feeling relaxed and good, the One is likely to take on some of the positive aspects of the Adventurer (Seven), becoming less critical and more self-accepting, noticing the good in a situation rather than immediately focusing on what needs to be fixed, and planning more activities simply for enjoyment. On the other hand, a Perfectionist who is stressed out is likely to take on some of the negative characteristics of the Romantic (Four), and turn her anger inward and becomes depressed, or longs for what she doesn't have and feels hopeless about ever getting it.

If you would like to learn more about the connecting points of your Type, we would recommend the book *The Enneagram Made Easy* by Renee Baron and Elizabeth Wagele. This book is deceptively easy to understand, but in fact lives up to its name and provides a thorough and very accessible guide to the nine enneagram Types. Alternatively, you can proceed to the next chapter – the beginning of the meat of this book, how each personality Type plays out in relationship.

CHAPTER FOUR

The Perfectionist (One) In Relationship

Probably my best feature in relationship is that you can trust me to be responsible, to be honest, and hardworking. I have high standards and it is important to me that my partner and I work toward improving ourselves and the relationship. At times I put my partner on a pedestal and I can be tremendously loyal to him, helping him overcome obstacles as long as he is committed to working on them. Some people say that I can be too serious at times and that I need to lighten up a little - that I need to decide whether I want to be right or to be happy. Probably my worst feature in relationship is my black and white thinking and my tendency to focus on what is wrong and to become critical if I feel like others are being irresponsible or getting away with something.

You may recognize the Perfectionist characteristics of the authors of the quotations below:

The time is always right to do what is right.
-- Martin Luther King

VIRGO (Aug 23- Sept 22): "Water that is too pure has no fish," wrote Zen teacher Ts'ai Ken T'an. Keep that advice close to your heart in the coming days, Virgo. Your clean, clear ideas will become sterile unless you mix in some quirky, unruly emotions. Your spiritual intentions may become awkwardly rigid unless you loosen up with a bit of

healthy blasphemy. So please, don't push for utter perfection. Be careful not to burn away every last flaw or banish every last messy doubt. In order to know the truth, you'll have to consort with B.S.
-- Newspaper astrology advice

Everything belongs.
-- Richard Rohr

Your tombstone will not only say, "I was right!"...but will also say, "You were wrong!"
--Husband of a One wife

Every time I've done something that doesn't feel right, it's ended up not being right.
-- Mario Cuomo

Perfectionists tend to be conscientious, discerning, ethical, fair, loyal, focused, have an intense sense of right and wrong, have personal integrity, honest, idealistic, inspiring, loyal, orderly, organized, productive, reliable, self-disciplined, wise. When a Perfectionist gets into a relationship, the characteristics summarized in Chapters Two and Three will be expressed in predictable ways that will both enhance and cause difficulties in the couple's interactions.

Characteristics of Perfectionists

Perfectionism
Ones want to "do it right," meaning the job not only gets done, but it gets done with a striving for perfection. All details are attended to, and (hopefully) nothing is forgotten. In Jennifer's career as an internal medicine physician, attention to detail is definitely a desirable trait: Remembering to phone a patient as promised is much appreciated by the patient; filing an abnormal lab result or CT scan in a patient's chart without taking action on it can lead to serious adverse consequences. Perfectionists are often the anchor, the solid underpinning in a relationship where they balance out a marriage to a partner who is a head-in-the-clouds dreamer, or a wandering adventurer, or some other less detail-oriented or less grounded partner.

In their quest for perfection, however, Ones tend to fall prey to perfectionism, which is excessive zeal to do it right. Of course, each Perfectionist has her own unique mental template that holds the idea of what is right and wrong to her. This template is then "cast" out into world and determines what the One will judge as good or bad, right or wrong.

Ones can be not only very responsible in the relationship, but also too serious. A partner of a One complained, "You are too detailed and serious. You always have to do everything to the nth degree – 98% is not good enough."

For the One, high expectations are not reserved only for oneself, but also for others. A Perfectionist reported that what kept her from effective problem-solving in her relationship was, "My expectations that other people should behave according to my standards and should be willing to change their behavior." Another Perfectionist reported that the challenges she brought to her relationship were, "Wanting a perfect marriage, expecting fairness, always!" High standards indeed! Julianne, a 49-year old Perfectionist, reported,

A big challenge for me in my relationship is wanting everything to be perfect and clean. This means I sometimes get frustrated that my husband isn't the neat freak that I am. Consequently, I wind up doing more of the housework and I can get resentful about this. Usually what happens is that we go along this way for some time until I blow up about carrying an unfair share of the load. Then he agrees to help more and he does for a while. Eventually this wears off and we are back to me doing most of the work unless I just go on strike and refuse to do it!

Julianne describes a common theme for Ones. Perfectionists feel they have to do all of the work while others are resting or even goofing off. The One's serious work ethics in the relationship can continue for a long time, initially reinforcing the One's goodness and their responsible nature while illuminating how irresponsible others can be. Resentments will usually simmer under surface, finally reaching a boiling point that will cause the One to explode. Julianne found a way to right the wrongs at least for a while with her husband. But because his values differ from hers, soon she is likely to feel again that she has to carry more than her share of the load.

Perfection paralysis

In other relationships the One's need to do it right is expressed in a form of "perfection paralysis" rather than a build-up of frustration. Jessica, a One married to another Perfectionist, describes a different form of perfectionism in their relationship:

When our daughter started piano lessons, we decided to buy a piano. My husband Brian set out to research pianos, in order to buy the best one –the best sound, whose wood would be least likely to be affected by seasonal temperature and humidity changes, etc. etc. He read everything he could find about piano construction, and made a personal visit to piano stores to inspect every brand. Naturally he was able to do this only on weekends, since he worked long hours at his job. By the time he was finally satisfied and chose a particular piano, 6 months had passed without our having a piano at home for our daughter to practice on. This kind of delayed decision-making was a recurrent problem in our marriage.

In the situation above, you can hear a tremendous need for the One to find the perfect piano. Perfectionists feel not only a duty and responsibility to get it perfect, but also a kind of ultimate satisfaction they strive for. Unfortunately, this seeking for perfection can be overwhelming, easily leading to perfection paralysis. If you think about it, seeking perfection can be an endless process. Trying to build the perfect house can cause it remain in the blueprint stage forever, or trying to find the perfect partner can cause us to be single for a very long time. When perfectionism paralysis sets in it is sometimes helpful for the One to do a reality check to see if what is happening is simply "good enough" for what is being called for. Striving for excellence, not perfection, is also important for Ones to remember.

Strong work ethic

Ones tend to be organized, orderly people with good follow-through and a strong commitment to finishing what they started. This translates into loyalty and commitment to the relationship, and a willingness to hang in there during bad times. But these same qualities can also be expressed as workaholism, which can also adversely affect the relationship. Sylvia, a 50-year old Perfectionist, related:

I was a severely work-addicted person for most of my life. I was into my "reform" work at the county hospital. I managed to do some really good things, yet it was very harmful to myself and my relationship. . . All I could think about was work and I wasn't present for my husband.

Ones' strong work ethic makes it difficult for them to relax and enjoy themselves. They believe they have to first finish the task before having fun. Sylvia described her type-related challenges as, "Time crunches due to too many projects to complete to a level that satisfies my very high standards."

As you can see, one of the gifts of the One, the strong work ethic, is also one of their biggest challenges as well. Planned vacations, regular getaways, and maintaining a sense of humor are necessities for Ones and their partners.

A strong inner sense of right and wrong

Because of their strong inner sense of right and wrong, healthy Ones are ethical people committed to justice, to bettering the world, and to doing things the right way rather than the expedient way. But the same qualities can also cause them to have high – sometimes unrealistic – expectations of themselves and others, and to be ready to criticize and correct others. The partner of a Perfectionist wrote that if her husband were to put a slogan on his T-shirt that describes his basic belief about relationships, he would write, "Do it my way and we'll get along just fine." Enneagram authors Baron and Wagele echoed this in their delightful book *Are You My Type, Am I Yours?* by using the humorous quote, "Let my conscience be your guide" to describe how strong this particular voice is for the One.

Disagreements can degenerate from problem-solving efforts into attempts by the One to prove that he or she is right and the partner is wrong. A 69-year old Self-Preservation One recognized that one of her biggest challenges was "needing things to be done a certain way – my way." She eventually realized that a much better personal slogan was, "I can only change myself and I don't have all the answers." Another Perfectionist, who struggled with this same issue, shared that she and her husband have a baseball cap that they take turns wearing while working on projects together. The cap designates who is the "boss" or who is taking the lead during a particular project.

The Perfectionist's right-and-wrong, black-and-white approach can result in a tendency to be rigid rather than flexible. This can be a source of conflict if the partner values spontaneity and last-minute planning. Ones' strong sense of right and wrong can also lead them to be impatient in problem-solving, since they may believe they know exactly what the solution is, and want to get right to it.

Self-improvement, partner-improvement, and criticism

In their quest for perfection, Ones are very motivated to improve themselves, others, and the relationship. But just because they are called

Perfectionists, it does not mean they think they are perfect. Quite the opposite. It simply means that they are constantly striving to improve themselves. Ones have a very strong inner critic that bombards them with such statements as, "You must…", or "You should…", or "You ought to…". Since they already work hard to better themselves and because they already have a strong inner critic, it's very difficult for them to hear criticisms from others. A criticism may feel like a stab in the heart. They may think, "I know I'm deficient! I'm already working on myself as hard as I can! I don't need to hear from you a confirmation that I'm imperfect." One Perfectionist wrote, "Being very sensitive and interpreting silence as blame causes some problems, which we work through much more easily as time goes by." This is a simple sentence, yet it speaks volumes to the sensitivity of Ones, especially when silence itself can be taken as personal criticism and blame.

As for improving others, it is important to remember that Ones truly want to help others, especially those they love. They tend to assume that others are as interested in self-improvement as they are, so they consider it a caring gesture to help the partner become a better person. As one Perfectionist put it, "Criticism is kindness, it means you care." Unfortunately, all too often the partner perceives this kind of "caring" as criticism and as a statement that "you're not good enough." Partners of Ones often complain that the One is too critical of self and others.

Perfectionism means that Ones not only expect too much of themselves, but also of others. Some Ones are constantly correcting their partner, pointing out little and big things the partner has done wrong and insisting it be corrected. This can result in an ongoing litany of nitpicking, which can erode the partner's good feelings and create resentments. Writing about the challenges she brought to her marriage, a 46-year old Perfectionist defined nitpicking as "really driving to fix myself and everybody else. Non-acceptance of the world as it is and people as they are." Another One wrote that a challenge she brought to her marriage was "my tendency to criticize and get uptight about how things are done."

When a Perfectionist finds that her relationship is having difficulties, she may become increasingly fixated in her personality "passion." A woman explained, "I gradually became more judgmental and less empathetic of him, and began criticizing him, which he found hard to tolerate." Ones who have fallen into nitpicking/criticizing behaviors need to explore their anger and assess their own wants and needs that are most likely not being met. They also need to remember to separate behavior from personhood. It is okay to ask for a behavior change from your partner, but it is not okay to attack another's core being.

Responsibility, dependability, and respect

Ones tend to be responsible and dependable people. They take promises and commitments very seriously, and work hard at keeping them. They expect the same of others, and will feel deeply disappointed and disrespected if others break the promises that they made to them. Being treated with respect is crucially important to Perfectionists. "My definition of love has to include respect," one Perfectionist related. "I don't see how you can love someone without respecting them." When someone else behaves irresponsibly, blows off a commitment, and doesn't follow through, Ones tend to interpret this as lack of respect. When at least one member of a couple is a Perfectionist, therapists often tell the pair that they may not necessarily have "fallen out of love" with one another during their difficulties, but they may have "fallen out of respect". They need work toward re-instilling respect in the relationship as well as toward each other.

Black-and-white thinking

Perfectionists are not wishy-washy people. Unlike Mediators (Type Nine), who can see the subtleties of any issue, Ones have definite opinions about the right way to do something, and this translates into black-and-white thinking. One mistake or negative characteristic in their partner or one serious disagreement or argument can make them reconsider whether the relationship is right or not. It's hard for them to love someone and be angry at the same time. If they feel bad about their partner, they tend to jump to the conclusion that they are in the wrong relationship – or else may feel guilty about feeling unhappy. Some Perfectionists believe that a good relationship should have only positive interactions. An argument may feel like the end of the relationship, so they may stifle their anger for as long as possible.

A positive side of being so highly principled is that it can lead to setting firm boundaries and limits with others. The negative side is that Ones have to be careful that they don't fall into an "off with his head" reaction over a minor mistake or failing.

Anger and resentment

Whether he or she is aware of it or not, anger is one of the primary issues of the Perfectionist. Simply put, the One is angry about all the wrong things in the world and resentful about how the responsibility of correcting those wrongs somehow fell on their shoulders while others seem to be getting away scot-free. Some Ones see their anger as being wrong in and of itself and so attempt to suppress it and view themselves as good people who never get angry. They may have a very hard time openly disagreeing with their partner. What they tend to do instead of overt anger is righteous indignation, judgmental put-downs, and developing resentments. Another kind of Perfectionist, whose personal template of right and wrong does not include that anger is wrong, may have no problem expressing anger when he believes he has a good reason or a just cause, and in such cases can appear more fiery and have a difficult time hearing the other person's position.

One Perfectionist related, "I have a tendency to repress anger and build resentment until it suddenly explodes." Another said, "I repress my own anger and my own desires in favor of what's 'best' and 'correct.'"

Ones at stress and at security

According to enneagram theory, Perfectionists have connections to two other types on the enneagram diagram – The Romantic (Four) and the Adventurer (Seven). When Perfectionists feel secure, for example on vacation, they can experience the positive traits of the Seven – adventurousness, playfulness, and relaxation. They will let go of trying to make things perfect, and they are more flexible about things. This is certainly true for Jennifer (one of the authors), a One. When she is on vacation, she doesn't even think about her work. She enjoys every minute of her "down time." Of course, at times Jennifer can be very One-like in her activities on vacation, trying to fit a lot of sightseeing or other fun activities into the day, but at other times she will be happy lying on the beach all day and watching the waves come in.

When Ones are stressed out, they will experience some of the negative attributes of the Four – feelings of depression and a sense of hopelessness about the likelihood that they or other people can ever measure up to their high expectations.

How Ones help their relationship thrive

Have you ever asked your spouse or partner what he or she believes are the gifts they brought to your relationship? We asked this in our survey we and here are some responses by Ones:

- Fairness, unconditional love
- I keep my promises

- I provided a solid grounding to our relationship as well as the financial support. I encouraged him to explore new career options when he tired of the old.
- As a perfectionist, I've always worked to improve the relationship – I want "more" and "better." He appreciates my integrity, ethics, and energy to get things done and carry out goals.
- Being practical and organized is a huge help next to his vagueness.
- Honesty, consistency. My husband knew he could always count on me.

Notice that the gifts Ones believe they bring to the relationship consist of their fairness, integrity, ability to keep promises, being organized and practical, and trying to improve themselves and the relationship. Partners of Perfectionists whose "want list" is heavy on romance may feel unappreciated. They need to recognize the ways in which Ones tend to express their love. This is true of all relationships; if we are going to be with someone, we need to respect and accept the unique gifts that our partner brings to the relationship.

Couples' expert John Gottman points out that one way a relationship gets off track is when partners can no longer see how their partner's positive characteristics and behaviors are contributing to the relationship. Especially during times of difficulty it may be a good idea to ask yourself what your partner has given to you and then to make a list of your partner's positive characteristics so as to have more realistic and balanced picture of him or her as you set about to work on things in the relationship.

How perfectionists feel about other personality types in relationship

In our survey, we asked, Which Type (including your own) do you feel most compatible with? Which types are likely to be most problematic for you? Not surprisingly, the responses were often strongly influenced by particular people with whom the responder had had either a positive or negative relationship – spouse, ex-spouses, parents, and friends. People also expressed familiarity with those types that represent a wing, a connecting point, or are from the same center as themselves.

Some responders mentioned the same Type in both the compatible and problematic categories. We might be both drawn and repelled by people who have the same but differing levels of health. For instance, we may really like being around a healthy Giver (Two) but detest being around an unhealthy person of the same Type. The three most commonly mentioned Types with which Ones feel most compatible with in relationship are the Giver (Two), Adventurer (Seven), and Mediator (Nine). Some of the reasons were:

The Giver: "I like their personality, humor, and depth of love." "They are easy to be with and you can feel the caring." "I enjoy the caring, helping aspect, and I connect because I have a Two wing." "Great friends, generous, giving, tuned in to other people. Because I have a Two wing, I share values with Twos and understand where they're coming from." "Warm, giving, human. My wing." "They want to help others." "So loving usually. It's easy to express affection to them."

The Two is a wing of the One, which could give a feeling of familiarity. Also if the Two has a One wing the two types would have an almost mirroring experience. Because Perfectionists can be so hard on themselves they may gravitate toward the Givers' love and compassion much like gravitating toward a warm fire on a cold night. The Two may also turn the One onto his or her feelings or help them access the heart space in general.

The Adventurer: "I want to have fun – and this can work unless the Seven is too superficial, as that will turn me off very quickly." "They're optimistic." "They balance me, and lighten me up." "They add and bring joy, zest, and love of play." "They make me play, and draw me out of myself." "Fun-loving, joyful, varied life." "I get to play without feeling awkward or guilty." "Stimulating, creative, responsive to my Seven connecting point. Someone to have fun with."

As you can see, Ones like how Sevens bring out the playful child inside of them. Sevens like to have fun and can teach the One how to play. Ones can also teach the Seven about discipline and structure – something the Seven can usually use help with.

The Mediator: "Nines are a wing of mine. I also want everyone to get along." "Peaceful." "Tolerant." "Most easy-going, least maintenance required." "They can be very low-ego, wonderful friends, easy to get along with, always ready to listen, able to consider all sides of every issue, loyal, not demanding, not into overt anger. Among my friends are many Nines." "They seem to get along with everyone, and they help me be more diplomatic and accepting." "Not critical of me, relaxed. This helps me to relax and enjoy myself." "They want to make peace." "I like the placidity, acceptance, equanimity." "They don't judge me, and make me feel valuable."

Nines can embody the serenity that the Ones are ultimately striving for through all the correcting and perfecting that they do. Mediators can make the Perfectionist feel loved for whom they are and not for what they do. For Ones, hanging out with Nines can feel like a refreshing break from both the inner and outer critic.

As we stated earlier, each of the most "compatible" Types chosen by Ones were those with whom the Perfectionist has some connection on the Enneagram diagram, and therefore some understanding of the Type: Two and Nine are the two wings of Type One, and Seven is the security point, which constitutes the direction of growth that Ones need to work on.

In answer to the question, "What Types do you feel you struggle the most with in relationships?" Perfectionists most commonly selected the Boss (Eight), the Achiever (Three), and the Romantic (Four), with the Adventurer (Seven) close behind. The reasons included:

The Leader: "They can be scary." "My way or else." "Too pushy, unempathetic." "Too much over/against energy." " I feel very uncomfortable with their overt anger, their impulsivity, their difficulty expressing feelings (other than anger), and their having to be in charge and in control. Their tendency to black-and-white thinking and to attacking disproportionately to the issue makes me want to run the other way. More true of an Eight with a Seven wing than an Eight with a Nine wing." "My Dad's an Eight and they can really punch my buttons when they have to be the boss and claim to always know what's right." "Bossy, overprotective, they feel threatened by the world."

For the most part, Ones want things to be nice and appropriate. Eights can make Ones feel uncomfortable with their bending and breaking the rules, especially when politeness and etiquette counts. Anger can also be a challenge for Ones, whereas Eights can't understand what all the fuss is about.

The Achiever: " Too busy." "Scarcity of emotional authenticity." "Unless they're Old Souls, I don't really trust them to do anything that doesn't benefit them." "Fake front, lack of integrity, out of touch with inner self." "No way to get to the real person." "It's all about them (image and achievement)."

While both Ones and Threes can be high achievers they will likely differ in how to get to the goal. Threes are usually not opposed to taking shortcuts whereas Ones believe that you have to earn it even if it means taking the long way around. When it comes to respect and integrity, they may seem to come from two different cultures with differing values.

The Romantic: "I'm never quite good enough for them." "They require lots of attention and seem so self-absorbed that I get impatient with having to deal with them." "They drive me nuts with their whining and sighing and hand-wringing. I just want to slap them and say 'Buck up'' and quit being a victim!'" "It's always about them – narcissism." "So temperamental. I see them as self-centered and overly dramatic, narcissistic."

Type Four is the stress point for Ones. A reason that Perfectionists have such a strong reaction to Romantics is that they can trigger the One's shadow side, the side Ones would prefer not to own. Some of the characteristics of Fours go against the grain of the Ones' focus on always being in control of their feelings and their responsibility to the world. The Perfectionist's spirit and will is not easily broken but when it is, the irony is that they can take on a Fourish melancholic, depressive aspect, and a victim-like loss of hope in their efforts to get things right.

The Adventurer: "I don't know who they are – too much talk, but not about feeling." "Not grounded." "It's hard to trust their staying power, so I can't depend on them." "A Seven, especially with a Sexual subtype, can have very different values from mine – they can be impulsive, lack follow-through, be unwilling to discuss painful issues, have difficulty with commitment to one partner, and forget tomorrow what they agreed to yesterday (because they feel differently by then). But they are great fun, and bring out the fun and playful Seven part of me." "As a sexual subtype I want them to care about me, but the Seven's narcissism is sometimes the stronger force." "Superficial, but they have lots of friends and great social lives."

Perfectionists identified Adventurers as both compatible and challenging as relationship partners. Ones can feel that someone needs to teach those Sevens the rules. Life is serious and not to be played with! Their relationship resembles that between the fictional Peter Pan and Wendy: Wendy wants Peter to be more grounded and grow up and Peter wants Wendy to be less earthbound and to let go and fly.

Perfectionists and listening

At times, it seems as if listening is a lost art in our society. Poor communication and feeling unheard is a common complaint among many couples. Women in particular tend to complain that men won't just listen and be supportive, but instead immediately jump to solutions and problem solving. This isn't just a gender issue, however. Certain personality Types may have more difficulty with listening than others. The Perfectionist is one of these. One

Perfectionist gave fellow Ones this advice, "Listen attentively. Be open, willing to learn. Don't assume you know everything." The minute the Ones feel they have a basic grasp of the issue, they may believe they don't have to listen any further -- they already have an idea of what to do about it and how to solve it. They are certain they are on the right path, and they are not interested in any more input.

If the Perfectionist gives his partner advice to which instead of immediately agreeing, she replies, "Yes, but," the Perfectionist might get upset and say, "I'm putting all this effort into being responsible and helping you solve this problem and you're not even grateful," and then proceed to criticize the partner. Unless both parties are aware of this kind of interaction, the One's partner could easily fall into criticizing him back. If taken to counseling, the issue may be presented as a problem with criticism in the relationship when the actual problem is in the listening and communication arena. Effective listening involves empathy and the ability to stay in the present moment with no agenda or no preparing for what you are going to say back. We will say more about this at the end of this chapter, in the exercises for Perfectionists.

Advice Perfectionists give other Perfectionists in relationship

Perfectionists are usually very interested in self-improvement. Although they tend to be very sensitive to criticism from others, they often are aware of what they need to change in order to better their relationships, especially as they get older. A 63 –year-old retired teacher, a Self-Preservation One, wrote the following detailed lesson for a young Perfectionist to follow:

- *Do enough enneagram work to understand that your Type and your instinctual habits can be consciously changed.*
- *Do enneagram workshops with your partner so that you can see their behavior as __different__ rather than as __wrong__. "Differences are not disasters."*
- *Practice letting go of faults and failings, yours and theirs.*
- *Don't dwell on the negatives, and recognize the constant inner critic for what it is – your perception that may reflect only your view or only a partial view of yourself or the world.*
- *See yourself and your partner as not perfect but as flawed, and honor and accept the shadow side of who you/they are. Share as much of what you see in yourself as "ugly," "sinful," "shameful," "bad," "wrong," with your partner, thus lessening its power over you and the destructive role it may play in the relationship.*

The responder's comments touch on many of the challenges that a One faces in relationship. Perfectionists can have tremendous compassion for those who they think are experiencing some form of injustice. But in their most intimate relationships, Ones can struggle with the differences their loved ones may have. Since partners can be seen as almost extensions of themselves, differences can feel negative or wrong. The responder recommends monitoring the inner critic, open communication, and striving for acceptance of self and others.

Another responder had specific comments with regard to the One's struggle with the inner critic and the idea of acceptance and letting things go:

Suspend conclusions about the other person – try not to judge, pre-judge, or allow your mind to get into a critical mode. Be discerning, but let the less-important stuff be just as it is. If you decide that it's too much to bear, say so. If it won't change, and you really don't like it, are you willing to let the relationship go? Do that, or be more willing to let him/her be who they are.

Another responder simply summed it up this way, "There are nine ways to look at the world, not just the One's way." No matter what type we are, we all believe we have a corner market on the truth. We feel we know the right way to live life and how to be in relationship. Type Ones most likely voice this more loudly because of their tendency to see things as right and wrong. Enneagram teacher Richard Rohr, a Perfectionist himself, says in his lectures that each of the nine types has only one-ninth of the truth but each think they have the whole truth.

Perfectionists also gave advice to younger Ones about how to relax a little in their lives:

Play, especially with your partner. Move to the Seven [Adventurer] space, build sand castles, take trips, get out of the house/work setting on a regular basis, leave the kids with a babysitter and go someplace for a weekend. You need to get away from the lists, the endless shoulds and have to's. Go there with no agenda except play, relax and enjoy each other – easier to do in nature where there are no rights and wrongs.

This is wonderful advice for how to learn to relax and enjoy the moment – it is also important for Perfectionists to remember that you don't have to have everything done before you can enjoy being together with your partner.

Partners of Perfectionists describe their mates as almost totally different people when they go on vacation. They seem to be able to go to type Seven and let their hair down as well as let go of all of the responsibilities which includes the have-to-do lists as well as all of the other musts, shoulds, and ought to's in their everyday life. Ones believe in work before pleasure, and the problem is that work seems to be never ending for them. Ones need to find a way to be able to go on "vacation" in their everyday lives through such things as meditation, yoga, massage and/or other practices that will calm the inner critic. Another Perfectionist summed it all up this way:

Realize it's more important to be happy than right. Recognize that most people don't __want__ the benefit of your insights about how they can improve themselves. Pick your battles – let go of the need to have the little things just so. Spend time at your Seven point – have fun with your partner, laugh, and do enjoyable things together.

What partners of Perfectionists need to know
- You can expect Ones to keep their promises and accept responsibility without really expecting anything in return. Ones say, "You do the right thing because it is just what you are supposed to do.
- Even though Ones are seen as the "critic," be aware of how sensitive they are to criticism. Also recognize living with a Perfectionist is somewhat like living with two people – the person and the critic.
- You can be helpful by assuring Ones that they do not have to be perfect and by giving them things that they would normally deprive themselves of because of their ascetic nature.
- Ones in relationship are sensitive about details. They appreciate partners who are on time and those who evince proper etiquette, responsibility, dependability, and respect.
- Ones want a partner who works on himself or herself, sets self-improvement goals, and is modest about accomplishments. You need to realize that the One's criticism can be a kind of compliment, a proof of caring.
- It is helpful to the One if you admit when you made an error, as this prevents resentments from building in the One.
- Ones actually have a good sense of humor, but it may be helpful if you can bring out the playful side in them. It is also beneficial if you can help alleviate their guilt by giving them permission to allow pleasure in the partnership.

The final section of this chapter consists of a series of exercises for the Perfectionist.

Exercises for the Perfectionist (One) and Your Partner

The following exercises are designed to take a look at some of the primary characteristics of the Perfectionist in relationship:

Would you rather be right or would you rather be happy?

Ones are naturally predisposed to judge and compare so as to determine what is right and wrong in a situation. In a positive light, this can give the Perfectionist a conscience with a strong sense of morality. Believe it or not, when it comes to being right or being happy, some diehard Ones will choose to be right. This actually makes sense considering that the Perfectionist's focus is on correcting and perfecting the world – it is not necessarily about finding happiness. Some Ones may relate more to, **"Would you rather be right or would you rather be peaceful?"** Perfectionists can usually relate to striving for improvement and perfection in hopes of eventually reaching a level of peace and serenity in the world.

Ones need to realize that a right-or-wrong approach in relationship can result in a win/lose outcome or relay a message to the partner that says, "I'm okay, you're not okay." This dynamic does not foster a healthy sense of interdependence and limits the depth of intimacy that can be achieved in the relationship. The agenda and goal of all healthy, loving relationships involves the striving for a deep connection and closeness. Being right has more of a tendency to separate than achieve a level of connection and closeness. Creating an environment of peace and happiness in the relationship, where both partners are concerned about each other's satisfaction and happiness, can create a level of closeness rather than the separation that a right-and-wrong approach generates. The One's need to be right in a relationship will most likely push people away. The actual mantra for the One, would read more like: **"Would you rather be right? Or would you rather be close and connected to your partner??**

Please do the following exercises below to see where you and your partner stand with regard to the above situation:

- Discuss between the two of you what role being right or even being self-righteous played in your childhood.
- Share with your partner why it is so important to be right.

- Does your overall posture toward your partner reflect rigidity or flexibility?
- Does your manner, tone of voice, and attitude show respect and kindness toward your partner when you are discussing issues in the relationship?
- Discuss with your partner how the desire to be right plays a role in your relationship – especially during arguments and disagreements.
- Does the desire to be right interfere with the ability to be close and connected to each other?
- Discuss how the two of you can commit to being close and connected as opposed to being right.

Always be sincere – but never serious

Perfectionists take things too seriously and need to lighten up a little. One of the ways to diminish the seriousness in a relationship is to implement fun. There was once a teacher who spoke to this very issue by saying, "Always be sincere – but never serious." His statement depicts a great way to take some of the seriousness out of the situation and yet not undermine the sincerity in the relationship.

- Do you feel you are too serious at times?
- Discuss with your partner the role seriousness plays in your relationship. Can you switch seriousness with sincerity?
- Are you and your partner able to find ways to laugh and to have fun in the relationship?

Being responsible

Ones often take on more than their fair share of the responsibilities in the relationship. Perfectionists may feel they are being overly responsible but say little about it, allowing their anger and resentment to simmer under the surface. The payoff for the One is that it can allow them to feel like the "good" person while their partner is the irresponsible one. In time the Perfectionist may finally explode, possible even cut the partner out of their life because of their "irresponsibility."

- Discuss openly and honestly with each other the responsibilities in the relationship and how they are being divided up. Do both of you feel it is fair?
- The Type One partner should state openly any responsibilities you feel your partner could take on to balance things out.

- Finally, air out any stuffed anger and resentment about this particular issue.

Workaholism

The Perfectionist's tendency to take on too much responsibility can result in a form of workaholism in the outside world. Taking on too many projects and becoming repeatedly over-committed can cause difficulty in the relationship as well. Usually, either the partner of the One will feel lonely and forgotten or both will be like two ships passing in the night.

- Both partners should assess the "balance" in the relationship. Is there a healthy balance between work and relationship/family time? Draw a picture of a pie and label the various slices with the activities in which you are both involved. What is the largest slice? How large are the slices that represent relaxation, fun, and relationship time? Are you satisfied overall with what the slices represent and the size of the slices?
- How can you both work toward building into the relationship more down time and more together time?
- What are you both willing to commit to with regard to time spent together as well as time spent toward nurturing the relationship?

The Inner Critic

Perfectionists have a strong inner critic that can cause them to be very hard on themselves as well as others. The inner critic's original purpose was to improve and correct all of the wrongs in the world. When this particular "gift" of the One is working appropriately it can make order out of chaos and it can truly right a lot of the wrongs in the world. When it comes to the Perfectionist's partner, the One will see criticism as a form of kindness and caring toward them. Unfortunately, if the One's gift is overused and ego and control are guiding the inner critic, you will beat yourself up and appear excessively critical toward others, possibly pushing them away. Ones who have fallen into nitpicking/criticizing behaviors need to explore their own level of anger and resentment as well as their needs not being met.

- The inner critic usually speaks in a language consisting in commands like:
  "You must... "You should..." "You ought to..." How would you complete the above incomplete sentence stems? Try completing them toward yourself as well as toward your partner.

- Now change the above demands into "preferences." In other words, you would prefer that you or your partner would do something, but it is no longer a demand or command. Hopefully there is some freedom in this different approach.
- With as little blaming as possible, share with each other how you feel the relationship has been affected by the criticism of the One's inner critic. Share with each other how the inner critic has personally affected each of you. Share with each other how it has served as a block in your intimacy with one another.
- Brainstorm together a strategy for diminishing the inner critic and the criticism in the relationship.
- Commit to primarily using "I" statements as opposed to "You" statements in your communication with one another. Commit to reducing as much as you cam any demands, criticism, blaming, or labeling toward one another.
- Allow for differences between you and your partner. You do not have to be exactly alike. Also, your partner does not have to fit into a particular template in order to be okay or for you both to be compatible. Differences can be stimulating to a relationship; just because something is different does not make it wrong. Try to come up with the many ways that you two are different from one another.

Why listen?

Perfectionists can struggle with fully listening to their partners. Ones are problem solvers at heart and once they feel they have enough information they can set about to solving whatever needs to be solved. If the One is caught up in being right or knowing they are right, they may see no reason to continue listening; instead they will begin formulating their agenda and comeback to their partner. Effective listening involves a mindfulness approach. Good listeners need to be able to stay in the present moment without an agenda, without preparing a response, and without assuming we know what our partner is going to say next. During difficult or sensitive conversations it is important that we reflect back or paraphrase what we believe our partner has said. It is only after we have truly heard and understood our partner that it is appropriate for us to respond.

- As a One, how difficult is it for you to stay in the present moment, actively listening to your partner, without preparing a response especially when you feel the need to be right?

- Discuss with your partner how well he or she feels heard on a regular basis.
- Brainstorm ways to communicate with each other so that effective listening takes place in the relationship.
- Practice reflecting or paraphrasing what your partner tells you and then ask him or her, "Did I get that right?"
- Commit to checking in with one another from time to time to make sure you haven't fallen back into old patterns of ineffective listening.

Falling out of respect

Ones fall out of love with partners just like everyone else. But before they fall out of love they most likely fall out of respect for them. Respect is a key issue in the Perfectionist's relationship. Ones strive to treat their partner with respect and want a partner who will treat them with respect. To make sure respect is thriving in your relationship, ask and answer the following questions with one another:

- List the ways that you truly respect one another. Give concrete examples.
- Does each of you feel you are being treated with the utmost respect in your relationship?
- How do you feel your efforts or your being overly responsible are connected with your attempt to get respect in the relationship?
- Do you feel there is anything undermining the respect in your relationship?
- If the level of respect toward one another needs to be improved, what specific changes are necessary?

Remember, respect and love go hand-in-hand for Perfectionists. If you don't have respect in the relationship, the love you have for each will be slowly eroded. Please be careful to not fall out of respect for one another.

CHAPTER FIVE

The Giver (Type Two) In Relationship

Probably my best feature in relationship is my ability to take stunning care of others. I have great radar for knowing what others want and need, and I am good at nurturing others' potential. Some people say that I can be too intrusive, thinking that I know what's best for others, and that I need to spend more time identifying my own wants and needs instead of putting them on the back burner as I have a tendency to do. Probably my worst feature in relationship is my tendency to give and give and give and then be resentful and emotional if others don't appreciate what I've done for them.

You might recognize the Giver characteristics of the authors of the quotations below:

Make yourself necessary to somebody.
-- Ralph Waldo Emerson

I want you to want me more than you want anything else.
-- Unknown

We could say that genuine receiving can be an even more sacred act than giving – because it requires humbling ourselves and melting open, giving up control, and making ourselves fully available to love as the great power that infuses us with life.
-- John Welwood

Twos, usually called the Giver or the Helper, are among the most relationship focused of the nine Types. In order either to give or to help, another person is required to be in the picture. If the Two's helping is not done in a truly altruistic way with no strings attached, they can fall into operating from a place of pride, with a giving-to-get agenda. These qualities will both enhance and create difficulties in their relationships.

A simple but insightful story provides an extreme "Twoness" example. Kirk, a Giver, had very recently married a woman from Thailand. One Saturday morning when Kirk and SIrikit got up, she immediately jumped into the shower. It was a warm Arizona morning, and as he waited for her to join him for breakfast, Kirk went to open the patio door for some cool, fresh air. He then reconsidered after thinking that his new bride might possibly get chilled after her shower. As he waited for her, and because it was so warm, he found himself going to the patio door several times to open it, only to close it back again after imagining her getting chilled. When Sirikit got out of the shower, she immediately remarked to Kirk, "Don't you think it's hot in here?" Her Two husband replied, "Yes, I went to open the door several times, but I was afraid you would get chilled." On her way to open the patio door, and in her best English, Sirikit murmured under her breath, "Too much helping… too much helping."

When he tried to explain the enneagram to her, Kirk would describe himself as a Giver whose goal was to be helpful. Once again, in her broken English, she asked, "Does that mean you are full of help?"

Characteristics of Givers (Twos)

Focus on other people

The various personality Types are sometimes referred to as either primarily self- focused or other-focused. Givers, who early on come to believe that their own survival and well being depends on the approval of others, definitely fall into the "other focused" category. Their mantra sounds something like this, "If you want to be loved, be lovable," or as the quote above states, "Make yourself necessary to somebody." A 56-year-old Giver described herself in relationship as "Caring, other-directed, and involved." Twos seem to have feelers for other people's needs. They remember special occasions, the partner's favorite food, color, or restaurant and sometimes specialize in finding the perfect gift for every occasion.

The downside, of course, is that they tend to focus too much on their partner and neglect themselves. One 40-year-old Giver said that the biggest challenge he brought into his relationship was "not knowing what I really want." Another described his challenge as, "Initially not stating my needs. Not setting appropriate limits and boundaries. Focusing on my partner instead of myself." And another Giver reported, "I felt I couldn't, wouldn't, or didn't need to pay attention to my own needs," which seemed to be driven by the idea that "everyone had to, or would, like me." This can be frustrating to partners of Givers. A 68-year-old Two wrote that his wife's chief complaint to him was "You never tell me about your own feelings." The husband's message or plea to his 58-year-old Giver wife, "You need to think of yourself and not give so much time and energy to others. What you want, not what you think I want." In many ways his message to her sounded so simple, yet to the Giver it can sound like a Zen koan. A male Giver, no longer in the relationship, seems to sum up the Two's main agenda, "The relationship was too important to me. I found my value and worth in another's love of me. " This appears to coincide with the following passage taken from the I-Ching, a Chinese book of wisdom. It beautifully and painfully sums up the Two's basic approach to life and relationships.

> Here the source of a man's strength lies not in himself but in his relation to other people. No matter how close to them he may be, if his center of gravity depends on them, he is inevitably tossed to and fro between joy and sorrow. Rejoicing to high heaven, then sad unto death – this is the fate of those who depend upon an inner accord with other persons whom they love. Here we have only the statement of the law that this is so. Whether this condition is felt to be an affliction or the supreme happiness of love is left to the subjective verdict of the person concerned.

Twos can bring tremendous amounts of empathy and compassion to a relationship. They see others' potential and can therefore inspire, support, and motivate. Givers put their own needs on the back burner and can lose themselves in a relationship; to be present for others and yet still be there for themselves is the challenge. Finding value and worth in another's love can be deadly for Givers. Bringing the focus back to themselves and becoming more self-validating can make all the difference in the world in their relationships.

Pride and control

Some Givers might be surprised to learn that pride is considered their core issue. If they look deeply within, they will realize that believing they are indispensable while having no needs of their own is a source of great pride. Self-reflective Givers may also recognize that their giving can be manipulative as well. "If I give them what they want, then I'll get what I want in return." Some Twos (especially those of the Social Subtype) might seek out people who are important – such as politicians, professionals, entertainers, or community leaders. By making themselves valuable to such people, Twos feel greater pride and expect to get greater rewards. When humility is operating, the Two's giving is compassionate and undiscriminating — they give because it is appropriate, without any strings attached.

Twos can be generous and altruistic in their helpfulness. However, one result of their willingness to give may be that partners and friends expect this at all costs. Nothing irritates the Giver more. The worldview of the Giver is basically, "Others have needs, and I don't (or at least I shouldn't)." Twos feel that they should be in control, that it's their choice. Some Givers probably experience enhanced self-respect from the giving; for unhealthy Twos this may become a sense of superiority, of being one-up. The Giver hopes the other person appreciates it and is grateful and, of course, gives back and meets their needs unasked. If they feel that the other person assumes they will continue to give, they can get upset and resentful, focusing on the other's lack of appreciation, while crying the Two's codependent blues, "After all I've done for you!"

Twos go down the wrong path when they think that the more energy and time they invest and the more perfect the gift, the greater will be the return on their investment. A formerly married 54-year-old woman wrote, "I needed to feel loved. The more I was rejected, the more hard and demanding and needy I became." Another explained, "I had a tendency to martyr myself by over-giving and settling for little in return, until I would get angry and confused and not like myself."

Givers often believe they know what others want, and they proceed to provide it (often with great accuracy). Sometimes, however, what they give is either not what the other person wanted or the gift is taken for granted. A 60-year-old psychologist, a Giver, wrote about his "unconscious habit of 'doing for my partner' and then being resentful that I'm not more appreciated and loved by her." Most people resent it if they feel unappreciated, but this is a particular issue for Givers. The psychologist added, "If I focused on my needs more consistently, I would not displace energy into 'helping' my partner with things with which she does not need my help." The challenge for Twos is how to feel loved without constant giving. In a nutshell, Twos need to contain the energy of giving when it arises by resisting the urge to act and then questioning their motivations. And then finally, knowing they are loved for who they are and not just for their giving.

The conflict between living for others and wanting their own space

Despite being focused on others, Givers who work on self-knowledge may discover a yearning for their own space and to spend time on their own desires. Initially this might feel like self-indulgence, yet the pride of the giver – denying they have needs while wanting to feel indispensable – makes it very hard for them to ask for such. Giving themselves permission to be a little self-indulgent is important. With so much going out and very little coming back in, Twos are susceptible to burnout. Suzanne, a 57-year-old Giver, wrote of experiencing "the push-pull of thriving in an abundance of love and attention – while at the same time struggling to be freed up lest I suffocate!"

Seduction: The art of winning people over

Givers are sometimes accused of practicing a form of seduction. Although this may include being sexy, it is more about paying intense and flattering attention to the other, knowing just how to meet his or her most intimate wants and needs. Ex-partners of Givers many years after the fact may say, "He understood me so well, I still miss the attention he used to give to me. He made me feel unconditionally loved." Givers can see the winning over of people as a challenge, where the pride and juice is in the chase until the quarry is won over. It is at this point that the pursuer may wonder whether he or she really wanted to "capture" the other person's heart and attention in the first place. If not, the person might be abruptly dropped because the relationship traps and smothers instead of satisfying.

Pride and Humility

For Givers, pride is a feeling of superiority, imagining oneself to be entitled to greater privileges than other people, or to be above all others. The antidote to pride is humility. The word humility comes from the Latin root word *humus*, which is the word for earth. It also comes from the word human. In other words to be human and to be rooted in the earth is to be humble. Being humble is not being above or better than anyone else. It means not having to have all of the answers, but instead, being able to operate with a "don't know" mindset when one really does not know the answer. Humility also means knowing limitations as well as strengths, where one ends and the other begins. Respectful toward others' boundaries, not intruding. Twos in particular need to know when it is appropriate to give and help. Sometimes, when we go to help someone, we are automatically sending him or her a message that says, "You are not able to do it; therefore I need to do it for you." This message is disrespectful if the person is really able to take care of things for themselves. In other words, Givers need to treat their helping and giving like powerful electricity - with the greatest respect.

Avoidance of confrontations

Giving and helping seem to go hand-in-hand with pleasing people. Twos like to be liked, and most don't like confrontations. They just want things to be nice and loving, to be in a relationship of sweetness. To accomplish this, therefore, Twos tend to stuff their anger and put their own needs on the back burner while barely expressing dissatisfaction or doing so passive-aggressively. Lorie, a Giver, said, "My need for approval/love and fear of disapproval keep me from rocking the boat." Another woman wrote, "Sometimes I need to be gently reminded to think of myself and not just give in to keep the peace."

According to Judy, also a Giver,

I have difficulty in directly communicating thoughts and feelings about important issues that I know will trigger my husband's anger or strong disagreement – wanting to please too much. As I've gotten older (and hopefully wiser and more integrated), being direct and standing my own ground about things I feel strongly about has sometimes provoked upsetting arguments. I realize the necessity of doing this, but only about issues I'm willing to die on the hill for.

Twos give and give until they reach a breaking point, when they are likely flip into their Type Eight (the Giver or Boss) stress point. They may explode in anger or tears and voice, in some way, the Two's codependent cry, "After all I've done for you!", but will also add an implied threat, something like, "Just see if you can get along without me!" This is the Two's pride at its highest (or lowest, depending on how you look at it). At times, blowing up can feel cleansing for the Two. It can be healthy if this time is used to reassess their wants and needs and their boundaries. Of course, it's preferable for Givers to stay more in touch with their dissatisfactions and desires and learn how to express them in an appropriately assertive way so that they do not need to explode. Twos need to regularly ask themselves, "What do I need at this time?" and then ask for it—being willing to risk confrontation if necessary. It will be easier for Givers to risk conflict and even the loss of love if they have sufficiently nurtured themselves.

The Givers in stress and security

In enneagram theory, Twos have a connection with Types Four (the Romantic) and Eight (the Boss or Leader). It is commonly thought that when Givers feel secure, they can experience and appreciate the positive traits of Romantics. They get in touch with their own feelings (both good and bad) and their own needs, and are less compelled to please others. They become more emotionally honest and are able to express their feelings.

On the other hand, when stressed, Twos might take on the negative characteristics of the Leader. Feeling used and taken advantage of, they want to punish people for ingratitude. They can become explosively and excessively angry at presumed injustices and thus demanding. Less commonly, Twos can go to their Four space or point and experience it negatively, becoming self-indulgent, self-pitying, and envious. . They can also approach Type Eight positively and benefit from the Leader's big energy, using it to set appropriate boundaries and say "no" when necessary.

How Twos see themselves in relationship – their gifts

When asked, "What is the one key thing you do/did that is related to your Type that you feel helps the relationship to thrive?" Givers replied,
*   Willingness and ability to change to accommodate my partner.
* Gift of bringing other people into our lives, understanding feelings, truly caring, being able to connect to others very quickly. I showed my husband how new people can enrich and not detract from our relationship. I also made our family the most important. [Social subtype]
* My ability to make my husband – a Four – feel so special, unique, chosen, and supported.
* My need for approval/love and fear of disapproval keep me from rocking the boat. [Her partner is a Five, who also doesn't like confrontation, so she believes she's helping the relationship by not being confrontational]
* I think that I am good at putting my own needs on the back burner (in a positive way) and making the other person feel truly cared about and honored.

- The genuine caring and devotion to our relationship and to my partner.

In many of the responses you can hear an ability and willingness to accommodate and change. Ron (co-author of this book), a Giver, recalls a dream he had several years ago: In the dream, he was a manager of a mini-mart, feeling special and important as customers would come into the store, and he was able to provide them with all the different things that they needed. When he awoke, Ron spent some time analyzing his dream. The mini-mart seemed to have symbolized the "many selves" that Twos can have, the ability to readily alter themselves, taking on the self that fits the situation or the needs of a partner. He recalls at the end of assessing the dream exclaiming, "I'm one-stop shopping!" The dream is a little humorous, but also represents a metaphor of sorts, describing and symbolizing how Twos like to show up in their relationships and the various gifts that they bring.

What partners of Givers can do to help the relationship thrive

When Givers were asked what their partners could do to support them and to help the relationship to grow and thrive, they responded, "Continually ask me if I'm aware of my needs." "Repeat that he loves me." "Support me unconditionally in my spiritual journey." "Be more demonstrative with affection." Givers felt it was important that their partners stay current with their wants and needs and yet remember to tell them that they are still loved.

How Givers feel about relationships with other personality types

When asked which Types they struggle with most in relationship, Twos commonly mentioned the Observer (Five) and the Leader (Eight).

The Observer (Five): "She stays too distant." "I can't get the 'connection' I'm after – I have to try too hard." "Going out of contact, not willing to invest in the relationship, avoiding confrontations."

The Two-Five relationship is definitely one of opposites attract. Observers tend to detach in relationship, whereas Givers strive to attach. This makes the Two-Five pairing challenging. Observers prize their need for self-sufficiency and independence, which can throw Givers back on themselves. Twos can become confused and frustrated as to how to relate to Fives as well as how to help or give. This is especially so if the Five sends a message of not needing help. If Twos can hang in there, they can learn a lot about self-containment and self-focus from the Fives.

The Leader (Eight): "I try to get close to them, but when they turn and are in my face, I want to run." "My father was an Eight – always angry." "I try to over people-please in order to stay out of the firing range." "He was very aggressive and verbally abusive. I was very afraid of him for good reason."

Some of this difficulty could be because the Eight represents the stress point for Twos. The stress point in general represents the Type's shadow side. For the Giver, this means embracing the usually suppressed anger and resentment. Givers need to confront their own shadow with its accompanying anger, aggression, and selfishness.

On the other hand, the most commonly mentioned Types that Givers reported feeling compatible with were the Romantic (Type Four) and, interestingly, the Leader (type Eight). The reasons were:

Romantic (Four): "They focus on getting out of me exactly what I most readily give – attention and 'selflessness.'" "They have apparently open emotional depth and aliveness." "They want to connect." "Creativity, idealism, never a dull moment."

Some of the compatibility Twos feel with Fours relates to their connection on the enneagram diagram. Four is the security point for Twos, and both share the same (Heart) Center. To some extent, Givers and Romantics speak the same language— both agree that the most important thing in the world is relationships. Fours can teach Twos about authenticity and the ability to go inward.

Leader (Eight): "They are good at asking for what they want, so they are easy for me to please." "They say what they think." "I like that what you see is what you get, and I also feel cared about in a protective sort of way." "They don't bullshit, are usually physically imposing, and have protective qualities." "Courage to go after a goal, righteousness."

Givers put Leaders in both categories – the Type they most struggle with and the Type they feel most compatible with. When Twos and Eights see eye to eye, Twos admire the Eight's honesty while Eights value the Two's heart connection. Twos feel that they can be themselves around Eights, for once not having to worry about having to please or guess at somebody's needs. Leaders can teach Givers about boundaries and limits, about saying no, and that anger, when it is channeled correctly, isn't all that bad.

Advice Givers give other Givers in relationship

- Observe how much you go "out," and try to stay within yourself a bit more. Take the time to know what you want and how to ask for it quietly.
- First, get to know yourself; then, don't "give yourself away" to your partner. Beware of the chameleon tendency.
- Spend some time alone – totally out of the relationship. Fill yourself up with yourself. Learn what your wants and needs are and meet them as you would with a partner. In relationship, learn to state your wants and needs, set boundaries, and continue to focus on yourself as well as on your partner.
- Develop inner awareness and self-observer skills. Use the relationship to develop your own self-love, not to impress or manipulate your partner. Practice telling your partner your own needs, not just attending to those of your partner.
- Be sure to learn how to practice self-care. Putting everyone else first is one of the biggest traps you'll struggle with.
- Keep in mind that when a giver meets a taker, it feels so right. You are a giver and need to remember that give and take on each side exist in a healthy relationship. Beware of narcissists, because they will be very attractive to you. For them, you can do what you do best, which is give. They will do what they do best, which is take. You will eventually be depleted and angry.
- Know yourself — particularly your tendency to give until you're exhausted (with the hope that your needs will eventually be met). Learn to be assertive and to say, "No" when appropriate. Use anger and resentment as a key to your own unmet needs, and do something about it yourself.
- Ask yourself repeatedly, what do I want?
- Listen to your own needs and fulfill them. Don't expect others to do it for you. Take good care of yourself.
- Be centered on life in some way other than the person who is your significant other. Be self-accepting and practice self-care.

These are all wonderful affirmations and teachings for both young and adult Twos in general. They start off with what is commonly recommended for Twos, which is spending time alone – filling your self up with your self. Twos can be like empty vessels, just waiting to be filled up with other people. In the enneagram classes that Ron (co-author of this book) teaches, he sometimes draws a stick figure with a triangular torso on a flip chart. Inside the empty torso, Ron draws several other smaller stick figures that represent the people Twos fill themselves up with. He draws another stick figure beside the original one, and then slowly colors in the torso part until it is completely filled up. This represents a Two who is filled up with his or her self – a whole person. The responders to our survey then go on to advise fellow Twos to stay inside themselves, to focus on their own wants and needs. They recommend looking at their anger as an indicator that they are not taking good care of themselves. And finally, practice self-care and don't put all their focus on their partner, but to have other interests as well. All good advice for the Giver.

Exercises for the Giver (Type Two) and Your Partner

The following exercises are intended to take a look at some of the primary characteristics and issues of the Giver in relationship.

Gifts of the Type Two

Before we tackle the more difficult issues, it might be good to talk about the gifts that the Giver brings to the partner and to the relationship overall. Probably the most famous of all the Twos is Mother Teresa. Obviously, she is the epitome of Givers, yet it is that distinct generous spirit of helping and giving while putting your own needs on the back burner that separates the Two from all the other types.

When doing a typing interview to try to determine a person's Type, and especially to see whether they are a Two or not, a revealing question to ask is, "Do you see yourself being able to take rather 'stunning' care of other people?" For the most part, only the Giver will answer this question "Yes" without batting an eyelash. This is the gift of the Two. Discuss the questions below together:

- For the partner: Do you feel your Two partner takes outstanding care of you? Describe what it feels like to you.
- For the Two: How does it feel to be able to help and give to your partner when they are in a place of truly needing your help?
- For the partner: What have you learned from your Two partner about giving, helping, and possibly even sacrificing for others?

Mother Teresa or codependency?

Here the source of a man's strength lies not in himself but in his relation to other people. No matter how close to them he may be, if his center of gravity depends on them, he is inevitably tossed to and fro between joy and sorrow. Rejoicing to high heaven, then sad unto death – this is the fate of those who depend upon an inner accord with other persons whom they love. Here we have only the statement of the law that this is so. Whether this condition is felt to be an affliction or the supreme happiness of love is left to the subjective verdict of the person concerned.

> -- I Ching

This is part of a quote we used earlier in the chapter. It speaks eloquently about the dynamic in a relationship where one's focus is placed on the partner. Please answer the questions below with your partner:

- For the Giver: Do you feel your approach with your partner is an "affliction" or the "supreme happiness of love?"
- For the Giver: Where do you feel your strength lies – in yourself or in your relation to other people?
- For the Giver: In your relationship, do you feel "tossed to and fro between joy and sorrow" depending on how your partner is feeling?
- For both partners: When you become focused on your partner, how are you each able to bring your attention back to yourself? How can you support each other in keeping a healthy focus on yourselves?
- For both partners: "The way that I've been able to take the focus off my partner and fully place it on myself is by…"
- For both partners: "I feel I am in touch with my own feelings and can express them to my partner when…"

Personal growth within the relationship

A healthy relationship for a Giver consists half of serving a partner's potential and the other half developing one's own self. Obviously, many times Givers' relationships primarily focus only on the partner and they forget about working on themselves. Discuss the questions below with your partner to get a better idea of where the focus is in your relationship:

- For the Two: Do you see yourself primarily serving your partner and forgetting about your own self?
- For both partners: How can you both work on serving your partner and working on yourself as well?

- For both partners: How do you each work on "filling yourself up with yourself" – not in a selfish way, but in a way that creates more wholeness in the relationship?

Is it really better to give than to receive?

We could say that genuine receiving can be an even more sacred act than giving – because it requires humbling ourselves and melting open, giving up control, and making ourselves fully available to love.

-- John Welwood

Obviously, Twos do believe that it is better to give than receive. Their primary task is to learn more about receiving and to experience relationship without feeling they have to give for the partner to love them. Being in a relationship without the necessity of giving, especially if giving has an agenda or strings attached to it, is usually foreign territory for the Two. Discuss the questions below with each other:

- For the Two: When you give in the relationship, is there either an agenda or strings attached? Is your giving based on not losing your partner or is it based on loving your partner?
- For the Two: State a time where you gave to your partner, hoping to get "something" back from him or her.
- For the partner: How does it feel to be given to when you know there is an agenda or strings attached on the part of your Two partner?
- For the Two: How do you recognize your importance to or love from your partner if it is not through giving and helping?
- For the Two: How do you feel your helping and giving protects you from your partner leaving or hurting you?
- For the partner: How do you show love toward your Two partner without participating in the dance of being given to?
- For the Two: Where do you show up in the relationship without the giving and helping – but just as yourself?

Don't just complain - State your wants and needs

Givers tend to believe that the way to be in relationship is to deny their own needs. Instead of stating their wants and needs, Givers often complain about and to their partners. To be able to receive, Twos need to state clearly what they want without complaining and without the hope that giving will result in getting their needs met in return. Discuss the questions below together:

- For the Giver: When you start complaining, ask yourself, "What do I really want and need?"
- For the partner: When the Two complains, ask him or her: "I know you are unhappy with me, but what do you really want?"
- For both partners: What comes up for you when you think about the giving and receiving in the relationship being more balanced?

Pride versus humility

The core issue for Givers is pride; the antidote is humility. We spoke about pride and humility earlier in this chapter, where we defined pride in this context as a feeling of superiority, imagining oneself to be entitled to greater privileges than others, or to be above all others. G.K. Chesterton stated, "All evil began with some attempt at superiority." In contrast, to be human is to be humble, which is not being above or being better than anyone else. It means not having to have all of the answers, but instead, being able to operate with a "don't know" mindset when one does not really know the answer. A humble person knows his limitations as well as strengths. Twos in particular need to know when it is appropriate to give and to help. If a person is really able to take care of things, it is disrespectful to imply that he is not able to do it alone and needs your help – but this in fact is what your action can convey.

- For the Giver: Based on the definition above, when do you feel you exhibit pride in the relationship? For example: A feeling of superiority – "I have no needs", intruding on the other's boundaries, knowing one's limitations, being able to say, "I don't know", knowing when it is appropriate to give and help – "They'll never make without me," or not asking for help.
- For the partner: Where in the relationship do you feel your Two partner exhibits pride?
- For the Giver: Where in the relationship do you feel you exhibit humility?
- For the partner: Where in the relationship do you feel your Two partner exhibits humility?
- For the Two: How do you work on both the pride and the humility in yourself? How can you ask your partner for help and support?

CHAPTER SIX

The Achiever (Three) In Relationship

Probably my best feature in relationship is that I don't like to fail at anything including relationships I'm in and I also want to be successful as a partner. In order for the relationship to be the best it can be, I can work hard at improving myself and I can be a good team player with my partner so that we can accomplish having a successful relationship. Some people say that my being a partner in a relationship can be like me playing a role and that the relationship itself can become a task for me to accomplish. I know I can sometimes confuse love with success and achievement. To me, love needs to be earned through working hard and being successful – two cars in the garage, a roof over our heads, and money in the bank. Probably my worst feature in relationship is that it is hard for me to get in touch with my feelings and it makes me anxious to share intimate moments with my partner, as I am not sure who I am supposed to be if we are not doing something. It can also be hard for my partner to slow me down enough to discuss things with me as I have a tendency to go, go, go. I hate to admit it, but at times workaholism has taken its toll on my relationships.

Achievers are ambitious, charming, confident, efficient, energetic, industrious, optimistic, popular, practical, purposeful, responsible, self-assured, and self-propelled. Not surprisingly, fewer Achievers than other types took the time to fill out the survey. But enough did that we still have an insider's view of this personality Type. Emily, an Achiever, who works as a therapist and has done a lot of personal growth work, wrote the following summary of her characteristics:

From my own experience as a Three, what stands out for me in my own life are the following: 1. Work is love made visible. (Also a farm family rule) -- when I work it is telling you I love you. I love my company or mission or organization, and I love the goal or mission of organization. 2. No matter what I accomplish, I still feel it isn't enough, so I over-extend myself and then get resentful. 3. I get resentful if when I am sharing a leadership role, I make a suggestion or observation and it gets ignored; somehow people know that they can walk over me. It often turns out that I have been right in my observation or suggestion – but that too gets ignored. 4. When I get overwhelmed, I have to accomplish a couple of things to get out from under that feeling, but then I fool myself into thinking I can do even more. 5. The main reason I do so much is to cover my fear of being really seen, that someone will figure out I don't know as much as I profess to know, that I will be asked to socialize in a large group (I prefer the one-to-one socializing), that someone will look over my shoulder and pronounce I am a fraud.

As children, Threes earned love through their achievements. They bring into adulthood the belief that their worth depends on what they produce. As adults, failing or unable to reach their goals may make them feel anxious about being unlovable failures. To Achievers, runners-up are unlovable.

Characteristics of the Three in relationship

Solution orientation

Achievers keep their eye on the goal. They have terrific follow-through. When problems appear, they tend immediately to move to solutions. This is great on the job, but can cause difficulties in a relationship. It's hard for many Achievers to just sit and listen – they value efficiency and tend to get impatient with "the process." When a problem occurs in the relationship, Threes want to "fix" it as soon as possible. Immediate action is a way to get rid of negative emotions they may feel. Kelly, an Achiever who is a retired educator, explained:

Not thinking aloud or processing with my partner sometimes leads to misunderstandings. I tend to think through an issue, come to what I believe is a "logical" conclusion, and sometimes I take action before discussing the issue with my partner. Also, I can move very rapidly from Plan A to Plan B without needing time to regroup, which can be uncomfortable for her. Finally, I unconsciously value efficiency too much – and I tend to finish tasks or projects before she's ready.

A 55 year-old business owner related:

My partner's central complaint was, "You're not emotionally engaged. You're a workaholic, too judgmental, too quick to jump to conclusions, never satisfied, impatient, demanding."

Workaholism

In order to get love, to be appreciated, to have self-esteem, Achievers believe they need to be successful – and to keep on being successful. For many Achievers, their work has the highest priority in their lives. Threes also express love through action. They see their hard work and long hours as the way they care for those they love. Threes come home late and tired and wonder why they're not appreciated. It's a real dilemma – they are afraid of rejection if they don't produce, and they in fact are rejected when they do. Looking back, Kelly relates,

"Workaholism" was a major problem before retirement – multi-tasking and having dozens of projects going at once. I had less need for interpersonal intimacy because many of those needs were "sort of" met in work and social arenas. My high energy, speedy talk, speedy decisions, speedy actions were stressful for my slower-paced, more deliberate partner. My partner kept complaining, "You never stop 'going."'

Jose, a Type Three salesman, wrote that a central complaint he heard from his wife was "You're insensitive, don't pay attention to details, are self-centered, and too busy." He admits he has been very task-oriented and not emotional, and that he gets his value from accomplishments.

Focus on projects

Achievers tend to focus on "projects." If the project is in the work arena, the relationship may take a back burner. According to Rita, a Three lawyer,

My marriage was rather incidental to my life, which was about work, accomplishment, and having the possessions I felt I should have in order to be considered a success (however one defines that term for him/herself). The

relationship can become an object rather than a process. It's sort of like, "Well, now I have a husband. I can check that one off my to-do list."

If the Achiever's focus is on the family, her full attention will be placed in that arena. After retiring, Kelly switched her attention from work to the relationship:

I've identified this relationship as the top priority, and I do whatever is needed to make it thrive. Threes know how to focus on a project and make it successful – and this is the most important "project" in my life. Our common commitment to mutual spiritual growth (and study of the enneagram) has been very good for our relationship with each other, our families, friends, and colleagues.

Difficulty relaxing

Achievers' orientation towards accomplishment makes it difficult for them to just unwind and relax. They often bring work with them on vacations, and their vacations tend to be filled with planned activities. A Three psychologist, Leslie, reported that her husband complained that she doesn't' relax and trust that everything will work out. Rather, that she wants to plan, manage, and control.

Focus on image

Like the other members of the Image or Heart triad (Givers and Romantics), Achievers want to project an image – an image of success, in whatever area they focus on. Rita, the attorney, wrote:

Troy felt I was much too concerned about the way things looked to others. In particular, he disapproved of how focused I was on how our home looked and functioned. I wanted it to look beautiful, elegant, and tasteful, and to be clean, orderly, and picture perfect, even with two young children running around in it,

He once said to me, "I saw you looking up at the ceiling and was going to ask you what you were thinking, but then I realized that your thoughts were probably not rising any higher than the roof of this house." He also commented that he wondered if I would spend so much time on the house if it were on a desert island where no one but me would see it.

This thoughtful Three understood that her husband recognized that her involvement with the house wasn't primarily because she enjoyed interior decorating, but because she wanted to show others a particular image.

When asked about the challenges she brought to her marriage, Janet, a 55-year old business owner wrote, "I had terror about not having enough money, always wanting to look good and be admired, extremely jealous over popular, beautiful people." The Achiever wants to project an image of success in whatever part of his life is the most important to him. If the priority is the home and family, the Three may want the home to look like something out of the magazine "House and Garden," and the children to look well-dressed, be polite, and be a positive reflection of their parents. If in the work setting, the image might include awards for having sold the most homes, having the most publications, or racking up the highest production in the factory. A Three in recovery from addiction once told us, "These days I want to look like the model of recovery. But back when I went to prison for drug dealing, I wanted everyone to know I'd been the most successful dealer around."

Other issues for Threes

"Can I be loved for myself?"
"I have difficulty trusting that I am loved for myself," wrote Leslie, a Three psychologist. Underneath the drive to succeed is the fear that they would not be loved but for their accomplishments. Endlessly focusing on the *appearance* of success means suppressing a lot of one's authentic self. Rita, quoted above, continued:

I want everything to look perfect, even where there are serious issues. I'll stuff my complaints, trying to "make nice" and get along, make everything look okay, then finally blow up (although I followed this pattern much more in the past than now).

I tend to hide who I am a lot of the time when I'm in a romantic relationship. I always fear that if I say exactly what I feel or think, the other person will be displeased with me and go away. I don't feel that a man would want me as a partner if I have any flaws or weaknesses. I fear that he will despise me for any weaknesses or failings.

My underlying belief has been that my value is in my ability to take care of myself (a form of "success."), and that if I need help (read: failure), then no one will want me. Certainly no man would want to take care of me. At its worst extreme, I have thought that asking for help is being "pathetic" or "needy" in the clinging-vine sense, and that a man would simply be disgusted by any helplessness at all.

Time pressure

So much to accomplish – so little time! That could be the mantra of many Achievers. They value efficiency, and may consider it a waste of time to "smell the roses" or spend time talking about feelings. A young college professor, Robin, wrote that the challenges she brought to her relationship included "Being future-oriented. 'Where does this lead to?' is part of the experience. Time is short for me." When she sensed there were problems in the relationship, "I asked what I did wrong and he stonewalled. I felt that my time spent with him and little efforts I carved out of my busy day were no longer appreciated." Robin also noted her tendency "not to give the other enough time (for him) to express what he was struggling with." Threes who consider their work their top priority may find themselves paying attention to the relationship only if they perceive something wrong, and may then get involved only long enough to put out the fire and return things to status quo, after which they will again turn back to their work.

The Three in security and stress

According to enneagram theory, Achievers have a connection to the Detective (Types Six) and the Mediator (Type Nine). When secure, Achievers may express the positive traits of the Detective. They become less concerned with prestige and success, or with being a leader, and become more humble and human. They get more in touch with their feelings, and can feel empathy and loyalty.

When stressed, Threes may express the negative characteristics of Type Nine, the Mediator. They may lose their focus and spin their wheels, going from one project or task to another without accomplishing anything and without feeling anything.

Threes describe how they make the relationship thrive.

As mentioned above, Achievers tend to approach their primary relationship as a project. When asked how they make the relationship thrive, their answers often reflected this orientation:

I accomplish a lot and my income has given us a lifestyle he likes. I've improved his status in life. I'm a high-energy person. I like to do things. We enjoy our free time. I'm game for socializing, travel, the arts – and he likes that too. I'm intellectually his equal and we're good in front of people together.

Other Achievers echoed this, "I like to share in our discussions and to get feedback and allow for us to make individual mistakes without taking things personally. When I do something hurtful and it is pointed out, I usually am forthright in apologizing. " "I'm motivated to make the relationship work. I have tools, such as fair fighting techniques, negotiation." "I bring structure, momentum, optimism, and decision making."

Note that there's very little about feelings in most of these comments – they're about *doing*. Achievers tend to be out of touch with their feelings, and much more comfortable about getting things done. They are likely to view their gifts to the relationship in terms of what they can accomplish. Because it is important for a Three to avoid failure and to maximize success, her primary goal for the relationship is to make sure it runs efficiently.

What the Three wants in a relationship

Achievers want their primary relationship to function well. They want their relationship to be successful, and to look successful. They want their partner to see them as winners. Rita described this well:

It's very important to me that my partner thinks I'm pretty, clever, talented, etc. etc. etc., and tells me so, at least reasonably often. Otherwise, I don't feel like I'm truly loved, and, in fact, I can start to feel like I'm just being used. I start to feel that I'm just a vehicle for fulfilling the other person's needs, and that my needs, wants, and vulnerabilities, are not particularly important to them. (Is there a bit of projection going on here?)

Martha, an Achiever formerly in relationship with a Leader, remembered,

I needed her to respect me and to value my work. I was hurt and angry at perceived or actual criticism. I sometimes played the role of a partner instead of being real.

How Threes feel about other types in relationship

When asked which Types they struggle with the most, more Achievers chose the Observer (Type Five) than any other type. Least-mentioned were The Giver (Two), the Achiever (Three), the Adventurer (Seven), and the Mediator (Nine). The Achievers' struggles with the Observer included: "Withdrawn, secretive, reluctant to commit." "They don't respond to me emotionally; I believe they always see themselves as intellectually superior, and I don't like it." "I'm not sure what he's all about – he's ambiguous." "At the low end, they may not want to DO anything, just talk or think about it. It can be maddening to a Three who wants to get things done."

Achievers like certainty in their primary relationship; they don't want to have to spend a lot of time figuring out what their partner wants and how to get them to act.

Achievers felt most compatible with other Achievers and with Adventurers (Seven). They reported:

Achiever: "We have a natural affinity. They're easy to work with, and understand." "At this stage of my life [age 39], I know what I want and need and I have little time to waste. I want someone who is committed to peaceful coexistence and meaningful work." "Achievers get things done, have good ideas, are great conversationalists." "They just 'get it.'"

Adventurer: "They appreciate lightness, are fun-loving, and have high energy." "They help me have fun, feel free, less responsible." "They like to do things, and are often willing to go along with any fun plan I come up with. So I get to be in control of the agenda and also have an enthusiastic companion." "Fun, spontaneous, not demanding, can help me be less serious." "They like to be busy too, have fun."

Many Achievers seem to be attracted to high-energy partners, other people who are focused on action rather than emotions. It is interesting that although they frequently chose Threes as "most compatible," a primary relationship between two Threes seems uncommon. This will be discussed in more detail later. In contrast, working relationships between two Achievers are likely to be common and successful.

Advice Threes give other Achievers in relationship
Achievers gave some very thoughtful advice that would be very helpful for other Threes. Their comments included:

Don't assume that everyone has the same sensitivities (or not) as you do. Really tuning into another person and actively responding to their needs is not natural for a Three and must be learned and cultivated.

Remember that admiration is not love and watch out for choosing some-one because you think they will lead others to think you have the qualities you admire in your mate. This is just choosing someone because he/she promotes your own self-image or what you want others to believe you are. Essentially, you need to be conscious of the risk that you are just using the other person to pro-mote your own public image rather than having a real, intimate relationship.

Look at yourself rather than what is the problem with your partner. Issues that arise are mirrors to look at yourself.

Don't let work or striving for personal success overshadow relationship needs.

Be sure to marry someone who lives up to your "image" or you'll be disap-pointed your whole life, but also be careful, because glitz isn't always character.

Exercises for the Achiever (Type Three) and your partner
The following exercises are intended to take a look at some of the pri-mary characteristics and issues of the Achiever in relationship.

Coming in second
Someone once asked Leonard Bernstein, the great composer and orches-tra conductor, "What's the most difficult instrument to play in the orches-tra?" He replied, "Second fiddle." Leonard Bernstein could have just as easily been asked, "What's the most difficult role to play in life and relationships for a Type Three?" Had he known about the enneagram, his answer would have been the same, "Second fiddle." When it comes to relationships, Achievers can have a hard time not competing with their partner, being honest about their vulnerabilities connected to their failures and inadequacies, and finally, surrendering to their partner. Life to the Three is about win/lose, not win/win. Taking off the mask and allowing someone to see them for who they re-ally are can be very, very daunting.

Gifts of the Type
Before we tackle the more difficult issues, let's talk about the gifts that the Achiever brings to the partner and to the relationship overall. Threes are known for their looking at the positive side of things, seeing the glass as half-full as opposed to half-empty. They can have a strong self-confidence about them and a "you can do it" attitude. These positive qualities can spill over

onto their partner, something that can be quite invaluable if the partner has a history of struggling with their own self-confidence and faith in themselves. Complete the unfinished sentences below to verify what the Achiever brings to the relationship:

- For the Three: I feel that what is helpful to my partner is...
- For the partner of the Three: When it comes to the positive gifts that my Three partner brings to the relationship, (s)he is especially good at...

A Three movie

Probably one of the best movies that exemplify a Three is "Jerry Maguire". Actor Tom Cruise plays the title role of a high-powered sports agent who joins one of his top clients in repeatedly screaming their mantra in unison, "Show me the money!" What makes this movie especially dynamic from an enneagram point of view is that the character Jerry Maguire is a Three who is in a Threeish profession, while Tom Cruise is most likely also a Three in real life. At one point in the movie, Jerry Maguire has a "crisis of conscience," something that Achievers usually need to have before they can take off their mask and become real with themselves and others. This is most often a point in their lives where the deceit has created a double life, where workaholism has usually destroyed their most important relationships, and where loneliness, fatigue, and ill-health are looming large. In the film, Jerry falls in love, which is sure to throw a Three even deeper into a tailspin of "Who am I? "What am I feeling?" and "What do I really want?" Love is about authentic feelings and about finding one's heart and soul, something that is not easy for an Achiever.

- For the Three: Does the movie "Jerry Maguire" and/or the different issues talked about above relate to you in any way?
- For both of you: Discuss with each other how these or similar issues have affected your relationship.

Love – given or earned?

"I know I can sometimes confuse love with success and achievement. To me, love needs to be earned through working hard and being successful – two cars in the garage, a roof over our heads, and money in the bank. I hate to admit it, but work has taken its toll on my relationships at times."

The above sentences are taken from the "identifying your Type" paragraph at the beginning of this chapter. Discuss with each other how the overall dynamic of the above sentences may have played a role in your relationship:

- How was love viewed in the family you grew up in? Were you loved for your "doing" or your "being?"
- In your current relationship, do you each feel that love is earned, given, or a little of both? Do you love each other for your "doing" or your "being?"
- How big a role do material possessions play in your relationship? Do you use possessions to express love?
- Has workaholism played a role in your relationship? How much distance do you feel exists between the two of you because of work or "doing" in general?

Authentic relationships

A classic quotation from an Achiever says, "Probably my best feature in relationship is that I don't like to fail at anything including relationships I'm in and I also want to be successful as a partner." Threes tend to approach their relationship as they would a work project -- with tremendous effort and a desire to succeed. Achievers who have committed to having a truly authentic relationship, either because they simply want to grow, or because their partner has called them on the carpet, or from hitting bottom – may find themselves approaching the relationship as a work project, with tremendous effort and a desire to succeed.

- Discuss with each other the level of commitment you each have toward the relationship and toward each other as partners and what you are willing to do to make sure the relationship is successful.

However, Threes also report, "Some people say that my being a partner in a relationship can be like me playing a role and that the relationship itself can become a task for me to accomplish." Achievers need to be careful about falling into a performance role, mimicking what they have seen with other couples. They are simply going through the motions, and even though their motions can seem quite accurate and powerful, they are not authentic and the true feelings are not really there. Discuss the issues below with each other:

- For the Three: How do you know when you have fallen into a performance role? How do you catch yourself and maintain an authentic approach to your partner and the relationship?

- For the partner: How do you know when your Three partner is operating from a performance position? How do you discuss this particular issue with your Three partner?

The "work" and competition versus team player

An Achiever related,

In order for the relationship to be the best it can be, I can work hard at improving myself and I can be a good team player with my partner so that we can accomplish having a successful relationship.

Achievers sometimes have a hard time truly working on themselves since the "work" involves dealing with one's feelings, something they really shy away from. Psychotherapists sometimes joke that Threes approach counseling the way a race car driver approaches having their tires rotated during a pit stop: it's quick and doesn't go very deep. Being a team player can also be difficult for someone who is very competitive. In this context, competition and team player are seen as an oxymoron of sorts. Remember, Achievers see themselves as needing to be first or the best. For the Three to become a team player takes quite an attitude adjustment.

- For the Three: How have you committed to working on yourself? Does your work involve feelings work?
- For both of you: How do you see yourselves as a team? Does the power in the relationship feel equal? Is there an overall interdependence in the relationship?

Intimacy? What's that?

Probably my worst feature in relationship is that it is hard for me to get in touch with my feelings and it makes me anxious to share intimate moments with my partner, as I am not sure who I am supposed to be if we are not doing something. It can also be hard for my partner to slow me down enough to discuss things with me as I have a tendency to go, go, go.

Achievers can feel as if there is a gap in their development. When it comes to feeling feelings and experiencing intimacy, their tendency is to jump and run at the first signs of it or conflict.

- Discuss how feelings and intimacy were handled in the families you grew up in.

- What have you both committed to do as a couple with regard to intimacy and feelings? What work are you involved in to deepen the level of intimacy between you and your partner?
- How will you know when you are running away from either feelings or intimacy?

Relationship mission statement

Mission statements were first designed for the workplace; they state the goals of the business and then commit to those goals and standards. Because of the Three's nature it might be helpful for both partners to write a personal mission statement stating specifically what you are willing to do to support and enhance the relationship. After that is done, both partners can then write a relationship mission statement together that describes the goals that each of you are committing to abide by.

CHAPTER SEVEN

The Romantic (Type Four) In Relationship

Probably my best features in relationship are my romantic nature and my eye for beauty. To me, relationships symbolize a meeting of the hearts, and having an emotional connection with a beloved can have a sacred quality about it --especially if the relationship includes an honest, authentic expression of feelings. I know that the possibility of love brings the possibility of rejection and abandonment, so I am sometimes guilty of preemption. Then, once the other person moves away from me, he or she again becomes attractive to me. Some people say that I am never truly satisfied in relationship, that I focus too much on what is missing, and that I have a hard time staying in the present moment, but instead use my vivid imagination to romanticize the past or future. Others say that it is important for me to be special and unique to my partner, and that if the relationship becomes ordinary, I might sabotage it with drama and intensity. Probably my worst feature in relationship is that sometimes I compare my relationship with others. I long for what they have and lose hope of ever finding my own true love. This can result in my becoming melancholic or depressed.

"Always remember that you are absolutely unique. Just like everyone else."
-- Margaret Mead

"When you do the common things in life in an uncommon way, you will command the attention of the world."
-- George Washington Carver

"If I never meet you in this life, let me feel the lack."
-- The Thin Red Line – Movie

Romantics can be compassionate, creative, emotionally honest, empathetic, expressive, introspective, intuitive, passionate, refined, self-aware, sensitive, supportive, warm, and witty. Far more Romantics filled out the survey than most other types.

Characteristics of the Romantic (Four) in relationship

Drama and intensity, strong emotions

Romantics are known for their intensity, strong emotions, and dramatic lives. They embrace the illusion that somewhere a great love will provide them with all that is missing in their lives. Fours seek perpetually all-consuming and passionate relationships. "I did everything with great intensity; it often became exhausting." "I can be blinded to the best solution if my emotions are running too high. I can be deluded by my personality into thinking my feelings are the truth of the situation." When asked about type-related challenges that she brought to her relationship, one Romantic replied, "Depth of feeling/emotion." Recognizing that her emphasis on her emotions was sometimes a problem, she added, "I learned through enneagram counseling that I need to be able to sit with big feelings without having to act them out."

Regarding their oversized emotions, one Romantic wrote that this trait keeps her from effective problem solving: "My 'emotionality' – It's hard for me to stay as logical and removed as him [her Observer husband]. I get overwhelmed with more and more information." Another Romantic wrote that what hindered his problem solving in the relationship is: "my emotionality, sometimes seeing patterns and problems that aren't really there, because I've been running scenarios in my head based on incomplete information." Yet another Romantic reported, "Just wanting things my way emotionally – not seeing his experience of things because I'm caught up in my own emotional experience." Seeing other people and situations primarily as reflections of themselves constitutes narcissism, a typical Four characteristic. Rob, a Four colleague of Jennifer's (an author of this book), lectures on narcissism, explaining humorously that he's an expert on the subject, having fought this tendency in himself all his life.

People generally have difficulty with what is at the core of their triad (feelings/image, anger or fear). Romantics, along with the Giver and the Observer, are members of the feelings, Heart, or Image triad. It's not unusual for Romantics to be confused about their feelings, and to have difficulty accessing them (especially Fours with a Five wing). Fours are in touch with their _emotions_, but not with their _feelings_. Emotions are like the superficial waves that rise and fall on the ocean's surface Feelings—real feelings—are the deep currents that can be so powerful they actually shift the ocean floor. Feelings are analogous to the foundation of one's being – those deep feelings what you definitely want to be in touch with. But most people are only in touch with their emotions. They can't access their feelings, or have trouble expressing them. Fours, the prototypic artists, look for other ways – such as through their art -- to voice the feelings that are locked up inside. Unless they've done a lot of work on themselves, they have a tough time having a straight exchange, instead becoming passive-aggressive, moody or critical. Therapy work with Romantics often involves helping them to get beyond the drama and emotions, and putting them in touch with their true feelings down there on the ocean floor.

Fear of abandonment/push-pull relationships

Most Romantics can describe a childhood experience of loss – a parent ill or dying, a divorce, some neglect or abandonment. That fear subsequently tends to color all their important relationships. A Four reported about her marriage, "I felt emotionally abandoned and misunderstood, which led to feelings of unworthiness and depression at times. Also crying jags and angry outbursts." When Fours actually find themselves in an intimate relationship, despite their longing for such, they assume they will be found lacking and abandoned again. It seems safer to reject the other person than to risk being rejected.

"My fear of being abandoned makes me either cut and run first or get emotionally demanding," admitted a Romantic. Another related, "I either want all your attention or I want you to leave me alone." Romantics' relationship history is often described as push-pull. They long for the unavailable or new person, but when they get to know him or her better, flaws may be magnified. For all committed relationships, with time, even the best ones tend to lose the passion and intensity of the initial stages. When the daily routine becomes predictable and the partner becomes less mysterious, the Four may pull back. It can be hard for Romantics to commit. A young Four wrote, "I long for other partners sexually, even when I feel deep love for the one I'm with." Another said her slogan is, "Love – can't live with it, can't live without it." The Four's feelings of affection seem to get stronger when obstacles to the relationship exist, such as enforced separation or uncertainty about its future. When the Romantic gets what she hoped for, she may find it difficult to maintain her interest. As a result, many Fours have a history of multiple relationships and recurring cycles of longing, intense romance, storminess, disappointment, and rejection of or by the partner.

Rosanne, a young Romantic, was initially very enthusiastic about Tim, a Giver. They were both attractive people who had many common interests. Tim quickly fell in love with Rosanne. He spent his time doing everything he could for her. Knowing she loved to travel, Tim told her he'd follow her to the ends of the earth. Everyone told Rosanne she was lucky to have met this loving, caring man after all the difficult men she had previously dated. But she found herself becoming increasingly critical of Tim. She said, "He's a total bore. I can't imagine spending my life with him. What would we talk about after two days? Boring, boring." Thus, Fours can repeatedly find themselves in difficult relationships with emotionally unavailable partners, since the nice ones are boring. The Fours, fearing intimacy, create their own reality – that of rejecting the available and living in the void.

One Romantic wrote that his partner's chief complaint is, "You're not available for a committed relationship." Another Romantic, three years into his current relationship, said his partner complained that, "You are never fully committed." He added, "I fear being absorbed and losing myself. When I feel that way, I retreat and push my partner away."

Specialness and uniqueness

Judy, a Romantic, was attracted to her partner because:

I paid more attention to what he said than to what he did, as he spoke so elegantly and said all the things I wanted to hear. He reinforced my sense of uniqueness, at being the only woman who had ever. . etc., etc.

This sense of uniqueness is often underlain with a deep feeling of being inadequate, not good enough and not wanted. This may sometimes appear as narcissism or self-absorption and also make them very sensitive to criticism:

I take my husband's remarks and actions too personally (i.e., I tell myself that he is abandoning me, I'm too unattractive, too needy, too . . .) rather than understanding he just needs some time to himself.

Sense of longing, attention to what's missing

Here is how Roxanne, a 40-year old Romantic, recalled her childhood:

I was a very sensitive child who absorbed the negative or positive energy that was around me. Sadness has played a large role in my life. I'd have times of depression and hopelessness. My father was an alcoholic, and my sister, my mother and I were very close. I was always angry that I couldn't do more for my mother and sister. I had a friend whose parents paid for art classes, and she didn't even finish them!

The chief issue for the Fours is envy, and in her account, Roxanne focuses on what was missing in her life and contrasts it with what her friend had and carelessly dismissed. An earlier version of our survey asked the responder to create a slogan he would put on a T-shirt to describe his basic belief about relationships. One young Romantic wrote (as we earlier cited), "If I never meet you in this life, let me feel the lack," explaining that this is a quotation from the film, "The Thin Red Line." It perfectly describes the Four's intensity and focus on what is missing. Geoffrey, a Romantic, wrote about the challenge he brought to his 14-year relationship:

Dealing with my longing for something that is missing in my life and projecting this onto my mate as her responsibility to be or become what I am creating in my imagination.

Although he was in a lengthy marriage, Geoffrey's focus still often went to what was lacking. This then was translated into dissatisfaction with his partner. Another Four, Clark, wrote that a challenge he brought to his four-year relationship was, "Staying in the present moment, not wanting something that's missing or longing for the past." Not surprisingly, the partner senses this. Another Romantic states her husband tells her, "You are never satisfied, you are always hungry for more of me." Writing of a five-year relationship, a 59-year old Romantic said, "My partner always felt I was demanding something from him, even when I wasn't. I expect that that would be my unconscious search for the missing, idealized thing."

When asked about the type-related challenges she brought to her marriage, one Romantic replied, "My mental model of how I wanted to be romanced is different from how things are (always missing)." This attitude can lead to chronic dissatisfaction with the current relationship, a feeling that 'the grass is always greener elsewhere' and can lead to the partner's feeling that they can never satisfy the Romantic. David Daniels, an enneagram teacher wrote in *The Enneagram Monthly*,

Thus it is really important for Fours to pay attention to that which is missing, and discern if this is old habit of mind or something vital. About 90% of the time it will be old habit, hence not something vital missing in your life. Since you are concerned that envy or longing – fueled by your Type Two sister "enjoying her kids so much" and the approval she gets from your Type One father – plays a role here, how can you know/discern your own real choice? [P.4]

Quest for authenticity

Romantics want to be known for who they really are. They want to be understood and appreciated. Their double bind is that on the one hand, as members of the Image triad or center, they want to maintain their artistic persona in public, which keeps them from admitting their limitations, while at the same time they want to be really understood. Gabrielle, a Romantic, had had several operations and suffered ongoing pain. She put up a good front in public, minimizing her medical problems. She related,

Because I'm very sensitive and emotional, I get my feelings hurt. Many people don't know what to say, and so they hurt me with remarks like, "Oh, you look good, so you must be feeling better." They have no idea how I'm feeling! They don't see me struggling—they don't know the real me.

When her effort to project a healthy image was successful, she wasn't satisfied; on the contrary, she hated being perceived as ordinary -- as though her friends were saying, "Cheer up, you'll get over it." Romantics don't want to be cheered up; what they want is your understanding and empathy.

This focus on authenticity sometimes results in inadequate attention to the realities of life. A Four related, "I tended to have a higher concern for emotional authenticity than for appropriate action." Healthy Fours spend time in their One Security point (see below) where they are grounded, notice what needs to be done, and take right action.

Judgmental and competitive

Some Romantics, especially those of the Sexual subtype, tend to be quite competitive and judgmental and can easily access their anger. Sexual Fours can appear like Eights (Leaders) -- aggressive, heated and competitive. One such man, Oliver, reported that his partner's central complaint about him was, "You are judgmental, competitive in the workplace—it colors the mood of our relationship, and work can seem to be a priority". He added, "I'm quick to judge and to be swept away by negative emotions before I can be objective." A Sexual Four woman wrote that her challenge in the relationship is that, "I can be very angry and hostile."

The Four in security and stress

Enneagram theory teaches us that the Romantic has a connection to Types One (the Perfectionist) and Two (the Giver). When secure, Romantics may express some positive traits of the Perfectionist, becoming more practical, with less focus on themselves and more on the outside world and getting things done. Then, as Don Riso and Russ Hudson put it, they are no longer controlled by their feelings but by their convictions, acting on principles rather than moods.

When stressed out, especially upon experiencing loss, Romantics evince some of the negative characteristics of the Giver, becoming people-pleasers and dependent. They also create more drama and histrionics in their relationships and demand more of others.

How Romantics see themselves in relationship

A Romantic man describes himself in relationship as "empathetic, willing to work on building the relationship," but he also reports that "I either want all your attention, or I want you to leave me alone." Another Four states he is "compassionate, caring, bohemian." A 54-year old Romantic writes she is "empathetic, passionate, sometimes too emotionally intense and/or demanding." Another describes herself as "high-maintenance, expressive, caring."

Fours describe how they make the relationship thrive

In contrast to Achievers, whose gifts to their relationship were mostly practical, Romantics focused on their emotions and sensitivity to their partner's needs.

- "I am compassionate and can go back to love in conflict, which helps to disarm and heal."
- "I listen very well, have a deep awareness and understanding of my partner's energy, and am very supportive."
- "I am willing to work through core issues, no matter how intense the emotions."
- "My empathy and sensitivity."

- "I have a keen intuition, warmth, an ability to be deeply intimate, a good listener."
- "Applying my intuition to problems around me, empathizing with others, particularly my significant other."
- "Helping us grow individually and in our relationship. I insist that we work on our issues."
- "I share my thoughts and feelings as much as he'll let me."
- "I keep the focus on our relationship. I challenge each of us and our relationship to be the best it can be. I can be romantic/passionate."
- "I've been using my love of truth to explore my own emotional depth and sensitivity."
- "I communicate, communicate, communicate (the good, the bad, and the ugly)."

The Four partner of another Four wrote, "My partner prefers me to be emotionally 'real' and hates it when I try to be even or less emotional (this is not always a good thing, as I'd like to be more even."). Her partner likes her intensity, but it can be a problem if partners have other personality types.

Darlene, a Romantic, describes the gifts she brings to a relationship as:

I'm willing to explore and understand motivations, to learn and grow; willing to take personal responsibility; aesthetics and love of beauty; sense of humor; compassion; clear sight and clear communication. I've been there, done that emotionally, and had deep compassion for and insight into the dark places of the relationship and the struggles my partner was facing. I knew that there was grace at the core of our problems, and was willing to hang in there through the tough times to experience it.

How Romantics believe their partner could make them happy
- "Touch me while expressing appreciation and admiration in a warm voice."
- "Give me space when I need it, but be there fully if I'm available."
- "Ask me questions about how I'm doing, especially where personal growth is concerned."
- "Call me even when we're far apart geographically and tell me, 'I love you. I adore you,' and make me feel special. Share intimately with each other. Fluidly move between physical and spiritual sharing."
- "Accept my faults as part of the package and worth the trade-off."

- "Share our thoughts and feelings, be open, making physical intimacy follow naturally."

How Romantics feel about other types in relationship

Romantics were most likely to struggle with the Leader (Eight), Adventurer (Seven), and Perfectionist (One). Here's what they wrote:

Leaders (Eights): "They take up all the air in the room. I can't match their energy." "Gruffness, yet I feel safe and protected." "I'm extremely conflict-avoidant (people often guess I'm a Nine), and Leaders can make me nervous; on the other hand, I've dated an Eight and that worked." "I dislike their bossiness." "They are too controlling of the partner and at the same time often don't pay adequate attention to them. They seem to be the least sensitive of the types." "I take everything personally." "Conflicts over power." "Their 'big energy' takes over and I don't feel seen."

Adventurers (Sevens): "I don't trust them. They have a weird kind of deceitfulness." "They are just plain opposites of my nature." "They are ultimately unavailable." "They seem superficial and it gets exhausting." "I have a hard time in the superficial." "I can't stand all that cheerfulness!" "They're too active. They want me to keep doing things that I am not interested in."

Perfectionists (Ones): "I'm morally relativistic and rebellious, and I don't take things too seriously; I can't understand why they get so tightly wound about things, so we don't communicate well." "Perfectionism and so many demands on me can make me feel imperfect, even worthless." "I dislike know-it-alls." "Judgmental nature – too harsh." "The "right/wrong" attitude is something I just can't get inside. Let's look at possibilities, feelings, instead." "I hate the arrogance of Ones. Perfectionists can be critical and judging, which makes me "shrivel." "It's incredibly painful to be criticized when one's self-esteem is low."

Romantics felt compatible with other Romantics, and with Observers and Mediators:

Romantics (Fours): "Because they are exotic and passionate and full of feeling." "Understanding each other's emotional issues and interest in the same things (emotion, spirituality, relationships, etc.). Most of my best friends have been Fours." "Because we're on the same wavelength and are sensitive and empathetic. We share many values generally." "I feel a beautiful resonance. We speak the same language." "They can be deep and introspective." "I think Fours need Four friends because they understand each other, especially when we're in emotional turmoil. Other types often think we're overly dramatic or they want to fix it. They don't understand the value of intense emotions." "Variety of interests and emotional capacity. They are creative people."

Observers (Five): "They are nonjudgmental and interesting." "I have a strong Five wing and grew up in an academic family. I love learning from people." "I love them and they are smart." "This was/is my great life partner and soul mate. With a strong Four wing, we share artistic spirit and a little out of step with societal norms. I value his work (composer) and I feel we bring out the best in each other, balance each other." "They are generally somewhat intellectual and well-read, which makes them compatible. They are fellow introverts." "I like the objectivity, non-judgmental nature. Steadiness, wealth of ideas, endless topics of interest." "We can talk about interesting, meaningful things." "I like their depth, they respect confidences and boundaries. I appreciate their knowledge and intellect." "They're sensitive, intelligent, clear." "I too like a lot of autonomy and privacy."

Mediators (Nine): "I can help Nines get in touch with their own needs." "We share conflict avoidance, and often have an interest in talking about the same things. " "I love their mellowness." "Nonjudgmental and kind, calming." "I love my Nine friends. They are kind and understanding, comfortable companions who listen well." "The vast majority of my relationships have been with Nines. I've accepted my 'fate' with them. The numbing behavior gets really old, but I do enjoy their ease with me. They're very accepting and I guess that's what has been the glue that kept me with them."

Advice Romantics give other Fours in relationship

It's interesting that when giving advice to others of their type, most people (of any type) had a great deal of insight into the challenges of their enneagram Type. Romantics, who spend so much time looking inward, were particularly good at nailing the issues and recognizing the direction of growth. They spoke of lightening up when it comes to drama and emotions, focusing on reality, understanding their own motivations, finish the sentence. Here are some of their suggestions:

- There are times when you will think that if you spend <u>one more minute</u> with this person you loved so much yesterday, you will die of suffocation. Take a deep breath, take a walk, listen to some music, gently disengage, and spend some time refreshing and renewing your emotional resources – and you will find that he or she suddenly comes back into focus, and you remember what it was that warmed your heart.
- Learn to appreciate the pleasures of true togetherness. Learn to define what togetherness actually is. There's a difference between two discrete beings sharing time and space and two beings joining together in one time and space.
- Remember that <u>you</u> are not your feelings and you don't have to amplify and dramatize all of them. Get over the <u>sturm und drang</u> of being a Four. You're unique (just like everyone else) so get over it. Don't be so into yourself and downplay the drama.

This, of course, is a fundamental lesson that Fours need to learn.

- Don't take what they say (criticisms) as personal.

Fours can be very sensitive to criticism, which may reinforce their deep sense of being inadequate or unwanted.

- Develop your awareness of others. Try not to take things too personally.

Out of a sense of their own specialness, Romantics may become narcissistic and self-absorbed.

- Try to have a sense of humor about your emotions and not take them too seriously; try not to create stories without checking in with your partner; be aware of your tendency to "not want to belong to any club that would have you as a member," and not push your partner away when s/he comes toward you.

Good advice to Fours regarding their push-pull tendencies.

- Focus on what is there (the good things), rather than what's missing. And don't settle.

David Daniels summarizes beautifully the personal growth tasks of Fours:

> Fours long for the ultimate ideal connection and complete fulfillment wherein nothing of substance is missing. In the process, attention naturally goes to what is missing, absent, or lacking that results in a blindness to what is present, positive now, and lovely. The primary task for Romantics is to realize that ultimately wholeness and completeness come with acceptance and appreciation of what is here now in the present moment, from the inside out, not from the outside in. Disappointments and deficiencies are part of the fabric of life, not an indication of a deficiency in being. [Enneagram Monthly, July-Aug 2004, p.4]

Romantics become happy in relationship when they come to believe they have enough, when their focus shifts from past losses and future longings to the present, and when they stop expecting others to fill them up and fulfill all their needs.

Exercises for the Romantic (Type Four) and Your Partner
The following exercises are intended to take a look at some of the primary characteristics and issues of the Romantic in relationship.

Gifts of the Type Four
Before we tackle the more difficult issues of the Four, let's talk about the gifts that the Romantic brings to the partner and to the relationship overall. Fours do have a romantic nature, focusing on beauty, the beloved, and the sacred in the relationship. They desire a relationship that has plenty of trust in it as well as honesty and authenticity. These are some of the gifts of the Romantic. Discuss the questions below with your partner:

- For the partner: What are the gifts you feel your Four partner brings to the relationship? Describe how they affect you.
- For the Romantic: What are the gifts you bring to a relationship?
- For the partner: What have you learned from your Four partner about the way to be in relationship, that you weren't aware of until you met him or her?

Ocean waves versus deep currents

Romantics are known for their intensity, their strong emotions, and drama. The Romantic's strong emotions can sometimes be a problem in the relationship. Many times people confuse emotions with feelings. In this chapter, we metaphorically describe emotions as similar to the waves on the surface of the ocean -- They rise and fall and are quite dramatic, but have little positive affect on the relationship. Feelings on the other hand can be described as the deep currents near the ocean floor that are so powerful that they can shift the sand on the ocean floor. People who are in touch, only with their emotions, have a drama-filled life. Those who are in touch with their authentic feelings, metaphorically those deep currents near the ocean floor, have a better understanding of who they are and what they want in life. Discuss the questions below with your partner:

- For the Romantic: How well are you able to separate emotions from feelings (as we define them)?
- For the Romantic: What roles do your emotions, which are represented by the rising and falling of the waves, play in your relationship? How do you handle your emotions overall? How do you feel your emotions affect your partner?
- For the Romantic: What role do your feelings, that are represented by the deeper currents, play in your relationship? Are you able to allow your true feelings to lead you toward a richer, authentic life?
- For the partner: How do your Four partner's strong emotions affect you? What is the one thing that would be helpful to you, which you would like to ask of your partner during the more emotional times?
- For the partner: How does your Four partner's authentic feelings affect you?
- For both of you: During the times that strong emotions get expressed, do you feel that they are detrimental to the relationship?
- For both of you: In what positive ways do you feel that the Romantic's deeper, authentic feelings affect your partnership? (Some Fours refer to these feelings as their intuition.)

The Push/Pull - Reject before being rejected

Romantics fear being abandoned. As one of them put it, "My fear of being abandoned makes me either cut and run first or get emotionally demanding." Fear of abandonment can lead the Four to choose relationships in which they either get rejected or where they reject before being rejected themselves. Rejection and abandonment come under the umbrella of commitment. A partner of a Romantic stated to her, "You are never fully committed." Another partner stated something very similar, "You're not available for a committed relationship." The possibility of rejection and abandonment can create a push/pull dynamic in the relationship, making it difficult for the Romantic to truly commit to someone. Discuss with your partner the following:

- For the Romantic: What comes up for you when you think about abandonment and/or rejection?
- For the Four: Where do you struggle the most when it comes to commitment?
- For the partner: What role do you play with regard to the aforementioned issues?
- For both of you: What is the dance that you both do when it comes to the commitment to each other? Does push/pull play a part?
- For both of you: What is the "classic fight" that you end up having time after time around these particular issues? What is the payoff that you get from your fighting?
- For both of you: At what point in your "classic fight" could you choose to stop and engage differently so that the fight ends differently? Are you willing to let go of the payoff?
- For both of you: After changing your "classic fight," in what ways can you both work toward a healthier commitment, one that includes trust and honesty, and one that leads to a more genuine intimacy and vulnerability?

Feeling unique and special

Romantics are drawn to feeling unique or special. This likely is a defense against their fear of abandonment, fear of being flawed: People who are special aren't flawed and don't get abandoned. Fours can also relate to feeling different and misunderstood –which can shift feeling special or unique. Discuss the questions below:

- For the Romantic: How does feeling special or unique show up in your relationship?
- For the Four: In what way does feeling special or unique protect you? In other words, what is the payoff?
- For the Four: How does being special or unique connect to feeling misunderstood? How do you feel it may block genuine intimacy between you and your partner?

- For the partner: What role do you see your partner's specialness or uniqueness playing in the relationship? How do you feel it may block genuine intimacy between you and your partner?
- For both of you: How can humility play a role in balancing the uniqueness and the ordinary so that the two of you can attain simple happiness?

Envy – Focusing on what Is missing

Romantics have an eye for what is missing. This probably comes from the Four's experience of early loss in their life and their preoccupation with what others have that they don't. Discuss the following:

- For the Four: How does focusing on what is missing and envy show up in your relationship? What is the payoff for this focus?
- For the partner: How are you affected by your partner's focus on what is missing and never being quite satisfied?
- For the Four: How can you catch yourself from falling into focusing on what is missing? What are your specific triggers? How can your partner support you?
- For both of you: How would staying in the present moment affect things overall? Ask yourselves, "Is what is missing truly vital in our relationship?"

Suffering versus happiness – or can they co-exist?

Romantics gravitate toward suffering and toward intense relationships. For them, this represents depth and meaning. To the Romantic, lightheartedness in the relationship can translate to being lightweight, void of depth or meaning. Balance for the Four is the key for both a meaningful and a happy relationship without many highs and lows. Partners of Romantics can sometimes be confused about how to relate to the Four during times of angst. Discuss with your partner the questions below:

- For the Four: How do you handle balancing the suffering and happiness in your life? What are your positive and negative payoffs from suffering?
- For the Four: How do you want your partner to relate to you during the times that you are melancholy or experiencing angst? Be specific. (Know that you can expect a level of acceptance and to be "met" at times – but not enabled or followed into the abyss.)
- For both of you: How do you create balance in your relationship, so that it contains both meaning and depth as well as a lightheartedness?

- For both of you: What do you want your relationship to look like overall? How do you use and respect the gifts of both of your Types in order to create balance, purpose, and meaning – to heal the reasons you were brought together?
- For the Romantic: How will you know when you are running away from either feelings or intimacy?

CHAPTER EIGHT

The Observer (Type Five) In Relationship

Probably my best feature in relationship is my ability to be logical and to stay calm and collected especially during emotional times. I pride myself on being low maintenance due to my self-sufficiency and independence. Even if I truly love someone, I may still give them the message that I can do without them. I can either be possessive of my partner, putting them on a pedestal and wanting them by my side at all times, or I can give them a lot of freedom to explore outside the relationship so that they can bring back stimulating information for us to talk about. Some people say I can be distant and hard to get to know and that I can really be frustrating, especially when I don't say much. Probably my worst features in relationship are my not taking an active role in the relationship, my difficulty expressing my feelings in the moment, and my tendency to withdraw and withhold my thoughts and affection. I also hate it when others intrude upon my personal space and privacy. To be honest with you, relationships can feel quite foreign to me – almost everyone else seems to know much more about them than me.

Observers can be analytical, caring, curious, excited by knowledge, idiosyncratic, independent, objective, observant, perceptive, persevering, self-sufficient, sensitive, reliable, smart, trustworthy, whimsical, and wise.

Characteristics of the Observer (Five) in relationship

Desire for privacy and solitude

Observers can be possessive and protective of their alone time. It is as if energy, time, and space are in short supply. They may feel easily invaded or intruded upon by others, and seek to escape. It is not unusual for Fives to have an "invasive" story to tell from their childhood, which demonstrates how they felt intruded upon. Observers tend to have very permeable boundaries through which everything seems to permeate, as if they've lost a layer of skin that other people have. Their main defense is to retreat, into their private space and into their heads.

Observers are considered the most introverted of all the types. Whereas extroverts thrive on contact with other people and feel replenished by it, introverts in general, and Observers in particular, feel depleted by interactions with others, and need alone time to process their feelings and to recharge their energy. Five is also probably the most self-preservationist of all the types. For the most part, they come from a position of scarcity, and feel a need to conserve their resources, including their energy, which requires them to be alone. This characteristic, which is accentuated in the Self-preservation subtype of Five, can significantly impact the couple relationship.

A psychologist who's an Observer reports that a complaint he frequently hears from his spouse is, "You don't like family gatherings or socializing." He explains, "My reclusive nature is the major challenge" in his relationship. Other Observers wrote that their challenges are, "Needing a lot of space. Tendency to withdraw to regain energy." "My withdrawal into my world." Even Fives of the Social subtype have a strong need for solitude.

Difficulty expressing emotions/difficulty communicating

Observers are in the "mental" or "thinking" triad or center; they tend to approach the world intellectually, and under-use their emotions. Some of them, especially those with a Detective (Six) wing, are out of touch with their emotions and feelings. Fives have a tendency for delayed reactions – they suspend their feelings until another time when they will "replay" the scenario and then attach feelings to the situation after the fact. This way the Observer can feel safer and more in control. One Five (with a Six wing) wrote that her partner's central complaint is, "You never show emotions. You don't touch me enough." Another Observer (who had a Four wing) wrote that her challenge was that "I didn't communicate my feelings."

Coming from a position of scarcity, Observers tend to hoard not only their time and energy, but also their words. They may prefer to express intimacy in nonverbal ways. Not only do they not express their feelings, they often don't communicate at all what they are thinking. One Observer wrote that a challenge to his relationship is "I often do not communicate what is on my mind, then I think that I did."

Ron (co-author of this book), a Two, once worked with a fellow counselor who was an Observer. Ron relates the following story:

Joe and I traveled around the state by car doing mediation work in various post offices, trying to resolve conflict. At the very beginning of our partnership-- after the first car trip I took with Joe -- I bumped into a mutual friend of mine and of Joe's. When she saw me she asked how our first trip together went. I said sarcastically, "Oh it's great if you like to be in a car for about six hours with someone who says about five words the whole trip!" She responded, "That's funny, I just spoke to Joe a couple of hours ago and asked him the very same question and he said that you guys talked up a storm the whole time you were away."

As our partnership continued, I was troubled by not only the lack of words but also by the lack of juice or the lack of feelings between us. It felt to me as if he wasn't really interested in me or our relationship. Eventually I told him that we might as well call off our friendship and partnership, as he really didn't seem interested in me as a friend or a partner. He was shocked. He replied, "What are you talking about...you don't know how much I think about you and our interactions in my private moments."

My relationship with Joe taught me a lot about a Five and also about the Two (my type) and the Five together. I learned that the Observer's lack of words and even lack of affect doesn't necessarily mean he doesn't care about you. As a Giver, I also learned that I didn't need quite as many words as I thought I did to have an intimate connection with another person. As for Joe, he worked hard to bring the emotions he would normally feel in his private moments into more current time and integrate them into our daily interactions.

Tendency to problem-solve rather than just listen

Observers are superb at applying their thinking ability to solve problems. They make excellent therapists, so it's evident that many of them are able to sit and listen. But in the personal arena, some Observers tend to jump to solutions, and to be controlling, rather than be willing to sit with a partner's feelings and listen. An Observer wrote that her husband's central complaint to her was "You are always too quick with an answer or analysis of me and others." Another wrote that "I am a good problem solver, but I can be too direct and stubborn," and a third admitted to, "Knowing the answer, believing I am right and he is not." A retired Five physician wrote that his partner's frequent complaint about him was, "I don't listen, I don't pay attention to details."

In Ron's psychotherapy practice, sometimes a client might drag in their Five partner for couples counseling; Observers can be somewhat reluctant to go to counseling. Psychotherapy usually involves the expressing of intimate thoughts and feelings, something most Fives are not comfortable with. A typical issue may consist of the Observer's partner asking for more of an emotional connection, a desire for the Observer to be there for them, to sit with them, and to listen. One Observer somewhat jokingly asked Ron if it would be okay if he dropped his wife off at Ron's office on a regular basis so that Ron could process her feelings with her and then he wouldn't have to. When the partner asks for more of an emotional connection from Fives, they can feel lost. An Observer may ask the counselor, "What does she want? Just tell me what to do and I'll do it so that we can move forward." It is sometimes difficult for the Observer to understand that feelings and emotional connections can't be problem solved. If the relationship is in serious trouble though, the Five may become nervous about the prospect of losing the partner. Fives do not attach themselves to others easily and they also do not let go easily. To the Observer, partners can seem like very precious possessions.

Criticism, competency, and withdrawal

When asked what Type-related traits keep her from effective problem-solving in her relationship, one Observer wrote, "I don't delve too deeply when problems arise. I escape into books, music, myself." Another noted, "My tendency to avoid, because complications of intimacy in the past have not been worth trying again."

Some Observers appear sweet and laid back, whereas others can be critical and judgmental, much like a Perfectionist. One Observer wrote that her husband's central complaint about her is, "I am too quick to be negative and judgmental." Some Fives can be grumpy and arrogant regarding the daily inconveniences and nuisances of life. It's as if they are annoyed and don't want to waste time or energy on such things; they would rather that we all be logical and use common sense to deal with life's everyday problems. Some Observers can put on a mask of sorts that gives off a know-it-all look. Fives have told Ron that the mask is meant to be off-putting so people will back off and not invade their personal space.

It is important to the Observer to appear competent. Fives need to be careful not to appear as all knowing. Healthy, loving relationships require us to be humble and to surrender at times. Many times it takes a Buddhist "don't know" approach to relationship problems before they can be resolved. In this state, we can become vulnerable and connect intimately with our partner, which is often difficult for Observers.

Wings

In Chapter Three we explained that each personality Type is likely to possess some characteristics of one of the two adjacent Types on the nine-pointed enneagram diagram, which are termed the *wings* of that type (see page xx). Fives with Four wings are like the coming together of two totally different worlds. The Observer comes from a world that prizes the intellect, whereas the Romantic revels in emotions. Some people feel that this personality combination can be the most self-absorbed and the most withdrawn and introverted of all the types, which can be hardest of all the types to try to reach. But when they come to terms with their intellectual uniqueness, it can be the richest and the most interesting of all the Types.

Fives with Six wings embody a combination of two fear types. Enneagram author Don Riso says, "Intimate relationships may be challenging for them because of the isolation tendencies of the Five and the suspiciousness of the Six." This combination needs to work on accessing their heart, their trust in humankind, and the importance of interdependence in relationships. The gift they bring to relationships is their undying loyalty, even to the point of blind loyalty.

Observers in stress and security

Observers have a particular connection to enneagram types Eight (the Leader) and Seven (the Adventurer). When feeling secure, Observers may express the positive traits of the Leader. They become more assertive regarding their needs and their boundaries, no longer feeling easily invaded. Instead of waiting on the sidelines, they will engage both physically and emotionally with others. They also become willing to take action without first knowing everything about the situation. On the negative side of Eight, they can become dominating and controlling of others, especially loved ones. When under stress, they may demonstrate the negative characteristics of the Adventurer, plunging into excessive mindless action. They feel overcommitted and stretched too thin by too many options, too much to do, and not enough time to reflect and consider. On the positive side, they can become more playful, putting themselves out there more, and accessing the imagination of both the Five and the Seven.

Gifts of Observers in relationship – how they help their relationship thrive

For all pairings, partners need to understand what the other person considers to be a gift to the relationship. This may differ from what you would like to receive. We saw this with Romantics, many of whom considered their intensity, drama, and emotions to be positive contributors to the relationship. In contrast, Observers believe that they help their relationship thrive by being low-maintenance partners who are independent and don't make many demands.

A Five psychologist writes, "I will adapt and accommodate unselfishly to keep things balanced and happy. I am sensitive to my wife's feelings and situation and don't take criticism too personally." A 34-year old Observer married to a Perfectionist, says, "We both like to do separate activities." Observers also point to their competence, objectivity, and problem-solving abilities. "I am very grounded and more discerning than he is." "I can understand and see patterns and problems develop, and can bring them out in the open early for discussion." "As a Five, I have enriched our relationship with information and many activities, educational and personal. My desire to be open and nonjudgmental about others."

How Observers feel about other types in relationship

Asked which types they struggle with the most, Observers most commonly mentioned The Perfectionist (Type One), the Giver (Type Two), and the Mediator (Type Nine). Some comments were:

The Perfectionist: "Too critical, which triggers my own inadequacy feelings." "They make me feel too guilty. I strive very hard to do the right thing." "They are too serious and I don't do perfection." "So rigid, both of us easily lose patience". Perfectionists and Observers are actually look-a-likes. Their similar characteristics can represent the shadow aspect in the relationship. The One's need for perfectionism mimics the Five's need for competence. Both want to be seen as being right or correct, the Perfectionist out of wanting love whereas the Five wants to feel safe in the world. The Observer's hold on his own competency is more tenuous than other people realize and the Perfectionist may tend to undermine it.

The Giver: "Doesn't leave me alone." "Too needy, doesn't allow me enough space". "I can see through the nurturing and doting to the basic self-serving." "I don't want them to intrude on my needs." Like most fear types, the Observer is skeptical and untrusting of the Two's giving. Observers, especially those with Four wings, look for authenticity and truth in others, and they question the motivation of all the giving that a Two does. The Observer may also feel annoyed with the Giver's constant intrusiveness and their seemingly knowing what is best for the Five.

The Mediator: "I never know what they're thinking." "They don't do enough to truly help themselves and don't get things done (at first) the way "I" think they should and could be." "I need more decisive." "Won't stand up to me – instead aligns too closely." "Not knowing what they want drives me crazy." Fives and Nines are a common pairing whose positive features will be described in a later chapter. However, the Mediator's "go with the flow, trust the universe, and everything will turn out okay" approach rattles the Observer's basic way of being in the world – competent and independent.

Observers reported being most compatible with other Fives and with Mediators (Nine):

The Observer: "I like people who think and feel. I like people who are reclusive like me. They understand the value and reason for solitude and don't judge it as something bad." "Just like me, can have quiet time together and read without being bothered, do separate quiet activities in one room." "They allow me to have space. They don't drain my energy." "This is the best ever! I feel understood, I don't have to work so hard to explain."

The Double-Five pairing clearly demonstrates the idea of collusion, which is the co-illusion about the world and relationships that the pairing brings. StarTrekkies would most likely call it the ultimate "mind meld." Unless one of the Observers spends time at their Eight (Leader) connecting point, this combination is usually filled with respect toward one another for their intellectual pursuits and non-intrusiveness When two Observers get together, they need to beware the lack of feelings and the lack of juice that can be present .

The Mediator: "They don't make any demands on me." "They are willing to fit into my agenda. Good listeners. Open to discussion." "They are capable of hearing what you say." "Flexible, easygoing." As stated earlier, Fives can be drawn toward Nines in both a positive and a negative way. There is an "opposites attract" to this pairing and both can be teachers to one another. Mediators will be sensitive to the Observer's need for privacy and independence, sometimes too much so. This pairing needs to be careful of the separateness that can grow between them both because of the lack of feelings and the independence that each prizes.

Advice Observers give other Observers in relationship

In their advice to other Observers, Fives emphasize the need to connect more with their feelings and to be more expressive of emotions with their partner. There is also advice regarding the tendency to withdraw. They wrote,

- Learn to share the experience rather than serve it.
- Listen. Be attentive to the other's needs.
- Try to be more open and spontaneous and show your love and affection.
- Explore your feelings and express them openly when it is appropriate.
- Don't withdraw from problems; be ready to discuss them.

These comments deserve careful attention from Observers. The emphasis on listening, feelings, and on recognizing and fighting the tendency to withdraw taps into the core issues that Fives bring to relationship.

What partners of Observers need to know

Friends or partners of Fives can feel frozen out by the Observer. At times there appears to be a clear "Do not Disturb" sign etched on the Five's face. His or her withdrawal can make you feel as if you are striving to speak to someone who is a great distance away. Partners of Observers need to know that the Five needs time to evaluate new ideas that differ from your own. Their first response to a new idea regarding the relationship may be a strong "no". Given time and thought, the Observer can actually come around to embracing new ideas that may be stimulating to the partnership.

Know that you are probably more loved by the Five than you'll ever really know. Losing a partner can be devastating to the Observer, causing more of an implosion than an explosion. Don't take personally the Five's reticence to engage. Observers have a difficult time expressing emotions. They often don't even know what they feel. When the partner of an elderly Five, feeling especially warm towards him one evening, said, "I sure do love you!" he replied slowly, "I don't really know what love is, but I love you too." If you are aching for more hugs and kisses from your Five, the solution is to model affectionate behavior. For example, hug him or her whenever you greet each other or leave the house. Tell him you want a hug first thing in the morning and last thing at night. When he initiates a hug, tell him how much you like it. It may take months, but the Observer is likely to learn eventually. Many Observers in fact have been touch-deprived and believe they are unlovable, so your affection is a corrective experience for them. Positive strokes and respect for the Five can go a long way in getting them to come out of their shell and helping them to make strides in the social arena.

Observers are thin-skinned and easily pushed away by strong emotions. Five's partner can inadvertently push away the Observer. You need to moderate emotions so as not to overwhelm him. Observers need space, time alone, and privacy. Recognize that this recharges their batteries, and don't crowd them.

Exercises for the Observer (Five) and Your Partner

The following exercises are intended to work with some of the primary characteristics and issues of the Observer in relationship.

Gifts of the Observer (Type Five)

Before we tackle the more challenging issues of the Observer, let's talk about the gifts that the Observer brings to the partner and to the relationship overall.

- For the partner: What gifts you feel that your Five partner brings to the relationship? Describe how they affect you.
- For the Observer: What are the gifts you bring to a relationship?
- For the partner: What have you learned from your Five partner about the way to be in relationship, that you weren't aware of until you met him/her?

I won't ask much from you – so don't ask much from me

As children, Observers report feeling either invaded and smothered or not given enough attention. Based on this, the childhood strategy becomes one of self-sufficiency. Later on in life and in relationships they have a strong tendency to withdraw behind boundaries that provide them with a sense of privacy and protection. All of this can make a partner feel frozen out or as if the Observer doesn't really need them. Discuss the questions below to see what role these issues play in your relationship.

- For the Observer: Do you at times claim or act as if you really don't need your partner – when in actuality, you would be quite lost without him or her?
- For both of you: Enneagram teacher Helen Palmer recommends that Observers work to overcome their three "S"s – Secrecy, Superiority, and Separateness. Discuss the role these three issues play in your relationship.
- For the Five: What role does your withholding or your need for privacy play in your relationship?
- For the Five: What is the payoff for the withholding or the withdrawing that you do? What are the negative consequences?
- For the Five: What role does generosity versus stinginess play in your relationship? Where could you be more generous as a partner?
- For the Partner: How does your Five partner's withholding or withdrawing affect you? Have you ever felt "frozen out" or not needed in the relationship?
- For the Partner: What would you like to ask from your Five partner that would help you feel more included or give you the feeling of having a more shared experience?
- For the Five: What comes up for you when you think about loosening your boundaries and allowing your partner more access to the personal, private side of yourself? How do you handle feelings of being invaded or smothered?
- For the Five: How do you feel about becoming more "attached" to your partner? What fears do you have around the idea of attachment and the possible loss that you could end up experiencing?
- For both of you: How do you define genuine intimacy between the two of you? How can you both work on creating a shared partnership where you allow each other in, making yourself vulnerable to one another, sharing your feelings – your wants, needs, fears, and desires?

Feelings: After the fact or maybe not at all

"An Observer in love is caught between being affected by strong positive feelings and the habit of not wanting to feel at all." Helen Palmer

Feelings can be scary for Observers. Many report feeling as if they had to leave their body and retreat into the mind in order to feel safe. This meant trading their feelings for analysis. Fives frequently detach emotionally during an experience, then later in private replay the experience and only then attach feelings to it. This keeps them from feeling in the moment, thus depriving partners and themselves of a shared emotional experience. The goal is for the Five to be able to integrate both feelings and experiences and to be able to share those feelings with partners in the moment. Discuss the following questions together:

- For the Observer: How well do you feel you integrate feelings with experiences in the moment?
- For the partner: Can you feel the Observer's presence during intimate moments or do you feel him or her detaching, afraid to have feelings? How does this affect you?
- For the Observer: What helps you be able to integrate feelings with experiences in the moment and in the presence of your partner? What would you like to ask of your partner that would be of help to you?
- For both of you: How can both work on increasing self-disclosure and feelings in your relationship? What are your fears? Where do you feel threatened? How can you increase your overall trust in your relationship?

Being there for your Observer partner

In the exercises above, we took a hard look at some of the issues the Observer brings to a relationship and how both partners can work with these challenges to have a better, more evolved relationship. At the same time, we want to honor the Observer's basic nature and not try to make him into someone he is not. As a partner, it is important to be discerning when assessing whether your partner's behaviors are harmless or if they are compulsive or excessive. Remember, it is important that a partner be accepted and cherished at a core level. If you are going to be with an Observer, don't forget to:

- Try not to crowd him. Ask your Five partner how you can respect his need for space, time, and privacy.
- Don't be demanding, although you can be direct, using as little chitchat as possible. If you are putting forth a new suggestion, ask the Observer if he needs time to evaluate ideas that may be different from his own.

- Appreciate the Observer's sensitivity. Since the Five can be thin-skinned, ask him to tell you when he may be overwhelmed by any strong emotions or aggressive tendencies you may have.
- Appreciate the Five's mind and intellect and the time he may need to spend alone, especially if worried or stressed out. His mind can also bring great objectivity.

CHAPTER NINE

The Detective (Type Six) In Relationship

Probably my best feature in relationship is that once I commit to someone, I can be tremendously loyal. If bad times occur, I'll stick up for my partner and for the relationship with great courage and determination. I can be playfully childlike or a little eccentric, which most people find endearing. Sometimes it may seem as if I won't let things go – I don't like things swept under the rug – so I'll try to get things out in the open by asking the "hard" questions. It may seem as if I'm negative or overly skeptical, but it is important for me to have clarity when there are unanswered questions in my mind. Probably my worst feature in relationship is that I can be paranoid, imagining worst-case scenarios, especially if I feel insecure or uncertain. If I feel threatened I may see you as the distrustful authority or even the "enemy," and I will either withdraw or approach you head on.

An unexamined life may not be worth living, but the over-examined life is hell.

--Abigail Thomas, *A Three Dog Life*

But you see, most of us are afraid to find out for ourselves what is true and what is false, and that is why we merely accept what somebody else says. The important thing is to question, to observe, never to accept.

-- J. Krishnamurti, *Life Ahead*

If a man will begin with certainties, he shall end in doubts; but if he will be content to begin with doubts, he shall end in certainties.
-- Francis Bacon

Characteristics of the Six in relationship

Detectives are the most complex type in the enneagram system, because there are two kinds, *phobic* and *counterphobic*. The phobic person is someone who senses some sort of threat and chooses the flight response – quickly running away or getting out of harm's way. The counterphobic Six senses danger and opts for the fight response – challenging the threat by moving toward it and confronting it that way. Note that both approaches have to do with feeling fear and are just the opposite sides of the same coin. Detectives can be a mix of phobic and counterphobic depending on the situation, or they might have been one or the other at certain times in their life. It is important to know the most often utilized approach, as this will significantly color their approach to relationships.

Fear, loyalty, and trust

Detectives approach the world from a position of fear and distrust. To "trust or not to trust" is their major quandary regarding relationships. Fear is the lens through which the Detective peers, and that lens is colored with worst-case scenario thinking, hyper-awareness, and loyalty versus betrayal. In relationship, Detectives fear silence; their doubting mind begins to ask, "Why didn't he call?" or "Has anything changed between us?" They want frequent reassurance and reality checks. Paula, a phobic Six, summed it all up this way,

I have extreme fear that can change to terror. Often, I fear I'm in a war zone and have to be hyper-vigilant. I'm always checking people for cues, to know what they're about. Authority figures can be terrifying to me. At times I've gotten in their face, but mostly I want to blend in and not make any waves. I'm loyal to a fault – in relationships and at work. Sometimes I let people walk over me. If I feel betrayed – for example if someone was dishonest with me – I am crushed. It's very easy for me to think of worst-case scenarios; I believe they're really going to happen. I have an over-the-top need for safety and security. I like to have structure, to know where I'm going and with whom. I scan the environment for danger, and I scan people's faces. I want to know, am I physically and emotionally safe?

The above provides valuable clues to how the phobic Six looks at life and relationships. The description describes how most of us felt in September 2001 when the World Trade Center was attacked. During that time, many Detectives felt that 9/11 substantiated their basic beliefs that the world is an unsafe place. Because it was a worst-case scenario of sorts, many of them also reported an almost calm feeling after it happened – Sixes can experience a kind of "eye of the hurricane" composure during such situations. However, for many who are not Sixes and who prefer living in a state of denial about anything bad happening, 9/11 became a wake-up call. If someone is receptive to experiencing the mindsets of the other types, the world of the Six became accessible to all of us during that time. In a relationship, partners of Detectives describe the Six as tremendously loyal, while occasionally feeling they are perceived as the enemy, both experiencing discomfort around authority figures. A counterphobic Six former military officer, Warren, explained;

Someone has to prove himself beyond a doubt for me to trust. If you expect the worst of people, you'll never be disappointed. I have a hard time making decisions. I look at all the alternatives, and it takes me forever to decide. Yes, this was a handicap in the Army. So was my problem with authority figures. I resented being told what to do. I just didn't have any respect for authority. I expressed my opinion, and I always questioned.

When a Detective's partner either tries to or actually does become the authority in the relationship, the reaction might be a "you are the enemy" attitude, The Detective questioning if they'll be safe. Authorities have the power to protect, but they also have the power to control, to oppress, and to betray.

Although fear is often seen as a tendency of the mind to jump to the worst-case scenario, some counterphobic Sixes may nonetheless view themselves as very positive, upbeat people who see the glass as half full rather than half empty. How can we explain this? The answer may be that Detectives don't like to stay in a gray area. If they feel depression, sadness or confusion – gray areas --they try to escape as soon as possible. Especially if they're counterphobic, their response might be to just do it! Take action! They might define this as being positive.

Trust does not come easily for Detectives. One of their core issues is betrayal, so the lack of trust can adversely impact a relationship. One Detective, married 23 years, wrote that her partner's central complaint is, "Why don't you trust me? You're never going to trust me." Another Detective wrote that if he were to put a slogan on his T-shirt, it would be, "It's a miracle that relationships work at all." A Six woman admitted that even after six years of marriage, she worried, "You're here today, but what about tomorrow?" Married 31 years, a woman related,

I have complete faith in my husband and the relationship we have built together. It took me 15 years to completely trust him. What did it was getting breast cancer and seeing how he responded to that.

The internal questioning to which Detectives are prone chips away at an initial message such as "you are loved" until it may slowly erode the relationship. Enneagram expert Helen Palmer, a Six herself, recommends "measured reassurance," repeating important messages. This can be valuable when it comes to building trust with Detectives. Another Six put it this way: "We only want to clarify what we believe to be true. Our questions are not because we don't believe you; it's because we need to be certain for ourselves."

Loyalty

In Paula's comments, she states that she can be "loyal to a fault." A male Six concurred, and added, "In other words, always make your partner look good in public and with the family." Once someone has earned the Detective's loyalty, he or she will be there through thick and thin. Detectives are known for their stable, long-term relationships. In the absence of someone or something to which one feels loyalty, the best defense a Six has against being betrayed is to seek his or her own counsel first and foremost, and to be discerning whom he or she allows in.

Many Detectives relate to the concept of the "committee" that we have inside our heads. Sixes seem to have assembled or "taken in" a team of people throughout their lifetime that serves as the greater authority, one they turn to for making important decisions. Sixes can become extremely loyal to or even dependent on an authority or protective figure. Whether it is a spouse, mentor, family member, and/or friend to whom the Six has become attached, he will be very loyal but also may rebel.

Rebellion

Detectives are prone to demonstrate rebellious or "the in-their-face" behavior in dealing with authority figures. A childhood message that Sixes frequently describe is their discovery of an authoritative or protective figure, attachment, loyalty, and subsequent safety. It may be in the form of aligning oneself with an institution or company that will provide all the necessary income and benefits, or it may be a partner who appears strong and safe. Whatever the actual situation, Six at some point frequently starts to question his or her dependency, perhaps ignited by what the Detective perceives as some act of betrayal. Sixes may also question whether they have given their power away by aligning themselves with this protective figure and the resulting possible worst-case scenario. When this happens, the partner of the Six may feel that unexpectedly she has become the enemy. Both parties need to recognize what is going on in order to more openly and directly address the fear and power issue lurking under the surface of the relationship.

Decision making

Although some Detectives can make decisions without having all the information, and subsequently do not question or regret their choices, many find it difficult to commit to a choice, since their "doubting mind" tends repeatedly to second-guess itself. Questioning what could go wrong is a part of the process, although they can be very good at quickly analyzing the pros and cons of an important project. A phobic Six woman wrote,

Decision-making is hard for me. There are so many variables that I get anxious that I won't make the right decision. I worry that one bad decision will snowball and lead to others.

According to another Detective,

"I have trust issues. I want to slow down and look at all possible outcomes before moving through on something. My husband complains, 'You always try to slow me down.'"

In a relationship, the upside of this tendency is that Detectives are really good at "staying current," meaning they are careful that issues don't get put aside and that problems that need to get talked about do. "Staying current" is an excellent way to keep a partnership healthy. Sixes dig for what is bubbling under the surface and question partners about what is going on. They have a good nose for something being not quite right. On the other hand, partners sometimes complain that it feels too negative, as if the glass is always half-empty, and that the questioning can feel intrusive or like an interrogation.

For example, an entrepreneur of Type Seven (Adventurer) talked about seeing himself as an "idea" person. He loved to fantasize about new projects and the positive effects they would have on others. When he enthusiastically presented these ideas to his skeptical Six wife, he felt as if she was taking a pin, sticking it in a balloon and popping all the air out of it. After a while, he became reluctant to tell her his ideas. He didn't realize that for the Detective, speaking what's on her mind and questioning her partner is anxiety-reducing behavior, her way of leaning into the anxiety and confronting it in lieu of running away and denying its existence. Through counseling, this couple was able to understand each other's approach to new projects. He learned that he scared her with his big ideas, and that she thought she was helping him with her questioning; she learned to allow him his fantasies and positive moments without seeming as though she was trying to take them away.

Anger, aggressiveness, and projection

Counterphobic Sixes may be perceived as prickly, aggressive, and easy to anger. In fact, some can be confused with Eights (Leaders), the Type generally associated with such overt behaviors. The anger is often a counterphobic response to fear. The Detective will project, react defensively, and protect herself with anger. Laura, a counterphobic Six offered an example of this. "My former boyfriend asked me to pick up his suit at the cleaner's, and I went into a rage! I said to him, 'I'm not your servant! Go pick up your own damn dry cleaning.'" Later, she realized that the worst-case scenario immediately came to mind, and she was off and running, thinking, "This is going to be a pattern in the relationship; he's always going to be asking me to do things for him!" Her boyfriend just listened for a couple of minutes, and then said calmly, "I'm only asking you to pick up the dry cleaning today." Laura realized she was overreacting.

Detectives have a tendency to project internal fears onto others in an attempt to head problems off at the pass. In the story above, Laura projected her stored-up fears about being controlled in a relationship onto her boyfriend. Feeling a lack of power along with thinking they are not being heard, Detectives overcompensate by becoming reactive.

According to a Detective, what keeps her from effective problem solving in her marriage is, "As a reactive type, my temper definitely gets in the way. I've learned many ways to calm myself down over the years and know I have to do that before I can effectively problem-solve. I respond proactively instead of reacting passively." Another wrote that her challenge in her marriage was "self doubt, attacking as a way to get reassurance of my desirability." A Six woman, married to a Nine man, wrote that his main criticism was, "You always argue with me."

Relationship expert John Gottman refers to these kind of overreactions as "harsh start-ups." His research shows that discussions that begin with a harsh start-up are pretty much doomed from the beginning.

Some Sixes become alarmed when things are too peaceful; they fear the "calm before the storm" and that some disaster is close at hand. They may precipitate a drama or disagreement as a way to get reassurance that they are still loved and that all is well. One Detective reported that his partner grumbled, "You always keep stirring things up so that we can never get settled down."

The Detective under stress and when secure

The enneagram teaches us that Detectives have a special connection with two other Types, the Mediator (Nine) and the Achiever (Three). When they feel secure, Detectives take on some of the positive qualities of the Mediator: They feel safer in the world. They begin to see people as friendly instead of unfriendly, and they trust more. Without the need to be on guard, they relax and perhaps take more risks. Their minds quiet down, they get out of their heads, and feel more at home in their bodies. If Sixes access the negative side of the Nine, though, they will demonstrate a merging quality in which they will lose appropriate boundaries with others.

When they are under stress -- primarily when their security is threatened and they feel unsafe –Detectives' behavior resembles the negative aspects of the Achiever (Type Three). Phobic Sixes might adopt flighty, manic behaviors or find themselves frozen between fight and flight. Counterphobic Sixes feel impelled to take action. Although still frightened, they too can take on a manic quality. Accessing Type Three can give the Detective an authoritarian front and make him or her more image conscious. In this case, they can become more confident, taking action in the face of fear.

Wings and subtypes

In Chapter Three we explained that each enneagram personality Type is likely to possess some characteristics of one of the two adjacent Types on the nine-pointed enneagram diagram (see page 11). Sixes with a Five wing are quite different from Sixes with a Seven wing. The former are much more contracted, steady and reclusive -- they don't want to go out into the world as much, nor take as many risks. In contrast, a Six with a Seven wing is more sociable, more comfortable interacting with others.

Detectives of different subtypes use specific strategies to mask their inner doubt. For example, the Sexual Six manages her anxiety by striving to appear strong, powerful, and attractive. Even a frightened person can feel powerful if people think (s)he is strong, beautiful, sexy, and/or smart. Self-preservation ("warm") Sixes get close to people by disarming their anger and allying in friendship. Their safety (self-preservation) is tied to other people, so they want to understand others deeply. Bonded by warmth, Self-preservation Sixes say, "We're in it together," and "You are not alone."

How Detectives help their relationship thrive

Detectives perceive their main gifts to their relationship to be loyalty and strength, part of which is keeping commitments. One Detective wrote, "I have reached out to his family and become close to his daughter. I have supported him with his health challenges; I see both of our needs as being important." A Six man reported that he brought to his relationship commitment, responsibility, determination, supportiveness, fairness, and reliability. He helped his relationship thrive by "honoring my commitments when things were not going well." Others explained, "I am incredibly loyal – a giver, a nurturer of others. I work very hard and support others to my own detriment." "I predict problems and talk about internal experience." It's clear that Detectives can make wonderful partners - loyal, caring, mentally stimulating, and self-sacrificing.

What the partner could have done to help the relationship thrive:

Because Detectives struggle with fear, doubt, and worst-case scenario thinking, they need a great deal of reassurance. Sixes wrote that what they their partner to do is "to be reassuring about me and the relationship – that I don't always have to have everything together." Partners also need to be able to handle strong emotions at times, to be committed to staying put. Sixes also asked that partners "acknowledge my strengths and talents." Although Detectives are strong, they want affirmation from their partner; being strong does not mean they always want to "drive the bus." Sixes can have a hard time recognizing their positive qualities. Their questioning and "amnesia" regarding their triumphs make it difficult for them to feel good about themselves at times, thereby undermining their self-esteem. Partners who can mirror how the Six has made a difference can help Sixes feel more positive about themselves.

How Detectives feel about other types in relationship

When asked which types they struggle with the most, more Detectives chose the Giver (Type Two), the Romantic (Type Four), and the Leader (Type Eight). Some comments were:

The Giver: "They seem false – don't share the same values. Too much emphasis on appearance." "Too much attention on me. Neediness." "I don't need you as much as you think I do." "I feel the manipulation destroys my being able to trust them -- like liars." It would appear that Sixes struggle with the "Image" types and their approach to relationships.

The Romantic: "They can be impossible to please." "My dad was a Four living in the past. We didn't share common goals – he wanted to withdraw from the world. He was self absorbed." "The relationship is never enough." "They don't seem to want anything to be different; they love their story too much."

The Leader: "I fear their assertiveness." "They come across as sullen." "They can be judgmental." "I can't bear the confrontational, angry expression." "They threaten my sense of control." Whereas some Sixes can feel intimidated by the Eight's power, others report that they feel safe and that they appreciate not having to look under the surface because of the Leader's "what you see is what you get" style.

Detectives reported being most compatible with Observers (Type Five) and Adventurers (Type Seven). In their words,

The Observer: "I have a Five wing. I respect their need for space and vice versa. I admire their intellectual bent." "Fives can also display quirky behavior. " "I know they respect my privacy." "I can have a rational discussion."

The Adventurer: "I have fun with them." "They can let go and move on." "My wing. I like adventure." "Pulls me to my Seven light side."

Advice Detectives give other Sixes in relationship
The advice Detectives give to other Sixes in relationship relates overwhelmingly to recognizing their fearfulness and tendency to project their fears onto others. One Detective wrote,

Recognize that FEAR (false evidence appearing real) is a major driving energy in your life. Look for ways to strengthen your relationship, rather than seeing his or her questionable or doubtful behaviors. Sixes have a tendency to see negative possibilities in a situation. It is important for us to look for positive possibilities.

Other recommendations were,

- "I would tell them to learn to identify their own feelings and needs, to check perceptions out with others (in order to avoid projections), to be open to support (as in therapy, groups)".
- "Become conscious of your projections and the many ways you mask your fear from yourself. Therapy helps."
- "Learn how to live with ambiguity and ambivalence in yourself and your partner."
- "Be aware of negative, defeatist thinking, assuming things won't work out."
- "Remember that not everything that is bad will necessarily happen. It's not always about you."
- "Don't get down on yourself for the doubt and fear; work with them, become friends, and try to see the good you bring with these qualities."
- "Learn to trust yourself, in order to trust a partner. Take more risks and trust people sooner."
- "Don't ignore your heart." [Because many Detectives so strongly seek security, some may make decisions based on whether it will increase their security rather than from the heart.])
- "Be aware of how much your security needs drive you to connect with and get in the way of connecting with another."
- "Deal with your own issues and be very aware of projection and fear. Know that you can always take care of yourself by yourself, and enjoy the relationship for the gifts it brings."

Exercises for the Detective and your Partner

The following exercises are intended to take a look at some of the primary characteristics and issues of the Detective in relationship. We hope the following exercises will help the Six and their partner to be more aware of what it is like to be in a relationship with a Six and how to illuminate and break unhealthy patterns embedded in the relationship and instead create more of an atmosphere of understanding, compassion, and love.

Gifts of the Detective

Before we tackle the more difficult issues, let's talk about the gifts that the Detective brings to the partner and to the relationship overall.

"Probably my best feature in relationship is that once I commit to someone, I can be tremendously loyal. If bad times occur, I'll stick up for my partner and for the relationship with great courage and determination."

Discuss the questions below together:
- For the Six's partner: Describe the gifts your Six partner brings to the relationship – especially the loyalty. Give a concrete example and describe how it made you feel.
- For the Detective : Describe the gifts you bring to the relationship – especially the idea of loyalty. Talk about why trust and loyalty is so important to you.
- For both of you: What role does commitment, trust, and loyalty plays in your relationship overall?

Fear

The core issue for Detectives is fear. Within a relationship, this fear can rear its ugly head in various ways. To set the tone for the exercises below, listen again to how one of our type Six survey participants summarized their fear:

I have extreme fear that can go into terror. A lot of time I fear I'm in a war zone and I have to be hyper-vigilant. I'm always checking people for cues, to know what they're about. Authority figures can be terrifying to me. At times I've gotten in their face, but mostly I want to blend in and not make any waves. I'm loyal to a fault – in relationships and at work. Sometimes I let people walk over me. If I feel betrayed – for example if someone was dishonest with me – I feel crushed. It's very easy for me to think of worst-case scenarios; I believe they're really going to happen. I have an over-the-top need for safety and security. I like to have structure. I like to know where I'm going and with whom. I scan the environment for danger and I scan people's faces. I want to know, am I safe physically and emotionally?

Remember, there are two different types of Detectives – phobic and counterphobic. Each handles fear differently. It is not unusual for counter-phobic Sixes to be out of touch with their fear. Discuss the questions below with your partner:
- For the Six: Do you believe you express your fear primarily in a phobic or counterphobic way? Please give an example.

- For the partner: How do you think your Six partner expresses fear and how does it affect you?
- For both of you: Together, what goal would you like to accomplish with regard to how fear gets expressed in your relationship?

"Has anything changed between us?"

Detectives can be great trouble-shooters. They can spot a potential problem miles away. In partnerships, these skills can assure them that matters don't just drift along or that issues get put aside and not talked about until they become relationship-ending problems. If, on the other hand, these trouble-shooting skills are carried too far, they can result in the Detective looking for or even seeing problems that aren't really problems. Many times a partner of a Detective will complain about the Six, perceiving only the negative in a situation and making mountains out of molehills. In an old enneagram joke regarding this situation, the Six not only sees the glass as half-empty, but also sees the glass as glass and that it can break. The joke refers to the sensitivity that Detectives have for what could go wrong, or for worst-case scenarios. Recognizing their extremes in perception and using moderation will help the Six balance his or her relationship.

- For the Six: Do you feel you are good at sensing potential problems before they become "mountains" in the relationship?
- For the Six: Do you ever feel that this "skill" is carried too far – seeing problems where there aren't any?
- For the partner: Do you appreciate your Six partner's ability to pick up on issues, especially before they become "mountains?"
- For the partner: Do you ever feel your partner makes mountains out of molehills?
- For both of you: Overall, do you feel that enough time is spent toward focusing on the positives in the relationship as opposed to the negatives?

Detectives constantly scan their environment to see if anything has changed in the relationship. They repeatedly ask questions such things as, Does my partner still love me? What is wrong now? What did I do? Is my partner upset with me about anything? Are they thinking about leaving me? How the Six goes about finding the answers to these questions is important. They need to make sure that their internal fear hasn't risen to the point where it spills out with a kind of venom, making their partner feel attacked or at the least accused of something they haven't done. The following topics and the accompanying recommendations will hopefully help the Detective and his or her partner deal with the fear in a healthy manner.

- For the Detective: Do you frequently question your partner's love for you?
- For the partner: How do you feel when your love for your partner being questioned? Do you ever feel "attacked" by your partner's questioning?
- For both of you: How can you improve your relationship using positive and measured reassurance?

Staying current

Because of the Detective's fear, "staying current" in a relationship with one's partner is very important. That way, hopefully the Six's fear will remain at a reasonable level instead of building over time. The Detective's fear, when at a manageable level, can be useful in assuring that problems in the partnership are discussed in a timely way. In this way, very little will be swept under the carpet and ignored. In order that the fear does not become excessive, take time to sit down on a regular basis with your partner and check in with each other about possible concerns that may be surfacing in the relationship without being talked about. Use the following questions to keep current in your relationship:

- For both of you: Is there anything we need to be talking about so as to stay current in our relationship?
- For both of you: Is there anything you are hesitant to talk to me about? Is there anything I can do to make you feel more comfortable in opening up to me?

It's all in the way you say it

When words reach the tip of your tongue, hold back half of them.
                    -- Chinese proverb

As we said earlier, because of the Detective's hyper-awareness and assertive questioning style, they need to make sure they are not perceived as attacking or interrogating their partner. Staying current in the relationship will help to keep the fear at a reasonable level so that the Six doesn't become reactive. As we also mentioned earlier (p .158), relationship expert John Gottman refers to these kinds of behaviors as "harsh start-ups." In a nutshell, this is about being very conscious of how you start a disagreement. Disagreements that begin with harsh words are usually doomed from the start. Use some of the following communication tips to help with this particular issue:

- To soften your tone, use "I" statements instead of "You" statements when communicating with each other. Try to eliminate harsh-start-ups" by committing to staying away from initiating a conversation with a loud, aggressive, accusatory style. Or at the least, try to catch yourself in the moment of a harsh start-up and take a time-out. Remember, harsh start-ups tend to scare and overwhelm the partner, causing them to shut down, and hardly ever end positively.
- Learn about Marshall Rosenberg's Non-Violent Communication techniques. Try to use non-violent communication that bans blaming, criticizing, labeling, and/or making demands of the other.
- Try coming from your heart. Detectives are head types, meaning that the primary bulk of their energy is held in the head area. It is sometimes important for Sixes to communicate things from their heart space so as to soften their energy. Try using the following statement:

"If I channel what my head wants to say through my heart, what I would like to say to you changes to…"

- Or, use the following technique: as you ask your question, make sure you ask it in a way that tells your partner that you still love him or her. For example,

"I love you and want to be close to you. But when you seem angry and accusatory as you ask me something, I feel distant and detached from you. Would you be willing to speak more softly to me?"

Dealing with the actual fear

It is important for Detectives to take responsibility for their fears. They also need to be aware that underneath most reactive behaviors is fear. The Six commonly projects the fear onto the partner, accusing them of being up to something. Couples may also find themselves fighting over "false Issues" – things that are not the real issue, usually because the real issue is too scary. When the Six feels strong emotions, it can be helpful for them to assume that these feelings are coming from fear. When addressed more openly, the fear will usually: (a) subside, because it is being talked about openly. Try using the following statements when experiencing strong emotions:

- "I'm feeling reactive so I believe that something is scaring me in our relationship. Would you please work with me so I can get to the bottom of my fears?"
- "If I were to guess what is scaring me, I'd say it has to do with..."
- "I think the reason this situation scares me is..."
- "The real reason this situation scares me is..."

Once the fears are recognized and worked with in a more productive way, they can be dealt with more authentically instead of being either projected onto the partner or fought about in a "false issue" way.

Worst-case scenarios

"Both optimists and pessimists contribute to our society. The optimist invents the airplane and the pessimist the parachute."
-- G.B. Stern

When something is frightening them, Detectives can easily go to worst-case scenarios. For example, one morning the wife rushes off to a business meeting, overlooking her usual ritual of a good-bye kiss for her stay-at-home Six husband. This causes him to jump to worst case-scenario thinking , which is to immediately worry about the relationship ending. Sometimes it is a good idea to just get the worst case scenario out in the open, to assess if it is truly rational. Try some of the following statements below to explore worst-case scenario thinking:

- I know it might sound a little ridiculous, but would you please bear with me as I try to express my fear at a worst-case scenario level?
- I need to check in with you about what I'm sensing or feeling. Please recognize that this is about me and not about you.
- When I think of the fear I'm experiencing, I know it might sound a little crazy, but I can easily imagine it becoming. . .
- Being as objective as possible, do you think my fears are rational, or not?

[Most of the time, there is some kernel of "truth" in the Six's thinking. Remember, fear can be a valuable tool to keep true issues from being swept under the rug.]

- Do you feel there is at least a kernel of truth attached to my worst-case fear?
- Now that I've said the issue out loud, and with your input, I can now see my fear in a more realistic light that looks more like. . .
- Would you be willing to work with me regarding the fears and concerns I have regarding our relationship?
- And finally, enneagram teacher Helen Palmer recommends to Sixes that they spend at least as much time in "best-case scenario thinking" as they do in worst- case scenario thinking.

Working on trust and faith

The antidote to fear is to somehow reach a level of trust with your partner and -- even more importantly for the Detective -- to reach a level of trust within themselves. Sixes need to realize that there are no guarantees in life how long a relationship will last or whether a partner will stay long-term. It has been said that Sixes have intolerance for uncertainty. Detectives who project this kind of distrust onto partners will most likely hear statements from their partners such as, "Why don't you trust me? You're never going to trust me? What is it going to take for you to trust me?" When partners of Sixes have demonstrated a more than reasonable amount of dependability, it is largely up to the Detective to find trust and faith both inside and outside themselves. Not to do this can cause a partner to take the Six's lack of trust personally. It can also limit and block the depth of intimacy the couple is able to achieve. To see where you are regarding trust, answer the questions below:

- I gain trust and faith in the world and in my intimate relationship through…
- When it comes to trust and faith in my relationship, I try not to put too much pressure on my partner by…
- When I can't lean on myself and I don't want to or can't lean on my partner, I lean on…
- If I could ask one thing of my partner with regard to trust, it would be…

Recommendations to partners of Detectives

Partners of Sixes need to be able to hold their ground and not to take things so personally when the Detective begins to doubt and question them or the relationship. They need to approach the Six with consistency and reassurance. Do not become an authority in the relationship or the Detective will likely rebel. Below are some questions you can ask your Six. These questions are in no way meant to imply that you should "care take" your partner in any way; the answers your partner gives you should be looked at as requests and suggestions rather than demands. All of us should ask ourselves, "Will what my partner is asking of me take away from me in any significant way if I choose to do it?" If it goes against your very nature or enables your partner in some way, do not do it. If it does not…please consider their request.

- During times when you doubt or question me or the relationship, how would you prefer that I handle the situation?
- If you lose touch with the trust and faith in me or in our relationship, how can I help you to regain it?
- In general, how can I give you reassurance in our relationship?
- How should I handle information or thoughts I may have that might scare you?

Finally, both of you together can discuss the following:
- What should we be willing to work on and commit to, both individually and together, given the core characteristics of our Types? How can we support each other in our journey together?

CHAPTER TEN

The Adventurer (Type Seven) In Relationship

Probably my best feature in relationship is that I am more fun than fun and I don't know if I will ever truly grow up. I like a relationship that includes lots of humor and endless adventures and good times. I'm good at uplifting my partner's spirit and helping him recognize his potential. Some people wonder whether I will ever commit to anything, as I seem to be like a butterfly flitting from one flower to the next. Probably my worst feature is that I hate being told "no" and I may make my escape if the relationship involves pain or limitations or becomes humdrum.

Happiness is the meaning and the purpose of life - the whole aim and end of human existence.
-- Aristotle

Everything has its wonders, even darkness and silence, and I learn, whatever state I may be in, therein to be contented.
-- Helen Keller

Characteristics of the Adventurer (Type Seven) in relationship

Adventurers seek fun, and they are fun to be with. With their gregariousness and sense of humor, they are often the life of the party. Their charm carries them a long way, and their optimism is infectious. They can see the positive side of almost every situation. They don't hold grudges, and their anger is usually infrequent and brief. Adventurers, as friends, can be a blast! Here are some characteristics of the Seven:

Charm and verbal skills

Adventurers think quickly and are very facile with words. Many become comedians, entertainers, and actors, known for their wit and their skills with language, as well as their ability to respond quickly on their feet. Sevens usually like to joke and talk, and are often more comfortable doing that than engaging in deep communication. Comedian and actor Robin Williams, most likely an Adventurer, was being interviewed on TV, where he deflected any personal questions with a joke. By the end of the interview, viewers, although entertained, had learned very little about who Williams really was. Like many Adventurers, he seemed to be more comfortable skating along the surface of life rather than probing into more serious matters. In another situation, the former wife of a well-known Seven comedian was asked if her ex-husband was as funny in his private life as he was on television. She remarked, "He's funny all the time." She added that his constant joking, although sweet at times, was also rather tiring and kept them from having a more serious and in-depth relationship.

Rationalization and reframing

When asked, "What helps your relationship thrive?" Susan, an Adventurer married for 30 years, answered, "My ability to rationalize difficult situations and accept them. I forgive easily, and I'm on to the next thing." Susan's approach can be both an asset and a liability. Adventurers prefer to focus on future options rather than to rehash the past, especially if the past involves pain. The positive aspect of their behavior allows them to let go and move on quickly during painful times, rather than being bogged down in negativity. Nonetheless, the downside of this is that they may miss the opportunity to address negative personality characteristics and consequences that get covered over when they reframe and rationalize the situation. This can render them oblivious to the effects of their actions on others, making empathy difficult for them.

A Seven psychotherapist, recalled her childhood and how she coped with pain and suffering through rationalizing and reframing:

I had abandonment issues in my childhood. My mother left me when I was seven. My response was to knock at other kids' homes and say, "Let's have a parade," let's move on, let's reframe. Now I'm an adult, a therapist, but I still don't dwell on the pain, although I feel it. I reframe, I'll find an opportunity. I call it a spiritual perspective. I can put things in perspective pretty quickly. Most of us suffer over things that aren't worth the suffering – they lost a boyfriend or something. As a therapist I work with clients to mourn the loss, but also help them not make things into drama that aren't. If you're still living, you learn to cope.

This is a good example of how a Seven child develops a positive coping strategy to deal with pain and abandonment. In her adult life, when some aspect of suffering comes her or her clients' way, she tries to incorporate her positive childhood approach of reframing and positive thinking. She sees her positive outlook as a kind of "spiritual perspective." She now allows herself to feel things, but still makes sure not to dwell on the pain.

Another huge issue for Adventurers is boredom. One man admitted that he often ended relationships because of this: "I think I'm not very suitable for long-term relationships. Of course I have a lot of affairs, but this damned 'getting bored' is always present, as are my Sevenish polygamous tendencies." He was then asked, "How do you react to other people saying they are hurt when you end a relationship because you've gotten bored with them?" He replied, "That hardly happens because mostly I find sophisticated arguments to cover the deeper reason of boredom…these are perhaps easier for them to accept than being told I'm bored." As you can see, he has found a way to reposition the actual reason he is leaving the relationship, while also hoping that his new perspective will ease the pain of the other person.

An approach that can be used to check if the relationship will suffer from this issue of boredom and most likely not survive is to ask the Adventurer, "Are you able to see the relationship as 'endless'? How will you handle things when the relationship becomes routine or even boring?" The idea of "endless" is defined as being willing and able to explore the many levels of depth that a relationship has to offer. Almost all relationships experience a routine quality as they mature, something Adventurers in particular might see as boring – so the question is about how he or she is going to handle things when that happens. Healthy Sevens find a way to stay put, usually by doing the work of the relationship and by exploring the richness that can come from a committed coupleship.

Adventurers are notorious for their boat rocking in relationships. When life is calm, the Seven may deliberately stir things up. A 37-year old Adventurer wrote that a challenge in her marriage is that she tends to "evoke massive changes to shake things up." What better way to bring excitement to a relationship when it has become a little humdrum! As we mentioned earlier, Sevens have been known to do on-again/off-again relationships so as to re-create a newness that may have faded in their mind. The Adventurer said that in her relationship they had done on-again/off-again to the point where even that had become routine! The Adventurer was also asked about rejection, "Did you ever get dumped first in a friendship or intimate relationship? How did that feel for you?" The answer was classic reframing:

> *Yes, I did. I think my reaction was pretty Sevenish: I looked at it in a positive way! For example, I thought, the friendship was dumped because it was not a real friendship any longer. So dumping brought me away from illusion, back to reality, and created new freedom for looking for other friends.*

Another Adventurer similarly escaped into other activities after an intimate partner dumped her:

> *Of course it feels horrible– but when I've been dumped I've tended to pretend I'm okay, and usually go off on some manic binge either with other relationships or shopping to dull the pain.*

Adventurers excel at making lemonade out of lemons. They are also great at seeing the possibilities and opportunities in certain situations. When a Seven is dumped, he may quickly turn it into an "opportunity" for new friendships. When experiencing pain, Adventurers can pretend that everything is okay and distract themselves with mind- numbing, addictive behaviors.

Avoiding pain and conflict

Because discussing difficulties can be uncomfortable for Adventurers, they often avoid dealing with problems head on. One Adventurer reported: "My need to be happy all the time can keep me from dealing with conflicts and pain." Another wrote, "I'm always looking for a stress-free life and sometimes I won't do the hard work required of me."

Along with a reluctance to spend time listening, discussing problems, and hammering out a solution, some Adventurers prefer to end the discussion prematurely. A man who stated he had difficulty dealing with problems head on added, "I try to problem-solve instead of listening – ironic, no?" Sevens may find listening and rehashing problems tedious and boring, whereas problem solving can be creative and interesting to them.

Another example involved Ryan, a 56-year old Adventurer of the Sexual subtype, who found himself living alone when his wife filed for separation after he had had a series of affairs. His wife still hoped they could work things out through counseling when he surprised her by saying, "I need to get a new start in life. I need to find a new woman with whom I don't have a long history, someone who will appreciate me for who I am now rather than reminding me of the past." His solution was to wipe the slate clean rather than work on saving his 20-year marriage. Ryan's viewpoint was that going to counseling and reviewing his relationship problems was just going to result in more pain and conflict. His form of escape, leaving the relationship, kept him from feeling pain and maintained intact his image of himself. His plan was to simply create a new beginning and move on to another relationship with the "newness" that it brings, with less need to dig into the past.

The "Monkey Mind" - constant activity and multiple options

Adventurers love to be in perpetual motion, whether externally or in their head. Because they have a constant chatter in their minds -- plans, projects, options, and jokes – their mental process is often referred to as the "monkey mind." This analogy compares the Seven's mind with the image of a monkey in a forest, swinging from tree to tree to tree; each tree symbolizes a different idea or plan. Most Sevens are very good at synthesizing multiple ideas into something better or more expansive than the original concept. One Adventurer told us that he thought of so many ideas every day, that he seriously considered starting a website titled "New Ideas for the Taking." Most of the ideas were about starting a new business. People who wanted to run their own business but couldn't come up with an idea for one could just come to his website and take whichever idea appealed to them.

The downside to the monkey mind is that the constant activity can be like a whirlwind that holds objects only for a short period of time before dropping them. It can also be a defense against having to stop and face their feelings, which may include painful ones. Adventurer usually do not want to spend time listening to their partner talk about problems and feelings. "You never listen" was the complaint of one woman, married to an Adventurer for almost 60 years. Another partner told his Adventurer wife that he felt depressed. She responded, "Are you sure you aren't being a little dramatic – maybe you're just a little sad and you need to get out more?" This is an example of problem solving before truly listening.

Some of the above interactions challenge us to ask: When is it appropriate to reframe, to move on, to think positively as the Seven encourages others to do? Certainly before "prescribing" a solution we need to make sure we have heard what the problem is. Feelings need to be felt, but not wallowed in. Losses need to be grieved, not stuffed or escaped from. Whether we are talking about our basic approach to life and relationships or how therapy should look, we don't want to discount the piece of truth and the gift that the Seven approach brings to the world.

Lots of energy, creativity, and attention to the big picture rather than details

Adventurers can be highly creative people, excellent at brain-storming solutions and planning projects. They like to focus on the big picture, leaving details to others. This can cause problems in a relationship. Sevens are often accused of having too many irons in the fire, with reason, as one Adventurer reported: "I have a tendency to take on too much and end up exhausted by my schedule." The central complaint of one Adventurer's partner was, "You start too many things you never finish." Another Seven woman reported that her (Type Nine) husband lamented, "You're always over- scheduling us." The Seven went on to say, "I want to do everything too quickly. I have great ideas and am interested in many different things and I sometimes have trouble completing a task before I become interested in a new one." Writing about her four-year relationship, an Adventurer related,

I get scared of being stuck. I'm always looking for freedom to explore new things. I'm changeable. I get caught up in new pursuits and distracted from my relationship. I tend to discount my partner's feelings.

Lest we forget, the Adventurer's core issue is fear of being limited, which can create a "noise" so loud that it can virtually drown out what their partner has to say. An Adventurer's worst nightmare is to be limited, to close down his or her options. Ironically, the fear of being limited itself can cause severe limitation. As Dr. David Daniels wrote in *The Enneagram Monthly*,

> "Deep in the non-conscious [of the Adventurer] is the fear that embracing pain will result in being trapped in suffering and not being able to ever again experience joy in life. . . You, as a Seven, deplore limitations, but you are indeed creating huge limitations in your life and perpetuating your pain by avoiding it. You will not lose your ability to create and see the positives in life if you allow in the full range of life." [June 2006, p 4]

Impulsiveness and spontaneity

Adventurers like to keep their options open. When plans are in place, some of the juice may be gone, and the Seven may then find a different option that is more appealing. Because long-term relationships can become somewhat stagnant with patterns and everyday routines, some people find the Seven's spontaneity fun and exciting. Adaptability also falls under this same category and is rated as a tremendous asset that a partner can bring to a relationship.

But with a partner who likes planning and order, the Seven may find that the constant changes do not go over very well. Joyce, an Adventurer, wrote about the challenge she brought to her marriage to a Perfectionist (Type One):

Early in our relationship I didn't recognize how differently we are wired. So my frustration level with my husband was high since I expected flexibility and adaptability – which isn't easy for him.

Being spontaneous and being impulsive may also be associated with a desire for immediate gratification as well as for pain avoidance. A partner of a Seven reported that after coming out of a business meeting he found a voicemail from his Adventurer wife. Unlike her usual upbeat self, she spoke in a rather depressed voice, stating that she was feeling down and that she was thinking about going home from work. The husband became concerned and rather hurriedly picked up the phone to return her call. As he did, the second message came on – it was she again, stating that all of a sudden she was feeling much better, that she had just learned that the county fair was happening, and that she had decided to pick up their kids from daycare and head to the fair. This experience demonstrates clearly how when something negative happens to them, Adventurers don't usually stay down for long. Their spontaneity can pull them out of the dumps. The only remaining question is whether it matters what the issue was that caused the Seven to feel down in the first place.

Reaction rather than action

It's ironic that many Adventurers, who are very active people full of endless plans, feel that they're not really in control of their lives. They get caught up in the adrenaline rush, the infatuation, and the fascination. On the surface they appear to be confident, going after what they want, but underneath it all, they are just trying to keep their head above water, responding to outside forces. They often feel they're being dragged along, that decisions are being made for them. They give away their power. They are said to have "an external locus of control."

Enneagram teacher and psychiatrist David Daniels asserts that our "energy follows attention." He means that each type has a particular view that contains a specific attention style, and energy usually quickly follows wherever our attention is placed. For instance, if you are a Type One, the Perfectionist, your attention goes to what is wrong or imperfect. Once your attention is in place, your energy will quickly set out to improve things in the world. To discover where your attention goes and to be able to "stay in your seat" so that you are not at the mercy of your personality is doing the work of the enneagram.

An Adventurer who was once explaining this particular theory became confused and stated, "Attention follows energy." She had it backwards – in a Freudian slip sort of way. She may have truly felt as if her energy was so big and captivating that at times it took the lead in her life and her attention then became secondary. If this is true, it substantiates why Sevens sometimes feel out of control. To paraphrase Daniels, if I'm spinning off in one direction or another, to do something about it I have to pay attention to where my attention goes.

Breadth versus depth

At times, Adventurers have acute insights into their behaviors and intend to do things differently, but they may have trouble retaining awareness, and soon thereafter revert. They may prefer living their life on a superficial level rather than practicing self-examination and taking charge. A Seven health professional admitted,

> My whole life has been about keeping things on a very superficial level. This has really bothered other people. When I was younger and was I dating someone I really liked, I thought we were having a great time together. Then she announced she was leaving the relationship because it was way too superficial for her. I was really struck by that – I thought, WOW, I really don't do depth."

It was a wakeup call for him. He still feels that breadth versus depth is a big issue for him.

Narcissism and gluttony (the self-involved consumer)

Therapists sometimes joke that the work of therapy is to turn clients into narcissists. What they mean is that people who seek counseling usually need a healthy dose of confidence, to focus more on themselves, to become more thick-skinned and to worry less about what others think of them. Adventurers do their own version of narcissism. They feel as if everyone wants to be like them, how could they not, and what's not great about being fun and happy go lucky? Sevens believe that everyone would be happier if they would only be more like them. At their unhealthiest, self-referencing Sevens think that people are there for their benefit, which of course can cause hurt and pain in others. An Adventurer who was looking back over her life stated, "I've left a lot of dead bodies along the side of the road." By this she meant that she had used people to get where she wanted to go and then had cast them aside.

Enneagram Types Five, Six, and Seven (the Thinking triad or center) operate from a scarcity approach to life, as if there is not enough of "something" to go around, whatever that something is to the person. To the Adventurer, it's as if life is a great desert with an occasional oasis here and there. When the oasis appears, the gluttonous Seven who thirsts for more feels that it 's time to get while the getting is good, that if he doesn't do it for himself, no one is going to do it for him. This can cause him to become the self-involved consumer. Gluttony is usually seen as a hoarding, an excess of things, or a very large appetite. For the Adventurer, it usually means an excess of stimulation and experiences - they can be the ultimate adrenaline junkies. To their thinking, the constant stimulation soothes the scarcity mindset and wards off pain and limitations. The healthy Seven combats the gluttony with a form of sobriety, which entails a single- minded focus that includes moderation, concentration, and commitment at the forefront. It is at this time that the Adventurer commits to staying put even in the face of possible pain and limitations. He opens his heart and finds empathy for others.

Multiple Options: Difficulty with commitment and monogamy

Adventurers want to maximize their opportunities and keep their options open. They are generally great on start up, less so on follow through. Commitment therefore is one of their biggest challenges. For the Sexual Seven in particular, monogamous commitment to another person can be an ongoing difficulty and for some even unrealistic. Commitment has been referred to as the "C" word, as Adventurers don't want to be pinned down. What about monogamy once they *are* in a committed relationship?

Thinking about this issue we are reminded of a scene from the movie "Out of Africa." In the film, Karin, a Romantic played by Meryl Streep, is very unhappy that the Adventurer (played by Robert Redford) is gone a lot and clearly has other women in his life. He tries to explain, asking, "What's wrong with me being in love with several people at a time? What's wrong with me wanting to go off and have a good time and then come back and be present with you?" He's telling her that one person can't possess another, that Karin is getting too attached to something she can't own. This may be a great example of the Adventurer's truth as he sees it. It begs the question: With our attachment to monogamy (that supposedly soothes our issues of jealousy and possessiveness), are we simply unable to handle the Seven's "truth" in our current society?

Helen Palmer says that One-to-One [Sexual] Sevens in particular can feel limited by only one relationship and that commitment for them is usually associated with pain. Because so much has been said about whether an Adventurer can commit and be faithful in relationship, we created an adjunct questionnaire to our survey that asked Sevens specifically how they felt about this issue. We asked the following questions:

* Have you found a way to adopt the more traditional view on relationships and how have you done that?
* Or have you marched to the beat of your own drummer and in doing that what has your experience been in relationships?
* If you have marched to the beat of your own drummer, do you feel you have brought your own version of the "truth" about how relationships should be done? If so, what is that particular "truth"?
* How has your partner played a role in your approach to finding your way in relationships and how do you think they have been affected overall?

According to our survey results, it appears that many Sevens, especially Self-Preservation Sevens with a Six wing, do not extend their interest in novelty to new persons. For example, one woman, a psychologist, related,

I am very traditional about relationships although I am politically very liberal. I am a Self-Preservation Seven with a strong Six wing. Even as a teenager I had one boyfriend at a time and liked long-term relationships (years, not months). In my 20's I was with a man who was unfaithful, and I refused to marry him for that reason. I am happily married for 24 years with absolutely no consideration of cheating. I really don't think I could if I tried; it seems completely foreign and out of the range of possibility even if I were in a terrible marriage. It is just not me.

Several Adventurers wrote that the key to success in their committed relationships was that they felt they had a lot of freedom and could be independent. Miranda, a 40-year old Self-Preservation Seven, wrote,

Once I'm in a committed relationship, I am very traditional. I don't really have a problem with commitment once I'm here. It's getting there that can sometimes be a struggle for me. You know, closing the doors to other potential opportunities. I will often maintain (platonic) relationships with ex-boyfriends, sometimes to my detriment. I am learning to be more discerning with whom I maintain such relationships. When in a committed relationship, I don't necessarily feel limited, as long as my needs are getting met, which they usually do. Maintaining my independence is KEY in being in a committed relationship. It helps a lot if my partner is also independent and not super needy. I am engaged to be married (first marriage). It's pretty scary, the idea of being with one man for the rest of my life, and also reassuring (I have a strong Six wing).

Miranda's wedding to Jim (a Perfectionist) took place three months later. After a few months went by, she wrote,

I am learning that there is "an other" to think about, not just me. Thankfully we both are pretty independent people and give each other the space we need. We lived together before getting married, but it does feel different. More secure. Not so easy to just walk away. I sometimes think about the so called opportunity costs for getting married – all the many men I didn't get a chance to meet and possibly find the one that, you know, is the perfect dream, who makes a million bucks, is thoughtful, caring, loving, giving, funny, smart, etc. But I also feel really committed to the relationship and happy to not be searching any more.

The very qualities that Sevens initially find appealing in a partner – that he gives them independence, doesn't make many demands, has his own life – may later turn out to be sources for complaints. This can make Adventurers feel they are not important enough to their partner, that their interactions lack intensity, or that they don't have enough quality time for one-to-one interactions. It's probably no accident that although Sevens listed type Seven as the type they like the most, Seven-Seven primary relationships are distinctly uncommon; Adventurers may have fun with other Adventurers, but they are unlikely to get their needs met. Additionally, both tend to like the spotlight too much.

Many Adventurers spend years in serial relationships before settling down. When they do commit to a single partner, what can help them stay faithful is thinking of the potential consequences of infidelity and the accompanying pain. A Seven woman (of the Social subtype) wrote,

I have adopted the traditional view of monogamy. The way I have "done" that is simple: Out of sight, out of mind. I don't see other guys as something I am "missing." People always think about Sevens as going after pleasure, as if we go after every pleasure we see, which is absurd. You have to remember that our main drive is pain avoiding. To me, the pain and guilt of being out of integrity and the potential pain of my husband if I were to stray are huge incentives to stay out of any trouble. No pleasure is worth it if pain is caused. You have to remember that Sexual Sevenness is about "fascination." I "fall madly in love" every day with books, music, authors, restaurants, etc. Who needs to fall in love with guys????

Many Adventurers with a Sexual subtype find it difficult to maintain sexual and emotional commitment to one person even after marriage. One wrote, "I have a difficult time being committed to one person, but we have stuck it out for almost 34 years." *Stuck it out* suggests that this has been a struggle for her. A significant proportion of Sexual Sevens, and most likely a smaller proportion of other subtypes of Seven, have other sexual or emotional partners while married or in a committed relationship. Because commitment and monogamy are important values for most married people, the perceptions, beliefs, and actions of Sexual Sevens are worth exploring in greater detail. A Sexual Seven woman wrote,

I feel that monogamy and jealousy (and also envy) are the result of scarcity thinking – that there is a finite amount of love to go around. My truth is that I can love (and have sex with) more than one person (of any gender) at a time.
Right now I'm in a traditional lesbian relationship. I've agreed to monogamy because it's very important to my partner. I'm a polyamorous person to the core, but I choose not to act on it. Doing lesbian monogamy is a novelty and a challenge. If it becomes a problem, I will propose renegotiation.
The only other time I've ever been monogamous was the four years I was married to my first husband. Ironically, he cheated on me. After my divorce, I regained my polyamorous nature and discovered women as sexual partners. I

had concurrent relationships that often ended when my partners couldn't han-
dle sharing me. Although they agreed to my terms initially, their jealousy (and
my lack of jealousy) would get the better of them. I never "cheated" – I was al-
ways honest about what I was doing and whom I was doing it with. Eventually
I married a gay man and we had a delightful open marriage for many years
(until I met my current partner). He's still my best friend. I still am polyam-
orous because I love him and my partner.

Some Sexual Sevens may find it difficult to understand why their partners are so possessive. "It has nothing to do with you," the Adventurer will argue. "I love you as much as ever, and this isn't about our relationship." Many
will keep their extramarital affairs hidden because they want to avoid pain
and conflict in their primary relationship. According to Anita, a Social Seven
married to a Nine (Mediator):

In the case of my husband and me, there is not a problem with monogamy.
Anil and I each have friends of the opposite sex. We don't have a traditional
marriage in that we each have our own lives. And we have our life together.
Our marriage is based on trust, loyalty, honesty, and genuine concern for the
well-being and happiness of the other that includes allowing the other to be
free – free even from guilt. If Anil doesn't want to go to a party with me, I go
alone. If I want to spend my time doing something he doesn't want to do, I don't
feel guilty about possibly neglecting him. I spent a year working abroad without
him; he came to visit twice and made sure that I had care packages from home.
We were in touch by email at least five days a week. Another key to our mutual
happiness is that we treat each other with a certain civility and respect.

Sexual Sevens who are themselves strongly lured by the attraction of a
new person report that they find the new person fascinating at first. The attraction can be so powerful that it soon becomes "intoxicating" for them.
Although each enneagram Type has an addictive aspect, meaning they have
an attachment to a particular vice connected to their Type, the Seven, especially the Sexual Seven, seems particularly prone to sexual or emotional
affairs. It's not surprising that the word "sobriety" is a growth word used for
the Adventurer.

It is understandable why for some Sevens, new relationships can be so
attractive. Falling in love, or falling into infatuation, is one of the most powerful and overwhelming experiences a person can have. Part of the power is
that it is so positive, so enjoyable, such a great escape from reality. Eventually,

however, this kind of love cools down as reality sets in. Life's problems, set-backs, disappointments, and disagreements intrude upon the previously idyllic relationship. Painful moments, days or months of ordinariness, occur. It's easy to wish for those early days of paradise again. Sevens (especially of the Sexual subtype), who strive mightily to avoid pain and limitation, are particularly vulnerable to pursuing the high of romantic love elsewhere.

For the Adventurer who sees this as a self-destructive tendency, a first-order change is to find novelty and variety in other arenas. Some possibilities are: travel to exotic places, a profession consisting of sequential different projects, a career that brings a variety of people into the Adventurer's office, or many friends. But this is only a superficial solution. A more fundamental change is about accessing the heart space so as to deal with any and all earlier experiences connected to pain and deprivation, which then allows the Seven to be able to commit from the heart. This will enable the Adventurer to attain a singular focus, to quiet the monkey mind and be able to live in the present, diminishing the fear of scarcity and increasing empathy for others while en-joying what he already has in his life rather than focusing on the future and on possibilities and options. This is not easy.

Adventurers under stress and when secure

According to enneagram theory, Adventurers have a particular connec-tion with the Observer (Type Five) and the Perfectionist (Type One). When they feel safe, or when they have made a commitment or chosen a course of action, or perhaps as they get older and recognize that indeed their options are limited, they express the positive qualities of the Observer. As one Ad-venturer explained it, "Going to Five is like crashing from a high I've been on – although it usually involves a soft landing." They become more focused on the internal instead of the external, centered and cognizant of the fact that their personal gratification is not what the world is about. Like Dorothy in the Wizard of Oz, they come to realize that the ability to "go home" was there all along.

Under pressure, when they feel limited, criticized and deficient, Adven-turers can demonstrate the negative aspects of the Perfectionist. They be-come angry, critical, and judgmental. Their negativity is focused on feeling deprived or frustrated by someone else. They notice when others have op-tions that they don't, and harshly judge the person who's preventing them from getting all they want. As enneagram teacher Tom Condon puts it, "When you catch a Seven with their hand in the cookie jar, they'll accuse you of being small minded about the cookies." But when the Seven accesses the positive side of One, it can create useful discipline and structure.

Wings

Wings sit as neighbors either to the right or the left of the primary type on the enneagram diagram and can color one's type. Sevens with an Eight wing are not to be denied! Dauntless in approach, they can overcome great challenges and achieve seemingly impossible goals– at times uplifting humankind. They want what they want, not to control (unlike an Eight), but to consume, to have. They can get assertive, even aggressive, about getting what they want – become mental bullies.

Sevens with a Six wing are less aggressive than Sevens with Eight wings and have a more endearing quality. They are more people-oriented and usually more helpful and loyal to their partners, similar to Twos (Givers). When unhealthy, there will be more neediness and a feeling of being deprived from their partner's affections.

How Sevens help their relationship thrive:

Adventurers consider their gifts to the relationship to be their adventurous spirit, humor, non-judgmentalism, ability to communicate, optimism, independence, and creativity. As a Seven wrote, "I'm creative and open to new concepts and committed to making it work. And I'm fun! I have warmth, humor, caring. I communicate well." As many partners will attest to, Adventurers can be fun in relationship, with never a dull moment. They are careful not to become a drag or to burden their partners with their problems. They are great at uplifting a partner's spirits and at recognizing and helping the partner actualize their potential.

What partners of Adventurers could do to make the Adventurer happy

A few Sevens gave their partners hints of how to make the Adventurer happy.

"Support my dreams and enjoy my strengths; be less competitive with me."

"Be more emotionally available and romantic" [Sexual Seven woman]. Because of the Seven's sensitivity to criticism, competition can feel threatening. They also believe that if you don't have anything positive to say to them, don't say anything at all. Bursting their dreams can feel downright cruel to the Seven. They thrive on plenty of attention and praise and love being the center of attention.

How Sevens feel about other types in relationship

When asked which types they struggle with the most, more Adventurers chose the Perfectionist (Type One) than any other type. They also singled out The Romantic (Four) and the Leader (Eight).

<u>The Perfectionist:</u> "Rigidity, high-gear attitude." "Too judgmental, critical, inflexible, serious to the point of painful. They'd rather be right than happy. Yuck." "I feel like I can never anticipate what 'right' is in their consciousness."

Even though Sevens gripe about Ones in relationship, this is actually a common pairing. Most likely both are trying to find a balance, Sevens wanting structure and discipline, Ones looking to be more playful.

<u>The Romantic:</u> "They are too difficult to understand. They want to be center stage too much." "Too much drama and self-preoccupation." "Too depressive."

In reality, Sevens and Fours can balance each other: The Adventurer can learn more about depth and feelings from Fours, while the Romantic can take on a less serious attitude thanks to the Adventurer. Both may go into this relationship griping about each other, yet end up better off.

<u>The Leader:</u> "Too bossy – they have to do everything their own way." "They tend to be invasive, and too pushy." "Lack of agreement."

Adventurers struggle with being controlled in any way, as it feels too limiting. They usually strive to balance any power inequity. Equality or shared power to the Seven means everyone ends up with more. Because the Seven and Eight are wings of one another, they understand each other and can come together to create big ideas with big energy. The downside is that it could be too much fun and too much excess…a somewhat dangerous combination.

The greatest number of Adventurers reported being most compatible with other Adventurers. They wrote:

<u>The Adventurer:</u> "We are lighthearted, kind, and understand each other." "Similar senses of humor." "Enjoys life. Knows it's not forever." "Fun, entertaining."

Fun ship cruises and costume parties are built on the idea of tapping into everyone's inner Seven. How could you not have a good time? Having fun all the time can be a little exhausting and superficial though. When they're not too busy being like two ships passing in the night, two Adventurers together are likely to fight over the spotlight.

Advice Sevens give other Adventurers

Adventurers with personal growth work experience had some very insightful suggestions for younger counterparts. Adventurers want to avoid pain and don't like rehashing the past, so a Social Seven man advised, "Look for someone who has done some inner growth work and is aware of their own personality dynamics. Be willing to commit to working on your own dynamics and to not be afraid of the pain that might entail."

Recognizing the Adventurer's tendency to bolt and look for novelty rather than staying with the present, one person advised, "Know when the need for freedom is a true need to be apart from that person and not just cold feet or a fleeting feeling of being caged, as this can pass. Don't be too critical of yourself or them."

Sevens lead a fast life, with multiple irons in the fire, ever ready to try something new rather than stick with commitments. A Self-Preservation Adventurer advised, "Slow down, calm down, get real, listen more and better, be more sincere, keep your commitments, say what you mean and mean what you say." A Social Seven woman agreed: "Go slower, hold your horses; the house is not on fire."

Concerning the Seven's tendency toward narcissism, a Seven woman suggested, "Try to remember that it's not all about you. Think about the other person's needs too. Find the balance." Another Adventurer wrote on the same theme: "Know yourself first; be the partner that you want to have."

This is all good advice from Adventurers to fellow Adventurers. To sum up, keep your promises and distinguish between true commitment and the feeling of being caged. Stick with things, slow down, practice honesty and integrity. Be empathic and try to find a balance between your needs and those of your partner.

Exercises for the Adventurer (Type Seven) and your Partner

The following exercises are intended to deal with the challenges and issues of the Adventurer in relationship.

It's all about fun

Adventurers seek fun, and they *are* fun. With their gregariousness and sense of humor, they are often the life of the party. Their charm carries them a long way, and their optimism is infectious. They can see the positive side of almost every situation. They don't hold grudges, and their anger is usually infrequent and brief. Adventurers as friends can be a blast! Before tackling the challenges that can be present in a relationship with an Adventurer, let's first appreciate the positives that they bring to a relationship. For the partner of the Seven:

- Share with your Seven partner the benefits of being with him or her.

What about the pain?

Where did all this humor and optimism come from? Many Sevens report a childhood that included pain, oppression, and deprivation, which resulted in the need to develop a coping strategy that compensated or over-compensated on the side of optimism and a no-limits lifestyle. In counseling, however, Sevens tend to want to talk only about the positive things in their life. At some point during the session, Ron finally has to ask them, "If things are going so great for you, why did you come in for counseling?" The Adventurer's optimism can also cover over things about them that the partner may not be aware of.

For the Seven: To make sure your partner sees you more fully, complete the incomplete sentences below with your partner:

- Beneath my comic nature and upbeat approach to life, the one thing you would not guess about me is…
- The one thing that I hide from you with my upbeat manner and really would like to let you know about me, is…
- If I were to be really honest with you about the core issues of my Type, I would try to share with you more about my feelings of insecurity… about my fear of pain and limitations… by telling you…

Dealing with rationalization and reframing

Here is an example of the Adventurer's rationalization and reframing:

I had abandonment issues in my childhood. My mother left me when I was seven. My response was to knock at other kids' homes and say, "Let's have a parade," let's move on, let's reframe." Now I'm an adult, a therapist, but I still don't dwell on the pain, although I feel it. I reframe, I'll find an opportunity. I call it a spiritual perspective. I can put things in perspective pretty quickly.

For the most part, this is a positive example of rationalizing. In relationship, the Adventurer can rationalize behaviors that affect the partnership in a negative way. Discuss with your partner how rationalizing plays a role in your relationship. For the Seven:

- Has your partner caught you with your hand in the "cookie jar?" If so, how did you try and spin it in a positive way?
- How can you and your partner put a plan in place that ensures honesty, openness, and integrity in the relationship?

The downside to optimism

Adventurers have a hard time dealing with the ordinary, the routine, or times of boredom, deprivation, and limitations. They may want to escape with their sense of humor or maybe just totally escape. Talk with your partner about how you deal with the daily challenges of the relationship. You first may want to acknowledge the benefits of humor and optimism in your relationship.

- What positive role do you see your humor and optimism playing in the relationship?
- When do you see your humor and optimism not working in the relationship?

Next, talk about the downside. For the Seven:

- If the relationship becomes boring or limiting in some way, how do you handle it?
- How do you deal with the escapism that generally accompanies your Type? Do you consider your tendency to escape as being healthy or unhealthy?
- Are you ever tempted to initiate on/again – off/again patterns in your relationship to "renew" the relationship?
- Are you able to see your relationship as "endless?"

Empathy

An Adventurer who was aware of her tendency toward narcissism suggested the following, "Try to remember that it's not all about you. Think about the other person's needs too. Find the balance." Another Seven wrote on the same theme: "Know yourself first; be the partner that you want to have." This is good advice for the Adventurer who at the unhealthiest can become self-absorbed and see people as extensions of them. To help you become more empathetic, consider the following questions:

- Do I make an honest effort to listen to my partner, trying to understand where they are coming from and what their current needs are.

- Do I make it easy for my partner to ask for what he/she wants?
- Would my partner say I make his/her needs a priority?
- Do I put forth a true effort each day to meet my partner's needs as best I can?
- Is my being pleased by my partner fairly balanced with me pleasing my partner?
- Before making decisions, do I ask myself how my decision will affect my partner and whether I should discuss it with them first?

Empathy means that I understand that my partner has entrusted me with their heart and that I will ask myself how my actions and behaviors may affect my partner's heart.

Committed or stuck

To some Adventurers, fear of commitment is defined as "the fear of being stuck." Commitment can mean a closing off of their options, which to them represents a form of pain and deprivation. It can also mean that when partners commit to one another in a relationship, they now have a right to ask for their expectations to be met. This can be troubling to those who don't like to take on such responsibilities. Not fully committing or being unsure of whether you are in or out of a relationship prevents the depth of intimacy that can be had with a partner when both people are fully committed to one another. The avoidance of this depth of intimacy may be a fear for the Seven as well. Discuss with each other the following commitment attitudes:

- Commitment to me means…
- When I hear such sayings as, "The grass is always greener…" or "Commitment means being stuck." – what comes up for me is…
- When I think about the pressure and responsibility that comes with commitment and that my partner now has a right to expect certain things from me with regard to her needs and expectations, I feel…
- I understand that fully committing to my partner will most likely deepen the level of intimacy between us, which makes me feel…

The Seven's aversion to boredom and their need for novelty can be challenging in a long- term relationship. Adventurers somehow have to find a way to make peace with this dilemma, and when they do, the relationship can provide much personal growth as well as a possible spiritual path.

CHAPTER ELEVEN

The Leader (Type Eight) In Relationship

Probably my best feature in relationship is that I tell it like it is – you can depend on me to tell the truth. I am quite powerful, and I use that power to protect the people I love. I demand honesty in a relationship, I can't stand B.S., and I like a partner who sticks up for himself and says what's on his mind. Some people say I'm too blunt or bossy at times and that I have a hard time hearing another person's truth. Probably my worst feature in relationship is that I can become controlling and possessive of those I really care about, and I have a hard time knowing when I've hurt someone's feelings.

We who in engage in nonviolent direct action are not the creators of tension. We merely bring to the surface the hidden tension that is already alive.
-- Martin Luther King

I am not interested in power for power's sake, but I'm interested in power that is moral, that is right and that is good.
-- Martin Luther King

He can who thinks he can, and he can't who thinks he can't. This is an inexorable, indisputable law.
-- Pablo Picasso

If you have an important point to make, don't try to be subtle or clever. Use a pile driver. Hit the point once. Then come back - and hit it again. Then hit it a third time – a tremendous whack.

--Winston Churchill

Leaders are motivated by the need to be self-reliant and strong and to make an impact on the world. They are very supportive and protective of themselves, family and friends and tend to act in an aggressive, often combative way. To those they trust, Eights can seem like two different people in one body – tough on the outside, but with a soft heart. They want to empower people, to test you and trust you enough to become a part of their lives. They bring excitement and intensity to a relationship. Healthy, they are courageous, determined and persistent, fair-minded, truthful, straightforward and unpretentious. With an Eight, what you see is what you get.

Characteristics of the Leader in relationship

Anger

Leaders' emotion of choice is anger that flares up quickly, is expressed easily and then may quickly be forgotten. Not only don't they fear it, they believe that it has many benefits. Unlike most other personality types, Leaders don't see anger as a big deal. Just as with primary colors, primary feelings exist as well – mad, sad, glad or scared, although society has a hard time seeing anger as a healthy emotion. Yet when channeled correctly, anger can help set appropriate boundaries with others and allow someone to say "no" when necessary. Anger also can help define values and identify where one person ends and another begins.

Leaders find anger useful in other ways, too. They think that the real person comes out in a confrontation, and that then you will know whether he or she will shrink back or hold fast to a position or opinion. Eights believe that power struggles in relationship provide vital energy that serves to test the partner's strength and honesty.

On the surface this sounds good. There is some truth to it, but a serious downside to the Leader's anger does exist. Leaders might believe that they have simply expressed the truth as they saw it, but they often don't understand the negative impact their over-the-top anger has on others. When partners are in discussion, the issue of anger often comes up, not always positively. It takes insight for them to recognize this. Lynette, a psychotherapist and recovering addict, wrote;

I have found that anger was, and sometimes still is, my most prevalent emotion and the one that got me in the most trouble. I have the Queen archetype. When people don't do what I want, I have a tendency to say "off with their heads!" In recovery I had to learn the hard way that just venting anger got me nowhere, and that I had better figure out a different way of working. It was LEARNED behavior to join the resistance and not just get into power plays all the time. It is also true for me that my fear or anxiety can come across as high intensity and anger. If I feel vulnerable, then no matter how much I know from an intellectual viewpoint, I can't always communicate that in a way that someone else can hear it. I tend to bark things out even now rather than be calmer about it.

Feelings and vulnerability

Like Perfectionists, who tend to criticize themselves unmercifully, Leaders can brutally beat themselves up. Drawing a picture of herself as a small child was tried as a therapy strategy to help a Leader named Marlene with this problem. It was hoped that her protective side would emerge and take a gentler and more protective role. She drew a wonderful picture of a child who looked like an angel. She colored her gold and titled it, "I'm Innocent." Not knowing the enneagram, Marlene was unaware that Innocence is considered the higher aspect of the Eight when it comes to personal and spiritual growth. She wrote the following affirmation about herself as a small child in the picture:

The ideas of openness, innocence, vulnerability all come to mind. She's sweet and open, unashamed and unaware of her vulnerability. She would never harm anyone or anything. She doesn't know enough to see that she is naked or that she should hide her body. She is happy and affectionate. There is nothing wrong with her. She loves her parents. She is very good.

What an effective description of a Leader's inner child! It should also be noted that female Eights in our society can have difficulty with expressing anger and believing it is acceptable.

Many Eights have difficulty accessing any feelings other than anger. If they feel sad, afraid, or vulnerable, it will emerge as anger. They perceive other emotions as signs of weakness. A Leader wrote that her partner's central complaint about her was, "You never show any feelings. I never know what is going on with you." Eights not only don't show their feelings, they often don't even recognize them. Here's what Myra, a former marketing executive, wrote:

Once I get angry or feel vulnerable, I say things I shouldn't. I don't lie, but I can be very hurtful in an uncontrolled manner. I've gotten much better at this. I try to explain why I feel vulnerable instead of getting angry. What keeps me from effective problem-solving is seeing my partner as one of "them" with whom I can't be vulnerable.

Leaders strongly fear exposing their vulnerability or feeling powerless. In an email discussion group, one man wrote, "Anger is nearly always an expression of powerlessness. A person who is confident that he can change a situation to his satisfaction would not need to waste the energy of getting angry." An Eight woman responded to this statement:

As an Eight, this is one of the most profound statements I have heard explaining what makes me angry. I had never really seen my anger as an expression of powerlessness, but it makes sense. When I feel unable to control a situation – involving me directly or indirectly; I lash out, find reasons to become angry at the people involved, and then use intimidation (i.e. the wrath of my anger upon these individuals) to try and gain control of the situation. Aside from these situations, I have Two-like tendencies and am very caring, my emotional connections with people being very central to my life. How can I stop this all-consuming need to go to battle?

Leaders protect their soft inner core, their vulnerability. They are wiling to reveal this only to those they love and trust. When asked to define love and intimacy, Leaders emphasized truth, trust, and vulnerability: "Love is supporting me and telling me the truth." "Intimacy is being able to allow someone to see my vulnerability." "Intimacy is a trusting place to be your complete self. "

Eights under stress may become more reactive, angrier. They might lash out at a loved one, even if he or she had nothing to do with whatever caused the Eight's anger. If the partner doesn't match the Leader's reactivity, but says something like, "It must be scary to deal with your current situation," the response might be, "I'm not scared at all." Several different approaches might be necessary before getting to the truth. Denial is expected from a Leader. It fits with hiding softer feelings and existing pain. It most likely will take a little while for him to access his vulnerability, as he instead channels his feelings into anger. Some Leaders recognize this dynamic. One of them would caution a younger Eight, "Recognize your intensity, dial it down, and get in touch with your vulnerability" (especially when anger flares up). Asked what they'd say to a younger Eight in relationship, one man wrote, "Learn how to talk about emotions. Learn how your body tells you what you are feeling." Another advised, "Do lots of therapy to become emotionally available."

Take charge; be in control

Leaders like to be in charge and are often perceived as controlling, but from their perspective, someone needs to step up to the plate. Leaders feel that if there is a problem, let's not beat around the bush, but instead, let's get it out on the table and take care of it. An anecdote from therapy illustrates this characteristic.

Rich, by day a blue-collar dockworker, in his off hours was a cowboy who loved bull riding. He had just lost his beloved wife to cancer. His emotions were bottled up, and he was hostile toward anyone who got in his way. He had tried traditional anger therapy, but it failed to pierce the hard outer shell that he had erected. Journaling had just become popular, so Ron, who was counseling Rick, thought it would be a good tool for him to access his feelings of vulnerability and loss. However, Ron was timid about suggesting journaling to Rich, afraid of his response, so he began the process by offering an overview of the journaling process and talking about the positive benefits. Then he slowly introduced the steps on how to do it. As the counseling hour drew to a close, Rich stopped the speech on the effects of journaling and said, "Let me see if I got this right. You want me to write down about how I'm feeling about my wife dying?" "Yes, that's correct." Rich then said, "Well, then I'll do it. But why didn't you just say so at the beginning of the session instead of taking the whole hour to say it?"

A significant event such as losing a spouse can make the Leader feel out of control and vulnerable. To him, his attempt to control is only a way to make sure that he is not being controlled by others or by the situation. One Leader explained, "I can be afraid to be weak. So I have problems surrendering, letting go of control." It's important for them to be seen as powerful and not vulnerable. They reveal their tender side only to those they completely trust.

Being right or believing they have a hold on the truth goes hand-in-hand with their controlling aspect. With regard to relationships, a Leader (who had a Seven wing) wrote about both control and the "possession" of her partner,

"I wanted to control his choices about career, friends, the ways he spent his time and his money, and how he dealt with his issues."

Eights can become impatient with discussion. When issues come up, they tend to quickly evaluate the situation and decide how to best handle it – their way. A central complaint might be, "You never discuss issues. You just make a decision." One Leader reported that the challenges he brings to his relationship are "too much energy, focus, directness, and not enough collaboration." He admitted that, "In the past, I have not recognized how I've controlled, crushed and micromanaged my wife. I haven't allowed her to 'partner' with me." Leaders are too ready to believe that, "it's my way or the highway." One Eight's advice to a younger person in relationship was,

Make enough time, listen well, and let the other know that you did listen, even if you still do things your own way. Tell them you understand instead of only thinking it in your head. Don't tell the other solutions; let them find their own. They can't cope with your solutions anyway. Understand that the other is a different person. Try to understand his/her personality as well as you can. Don't give too much advice; let them do it their own way.

This statement gives good advice about how to handle the aforementioned issues.

Truth, Justice, and Fairness

Truth and justice are key values for Eights, often based on memories of an earlier time when they were dominated or, as one Leader described it, "squashed." It seems that it was in that moment that he lost innocence and experienced ultimate vulnerability. He lost faith that justice would prevail and that others would treat him with fairness or be completely truthful with him. Another Leader said her challenge in relationship was "I'm afraid to trust and have too long a memory about forgiveness." Eights sometimes have difficulty trusting others until they have proved themselves. How she helped her relationship thrive was to "keep good boundaries and tell the truth." Love and intimacy for the Eight depends on these values.

Excess and Intensity

Enneagram teacher Helen Palmer defines lust as "a great upwelling of force, power, and anger in order to get what is good in life. An excessive use of energy and anger in the interest of personal survival." Lust for the Eight most likely kicked in during the time when innocence was lost. The fear of being "squashed" by someone more powerful grew to the point where the life force was threatened. A passion for excess, intensity and power is an attempt to compensate for these earlier feelings of feeling dominated. Lust becomes a desire for more, for the maximum. Leaders enjoy a lot of food, a lot of sex, a lot of alcohol and basically more of whatever appeals to them. The view that, "If some is good, more is better" not only leads to excess consumption for enjoyment, but also serves as an escape from difficulties. This makes them vulnerable to addiction.

Lori, an Eight, wrote;

The key thing I did that has helped everything in my life is to learn to stay with my own pain. Stay there until I understand what is going on and see it through. Prior to this understanding, I would escape pain through alcohol and drugs. I learned that does not help, only hinders the awareness process.

The lust of the Leader also manifests as intensity. A female Leader, Sexual subtype, wrote that a challenge for her relationship is "my high sexual needs/ desire and relational intensity. My drivenness." Another wrote that her challenge is "not to bowl over my partner with my intensity and strong energy." According to yet another woman, "I'm not aware of the impact I have on others – either from my intensity or from my speed."

When asked what advice they would give a younger Eight in relationship, several spoke to the issue of power and intensity. One wrote, "Beware that your strong energy can be intimidating." Lori advised,

It is important to understand how fierce we can be and to monitor our behavior so we don't scare the . . . out of our partner. Instinctively, I knew when I met my husband that I could scare him away, and I did not want that to happen. In my past relationships, I would test their love with my fierceness and my lusty behavior – and if they were able to weather that, then we could move on. I knew that this was not an option in my current relationship.

What Leaders do to make the relationship thrive.

Leaders see their gifts to the relationship as their tell-it-like-it-is attitude, their tenacity, decision making and problem-solving skills. As they put it, "I stay regardless of the problem." "I like to get issues on the table and get them over with before they fester. "If I put my mind to it, it will get accomplished." "I'm enthusiastic, determined to make the relationship work, and I'm willing to invest all my energy."

Note that Eights do <u>not</u> generally see themselves as helping their relationship with listening skills, depth of feelings, or ability to just sit with their partner. They consider themselves action-oriented, problem-solving people, and their gifts are practical. As some of the statements above verify, they can be extremely loyal, and if problems emerge in the relationship, they are not reluctant to get the issue out into the open and then attack it with great force – much like they would an enemy of sorts.

Help the Leader to feel happy.

Leaders want their partners to know that they would like directness from partners. They ask their spouse to, "tell the truth about what you want," "Don't make excuses," and "Speak up to me." Although Eights want to dominate, paradoxically, they also want their partners to resist and stand up for themselves. One Leader wanted his partner to recognize his vulnerability. He said, "I need my partner to allow my needy side." Even with all their toughness, Eights seem to know that the work for them is to eventually get back to their original innocence. They want partners who can help them expose this softer side of themselves, so that true love and intimacy has a chance of blossoming.

How Leaders feel about other Types in relationship

When asked which types they struggle with the most, more Leaders chose the Giver (Two) and the Romantic (Four) than any other type. Some comments were:

The Giver: "I have not been in an intimate relationship with a Two, but I've worked with some. I hate their tendency to seduce and manipulate but not to own up to their own needs." "I do not like help unless I ask." "Manipulative – they give to get."

As you can see, the Eight's necessity for truth and honesty conflicts with the image-oriented Two. Leaders struggle with the Two's indirect approach to getting their own needs met. Even though Eights gripe about the Two's tendencies, this pairing is not uncommon and does have a teaching element to it – Twos can turn Eights on to their heart space, whereas Leaders can teach Givers to be more upfront about their wants and needs and feel okay about it.

The Romantic: "I have no patience for the drama. Get real! " "Roller coaster rides and emotional turmoil."

These comments by Eights about the Four, another Image type, are harsh. Ironically what Leaders complain about with the Romantic are the very things that will drive them together. The intensity that each can bring to a relationship might provide its own form of excess. Also, both of these types search for truth and authenticity in their own way.

Leaders reported being most compatible with Observers (Five), other Leaders (Eight), and Mediators (Nine). They reported:

The Observer: "I like them in a social situation – their minds and thinking process." "They help bring down my energy level. Stay calm rather than withdraw or match me." [A great observation!] "They allow me my space; they make space for my energy." "Not intrusive – but fairly clear." Leaders can be charmed by the Observer's style. It seems Eights want to be more like Fives, and Fives want to be more like Eights.

The Leader: "There is a very bottom line that we know where we are with each other. I love the lusty, high energy." "They know what they want." "We have an understanding of energies." "Honest, tell it like it is, colorful." "My own type – understandable and straight." "If they have experienced enough to mature." All of the preceding comments make sense in a practical, earthy kind of way as to why Eights are attracted to Eights. However, it they "haven't experienced enough to mature," the combination is likely to be volatile and temporary. Long-term pairings of two Eights are very uncommon.

The Mediator: "Easy to be with. "Acceptance and rhythm." "Peacemaker, creative, aware, nonjudgmental." These statements may help explain why the Leader-Mediator was one of the most common pairings in our survey. Even if they would not admit it, Eights for the most part have felt shunned and unaccepted by others much of their lives. Nines bring a level of acceptance to the relationship that must feel warm and loving to the Eight's battered inner child. Nines, whose approach to life consists of putting one foot on the brake and the other one on the accelerator, love the full-throttle-ahead style of the Eight.

Exercises for the Leader (Type Eight) and your partner
The following exercises are intended to take a look at some of the primary characteristics and issues of the Leader. But first here is a story about celebrity Rosie O'Donnell who is most likely an Eight. After the tragedy at

Columbine, Rosie stated that she called Oprah in the middle of the night and told her, "We have to form a union and save the children of the world." She connected her behavior to when she had been a very successful talk show host. She said, "I had this illusion that fame came with a magic wand and it would be able to cure all social ills. So when a national tragedy happened on what I considered to be on my watch, I had to get the other super-hero women to form a justice league."

Later, Rosie talked about a disagreement with TV personality Barbara Walters. Rosie described a certain behavior she has at times when she is in an intense argument with someone – it involves her "standing up." Rosie said, "I tell people I love – if you are ever in a fight with me and I stand up, leave the room…if I stand up that's a sign that the rage is too big for my body. I have to move to readjust the rage and the pressure of the past." She went on to say that she really regretted that she most likely scared Barbara Walters. "Words are like weapons to me," stated Rosie. If I had been braver, I would have just cried and said to her, "You hurt my feelings. Because (when you cry), you are vulnerable…the authentic feelings were pain, hurt, and rejection."

This story describes core attributes of Leaders. One is the almost over-whelming anger and power that can rise up in Eights around social ills and the injustices mirrored in a tragedy such as the Columbine shooting. It describes how big that anger is as it is held in the body of an Eight, where it can be used both to protect the innocent and also to bully and intimidate an enemy of sorts. It also speaks to the Leader's fear of being vulnerable and how bravery does not always mean being strong in a traditional way, but rather to share one's tender side. In an intimate relationship, Leaders need to deal with these core issues -- anger and fighting, power and control, listening and collaboration, feelings, vulnerability, and innocence.

Gifts of the Leader

Before we tackle the more difficult issues of the Eight, let's summarize the gifts that the Leader brings to his or her partner and to the relationship overall. Eights are known for their "what you see is what you get" approach to life. This characteristic can produce an honest and open relationship. Leaders both protect and champion their partner, helping them reach their goals. If trust can be established in the relationship, the Eight and their partner can share a genuine intimacy that can include a sense of innocence and vulner-ability.

Complete the unfinished sentences below to verify what the Leader brings to the relationship:

- For the Eight: I feel like the gift I am able to bring to the relationship that is hopefully helpful to my partner and the relationship overall is...
- For the partner of the Eight: I feel like the gifts that my Eight partner brings to the relationship are...

Anger and fighting

Rosie O'Donnell's description of her fight with Barbara Walters demonstrates how Leaders fight and the issues with which they struggle. First, Eights don't usually avoid anger and fighting. On the contrary, most Leaders believe that the "truth" comes out in a fight. In other words, if you want to know where someone stands, test them a little bit by stirring things up. Leaders don't want their partners to be pushovers; they expect others to resist the Eight's domination and to stand up for themselves. Leaders in our survey put it this way, "Don't make excuses." and "Speak up to me." Rosie stated that she now knows that she most likely scared Barbara during their fight and that she regretted it. As with most Leaders, Rosie most likely was just testing Barbara to see where she stood in the matter they were quarreling about. Withstanding the Leader's hurricane-like force, though, is easier said than done. Rosie admitted after the fact that she should have shown more vulnerability and expressed her authentic feelings during the confrontation instead of just overwhelming anger.

Answer the questions below about your fighting style with each other:

- Is it important for one of you to win during arguments? If your answer is yes – what is the payoff for winning?
- Like Barbara, does either of you feel uncomfortable or scared while fighting? If your answer is yes – make "safety and respect" your first rule of fighting fair.
- Like Rosie's "standing up" cue, are there specific signs you are aware of that your anger is getting out of control? If this happens – take timeouts or table your discussion for another time.
- Like Rosie, are your "words ever like weapons" with which you attack your partner? If yes – build in "safety and respect" as a guideline.
- Is the end goal of your fights to "be brave" and explore and access authentic feelings, innocence, and vulnerability with yourself and with each other?

Power and control

> "Power is good for one thing only: to increase our happiness
> and the happiness of others."
> --Thich Nhat Hanh

Leaders believe that their reason to control is that they are only trying to avoid being controlled by others or by the situation. They have told us that they have problems surrendering and letting go of control. It's important for them to be seen as powerful and not vulnerable. Eights reveal their tender side only to those whom they trust completely. Being right or believing they have a hold on the truth goes hand-in-hand with the controlling aspect of the Eight. Discuss the following questions with each other:

- Who would each of you say "controls" the relationship?
- Are there power struggles between the two of you? How do you make decisions? Is there ever a discussion about who has the truth?
- Does the Leader's partner ever feel that the Eight "possessed" her or is trying to control her and her choices?
- Do control issues and resistance to letting go make surrendering difficult so that vulnerability and innocence are hard to access? What can each of you do to achieve this?
- Do you each feel you can trust each other to the point where you can reveal your tender side to one another?

Collaboration and Listening

In our survey, a Leader reported that he has "too much energy, focus, directness, and not enough collaboration." He admitted that, "In the past, I have not recognized how I've controlled, crushed, and micromanaged my wife. I haven't allowed her to 'partner' with me." With regard to listening, another Eight's partner's central complaint is, "You never discuss issues. You just make a decision." Another Leader reported that her husband's central complaints were, "I decide things on my own, without properly talking about it with him. I work too much. I don't listen enough, especially when I am too busy." Answer the questions below together:

- Do you feel you are each making an earnest attempt to hear the other's current wants, needs, and goals?
- Does each of you feel heard when trying to communicate with your partner?

- Is there anything you would like to ask of your partner that would make communicating more effective?
- Are you are both working on expressing genuine feelings with one another and exploring with one another your vulnerabilities and innocence?
- Do you both feel you are striving for a partnership that includes an equal collaboration plus the upmost respect and recognition for one another?

Together, create a Relationship Mission Statement that speaks to how you will handle the issues of anger/fighting, power/control, listening/collaboration, feelings, vulnerability, and innocence in your relationship with one another. Post it where you can see it daily and commit to honoring these guidelines for your relationship.

CHAPTER TWELVE

The Mediator (Type Nine) In Relationship

Probably my best feature in relationship is my easygoing, laid back style and my ability to totally be there for someone. It's as if I can become one with them. I can also be accepting and non-judgmental, which makes them feel comfortable and safe. Some people say they become frustrated with me because I'm not fully present when they want me to listen or to participate in a project. They would probably also say that I can become quite stubborn, especially if I'm being pushed to do something. Probably my worst feature in relationship is that I have a hard time knowing what I really want, and then I tend to blame others for not seeing me for who I am.

"I always procrastinate whenever I get around to it,"
-- A Mediator

But let there be spaces in your togetherness,
And let the winds of the heavens dance between you.
Love one another, but make not a bond of love:
Let it rather be a moving sea between the shores
of your souls.
-- *The Prophet* by Khalil Gibran

"I'll agree with whatever he says, but I'll do what I want."
-- A Mediator, quoted by Baron & Wagele

Characteristics of the Mediator (Type Nine) in relationship

Ability to see all sides – Accepting/peacemaking/mediation

Nines are easygoing people who give others the freedom and encouragement to unfold in their own way. They value peace and harmony. They can see both sides of an issue and can therefore mediate between people with opposing points of view. A prominent characteristic of Mediators, one that helps explain why they are typically so beloved by their friends, is that they are accepting and nonjudgmental. They can also be very kind and giving, and when Nines give, they generally do not keep score. They come across as low-key, low-ego people who have few expectations of others. Embedded in the following stories are some core characteristics of the Nine being formed at an early age.

When I was growing up, my parents made me the mediator, the peacemaker of the family. When my older brother ran away, my parents basically forgot about me for several years. It was as though I'd disappeared. I love to laugh and have fun, but I think comfort and peace are more important than fun. Unity and harmony are really important to me, and so is nature. People always said I was easygoing, but I was stifling what I wanted to say. My head's always going.

A 32-year-old man recalled,

As a kid growing up, I was the quiet type. I didn't draw any attention to myself. If there were any trouble, I'd walk away. I always hated arguing and fighting. Even today I'd rather leave than fight. I'm still pretty quiet with people I don't know. It takes a lot to get me mad, but when I do, I explode. I'm a good listener, and I bend over backwards to help a friend.

People who hold jobs as real-life mediators in the workplace or who work with partners in conflict are usually skilled at being able to forget their own agenda. Instead they can hold equally the different points of view of the people they are trying to assist. They can be almost invisible in their work, and most of the time they take little credit for successfully bringing two opposing sides together. Enneagram Type Nines, called by some Mediators and by others Peacemakers, have similar characteristics. Many of them report that as children, they felt largely invisible in their families. Their childhood coping strategy was to merge with other family members or with the family system as a whole, thereby gaining an identity from the blending. Unity and harmony are very important, and the Mediator often plays a stabilizing role in the family dynamic.

As a little girl, Audrey's mom and dad fought constantly, always on the verge of a divorce. At age eight, she decided to start going to church. She called a nearby church and asked if someone would pick her up in the church van. Every Sunday morning while her parents fought, Audrey got up, put on her Sunday school dress and waited for the van. After some time, one Sunday morning her parents got up and, tired of the fighting, followed her to church in their car. They eventually reconciled their differences and ended up staying together.

This story illustrates how a little Mediator subtly and without recognition mediated the conflict between her parents and brought peace and harmony to the family. Audrey later became a successful administrator of non-profit programs for the developmentally challenged and disabled. She worked tirelessly, with little recognition, trying to provide services for all who needed them. Eventually, at mid-life, she experienced depression and burnout. She entered therapy and explored her unresolved childhood anger issues and her feelings of being overlooked while her parents fought. As an adult, Audrey knew she had been successful in the outside world, yet inside, deep down, she felt unhappy. Finally, her work was to find out who she truly was and what she really wanted in her life – following her own agenda.

Mediators recognize that the gifts they bring to their relationship are patience, acceptance, unconditional support, non-judgmentalism and compassion. One Nine cited her "Ability to compromise. Kindness. I'm able to see all sides of an issue and consequently, adapt to circumstances." Another wrote, "I have an ability to live in the moment, to find good in every circumstance and be encouraged by it, to make people laugh and want to play."

Self-forgetting and detachment

As adults, it's easy for Mediators to adopt another person's agenda. Sometimes they have trouble even recognizing what they really want; it's easier for them to know what they don't want. In their family of origin, Mediators were probably not demanding. They went along with everyone else and tended not to speak up for themselves. They were usually unseen and unrecognized. They are described as being self-forgetting. Some Nines describe themselves as detached or distant in their primary relationship. Partners complain that they don't even know what the Mediator is thinking or feeling. One Nine said that what keeps her from effective problem solving in her relationship is, "not knowing what I want." Another woman, 57 years old, wrote,

I oftentimes do not state or express what it is I am thinking or feeling, and I automatically think my partner already knows this. Then when she doesn't do what I think is appropriate for the situation, I will say something, only to find out she had no idea what I was thinking or feeling – this was news to me!

Nines are not deliberately trying to frustrate their partners by withholding their thoughts, feelings and desires from them. They usually are just not in touch; it's simply unfamiliar territory. Just like Audrey's story above, the primary focus is outside them, keeping the peace and making sure the connection stays in place. In the Mediator's mind, you don't safeguard a connection by rocking the boat -- which is what stating one's own wants and needs feels like. Unfortunately, what the Nine misses with this perspective is that most people in relationships want someone who will meet them halfway and also present a challenge.

Healthy, spiritual relationships are said to comprise three elements – nurturing, challenging and transforming. A relationship needs a foundation of love and nurturance. Once that is in place, partners are then supposed to challenge each other as if holding up a mirror and asking if this is who they really want to be. And finally, the combination of love/nurturing and the healthy challenging of each other creates an opportunity for self-transformation. Stan, a Mediator, in conversation about relationships with a therapist, stated, "I really like that idea that relationships have three elements – love/nurturing and...and...and transforming." He then asked, "What was the second one?" When Stan was reminded it was about challenging one's partner, they both laughed at his typical Nine's reluctance to remember something that truly rocks the boat in relationship.

Sloth and self-forgetting

Another Mediator, Vivian, became so overwhelmed and stressed out in the everyday busy-ness of her life that she decided to move temporarily to South America. When she returned, she spoke of the sloth that lives there. Vivian described sloths as endearing and cute. They would sometimes begin crossing the road, but about midway would stop dead in their tracks as if they had fallen asleep or had simply forgotten where they were going. She claimed they would stand upright, perfectly motionless, sometimes with one paw up in the air as if someone had pressed the "pause" button. People would get out of their cars, pick up the sloth and carry it across the road and set it down on the other side.

The core issue of the Mediator, put in spiritual terms, is termed "sloth." Many use this rather harsh word to describe someone who is generally lazy, a procrastinator or a couch potato. In the context of the enneagram, the word sloth is defined as a "laziness toward the self," a self-forgetting or self-neglect. The Nine's childhood coping strategy of merging with another is an effort to have an identity or a sense of self. This means, though, that one must empty oneself out to make room for the other. This strategy develops into both a gift and a liability.

The Nine's gift is a tremendous capacity for empathy. The downside is getting so focused on others, "laziness" or self-forgetting, that shows up in several different ways. One is the stereotypical procrastination or inactivity, but some Nines work compulsively. In fact, they may even use excessive physical activity as a way to numb themselves. Sloth is a form of narcotization, a way that the Mediator "falls asleep" in his or her own life and in the lives of significant others. No matter how sloth manifests, it's important to recognize that the underlying motivation is that the Mediator finds it hard to remember and honor him- or herself. A young man talked about self-forgetting in the form of procrastination and distraction in his life:

Procrastination is a big problem for me. If there's something I need to get done, I'll do everything and anything else instead. I'll get busy with other things. Sometimes it's hard for me if there's more than one thing going on around me. I tend to start something, and then I won't finish it because I get distracted.

These core issues can interfere with the Nine's ability to accomplish tasks efficiently. First, because of their desire to merge and go along with what others want, they agree to do more than they have time for and are frequently overcommitted. Also, because they are easily distracted and have difficulty prioritizing, their good intentions, completing a particular project may get hijacked by the inevitable other things that get in the way. The result is that even though Mediators seem constantly in motion, things are done late, if at all. This characteristic can be very frustrating to a partner, especially when he or she has a task-oriented personality style.

A Mediator reported that one of her challenges is that "I'm not focused. I spin my wheels a lot, and my partner has to pick up the slack." One man recognized that it would help his relationship if he were "present on a more consistent basis; sharing feelings. Sharing relationship issues."

Anger and resentment

Mediators are generally seen as sweet and non-threatening. But under the surface, anger and resentment frequently lurk. Mediators are in the anger triad or center along with Perfectionists (Ones) and Leaders (Eights). Anger is dealt with in different ways by each of the Types in this center. The Mediator's anger is about not being truly seen or heard. This non-recognition has resulted in an approach that says, "Just go along to get along." A common consequence is that resentments build up, which eventually may result in an explosion. In her article, "Nine Story" in *The Enneagram Monthly*, Joan Ryan writes,

I have always been aware that once in a great while a huge explosion will burst out of me that I can't stop even if I try. I am almost always surprised when it happens; I don't feel it rising; there is no logic to when, where and what will touch it off. These explosions are almost invariably triggered by small and relatively unimportant causes. I finally realized (after wading through tremendous resistance) that I actually store it all up and the match of a slight aggravation or insult will light a huge hidden bonfire instead of a single flame. . . [Afterwards], sometimes my apologies are subject to extremes – either I over-apologize or I refuse to apologize at all; there is no in-between. I now feel that this pattern allows me to cover up or withhold, even when there is an explosion, both from myself and others, the real sources of my anger (the parts that feel really risky to expose). I am slowly learning to remember that if I really look, I can find many layers underneath each piece. The anger is never just about the surface cause or even the obvious second layer. [March 1996, p. 1]

Some Mediators do not release their anger in explosions; they may store them up until one day they finally decide to end the relationship, leaving their partner baffled. Joan Ryan concluded, in her article,

I have noticed that my reasons and fears for not expressing anger seem largely unfounded. So little by little, I am beginning to risk expressing some anger in the moment. This way it stays a little flame and does not grow into an enormous destructive bonfire.

Tuning in, tuning out

The tendency to tune out and not be fully present in their relationship is a source of unhappiness for the Mediator's partner. A 75-year-old man, married over 50 years, wrote that his wife would describe him as "missing

– removed – talks too little." One Mediator wrote that when his Leader wife starts to fight, "I feel a disconnection. I have tried and keep trying to be aware of the disconnection feeling when situations start to get tough. With that awareness, it is easier to recognize my feelings for what they are, feelings in me that will pass, and to recognize that my wife is not experiencing the situation the same way I am."

Despite the tendency of Nines to disengage in their primary relationship, they are often described by friends as being empathetic, energized, caring, willing to listen and see the other person's side, and very supportive. It can therefore be confusing to learn that their primary partner often sees these same people as detached or just not present. The answer seems to lie in the difference between casual friendships and long-term relationships. At the beginning of a romance, the Mediator can be very enthusiastic, present, and engaged. When contact is intermittent, such as in most friendships, the Nine may feel comfortable maintaining this interaction. But in their primary relationship, they tend to lose steam. Their inertia increases and the ongoing relationship seems to wear heavily. For Mediators of the Social subtype, interactions with friends and colleagues energize, but also bleed off energy so that little is left for the primary partner. Spouses will complain that the Mediator seems to "be there" for their committee meetings and social activities, but then crawls into his cocoon once he gets home. Nines tend to gradually take their primary relationship for granted. With time, power struggles can intensify.

Difficulty making decisions

"You can't make decisions" was a central complaint by one Mediator's partner. This difficulty arises from the Nine's ability to see all sides of every issue, as well as their tendency to "self-forget," meaning that they often don't actually know what they want. More than one Mediator wrote that a major challenge was indecisiveness. Here is what two said:

#1 Sometimes it's hard for me to make up my mind. If there's something I want and there are several choices, I might decide and then change my mind two or three times, thinking that maybe something else would be better.

#2 Making a decision is hard because once I decide, I might find out something that might make me feel different about it.

The Mediator's struggle with decision-making can become quite an issue. A partner can become frustrated with the indecisiveness, and eventually might say, "Just make a decision for gosh sakes!" But it's not that easy because of the Nine's long history of merging with others' points of view, fear of conflict and separation, and self-negation. If the partner steps in and makes the decisions, on the surface the Mediator appears to go along but inside he becomes resentful and angry. But inside he feels unrecognized and disrespected and can resort to a stubborn stance, digging in his heels. The thinking is, "I may not know what I want, but I'll be damned if I let **you** tell me." The couple can soon find themselves in a power struggle without realizing it.

Conflict avoidance and withdrawal

Mediators make wonderful friends. They generally don't insist on having their own way; they don't make waves, and they try to avoid conflict. In their primary relationship, though, in their reluctance to get into confrontation means they tend to not want to talk things out. One Mediator related that "not being able to communicate effectively so as to avoid criticism" keeps her from effective problem solving. An alternative is to minimize any communication about feelings, desires and complaints.

A 49-year-old Mediator wrote that what keeps him from effective problem solving is that "my energy goes to avoiding problems and problem solving." A 75-year-old man wrote that he is "too laid back. Too peaceful. Too easily relaxed. Too conflict-avoiding. Too passive." A woman reported that her husband's central complaint is, "You never tell me when you're upset about something. The first I know of it is the pots slamming in the kitchen."

A Mediator married to a Leader wrote that a challenge for her is, "being able to be honest – not afraid to bring up things that might be uncomfortable. I'm afraid of his reaction, so I don't bring things up." Another Nine married to an Eight wrote that a problem for him is "my reluctance to confront. It's very difficult for a Nine. Nines don't believe in win/lose confrontation. Nines want calm discussion which seeks to uncover the truth and leads to a mutual understanding."

Many Mediators feel that they were not seen or recognized enough during their childhood; as adults they suffer from an inner sense that they're not important. They are very sensitive to being treated as unimportant, yet their style in the world tends to be quiet and unnoticeable, likely to bring about exactly what they fear.

Telling a long long story

The difficulty some Mediators have in prioritizing and their self-forgetting sometimes extends to conversations and relating to others. It might show up in their storytelling where they have a tendency to go on and on, focusing on the non-essentials. Meanwhile their listener's attention drifts away. One Mediator explained,

> *Even though my Two* [Giver] *partner is process oriented, she does not like as many details as I am more than willing to put into the "story," so she tends to tune out. I realize I can keep her more engaged if I keep the conversation to bottom line feelings and thoughts.*

In many ways this behavior serves as a metaphor for Mediator's basic approach to their life — how they reinforce their feelings of unimportance, and how they focus on the non-essentials and distract themselves from what is truly important. Roxy, a Nine client of Ron's (one of the authors of this book), was working on this aspect of her personality. As she talked about her issues during a session she would stop the conversation from time to time and ask Ron if he was getting bored. It was as if she saw herself as boring or that she was determined to bore someone to prove to herself her unimportance. Roxy also got distracted as she talked and her conversations tended to go off on tangents. She referred to this as "going down the rabbit trail." What she meant is that a larger path represented her primary conversations, and when she got distracted her thoughts would go off on smaller trails that generally led nowhere. The metaphor is about how she shows up in her life. Ron also generally asks clients at a certain point during the session if they have talked about the things they wanted to talk about. The first time Roxy was asked that question, she took a hidden list out of her pocket, and then after scanning her list, she said she had brought up only the unimportant issues on her list. All of this mirrors the Mediator's difficulty in honoring and remembering themselves.

Wings

In Chapter Three we explained that each personality Type is likely to possess some characteristics of one of the two adjacent Types on the nine-pointed enneagram diagram, which are termed the *wings* of that type (see page 52). For The Mediator, the wings are the Leader (Eight) and the Perfectionist (One).

The same people who are surprised that a Mediator would ever get together with a Leader in a primary relationship might wince about this personality combination. But just as Mediators do sometimes get together with Leaders — because if nothing else it works to have someone handy to jumpstart their battery — something similar happens internally to Nines who have an Eight wing. They are usually a bit more earthy and blunt, sometimes referred to as a "grumpy" Nine and a little less afraid of hurting others' feelings, although they are still gentle. When healthy, Nines with an Eight wing can be leaders who bring others together with their calming, reassuring presence. They also tend to relate less to some of the stereotypical Mediator characteristics such as merging or not knowing their own agenda. These features are still a part of them, but not as readily apparent.

Mediators with a One (Perfectionist) wing often have their typical characteristics overlaid with a nitpicking quality, usually turned more toward themselves than others. They are less grounded and have more permeable boundaries than the Nine/Eight combination and therefore can find themselves being carried away at times by negative external forces. They are likely to react with an "Oh clumsy me" response. The One wing can help the healthy Nine to stay awake, so that they can assert themselves in the world in a truly "right action" way. They can be a true "mediator" in the world who brings things together for the moral benefit of all.

What the Mediator's partner could do for the Nine's happiness

Although they are so accommodating, Mediators actually crave their own space and want to feel independent. One of them advised, "Balance being a couple with being independent." Another suggested, "Give me both space (independence) and recognition of my importance as a person and in the relationship." Mediators often feel forgotten or not seen, so it really helps if the partner recognizes and honors them.

How Mediators feel about other Types in relationship

When asked which types they struggle with the most, more Mediators chose the Leader (Type Eight) than any other. (Interestingly, this was by far the most common pairing in our survey!) Next was the Perfectionist (Type One). Some comments were:

The Leader: "They scare me, because their aggressiveness threatens to put me in touch with my anger." "Too direct and powerful." "I don't like to be dominated." "My Dad was an Eight. I was scared of him. I also get intimidated and overwhelmed." "They want it their way all the time." "Inability to see different sides."

Nines view anger as similar to electricity — if you don't know what you are doing, it is best to just stay away from it. Eights are the electricians in the world. When Mediators hang out with Leaders, they discover the power and benefit that anger can provide, and yet it's still scary. The Nine-Eight pairing can be fraught with power and control issues: This relationship has a love/hate aspect to it. If these two Types can find some respect for each other's power, it can be dynamic and powerful – if not, they might as well stop beating up on one another and go their separate ways.

The Perfectionist: "The perfectionist is a tad more perfect than I am, and the difference is that they won't stop until it is 'perfect' in their minds, whereas 'good enough' is perfect for me. The extra time to attempt perfection is a waste of time to me." "Self-righteous bastards, all black or white (the real world is shades of gray). Probably because it's what I like least in myself – the judgmental, self-righteous attitude." "Their critical nature pushes my buttons."

Even though Nines in our survey claimed they struggle with Ones, this is another quite common pairing, a little bit like the "Odd Couple", always sniping at each other. Perfectionists need to be careful that their constructive criticism doesn't undermine the Mediator's attempt to be visible in the world, and the Mediator needs to stop being so stubborn toward the Perfectionist's attempt to be helpful. When they are on the same wavelength, the Nine can help the One to feel free of all of the judging, and the Nine can get organized, disciplined, and possibly find a cause to pursue with the One's help.

Mediators reported being most compatible with other Mediators and with Detectives (Six).

The Mediator: "General harmony. " "Comfort and understanding." I accept them easily. They're not making demands for change and attention. They are accepting." "We are compatible." "Very accommodating – not demanding." "We think alike."

During the course of an enneagram interview of a couple, after realizing both were Nines, the questioner exclaimed, "How do you guys ever get out of bed in the morning!" Partners in relationships generally collude with each other about how the world works. This is sometimes referred to as the co-illusion. Two Mediators together, although there is probably no sweeter pairing, need to be careful that they still present a regular challenge to each other.

The Detective: "Loyalty, someone to always 'cover my back,' and a way of merging intensities." "I admire the courage and enjoy the loyalty and loving heart." "I think I understand the paranoia, and for the most part, it does not bother me. Sixes are clever, relational, and quick to let go of the stuff that doesn't really matter."

Although there is much good about this pairing, it can also have a bit of an "Odd Couple" look to it. The Detective can't understand how the Mediator can have all that trust in the universe, and also wonders how they can possibly go so long without questioning everything. The Mediator wonders what all the fuss is about. Doesn't this person ever stop talking? Together the Nine teaches the Six how to have faith in the universe, and the Six teaches the Nine how to ask the "who am I" questions that lead to having a solid self in the world.

Advice Nines give other Mediators in relationship

In advising younger Nines, the Mediators' powerful comments cut right to their core issues: their "self-forgetfulness," tendency to withdraw rather than be fully present, reluctance to ask for what they need, unawareness of their own wants, and avoidance of conflict.

- *I would say to anyone: Develop self-awareness and a sense of humor, assume responsibility for yourself and your behavior, and have reasonable expectations of others. For Nines especially, take yourself seriously and address a problem directly when it arises. Avoid avoidance.*
- *Be clear about your own needs, what those are. It is easy to get lost in the relationship. It took me years to start focusing on the things I need to do for myself.*
- *Stand your ground and stick with what you say you want and need from other people. Don't allow the fear of conflict to make you overlook your feelings, wants and needs. Reflect long and hard on all the qualities you want in a partner and don't settle for less than what you want.*

Another lesson many Mediators need to learn is to be fully present in the relationship. One advised: "Get your priorities straight; be sure to keep in mind that your relationship is of utmost importance to you and that you cannot take it for granted." This is excellent advice for a Mediator, who tends to go to sleep in a relationship. Their partner can get really irritated. Sometimes they haven't had sex in years – they think it's just too much work.

What partners of Mediators need to know:
- Once a Nine merges with another person, it is hard for them to separate themselves from that person. Nines can know other people's wishes better than their own and support the lives of others accordingly.
- Mediators in relationship can be giving, compromising, adaptive and receptive. They can be caring and attentive, often aware of what is essentially good about other people.
- Mediators may divert attention from certain feelings by becoming preoccupied with nonessentials. They may avoid arguments by being uncommunicative about how they really feel. They question whether taking a position is worth risking the relationship and possible separation.
- Nines will often say back what you want to hear. This does not mean that he or she agrees with you. It's hard for them to say no because your needs sound louder than their own.
- If Nines feel coerced, they may become stubborn. When they feel pushed to make a decision, they control through non-action (passive-aggressive).
- Relationships deepen when the Nine no longer risks the loss of personal identity. The most intimate task of relating to them has to do with supporting decisions that come from their own being and allowing their choices to become their own.

Exercises for a Mediator (Nine) and your partner
The following exercises are designed to work with some of the primary characteristics and issues of the Mediator.

Gifts of the Mediator
Before we tackle the more challenging issues of the Mediator, let's discuss the gifts that the Mediator brings to the partner and to the relationship overall.

Nines are known for being empathic and for bringing unconditional love and acceptance to their partner. They can be very supportive, merging with their partner's life as if it were their own.
- For the partner: Discuss with your Nine partner a time or two when his or her love and support truly felt empathic and unconditional.

- For the Nine: Discuss with your partner the gifts you feel you bring to the relationship.

Neither seen nor heard: Recognition versus non-recognition

Many Mediators report feeling overlooked as children. This kind of non-recognition caused them to merge with others' identities and to put other people's agendas before their own. This can create the gift of love and empathy but it can also cause the loss of oneself .

Movie actor Adam Sandler, most likely a Nine, stated in an interview once that early in his career, when he walked down the street he would murmur to himself over and over again, "Please recognize me. Please recognize me." Most Nines have a love/hate relationship with recognition. A part of them would love to get it whereas another part doesn't think they deserve it. Or they may think that others might perceive them as trying to inflate their importance.

Please complete the incomplete sentences below. The purpose of the questions is for each partner to "recognize" the other:

- Some of the things I really appreciate about you as a person are…
- Some of the things I really appreciate about you as a partner are…
- The strengths I feel I possess are…
- The strengths I feel I bring to the relationship are…

Avoiding conflict

In an Oprah Magazine article, author and psychiatrist Mark Epstein described the feelings he had experienced in his relationship, "I did not want to be angry. I did not want her to be angry, and I did not want our marriage to have anger within it. I wanted peace and harmony and attunement and sex." Mediators would describe their feelings similarly – they usually avoid conflict at all costs. Yet healthy conflict and anger has the potential of balancing out a relationship. If the relationship has favored one partner's wants and needs, a healthy argument can balance things out and make sure that issues that need to be talked about, get talked about. To emphasize how important this issue is for Nines, listen again to what one of our Mediators said earlier in this chapter.

I didn't draw any attention to myself. If there were any trouble, I'd walk away. I always hated arguing and fighting. Even today I'd rather leave than fight. I'm still pretty quiet with people I don't know. It takes a lot to get me mad, but when I do, I explode."

To speak to your issues as a Nine, complete the following sentences:
- The thing that scares me the most about bringing up issues and the possibility of conflict, is...
- Something that would make me feel safer and more comfortable in bringing up issues that might lead to conflict is...
- An issue that I have put off talking about because I haven't felt comfortable talking about it, is...

Remember, conflict for the Nine with those they love brings up separation anxiety.

Merging versus personal agenda

Once a Mediator merges with a partner it is hard for them to separate themselves from that person. Nines can know other people's wishes better than their own and support the lives of others as their own. Merging and being so focused on others makes it difficult for them to recognize what they really want; it is sometimes easier for them to know what they don't want. This is what is described as being self-forgetting or self-neglecting. To bring to light the Nine's own agenda and personal desires, complete the sentences below. We recognize that this is not familiar territory to you and it may take you some time to truly get in touch with some of the following:
- A personal desire I have that I have not spoken about is...
- If I were to take the focus off my partner and allow myself to focus entirely on myself, what would come up for me would be...
- When I think about my own personal agenda, possibly even separate from my partner's agenda, what comes up for me is...
- If I were to care about myself the same way I support others and their goals, what I would most likely discover about myself and my own personal agenda is...

Zoning out and other-neglect

Mediators tend to tune out or not be fully present in their relationship, which causes great unhappiness for their partners. Jerry, a 75-year old married over 50 years, wrote that his wife would describe him as "missing", "removed", and "talks too little." In an earlier exercise, we focused on the Nine's tendency for self-neglect; here we'll deal with the Nine's neglect of others. Healthy relationships take a lot of work. The opposite of "the work" of relationships is a form of "laziness." Laziness is defined here as a kind of self- or other-neglect. This neglect can include indifference, apathy, and any distraction that causes the Mediator to check out. The antidote to this form of other-neglect is to stay awake, pay attention, participate, and stay in the present moment.

To work on this issue, we first ask the Mediator's partner to complete the following sentences and question:

- As your partner, I sometimes feel you tune me out when I'm...
- As your partner, when I feel tuned out, what comes up for me is...
- As your partner, is there something I can do that would help us to stay connected and in the present moment?

"He is less involved in his life - more than anyone I've known."

-- Anonymous

The above quote could easily refer to the Nine's not showing up and also not being involved in their life. This is often the chief complaint of a partner of a Nine.

- For the Nine: Where do you have the hardest time showing up and fully participating in your life and/or relationship?
- For the partner: Where does your Nine partner have the hardest time showing up in life and/or relationship?
- For both: What can both of you do to make it more likely that the Nine will show up? What can you do to decrease the likelihood of the Nine's getting into a power struggle with the partner?

Most couples engage in a recurrent "classic fight." Take a close look at your own classic fight and consider what roles each of your Types play. Try scripting out a beginning, middle, and an end to your typical argument. Try playing each other's role in the conflict, taking on your partner's Type. Brainstorm creative ways with each other to handle the conflict differently. Ask yourselves how different Types would handle your classic fight. Finally, try to come up with a different conclusion than the one to which your Types usually gravitate.

CHAPTER THIRTEEN

Putting your Knowledge to Work In your Relationship

The primary goal of this book is to help couples better understand and improve their relationship. You have just finished reading detailed characteristics of each of the nine enneagram personality Types. Each chapter ends with suggested exercises specifically designed for the reader of that Type and your spouse or partner, no matter what his or her Type is. We hope that both of you have discussed the questions at the end of the relevant chapters. By now both you and your partner may have concluded which enneagram Type describes each of you. There are 45 possible pairings of the nine personalities, and in Section Two of this book you will meet each combination and learn how they interact.

One of the strengths of this personalilty system is that understanding your style will enable you to perceive why people of your Type are likely to exhibit a similar set of strengths and challenges in their relationship no matter what Type your partner is. This is why, in addition to the specific exercises at the end of each chapter, we would now like to offer you a series of exercises for you and your partner to do together after you each finish reading the chapters in Section One and have a good idea of which Type best describes you.

If at the end of Section One you are still uncertain of your style, we suggest you look online, where there are multiple websites that provide screening tools to help you determine your Type. You can find a listing of recommended books in the Appendix.

Once you have each identified your enneagram personality Type, sit down in a comfortable place with your partner and carry out the exercises below. During the exercises we will refer to the two of you as Partner A and

Partner B. Partner A is the person who whose personality Type the preceding chapter just described. Partner B is the significant other of Partner A.

- Both partners should review the paragraph at the beginning of the chapter that describes the personality Type in a nutshell.
- Next, Partner A shares with B the parts of the paragraph that resonates with him or her as well as the parts that don't. (Note: Most of the paragraph should speak to Partner A if he or she is truly of that Type. Also, if you are both the same Type, simply take turns doing the Type-related exercises.)
- Partner B now shares with A the characteristics in the paragraph that they see pertaining to their partner.

Early childhood:

As children, personality type can be seen as both an identity and a coping strategy that we utilized in the family we grew up in. This childhood strategy provides a way to either win your parents' love or, in severely dysfunctional families, as a way to survive. Because early childhood patterns are carried over into adulthood, understanding them can help us identify current patterns in our relationships. The questions below will help you and your partner get more in touch with your Type and the childhood patterns that may be affecting your current relationship.

- Knowing what you now know about your personality Type, how do you think your Type showed up in childhood?
- If you can, tell your partner a childhood memory that you feel relates to your Type.
- What purpose do you feel your Type served in childhood – kept you safe, helped you get the goodies, provided recognition, etc.?
- Do you feel your Type was connected to a wounding experience in childhood? (Ex.: For Ones – Having to be "good", trying to correct, etc.)
- How does the role you played in childhood mirror the role you now play in your current relationship?
- How does your Type or childhood coping strategy show up in your current relationship in both positive and negative ways?

The agenda:

Each personality Types enters into relationship with an agenda connected to one's childhood experiences. It's as if our inner child is saying, "I may not have gotten it right with mom and/or dad, but I'll be darned if I don't get it right with my partner!" "Right" is whatever frustrated you or caused you pain as a child, which results in a pattern that continues to frustrate you or cause you pain in your adult relationships. Childhood coping strategies that were useful or even necessary at that time usually become worn-out or no longer needed in our adult relationships. Yet we continue to use them until we gain the necessary insight and healing takes place.

- Discuss with your partner the role or the agenda your Type had in previous relationships, both the positive and the negative aspects.
- How did your Type cause you problems and frustrate your ex-partner -- a part of you that keeps coming up over and over again.?
- Do you feel you and your current partner selected each other to complete unfinished business that is connected to both your Type and your childhood issues?
- Is there a frustration connected to your Type or childhood coping strategy that mirrors a frustration in your current relationship?
- When does your partner feel that your Type or childhood coping strategy causes both of you difficulty in the relationship?
- When do you feel like your partner pushes the buttons of your Type?
- What are some of the outdated or no longer useful aspects of your Type's childhood coping strategy that you believe would be a good idea to let go of in your current relationship?
- What do you feel are the payoffs of your Type's coping strategies in your current relationship that would make it difficult for you to let go of?
- What other resistances do you feel would come up for you if you were to try to let go of some of the outdated and no longer useful aspects of your Type?
- What Type-related behaviors are you willing to take responsibility for and commit to being mindful of especially during moments of conflict or power struggles?
- Discuss with your partner ways he or she could support you in letting go of these outdated and no longer useful aspects of your Type without using criticism, sarcasm, or blame.
- Together, discuss how each of you, now knowing what you know about your partner's Type and childhood coping methods, can commit to not pushing your partner's buttons nor taking advantage of the natural characteristics of their Type.

The emotional bank account

Each partner in a relationship maintains an emotional bank account into which the other partner can make deposits or from which to make withdrawals. A deposit is a "gift" that the other person feels is nurturing or just something they really like. A withdrawal is something that takes away from your partner or is something they just don't care for. When a relationship is struggling, one or both bank accounts are usually close to being bankrupt. Regular deposits nurture the relationship and help to make each partner feel that your wants and needs are being met.

In this exercise we encourage you and your partner to consider deposits and withdrawals as things that speak to your Type in a particular way. It is essential to make sure you know what your partner considers a deposit as well as what constitutes a withdrawal. Ron (an author of this book) states that he has at times challenged clients to come up with three things they are certain are deposits to their partners. When the partner is then asked if those things are truly a deposit, it often turns out that they are not! Take time to share with each other what is a deposit and what is a withdrawal to each of you, especially from an enneagram Type perspective. Ask each other the following questions:

- Given your Type, what would you consider a withdrawal in your relationship?
- How does this specific withdrawal take away from your Type?
- Are there withdrawal(s) that could eventually become a deal breaker?
- Given your Type, what would you consider a deposit in your relationship?
- How does this specific deposit relate to your Type?
- Is there a deposit that could even be considered healing to your Type?
- What could you both commit to on a regular basis that would be considered deposits and that would be nurturing to each other?

Relationship Contract

A relationship with someone includes our wants, needs, hopes, dreams, desires, goals, and expectations, preferences that are colored by our enneagram Type. All too often these personal preferences are never spoken aloud to our partner. Instead, we may just assume that our partner will naturally think the same way we do. Most of us think that other people see the world the same as our Type does or, at least, that they *should* see the world as our Type does. Many times a partner will not even be aware of your various wants and needs, much less realize that they are not fulfilling your personal desires.

Our personal preferences may only surface after we have become frustrated with our partner and the relationship has begun to get off track.

If the relationship is struggling, it is useful to try to identify where our preferences are not being met. If we understand the unspoken preferences and expectations that our partner had when they came into the relationship, we have the potential of being able to consciously fulfill them. It is also important for us to update the relationship contract so that it meets the current wants and needs of each of the partners. To get more in touch with both your original and current relationship contract, answer the following questions and share the answers with your partner:

The Original Relationship Contract
- Share with each other what you feel the original contract of your relationship contained. In other words, what wants, needs, desires, goals, and expectations did each of you bring to the relationship?
- Do you believe you were aware of each other's side of the contract that contained their personal preferences and expectations?
- How good of job do you feel each of you did in trying to meet the preferences and expectations of the other?
- How many of your personal preferences and expectations are Type related? Discuss with each other how your Type influences the importance of each of them.
- Now that you know each other's Type, how do you think it will affect your acceptance of and ability to meet your partner's wants and needs?

The Current Relationship Contract
- How do the wants, needs, personal preferences and expectations of your current relationship contract differ from your original contract? What personal preferences and expectations need to be updated and what new information do you need to make sure you share with your partner?
- How many of your personal preferences and expectations are Type related?
- How have the ways you grown and changed within your Type affected the current contract? How can you support your partner's personal and spiritual growth related to his or her Type?

- Are there ways that your partner could help fulfill your current preferences and expectations so as to create more happiness in the relationship and in your life in general?

Relationship Mission Statement

Most of us have heard about a business mission statement that describes the values and mission of a particular business, hopefully keeping it on track. A relationship mission statement is similar; it too is a powerful statement that summarizes each partner's values and goals of as well as the healing and growing that both hope will take place individually and as a couple. After reading the chapters about each of your Types and then doing the exercises at the end of each chapter, together create a relationship mission statement that embodies (1) the core characteristics of your two Types and (2) how you will both work to grow in the relationship and to increase the understanding and compassion you have toward each other. As you write your mission statement, consider:

- The core characteristics and gifts you each bring to the relationship
- How you will support one another
- How you will grow
- How you will love
- Future goals
- What you are committing to

The enneagram can be a powerful tool for understanding yourself and others. Through this understanding, we can gain even more love and compassion for ourselves and others. Through this, our relationships can thrive and provide us with the healing, and personal and spiritual growth we have been looking for.

If you have finished the exercises above:

Congratulations! You are now prepared put your information to use in your most important relationship(s). Section Two contains separate chapters of each of the 45 possible pairings of each type, once again based on the research the authors did on couples who knew their enneagram personality Types. As with Section One, each chapter concludes with some exercises, but this time they are specific exercises that you and your partner should do together regarding your particular relationship issues.

Section Two

Understand Yourself, Your Partner, and Your Relationship

CHAPTER FOURTEEN

Introduction to Section Two

Section One of *Understand Yourself, Understand Your Partner* presented a personality system, the enneagram, which consists of nine basic Types, each of whom views the world through a different lens, has different priorities and goals, and different but predictable struggles. To review, the enneagram diagram (See Figure below) visualizes the nine Types as points along a circle. Each Type has a connecting line with two other Types, and each Type also demonstrates some features of one of the adjacent points on the diagram (called the wings of that type). Additionally, the nine personalities are divided into 3 triads or centers, each consisting of three adjacent Types. All Types in each center have the same basic issue but each a different coping strategy – anger (Eight, Nine and One), their image (Two, Three, and Four), or fear (Five, Six, and Seven). You might want to review Chapters One through Three which describe the features of each of the Types and the various subtypes.

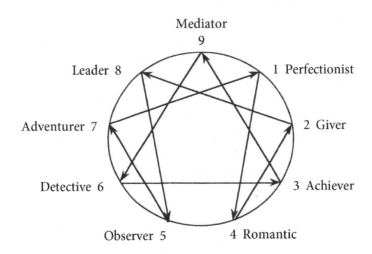

Mediator
9

Leader 8

1 Perfectionist

Adventurer 7

2 Giver

Detective 6

3 Achiever

Observer 5

4 Romantic

Once you learn the basics of the enneagram personality system, you probably will quickly start to reflect on the various relationships in your life, usually trying to figure out the Type of that partner or family member that you either love and/or struggle with. You might actually gasp as you recognize the enneagram Type of your ex or some other past relationship. You are likely to think, "Oh…now I see why we had the problems we did!" We can live five, ten, or even twenty years or longer with someone and really not see where that person was coming from until we begin to study the enneagram and its explanation of personality Types.

Another likely question you may ask yourself is "I'm a Type Four (for example), so what Type is the best type for me to be with?" The correct answer is: a healthy, mature person of any Type. In this chapter though, we will try to answer that question in greater depth. We'll pair up the various combinations, explain what those pairings look like based on our survey, and hypothesize what can make some pairings more or less challenging.

First, however, you must recognize that how well any couple does in relationship does not just hinge on personality. Whatever their Type, the psychological/emotional health and maturity of each person is critical. Additionally, even the healthiest relationship can sink under the weight of enough stress. Some other factors include general compatibility and their skills with problem solving and communication. We will assume in our discussion that the people who replied to our survey were at least of average emotional health and were probably not overwhelmed with stresses, at least at the time they completed the survey.

Even though personality type is only one factor in a relationship we believe it can be huge. Knowing our own personality Type can lead to tremendous self-awareness and can keep us from getting stuck in our same old relationship patterns. Knowing our partner's Type can help us move from confusion and frustration to acceptance and compassion during difficult times. A person's Type is an aspect of him or her, not of the relationship, so it is likely to be expressed no matter who the partner is. For example, partners – no matter what their type – mention the Leader's overt anger and tendency to control. Mediators' partners, regardless of Type, were likely to complain that much of the time the Nine was not really present in the relationship. However, an interesting finding about different pairings is that the features of any enneagram Type may cause difficulties for one particular Type but not for another, who might actually find those same characteristics endearing. This is why particular combinations of Types are inherently more or less challenging. Most relationship experts believe that the more similarities you have and the fewer differences you have, the more compatibility you are likely to experience. Pairings that are more similar and feel less as if they come from totally different worlds are those that:

- Belong to the same Center or Triad (gut, heart, or head) so that they share the same core issue, which may feel like coming from the same culture
- Share a common wing (the Type on either side of your Type on the enneagram diagram), which is similar to being next door neighbors
- Share a common connecting point, so that you will see a part of yourself in the other person (See Chapter 3)
- Have the same subtype (Sexual, Social, or Self-Preservation), so that their priorities are similar.
- Are "look-a-likes," creating familiarity through similar behaviors but not necessarily the same motivation

Interestingly, pairings that share the same enneagram Type are fairly uncommon. This may have to do with too many similarities and not enough differences. In our study, we had the greatest difficulty obtaining surveys from same-Type couples. Most people report that they get along very well with people of their own Type, mainly because they understand them so well. However, people seem less likely to be attracted to same-Type romantic partners. One reason is that in choosing a romantic partner, we usually try to find just the right balance of similarities and differences. It could be that same-Type pairings do not provide enough contrast for most people. We will explore same-Type pairings in greater depth when we discuss the pairing of all 45 combinations.

CHAPTER FIFTEEN

The Double Perfectionist (One-One) Couple

Logically, you might think that same-Type pairings would be ideal. Most relationship experts, as well as Internet dating sites, suggest that similarities lead to compatibility. That's true to a point, but too much can have its own set of problems. The old saying, "birds of a feather flock together" might be more appropriate for friendships than romantic interests. In our survey, people often listed their own Type as most compatible, but it's likely they were talking about hanging out with friends (as in "birds of a feather") and not necessarily marrying them.

Same-Type couples intuitively understand each other, have similar worldviews, goals and fears and often feel an instant connection. But we probably want our partner to be different, more challenging than what a same-Type lover can bring to a relationship. There is nothing as difficult in relationship as seeing a version of ourselves at the other end of an argument or at the end of a stressful day when our same-Type partner complains about the same gripe we expressed just the other day. Now we see how ridiculous we must have sounded. Seeing one's shadow side is usually hard to take and especially hard to live with. Whatever the reason, we have found that same-Type couples of any of the nine enneagram Types are relatively uncommon.

Another potential problem with same-Type couples can be the lack of "juice." Passion is more likely to be present when there are significant differences. It's not surprising, then, that two people of the same Type who do choose to establish a committed relationship often differ in their wings and/ or subtypes (See Chapter Three). What often happens is that subtype and wing differences loom large and may be perceived as significant causes of obstacles the couple face. A same-Type couple, two Perfectionists, is the first of the pairings we describe in this book. Janelle relates this story:

When Brian and I first met, we both felt an instant affinity for each other. It felt so good to spend time with someone who felt as strongly as I did about what's wrong with the world and how to fix it! We spent hours discussing the current political situation and which candidates could best turn things around. We became very involved in brainstorming ways to prevent the projected closing of our city hospital's Poison Control Center hot line. Brian never found it boring to listen to my righteous indignation over this or that injustice.

A few years later, things looked very different. We had two young children and we were both very busy with careers. Brian, a Social subtype, was teaching at the university, focused on getting tenure. He also attended committee meetings, helped his students, and did research. His work became his highest priority. Household chores went undone, because he had more important things to do. As a Sexual subtype, I felt that our relationship and our family seemed to have the lowest priority for him, and I resented it.

Perfectionists operate with an internal template, and whatever fits into its confines, the One sees as good or right. Early in their relationship, Janelle and Brian had a similar template that they cast out into the world so as to determine what needed correcting. For a One to find someone else who sees the world the same way can feel exciting. As time went by, their paradigms began to shift; what appeared to one to be the right way to approach the world and relationships no longer necessarily match the other's view.

It took forever to get anything accomplished. When I wanted to buy a piano for the kids, Brian had to first research the best piano; this took a year. When an outdoor electric lantern in the back yard went dark and he discovered faulty wiring, he took down all 12 lanterns in order to do the job right, but five years later he still hadn't replaced them.

In the meantime, I was attending graduate school during the day and caring for the kids and the home before and after classes. I cooked, cleaned, and played with the children – and my study time began only after they were in bed asleep. Brian and I had very little time together. He repeatedly promised to be home on time for dinner so he could eat with the kid sand me and we could have a little quality time together, but other things always interfered, because he had to do them "correctly" before he could leave work. The grass in the back yard got so tall that a lawnmower could no longer handle it. When I tried to pin

Brian down to agreeing to a specific division of labor, he said, "I can't make any promises such as to mow the lawn on Saturdays – after all, I might have to go back to the office. All I can say is, I'll try to do it if I have the time."

Since Perfectionists usually don't express their anger overtly, it smolders under the surface. With time both partners might find their positions becoming entrenched. Each is confident he or she alone has the right way. One of them struggles with procrastination, needing perfection before going forward. The other resembles a Type Three: to her, the way to be the "good little girl" and to be responsible is to be punctual and to approach things full steam ahead in order to correct as much as possible.

When my resentments would reach a boiling point and I'd confront him, Brian would respond with lengthy justifications for his point of view. The problems never got resolved. Instead, we'd end up in a long standoff, barely talking to each other for days, until we gradually re-engaged. We never seemed to have any time for each other. We became more and more emotionally detached. When I finally insisted we go to counseling, the counselor listened to us and then asked, "Would you guys rather be right or happy?" We were each more committed to proving to the other that I'm right, you're wrong, than to solve our problems. Eventually we divorced.

You can see the anger breaking through. Yet it resulted only in each becoming more deeply established in their power struggle. As with all couples, but in particular when at least one of them is a Perfectionist, the couple can reach a point of no return. Justified in their anger and feeling disrespected, they forget the warm feelings they once had for each other. The therapist was right in pointing out that they were choosing to be right instead of happy, but his advice was too little, too late.

Positive aspects of the Double Perfectionist relationship

Meeting another Perfectionist can be a heady experience. Finally, you have met someone who feels the same passion you do for educating others about the dangers of global warming or the need to preserve our natural resources or stop abortions or legalize medical marijuana – someone who admires you for devoting yourself to a worthy cause. As interested as you are in self-improvement, he shares your strong work ethic and understands that your motivation for criticizing others is to help them be better people! This person values the importance of being ethical, of doing things the right way rather than the expedient way, of putting work before pleasure, of being fair and expecting others to behave fairly. Others may be willing to cut corners or prefer to live an indulgent lifestyle, but you have finally met someone who really understands and shares a strong inner sense of wanting to right the wrongs of the world.

One of the problems with same-type pairings though, is that because they may collude around the core belief, neither represents a dissimilar view of the world. This can create a paradigm with the pairing that never gets questioned. They may, for instance, agree that work always comes before pleasure -- and then never get around to playing. Lloyd, a Perfectionist, describes how he and his One girlfriend Kathleen were able to access the Adventurer (Seven) connecting point and the Giver (Two) wing that are available according to the enneagram diagram. He recalled the good times:

We both played well and when in our Seven space [their security point], things were really great. This was true when we went on vacations with little or no agenda. We were both hard workers and very responsible, both willing to do things for each other, and that Two wing meant we were both willing to give of ourselves to make the other happy. There was a sense of self-sacrifice in the early stages that was really good.

As Lloyd and Kathleen demonstrated, Ones can have a very enjoyable time on vacation. Both can forget work and responsibilities and just relax and have fun. When agendas and responsibilities are shed, they take on a Sevenish (Adventurer) quality. Lloyd also felt that his Two (Giver) wing helped him and his partner access their hearts and feelings, allowing them to give of themselves more freely. The ability to access one's connecting point and wing so as to become more multi-dimensional is probably especially important with same-type pairings.

Challenges of the Double Perfectionist pairing
Recalling his One-One relationship that failed, Lloyd wrote,

My biggest challenge was my tendency to be critical of myself and my partner – to see only her flaws. I did too much right/wrong thinking and Have To's, as in "I have to get this work done, this crossed off the list, before we can play." As a result, we didn't play enough. I was too responsible, especially financially, as in, "We can't afford this" – when we could.

Sue, a One, summarized her husband William's complaints about her:

I am inflexible. I need to be in control, have things my way. I don't listen. I do too much problem solving. I need to be right all the time. I'm too critical of myself and others.

William was probably very sensitive to Sue's personality flaws because he had similar ones himself. Sue wrote that if William were to put a slogan on a T-shirt describing his beliefs, it would say, "Do it my way and we'll get along just fine." She also said he tended to be judgmental and angry.

Anger and resentment

The major issue for the Perfectionist, as we discussed in earlier chapters, is anger. One typical comment is, "It says that anger is the core issue of the One, but I <u>never</u> get angry!" Only later will someone recognize that her righteous indignation and resentments were rife; they were the way she expressed the anger that "nice girls" don't have.

Many Ones, especially the introverts, rarely express overt anger and instead tend to withdraw and nurse resentments. But some (especially extroverts) do express their anger more easily, because it's in the service of a righteous cause rather than a personal issue. Even those Perfectionists, however, are less likely to favor direct anger such as shouting or use of epithets. They are more likely to express sarcasm, indignation, passive-aggressive behavior and words to the effect that "I am right and you are wrong." Below Lloyd describes how easily a situation between two Ones can degenerate:

On our last vacation, the planning went really, really well. Kathleen wanted me to do all of the driving and said she would be the navigator. On the second day she got us lost, and I got angry and expressed it by driving too fast for her. She got angry and scared but didn't want to drive. Kathleen wanted to relax but also wanted to see and do a lot of things. I wanted to see and do a lot of things too, but instead I did all the driving, got tired, drove "too fast," and resented her criticism. On the last day I drove maybe 200 miles, and we had a gloriously romantic dinner with a sunset over a bay filled with sailboats, at which she said, "This is the best and most romantic vacation I've ever taken."

Then it got dark and I had to drive another 50 miles (on unfamiliar roads) to the airport hotel. When we got there, we disagreed on how to repack our belongings for our forthcoming flight. Kathleen wanted to go to the hotel room and repack everything for both of us; I wanted to just leave everything in the car. We exchanged some unpleasant words. I took all the baggage from the car to the lobby, I left with the car to fill it up with gas (we had a 5:30 AM flight), and she walked away, supposedly to repack. When I came back, our entire luggage was still in the lobby. Kathleen lit into me in a 20-minute tirade that made me sympathetic to all three of her prior husbands. To myself I said, "This is over – just get me home." I almost left for the airport at 2 AM to try to get an earlier flight home. I was that angry.

I just kept it in until we got home. She paid what she owed on the trip, we got the pictures developed, and then I ended it.

In this story, two people who had warm feelings for each other got off the track. What stands out is the trivial nature of their "fight." A minor disagreement turned into a major argument about who's right and who's wrong. Instead of expressing their feelings and trying to resolve their differences, Lloyd and Kathleen each withdrew and acted passive-aggressively. One then lashed out while the other threw in the towel about the entire relationship. Their positions were rigidly maintained. Their earlier warmth evaporated before their need to remain entrenched in their positions, as they preferred to nurse their resentments rather than trying to solve the matter at hand.

It's typical of a Perfectionist's ongoing experience that everything becomes huge and small problems get blown out of proportion. The One's tendency is then to want to reinforce his or her position. If both partners understand this dynamic early in their relationship and are really committed to recognizing it quickly and stopping, a Double Perfectionist relationship can succeed. If not, resentments will build up, and then the explosion occurs. Sue, who has been married over 30 years, described how she and her husband William have dealt with this.

There used to never be an end to any disagreement as we both needed to be "right." With self-awareness, we have both been able to decrease this bantering. We especially had a problem when we were working on projects. At the hospital where I worked, we had many interns and residents who would rush to the bed of a patient who needed to be resuscitated. The doctor in charge would wear a baseball cap so there would be no confusion. Now, we decide who is going to wear the cap whenever we begin work on a new project, so we know who has the final say. It works very well.

Sue provides a good solution for the issue of leading and following as well as showing respect. As long as, in this case, roles are well defined – who will lead and who will follow -- and as long as respect is shown toward both the leader and follower, Perfectionists will generally honor this process.

Need to be right

Ones' need to be right can interfere with their willingness to listen to other points of view. Sue's husband's chief complaint about her was, "You don't listen to me – you zone out." Once they have made up their minds, they may tune out others' opinions or input. Another common communication error is to begin preparing our response while the other person is still talking. The result of course is that we aren't really listening. Ones, who place a huge emphasis on being right, may have even more of a tendency to formulate the "right" response, so the shutting down of communication and the need to be right isolates each partner.

Criticism/perfectionism

Lloyd wrote about Kathleen, his former girlfriend:

She was too obsessed with neatness and cleanliness, too critical and verbally blaming. She said she adored me, but then in a relatively short time span would bite my head off. I tended to take her critical judgments too severely instead of seeing it as just blowing off steam. She was much more of an extrovert. I kept my anger in. Eventually I just left.

Perfectionists have high expectations of themselves and others and criticize across the board (as it were). They are highly critical of themselves. They are also sensitive to others' criticisms, which make them feel like failures in their quest to be as good as they can. A relationship between two people who are each looking for perfection in themselves and in the other, who is quick to criticize, yet reacts poorly to the other's criticism, can be very problematic. Ones feel they won't get or don't deserve love if they aren't perfect. For them, criticizing their partner is a form of caring. Two Perfectionists together can exacerbate this issue. Since they both come from the same perspective, they may have a hard time finding a way out of the dilemma.

For a relationship to thrive, both people need to be able to accept and handle healthy, constructive criticism. For us to grow in relationships, we need to feel loved, and at the same time, the partner needs to act as a mirror, reflecting an accurate image of who we are. "This is how I see you. Is this who you want to be?" This interaction should be done with as much love and as little blame or out-and-out criticism as possible.

Workaholism/Focus on Action.
Sue, a Perfectionist with a Social subtype, wrote,

I was a severely work-addicted person for most of my life. I was into my "reform" work at the county hospital. I managed to do some really good things, yet it was very harmful to myself and my relationship. I have been in recovery for 15 years and have actually made significant changes in my life in the past two years. In the past all I could think about was work, and I wasn't present for my husband (who also deals with work addiction). Now I'm learning to have fun – I just bought a bright yellow car for my birthday and am having lots of fun with it.

The work ethic of the Perfectionist can interfere with relationship, and a Double- Perfectionist couple can be like two ships passing in the night. If it's not obsession with work, then it may be intense involvement in fighting for causes, leaving no time for nurturing the relationship or for having fun and relaxing. Two Perfectionists together need to make sure that the relationship and partner is a priority. They need to commit to the relationship as if it were a cause, a cause that they fall in love with, and one that deserves a tremendous amount of their time and energy.

Respect
Respect is a critical value for Perfectionists; for the One-One couple, respect is a major issue in the relationship. The story below illustrates this:

*My former husband was an electrical engineer. He believed he could solve any electrical problem in the house. One evening I got a tremendous electric shock when I touched the kitchen stove. When he came home I told him about it, and that I'd almost gotten killed. He got out his voltmeter, probed the stove, and told me there's nothing wrong. I told him, I **know** there's something wrong, but he said, well, there's nothing wrong now. A couple of days later, same thing. Again he checked out the stove and told me there was nothing wrong. I was upset – I told him if he couldn't figure it out I'd call an electrician. He insisted that I shouldn't.*

The third time, he was home. I got such a strong electric shock that I involuntarily let out a blood-curdling scream and he came running into the kitchen. I was hysterical, crying and screaming, very unlike my usual calm self. This time I really got his attention. He checked the stove, then did some thinking, and within a few minutes he diagnosed the problem: a short between the stove and the adjacent fridge, but it was live only when the motor of the fridge was on, which was very intermittent. He needed to ground the fridge better, which he immediately did, and solved the problem. I was absolutely furious – I felt that I'd endangered my life several times and he hadn't taken me seriously. I felt he didn't care, that he didn't respect me, that my needs weren't important enough to him, that he thought I was stupid. We went to counseling over this. I still remember! In my opinion, the first time I told him about this problem he should have approached it seriously.

In this scenario, the One husband gets caught up in what is right according to him. What really bothered the wife was that her husband was not treating her complaint with respect. He wasn't really listening to her, taking her seriously, and as a result, was endangering her life. On the other hand, most likely her husband felt that by threatening to call an electrician, his wife was not respecting him and his expertise. Both spouses felt disrespected. In therapy both needed to work on how to feel more respected and heard.

Disrespect was also an issue in the Double-Perfectionist story about a vacation gone sour. In that story, Lloyd perceived that he was doing all the driving, while his girlfriend was having all the fun. Here he was, the tired good guy, having done all the driving, and she was doing this and that and not appreciating all the work he did. He felt disrespected.

The moral to all of these stories is that, for Perfectionists, love and respect are synonymous.

How to improve the Double-Perfectionist relationship

Sue wrote that what helps her relationship is, "When I make a mistake and admit it, it allows my husband to make mistakes as well." Admitting we're wrong is difficult for Ones, but can be very beneficial for the relationship, allowing each to soften their "I'm always right" tendency.

What follows below is Lloyd's perceptive advice for younger Perfectionists in relationship. It is particularly applicable to One-One pairs.

Do enough enneagram work to understand that your Type and your instinctual habits can be consciously changed. Learn to see your partner's behavior as different rather than wrong. "Differences are not disasters." Practice letting go of faults and failings, yours and theirs. Don't dwell on the negatives; recognize the constant inner critic for what it is – your perception, which may reflect only your view or only a partial view of yourself or the world. See yourself and your partner as not perfect, as flawed, and honor and accept the shadow side of who you/they are. Share as much of what you see as "ugly," "sinful," "shameful", "bad," or "wrong," with your partner, thus lessening its power over you and the destructive role it may play (has the potential to play) In the relationship.

Play, especially with your partner. Move to the Seven space, build sand castles, take trips, get out of the house/work setting on a regular basis, leave the kids with a babysitter and go someplace for a weekend. You need to get away from the lists, the endless shoulds and have to's. Go there with no agenda except play, relax and enjoy each other – easier to do in nature where there are no rights and wrongs.

Exercises for the Double Perfectionist couple

The following questions highlight the classic issues that challenge the One-One pairing:

The power struggle

When couples are entrenched in a power struggle, therapists will sometimes use the saying, "Do you want to be right or do you want to be happy?" Due to their focus on being right, no other pairing will struggle with this dilemma more than two Perfectionists together.

- How does needing to be right get in the way of your having a loving relationship?

No time for love

Correcting the ills of the world can leave little room in the relationship for warmth and affection. According to Perfectionists, things have to get done – and get done right - and there is no time for playing.

- How do you make sure that the warmth and affection in your relationship does not get sacrificed to your need to correct all of the ills of the world?

Is it love or is it perfectionism?

Perfectionists confuse perfectionism with love. They feel that being perfect will win them love from their partner. Ideally, acceptance creates the path to true love. Accept each other for who you really are and then see the perfection within that acceptance.

- How do you find both perfection and acceptance with each other – creating true love between the two of you?

CHAPTER SIXTEEN

The Perfectionist-Giver (One-Two) Relationship

Susan, a Perfectionist (with Social subtype) and John, a Giver (Sexual subtype), organized a dinner party for some friends. Susan invited several social-activist friends and anticipated an evening of animated political discussion, by the end of which various group members would have come up with suggestions to make the world a better place. John looked forward to getting to know Susan's friends – he had heard the names of some and met others, but he had never had a chance to sit and talk with them and find out about their lives.

At the dinner, Susan brought up hunger in Africa (one guest had grown up there), the need to prevent dehydration-related deaths in illegal border crossers from Mexico (another guest was a lawyer involved in this cause) and the imprisonment and death of North Koreans who tried to escape their country, were caught in China and returned home (another guest was a South Korean with strong feelings about this issue). Everyone bemoaned the existence of so much bad in the world, leading to a discussion of whether evil is inherent in humans or results from being mistreated in childhood.

At the end of the evening, Susan rated her party as a huge success. On the other hand, John, who had said very little and devoted himself to making sure the guests were comfortable and had all the food and drink they wanted, felt disappointed: Other than their views on the above world issues, he knew no more about any of them than he had before they arrived on his doorstep. He hadn't made any personal connections. He knew nothing about their personal lives, their careers, their children or how they liked to spend their time. He also felt somewhat unappreciated – it seemed to John that because he didn't have a "cause" to champion, no one paid any attention to him. Susan couldn't understand why John was not satisfied with how the party had gone.

This story illuminates the dissimilarity that can occur between partners who are different types and subtypes. Susan, a Perfectionist, was focused on correcting and perfecting the ills of the world. As both a One and a Social subtype, she was in her glory, surrounded by people who were equally interested in either talking about or taking on world causes. As with all of us who discover our Type and subtype niche, it can feel heavenly. We may also have a hard time understanding why everyone else, (especially John), wouldn't also want to ascend to this level. But John, a Giver with a Sexual subtype, did not experience the same kind of nirvana. His personality lends itself more to an intimate, in-depth connection with others. He wanted to be appreciated for his deep caring for others.

If John and Susan's relationship happens to be a little rocky, these different worldviews and the disparity in each partner's perspective on what is the right way to be in the world could cause a misunderstanding. But if Susan and John are able to tap into their love for each other, they may bring understanding and compassion to these differences. They will make sure that their relationship is balanced, meeting their specific needs.

The Perfectionist-Giver relationship can work very well, especially because each type might have a wing of the other.

Positive attributes of the Perfectionist-Giver relationship

Perfectionists and Givers share a concern for others, high energy for giving and helping people improve. Each feels a commitment to and responsibility for their relationship. Twos can feel less burdened by the Ones' apparent lack of problems and needs and can appreciate their responsible, adult approach to the world. Both want to be "good" people and appreciate "goodness" in the other.

Helen Palmer, in her book *The Enneagram in Love and Work*, gives a lovely description of the positive aspects of the Perfectionist-Giver relationship:

> Ones deal with practicalities and Twos relate through feelings and style. Twos carry the social ball. They initiate . . . which cuts through Perfectionistic criticality and social anxiety. One's needs shine like a beacon to Twos. . . Ones are guilty about having needs, but Twos aren't guilty about meeting them. Twos are attracted to steady, dependable

mates who express love through responsible action. Perfectionists can be anchors during emotional turbulence, and Twos will seek that safety when the world starts to shake.

The couple meets at Four and may therefore have a mutual understanding of disappointment and depression. . . This couple often expresses a wish to shield each other from shame and disappointment. Four can become a point of solidarity for the couple. Ones respect people who struggle, and Twos are helpful when they see pain. (p. 256-257).

In our survey, Perfectionists ranked Givers high on their list of Types to whom they're most attracted. They commented about Twos: "I like their personality, humor, and depth of love." "They are easy to be with, and you can feel the caring." "I enjoy the caring, helping aspect, and I connect because I have a Two wing." "Great friends, generous, giving, tuned in to other people "So loving usually. It's easy to express affection to them."

One and Two can be each other's wing, Wings, the adjacent types that each of the nine enneagram Types has, are like a next-door neighbor or a bordering country -- familiar to us. Because Perfectionists s can be so hard on themselves, they may gravitate toward the Givers' love and compassion like a warm fire. The Two may also turn Ones on to their feelings and help them access their heart space.

When asked what gifts they thought their Giver partners brought to the relationship, Perfectionists responded with such sweet statements as: "He brought a gift for relationship – caring – understanding." "She brought constancy, warmth, dependability, very caring." "She was very caring, always giving and sending gifts and cards. She even sent gifts for my kids and friends she had met.

The Perfectionist-Giver couple usually does very well on vacation. The Perfectionist can go into a Seven (Adventurer) mode, forgetting about obligations and about doing everything right, and becoming more flexible and joyful. Givers have no trouble being spontaneous and creative, and Perfectionists on vacation are able to do this also. Lloyd, a One, related,

We went on a vacation to Key West, and it was wonderful. Very laid- back, relaxed, flexible, sexual, romantic, wild, and totally connected – for just the two

of us. She is fine with alone time, and at times when I need my space, she gives it to me. We are both very caring and compassionate.

Challenges of the Perfectionist-Giver pairing

Ones' tendency to criticize, correct, and assume that their way is best can be a challenge for them in relationship with Givers and with most other Types. At the same time, Perfectionists are very sensitive to criticism, and may react defensively to the Giver's attempts to be helpful by giving good advice.

In our survey, Perfectionists were brutally honest about their Giver partner's complaints, such as, "You're very critical of yourself and others." "You are inflexible. You need to be in control and have things your way. You don't listen. You do too much problem solving. You need to be right all the time. You are too critical of yourself and others." Since Perfectionists are usually harder on themselves than on others, they acknowledged that their marriages were sometimes challenged by these very things, such as, "Needing things to be done a certain way (my way)." "My tendency to be critical of myself and my partner – to see only the flaws. Too much right/wrong thinking, as in, 'I have to get this work done, this crossed off the list, before we can play'. As a result, we didn't play enough. I was too responsible, especially financially, as in, 'We can't afford this' – when we could." It is important to remember that Ones equate criticism with caring and that they see the problems of the world as their responsibility. It is a huge burden to carry.

Ones in general — and Social Ones in particular — are focused on correcting the wrongs of the world. The Two partner may feel left out. Janine, a Two, wrote this about her marriage with Saul, a One:

When we go out to dinner Saul frequently gets on his soapbox about all the ills in the world. As a Two with a One wing I usually go along with him. At times I feel like I can't stop myself. I want to bond with my husband, and I feel that the One part of me is being triggered. When I try to re-direct the conversation, Saul will sometimes feel disrespected and think that I don't like how he thinks. If I don't say anything, anger and resentment (my Eight connection) begin to build in me over time until I eventually explode. When I talk to Saul about this he says that he has a hard time not taking on all the responsibilities of the world. In fact he says he feels guilty if he doesn't spend a certain portion of his life around such things. I feel my husband is not growing (and also not having any fun) but instead is staying stuck in his trying to change the world. It feels like a loop that we are caught in.

Twos' desire to help people is initially very attractive, but can cause difficulty in relationship with a One, because it sometimes results in inadvertent neglect.

Perfectionists' chief complaint about Givers included: "He was so invested in pleasing others, he wasn't always present to me." "She was involved with her parents as their sole caregiver as they aged. This and other commitments always seemed to come first. " "She would make promises to do something with me or meet me somewhere and then something would come up for her that would involve another person, commitment, or relationship, and she would put that first and back out of her promise to me." Ones set great store in having others keep their commitments. In fact, two of the Perfectionists wrote that the Giver's focus on others could be a deal breaker. They wrote they would leave the relationship "If I felt I no longer came first to her," and "if he were no longer present and didn't truly hear me."

As we reported previously, Givers often tend to avoid conflict. Ones don't like overt anger either, but even more, they dislike indirectness and manipulation; what they do like is a straightforward discussion about the issues. Karen, a Perfectionist, complained that, "Jon [the Giver] did not express anger and left me feeling unheard, when he couldn't or wouldn't express himself." Unfortunately, Perfectionists can be overwhelming to Givers in their directness, rigidity, and certainty about positions. Karen wrote that a challenge in her relationship with Jon was

> . . . my need to immediately discuss my feelings and resolve the issue, and Jon's need to have time to think about what he is feeling and to become willing to tangle unpleasantness. I tend to come on too strong, which can overwhelm him and shut him down, which in turn will shut me down. When we agree to listen, check back in and be real honest, it helps (sometimes).

In addition to the reluctance to express anger, the Two's inability to express his or her own needs and desires can also drive a One partner crazy. According to Karen, "Getting Jon to express his needs, anger, disappointment, wishes, dreams and desires was a real challenge." Ones are very aware that they are not mind readers. In fact, unlike Twos, Ones have difficulty intuiting other people's needs (especially Ones with a Nine wing), so they get very frustrated when a Two declines to directly express his or her needs. Givers sometimes don't even know what they want; they are so focused on recognizing others' needs that they lose their own sense of self. Karen wrote about her Giver husband, "Jon didn't always know what he felt, and when he did, he didn't know what to do." Lloyd, a Perfectionist, described a similar situation with his girlfriend Sherry: "She wasn't real big on going into depth or doing things that would work through problems. She didn't have a strong sense of self.

Perfectionists are hard workers, ready to put in extra time to get the job done, and Givers crave lots of attention. Twos want to spend quality time with their partners, but Ones' work ethic usually puts work before pleasure or relaxation. Twos may feel unappreciated and taken for granted. This is especially true if the One has a Nine (Mediator) wing. A One with a Two wing tends to be warmer and more giving, making it easier for the Giver to be in the relationship than coupled with the cooler One who has a Nine wing.

Givers feel good when they help, but Perfectionists often feel criticized when the Giver offers help, concluding that they must not be doing the job well enough. According to Terry, a Perfectionist, "what prevents me from effective problem solving is my fear of saying the wrong thing and making a mistake." This perspective distorts Perfectionists' perception of what their partner says and can make them react defensively when there's no reason to do so.

Exercises for the Perfectionist-Giver couple
The following questions highlight the classic issues that challenge the One-Two pairing:

When the attention goes away.
Both types can feel as if the initial attention or attraction has gone away once the relationship has been established. Perfectionists can feel the need to focus their attention on other things that need correcting, making the Giver feel no longer needed. On the other hand, Twos can focus on other things that need their helping, making the One wonder where did the all of the flattery and compliments go? Both need to make sure to tend to their partners as they expand their horizons.

- How do you make your partner still feel he or she is a number one priority to you – especially when you expand your horizons?

How could I forget the good things about you?
When a relationship gets off track and struggles, we usually stop seeing the positive in our partner and mainly focus on the negatives. For example, instead seeing the Perfectionist as hard working and responsible, the Giver will start to see them as not spontaneous and way too serious. Meanwhile the

Perfectionist can start seeing the Giver's helping and good nature as manipulative and needy.

- How can you take time each day to express appreciation for each other's positive characteristics – especially those that attracted you to them at the very beginning of the relationship?

When things fall apart – things become real.

During times of hopelessness and despair, (experienced enneagram students call this "meeting at Type Four"), both Types can find this time as being truly authentic and deeply intimate. Perfectionists will give up trying to correct everything and accept their imperfections and needs. Givers will give up trying to help everyone and recognize their own wants and needs.

- During times of despair, how can you both move from blame and criticism to moments of authenticity and true love?

CHAPTER SEVENTEEN

The Perfectionist-Achiever
(One-Three) Couple

The combination of our Types has allowed us to plan and carry out finan-
cial planning in a very effective way—and has given us a relatively com-
fortable retirement despite very low retirement incomes from our years as
public education employees. We travel together very well— Leeann, my One
partner, moves to Seven and becomes very light and playful when she's out
of town. I take on responsibility for planning, logistics, and details. We have
evolved an unconscious "dance" that results in all parts of a mutual proj-
ect being handled competently. Over time we have naturally specialized in
different activities and now have a very comfortable routine for daily life,
entertaining, travel, and projects -- which reduces stress and ensure that all
the jobs get done.
>   -- Kelly, an Achiever

In the above description, you can almost hear a "cleanliness" about the
relationship. No mess or fuss, well organized and comfortable. Perfectionists
and Achievers collaborate very well as a no-nonsense, goal-directed team.
Kelly, the Achiever, described succinctly how this worked in various aspects
of her long-term relationship with a Perfectionist. Achievers and Perfectionists are attracted to each other because both are high-energy types who work
hard and accomplish a great deal, drawing their identity from their work.
Both value productivity and efficiency. Both want to look good and worry
about what others think of them.

Bob and Elaine were an attractive Perfectionist-Achiever couple, exud-
ing an air of having it all together. Bob, the Three, was a prominent minister
in the community who preached at a large church. He had a huge following

at his Sunday sermons where he was quite the showman. Elaine, a One, was a housewife and mother of several children, but as a minister's wife and because of her Perfectionist nature, she headed up numerous projects at the church. When they came in for their first counseling session, Bob and Elaine were clearly operating on overload. They were hesitant about the counseling process. In their previous attempts at problem-solving themselves, neither could clearly express their feelings to each other and neither was a good listener.

It was Elaine who suggested that they get counseling, not because she felt that her emotional needs weren't being met -- as a One she wasn't particularly adept at identifying such -- but rather because she felt they just weren't spending enough time together, that it wasn't right if they were going to really be the happy couple they projected out into the world. She liked being with Bob because he was able to help her see the glass as more than half full and also because he wouldn't allow her to criticize herself excessively. Elaine chided Bob about his workaholism and was also upset at him because she felt he was living a double life.

Bob's main complaint was that he was very unhappy with his work, and he felt Elaine criticized him too frequently. Every Sunday, he appeared in public as a passionate religious leader; yet at home he'd complain how much he hated what he did for a living. As a Three, he had gotten caught up in the image he was projecting, loved receiving the congregation's praise, and enjoyed the generous salary the church paid him. Elaine felt that all of this was very wrong.

Eventually, Bob was able to quit his job at the church and find another profession that was better attuned to his authentic self. With Bob's job change, both have lighter workloads. Elaine felt she had gotten her husband back and that they were no longer living a lie. They also improved their listening skills, and they worked on identifying their feelings and ability to share them.

Three and One can be a very good combination. Both are high-energy Types who get involved in many activities, and both have a strong work ethic and value accomplishment and productivity. Each values and supports the other's achievements. Both are very concerned what other people think of them; Achievers are careful to project a good image, and Perfectionists appreciate the good impression their partner makes.

Challenges of the Perfectionist-Achiever relationship

Both the Perfectionist and the Achiever are concerned about public image. For Bob, the Three, this was more from a "showman" style that made him the success that he was even though it wasn't really him, whereas Elaine, the One, worried about the incongruent aspects of their relationship in their private life compared to their public life. Here's what Helen Palmer, in *The Enneagram in Love and Work,* has to say about this dynamic:

> Both types are very concerned about what other people think, but they act out that preoccupation in different ways. Ones compare themselves with other people and are scrupulous about the difference between an actual accomplishment and an impressive image. . . Ones rarely puff out their image, whereas Threes project an exciting public façade. . .Threes' public self-presentation can be a source of irritation. (p. 259)

Her words are supported by the results of our survey, in which Perfectionists cited the Achiever as one of the types they most struggle with. Their reasons included: "Too busy." "Scarcity of emotional authenticity." "Fake front, lack of integrity, out of touch with inner self." "It's all about them (image and achievement)." In our story, Elaine the Perfectionist was turned off by Bob's efforts to impress people, by his willingness to take short cuts to get to the goal rather than "doing it right," and by his tendency to subserve everything else to his work. Threes' behavior can look deceitful to Ones.

On the other hand, Bob, the Achiever had trouble with Elaine's tendency to criticize him and with her self-righteousness about doing things her way. Achievers want to get to the goal, and may be very frustrated by the Perfectionist's need to spend extra time doing it perfectly. Kelly, another Achiever, complained about her Perfectionist partner, "She is too detailed and serious – she always has to do everything to the nth degree – 98% is never good enough." Her partner, Leeann, had the reverse complaint: "Kelly tends to gloss over details, thinking everything will work out smoothly without a lot of work or effort. She always looks at the big picture and misses the fine points and nuances."

Conflict resolution is an area of difficulty for Ones and Threes. The Perfectionist wants to dissect problems with all their details, whereas the Achiever avoids conflict and introspection and much prefers a rapid solution and then getting on with the "real" tasks in their life. Rehashing the past is a waste of time and energy from the Three's perspective, whereas Ones want to do it right!

Both Perfectionists related that their partner's chief complaint was "You are too rigid." Donald, a One, stated that his Three partner recognized "my

need to point things out that didn't fit my image of right and her need to protect her image of herself. There was no resolution." This couple parted after a
few years. Again, if we relate this to Bob and Elaine, Elaine (the One) had a
hard time with the image Bob projected and the image that she had of herself
about being good and right.

With their shared work orientation, Perfectionists and Achievers can be
like ships passing in the night. Each may be very involved in activities and
projects that leave very little time for the relationship. Even when they do
things together, the emphasis is likely to be the goal rather than an intimate
connection. They tend to connect around projects rather than connect emotionally. Threes, in particular, might have trouble making time for the Ones
on an emotional level. Kelly, the Achiever, wrote, "Really tuning in to another
person and actively responding to their needs is not natural for a Three – it
must be learned and cultivated." She wrote this about her workaholism:

*Workaholism was a major problem before I retired — multi-tasking and
having dozens of projects going at once. I had less need for interpersonal intimacy because many of those needs were "sort of" met in work/social arenas. My
high energy, speedy talk, speedy decisions, speedy actions were stressful for my
slower-paced, more deliberate partner.*

Leeann, her One partner, gave us the other side. She complained to Kelly,
" You go too fast in making plans – it makes me anxious to feel like all the
decisions are made, and I didn't have enough time to think it through or have
enough input." This Perfectionist was of the Self-Preservation subtype, which
has been called the "Worry One." They can look like Detectives (Sixes) in that
they are anxious and need time to process decisions and consider various options. Kelly listed her Achiever-related traits:

*Not thinking aloud or processing with Leeann sometimes leads to misun-
derstandings. I tend to think through an issue, come to a "logical" (to me) conclusion, and sometimes take action before discussing the issue with her. I can
move very rapidly from Plan A to Plan B without needing time to regroup,
which can be uncomfortable for Leeann. I unconsciously overvalue efficiency
and finishing tasks or projects before she's ready.*

Leeann, the One, was also very busy. She wrote that one of her problems
was, "Time crunches due to too many projects to complete to a level that
satisfies my very high standards." Perfectionists generally do recognize their

difficulty unwinding. Leeann would advise a younger Perfectionist to, "Learn to relax and enjoy the moments – you don't have to have everything done before you can enjoy being together." Donald, another Perfectionist, suggested, "Relax more." Donald, whose relationship had ended, wrote about his Three partner, "Jacqueline was never home. She started a million projects but rarely ever finished them."

Subtype Issues – Social v. Self-preservation

Leeann and Kelly, a Perfectionist-Achiever couple, had different subtypes – Self-preservation and Social, respectively. Their differing subtypes probably magnified their differences. Leeann, the One, wrote,

As a Type One/Self-Pres individual, I have less need than my partner for social activity and greater need for privacy, quiet time and alone time to complete projects on my list. Over time we have learned to compromise and to agree on which social events I will attend (or host) well in advance. Kelly feels free to go to social or volunteer events alone or with other people and I enjoy the time at home alone. When we do social activities together we often limit the amount of time and often leave earlier or participate in only one part of a larger event.

Writing about the same relationship, Kelly, the Social Three, related,

Our different needs for social contact have been resolved with age and compromise. My need for an audience has lessened over time, especially in retirement, and I don't need to be out in the world nearly as much as I did in my 40's. Now I volunteer with groups that give me satisfying social contact and offer service to the educational community while taking advantage of my skills and training. I also go to social events and movies alone or with other friends and don't expect or pressure Leeann to do "everything together." I meet weekly with a Writer's group that requires introspection and reflection and gives me both an audience and expert feedback. This weekly group gives Leeann scheduled and predictable time alone—a win-win situation. We try to schedule and plan a month or two ahead so any social or calendar commitments are posted and there are few surprises.

In the above quotes about their relationship and socializing, you can really hear the differences between the social Three vs. the non-social One. It's a great example of taking an issue in a relationship and trying to resolve it with acceptance of each other, through compromise, and finding ways to meet one's own needs outside the relationship. The only real caveat in this situation is that these two types need to be careful that their relationship doesn't become like two ships passing in the night. Both need to take time to connect. Perfectionists in particular need to avoid becoming too reclusive. Some Perfectionists can almost give up on life, the correcting and perfecting of it, and become hermit-like . . . creating their own little world of perfection and serenity.

Exercises for the Perfectionist-Achiever Couple

The following questions highlight the classic issues that challenge this pairing:

Human being vs. human doing

Both Perfectionists and Achievers can get into overdoing it. Some people refer to this as becoming a human doing vs. a human being. Both Types need to find time in their busy lives to make sure feelings can surface and then can be shared with one another.

- How do you go from "doing" to "being" – in touch with your feelings and sharing those feelings with each other?

Getting to the goal - differently

Both Types can find their identity through their work and can take pride in their partner's effort and success in their own ambitions. How they reach that goal can be quite different for each of them. Perfectionists want to make sure their work is held to the highest standards. Achievers don't mind cutting corners on the way to the end goal.

- How do you continue to value each other's work and successes even though your approaches to the work may be quite different?

Honesty vs. Deceit

Honesty vs. deceit is one of the biggest challenges for the One-Three pairing. As Helen Palmer states, "Threes want to look good to people while Ones want to look right." Achievers will most likely not understand what the big deal is as long as they are achieving their goal and receiving accolades. The Three's deceit can stimulate anger in the One which can be freeing to the Perfectionist. Both need to realize that gaining love from their pursuits is the ultimate goal for each of them.

- How can you each help one another to realize that unconditional love does not come solely from your work efforts?

CHAPTER EIGHTEEN

The Perfectionist-Romantic (One-Four) Couple

We used to work quite well together, as long as there was no emotional is-sue at stake. Once we took on the presentation of a large talent show for our community, and the combination of my people skills, flair for presentation, and emotional intuition, with his passion for order and follow-through, made us a very effective team.

-- Louise, a Romantic

Buying a house is a good example of what we could do together. We make great decisions together when it comes to looking at what matters most. I can easily identify what's missing by his follow-up of what is critical that we need to pay attention to. I'm creative, a big picture thinker; he is practical and tactical, so together we see all angles, long and short.

-- Rosa, a Romantic

The combination of the Romantic's artistry and vision and the Perfectionist's groundedness and practicality can make for success in planning things together. It is probably not hard to imagine the above scenario, where the two Types make for a great pairing when a mix of creativity and order is required. Collaborating on a project or business-type enterprise, it is easy for them to appreciate each other's gifts. "I have the vision, and he has the ability to make a realistic plan and a goal-setting strategy. "

But can they both appreciate the gifts that each brings to an intimate, romantic partnership? That's a question for all of us. Most people can recognize and value another personality Type's gifts and uniqueness when it comes to projects and friendships, but in relationships, it is sometimes a different story. Take a look at another scenario where the Perfectionist's and Romantic's differences work well together. Tiffany, a Four, recalled,

I've wanted to make some changes to my daily routine to try to fit in more open creative time. I couldn't figure out how to write, do administrative work, meditate, exercise, participate in our marriage, and have open creative space all in one day! (Who can?) I was getting more and more despondent about this. A friend who knows Steve, my Type One husband, suggested I ask for his help in figuring this out. That had never occurred to me. So I did, and his linear, clear thinking helped enormously. Steve laid out a grid of the week and built a schedule for me. It's a great schedule, and I was so appreciative of his help. My wish for space and accomplishment met his ability to structure and ground ideas. Very wonderful.

As the above scenario illustrates, Perfectionists can help Romantics structure and organize. Notice, however, that Steve's strength in this situation had to be pointed out to Tiffany by her friend. This has nothing to do with Type or this particular pairing; it is quite common for anyone not to truly appreciate the gifts and strengths the partner brings to a relationship. The One's practicality and groundedness can provide an anchor for the Four's emotional expressiveness and help him or her maintain a balance between inward focus and the realities of day-to-day life. Romantics may see the mundane as boring, and may also make simple situations more complex than they really are. In the above vignette, the Perfectionist takes the Romantic's dilemma and treats it in a logical and ordinary time-management way, yet it seems "very wonderful" to the Romantic. At the same time, Fours can help Ones get in touch with their feelings and creativity. Ones feel a need to be responsible, focusing more on the externals, such as "Is that right?" or "What would a responsible person do in this situation?" Rarely would they ask, "What am I feeling?" or "What do I desire?" Feelings and creativity can lie dormant for the One, and Fours can help access the inner self.

Perfectionist and Romantics share a connecting line on the enneagram diagram, so they intrinsically understand each other. Both have high ideals and appreciate this in a partner and both can be playful and witty. In times of trouble, the Four will be a compassionate companion for the One, unafraid of strong emotions a One may experience. Louise, a Romantic, formerly in a five-year relationship with a Perfectionist, wrote,

I've been there, done that emotionally, and had deep compassion for and insight into the dark places of the relationship and the struggles Jim was facing. I knew that there was grace at the core of our problems, and I was willing to hang in there through the tough times to experience it.

The Perfectionist will champion the Romantic in a straightforward way, encouraging and empowering the partner who is facing a challenge. On the other hand, the Romantic will be there for the Perfectionist in a deeply emotional way. A gift that the Four brings to the relationship is the ability to go into those dark places that other Types may resist. It is as if the Romantic has truly "been there, done that" when it comes to loss and the deepest feelings that come with it. They'll do it without flinching. When asked how they helped their relationship thrive, Romantics wrote, "I am compassionate and can go back to love despite the conflict, which helps to disarm and heal." "I practiced appreciating what is present right here and now. I count my blessings."

Fours are attracted to the One's groundedness and practicality. Ones can bring structure and direction to the relationship. Tiffany (a Romantic) wrote, "Steve has clarity and an unfailing bullshit meter. He has an enormous ability to hang in here, confront problems and keep talking/relating until the energy shifts. I would just run away, but he makes me hang in there." Louise (also a Romantic) reported, "Jim believed it was the right thing to do to work out the problems of the relationship, so he spent a lot of time studying how we might be together and was willing to sit down and discuss the situations that arose."

The combination of the Four's artistry and the One's practicality can make for success in planning things together. According to Gabrielle, a Four, "I have the vision, and Ted has the ability to make a realistic plan and a goal-setting strategy. "

Challenges of the Perfectionist-Romantic couple

Perfectionists and Romantics can push each other's buttons over certain shadow aspects in their relational styles. Ones criticize to perfect and correct, whereas Fours do so because they feel that something is missing either in the partner or in the relationship. Melancholy can also play a role in the Romantic-Perfectionist relationship: Romantics can be despondent, losing hope in the relationship, whereas Perfectionists, who generally do not give up easily, can at times travel along the connecting line on the enneagram diagram that takes them to the romantic, gloomy Four.

Not surprisingly then, in our survey, Ones considered Fours one of the three personality types they most struggle with, and Fours felt the same about Ones. The reasons Ones gave included, "They require lots of attention and seem so self-absorbed that I get impatient with having to deal with them." "They drive me nuts with their whining and sighing and hand-wringing. I just want to slap them and say, buck up and quit being a victim!" "I see them as self-centered and overly dramatic."

Romantics, in turn, struggled with Perfectionists because "I'm morally relativistic and rebellious, and I don't take things too seriously; I can't understand why they get so tightly wound about things, so we don't communicate well – but I have many Ones around me." "Perfectionism and so many demands on me can make me feel imperfect, even worthless." "The 'right/wrong' attitude is something I just can't get inside. Let's look at possibilities, feelings, instead." "It's incredibly painful to be criticized when one's self-esteem is low." "Too much attention to detail." Much like the harsh statements of the Perfectionists, Romantics can be quite critical of Ones. Yet Fours who either travel the connecting line to One or who pair up with Ones can learn much about discipline and about getting outside themselves to work for the betterment of the world.

Romantics feel shame about their worthiness, and the criticism, disapproval, and self-righteousness of the Perfectionist can accentuate this. Ones can seem very unfeeling to Fours, who can see all shadings of issues and have trouble with rigidity. A One's need for order and structure, for permission to do or not do, for correct behavior, can conflict with a Four's self-absorption, elitism, belief she is her own authority, and higher concern for emotional authenticity than for appropriate action. Louise, a Romantic who spent five years with a Perfectionist, wrote about their struggles:

I believe it's possible for Ones and Fours to come to agreement on situations that trigger these hot buttons. Sometimes my partner and I were able to laugh at our differences and chalk it up to type. It was usually easier for me to do that than it was for him, because I wasn't operating on a set of "divinely-bestowed" universal standards of behavior. It took him longer to get off his righteous position and loosen up enough to be accessible.

Louise walks a fine line, pointing out the shadow that underlies Ones' and Fours' dealings with each other. She seems to be able to stay out of it earlier in her description of their relationship but then comes close to it near the end. Her description of his "divinely-bestowed" behaviors and his "righteous position" seem to reflect her own shadow in her description of herself when she talks about her "elitism" and a "belief she is her own authority."

Both Perfectionists and Romantics need to understand that they criticize because they care. For Ones, who criticize because they truly care about the other person, this is a sign of love. Fours criticize because they truly care about the relationship. Romantics don't usually start criticizing until they are invested in the relationship and then not until they feel safe. Both need to get beyond this and try to see what it really means to each of them, what is the real message embedded in the criticism.

Feelings: The Romantic's big emotions and the Perfectionist's suppressed feelings

Another frequent source of difficulty for the One-Four couple is the One's discomfort with the Four's big feelings. Gabrielle, a Four, related,

I get upset, Ted tries to control me, then I get frustrated and angry and throw things, like dishes, then he gets angry and tries to restrain me physically, and then I get more physically dramatic and enraged. We found through enneagram counseling that I need to be able to sit with big feelings without having to act them out. And Ted needs to not have to control his surroundings if it means interfering with my process.

To the Romantic, the Perfectionist seems to be trying to control her rather than recognize her feelings. Gabrielle wrote, "Ted always tries to manage me when I get emotional instead of trying to understand and support me and see me for who I really am." But it's effective to attempt to closely match the first person's level of emoting. For the Perfectionist-Romantic couple, this can result in some very volatile exchanges.

When asked what behavior of hers would most likely cause her husband to leave the relationship, Gabrielle (a One) replied, "Wallowing too deeply in self-created pits of despair and unproductive fits of rage." Whereas the One is uncomfortable with the Four's big feelings, some Fours complain about the One's understated emotions. Louise, a Four, complained that her former partner was "emotionally rigid." At the same time, one Romantic would advise younger Fours, "Remember that you are not your feelings and you don't have to amplify and dramatize all of the them." Tiffany, another Romantic, wrote about her Perfectionist husband,

Steve has no idea what he's really feeling most of the time. So he has a tendency to get angry at really strange times, for really strange reasons. I find it very hard to cope with his unconsciousness – it scares me. His anger scares me.

These powerful statements describe the two very different emotional styles that Ones and Fours bring to a relationship. It is up to them whether they are opposites who attract and then frustrate each other, or whether they are opposites who are teachers. Relationships can be like being in traffic, where other people can first confuse us, then frustrate us, and then anger us to the point of road rage. The enneagram helps us with the confusion. We gain insight about people as to who they are to themselves, not how we want or expect them to be. The rest involves the "work" of relationships. We need to work on accepting our partners for who they are, and we also need to work on changing ourselves in places where our partners have challenged us to take a hard look at ourselves.

Rationality versus emotions in decision-making

Related to the Type difference above is how Perfectionists and Romantics make decisions. All of us want to know that we can trust our partner's judgment; we want to know if our partner's decision-making makes sense to us. Ones like to reason things out logically; Fours give a higher priority to their emotions. A Romantic, Rosa, wrote, "I change my mind about things because my feelings fluctuate." This can be irritating to the Perfectionist, whose tendency for black-and-white thinking and focus on being "right" means that once they make a decision they are reluctant to consider changing it. Louise, a Romantic, recognized this about her decision-making,

I think my view of things is the way things are . . . I see the ideal, why bother with the rest? I can be blinded to the best solution if my emotions are running too high. I can be deluded by my personality into thinking my feelings are the truth of the situation.

Gabrielle criticized her One husband, Steve, because "he gets rigidly stuck on an ideal and cannot see beyond to the myriad of influences, usually emotional, that are impacting the situation."

Probably even more important than what our partner thinks of our decision making process is how we view it ourselves. We need to know that we can trust ourselves. Ideally, Fours need to be more in touch with their heart intuition, and Ones need to be more in touch with their gut intuition. This means that Romantics need to be able to separate out authentic feelings that arise in their hearts from emotions that come and go like storm clouds. Perfectionists need to get out of their heads where their beliefs about how things should be can run amok. Instead they need to turn to their gut where they don't know why they know the things they know, but the things that they do know correspond with a higher truth of the universe.

Both can be critical and judgmental

Probably the biggest difficulty for Romantics in relationship with a Perfectionist is the One's tendency to judge and criticize. The shame-based Four is particularly vulnerable to being criticized. But Fours, who have a connecting line to One, can also be critical and judgmental. And Ones, whose judgment of others is exceeded only by their self-criticism, are also exceedingly sensitive to being criticized. This can be a volatile combination. Gabrielle wrote that a central complaint she has for Steve, her Perfectionist husband, is

STOP CRITICIZING ME!!!: That is by far my number one complaint. Stop paying so much attention to my every move around the house and elsewhere. Once I've screwed something up, you think I'm always going to screw it up. You want things done a particular way and it seems way too picky."

Interestingly, when asked what her husband complained about her, she replied that Steve says, "You always make me feel that I'm wrong and you're right."

The dissatisfaction of the Perfectionist-Romantic connection can be a shared dissatisfaction with life. Romantics suffer because something is missing and Perfectionists see the flaws. The relationship can be animated by focusing on the good things in the present moment and by taking pleasure in the satisfactions of here and now.

Subtype and wing Issues

In some relationships, difficulties with the partners' differing subtype can eclipse challenges related to the Type. For example, Tiffany, whose vignette was described at the opening of this chapter, was a Four with a Five wing, reinforced by a Self-preservation subtype. Her 11-year partner, Steve, was a One with a Two-wing Sexual subtype. One might predict that in this relationship the Perfectionist would seek a lot of closeness, whereas the Romantic would want a lot of space. Tiffany, whose Self-Preservation subtype translates into a desire for space and alone time, wrote that Steve's central complaint to her was, "Your number one priority in life is yourself; my number one priority is us. You never want to spend as much time with me as I want to spend with you." She explained,

I am uncomfortable with open-ended exposure to any single person. I need to have a cap. I just started living with Steve a couple of years ago. Before that we lived in different cities. I liked that. Living together has been an extraordinary exercise in stretching and including. It's been quite uncomfortable but—in the last six or so months—has really been a breakthrough for me. I've learned to find genuine pleasure in companionship. I've learned to tolerate the discomfort of togetherness, and it's really been like the proverbial pearl in the oyster. Really given me a new understanding of what love is. My nervous system seems wired to relax only in solitude. Any companionship, even if the person is asleep, keeps me from really letting go into my own mind and being. Even though I'm self-employed and could work at home, I rent an office outside the house. This has been very good.

Her advice to other Fours in relationship is,

Cultivate the ability to remain seated within your core while going out to the other person. In other words, learn to work with energy going in two directions as part of the same cycle: inward and outward, like breath. Insist, insist, and insist on private time. Don't be guilt tripped or shamed out of it.

Helen Palmer, in her book *The Enneagram in Love and Work,* beautifully summarizes the challenges and the work of the One and Four in relationship:

Four's dramatic moods can become repellent to serious and practical Ones. It looks like self-indulgence. Ones see emotional exhibitionism and Fours' need to be special as traits that should be brought under discipline. . . The critical cycle can be interrupted if Fours see why Ones are driven to control a "bad" emotion. From the One side, it helps to see the integrity of deep emotional connections, that rules cannot govern matters of the heart. (p. 263-264)

Exercises for the Perfectionist-Romantic couple
The following questions highlight the classic issues that challenge the One-Four pairing:

Water and Fire

The Perfectionist and the Romantic relationship can be like fire and water. Fours can both annoy and frighten Ones with their seemingly dauntless attitude toward their connection to their strong feelings. The One's criticism of the Four's undisciplined drama can create a cycle where Fours shame Ones for their lack of connection to their feelings of substance and their right and wrong thinking.

- How does the cycle of shame and criticalness show up in your relationship?

Teachers to one another

Perfectionists and Romantics can become teachers to one another if they can see the value in what each of them brings to the other. Fours can turn Ones onto their emotional strengths, loosening the shoulds and the black-and-white thinking. Ones can turn Fours onto their connection with discipline and integrity, balancing out the highs and lows of their emotional side.

- What can learn from each other? How can you be teachers to one another?

The spiritual side of things

Perfectionists at their highest self gain a sense of serenity – but they do this only if they can accept both their positive and negative feelings. Ones can gain this understanding through the help of the Four. Romantics on the other hand, at their highest self, gain a sense of equanimity. Equanimity can come about through the structure and discipline that the One has to offer.

- How can equanimity and serenity play a role in the spiritual side of your relationship?

CHAPTER NINETEEN

The Perfectionist-Observer (One-Five) Relationship

Our only problem is probably that we are both dominating and both always know better. Oscar knows the only perfect or right way, and I feel that my studies and experience tell me to do it my way. We both feel, however, that we are matched really well. The great thing about our relationship is the space we're able to give each other so we can each pursue our interests. Our interests are often in the same areas, but we do like to do what we do alone, whether in the same room, or nearby. We don't bother each other with too much neediness and needing assurance etc. That works great. We really love and trust each other and love to be together -- we can be together all day, actually -- but we don't need the constant interaction.

-- Stephanie, a young Observer married to a Perfectionist

Perfectionists and Observers have much in common. In relationship, they can be look-alikes, at least on the surface. If we think of compatibility as the state of being similar in thoughts and behaviors, then the Perfectionist-Observer pair can be quite compatible. Both value independence, don't mind working alone, and neither wants feelings to be too important in the relationship.

The relationship will have a practical, well-organized and down-to-earth quality, with both partners working to solve problems as soon as they arise and then to quickly move on. The romance in the relationship will likely be minimal. However, they may both become heavily invested in an intellectual project or cause in which they work together. In this case, they really appreciate each other. Even though Perfectionists are not in the thinking/head center, they can resemble head types, and they can very much appreciate the intelligence and the knowledge of Observers.

A young Perfectionist wrote approvingly of her relationship with an Observer: "We both like separate activities." A Perfectionist-Observer couple might lead parallel but separate lives, each content with the status quo but with minimal emotional engagement. Eventually this could become problematic. Neither partner accesses anger easily nor likes conflict or fighting. Ones avoid conflict because it just doesn't look "good," nor does it hold the serenity they try to attain. Fives don't find anger a comfortable feeling — it scares them. Thus, when issues occur, Ones and Fives may both simply stuff their feelings. As a result, neither stays current with personal wants and needs. Unfortunately, some Perfectionists and Observers believe that the approach to most problems is to solve them as soon as they arise, all the while neglecting their own emotions. They don't realize that sometimes the real issue may be being out of touch with feelings, needing to listen and support and not to rush to fix.

Observers don't want to see themselves as having needs; it's more comfortable to be self-sufficient and not vulnerable. They have a strong attachment to independence and believe they shouldn't need anything. Observers who express emotions may see themselves as "whiners." Perfectionists may feel they don't have the right to ask for anything, that they don't deserve to have wants, needs and desires. Remember, the One's role is to correct and perfect everything that is imperfect in the world; personal wants and needs do not fit into that particular paradigm. Both Types need to be given permission to verbalize their desires and feelings. It is important to note here that when Ones or Fives begin to express anger or say their needs, they begin to make themselves vulnerable, to demonstrate a strong investment in the relationship and an attachment to the other person. This is a positive outcome.

Perfectionists and Observers can benefit from building some vigorous physical activity such as bowling or racquetball into the relationship This will help them to stay more physically, sexually, and emotionally connected.

Strengths of the Perfectionist-Observer relationship

When asked what gifts their partner brought to the relationship, Diane, a Perfectionist, wrote of Aaron, an Observer to whom she's been married for 50 years, "deep love, no judging mind and original wit and great intellect." These are Five qualities that are much valued by Ones. Lloyd, a Perfectionist, had a very similar list about Lonna, his Observer wife of 26 years: "She brought knowledge and wisdom. A fantastic memory. Very good intuitive skills. She was a great listener. Very accepting and patient with me. Lonna enjoyed going to workshops and learning new things." Stephanie, the young Five woman, said of Oscar, the One: "He does things right, is reliable and follows through, I can trust him."

Ones value the steady, knowing presence in Fives with the lack of judgmentalism that detachment often brings. Observers can resemble Leaders in that you can say things usually without fear of upsetting them or of repercussions. For the most part, Fives will simply take what you are saying as information and process it from an objective viewpoint.

Ones will most likely be equally comfortable around Fives in that they don't feel they have to be perfect and don't have to worry about being judged. Because of their strong inner critic and never ending search for unconditional love and acceptance, this quality of the Observer can be a huge relief for the Perfectionist. At the same time, the Observer will value the Perfectionist's ability to be in touch with their gut, that part of them that can move mountains at times without running out of energy. Ones can jumpstart Fives into action and teach them about the infinite amount of energy that the universe provides for getting things done.

Ones and Fives, like Threes (Achievers), can be great problem solvers. Obviously, one of the partners could become upset if they just want to be listened to without attempts to "fix" them, but when there truly is a problem that can be solved, Ones and Fives make a great team. Here's an example where the One's problem-solving skills helped a reclusive Five feel more comfortable in a group. Julian, an Observer, reported,

I greatly dislike social gatherings, and Beth is able to find ways to make them work that make it easier for me to get through them. She will actually think about them in advance and present me with very practical ways to overcome my reclusive nature while respecting it at the same time. It amazes me.

The One-Five pair can work well together on projects. Stephanie, the young Observer, related,

Typically we both get excited about certain projects together. Oscar has more follow-through than I have though, and he will push me further than I could go by myself. He makes me get it right and perfect, where my way is just "good enough." I tend to flake out after my curiosity is satisfied. I do enjoy getting things right too, but they come out better with Oscar involved.

Another "project" that a One-Five pair may do better at together than alone is parenting. Lloyd, a One, wrote about his wife Lonna,

She would bring a lot of patience when our son (probably a One) would get so frustrated over doing an assignment or big project. I tended to get angry and judgmental, but Lonna would just sit with him and help him through the steps. When it came to sports, I would go with him to games or teach him to ride a bike, play basketball, etc. She would get involved in their schools and with teachers and know intuitively what was best for each son. I would play games with them, work puzzles and tell goodnight stories.

The Observer's broad view can balance the Perfectionist's detail orientation. As Diane, a One, wrote,

Looking through my partner's eyes and broad perspective, I can rethink my own detail-oriented traps, gaining more opportunities to enjoy life in the moment. Relaxing my narrow focus improves problem solving.

Challenges of the Perfectionist-Observer pairing

About the One: Challenges, complaints, and type-related difficulties
In our survey, Fives chose Ones as one of the types they have the most difficulty with. Yet, as we stated earlier, these two types are look-alikes, compatible in many ways. Fives' complaints about the One were primarily about the Perfectionist's critical nature: "They are too critical, which triggers my own inadequacy feelings." Observers resist when they believe their competence is being challenged. Both types are very sensitive to criticism, in somewhat different ways: The One feels sensitive when not seen as being perfect, whereas the Five is sensitive about being seen as not competent. When the Perfectionist criticizes the Observer, it most likely goes to the very core of the latter's self esteem, when in all actuality, the Perfectionist is most likely showing concern for the partner.

Stephanie, the Observer, wrote about her Perfectionist partner: "Sometimes Oscar forgets about my needs because he's so involved with Oneish stuff. Also he is very dominating and wants me to do things his way, the right way. He thinks my ways are pretty good too, but not as perfect as his, of course." The Five is also sensitive about anything that feels like an intrusion into personal space or any kind of smothering behavior. Ones need to be careful that when they are showing their particular kind of caring, it is not perceived as critical or invasive. Lloyd, a Perfectionist, had this to say about his long-term marriage with an Observer:

My biggest challenge was my tendency to be critical of myself and of Lonna – to see only the flaws. Too much right/wrong thinking and Have to's, as in 'I Have to get this work done, I have to get this crossed off the list, before we can play.' As a result, we didn't play enough. I was too responsible, especially financially, as in, we can't afford this – when we could."

Lloyd's regretful recollections make a good point about the need for play in the relationship. Both Perfectionists and Observers can get caught up in their heads or the need to accomplish things and forget to play. Lloyd remembers his deceased wife's central complaint about him: "Lonna told me I am inflexible. I need to be in control, have things my way. I don't listen. Too much problem solving. I need to be right all the time. I'm too critical of myself and others."

About the Observer: Challenges, Complaints, and Type-related difficulties

According to authors Baron & Wagele, Perfectionists have trouble with Observers because they resist going to functions the Perfectionist considers obligatory, become quarrelsome when the Perfectionist challenges their logic or disagrees with them, often have a slower pace and try the Perfectionist's patience and become silent and withdraw instead of working things out with the Perfectionist.

A recurrent complaint by Perfectionists is that the Observer is too solitary, too uninterested in get-togethers with family and friends. Julian, a Five, wrote that his wife Beth's major complaint about him was that he didn't like family gatherings or socializing, and he conceded, "My reclusive nature is our major challenge." Fives tend to feel their emotions only after the fact – after the interaction has taken place and it is safe. Even when they are together, the partner may feel that the Five is not emotionally present. One Perfectionist wished that her Observer husband could "share our experiences rather than observing them."

Diane, a One, reported that her long-term Five husband, Aaron, had an "attitude of superiority, not crediting other points of view as valid." In their focus on competence, Fives can thoroughly research something, draw a conclusion about it and then not be open to other perspectives. Actually, Ones can do exactly the same thing. Lloyd, the One, wrote," I make up my mind too quickly without listening to her side. Then I cling to it as 'the only right way.'" At its worst, this tendency in both partners can lead to significant clashes and power struggles.

Some Observers can be quite possessive of a partner; this may be part of their avarice. They do not want their partner to be too far away. For example, they might be comfortable giving the other a lot of space, as long as it is happening in the same house. The Perfectionist may begin to feel tied down. Although Observers can be very independent, a committed relationship can become very precious and like oxygen to them. A Five who wrote he would leave "if she put our relationship second to other things" demonstrated the importance of this.

Perfectionists tend to interpret silence as criticism and judgment. When Observers disengage, Perfectionists start worrying about what this means. Fives can detach emotionally for days at a time, thinking nothing about this. Meanwhile Ones get increasingly upset, just waiting for the bad news to be revealed. Ones need ongoing communication.

Perfectionist-Observer Interactions

In the book *Grace and Grit,* the heart-wrenching and deeply moving account of the five-year journey of philosopher and writer Ken Wilber (most likely a Five) and his wife Treya (probably a One) through her fatal breast cancer, Wilber described what happened during a period of great stress when her cancer recurred. Ken had given up what was his lifeblood, writing books, to be the primary support person for his wife. Although they were deeply in love and had great admiration for each other, they found themselves interacting so negatively that each thought of leaving. Wilber wrote,

> Our own individual neuroses were surfacing, exaggerated and amplified by our fairly grisly circumstances. In my case, when I become afraid, when fear overcomes me, my ordinary lightness of outlook, which generously might be referred to as wit, degenerates into sarcasm and snideness, a biting bitterness towards those around me – not because I am snide by nature, but because I am afraid. . . I end up with Oscar Wilde's epithet: "He has no enemies but is intensely disliked by his friends." And in Treya's case, when overcome with fear, her resilient strength would degenerate into rigidity, into a harsh stubbornness, an attempt to control and monopolize.

And indeed that is what was happening. Because I couldn't express my anger at Treya openly and directly, I constantly undercut her with sarcasm. And in her unyieldingness, she had monopolized most of the central decisions in both of our lives. I felt I had no control over my life at all, because Treya always had the trump card: "But I have cancer." [P.153]

This is the One and the Five at their worst. Rather than expressing their feelings, each acts them out in destructive ways.

Even when the life circumstances are far less serious, similar type-related problems with expressing feelings can adversely affect the Perfectionist-Observer relationship. Both Types may have difficulty accessing and expressing feelings. Both are great problem solvers and both prefer researching and thinking about the problem (especially the Five) and taking action (the One), rather than sitting with the feelings. June (a Perfectionist) wrote that the challenges faced by her Observer husband, Jack, are "withdrawal, privacy needs, lack of interest in personal growth and discussion of feelings." Lloyd, a One wrote about his Five wife's challenges, "She had trouble and problems with being touched, with expressing her feelings, with being sensual and sexual. She kept a lot of her feelings inside. This often resulted in a "No, I just don't want to do that." Diane, a One, wrote, "Aaron doesn't complain – he leaves. He doesn't easily stay present for an intense, anger-based discussion." It may be hard to engage a Five in an emotional discussion.

A recurring disagreement in this pairing can arise when the One's need for "right action" conflicts with the Five's need for space and solitude. In a 2004 lecture on couple relationships , enneagram therapist Mona Coates presented a video of a One-Five couple caught in a recurrent disagreement. The situation was that every year the Perfectionist invited his parents to stay with them for a month, which made his Observer wife very unhappy. She complained,

I really feel invaded, my territory invaded, and that I've lost control over my life. I need my time alone, because that when I get to think, and walk, and read about subjects that are interesting to me, and I recharge my batteries. When I don't get to do that, I get very uncomfortable. Instead of having my alone time, I have to be real busy, entertaining these people, and I didn't even invite them. Just want control over my time, my home, and myself. I feel emotionally abandoned because my husband doesn't seem to hear me, and he doesn't respect my needs.

The Perfectionist husband replied,

How I feel is that these are my parents, after all. They raised me, they put me through school, they spent a lot of money doing that, and they made me everything I am today really. I want them to be able to visit me, to return to them some of what I owe them. To be able to show them some of the caring they gave me. It wouldn't be right to cut them off from that now that they're old. And besides, they drive 2000 miles to see us! Shouldn't we consider that an honor in some way that they want to see us? I grew up in their home, and now I want to offer them my home, that would be the fair thing to do – I don't want to tell them to go stay at a hotel! What are they going to think about me if I don't let them stay a little bit of time here?

The wife responded,

As far as fairness goes, it's not fair to me! I feel invaded and overwhelmed to be with people all the time. It's my home and my family, and people don't have the right to just decide when to come and how long to stay.

Mona's solution, which the couple accepted, was to have them stay in a nearby hotel and schedule some time together for both couples, while at other times the son alone would visit with his parents. Both partners had to compromise.

Ones and Fives both see themselves with good problem-solving skills. When they come to therapy they say, "Just tell me how to fix it and I'll do it." One Perfectionist explained it this way: "I see myself as a solution-focused person. When something goes wrong, I identify the nature of the problem and try to come up with solutions, so the same thing doesn't happen again. As I see it, there's a lesson to be learned from every bad outcome."

Exercises for the Perfectionist-Observer couple

The following questions highlight the classic issues that challenge the One-Five pairing:

Perfectionists and Observers in Enneagram language are called "look-alikes," sharing many similar behaviors. For instance, both can be perfectionists in their own way. It's also very important for them to be led by competent bosses whom they respect. They also both like to be in control of their emotions. Paired together, these two Types can give energy primarily just to those behaviors that they both value, suppressing those that they don't value. When look-alike types pair up, they can become so focused on what they believe in together that they fail to balance out their overall approach to things.

- When do you feel that you and your partner may be losing a sense of balance, suppressing emotions with which you don't feel comfortable?

Ones and Fives can have completely different approaches to working out their difficulties when they arise. Ones will move toward discussing and resolving problems, whereas Fives will usually detach.

- How does responding differently to challenges in the relationship cause difficulties?
- Brainstorm with each other possible strategies to constructively discuss and resolve the inevitable problems in your relationship?

Observers are often out of touch with their feelings, and even when they are aware of them, they are reluctant to discuss them with their partner. Meanwhile, the Perfectionist, who is very sensitive to criticism, tends to interpret the Observer's silence as dissatisfaction.

- How can you work together to overcome the Observer's reluctance to bring up emotionally charged issues and at the same time to calm the Perfectionist's habit of concluding that silence implies criticism?

CHAPTER TWENTY

The Perfectionist-Detective (One-Six) Relationship

We troubleshoot, problem-solve, and brainstorm together beautifully – this has always been a strength, but has gotten better over time as we have fewer misunderstandings. We've gotten through life-threatening illnesses, writing a book together, house restoration, and traveling.
-- Cecilia, a Detective writing about her relationship with Jeff, a Perfectionist

Perfectionists and Detectives share many values. In fact, they are considered look-alikes, and people sometimes have trouble telling them apart. Both are responsible, capable, principled and loyal, and will hang in there when the going gets tough. Hard working, especially for favorite causes, they can make a great team. The One's sense of ethics and certainty about the right course can make a Six feel secure. Detectives would love to be sure that there is some rhyme or reason to the way the universe works, and that acting a certain way will bring about a particular outcome. On the other hand, Sixes, who struggle with uncertainty, also have a hard time not questioning someone who can be preachy and seems to have all the answers. Sixes tend to rebel against authority and may in particular resist the One's authoritarianism.

Strengths of the Perfectionist-Detective pairing

Perfectionists, as partners, will strive to do the right thing -- to be ethical, loyal, and trustworthy. The Sixes in our survey wrote that their One partners' gifts were "Commitment. Desire. Belief in equality and fairness. Generosity in terms of my family and children." And "Honesty, humor, depth, truly seeing who I was on the inside." Trust is a fundamental issue for the Six, so having a trustworthy partner is both appealing and reassuring. Anne, a Perfectionist, reaffirmed this when she wrote, "I keep my promises, a big thing for a Detective. My husband Tom can count on me." It is commonly thought that Detectives like to link up with Perfectionists (as well as Leaders) because of their "what you see is what you get" approach.

Ones and Sixes are usually detail-oriented people, determined and committed to seeing any project through, working together effectively and efficiently. The dutiful, loyal Six is very compatible with the One and his or her "right thing to do" attitude, so the couple tends to be on the same side of many situations. Both are often committed to a cause. Sixes, besides challenging authority in general, will stick up for the oppressed, and Ones will champion unfairness and the underdog. A Perfectionist related the following story in which both she and her Detective sister took on a cause for the sake of principle:

When my father's former wife contested his will, despite having signed a legal agreement that she would never do this, my Type Six (Detective) sister and I were in complete agreement that despite the costs, we would continue to fight her to the end. My Type Seven (Adventurer) husband pointed out that much of our estate could be eaten up in legal fees, and advised us to cut a deal so we would have some money to enjoy. But my sister and I both agreed that it was a matter of principle, it wasn't about money.

Here's another example: When the local Poison Control Center announced it planned to eliminate its telephone hotline, a Perfectionist-Detective couple mounted a campaign to keep this community service going. When the university planned to downsize the department headed by one of the pair, both fought to prevent this. Being equally engaged in their campaigns brought them even closer together.

Interestingly, although both Types may pursue a common cause, their underlying motivations often differ. Regardless, although Sixes may work to change things out of fear whereas Ones seek to change things out of a sense of responsibility, both can be motivated to correct things and can work well as partners. This is the true definition of look-alikes: Even though surface behaviors may be the same or quite similar, the motivation for those behaviors can be totally different. How many people side with another because they believe they are thinking about the situation in the same way, but in actuality they seek the same outcome for different reasons? Do couples ever get around to talking about *why* they want things to change?

Even when not specifically fighting for a cause, the One-Six couple will do very well when working on a joint project or pulling together in crisis. When a Detective had to move her office from one building to another, her Perfectionist husband was right there, spending weeks helping her to pack and then helping her to set up her new space.

Perfectionists generally don't want a lot of praise for their efforts; for them, it simply is the right thing to do. The movie "Pay It Forward" may have depicted the principles of a One with a Two wing. The film is about a man who helps someone out, and in return asks that person to "pay it forward" by helping someone else out sometime in the future.

One gift that Sixes bring to a relationship is questioning. In fact, another name for the Detective personality type is the Questioner. Sixes like to talk about potential problems, to get things out on the table so that they don't remain hidden. Because of these qualities, the couple's chances of staying current in regard to relationship issues are increased, which not only is healthier but also can be very helpful to Ones, many of whom are reluctant to get into conflict and prefer instead to withdraw. Anne, a Perfectionist, described this very challenge in her marriage:

I don't want to make a fuss about 'small things' – I'm reluctant to speak up or show anger about what Tom is doing that bothers me. He invites communication, so it's not as threatening as it was in past relationships, to broach difficult subjects. I'm learning to trust the process, but I still don't feel entirely comfortable with it.

Perfectionists can be great at looking outward and seeing what needs to be fixed or improved, and they can be just as great at championing the underdog. But when it comes to their own desires, they can have a hard time moving forward. Sixes can help by either asking the One partner what he or she wants or by teaching how to pose occasional questions. Eventually, Ones can learn that they have a right to their personal desires and also to pursue them.

On the enneagram diagram, Ones and Sixes share a common connection to Type Seven, the Adventurer. Seven is the "heart point" for the One (usually the place they go when relaxed), and it's a wing for the Six. Perfectionists and Detectives who are able to take a break from their work and responsibilities can have a good time together. A Detective can be playful at times, even childlike, and will try to get the Perfectionist to loosen up. This might be a source of disagreement, but it can also be good for the Perfectionist.

Cecilia, a Six, mused, "I think my Seven wing is often my saving grace – We [she and her partner] definitely connect at Seven." Although the usual perception of Ones is that they are very serious, sometimes people misinterpret their great sense of humor because it can be dry and eccentric. As long as others are not poking fun at or disrespecting them, they will gravitate quite easily to the lighter side of things, almost as if they know being too serious is not good for them. In a nutshell, Detectives will literally poke Perfectionists in the ribs to get them to lighten up, while Perfectionists will amuse the Detective with their off-the-wall wit.

Challenges of the Perfectionist-Detective relationship

Difficulty expressing feelings

Ones and Sixes generally value thoughts over feelings; expressing emotions may not be easy. Ones are often more comfortable responding to their partners' concerns with solutions to the problem rather than with a listening ear.

Both Ones and Sixes also can have trouble accessing their anger. Ones tend to choke it back because it doesn't look "right" or isn't perfect. Sharon, a Detective, says of her Perfectionist husband, "Stephen doesn't express his complaints verbally very often. He'll look angry, even throw something down, but he'll deny he's angry." Sixes are much more afraid of the unknown than of what is directly in front of them. If a One suppresses his anger, it can make the Six nervous. "How angry can my partner get? What will he do if he really does get angry?" The indirectness can escalate the Perfectionist's fear or paranoia, resulting in frightening imagined worst-case scenarios, which cause him or her to test the One to see if they are in fact angry. This might be done in a passive-aggressive way that will irritate the Perfectionist even more. Therefore, Perfectionists need to be given permission to express anger, while Detectives need to know that the One's expression of anger doesn't mean he's going to leave and that the Six will be physically safe.

Worry and anxiety

Ones of the Self-preservation subtypes have been termed "Worry Ones" because they experience much anxiety. Sharon, the Detective married to a Self-pres One, wrote, "Our similar personalities can get us worrying over security issues in ways that are not helpful." As you can see, both Types tend to either point to all the injustices just waiting to happen or think up all kinds of worst-case scenarios.

When not sharing the Six's anxiety, a One can react negatively to it. A One woman married to a Self-pres Six wrote,

Tom's work comes first and his anxiety about getting everything done is exhausting and leaves little or no time for fun. He worries and is anxious about things. He is mentally preoccupied with being ready for anything and is focused on that, rather than being alive in the present and planning for future pleasure.

The One's embedded criticism in the above quotation is most likely about control. A One who is critical of her Six partner's worries and anxieties may have fallen into a "snap out of it" approach. Basically she is saying, "How dare you allow something to get you down. This would never happen to me with my strong will. Why don't you just change your thinking?" For the most part, though, the above quote could have just as easily been written by a Self-pres One or by a One who has gotten caught up in her workaholism and in being overly responsible.

When the Perfectionist or the Detective falls into the trap of their own personal compulsions, the relationship becomes tedious and exhausting, something the Perfectionist wants to avoid. Paraphrasing Helen Palmer's recommendation to Detectives, "You need to spend as much time in best-case-scenario thinking as you do in worst-case-scenario thinking." This advice may be good for both the One and the Six, especially when they are both at their worst.

Tell me everything. ... You're scaring me

Living up to their name, Detectives seek to ferret out all the potential negatives associated with any situation; the knowledge alleviates their fears. Married for many years, a psychologist related,

My Six wife said to me more than once, "Tell me everything. If you leave things out, it scares me." So I would tell her something, something personal, and then she'd say, "Oh, that scares me." At other times, if I told her I was feeling insecure about something, she'd say, "Oh, no, I'm scared." It's that contradiction of the Six: You can't have it both ways. You can't tell me to be totally honest about things, and then when I am, you tell me it scares you. That was my experience with a Six wanting total honesty.

In our earlier chapter in Section One on the Detective in relationship, we described the differences between the phobic and counterphobic Six:

The phobic Six, very aware of her fears, tries to avoid dangerous situations and seeks a strong protector. The counterphobic Six has a different strategy – when she ferrets out (or imagines) danger, she will go on the attack, aggressively defending herself. Counterphobic Sixes can resemble Eights (Leaders) in their assertiveness. They are more comfortable with perceived dangers than with the unknown. The relationships of counterphobic Sixes are full of confrontations. The following description by a counterphobic Six illustrates this:

Some years ago my husband became very friendly with one of his graduate students. At at some point, when I suspected there might be more to the relationship, I confronted him and he admitted they'd been having an affair. I lashed out at him, grilling him for all the details. I kept going back to this for days, assaulting him with endless hostile questions. Looking back, I realize it was because I was terrified. But the result of fighting my fear so aggressively is that I believe that was the last time he ever told me the truth about anything important.

The Six's attempts to feel safer by asking for the truth with all the details – and then responding with fear – constitutes a double blnd for the One partner. "How much do I tell?" "How do I then deal with my partner's fearfulness?" This dilemma, which is likely to be a recurrent one for partners of Detectives, can be an ongoing challenge in the relationship.

Criticizing is caring, criticizing reflects fear

A counterphobic Six married to a One relates,

My desire for autonomy clashes with my husband's desire for doing things correctly. When I drive and he's the passenger, his continuous instructions bring out my strong desire to drive in a way I feel is best for me – It also brings out my orneriness (often unconscious). I think he is righteous, controlling, arrogant. He thinks I am careless, obstinate. . .

Being critical is part of the Perfectionist's personality. Many times, they see it as wanting to help their partner be a better person, i.e. a loving gesture. The partner usually sees it differently. Sharon complains to Stephen, her Perfectionist husband: "You criticize me. You w ant things done your way. You don't give me enough space to experiment, to be spontaneous. I often feel stifled." Cecilia, another Detective, says of her Perfectionist husband: "Jeff has a tendency to correct me. I mostly tease him about it now, but it was definitely a bone of contention in the past." Their tendency to correct makes the Perfectionist seem like an authority figure in the Detective's eyes. For a partner, it can sometimes feel good to be looked up to or really respected as someone who has the answers. But with a Six, it most likely won't be long before he or she will rebel against that authority. Helen Palmer states that, "Sixes either fall at the authorities' feet or go for the authorities' throat."

When Anne, a One, was asked what advice she had for a younger Perfectionist, she spoke to the issue of criticism.

Suspend conclusions about the person – try not to judge, pre-judge, or allow your mind to get into the critical mode. Be discerning, but let the less-important stuff be just as it is. If you decide that it's too much to bear, say so. If it won't change, and you really don't like it, are you willing to let the relationship go? Do that, or be more willing to let him/her be who he/she is."

Ones and Sixes are look-alikes in several ways, including a tendency to be critical. However, their motivations are different; whereas Ones criticize to help or improve their partners, the Six's criticisms are most likely based on fear. A Perfectionist related to one of us her difficulties with a counterphobic Detective husband:

My partner seems to frequently go on the attack. He thinks it's just gathering information, asking questions, but his tone is so aggressive that I just want to leave the room! It makes me extremely uncomfortable. It feels to me like constant conflict, although he doesn't perceive it that way. I feel I need to walk on eggshells around him, since if there's a way that something I say can be interpreted as offending him, -- attributing to me the worst motives -- that's the way he'll take it. So I have to be very careful how I say things. I've tried explaining this to him, but he just doesn't see it.

Ones can react badly to Sixes' aggression. One Perfectionist explained, "I'm defensive about being corrected, instructed, and having to respond to the other person's anxieties and projections about what could be better about me. I hate to be told what I already know!" Ones are alrelady hard enough on themselves. It's like putting gas on the fire. And who's better than a Six to come in all laser-like and tell the One what he or she is doing wrong!

Another problem with the Perfectionist's tendency to criticize is that the Detective may perceive the criticism as an attempt by the One to set him- or herself up as an authority figure. Sixes, especially counterphobics, have difficulty with authority figures and are very likely to rebel against them. A power struggle can be deadly for the relationship. If the One points out how the Six is wrong, it will set off a dance that can become a never-ending loop, with each defending their position. What the Six is feeling is, "I really don't want you to be the authority in my life." The One feels, "I was just trying to give you information about what's right." If this dance is repeated, the relationship can get off track.

Improving the relationship

According to one Detective, her challenges to the relationship included: "Lack of trust (you're here today, but what about tomorrow?), judgment (If he acts in an unfriendly manner, I sometimes interpret his behavior as having to do with me, without checking it out first.)" She acknowledged that her distortion of her partner's motives is fear related, and continued: "As a reactive type, my temper definitely gets in the way. I've learned many ways to calm myself down over the years and know I have to do that before I can effectively problem solve." Another Detective had this advice for a younger Six: "Learn to identify your own feelings and needs, to check perceptions out with others (to avoid projections), to be open to support (as in therapy, groups, etc.)."

John Gottman, a relationship expert who offers non-violent communication training, advises against what he calls a harsh start-up, which is when one or both partners addresses the other in a loud and abrasive manner. His research shows that couples who begin interactions that way are doomed right from the start. Being careful and conscious as to how to talk about disagreements, especially at the very beginning, is important. Sometimes it's necessary to take time out and start over again. Gottman considers violent communication to be language that consists of criticizing, blaming, and diagnosing as well as making demands of your partner. Couples who can eliminate this from their dialogues have a better chance of hearing each other without becoming defensive.

Exercises for the Perfectionist-Detective couple

The following questions highlight the classic issues that challenge the Perfectionist-Detective pairing:

Perfectionists can have a moral superiority about themselves which can trigger the Detective's natural tendency to question authority. Both types need to make sure that a pattern doesn't get established where Sixes feel judged and Ones feel they are being undermined.

- How do you handle the judging nature of the Perfectionist and the rebelling tendency of the Detective, to prevent establishment of an unhealthy pattern?

According to enneagram author Helen Palmer, "Anger frightens Sixes, and Ones think anger is wrong." Especially if handled correctly, anger can be freeing to Ones and it can help Sixes to say what they really want to say.

- How do you handle anger in your relationship?

Perfectionists naturally look for flaws while Detectives can question things in general.

- How do you protect your relationship, making sure that you don't undermine it by nitpicking it through criticism and questioning?

Ones and Sixes are look-alikes in that both can focus on "righteous causes," Ones because it's their nature to try to improve the world, Sixes because they look for potential negative outcomes and try to prevent or fix them. When the One-Six pair become intensely involved in correcting some perceived injustice, they may become excessively involved in supporting each other; there is no one to provide a more balanced view.

- **For both of you:** Think of some cause or goal you both may have put a lot of energy into in the past. Did you try to get information on all sides of this issue? How can you balance your involvement in various activities in which you might be excessively zealous as couple?

CHAPTER TWENTY-ONE

The Perfectionist-Adventurer (One-Seven) Relationship

The Perfectionist and the Adventurer are opposites in many ways –each has the potential to give the other a better sense of wholeness and happiness in the world. Iris, a Perfectionist who was married to an Adventurer for 20 years, explained how they were able to balance one another out.

When we married, we became blended family of eight. Our types worked very well in managing this brood. Being the Perfectionist, I had a demanding career with many responsibilities, and I provided structure, stability, and the financial resources for our family. Harold, an Adventurer, had had a series of careers, and now became a homemaker. Harold was lighthearted, liked to cook, was a loving and devoted parent, planned fun activities, and was always there for the children. I was able to go to the office reliably each day and concentrate on my work, knowing that Harold was handling things well at home.

In our relationship, our types worked well together for much of the time. Harold's spontaneity, humor, quick wit, and love of fun moved me out of my tendency to be too serious and overly responsible. I wanted things arranged in advance, and he loved to plan and organize fun activities. All I had to do was show up, as we traveled all over the world. We went on cruises, which I'd never done before. On these trips, my connection to type Seven emerged and I thoroughly enjoyed myself.

Also, since we were both Sexual subtypes, we were very compatible in our focus on the one-to-one relationship. We enjoyed our time together. With his interest in everything around him, our conversations were never dull. I constantly learned new things from him, and he was interested in everything that happened to me on the job.

The preceding story describes the best of a relationship between a One and a Seven (later on we will learn more about the challenges faced by Iris and Harold). Taking on a large family is a good example of how Adventurers can really rise to the occasion. Others might consider this stressful, but Adventurers see a complex life as an opportunity for welcomed variety. They like to be on the go, keeping busy, and they can even see a crisis as one big adrenaline rush. Such involved scenarios can work for a Seven, whereas others might just collapse under the pressure. Adventurers are high-energy people who can see every situation as interesting and full of options. Perfectionists, who tend to be overly serious, can learn from Adventurers how to be flexible and spontaneous, how to enjoy life and have fun. Ones, like Sevens, are lifetime learners and appreciate having a partner who also seeks new knowledge. Sevens are eternal optimists who can reframe negative experiences. They can also bolster the spirits of Ones who sometimes get discouraged at how imperfect the world is.

At the same time, Sevens can learn discipline and follow-through from Ones, how to complete the tasks they don't like very much and find boring. Sevens like the stability that Ones bring to their lives, and welcome their reliability and commitment to the relationship. Although Sevens like to fly, they appreciate the anchoring that Ones provide.

In our survey, we asked what would make the respondent's partner leave the relationship. Marla, a Perfectionist, replied, "Maybe Manuel would leave if he thought I'm not enough fun for him, but again, I can't really imagine him leaving me. He really does need me to help him stay focused! We are a good team, and we bring out the best in each other." Marla seems a little worried that as a One she may not be fun enough for her Seven partner. She also soothes herself by knowing that she provides that other "half" for Manuel mentioned at the beginning of this chapter. Of course, there's a downside to being the ballast in a relationship.

A One and Seven split up because the Seven wanted to play the field, while his wife waited and waited for him to return. After about a year, he finally did. As they sat in a café and he asked her to take him back, she asked him one last question before deciding. "Why do you want to come back to me?" He answered, "Because I have discovered that you are good for me, that my life just works better when you are in it." At that moment, the woman realized that for her, the relationship was over. Although she recognized that she was the stabilizing influence in her Adventurer's life, deep down a Perfectionist wants to know that her husband is staying because he loves her, not just that she's good for him or his life works better when she's in it. This represents the heart of the dilemma for a One who is loved for "being good" for her partner instead of just for being herself. Love and respect are key issues for the Perfectionist; in this situation she had discovered during her time away from her husband that she did not need to earn love.

Strengths of the Perfectionist-Adventurer relationship

In our survey, Perfectionists chose the Adventurer as a type with which they are most comfortable. Their reasons were: "They're optimistic." "They balance me, and lighten me up." "They add and bring joy, zest, and love of play." "They make me play, and draw me out of myself." "(They are) fun-loving, joyful, (and provide a) varied life."

Asked to describe how she helped the One-Seven relationship thrive, Iris, the One, wrote, "I provided a solid grounding to our relationship as well as the financial support. I encouraged my husband to explore new career options when he tired of the old." On the other side, Miranda, an Adventurer, listed her husband's gifts as "his intelligence, commitment, ethics, stability, loyalty, and dutifulness." These are stunning qualities indeed.

"Harold's optimism, his positive attitude about things, his ability to plan vacations and other fun activities, his social skills, quick mind, charm, and willingness to quickly forgive" were what Iris valued. Regarding the Seven's ability to "quickly forgive," it makes sense that Adventurers would have this quality; given that Sevens don't like pain and suffering, what better way to move away from anger and resentment than to forgive. Holding grudges against others, done often enough, shrinks horizons. Adventurers want more and always move in the direction of expanding their world. Forgiveness has a natural expansive quality that reopens a person to everything they excised from their life when angry. Perfectionists, with their black-and-white thinking and right-and-wrong approach to situations can have difficulty forgiving. Adventurers can help them to see the benefits of letting go of inhibiting daily resentments.

The flexibility of the Adventurer can counterbalance the Perfectionist's tendency to be rigid and can help him or her cope with the One's quirks. Miranda, the Seven, explained that what has helped her relationship is "my flexibility to adapt to Jim's type rather than expecting him to change." Relationship experts see flexibility and adaptability as one of the major strengths a partner can bring. Conversely, rigidity and stubbornness are destructive. In healthy partnerships, we need to be able to let go of the everyday crazy-making idiosyncrasies of our partners. Some Adventurers adapt to the extent that they lose themselves and eventually become very unhappy, so good at turning lemons into lemonade that healthy boundaries can slowly disappear. But being adaptable in relationship can be beneficial unless it is done too often.

The One-Seven combination is unbeatable for joint projects. The Seven provides the creativity and multiple options, while the One provides the practical grounding. Marla, a One, reported,

When we jointly set our minds on acquiring something new for the house or for recreation, Manuel is really great about exploring all the options. Together we weigh the pros and cons of the various choices and come up with the best choice considered from a variety of angles (usefulness, reliability, sustainability, costs, etc).

The juice for the Seven is the novelty of the purchases, whereas the One is focused on the practical aspects.

Challenges of the Perfectionist-Adventurer relationship

About the Perfectionist: Complaints, challenges, and Type-related difficulties

Even though Sevens and Ones balance each other and are a common pairing, Adventurers in our survey count Perfectionists as one of the types with whom they have most difficulties. Their reasons included, "They're critical and inflexible." "Too judgmental…serious to the point of painful. They'd rather be right than happy. Yuck." "One is sometimes too rigid for me."

Perfectionists have a clear inner sense of right and wrong, and the way they deal with this certainty can be detrimental to problem-solving. Iris says, "It took me years to realize I needed to focus on solving the problem rather than on making him acknowledge that I was right."

Some difficult challenges a One can bring to a relationship with an Adventurer were admitted by Iris, the Perfectionist who is no longer married to Harold. She related,

I had high expectations of Harold as well as of myself, and he felt he couldn't meet those expectations. I was judgmental about his personality traits; he felt criticized and reactive, and we ended up too often in a parent-child dynamic. I felt more comfortable with careful planning and was reluctant to support his impulsive decisions. My inability to express anger openly meant I accumulated resentments, which resulted in my becoming more rigid in our relationship.

The Adventurer's perspective on this issue is from Miranda, married two decades to Jim, a Perfectionist. "In the early years I didn't realize how differently wired we were, and I got frustrated at his lack of flexibility in changing plans. He is rigid even when it actually is not in his best interest. He expresses anger and frustration when things don't go as they should."

A Perfectionist's high standards and unmet expectations can cause increasing inflexibility and judgment and can risk becoming parental, and the Seven can respond with conduct that results in a destructive parent-child dynamic. Ones can potentially fall into the deadly situation of taking on the parental role in an attempt to change the Seven partner. This unhealthy pattern brings out the worst in each – the resentful controller and the acting out, rebellious child. Iris, the Perfectionist, recalls:

Another issue was that the more judgmental I became, the more defensive Harold was and the more he felt he was the bad child and I the controlling parent. This fueled his desire to flee into a more fun relationship, and I, of course, developed more "righteous indignation." Our interactions increasingly brought out the worse in each of us. I just didn't like the person I was becoming. We ended up getting divorced.

About the Seven: Complaints, challenges, and Type-related difficulties

Perfectionists in our survey chose the Adventurer as one of the Types they are most comfortable with, but also as one they struggle with the most. They wrote, "I don't know who they are – too much talk, but not about feeling." "A Seven, especially with a Sexual subtype, can have very different values from mine – they can be impulsive, lack follow-through, be unwilling to discuss painful issues, have difficulty with commitment to one partner, and forget tomorrow what they agreed to yesterday (because they feel differently by then)." "As a sexual subtype I want them to care about me, but the Seven's narcissism is sometimes the stronger force." "Superficial, but they have lots of friends and great social lives."

From their love/criticize viewpoint, Perfectionists can feel that someone needs to teach those Adventurers the rules! Life is serious, not to be played with. Their relationship can resemble the one between Peter Pan and Wendy. Wendy wants Peter to be more grounded and grow up, whereas Peter wants Wendy to be less earthbound, to let go and fly.

Marla, the One, wrote about her Seven spouse, "Manuel tends to get fascinated with an idea or concept or toy and *must* have that thing, but then he loses interest in it." As we described in Chapter Ten, "The Adventurer in

Relationship," Sevens can have difficulty with the big "C" – commitment. When a project, job, or relationship becomes routine or, God forbid, a little boring, their thirst for novelty—for exploring new options -- might overcome their commitment to follow through.

Although temporarily infatuated with a "toy," a project, or a person, Adventurers always leave themselves open to better possibilities. They are not really attached. To be attached to something or someone means you are vulnerable to feeling pain when the object of attachment is no longer there, and Adventurers want to avoid pain. The problem therefore is that it's not possible to be simultaneously non-attached and intimate. Intimacy is a willingness to be vulnerable, a kind of getting "naked" with another person, not only physically, but also mentally, emotionally, and spiritually. Sevens have a hard time doing that, and their partners may chafe at the detachment they perceive. One partner explained, "You can have fun with them, you can have a parallel life, but not intimacy."

[As we also discussed in Chapter Ten, Sevens of the Sexual subtype tend to have difficulty with monogamy. Adventurers who begin to feel bored with the routine of their marriage may use criticism toward their partner as a way of expressing their limited or bored feeling and as an excuse to free themselves up to seek out stimulation and excitement elsewhere. Sevens will sometimes fall into an "on again – off again" cycle so as to be able to repeatedly experience the partnership as new.

Adventurers can also operate with a form of amnesia or unwillingness to explore the past that can have a detrimental effect. This happened to Iris and Harold. She explained,

I believed that to change the future, we'd have to review the past and set in place some "relapse-prevention" strategies and contingencies. I also wanted Harold to acknowledge the pain he'd caused me with his affairs. Without remembering the past, how are you going to change? One of Harold's central complaints about me was, "You keep bringing up the past instead of just enjoying the good time we're having in the present. I'm acting trustworthy now, so why can't you let go of the past and trust me?" When we went for counseling, he absolutely did not want to discuss the past; he preferred to think about the positive possibilities for us for the future. He also admitted he really didn't understand the pain he'd caused me.

In their desire for change, some Sevens work at a series of jobs or move to different houses or cities. Iris wrote,

Harold frequently changed jobs. I was the major wage earner in the family. At one point he said there were job opportunities for him in another state and we should move there. I felt I couldn't be sure how long he'd stick with the new job. I balked. I said, 'It would be a huge deal for me professionally. I'd have to give up my job, get licensed in the other state, and start all over. It'll take me years to get to where I am today. How about if you move there, and if after months you still like it and want to stay, then I'll consider making the change.' Harold got angry with this. He accused me of not being supportive of his career aspirations.

You might notice in the above scenario that the One has come up with a strategy to try to keep herself from jumping every time the Seven's boredom led him to ask for change. But called on this behavior, the Adventurer can become quite critical. Paraphrasing enneagram teacher Tom Condon, when Sevens are caught with their hands in the cookie jar, they will label you as small-minded about the cookies.

Please don't give up hope after reading the preceding stories and information about the One-Seven combination. What follows are exercises to help you and your partner work through some of the issues we have presented and to also to appreciate the gifts both the Adventurer and the Perfectionist bring to their relationship and to value the "better" half that each of them represents to the other.

Exercises for the Perfectionist-Adventurer couple

The following questions highlight the classic issues that challenge the Perfectionist-Adventurer pairing:

Perfectionists and Adventurers are an interesting mix of yin and yang. The initial attraction usually requires each of them to find the balance between the discipline of the One and the fun of Seven. Unfortunately, this couple can find themselves in a power struggle if they aren't careful.

- How do you the two of you balance the fun of the Adventurer and the discipline of the Perfectionist?

This pairing many times finds itself in what is referred to as a parent-child pattern. Ones try to rein in the Seven, much like a parent will do with a rebellious child. The Seven, on the other hand, tries to resist the stifling limits that he or she feels the One is imposing.

- How do you resist the parent-child pattern in your relationship and instead be teachers to one another, striving to integrate the best you both bring to the relationship?

Adventurers of the Sexual subtype commonly search for novelty in their sexual relationships, a situation that is painful for most spouses, but is particularly unacceptable to Perfectionists, who believe people should "do the right thing," control their impulses, and keep their promises. The Perfectionist also considers the lying that usually accompanies cheating to be extremely disrespectful to her or him.

- Brainstorm with each other how each of you can get your needs met regarding your commitment to your relationship and what the potential consequences might result if this does not happen.

To do away with a lot of heartache in this relationship, both types need to focus on their own personal growth and spirituality. It's uncanny how this becomes almost the opposite task for each. Sevens need to focus on sobriety – along with single-minded concentration, moderation, and commitment. Ones need to focus on relaxation and pleasure, finding the joy and perfection instead of the flaws in all things.

- What do you think will happen in the relationship if the Perfectionist is truly able to focus on relaxation and pleasure while the Seven focuses on moderation and commitment? (As you will notice, this is almost a role reversal.)

CHAPTER TWENTY-TWO

The Perfectionist-Leader (One-Eight) Relationship

Ruth, a Perfectionist, gave a bird's eye view of a one-year-long relationship between a Perfectionist and a Leader:

> *Warren and I were both high-energy people who liked adventure. Our best times were when we were having fun – going to movies, plays, concerts; traveling far and wide; going to restaurants; hiking. We had an active sex life. I enjoyed his company and his leadership on our travels, and he valued my enthusiasm and my interest in always learning more. He liked my detail-orientation and appreciated my honesty, trustworthiness, and high ethical standards. My profession put me in a position to give him technical advice on the value of new products in which he was interested.*
>
> *Our "classic fight" was about his anger outbursts and inability to see any other perspective. The anger wasn't directed at me, until the end of the relationship, but it often took place in public, and as a One, who likes to appear a certain way, it was embarrassing and humiliating. For example, one evening Warren and I were to have dinner with an important professional colleague of mine, Roland, to whom I wanted to introduce Warren. It was important to me that Roland, a peaceful Nine, would like Warren. Warren had reserved a table at a prime location – the picture window facing the ocean -- but when we got to the restaurant, there were no vacancies at the window. Warren wouldn't take no for an answer and insisted*

loudly that we get a table at the window. He refused every suggestion the manager made to make up for the table's unavailability. He made a huge scene, attracting everyone else's attention. As a One, I was so embarrassed, I wanted to sink through the floor and disappear. I cringed inside, imagining how others were perceiving/judging me and what kind of impression he was making on my colleague Roland. But Warren seemed oblivious to what anyone else might be thinking. In my mind, I was sure Roland was also judging me for choosing such an impossible man.

I was so angry about this incident and frustrated by my inability to make Warren understand why he had ruined an important event for me that I dragged him to a therapy session with me. He explained to the therapist that he'd felt it was his responsibility to take good care of me, and at that restaurant that meant getting us the best table. He was just trying to protect my interests. I guess because he wasn't able to fulfill his commitment to me about the location where we sat, he felt he was a failure. Nothing else mattered at the moment. He never understood the impact of his behavior on me, nor recognized that he had over-reacted. We experienced similar situations the whole time we were dating. He embarrassed me in public several times with his angry outbursts and I kept trying to change him. We never resolved it.

It has been said that Perfectionists want the people close to them to "show well." Ruth wanted her partner to behave appropriately and to be socially correct. She needed to get her professional colleague's approval of the choice she had made in a romantic partner. Warren's focus was very different – he was not invested in looking good, but instead wanted to protect her, to fulfill his commitment. As is typical for many Leaders, he approached the situation with all guns blazing, oblivious to the reactions of observers or his partner's feelings. He also felt disrespected – he had been promised a nice table, and then offered a worse one. He had to stand up for what in his mind was a form of injustice!

About the One-Eight pairing, Helen Palmer wrote in *The Enneagram in Love and Work,*

If there's such a thing as enneagram opposites, this is it. The relationship is going to produce fireworks: Both are anger types, prone to black-or-white thinking, and convinced they're right. Initially Ones are mesmerized by the force and sexuality of the Eight persona... Eights are often attracted to the discipline and good intentions of Ones." (p. 274)

Not surprisingly, this is a common pairing. Enneagram teacher Dr. David Daniels, in his Touchstone column in the *Enneagram Monthly* confirms this and adds,

The One-Eight combination is not so uncommon. Both bring intensity, self-reliance, practicality, and the concern for fairness, justice, and truth to the relationship. The One's restraint, consistency, and self-control complements the Eight's directness, expression of desires, and impetuousness. (Nov. 2004, p. 4)

Eights and Ones are therefore basically similar and also quite opposite. Perfectionists and Leaders can balance each other as long as they respect each other's power and don't step on toes – not always an easy task.

Positive aspects of the Perfectionist-Leader relationship

Ones and Eights find many things to admire about each other. Ruth, the Perfectionist who told her story at the beginning of this chapter, described being attracted to her Eight partner because of "his high energy, interest in the world, encouraging me to join him in many fun activities — and initially, his black-and-white thinking when it meant he thought I was the best thing to come along in years." Other characteristics of Leaders that Perfectionists appreciated were, "Honesty, commitment, forthrightness, energy, humor, generosity/expansiveness." Perfectionists were attracted to Eights' sense of freedom and expansiveness, enthusiasm, high energy and ability to take the initiative, plus a willingness to stand up for what they believe, as well as for putting Ones in touch with their anger and allowing them to express it, something that is not easy for most Ones.

The Leaders on their part wrote that they respected the Perfectionist's "openness about feelings, communication, calmness, acceptance, and willingness to talk about issues." Leaders also admire Perfectionists' honesty, courage, and ability to stand up for themselves – traits shared by Leaders.

As well, Eights appreciate Perfectionists' sense of responsibility and follow-through on their commitments and self-discipline. Nicole, a One, said this about her relationship with Ray, an Eight: "As a Perfectionist, I've always worked to improve the relationship – I want 'more' and 'better.' He appreciates my integrity, ethics, and energy to get things done and carry out goals.

Together, they can make a good team. Angelo, a Perfectionist, described his partnership with a Leader this way: "Dana provides an expansive or plentiful approach and I supply research and carefulness." Other respondents painted a similar picture of a successful team effort. Nicole, a One, wrote,

Raising a family, building a house, throwing parties, extended vacations – I think the Eight's energy plus the One's attention to detail and perfectionism works well together.

Sally, also a Perfectionist, explained,

High energy, focused goals, ability to adapt to a challenging environment allowed us to build a cabin in the woods on an island with no road into the site, no electricity, phone or running water and two young children. We teamed up to clear the land without power tools, to prepare the site and build the structure with very little outside help. It was an experience that was difficult at the time but one we all remember vividly and cherish.

Eights and Ones can help each other get through what would be very difficult times alone. The One can help temper the Eight's occasionally excessive forcefulness, while the Eight can bring out the fight in the One when the situation calls for going against social etiquette. Following are situations where the Eight and One supported each other even when family and friends turned their backs or when the Ones were afraid to speak up.

We had a major family tragedy involving my adopted son. My husband Roberto – not the boy's father -- was protective and had stick-to-itiveness through very difficult, trying times. He was very loyal and kept up the relationship with my son where others would have vanished. – Eleanor, a One

We work very well together. We both have elderly mothers. Until 15 months ago, my mother lived 3000 miles away. She could be quite vicious to me. Neil [A One] would always travel with me to visit her – to support me and also to be a calming influence in the household. I am very good at gathering resource

material and finding solutions for problems, and these skills have been used in both situations. I also travel with Neil to visit his mom because, she too, can be nasty, and I try to protect my partner. I don't have a problem telling his mother when her behavior is inappropriate. No one in Neil's family is willing to tell his mom she's out of line. However, one and all are glad when I do say something.
– Lois, an Eight

Once a Leader has committed to a relationship, he or she can be very loyal and accepting, with a remarkably nonjudgmental quality, perhaps because what they've done in their lifetime has made them quite tolerant and non-judgmental. An analogy might be made between the Leader personality and the spirit of Alcoholics Anonymous. AA meetings are usually comprised of a mix of unconditional acceptance of others, while at the same time calling members on their B.S. AA meetings sometimes take on an Eight-ish quality. Members say, "You can tell us anything, we're not going to shame you, although we may challenge the hell out of you if you drink, but we're never going to abandon you."

Challenges of the Perfectionist-Leader relationship
Ones and Eights are both members of the Anger or gut triad. Eights express anger easily, and so do some Ones, whereas others divert it into righteous indignation and resentment. Nonetheless, anger in various forms is usually a big part of a Perfectionist-Leader relationship. In several areas of life there can be major disagreements and at times loud arguments. Some of these are:

Following the rules versus bending or breaking the rules
Steve eloquently expressed one of the biggest sources of friction in the Perfectionist-Leader relationship:

I'm an Eight, and I often struggle with Ones, who, truth to tell, make me feel a bit like a bull in a china shop. I always feel like Ones are monitoring the social atmosphere with an "appropriate-meter," and of course, such a device is likely to sound off a warning if I'm around and mixing things up a bit. At a recent conference, one attendee commented that he thought the best metaphor for the One and Eight was the matador and the bull. Interesting. All I know is that I often feel stifled if Ones are making the rules.

For the most part, Perfectionists want things to be nice and appropriate. Leaders can make Ones feel uncomfortable with their bending and breaking the rules, especially when politeness and etiquette counts. In a successful One-Eight relationship, the One needs to learn to choose his or her battles and lighten up about toeing the line when it doesn't really matter. Nicole, a Perfectionist in a 26-year marriage to a Leader, explained: "Ray is frank to the point of being tactless. As a Type One, I find his tactlessness clashes with my social 'correctness,' but I've learned to let it go."

Sometimes this isn't easy. Ruth, a Perfectionist, described an ethical dilemma she encountered with her Warren, the Leader, over his willingness to break a rule.

I was recovering from a fracture, so I had a Disabled Parking permit. Once when I was leaving town for a few days, Warren asked me to lend him my permit during my absence so he could find a parking place for his car in an area where parking spaces were difficult to find. I really didn't want to, because I felt it was absolutely wrong, but he insisted. It really bothered me, but he simply saw it as a great opportunity to find easy parking. I felt I was abetting him in morally reprehensible behavior, depriving a disabled person from obtaining parking. It made me think less of him. He thought I was just being a fuddy-duddy.

It is not hard to see how Eights and Ones interpret the "rules" differently. Although Leaders see rules as something that can be bent or broken to their satisfaction, Perfectionists try to figure out what they are so that they can abide by them. But the One's statement, "It made me think less of him," is the most important piece of the quotation. Respect is a cornerstone of all relationships, so when the Perfectionist starts to lose respect for a partner, it can be a downhill slide, ending with the One cutting the person out of their life, while the bewildered Eight wonders what the big deal was.

Respect

Respect is a core value for all members of the "gut" or "body" triad, meaning that both Ones and Eights have a special sensitivity about being treated with respect, as well as heightened awareness when treated with disrespect. One Perfectionist wrote, "I became increasingly rigid in my type as his anger outbursts, narcissistic demands, and disrespect of me increased. I became more judgmental and less empathetic of him, and began criticizing him, which he found hard to tolerate."

Both Perfectionists and Leaders need to ask themselves on a regular basis, "Where do we have a tendency to fall out of respect with one another?" When such an area is identified in the relationship, even if it seems trivial, both people need to work on bringing greater respect to that aspect of their relationship.

Control

A question that almost all couples have to answer is — who is going to control the relationship? Some couples seek a sense of equality by giving each partner an equal say in the making decisions. Others might take turns when decisions need to be made. Other couples might recognize the specific areas of expertise, deferring to that partner. And lastly, some partnerships may be okay with one of the partners as the designated leader while the other follows. Both Ones and Eights tend to be controlling. Ones, with their strong inner sense of right and wrong, are at times all too ready to make others change to what the Perfectionist sees as "right."

Perfectionists complain that Leaders can be narcissistic, focusing on their own needs. A One woman wrote, "You don't factor in my needs. You want me to fit your concept of a wife rather than seeing me for who I am as an individual, as a woman." Another Perfectionist said, "He always wants to be in charge and command everybody. He sees others as extensions of himself. He's possessive. He will never openly apologize for anything." A third Perfectionist related, "He's bossy. He's domineering. It's his way or no way."

An Eight who readily admits that a major goal of his life is not to be controlled frequently ends up controlling others himself. Nicole (a One) said of her Eight husband: "Ray always thinks he's right – his opinion is **it**. He doesn't see how his 'protecting' is also overbearing." Other Ones complain of the difficulty of getting an Eight to hear their point of view and consider different opinions.

Excess

The Chief Problem of the Eight personality Type is excess (also termed lust). Moderation in anything can be difficult for them. This can be a problem for Ones, who believe in doing things "the right way." A Perfectionist wrote that a problem his Leader wife had was "excess related to food and intoxicants." Another Perfectionist wrote of her Leader partner:

If some was good, more was better. This went for food, sex, alcohol, social activities, and money. When the stock market went down a few years ago, he was terribly depressed, saying he was broke when in fact he lost far more money than I'd ever earned, and had plenty more to spare. All this 'more, more, more' has been very uncomfortable for me.

Anger
An Eight woman related,

It's important to understand how fierce we can be and to monitor our behavior so we don't scare the .... out of our partner. Instinctively, I knew when I met my partner, that I could scare him away and I did not want that to happen. In my past relationships, I would test their love with my fierceness and my lusty behavior – and if they were able to weather that, then we could move on. I knew that this was not an option in my current relationship.

Most Ones are uncomfortable with overt conflict in their relationship. According to a Perfectionist married to a Leader, " My reluctance to express anger openly and my avoidance of angry people made me very uncomfortable with him and his overt anger." Another Perfectionist related,

I feel very uncomfortable with their overt anger, their impulsivity, their difficulty expressing feelings (other than anger), and their having to be in charge and in control. Their tendency to black-and-white thinking and to attacking disproportionately to the issue makes me want to run the other way.

When Ones finally do blow their stack and forcefully express anger to an Eight partner, the results may be different from what they might expect. A One woman in an Enneagram discussion group related,

After keeping untold anger toward my Eight husband bottled up for maybe ten years, I broke down one day and had a fit of rage, wherein I told him exactly how I felt. I don't believe I had ever expressed anger like that in my entire life! I was enraged and felt like a cat, hissing and spitting at him, choking out stuff from deep down. Afterwards I collapsed on the sofa, exhausted and embarrassed, imagining the worst possible response from him, apologizing for my horrible outburst. To my amazement, he just chuckled at me and assured me there was no need to apologize, that he understood how I felt and, furthermore, had a lot of respect for my position! "Anger doesn't bother me," he announced, "People speak the truth when they're angry." Well, I learned a lot that day. That's what I love about Eights. They are not afraid of the truth, nor of standing up to face it.

Choked-off anger can tamp down the life force of the One. For Eights to give their One partners permission to express their anger can be quite liberating. Resentment and rigidity are embedded in the stuffed anger of the Perfectionist, so accessing this frees them up to be able to express their desires and passion – not an easy thing for the Perfectionist.

Exercises for the Perfectionist-Leader Couple

The following questions highlight the classic issues that challenge the One-Eight pairing:

The Perfectionist and the Boss constitute a dynamic pairing. For the most part, it is a partnership of opposites (although they are both from the same enneagram Center, the gut). Some students of the enneagram joke that the Eight doesn't "show well" and therefore would be quite a challenge for the One's perfectionism.

- How do you both deal with this so-called "attraction of opposites"? Where do you see some similarities? How do you balance the differences with the similarities?

For this pairing to be successful, they must do at least one thing –treat each other with respect. If they fail, they not only fall out of love with each other, but they fall out of "respect" as well.

- Since respect is so important in this relationship, how do you show respect for one another? How do you each define respect? What is a deal breaker with regard to respect? How can you gain respect in each other's eyes?

Perfectionists can feel free when in contact with the unbridled power of the Leader, especially anger. Eights can feel the overall goodness that comes from the well- intentioned and disciplined nature of the One. Both types need to learn how to transform their anger. For Perfectionists and Leaders, anger is synonymous with control. Ones first need to embrace their anger/control before they can truly make peace with it. Eights on the other hand, sometimes need to be driven to their knees before they'll give up their sense of anger/control.

- How can you each help one another transform your anger/control – the One finding serenity while the Eight regains a lost innocence?

CHAPTER TWENTY -THREE

The Perfectionist-Mediator (One-Nine) Relationship

In running a household, Henry trusted me to make most of the financial decisions and he did most of the cleaning. We both had full time jobs. He was not "macho" and didn't mind ironing a shirt. I was good at details and providing structure for our social life as well as our financial affairs. We were a good team, had the same values, so we agreed on all the important things regarding rearing our child and major goals in life. We rarely competed with each other, even to the point where we didn't want to play chess because neither wanted to beat the other. We could compete on opposite teams if there were others involved, because then it became fun.

-- Jean, a Perfectionist (One) married 50 years to a Mediator (Nine)

Joanne's acceptance and tolerance have allowed me to see how damaging being an inconsiderate, demanding person can be. My support of and loyalty to her has allowed her to focus on her need to have better boundaries and to be more assertive. Early in our marriage I spent a lot of time and energy getting frustrated and angry because she was not doing things "efficiently" or to my liking. This created a lot of friction, as I would attempt to "advise" her. (I did not realize how much willpower this woman has!) With the help of personal growth work, I have developed my inner observer. I still get frustrated and angry. However, I now have enough objectivity (at times) to back off and take more responsibility for my own comfort.

-- Kyle, a Perfectionist (One) married to a Mediator (Nine)

The strengths of the One-Nine pairing are made evident by the fact that Perfectionists list Mediators as among the personality types with which they are most comfortable. The correcting and fixing that Ones forever do is in the service of serenity, and Nines can embody that serenity. Nines can make Ones feel loved for who they are and not for what they do. For Ones, hanging out with Nines can feel like a refreshing break from both the inner and outer critic. Nines value Ones for their high energy and ability to stay focused.

Perfectionists and Mediators have a lot in common. Both are in the Anger ("gut" or "body") triad (Eight, Nine and One) but tend to repress it. The conflict avoidance may even extend to the point of avoiding competition in games. Both types appreciate routine and like peace and stability in their homes and their lives. Nines are usually accepting, agreeable and nonjudgmental, and this reduces the One's anxiety about being right. Ones tend to be detail-oriented people, most comfortable with discrete structure rather than shades of gray. Nines appreciate Ones' organizational skills, which help them clarify their sometimes disorganized, perhaps chaotic life. In relationship with a Mediator, the Perfectionist often assumes the role of organizing and managing the plans, details, and finances, while the Mediator tends to go along agreeably, tending to the big picture. Adina, a One in her 70s about to be married to Dennis, explained,

Arranging our wedding (in progress), I can do the details and organizing. Dennis can think of wonderful passages from religious material to include. All the while he can remain very romantic in the face of all the decisions to be made.

Both types prefer stability to rapid change and both like structure in their lives. Adina described Dennis, the Nine, as "easygoing, floats, doesn't push the envelope. He's very principled and philosophic, deeply religious and intelligent. He also has a sense of humor."

In the Perfectionist-Mediator relationship, each can compensate for areas with which the other has difficulty. For example, Adina related, "Being practical and organized is a huge help next to his vagueness." A Nine woman, Marcy, aware of her tendency to procrastinate, wrote of her One partner: "Raquel had strength and purpose and was task oriented until completion." The nonjudgmental Mediator, in turn, can temper the Perfectionist's tendency to be critical and judgmental. The Mediator shows how to slow down and take it easy.

Challenges of the Perfectionist-Mediator relationship
Although Ones and Nines are often attracted to each other because of their complementary personality traits, those very same traits – the perfectionism and the rigidity of the Ones and the distractibility and lack of focus of the Nines – can turn into their biggest challenge and recurrent area of disagreement. Ones are action-oriented people who want to get things done once they are committed. Nines like to reflect and consider multiple options and are slow to act even after they agree to a particular decision. A One's tendency to take action can either jumpstart a Nine or else create resistance. Ones find it hard to relax, whereas Nines like to savor the moment.

Ones and Nines handle their energy differently, although both like to avoid direct anger. When angry, many Ones will react with righteous indignation, irritation and logical explanations as to the correctness of their position. Angry Nines will become stubborn and passive-aggressive, agreeing to do something but then not taking action or simply emotionally or physically withdrawing. Both types take criticism very personally and therefore need to learn how to access their anger and express it constructively.

A common consequence of these contrasting approaches is One becoming frustrated at Nine's inaction and attempting in various ways to motivate him or her, with the opposite result – the Nine digs in and becomes immobile. Jean, the 71-year old Perfectionist widowed after 50 years of marriage to a Mediator, recalled:

I would be demanding and press for something I wanted and Henry would withdraw. Also, I was critical of him sometimes for wasting time watching TV. We resolved some of this with counseling. I learned to back off as I recognized my tendency to judge. I still use one phrase - I say to myself every day...."I walk my own path and I allow others to walk their path." My husband also made resolutions to not watch TV as much and began keeping lists of books he had read. It was a work in progress; we were a work in progress until he died.

Power struggles can be quite deadly for the One-Nine pair. Both are stubborn in their own way – Perfectionists because they are "right" – Mediators because they are determined not to be controlled.

Conflict over their dissimilar styles is most likely when the One and Nine collaborate on a major project. Once Perfectionists get going on a project, they become laser-focused, wanting to continue non-stop until it gets done. Mediators, in contrast, are easily distracted, overwhelmed by large tasks and prone to lose focus. When working together, the One tends to push the Nine, while the Nine resists. This can be a recipe for disaster. The couples that dealt with this issue successfully were those who recognized this "classic fight" and worked out a strategy for defusing it. Phil, a Mediator, described how he and his wife Gina handled this situation:

We've agreed on a division of labor – Gina paints, I wallpaper. We do not try to do work projects together, because we always go about them differently and do not understand the other's methodology.

Complaints, challenges and Type-related difficulties for the Perfectionist

In their quest for perfection, Ones can be critical and judgmental, especially of their spouses, whom they want to help to improve. Marcy, a Nine, complained about Ruth's judgmentalism and unwillingness to concede or consider other points of view. She said, "After six years I left this relationship as I had begun to withdraw and feel depressed by constant criticisms and put downs. It's not easy for a Nine to take 'right action.'"

Mediators can suppress their anger, sometimes for years, and then finally make an irrevocable decision, for example, to end the relationship. Perfectionists need to learn to lighten up and let go of the need to be right and to improve their partner. Joyce, a Perfectionist, would advise another One: "Being good doesn't work. Be willing to let your partner's tasks remain undone and let your partner accept the consequences. Don't live your partner's life for her/him." Another Perfectionist, Adina, echoes this: "Give all the intensity a rest. Try to remember what the enneagram tells you: All is well, operating as it should."

Nines, who like to relax and take it easy, can be critical of the One's intensity and his need to ask about and talk through everything. Adina related, "I am so efficient, focused, list-making, that he feels guilty. In an argument, I probe, analyze, and I want to progress towards improvement. He just wants to blow off steam and let it go."

Jean, a One, speaking of difficulties she caused in her relationship, said, "It is when I start assuming I am right and that there is only one way." Perfectionists have a strong inner sense of right and wrong. Having determined what the right way is, they can be very resistant to looking at another perspective and possibly being convinced to do it differently. For the Mediator, who instinctively sees the many sides of most issues, this can be very frustrating.

Another challenge for Perfectionists in relationship is their planning and ruminating about future actions and how to best accomplish something.

Ones are inveterate list makers and, while doing one thing, may be more focused on the next. Phil, for example, complained to Gina (a Perfectionist):

You act as if you are being attentive to me when you are really preoccupied with thoughts of preparing for your teaching day ahead. Just tell me what you are thinking. Don't go through the charade of asking about me when your mind is really elsewhere. It is a big-time insult.

Complaints, challenges, and Type-related difficulties for the Nine

Despite their passivity, Nines have been called the most powerful of the enneagram Types, most likely because they can be very stubborn in a passive-aggressive way. However, the Mediator's difficulty in focusing, prioritizing, and getting tasks done can be frustrating for the goal-oriented Perfectionist, who might get tired of feeling like the responsible one in the relationship. A One, Joyce, complains about "falling into completing his tasks. Taking all of the initiative, including initiating sex. Acting as if I can accept poor treatment." She wrote that if she were to put a slogan on her T-shirt about her relationship, it would say, "Why am I doing all the work? At some point this *has* to be fun." The result is likely to be resentment and criticism by the One, who feels disrespected when it looks like the Nine isn't pulling any weight in the relationship.

Ones like direct communication, so a Nine's passive-aggressive approach to anger can be a real challenge. So can the Nine's difficulty with expressing – or even recognizing – his or her needs. Adina complained about her fiancé Dennis. "He won't tell me clearly what he wants. He's indecisive and hides his wants." So how do you resolve this issue? Phil, the Nine, simply and concisely advises fellow Mediators to, "Learn what your wishes are and how to speak them assertively." This might be easier said than done.

When a One's perfectionism includes a tidy home, the Nine's relaxed style can create problems. Here is how one couple resolved their difficulty over the condition of their house, according to Marcy:

As a Nine, I was unconcerned about putting things away and could easily – unconsciously -- clutter up every available surface. We resolved the situation by agreeing on three locations that I would not clutter – but would keep things in their proper place."

Probably the biggest complaint that partners of all types have about the Nine is the Mediator's difficulty remaining present. Joyce, a One now divorced from a Nine, said, "He didn't 'show up'. He didn't really commit to the relationship." And from another Perfectionist:

When talking with a Nine, I sometimes feel he is going through the motions of listening but is really not present. He just mouths the appropriate responses, but I don't feel I'm really getting his attention.

When asked, "What is the one thing your partner could have done on a regular basis that would truly help you feel happy and satisfied in your relationship? Joyce, replied, "Be present." She added, "The sense that Dave was not there, not in the relationship, was very distressing for me."

Another common problem area in the Perfectionist-Mediator relationship is the Mediator's preference for avoiding conflict and putting off dealing with problems. Perfectionists, on the other hand, are problem solvers and prefer to address issues directly. Kyle complained about his Nine wife: "Joanne has a highly developed capacity to avoid personal conflicts." Joyce recalled: "In Dave's desire to keep things smooth, he resisted work to gain insight. Without insight into his behavior, thoughts, emotions, he lacked the ability to problem solve regarding our relationship."

Working it out

When a Perfectionist-Mediator couple identifies core personality traits of each other which are unlikely to change, they hopefully can develop strategies for getting through what could otherwise turn into yet another episode of one of their "classic fights." For example, the laissez-faire attitude of the Mediator can drive the Perfectionist a little crazy. Phil, a Mediator, described how this played out when he and Gina entertained and how they worked it out:

I'm a sociable guy. I like to invite people over and give them little jobs to do so that they feel a part of the process and are not left to stand around being self-conscious. Gina likes to do everything so that it will be perfect. These days, when I have my groups over, she leaves the house until we finish. When we have joint friends over, I allow her to lead because I am the more flexible of the two. Working out a strategy for this situation has eliminated what used to be a big area of unhappiness for us.

Sitting down and seriously brainstorming how to increase each member's comfort level in situations where their personalities clash can significantly improve the couple's relationship. Below are exercises regarding some common difficulties that the One-Nine couple is likely to encounter.

Exercises for Perfectionist-Mediator couple

The following questions highlight the classic issues that challenge the One-Nine pairing:

Perfectionists and Mediators are prone to getting into power struggles. Ones think they know what's right for Nines – especially if the Mediator is wallowing in confusion about something in their life. Sensing that the One is trying to change them, Nines will dig in their heels and refuse to budge. The Mediator's motto becomes, "I may not know what I want, but I'll be damned if I let *you* tell me what I want!"

- Where in the relationship do the power struggles crop up? How do you deal with them in both a positive and a not so positive way?

The core issue for Perfectionists is their tendency to try to fix the flaws around them. The core issue for the Mediator is their sloth and their tendency to let things go. Understandably, the aforementioned power struggle can easily rear its ugly head once again with regard to these core issues.

- How do you deal with your perfectionism and sloth in a way that is healthy and positive for both of you?

Perfectionists and Mediators both belong to the gut or body center, whose main issue is anger. Neither Type is comfortable with conflict or direct expression of anger.

- Brainstorm how you might constructively let your partner know how you feel when something is bothering you and how you can work together to resolve a disagreement.

Nines bring a sense of flow and a connection with unconditional love that can be truly helpful to Ones. Ones can bring a sense of structure and a knowing of right and wrong that can be helpful to Nines.

- How can the Mediator take "right action" a little easier with the Perfectionist's support? How can the Perfectionist find love and serenity through the Mediator's support?

CHAPTER TWENTY-FOUR

The Double Giver (Two-Two) Relationship

How do I feel about linking up with another Two? I could see us being friends, both of us hanging out together and telling "war stories" about how we've taken stunning care of others and how our partners have not really appreciated our helping, but a committed relationship with another Two is just not that attractive to me. It would probably be a little boring. Another Giver just doesn't have any needs or problems to solve -- or at least none that are easily identifiable. How is that going to work? Where is the juice going to be in the relationship?

-- A Two man

I have trouble with Twos because I'm on to them. It's exhausting to be catered to by someone who doesn't take care of himself. It's like competition, each catering to the other.

--A Two woman

Double Giver couples are distinctly uncommon. The explanation above might just be why this is so. Twos for the most part form relationships with people who have problems and issues. They gain a sense of importance and worth through helping and giving, possibly even feeling indispensable. The Two's core issue of Pride means he wants others to believe that while indispensable to others, he has few needs of his own. The Two is therefore likely to choose a partner who welcomes being the frequent recipient of attention and gifts and is appropriately appreciative. This is unlikely to be another Two.

In the Double Giver pairing, each partner studies the other, trying to find where he or she can be of help. Givers just don't see themselves as having any problems. Their motto is, "Other people have needs, but I don't." A Giver linked with another Giver is most likely not going to feel sufficiently needed or important.

Another issue for this pairing is the Two's belief that you have to give or help in order to receive love. Each Type has its own way of establishing its role in a relationship, as well as a way to "win" love from the partner. This of course was set up in childhood when the child learned what would gain his parents' approval and recognition and therefore win their love. If we have not worked through this childhood issue, it continues into our adult relationships. The way that we "win the love" is embedded in the childhood coping strategy of the personality type, and it rears its sometimes ugly head later, making it difficult for a Giver who is paired up with a partner who resists being on the receiving end.

Overcoming this difficulty takes a great deal of personal work. If the Two has resolved some of the aforementioned issues, he may be able to enter into a relationship free from the personality dynamics that keep him stuck at the lower end of the relationship health continuum. For the Giver, that consists of such unhealthy behaviors as manipulation, giving to get, codependency, and living one's life through another. If neither Two partner exhibits these behaviors, they have the opportunity to support each other in redefining their role in a relationship, and as a couple they can enter into the "nurturing, challenging, and transformative" model. Both partners are committed to working on their Type and looking to transform themselves through the mirroring and love that only relationships can provide.

Occasionally a pair of Twos might find themselves in a relationship when one or both feel wounded and in need of help. In such a situation, what better person to give that to a Giver than another Giver? Here is a case in point: Shortly after meeting, a Two-Two couple who had both been abused in childhood and had had difficult and painful relationships as adults were able to make each other feel safe and comfortable. They gave each other permission to identify and state their needs openly. He would run a bath for her when she came home from work, and she would massage his head just like his mother used to do before she died at an early age. They knew how to meet each other's needs perfectly, and they enjoyed doing it. They were also mutually protective, giving others a message that no one would ever hurt their partner again.

Another Two-Two couple has been together for 10 years. Not surprisingly, they differ in their wings and subtype, which may provide enough difference that they may almost feel like another Type. Twos do well when both are working toward a common goal – such as raising children or running a business together – as long as they don't become competitive. Sometimes Givers can compete: Who is the best parent, who knows the kids' needs the best? In this partnership, the husband, Tom, explained that he and his wife, Rochelle, "did very well raising children (who by nature are very needy). "We do well at really any goal that we both embrace freely and willingly." Twos are also adaptable to whatever their partner wants and needs and can alter themselves to meet those needs. "My willingness/ability to change to accommodate Rochelle " was what Tom identified as what he brought to the relationship that helped it to thrive. At the same time, he characterized his wife's role as "caring, giving and considerate." As you can see, both are good at giving and will need to be careful to not lose themselves in the relationship while trying to meet their partner's needs.

During an interview with Tom, he recalled a time when he and his wife were on vacation. They went for a walk on the beach, which he didn't particularly want to do, but did it because he thought she wanted to. While they were walking, Rochelle said to him, "I hate walking on the beach." He replied, "Oh, I just assumed you wanted to." It is a classic example of how Givers assume that their partner wants what they themselves want, when in actuality their radar may be way off target; too often neither of them is willing to check it out in order to avoid hurting each other's feelings.

Tom also mentioned, "At times Rochelle doesn't take good care of herself . . . stretching herself too thin for her own good." Of course, he admitted that he, too, has difficulty with self-care, and in fact, he stated that it drives him a little nuts to see her Twoness emerge right before his eyes. He recalled listening to Rochelle, a Social subtype on the phone saying "yes" to someone asking her to sit on several committees. Tom fumed inside when he heard her taking on too many projects, unable to say no. Then he thought of his own life and how what she was doing was very similar to how he has handled things, and he realized that he too found it very difficult to decline.

In all same-type pairings, the partners can either collude around the issues of their Type or they can turn it into an opportunity to challenge each other to avoid falling into the trap of their Type. Embedded in double pairings is the opportunity for us to be thrown back on ourselves, similar to looking into a mirror. What we do with that reflection is what's important. Do we just gripe at our partner, or do we take responsibility for our own issues and support our partner in seeing their own self?

Positive aspects of the Giver-Giver relationship:
- Because they have the same orientation to relationships, they can help each other feel loved and appreciated.
- If both are working on themselves, they may help each other identify wants and needs and learn how to receive.
- They may stand together against the world, helping each other, or unify around a common venture.

Challenges of the Giver-Giver relationship:
- With two Givers, there is no one to receive and each is embarrassed to be the center of attention.
- Twos live somewhat vicariously through others so as to avoid the risk of losing face. With two Givers, one will have to put him- or herself "out there."
- Givers may feel bored with the relationship because there is no one to actively "fix."
- Givers compete with each other as to who is more important or most needed, who's the best helper.

Twos like to be "the power behind the throne." In a Double Giver relationship, each may wait for the other to take action and to have needs. Both can end up feeling bored. Each may have trouble admitting their needs or even knowing what they want. A man in a Double Giver relationship admitted that he had trouble recognizing his needs, as did his wife; having such a partner is surely frustrating for both! Also, both may be overly concerned with what their partner or other people think, and with projecting the right image. In their focus on the other, Twos may neglect themselves.

Exercises for the Double Giver couple
The following questions highlight the classic issues that challenge the Two-Two pairing:

This pairing is uncommon. Twos naturally want to link with people who need help and it goes against their nature to admit to needing help. A Two may be attracted to a fellow Giver if one or both had been wounded earlier in life and now need some nurturing. Two Givers might also get together if they had different subtypes and possibly different wings as well – making them appear almost as if they were two different Types.

- Since the core issue for the Giver is to link with someone to whom they can give – how does helping show up in your relationship with one another? What do you hope the payoff will be from your giving? How do you recognize your importance to one another if it is not through giving and helping?
- A Two's relationship may be seen as partially serving a partner's potential and the rest developing their own self. How do you serve your partner without losing yourself? How do you serve your partner and work on yourself as well? How can you support each other in keeping a healthy focus on yourselves?
- Being in relationship doesn't mean that you have to deny your own needs. How are each of you able to state your own wants and needs to the other? Without trying to fix one another - talk about a current want and need that you have had trouble talking to your Two partner about.

The Two's core issue or challenge is Pride, relating to their sense of being indispensable to others while having no needs of their own. In relationship with another Two, a Giver may find himself competing with his partner as to who is the better Giver.

- How do you handle any competitiveness related to your helping and giving to your partner?

CHAPTER TWENTY-FIVE

The Giver-Achiever (Two-Three) Couple

Givers and Achievers have much in common. They are adjacent on the enneagram diagram, meaning they are each other's wings, and both are in the heart or image center. Being "next door neighbors" on the diagram, and from the same center means that their beliefs, approaches to the world, and relationships are familiar. They may appear differently in the world, but if they were to have an intimate conversation, nothing would shock either of them. When Two wonders what type is best for him or her, the correct answer is always, "A mature, healthy person of any Type." But in reality some pairings have more challenges than others. When such partners have a conversation, they may say "Wow, I don't think I would have ever thought of that idea or approach to relationships quite like he just said." But this is not true for the Giver-Achiever pairing.

Both Types are optimistic, energetic, hard working people who value success. Both want to make a good impression on others and know how to fit in with a group. Twos may value Threes' independence; Threes may value the Twos' warmth, affection and understanding, and the Threes appreciate the affection and attention they receive. Twos would most likely enjoy being behind the "throne" as they say, helping the Three become successful, and Threes enjoy the attention and support they get from the Two. This couple often bonds in a relationship of "successful love." The Achiever is the wage earner, while the Giver becomes the emotional center of the home. If all of life were a stage, the Giver would make a great behind-the-scenes director, helping the Achiever give his best performance. Threes are generally good at being mentored and making the most of it . . . sometimes achieving success even beyond the Two's expectations.

We heard from one Giver-Achiever relationship, Jose, a Three with a Two wing, married almost four decades to Margarita, a Two with a Three wing. Jose wrote that one thing they had done well together was raising their children. He stated briefly but insightfully, "We are a puzzle fit between goal-oriented (me), people sensitive (her)." This partnership works best when the Three allows the Two to teach him about feelings and the Two allows the Three to teach her about non-emotional areas such as goals and efficiency. Jose and Margarita were able to bring these strengths to their relationship and most likely were great parents to their children.

Challenges of the Giver-Achiever couple

The biggest challenge of the Two-Three pair is their differing goals. Achievers are focused on professional success and accomplishment. Frequently they will get so involved with their work that the relationship becomes secondary. They keep long hours, come home tired, don't have time for vacation and may take their partner's support for granted. They might resent the Giver's demands for attention and tendency to pout when they don't get what they want.

Twos are often reluctant to state their needs and indeed may not even recognize them. At the same time, they can become resentful that all their giving and support isn't appreciated. And when they are aware of their own needs, they may try to get them met through manipulation rather than open discussion. It's much easier for the Achiever if the Giver can state their wants directly. Achievers aren't big on expressing feelings, whereas Givers want words of affection and love. Twos may feel as if the Three's career is the "other woman" or "other man."

Jose wrote that Margarita's central complaint about him is "You are insensitive, self-centered, don't pay attention to details and are too busy." One of the core issues for a Giver is his or her need to feel important to the partner. The Achiever's business-like approach to relationships can sometimes make the Giver feel she is being taken advantage of and not appreciated for all she brings. Jose lists his own challenges as, "I'm very task oriented. I get my value from accomplishment. I'm too self-contained, not emotional." Even though an Achiever may be insightful about his own struggles, he may still have a hard time avoiding innate patterns and beliefs and may feel that the Giver wants too much attention from him. Margarita's demands may feel to Jose much like messy feelings that don't really serve a purpose or have any value.

Threes can be very sensitive to criticism and conflict, and they don't like to spend much time discussing the relationship. Twos who feel neglected can get very angry, whereas Threes don't like strong emotions; to the Achiever, they are messy and inefficient. Jose wrote that he might leave the relationship if Margarita were to "stay angry," which shows just how resistant the Achiever can be to emotions and conflict. A Giver-Achiever couple whom Ron had counseled had difficulty resolving conflict because of the Achiever's avoidance: He would either leave the house early in the morning before his wife got out bed or sneak out the back door to avoid her.

Jose's complaint about Margarita was "You don't take care of yourself. You procrastinate." He believes that she is "too distracted by people's needs and concerns." This is a good example of how our partners can sometimes know us better than we know ourselves. Unfortunately, the Three may find it next to impossible to get the Two to see these things about him- or herself, because of the Achiever's avoidance of conflict and the Giver's disowning of her own needs.

Twos are very sensitive to people's feelings and may get angry if they observe a Three stepping over people to get to his or her goal. Givers bring the "heart" to the relationship, whereas the Achiever's lack of caring about others while getting to a goal will bring out the fight in the Giver. Twos will understand the benefit of setting and accomplishing goals, but they can't condone doing this at the expense of others. This may be where Twos and Threes will disagree the most. Threes do have a heart and, like Twos, are trying to win love by "doing," -- Twos by giving and Threes by achieving. Both need to recognize that they come from the same place at the core. Each needs to remind the other that they are loved for their being and not their doing. Both need to remember that genuine love is given freely, and it never has to be earned through anyone's "doing."

When asked about a recurring argument, and how they resolved it, Jose wrote: "The problem was about coordination of schedules to accommodate activities (me) and people (her). Now we meet weekly to discuss our respective schedules and to agree on priorities (compromise on both our parts is required)." Threes may be most comfortable when they can organize their home life into a business-like relationship, with clearly delineated schedules and responsibilities.

In some ways, Achievers are correct that sometimes relationships work best when seen as a business of sorts. It is an "emotional" contract that partners form with each other and -- like all successful businesses --discipline, hard work, structure and communication are important for the business or relationship to thrive. The Three needs to remember that integrity, vulnerability, and feelings are important in the business of relationships.

Exercises for the Giver-Achiever couple

The following questions highlight the classic issues that challenge the Giver-Achiever pairing:

This pairing can easily look like the "ideal" couple – or at least they can hold the image of the ideal couple. Twos and Threes come from the same center, a center that for the most part promotes image and status. Twos can exude love and sweetness while Threes can broadcast their success. Twos can both admire and help Threes attain the success that is so important to them. As for Threes, they can heap lots of praise and monetary gifts on the Two for helping them – or at least they should do so; there is nothing worse than an unappreciated Two, which my well happen when the Three is distracted with work and success.

- How close do you come to being the ideal couple, balancing success and love? How do you meet each other's needs – the Two's need to feel important in the relationship and the Three's need to feel successful? Are you able to see the Three's material rewards as a sign of affection and the Two's helping as a sign of needing to feel important and gain approval?

Feelings that aren't positive can be easily discarded by both of them. Promoting the image and the feelings of being successful and being loving are what's most important to this couple. Both can find themselves wearing a mask of sorts. This pairing can look good in the world – attractive, successful, and with no apparent problems. The real question is: "Just how authentic is this couple?" This is a couple that can struggle with genuine authenticity. So what is authenticity? The answer is, it's when the outer expression of who we are matches our inner self.

- Are you just trying to impress each other? When you each ask yourself, "Who am I - really?" Does your inner world - your beliefs and values, your purpose - align with how you live your life on the outside? Does it feel false or real? How can each of you support your partner in developing their "real" self and their potential apart from the relationship?
- Are you just trying to impress others? Others can sway the Giver and the Achiever. To maintain the right "mask" or the right status and

image, Twos and Threes can find themselves doing things to please others instead of pleasing oneself. How important is it to you for people to see you in a certain light? If others saw you differently from how you wanted them to see you, what lengths would you go to in order to change yourself?

The core issues for this couple are deceit for the Three and excessive pride for the Two. This pairing can collude, which means they can work in tandem to keep up a co-illusion that continues to promote the masks they each can wear, or they can support each other in their personal/spiritual growth.

- How can you each support your partner in dealing with their core issue – for the Three: deceit and for the Two: pride. Achievers can get caught up in their doing and achieving to try and gain the love while Givers can get caught up in their giving to gain the love. At the highest level, Twos need to shed their pride and instead access a sense of humility. Threes on the other hand, need to let go of the deceit and gain an honest expression of themselves.

CHAPTER TWENTY-SIX

The Giver-Romantic (Two-Four) Couple

Twenty years ago my husband Carl was laid off from a job he'd had for many years. He did antique clock restoration and repair as a hobby and found it fun and fulfilling. I proposed that he turn his hobby into a full-time business, and convinced him that it would work. I made a plan and we walked through it together. Now Carl makes a good income, and it has allowed me to quit working outside the home and pursue activities I love while he works at an art he loves. He gets to be a "special, one-of-a-kind artisan," and I get to be "the power behind the throne."
　　　　　　　　-- Lisa, a Giver, married 24 years

Annette, a young Romantic, 27 years old, had a string of problematic relationships, with men who didn't treat her very well. Then she met a Giver, very caring, very committed. She loves to travel, and he said he'd follow her wherever she went. All he wanted was to be with her and do things for her. Everyone told her she was lucky to have met this loving, caring man after all the difficult men she had dated before. Annette told her mother she couldn't see them getting married, because "He's boring. I can't imagine spending my life with him. What would we talk about after two days? Boring, boring." He wasn't a challenge for her.

These two stories describe in a nutshell the dynamics, strengths and challenges of the Giver-Romantic relationship. In the first story, Lisa (a Giver) is able to identify the wants and needs of her Romantic husband. She is also able to see the positive potential in Carl, something for which Givers have a knack. She devises a plan with her organizational skills and a practical approach that complements the creativity and passion of her Four husband. Twos love being the "power behind the throne," enthusiastically encouraging their partners to soar and triumph in practical and emotional ways. Also embedded in Lisa's story is that she ends up getting her own needs met, something that could have been motivating her from the beginning, since Twos often give to meet their own needs. We also assume that Carl loved having his uniqueness recognized and felt special being so supported by his wife.

The second story describes a Four, Annette, who is bored with a Two suitor. No matter how much he dotes on his partner, it seems too humdrum for her. The stereotypical Romantic's drama has her pursuing push-pull relationships where she longs for the unavailable and pushes away the person who is very much present. She is bored with the ordinary. Romantics who have not resolved this dilemma may repeatedly get involved in unrewarding relationships. They create a reality that confirms an abandonment scenario. Nothing will improve for Annette until she becomes conscious of her own relationship patterns.

Givers can get caught up in their giving, trying to make themselves important or even indispensable to their partner. When so compelled, the Giver feels that this will get someone to love them, and that it will serve as a sort of guarantee to ward off being rejected. If you are needed — synonymous with being loved — people stay attached to you. Givers need to learn that people love you because they love you, not for what you do for them.

Positive aspects of the Giver-Romantic pairing

The Giver-Romantic pairing can work very well, as reported by Judy, a Two.

We are a great match because Frank is creative – the kite – and I am solid and predictable – the anchor. We get great ideas from him and logic and steadiness from me. Without each other, he would go off "half cocked" and be ineffective, and I would never get off home plate and be rigid. Somehow we each work our angle effectively with the other so we have a great deal of success overall.

This is a relationship that honors the gifts each brings to the partnership. They appear to see each other clearly, and their personal symbols, the "kite" and the "anchor," denote their roles. The enneagram system can be helpful in letting others know who we are and how we will most likely manifest in the relationship. That information can help us honor and accept our partner.

In our survey, Givers chose the Romantic as one of the types to whom they are most attracted. The reasons included: "Romantics appreciate my deeper side." "They focus on getting out of me exactly what I most readily give – attention and 'selflessness.'" "It is easy for me to sense the Four's abandonment or engulfment places and respond accordingly (although I only figured this out after several years of living with one and finally realizing I needed to stay in one place emotionally while he moved in and out around me until he knew I was safe)." "They have apparently open emotional depth and aliveness." "Romantics want to connect." "Creativity, idealism, never a dull moment."

In the preceding comments by the Twos, the depth and the focus on relationships is apparent. The Two and the Four are both in the "heart" or "emotion" triad on the Enneagram diagram. They also share a connecting line, and both deeply value relationships and romance. Ron (this book's co-author), a Giver himself, remembers feeling drawn to Romantics when he first started studying the enneagram. He felt that their introspection would be good for him and possibly help with his tendency to be outwardly focused – they could be his teachers, replacing his other-directed doing and helping with self-fulfillment.

According to Baron & Wagele in their book *Are You My Type, Am I Yours?* Twos like Fours because they are warm and compassionate and are willing to share their inner life. They can be very funny and often have a unique sense of style and aesthetics. Fours like Twos because of the quality time spent, and how they can praise their partner's creativity and good taste. They energize the Two with their enthusiasm and can make the other feel truly loved.

About the Romantic, Eileen, a Giver, wrote that her husband Bob brought "a true understanding at a deep level of feelings and emotions, excitement and insatiable thirst for discovering new things, and incredible integrity." Judy, another Two, valued her Four husband's "availability for an intense, loving connection." Writing about himself, Dean, a Four related, "I listen very well. I have a deep awareness and understanding of my partner's energy. I'm very supportive." He also cited "My willingness to work through core issues, no matter how intense the emotions." Again, in most of the preceding comments, we hear a strong connection between the Two and the Four through the depth of intimacy that the two types can share.

Regarding his Type Two partner, Dean wrote, "Monica has a huge capacity to understand people. She is very responsible with money. She is warm, funny and wise." Arthur, a Two, listed his gifts as "love and willingness to support and encourage." Another Giver, Eileen, said, "I brought new people into our lives and showed how they enrich and not detract from our relationship. I made family the most important thing in my life." Twos can mirror the Fours, supporting the Four's need to feel special and unique. Fours, who have a tendency to focus only on the beloved and to be self-absorbed, can be helped by the Two to broaden relationship horizons to other people.

Challenges of the Giver-Romantic relationship

Baron and Wagele in their book sum up the differences and the complaints between Twos and Fours as follows: Twos have trouble with Fours because Fours (especially if introverted) don't like to be with people as much, have a push-pull habit in relationships, act superior, and can be angry, biting, and over-reactive. Romantics wallow in their feelings and can be depressing to be around. Givers complain that Romantics give too much energy to processing their feelings. A Two can be critical of a Four's style and melancholy. On the other hand, Romantics, according to Baron and Wagele, have trouble with Givers because they are seen as being too positive, nice, and smiley, and also because Givers are too ready to offer advice when the Romantic just wants to be listened to and understood.

In our survey, Romantics reported that Givers were among the personality types they most struggled with "Twos seem false – they don't share the same values. They have too much emphasis on appearance." "Too much attention on me. Neediness." "I don't need you as much as you think I do." "I don't trust Givers' motives and boundaries and neediness." "I feel the manipulation destroys my being able to trust them; they seem like liars." These are rather pointed comments given by the Fours, yet Ron (a Two himself) admits that given the "right" or "wrong" situation, and especially if he were under extreme stress, he could possibly do all of the things the Fours describe above. As we stated earlier, Twos and Fours share a connecting line on the enneagram diagram, meaning they have traits in common and can empathize with each other. This line can allow us to see the shadow side in the person at the other end. Under stress Romantics can travel down the connecting line and take on the shadow side of the Giver, with the very same negative qualities.

Importance versus uniqueness – core characteristics

Early on, the Giver and the Romantic can fit like lock and key: the Two devotes endless energy to pleasing the Four, and the Four soaks up the attention and eats up the Two's message that, "You are the only one for me, you are special; you are unique." The Two feels important and loves the Four's appreciation and positive feedback. But these same qualities – the Two's proclivity for giving and need for importance and the Four's desire for uniqueness — eventually tend to cause the most common "classic fight" for this pairing. According to Eileen, a Two with a Social subtype, here is one version of what can happen:

My family is too involved in our lives, but it is hard for me to pull back. They call too much, come to visit too much, walk into our home and use things without asking, and make judgments on our lives. I didn't see how that was bad because it was how I was raised. I could not set boundaries. My husband Bob wanted to know that he, and not the rest of the family, was Number One. We work on this all the time, try to set limits on phone calls, and visits, and it is better, but I have to watch all the time and pull back when I am out there too much.

Bob, Eileen's Type Four husband complains, "You don't pay enough attention to me. You are always on the phone, and your family is too involved in our lives." Another Giver, Lisa, described a very similar situation,

This is the second marriage for us, and we each have children from previous marriages. My children lived with me when Carl and I got married (and continued to until they were grown). Entering into our relationship, Carl was jealous of the attention and love I gave my kids and would do things just to get attention – like a child himself! Now, after 25 year of marriage, he does the same thing with my adult children, friends, even family! I made it plain (and it was not easy for me to do this) that I would always choose my kids over him until they were on their own, their needs would always come first, and he was making an ass of himself. Now I just say, "What do you really want?" "Why are you acting like this when you know it doesn't work on me?" Carl pouts, thinks it over and then can express what it is he really needs – most often it's that he was jealous and feeling second-fiddle. My Two personality has me make everyone special while his Four nature makes him the Only One!

Lisa, the Giver, has come to realize the dance that she and Carl have learned to do and recognizes her role in perpetuating her current complaints:

A key thing that in the past helped our relationship thrive has been my ability to make my Four husband feel so special, unique, chosen, and supported. But one outcome is that now when he walks into the room, Carl doesn't pay

attention to what I'm doing. He just starts talking without checking to see if I'm reading, on the computer, or have my attention elsewhere. He just assumes my attention is always on him. I've trained him that way. As I've become more aware of my propensity to ignore my own wants and needs and put others' first (and the associated costs), I have seen that Carl always wants and needs to be First.

As mentioned earlier, the Giver and the Romantic are shadows of one another - they have similar issues. The Romantic needs to feel unique; the Giver needs to feel important. That's quite a volatile combination. An exacerbating factor is the Romantic's predisposition to melancholy and the Giver's tendency to take it personally. Judy, a Two, describes this dynamic in her relationship with Frank, "The attraction to melancholy originally felt like being with me wasn't enough for him to remain happy. I used to feel angry and abandoned when he would go into his melancholy place." Drama and longing are part and parcel of the Romantic's personality. It's as though whatever the Giver does, it's never quite enough for the Four. It's difficult for the Two not to take this personally. A Giver who responded to our survey explained why he couldn't see himself in a romantic relationship with a Two: "I could never be enough, and that would really wreck my pride. If she said, 'If only you were different, if only you were more, whatever.' I would say, 'I'm out of here! I'll find someone else who will find me 'more.'"

When the Giver feels he can't meet the Romantic's needs, his pride is wounded. The Four says, "I need to feel unique, and you're not making me feel special." The Two says, "After all I've done for you!" and the subtext is, "You're not making me feel very important." This is the genesis of the classic fight. Commitment and humility have vanished at this point.

What makes the situation worse is another characteristic many Twos have -- their own form of push-pull. Even if the Four appears satisfied, the Two might lose interest once someone has been won over. For some Givers, the juice is in the chase, in winning over someone who is hard to win over, as is the case with many Romantics. When it comes to dating and relationships, most people first spot someone they are attracted to and then begin to date him or her, hoping that things will work out long term. For a Giver though, it is a little bit backwards, especially if his or her need to feel important to someone as well as to avoid the possibility of being rejected is paramount. The Two will start the dating process with a focus primarily on winning the other person over, and then once successful it's as if at the end of the pursuit, the question is, "I really do want to be with this person, don't I?" It's like that statement, "Be careful for what you wish for, you just might get it." Below is an example of a conversation that illustrates the Two's courting behavior:

The Giver: "I really want to be with Judy."
A close friend: "But you told me you really didn't like Judy when you first met her."
The Two: "Well…I didn't really want to be with Judy until I found out she didn't want to be with me."
The friend: "It sounds like you just want to see if you can make her want you and then if you do get her to want you, does that mean you'll no longer really want to be with her?"
The Two: "Maybe…I guess I'll decide whether I really want to be with her after I find out she really wants to be with me."

It's easy to condemn the Giver as being horribly manipulative. But in fact, this is just his coping strategy, his attempt to protect his heart and avoid rejection. Also, because the Two's heart is very malleable, he is prone to fall in love with the other person while trying to get her to want him. This then leaves him vulnerable to being rejected just like everyone else. If indeed the Two does lose interest in his partner at the end of the pursuit, the chase can then begin all over again. He could go outside the relationship and try to win over other people, especially if he is of the Social or Self-preservation subtype. He may focus his attention on other hard-to-get people or toward important persons with whom there might be a payoff in recognition or favors. The Four will then complain, "Where did all the attention go? I thought I was unique and special, and now I'm no longer getting the same kind of attention I was earlier."

Insightful Twos recognize that they, too, are ambivalent. The Two can be so focused on winning the person over that once the relationship is attained, he or she might start to question the desirability of the relationship and its emotional intensity. Lisa, a Two, describes this experience as "the push-pull of thriving in an abundance of love and attention – while at the same time struggling to be freed up lest I suffocate!" She advises younger Twos, "First, get to know yourself; then, don't 'give yourself away' to your partner. Beware of the chameleon tendency."

Challenges of the Giver

Twos frequently neglect their own needs and desires. Lisa, a Giver, admits, "I try to figure out his needs and then shape my behavior to fit that, instead of trying to figure out what I want." Another Two, Judy, wrote: "I bought the tendency to martyr myself by over-giving and settling for little in return until I would get angry and confused and not like myself." She reported that her Four husband advised, "You need to think of yourself and not give so much time and energy to others. What do YOU want, not what do you think I want." This is good advice from the Four.

The changeability of the Giver is a red flag for the Romantic, who intensely values "authenticity" and may see the altering that Givers can do at times as a lack of emotional depth and authenticity. Also, all this caring and giving by the Two may feel smothering to the Four, and perhaps even like manipulation, not like deep abiding love. Judy, a Giver, wrote:

Keep in mind that when a giver meets a taker it feels so right. You are a giver and need to remember in a healthy relationship there is give and take on each side. Beware of narcissists: they will be very attractive to you because you can do what you do best, which is to give. They will do what they do best, which is to take, and you will eventually be depleted and angry.

Challenges of the Romantic

Fours are attracted to drama and excitement. A Two, Eileen, had this to say about her Four partner and the drama: "When things get too calm, Bob messes things up just for something a bit different." Fours can be intensity junkies. Romantics at their core have abandonment issues. Abandonment can feel like death, and what better way to fend off feelings of death but to create drama and intensity, even if it means "messing things up."

Twos and Fours together can make for a very heart-filled connection. As in all relationships, they can be good teachers to one another. Their core characteristics of importance and uniqueness need to be diluted with a big dose of humility. Truly committing to one another will erase the common push-pull tendency, especially when the possibility of rejection arises. Staying centered and being in the moment will allow each of them to experience the depth of intimacy and connection that they have both longed for.

Exercises for the Giver-Romantic Couple

The following questions highlight the classic issues that challenge the Two-Four couple:

Both types in this pairing do their own version of push/pull. The Four's push/pull is a repeating cycle consisting of desire, acquisition, disappointment, and rejection. This pattern can strongly affect the Two's pride and fear of rejection. On the other hand, the Two's push/pull has more to do with withdrawal, a withdrawal of their giving or a withdrawal of their presence in general. This push/pull can be especially effective on Romantics, who have a natural sensitivity to things that are missing or unavailable. As you can see, these two Types can get into sneaky, vicious power struggles with each other.

- Discuss each of your versions of push/pull with your partner and the effects it has on each of you. How do you think your push/pull keeps you from feeling vulnerable and at the same time blocks you from true intimacy? What effect do you think truly committing to one another would have on the power struggles and the relationship overall?

This pairing shares a connecting line on the Enneagram diagram, meaning that each will see a part of themselves in the other. This can be good if you are trying to encourage in yourself a characteristic that the other one has. At other times though, Twos and Fours will get on each other's nerves. Romantics will find themselves irritated at the flattery and manipulation of the Giver, and Givers will find themselves irritated at the drama and the recurrent unhappiness of the Four.

- How can you focus on the positives you each mirror to the other and enhance that particular characteristic in yourself? How can you work on the negatives of your personality that shows up in your partner's mirror – diminishing it in a way that is similar to how your partner holds it?

Both Twos and Fours are in the same Center, one that for the most part is about image and status. The Romantic feels unique and special while the Giver feels important and prideful. Both can collude to keep these personality characteristics going.

- How can the higher core aspects of your Type -- Humility for the Two and Higher Power (Original Source) for the Four -- diminish your negative personality characteristics and bring about a more spiritual approach overall?

CHAPTER TWENTY-SEVEN

The Giver-Observer (Two-Five) Couple

We work well together by discussing problems together - Gary brings the logic and I bring the heart to the table. It's a nice balance when we respect and value each other's position.
-- Nancy, a Two - in relationship with a Five

The Giver and Observer form a relationship of opposites, which can balance one another out when they respect and value each other. Givers indeed "bring the heart to the table," as they are in the Heart (emotional) triad or center on the enneagram diagram, whereas Observers – who are in the Head (mental) triad -- "bring logic" to the relationship. Givers move toward others, so are most commonly seen as extroverts, whereas Observers, with their contracted style, are usually thought of as the most introverted of all the types. Givers' lives are focused on other people; Observers require a lot of alone time. But when the relationship works, the good qualities of each member can balance the other and provide a combination that works very well. The biggest challenge for the Two-Five pair is that the Two's need for attention and desire to be with other people may clash with the Five's desire for privacy and space.

Positive aspects of the Giver-Observer relationship

The gifts that Twos give to their relationship, according to our survey respondents, included, a "genuine caring and devotion" to the relationship and to their partner, and "nurturing me." Anthony, an Observer, described his Two partner's giving behaviors in the following way: "Mark is caring and is willing to change his schedule to fit my needs. He's an excellent listener. He has a strong set of values." As you can see, Twos often put their own schedule on the back burner so as to meet the needs of their partner. Because Fives have a fear of scarcity, they will be intrigued by the Twos' generosity and general philosophy of "what's mine is yours." A Giver's social and communication skills make him or her a natural to represent the couple in public, letting the Observer monitor rather than actively participate. The Two will also most likely get a kick out of teaching the Five how to socialize.

Several Fives described their gifts to a relationship as: "not being demanding of the other person" and "My ability to sit back and try to understand what's happening; my delayed reactions." Judy, a Giver married 37 years to an Observer, related:

Frank is patient, solid, reliable, intelligent, has a sense of humor, is trustworthy, and independent. He accepts all my new explorations, and understands and supports them, but doesn't join me in them. He helps me and takes of me using his many different kinds of expertise – computer support, repairing things, taking care of cars, making household repairs and maintaining our garden, and financial support.

Nancy, a partner of an Observer, describes him as, "calm, analytical problem-solving. Steady, attentive." These characteristics can be very soothing to an overly emotional Giver. In fact, Talia, a Giver, stated this about her former spouse Eric, an Observer: "He was a great mirror for my issues." One of the responsibilities we have in a relationship is to reflect our partner. It is as if, metaphorically, we hold up a mirror and say to our partner, is this how you want to show up in relationship and the world in general? Because Givers and Observers are profoundly opposite, the contrast allows each of them to mirror each other even more clearly.

The Observer's detachment will make it clear to the Giver how deep is her attachment. Fives can provide a steadying influence on the Twos, encouraging them to look inward more than is usual for Twos. They will marvel at a Five's independence, objectivity and detachment. Perhaps they can't believe that a person can actually be that detached in the world when there are so many needy people. Ultimately, the healthy Giver-Observer relationship is one in which Givers teach Observers about attachment, while Observers teach Givers about detachment.

Challenges of the Giver-Observer couple:

In our survey, Fives listed the Two as one of the types they most struggle with. Here are their reasons: "Doesn't leave me alone." "Too needy, doesn't allow me enough space." "I can see through the nurturing and doting to the basic self-serving." "I don't want them to intrude on my needs." "I have seen their meanness too often." Observers, as these comments show, tell it like it is. For many Givers, the quotes above hit the nail on the head when it comes to some of their core issues as well as some of their annoying behaviors.

Interestingly, Twos listed Fives also as one of the types they struggle with the most. They explained," She stays too distant." "I can't get the 'connection' I'm after – I have to try too hard." "Always withdrawing – barrier to emotional intimacy." "Going out of contact, not willing to invest in the relationship, avoiding confrontations." As you can see, the Givers' complaints have a lot to do with their need for relationship and intimacy – something they feel Observers withhold from them.

These complaint lists by both types make clear what are the recurrent issues between these two very different personalities, one of whom strongly seeks connection, the other a seeker of space and fearful of intrusiveness. Twos' biggest complaints are that they don't get enough attention from Fives. The Two tends to react by pursuing the Five, who will then withdraw. "The more I tried, the farther he retreated," wrote Talia, whose marriage to a Five ended after 18 years. She recognized that they fell into a vicious circle, adding, "The more he rejected me, the more demanding and needy I became." On their side, Fives can see Twos as intrusive, impinging on their space. Cindy, an Observer, complained about her (former) Giver partner, "Francisco was too smothering, too needy. He wanted to be together too much. He wanted too much of my time and energy and space." With their high need for validation and interaction with their partner, the Two can be seen by the Five as a "high-maintenance spouse," who leaves him or her feeling emotionally and physically drained.

One challenge is based on the Two's need for other people and the Five's need for solitude. Talia, the Two who ended her relationship with a Five, writes, "I would entertain, Eric would be in his room. It was impossible to resolve as he felt I was 100 percent responsible for all problems, and he was fine as it was." No matter what type we are, it is important that if we are in relationship, we need to allow ourselves to be influenced. Nothing breaks a power struggle between two people better than being receptive to the other's point of view. When we think that we have cornered the market on how life is to be lived, that is when we've gone down the wrong path. The enneagram at core is about learning and accepting the other eight different approaches to the world and to benefit from that understanding.

"I needed time alone while he needed more time together," explained Cindy, a Five, about her former relationship with a Two. Her chief complaint about Francisco was, "You are too smothering, too needy," while his about her was, "You never show emotions. You don't touch me enough." She admitted, "I need a lot of space, and I have a tendency to withdraw to regain energy." Another Observer in our survey, Anthony, reports that he and his partner of eight years live in separate homes. Both of them are retired professionals, and it should be noted that many older people prefer to continue living separately anyway.

This issue looms particularly large when the Observer is of the Self-Preservation subtype, which accentuates many of their personality traits. Judy, a Giver of the Sexual subtype, wrote about her decades-long marriage to a Self-Pres Observer :

Frank is too reclusive, too uncommunicative, does not express feelings and emotions, and doesn't like to talk. Worst of all, he doesn't like touch, holding, and snuggling – either to give or to get – and these are extremely important to me.

I need more communication and physical touch and physical expressions of affection while he needs quiet, routine, and home as a "safe haven." He doesn't have "fights" with me or complain except in minor ways; I capitulate in a lot of things, go along with the quiet, the routine, etc., and I find my opportunities for growth elsewhere. I have not resolved getting the touch or expressions of affection I need. I get by with daily dinner-table conversation, which is an important way for us to come together, even though the talk is almost always about issues in our work or about our son and other people and never about ourselves. I no longer expect much in the way of deep conversation, but he seems to understand in a general way the paths of growth that I am pursuing, and accepts them without participating. He has a full and rich life at work that he tells me about; maybe he has nothing left for home except to recover from the fatigue of work.

Reading Judy's words, most of us can relate to how difficult relationships can be. We want them to work so much, to have our wants and needs met, to be loved, yet if we have linked up with a different Type and possibly even a different subtype than our own, we are living with someone who is different from us all the time. We like to think that even people who are unlike us approach the world similarly. Yet, as the enneagram teaches us, different types of people have a different view of the world. So what does Judy recommend? Her advice to a younger Giver is: "Don't expect the person you get together with to change in any basic way. Don't expect one person to fulfill all your needs and wants."

When we stop accepting our partner's core personality and the various behaviors that go with it, the relationship is in serious trouble. This is not to say, though, that we cannot challenge our partner to grow and transform within the boundaries of their type. Nancy, another Giver, describes how she and her husband Gary have worked out this classic dilemma:

We both came from previous long-term marriages. "The Five's need for privacy clashes with a Social Two's desire to entertain" is a classic way we would have clashed. Learning about the enneagram has helped immensely. We can see each other's viewpoint and appreciate our differences. We resolve dilemmas that come up by recognizing that our styles are different and reminding ourselves of the differences. I know I acquiesce more, but that's my nature. I've learned not to default to this position and to ask myself what I need. It's hard, but I'm getting better at it (Happier too!)

You can see how beneficial the enneagram is not only for recognizing the other's primary personality type, so that you know what you are getting, but also to reach a level of acceptance of the differences. Nancy, who writes that her relationship is going very well, describes the lessons she learned;

I had to get used to Gary's pulling away to have solitary time alone. I took it personally at first. Now I know it's just what he needs, not rejection. I will never be 100 percent okay with it.

When Observers withdraw, Givers tend to feel rejected. For a Two-Five relationship to thrive, the Two has to learn not to take it personally, to recognize that the Five's need for alone time is an integral part of who he is and doesn't mean he doesn't love the Two.

Observers have another personality trait that may cause a Giver to feel rejected -- their tendency to get involved in their studies or their projects. In social situations, they tune out unless their particular interests are the subjects of discussion. At home, when the Two tries to converse about other matters, the Five spaces, out, not hearing what the Two is saying.

Observers place a high value on competence. If they feel their partner is lacking in some area, they can become critical, even demeaning. Often they have no problem "telling it like it is," even if their words hurt the partner. Twos, whose chief problem is pride, can feel humiliated by the Five's criticism. Talia (a Two) wrote that, according to her former husband, "I can never do anything right." Nancy, another Two, wrote that her husband Gary's "stubbornness and attachment to his perspective" was a real challenge. Once the Observer has studied and assessed a situation, he is likely to remain attached to his conclusion or his point of view, and become quite arrogant

Givers are people who find it much easier to give than to receive. This may seem paradoxical, as they can be sponges for appreciation and positive reinforcement. But the feedback they seek is for their ability to satisfy other people's needs. Twos tend to ignore themselves and to be overly dependent on attention and rewards from their partner. An important personal growth goal for them is to learn to identify their needs and ask to have them met. When queried about what advice he would give to a younger Giver, Lance wrote, "Stay independent and watch out for your own well-being." Nancy echoed this, "Be sure to learn how to practice self-care. Putting everyone else first is one of the biggest traps you'll struggle with." This is good advice for the Giver, which brings us back to why Twos are attracted to Fives.

Exercises for the Giver-Observer couple

The following questions highlight the classic issues that challenge the Two-Five couple:

Some say that this pairing is about "attachment" vs. "detachment." The Two needs to learn about "detachment" whereas the Five needs to learn about "attachment." The Two can become needy and can pull strongly for emotional contact. In contrast, Fives can become almost phobic and can contract and withdraw from other people. One Observer, paired with a Giver, put it this way – "I needed time alone, while he needed more time together."

- How does your relationship deal with the varying emotional contact needs of the Two and the Five? How do you not take the your partner's approach personally – intrusive and smothering to the Five and depriving and rejecting to the Two?

Givers' identity can get bound up in their emotional connection and their need to help. When an Observer contracts and withdraws and leaves the Giver alone, it can provide the time that the Two can use to reflect on wants and needs and to answer the "Who am I?" questions. On the other hand, Fives can use the Two's abundance of contact and feelings as a way to become more familiar with feelings with less discomfort.

- How do you each use your unique personalities, with their differing approaches toward emotional contact, to find ways to grow personally?

On a spiritual level, the Giver's connection to their essence can be attained through using the Observer's withdrawing and contracting as a catalyst. The Observer's contact with their essence can be attained through using the Giver's abundance of contact and feelings as a catalyst.

- How can you use your partner's gifts that they bring to the relationship as a way to evolve spiritually?

CHAPTER TWENTY-EIGHT

The Giver-Detective (Two-Six) Couple

Whenever I have had an idea for growth in my work or profession, she has always encouraged me through the fears I have surrounding change.
-- Ronald, a Detective

Givers can help Detectives overcome their doubts and make them feel safe and comfortable, giving them the real warmth and caring they have always longed for. Detectives can encourage and support Givers to be their own inspiring figure. Sixes are in the "mental" or "head" triad or Center, meaning they spend a lot of time thinking about things, evaluating and questioning. Twos can also help Sixes lighten up. Twos need to be encouraged to do more internal focusing and question who they really are. What are they really feeling? Sixes can shine in a crisis (facing a real crisis is often less fearful than imagined difficulties) and can support their partner in getting through a difficult situation. Both value each other's sense of humor.

Giver and Detective is a pairing of two very different people, Mars and Venus. This characterization doesn't necessarily refer to gender differences between men and women and their difficulty communicating with one another, but rather about enneagram personality types that are not wings of each other, have no connecting lines, and belong to different centers.

Despite these differences, this partnership is rather common. (As an aside, we believe all of the combinations can have a successful relationship as long as they are mature, healthy people of their type and as long they relate to one another in a conscious way). But if it is true that the Giver and the Detective do come from largely different worlds, and despite all the challenges that this combination creates, why are they attracted to each other?

One explanation is that their coping strategies mesh. The early childhood message for most Detectives is that the world is a dangerous place, and the way to deal with that is to find a person or organization you can be loyal to, someone who will protect you and keep you safe. The Giver fears rejection and deals with their fear primarily by giving and helping, hoping that this will tie them to the other person out of the other's need. The initial emotional agreement is that the Giver will help the Detective with their fears and insecurities in the world while the Six will make the Two feel important. The loyalty of the Six will also make the Two feel secure or almost guarantee that the Six is not going to leave.

Positive characteristics include: The Giver suppresses wants and needs and the growing resentments that come with always giving, but he or she avoids expressing anger, and the Detective will often keep the relationship from going off track by confronting the Giver. Also, pride doesn't allow Givers to experience much fear, but they usually expect that doing good in the world will bring good back. This belief in universal benevolence can rub off on the Detective and help him or her to trust. A Giver can fall in love with a Detective's mind, and the Detective can become curious about the emotions and relationships that the Giver freely discusses. This is a pairing with the head and heart coming together. Head types (Five, Six, and Seven) are often encouraged to access their hearts and see what that tells them, whereas heart types (Two, Three and Four) are usually encouraged to use their head and logic, especially regarding relationships. Twos and Sixes in relationship can come to appreciate and experience foreign aspects of themselves.

Not surprisingly, the Giver-Detective couple might gripe at each other about their differing worldviews. The Six is in his or her head too much and doesn't care about the relationship. The Two is too focused and needs to give it a rest. The main problem in this pairing, however, is the Two's tendency to take on an authority role and the Six's rebellion against that. The Two may project that he or she knows what is best for both of them, while the Six will question why that would be.

Our surveys gave us information about several Giver-Detective couples. Gerald, a Detective with a Self-preservation subtype, said what he brought to his relationship was, "I honored my commitments when things were not going well," — a reflection of his loyalty. About his Giver wife, he related, "She kept a positive focus on how our relationship is going." He also valued that she was "compassionate and caring, sensitive to feelings." Alex, a Giver, commented about his Detective wife, "She brought intellectual stimulation and the ability to ask the hard questions, to not let things drift; a sense of loyalty."

Alex described himself: "I think that I am good at putting my own needs on the back burner (in a positive way) and making my partner feel truly cared about and honored."

Challenges of the Giver-Detective relationship

A big challenge for the Giver-Detective couple relates to the Six's doubts about the Two's motivation and giving. Twos can give to receive. Sixes have difficulty trusting and may doubt the Two's sincerity. In our survey, Detectives chose the Giver as one of the personality types they most struggle with. Their reasons included: "They seem false – they don't share the same values. Too much emphasis on appearance." "I feel the manipulation destroys my being able to trust them --like liars." They also distrusted the Two's desire to help: "They put too much attention on me." "I don't need you as much as you think I do."

Detectives need frequent reassurance in their relationship. It's hard for them to accept things at face value –they keep questioning and analyzing. Gerald, a Detective, recognized being "a person who is suspicious about others' motivations (not just my partner) when it serves no purpose." When a Giver does something for him, the Detective may wonder what he or she is trying to get. Alex, the Giver, complained about his former wife, Elena: "You always question everything. You never let anything go. Nothing is ever enough. You are a bottomless pit with regard to reassurance." Givers pride themselves on their ability to figure out others' needs and fulfill them, so they may become frustrated and angry at their apparent lack of success with Detectives. Twos' pride is injured when they seem unable to "fix" the Six's insecurity. At worst, Twos may decide they might be better off with a different partner, one who can appreciate all the things someone does for them.

What the Detective asks for can be difficult for the image-type Giver, who may not know the answer to, "Who am I and what do I really want and need?"

If a Six becomes needy, and a Two tries to fix or to take care of her needs, the former may see the latter as the authority, react negatively and push her away. Sixes have a classic dependence-independence conflict. They seek a protective figure, but as soon as they get one, they anticipate a bad outcome and react negatively. The perplexed Giver will say, "What happened? I thought you wanted me to help you!" The Detective may reply, "Well… who appointed you God?" The exasperated Giver, probably heading toward type Eight (the Leader), may then state angrily, "Just tell me what you want from me!"

Sixes tend to second, third, and fourth-guess themselves and end up paralyzed. Ronald, a Detective, related "I have fear-based decision making." The following story is a classic Giver-Detective scenario in which the Detective becomes immobilized with so much self-questioning about what to give her partner that she ends up giving nothing, while the Giver feels confused and unloved because he expected a gift:

A Two man, Jim, who prided himself on giving to his Six wife, Julianne, would always bring back a special gift to her when he returned from business trips, so as to let her know how much he cared and thought about her while he was away. He recalled feeling hurt on one occasion when Julianne went away on a trip by herself and returned empty-handed. She noted his disappointment, and asked him if he was upset at her for not bringing him back something. Jim replied, "Well . . . it's not about the gift, the gift just symbolizes that you care about me and thought about me while you were away."

Julianne responded defensively, "You don't know how many times I thought about you and what you would like and not like, how many stores I went into, and how much time I spent trying to find you the right present. But every time I would think of something, I would question how you would probably not like it or think that I didn't put enough thought into it. You just don't know how much time I spent going around and around in my mind about the whole situation!"

Jim struggled with understanding where Julianne was coming from. From his perspective, it was the results that counted. As a Giver, he had had plenty of practice getting people gifts, and he wondered what the big deal was. You just intuitively know what people want and need, and you give it to them. What's so hard about that? He felt unloved, that Julianne most likely didn't really care about him if she didn't know what to get him. Julianne, on the other hand, didn't understand why Jim didn't realize how difficult this was for her! All of her efforts went unappreciated.

This couples' story is a simple one, but it points out the true difference between Types. They are motivated by different core issues and have different needs and fears. If you are a Two, imagine that you are a Six in this couple scenario. If you are a Six, imagine yourself as a Two. Allow yourself to feel how invested you are in your position and the outcome of the discussion. Imagine yourself blocking out any other way to see the world other than in the way you see it.

Endless analysis

A Detective's desire to analyze and discuss everything, to ask many questions, can wear down a Giver. Six tends to keep testing Two's loyalty, pushing hard to see how much the partner will take. They may ask, "What if I had an affair – would you still be there for me?" To the Two, who's already working overtime to be reassuring and loving, the Six may appear to be a bottomless pit of needs. Sixes who act this way need to recognize the damaging effect it can have on a relationship.

Aggression

At times, the Detective can view others with an "us versus them" approach and the spouse as "me versus you." Alex (a Giver) recalled telling his Detective wife, "We may disagree, but I'm not the enemy! I'm really on your side." Some Detectives, especially counterphobics, tend not only to question, but also to do it in an assertive, aggressive style (in tone, body language and choice of words) that can come across as an attack. A Detective might be completely unaware of his style of discussion, and even when it is pointed out, have no awareness of what the other person is talking about.

Feelings

Certain other Sixes might avoid overt conflict, preferring to withdraw, but perhaps express their displeasure with sarcasm. Gerald, a Six, reported that his Two wife complained, "You're always sarcastic and/or withdrawn. You avoid conflict." Ronald, also a Detective, wrote that his wife Michelle complained about his lack of sensitivity to feelings. Some Sixes may be more comfortable intellectualizing things rather than allowing or recognizing feelings. On the other hand, Sixes can have a similar complaint about the Two. Gerald wrote, "She's more comfortable fixing things rather than listening to me."

Recognizing one's needs

To the Detective, Givers can appear as possessive and needy. Actually, Givers often neglect their own needs as they focus on those of others. Type Two Alex described his "inability to state my wants and needs and to focus on myself as well as my partner. Filling myself up with her instead of myself." As part of the "Image" or "heart" triad, Givers tend to be concerned about making a good impression on others. Ronald, a Detective, wrote about his wife, "Michelle cares too much what others think of her. She's not in touch with her own feelings. When stressed, she becomes like an Eight (the Leader), very judgmental."

Exercises for the Giver-Detective couple

The following questions highlight the classic issues that challenge the Two-Six pairing:

A Giver reported that on a hectic, got-up-late Monday morning, he rushed out of the house for an important meeting at his office...kissing his Detective wife hurriedly before leaving. About halfway to his office, his cell phone rang with his wife on the other end sounding angry and dejected. She stated critically, "I didn't like how you kissed me this morning. Is something wrong?" The Giver, now preparing mentally for his meeting and so somewhat distracted said, "Oh, I'm sorry honey...no, no, no...I was just rushing for this meeting...I'll talk to you later...got to run...okay?" She immediately called him back and caught him just as he was getting out of his car. She stated, "I didn't like how you hung up on me...I didn't think it was very respectful." Soon their conversation took on a yelling and blaming quality.

For some of you, the above exchange may have an almost comical aspect to it. Unfortunately, this scenario can tap into core issues for each of the types. The Six's fear can take on an accusatory, attacking quality, while the Two's pride can get wounded to the point of ultimate deflation. Done time and again, and done enough, wounds and damage will take the relationship down.

- This couple must have a preventative tool in place to keep the damage control in check. Committing to a non-violent communication model might not only save but enhance this relationship. How do you think vowing to no blaming, no criticizing, no diagnosing -- as well as no demands placed on the partner will affect the relationship overall? Try it for thirty days and see if it doesn't make a believer out of you.
- This relationship must stay away from the parent/child dynamic. Share times being the authority, or be the authority in your own life, taking responsibility for all of your actions.
- Be teachers to one another. Sixes, with their innate sense of humility, can help Twos with their pride. Twos need to let them. Twos with their innate sense of genuine helping and giving plus seeing the positive in others, can help Sixes with their fear of others and their learning to trust.

CHAPTER TWENTY-NINE

The Giver-Adventurer (Two-Seven) Couple

The Giver and the Adventurer often find each other very attractive, which is not surprising since both are optimistic, enthusiastic and sociable, with many interests that provide zest for a relationship. The Giver expects excitement and passion, while the Adventurer anticipates fun, so the relationship will likely be lighthearted, stimulating and exciting, in addition to typically complex and challenging.

Sevens and Twos both thrive on receiving attention and where, at least in the beginning, each wants to give that to the other. Being with a Seven can feel as if a powerful spotlight is shining on you. They become infatuated with a new person, seeing him or her as an intrinsic adventure. Adventurers hang on to the other's every word, fascinated by the partner's previous experiences. This can make Givers feel important — which is what they look for in a relationship. The Adventurer can also feel special being on the receiving end of the attentiveness the Giver is so good at providing. The Seven appreciates the unconditional love and acceptance of the Two, which helps alleviate the Seven's natural sensitivity to criticism. Overall, this pairing falls into what relationship experts label as a "pedestal relationship," where early on, each partner puts the other up on a pedestal.

Sevens have many interests and talents, and Twos enjoy entering their world, going along for the ride and being supportive. Sevens can keep Twos interested, and Twos want to help the other fulfill his or her dreams. If the Adventurer has problems, the Giver can help with getting in touch with feelings. Before meeting the Two, a Seven may have been reluctant to face problems and feelings. But finally, sensing the Two's helping nature and non-judgmental mindset, the Adventurer may be willing to try to resolve unfinished business. Like a scuba diver, he or she will dive under the surface and into the psyche, pulling up memories that have long been buried because of avoidance of pain and suffering. The Two will patiently hold the Seven's hand all the while, until he or she emerges. Because Sevens aren't known for wallowing in their problems, this won't take long.

Marjorie, a Two married for 21 years to Roy, a Seven (with an Eight wing), wrote that they work well together to meet a challenge:

. . .whenever we're able to bring both sets of our strengths together to bear on a problem. Roy [the Seven] has a superb analytical mind, is generous and very tactful. He has no lines to the feeling types and lacks strength in just listening and being there for someone without thinking he must solve the problem. As a Two, I have no lines to the thinking types but superior insight and strengths into people's needs and emotions. I can easily just be with emotional pain. We are both generous, intelligent, and relate very well to a wide variety of people.

In this coupleship, the Adventurer analyzes and problem solves while the Giver tends to the emotional aspects of the situation. Despite the absence of connecting lines on the enneagram diagram, they are considered look-alikes, personality styles with similar behaviors driven by dissimilar motivations, because they both really want people to be happy.

Our survey taught us about several Two-Seven relationships. When asked about the ways they helped the relationship thrive, the Givers replied, "Being a really considerate partner who is deeply tuned into my husband's needs." "Having a caring supportive attitude toward my partner's development and self-discovery. I bring humor, caring, insight about people, thoughtfulness, reliability, and fun."

The Twos wrote that their Seven partners brought "bright enthusiasm for our happiness" and "Positive attitude, uninhibited, and outgoing." "He's sexy, highly intelligent, generous, respectful, knows what he wants and goes after it. He is an Alpha male, which I find very attractive." "Sevens champion people in their own way, recognizing people's strengths and wanting them to actualize those gifts so that they bring more to the world and have more."

Challenges of the Giver-Adventurer relationship

Givers in love may feel that they can live on love, and that this will suffice to solve all problems. In the film *When a Man Loves a Woman*, Alice, an alcoholic Adventurer in early recovery (played by Meg Ryan), tries to explain to her husband Michael, a Giver (played by Andy Garcia) about some of her challenges staying sober. Michael's less-than-understanding response is to seductively suggest they go away to a romantic spot for the weekend to forget their troubles. Adventurers think similarly – let's just have fun, let's not have any pain. So the Giver-Adventurer couple may collude to avoid addressing serious problems. This is also a couple who both treasure the romantic high and wish to prolong this stage in their relationship. For Twos, the way to be a couple is to just be loving; Sevens avoid dealing with problems because they fear pain and suffering.

If the Two partner becomes frustrated in the relationship, it will likely be because he feels that his partner has taken him off the pedestal and dimmed the spotlight that warmed him early on. If the Seven becomes frustrated, it likely will be because the Two wants to hang on to the original status quo, whereas the Seven becomes bored by the daily routine and limitations of the relationship.

Givers become frustrated because, even if they point out a problem, the Adventurer may prefer to ignore it. Marjorie, a Giver (whose Adventurer husband Roy has an Eight [Leader] wing and is therefore more in touch with his anger) wrote,

I think the Type-related issue that we've confronted most often is Roy's reluctance or refusal to face difficult and/or painful issues. Problems cannot be solved until they are acknowledged as real. He has strong resistance to recognize and talk about hard issues until anger sets in. He strongly avoids any kind of potential emotional pain, reframing genuine problems into non-problems. I made futile attempts to point out real areas of difficulty in our children that Roy just doesn't want to see or deal with. His avoidance of pain and genuine difficulties, to either rationalize or deny reality, has sometimes been very painful.

Paul, a Two who is a counselor, had a similar assessment of his Seven girlfriend whom he dated for two years: "She never really wanted to go very deep to solve things. She wasn't motivated to do the work of relationship, especially if it wasn't very interesting or exciting." Sevens prefer taking action and problem solving rather than just sitting and listening to a recounting of their partner's daily issues. Another Two, a psychologist named Jay, reported the problem below and how he and his wife solved it:

Initially in our relationship, I (the Two) wanted to complain at home after work about work-related conflicts. Rebecca, (the Seven), didn't want to listen to my "whining" and said, "So what are you going to do about it?" instead of just

listening to me. This created problems for us: She didn't want to hear negatives; I wanted her to listen. The enneagram really helped – just knowing the types allows us to get past this natural conflict. Now I announce when I want to complain and Rebecca listens attentively for five minutes.

Givers also complain that Adventurers, who live in their head rather than their heart, may not offer as much affection and nurturing as the Giver would like, and the feeling of importance they need in the relationship is lacking. For a Giver, if one of the primary reasons to be in relationship is to gain the love of the other, the idea of being rejected, abandoned or just losing the love in general is distressing. Twos' basic fear is rejection. They give to other people so that they won't be rejected, but instead they'll be needed.

The following statements most likely reflect the Two's sensitivity to rejection and/or the Seven's desire for stimulation. Paul, a Two, complained about his Seven girlfriend, Ellen: "You always have to talk to everybody." Her flirting, by projecting a feeling that she was uncommitted to him, that she would just fly away one day, disturbed him. He said, "We referred to her as the 'butterfly.' She was easily distracted. There was a lack of loyalty. She focused too much on herself. She was easily bored. She had a fear of pain or fear of being deprived."

Givers also struggle with what they consider the Adventurers' lack of discernment. The Adventurer wants to do many things with many people, whereas the Giver wants to feel special. The Giver's plea to the Adventurer often is, "Just talk to <u>me!</u>" Rosanne, a Giver, explained, "I over focus on my partner's moods and needs and not enough on my own needs. As a Sexual subtype, I want more one-on-one time than my Social Seven partner. I have an unconscious habit of doing things for my partner and then being resentful that I'm not more appreciated and loved by her."

Givers have difficulty expressing their own needs, which makes it harder for Sevens to discern what they want. Marjorie, a Two, wrote,

My challenge has been the inability to honestly identify my own needs and convey them to my husband – to ask for what I need. Although as I've gotten older (and hopefully wiser and more integrated), being direct and standing my own ground about things I feel strongly about has sometimes provoked upsetting arguments. . . I still have difficulty in directly communicating thoughts and feelings about important issues that I know will trigger my husband's anger or strong disagreement – I want to please too much.

The Givers recognized that they should work on expressing their needs. A Two's advice to a younger Giver in relationship included, "Develop an inner awareness and self-observer skills; use the relationship to develop your own self-love, not to impress or manipulate your partner; practice telling your partner your own needs, not just attending to the partner's needs." This man said his partner's chief complaint about him was, "You try to be too helpful." Another Giver wrote, "If I focused on my needs more consistently, I would not displace energy into 'helping' my partner with things she does not need my help with." Another woman wrote, "Know yourself and particularly your tendency to give until you're exhausted with the hope that your needs will eventually be met. Learn to be assertive and say "NO" when appropriate. Use anger and resentment as a key to your own unmet needs and do something about it yourself." Two Givers told stories about their Adventurer partners:

*My Seven partner bought me an expensive hot air balloon ride for Christmas, something I had no desire to do. I don't want a ride. **He** wanted it! He gave it to me so that he would get to do this. But, as usual, I thanked him and went along on the ride.*

Last night my Seven girlfriend Renee and I stopped at a gas station. I offered to pay for the gas and for a pack of cigarettes, gave Renee the money, and suggested that she go inside the store to get the pump turned on and buy the cigarettes while I filled up the tank. She went in and began to flirt with the clerk, a very attractive man. Wearing a low-cut blouse, she pointed to the cigarettes she wanted, leaning over the counter and exposing much of her breasts. It was raining out and Renee, in her flirting, forgot to ask the attendant to turn on the pump. Eventually she did. By the time Renee returned to the car, I was really upset! I see my role as giving to her, but all she does is flirt and keep me standing in the rain. I complained to her, but she blew it off, saying, "What's the big deal? Life is about having fun and taking care of yourself!" I guess she and I have different expectations in the relationship.

The first story illustrates that Adventurers tend to be self-focused. It's easy for them to assume that a gift that they would like to receive will please the partner. In the Giver's attempt to please, they make great efforts to get the partner exactly the right gift, one that the partner really wants.

In the second story, a discussion took place after the situation occurred. The Giver wanted the Adventurer to feel guilty about her actions and to recognize that she had indulged in a guilty pleasure and did not take her partner's needs into consideration. Her main argument was that she actually did give to her partner in her own way. She felt that we are all responsible for ourselves and that he should have taken better care of himself so that he didn't feel resentful and so that he would overall be happier in his life.

We tell this story because it points to the differences and challenges in the Giver-Adventurer pairing. Each defines giving and taking differently, each defines fun differently, each defines taking responsibility for one's life differently, and then finally, each defines relationship differently. These simple stories illustrate a major point of this book – that each of the Types are like different cultures with different traditions and rules. Each has a "truth" that they bring to the world and to relationships and each of us can learn, but at times these two very different worlds collide. Twos believe you should always "give" even at your own expense, whereas Sevens are convinced that you should "get" while the getting is good before being deprived. In the end, the Giver will feel taken advantage of, and the Adventurer will feel criticized and limited. With the insight that the enneagram brings, the two types will change and grow in ways where they can intimately and lovingly connect with each other.

In summary, the challenges of the Two-Seven pairing include that both may avoid difficult issues; that Twos need to make sure that they do not make Sevens their only project and wait at home for them; Twos may demand more attention than the Seven is comfortable giving, and the Seven may feel stifled by the Two's needs. Each of the pair needs to define commitment and determine how much outside attention they will ask for.

Exercises for the Giver-Adventurer couple

The following exercises highlight the classic issues that challenge the Two-Seven pairing:

The Two/Seven couple make for a rather "feel good" pairing. The Giver wants to help the Adventurer feel good about their potential plans as well as diminish any pain or fear they may be dealing with. The Adventurer likes to share their innate sense of fun and enthusiasm with their Two partner.

A Giver told us a story about his relationship with an Adventurer. One day this "fun couple" decided to go for a hot air balloon ride. The balloon took off and after reaching a high altitude, the pilot noticed that there was not even a slight breeze in the air. After staying aloft for several minutes, he decided to start bringing the balloon down. As the balloon approached the ground, the pilot challenged himself to land balloon in the very same footprints that they had taken off from, and in fact succeeded. This was quite unusual according to the pilot. The Giver who related this story said that the balloon ride served as a metaphor for him and the relationship –as if in many ways that the relationship had also landed in the very spot from which it had taken off.

- Try not to get caught up in the fun aspect of the relationship. Be sure and discuss long-term plans that include purpose and meaning. Both the Giver and the Adventurer need to assure that their plans for the future not only encompass fun but also include purpose and meaning. Otherwise the relationship will be like a hot air balloon ride that goes up and comes down in the very same spot.

- Both Twos and Sevens need to define the idea of commitment. Both Types like to be in the company of other people. Sevens can be charming and do not like limitations and restrictions and Twos can be seductive and rationalize love and intimacy. Discuss with each other the ideas of freedom with limitations regarding others, fidelity, deal breakers – most importantly, what encompasses healthy boundaries with others while still respecting the idea of commitment between you and your partner.

- For Givers and Adventurers who are on a spiritual path, in many ways their paths can complement each other. For the Two, it is about excessive pride or an inflated sense of self-worth, the antidote for which is humility. For the Seven, it is about gluttony for the pleasures of life, the antidote for which is sobriety. Discuss between the two of you how humility and sobriety are similar, how for the Two needing to be indispensable can lead back to pride, and for the Seven having feelings of entitlement can lead back to gluttony.

CHAPTER THIRTY
The Giver-Leader (Two-Eight) Couple

We usually complement each other well, but the challenges show up mainly in the parenting of my [Leader] husband's 16-year old son. I judge my husband Glenn's words and behavior as too harsh at times, and my efforts to connect and understand can be annoying to him. But here's an example of when our differences worked well together. Our 16-year old had a teacher who was unreasonable, and one day would not allow him to go to the bathroom. The teacher called our house to complain about our son and warn us that a failing grade was imminent. Glenn called him an asshole and hung up on him. I prevailed on Glenn to deal more effectively with the situation. The next day he went to the school and stayed in control of his rage, handled the situation well, and had his son transferred out of the unreasonable teacher's class.

-- Gail, a Giver, married 4 years

This vignette is a good illustration of the Giver-Leader couple balancing each other and accomplishing something together more effectively than either could have done alone. Glenn, on his own, with his direct, tell-it-like-it-is manner and earthy language, would most likely have created animosity and anger at the school, whereas Gail might not have been forceful enough. But instead, the Two was able to temper the Eight's approach so that he negotiated an acceptable solution for his son. Givers have the ability to soften Leaders; Leaders can jumpstart Givers into action, especially when it comes to defending the defenseless. On a deeper level, you might say that the Two is helping the Eight to access his heart space, to maintain composure, and to see the whole picture. If the Eight trusts the Two, in this situation it will mean that the husband will be willing to listen and recognize the value of his wife's words.

On the enneagram diagram, Eight and Two share a connecting line, which makes it easier for them to understand each other's point of view. Their connection gives them a mutual respect for each other. Two will respect Eight's power and boundary-setting style, while Eights will respect Two's trusting kindheartedness.

Of course, the part that they see might lie dormant inside of them and require the other type to act as a catalyst to bring out, just as the Eight brought out the Two. To carry the vignette a little further, if Glenn had not been able to go to the school that day, he could have possibly helped Gail find the Eight inside her so that she could have then taken the necessary strong action. This is how they relate to each other: Twos like the Eight's energetic leadership, such as the ability to be themselves, and for once not having to guess about another's needs. Eights like the Two's heart connection, and appreciate support and help.

According to Helen Palmer, writing in *The Enneagram in Love and Work*,

> The desire to be central in a partner's life is familiar to both types because they meet at Two. Both want attention, but their manner of earning that attention is radically different. Twos adjust their feelings to meet the need of others, and Eights insist that their own needs be met. Physical attention is significant in the relationship, as Eights are sexually expressive and Twos often equate sexuality with love. (p. 293)

In our survey, Givers chose Leaders as one of the types with which they feel most compatible. One of the reasons was: "They are good at asking for what they want, so they are easy for me to please." When Twos are with Eights, they may be able to give their helping radar a rest, feeling assured the Eight will tell them what he wants and needs. Another Giver said,

My best friend is an Eight. Absolutely loyal. Totally, solidly there for me. The contrast of her power, solidity, uncompromisingness, ability to see the big picture, pushiness and out-there passion versus my own very opposite traits such as meticulousness, attention to detail, focus on relationships more than principles, shyness (as well as other contrasts) makes for a very rich friendship that has gone on for 40 years. But she's hard to live with for long!

Other Twos said: "They say what they think." "I like the 'what you see is what you get,' and I also feel cared about in a protective sort of way." "I love their devotion and innocence and challenge." "They don't bullshit, are usually physically imposing and have protective qualities." "Courage to go after a goal, righteousness." Overall, Twos feel comfortable with Eights, if the Two gets enough attention. In many ways the Eight frees up the Two to feel they can say anything and not be rejected.

Gifts they bring

Givers described their contribution to the relationship as "sharing my heart – as a spacious holding environment for extended family, friends, and home." "I care so much about our relationship that I learn and understand my husband's motivation and style so I can bridge our differences and communicate effectively." Melody, an Eight, described her Two husband Lars in the following way: "Emotions, feelings, willing to talk things out." Another Eight, Julia, characterized her Two husband Zack as "sweet and affectionate." In the preceding statements you can hear the tremendous focus on relationships, caring, and communication — all very important to the Two.

When it comes to the gifts Leaders bring to a relationship, Melody wrote, "I keep good boundaries and tell the truth. . . If I put my mind to it, it will get accomplished." Julia, another Leader, wrote that her gifts were "organization, direction and decision-making." Twos bragged about their Eight partners by saying, "His energy holds me and gives me a sense of protection." "He has integrity, courage, strength, steadiness, assertiveness." And then with great pride, Amina, a Two, exclaimed about her Leader partner Norma, "She wants to be in relationship with me!"

Challenges of the Giver-Leader relationship

In our survey, although Givers chose Leaders as one of the types with which they are most comfortable, they paradoxically also chose Eight as a type they struggle with the most. The Twos' comments were quite fiery, indicative of the difficult relationship Twos and Eights can have if they are not getting along: "They give me little room for me to find myself." "I try to get close to them, but when they turn and are in my face, I want to run." "My father was an Eight – always angry." "Their quick, blunt judgments. I get reactive and fire back with equally blunt counter-judgments." "They sometimes don't understand others." And then finally, Jessica, a Giver, described her former Leader husband as, "overbearing, insensitive, aggressive, rude," adding that she believes that during their marriage he would have left her "if I ignored him and refused to satisfy his needs." The preceding statements aren't very pretty and contrast greatly with the Two's statements about their feelings of compatibility with the Eight. Eights love big and they fight big, and as the saying goes, one's light usually matches one's shadow. Twos need to be able to take the good with the bad when linking up with Eights. People love Leaders' energy, power, and passion, but then have a hard time accepting all of the other things that come with the personality.

The Leaders in our survey also chose the Giver as one of the types with which they most struggle. They did not mince words in describing what bugs them the most about being in relationship with Twos: "I hate their tendency to seduce and manipulate, but not to own up to their own needs." "Lack of sincerity." "I do not like help unless I ask." "Because my mother was type 2 – I can feel controlled" "Manipulative – they give to get."

Eights seek the truth and value directness; they would prefer their partner to stand up to them, but instead unhealthy Twos can be indirect and manipulative. Eights will see the Two's behaviors as phony and as an attempt to control them. Leaders aren't particularly good at figuring out people's needs, so the Giver's reluctance to express their own can drive the Eight a little crazy. Jessica, the formerly married Giver, wrote that her Leader husband used to complain, "You don't assert yourself." What he is saying to her is, "Just tell me what you want!"

Twos feel important when an Eight wants to protect them, but their pride also demands independence. Over time, the Giver may tire of the Leader's domination of the relationship and seek more autonomy. Power struggles can ensue. At other times, when Eights are focused on themselves, Twos may feel unloved and find themselves in pursuit, acceding to the Eight's agenda and seeking more overt expressions of love. The Two's dilemma consists of dependence versus independence. Givers are exquisitely aware of others' needs and feelings. They may also tire of the Eight's self-referencing and seeming disregard for what others want or how they are impacted. Givers want Leaders to be more feeling and less demanding, and might get upset at the Leader's brusqueness and apparent lack of empathy or discomfort with just sitting and listening. As an image type, the Giver might feel embarrassed by the Leader's public outbursts or inappropriate behavior.

In our survey, Melody, an Eight, wrote that she hears from her Two husband Lars, "You never show any feelings. I never know what is going on with you." Melody stated that she recognized her own difficulty with emotions and advised younger Eights to "learn how to talk about emotions. Learn how your body tells you what you are feeling." To be fair, both Eights and Twos may have problems discussing their feelings. Melody listed her complaint about Lars, the Giver, as: "You never tell me what is really going on for you, and then you get passive-aggressive." Twos have a tendency to act as if things don't matter to them and then reach a tipping point where they become resentful over not being appreciated. Here is an example of a "classic fight" between Mary, a Giver, and her husband John, a Leader. Mary reported,

Yesterday evening John and I were eating dinner at a restaurant. When we finished, I mentioned that before we returned to our hotel, I'd like to stop by a nearby curio shop we'd walked past earlier, and buy a statue I saw in the window. John simply ignored my request and began walking back at full speed to the hotel, saying he was tired. I followed him, and when we got back, he acted like everything was fine. It wasn't. I was really upset. It was as though John simply hadn't heard me! And this isn't the first time. We've been married for 30 years, and it seems I'm always trying to please him, always deferring to him, always catering to his needs. It seems like a one-way street. It throws me back to the little girl who wasn't seen. What more do I have to do in order to feel heard by him??!!

John described his perspective:

This is all news to me. I never heard her asking me. I was tired and just wanted to get back to the room. Yes, she was pouting when we got back, but I'm used to that. She often goes around looking put-upon, which seems silly to me, so I don't do anything, I just wait until she gets over it. But I can tell you, it's frustrating for me. If she wants something, why doesn't she just ask me straight out? Direct questions work better with me than subtle hints. I think she thinks I should know what she wants, but I'm not a mind reader. It's not my fault.

Eights value direct communication. Mary, a Two, has behind her a lifetime of denying her own needs, feeling pride in her ability to satisfy others' needs while minimizing her own, and expecting others to fulfill her needs without being told what they are. Some spouses might be intuitive enough to pick up on Mary's needs without being told directly, but a person like John needs clear and direct statements. Mary needed to learn how to focus more on herself and to state her needs more directly. In the restaurant the day before, if John appeared not to have heard her request, she could have repeated it more loudly. She could also have reframed her request. Instead of asking, "Would you mind if on our way back we stopped at the curio shop?" She could have said, "On our way back I'd like to stop at the curio shop and I'd like you to come with me. I want to buy that statue."

Possessiveness and control vs. freedom and independence

Givers like protectiveness, but do not like the Leader's possessiveness and the control that can accompany it. Jessica, who chose to leave her marriage, wrote that her Leader husband Walter "had to be right, had to win, had to control." Givers actually need more freedom than they may recognize, in order to explore and experience the many selves they have inside that help them to link up with all the people they befriend. They can also spend time winning over a partner, but once the chase is over, they want it and their and privacy back, causing questions about their loyalty. They may find themselves torn between the desire for relationship and the wish for independence. In fact, an aspect of self-improvement for the Giver is to learn to enjoy time alone.

In response to the Two's pulling away, the Eight may feel threatened and may react by increasing control. The Two might then explode, accessing the connection, and begin to forcefully fight back, protecting their right to be free. The result of a Giver's retreat might be more control by the Leader. This could escalate into an out and out argument, instead of direct manipulation by the Giver, which could be a relief to the Leader. Direct words will bring the couple closer together, because it can clear the air and instill a sense of passion. Ruby, a Two, describes the dynamic in her relationship with an Eight in the following way,

Scott sets some sort of boundary – usually something small --and I respond by feeling trapped and fight against this. He doesn't understand because it is such a small thing – and then he reacts too. If I could recognize my need for both protection and freedom, and let him know this – it might help!

This dilemma is similar to when the Giver speaks about the idea of having sex with someone attractive. He or she doesn't necessarily have to have sex with that particular person, just wants to know that the other person is willing. Protectiveness is similar: The Giver wants to know their Leader partner cares enough to offer protection, but they don't want the confines that come with the Eight's possessiveness.

Too much giving

A typical complaint by a Leader to her Giver partner was, "You don't do anything wrong." As with the One (Perfectionist, who is a wing of the Two), there's a desire to be perfect – in the case of the Two, it's to be the perfect, loving person. The partner may complain that the Two has a Mother Teresa aspect – always giving, ignoring her own needs. The Eight might think, "Be real! Have needs! Screw up occasionally! Get angry at times with what I'm doing!" He wants her to be more human.

The Givers in our survey recognized their need to stop being perfect Givers and lovers and become more human, thus humbler. They need to embrace their shadow side – the anger and resentment they can feel -- and to get to know themselves better. When asked what advice they'd give to a younger Giver, Amina wrote, "concentrate on your own motivations. Pay attention to the fact that you are not as loving as you might assume." Jessica's advice was, "Ask yourself repeatedly, what do I want?" And Gail suggested, "Do the work of learning how to recognize and meet your own needs, and avoid people-pleasing patterns that diminish you."

Exercises for the Giver-Leader couple

The following questions highlight the classic issues that challenge Giver-Leader pairing:

Because these two Types share the Two – Eight line on the Enneagram diagram, they are going to see a part of themselves in each other. Depending on the stress or security of the situation will influence each type dramatically.

A Giver in a relationship needs to be able to check the health of their pride, whereas a Leader needs to be able to make himself or herself vulnerable and at the same time check in with the partner's feelings. The two partners need to make sure they are being both conscious and respectful toward one another.

- For the Eight: Because your Type fosters autonomy rather than connection, as well as a likelihood of self-referencing, how do you stay conscious of your Type Two partner's feelings, making sure you are not running roughshod over him or her? Ideally, the Giver needs to take responsibility for his or her feelings and pride, although depending on the level of hurt, this may not always be the case. "Staying current" in the relationship, so that all the cards are on the table, will go a long way towards not having to do damage control. Checking in with each other on a regular basis – and being honest during those check-ins - should help you both to stay current with one another.

- For the Two: How do you take the temperature of your pride on a regular basis, to make sure it is not either inflated or deflated to the point of affecting your overall mood and ego in the relationship? Using your pride as a barometer for how you are feeling can be useful. Allowing your pride to control you and your relationship will only create immature relationships. How do you keep your pride from controlling you and your relationship?

- For both: For those Twos and Eights who are on a spiritual journey, we recommend that you "melt down" the lower aspects of your types – pride for the Two and power for the Eight, and turn them into antidotes – humility for the Two and vulnerability/consciousness for the Eight. How do the benefits of humility and vulnerability, plus staying conscious on a regular basis, affect the spiritual aspect of your relationship?

CHAPTER THIRTY-ONE

The Giver-Mediator (Two-Nine) Couple

The Giver-Mediator relationship can be very sweet . . . a match made in heaven, some would say. The Two looks for someone to love and give to, and the Nine seeks harmony and closeness with another. In fact, this might be their biggest problem, since both would most likely prefer a "head in the clouds" relationship versus "feet on the ground." A Two-Nine couple would lovingly "argue" with one another about who loved the other the most. One would start out by saying, "I love you the best." Then the other would quickly chime in and say, "No . . . I love you more." They would go back and forth like this for a while. They may also compete with one another through their gift giving, with a "Guess what I got for you today, honey?" while the other would state, "Well . . . guess what I got you?" Some of you might find this syrupy sweet and ideal, but problems can occur with this kind of mutual enmeshment as with any other relationship.

What might draw the Giver and Mediator together? The Two wants to help the Nine find life's purpose and meaning, especially if the latter appears a little lost. Upon linking up with the Mediator, the Giver's radar will be on the lookout for how to help maximize the other's potential, noticing any underachiever qualities. Both Twos and Nines have an uncanny ability to love people for who they are, while at the same time encouraging them to pursue their innermost desires. Since both Types largely live their lives through others, this pair will enjoy each other's successes almost more than their own.

A Giver molds herself to please the Mediator, while the Mediator wants to merge, listening and supporting. The Giver checks out what the Mediator needs. The Mediator looks for the Giver's agenda. Each can make the other feel special. These two types are look-alikes, yet deep down different core issues motivate them. Both are huge givers for whom relationships play a primary role. Twos and Nines often give the same answer the question, "If you had to boil life down to one thing, what would it be?" – it is about love. For the Two, love gets expressed through giving and being there for others, while the Nine expresses love in a kind of oneness with others (merging).

Givers and Mediators usually enjoy expressing their love for each other through physical affection. Givers feel important and cared about through sex, and Mediators can come alive and feel at one with their Giver partner.

Giver-Mediator couples are very common. Craig, a Two, wrote, "I brought joy and entertainment into the relationship, seeing the glass half full instead of half empty." From the Giver's perspective, we all have a choice - to approach things from a positive or a negative way; It is the same with relationships -- we can be kind and caring toward others or not. The Giver's motto is, "Why can't we all just be kind to one another?"

At times Mediators can become quite grumpy. Life can seem like a major inconvenience, with all its conflicts and choices to be made, when all he or she really wants is some peace and quiet. Givers in relationship with them can shield them from some of the oncoming flak, make decisions, and do some of the grunt work, while at the same time keeping a positive attitude.

Another positive feature Twos report is their ability for intimacy. Craig, the Two, reported his strengths: "My giving and the ability to be in relationship and not fold. I think I was supportive and helpful to my (Nine) wife and because of my relationship orientation, I could participate in a fairly deep level of intimacy." Twos thrive on relationships. For a Two, being in relationship can feel like the most familiar thing you can experience. And even though Twos may have their own set of problems, they can easily put their focus on their partner, helping them to discover who they are and what they really want.

Givers can get caught up in the everyday hectic pace of life. Suzanne, a Two, related to people and their problems essentially the same as a juggler who starts his act by spinning one plate on the top of a broomstick. The juggler quickly increases the complexity until he has about a dozen plates spinning on the top of a dozen broomsticks. When one plate starts to wobble, the juggler has to run back to that plate and give it another spin before it falls and breaks. As the juggler sets up more and more broom sticks with spinning plates, it becomes a mad dash back and forth across the stage to keep the plates spinning. Suzanne stated that in her mind people and their problems were much like the spinning plates. She tended to attract more and more people with problems and found herself running from one to the other, making sure they were okay. Her partner, a Mediator, helped her to learn to trust the universe more to provide for others. This gave her a sense of peace. He helped her to see how she could sometimes inflict her own agenda onto others, instead of allowing them to find their "own life."

Angela, a Nine, described the Nine's nonjudgmental love and acceptance; "I unconditionally support my partner who is (uncharacteristically) taking on being a leader of her own company and standing out as that leader all by herself." Twos can learn about the unconditional aspect of helping from Nines. To be able to help without strings attached or expecting anything in return can be huge for the Giver.

This story is about the Mediator's loving unconditionally:

I was once teaching a class where there was a very difficult student. Having a wealth of experience to draw on, I had tried a variety of techniques and teaching approaches to resolve the problem. When none of them worked, I diagnosed him with a disorder so that I could try and help him in a more sophisticated way. But nothing seemed to work. I finally decided to ask my Nine wife what she would recommend. As she listened, I went over everything I had tried with this difficult person. When I was finished telling her what I had tried to no avail, she thought for a moment, and then suggested, "Why don't you just love him?" I took her advice: The next day as I taught the class, I no longer saw the student as being difficult or having a disorder. With my Nine wife's advice, I imagined myself as a full length mirror, and I simply reflected back to him without judgment what I saw and heard. I felt a bond with him and compassion toward him. Thanks to my Mediator wife, my new approach broke the power struggle that had been created between us.

Challenges of the Giver-Mediator relationship:

Despite the sweetness of the Two-Nine relationship, challenges can be present. Many of them can be hidden under the surface. When this relationship gets off track, it may be hard to discern what the actual difficulty is. Both are "other-focused" personality Types. Remember the couple at the beginning of this chapter who played a game in their relationship called, "I love you more"? This is an example of being other-focused. The problem with it is that they may know what the other person wants and needs, and they may live vicariously through the other, but they have a difficult time staying centered in themselves. Life and relationships eventually demand that we know and are true to ourselves in order to be satisfied and fulfilled. Happy, healthy relationships require each party to be a whole person, not an empty shell or merely half. Givers and Mediators will very likely struggle with this aspect of relationship.

Expression of love versus reluctance to engage

How do intimacy issues play themselves out in the Giver-Mediator relationship? A recurrent problem is that the Giver states a desire for intimacy and connection, whereas the Mediator tends to withdraw and turn to other activities. Twos in relationship with Nines repeatedly complain about the partner's reluctance to emotionally engage. For example, Michelle (a Giver) described her frustration with Eric, her Mediator husband: "I feel a need for more intimacy, for him to share more of his thoughts and feelings with me. But the more I ask for it, the more he experiences it as a demand and draws back." Twos keep trying to squeeze feelings out of Nines, but it's likely that Eric truly doesn't understand Michelle's request and can't do what she wants. A recurrent complaint of many partners of Mediators is that the Nine is simply absent from the relationship. A Two woman explained,

My complaint to my husband is, "You never want to resolve or try to change our lack of physical and emotional intimacy. You never want to talk about or confront our problems head-on. You always avoid opening up and showing your feelings and emotions." Because he's passive – non-confrontive and wants always to keep the peace – the challenge for me has been to awaken some thoughts and actions that make him more responsive to the needs and concerns that I express I need from our relationship.

Another Giver had a similar description of her husband,

I would say to him, "'I very much miss intimacy, sharing your inner thoughts and feelings with me. Your dreams and fears, your wishes and expectations about life and our relationship.'" He doesn't give straight answers to questions, mostly saying, "I don't know." He avoids confrontations and conflicts, so that we do not really solve our problems. Sometimes I hear old reproaches from long ago which are still there and not forgiven. He says "yes" but does "no,"

Unless they have done a lot of work on themselves, Nines generally don't realize how absent they are. The Two may experience a huge void, no stimulating conversation, big blanks in the relationship; the Nine is simply "not there." The Nine can be so closed that even the normally intuitive Two can have difficulty figuring them out. Below, a Mediator describes what her Giver partner told her:

She [the Two] tells me that I often do not express what I am thinking or feeling. I tend to automatically think she already knows this. Then when she does not do what I think is appropriate for the situation I will say something, only to find out she had no idea what I was thinking or feeling. . . . news to me!

Craig, a Giver, wrote about a past relationship with a Mediator,

Marian did fundraisers for humanitarian causes. They were really draining, so she had no energy left for the relationship. She would immerse herself in her work and I would feel unimportant. I couldn't get her to understand how it made me feel – she would hold up her work like a shield, because it was a noble cause. Marian would tell me, "I'm doing this for a good cause! I'm raising all this money for people who need it." It was her way of not showing up in the relationship. I felt discounted, and she was stubborn. But in the end, it wasn't all bad, because I recognized I had to live my own life – I went to school, got a degree, and got a job I enjoyed. But even more than that, I was able to find my true self.

Mediators of the Self-preservation and/or the Social subtype may numb themselves through work. Angela, related,

For me, my attention to sloth is that I "overwork the sloth," and I am a workaholic. I tend to use work as a way to show my love. The more I want to show love and attention, the more I physically work at a task to complete it successfully so I can start another one in rapid succession.

Similar to Craig's complaint, the unfortunate result is Angela's absence from the relationship. Another Two, Manuel, a clergyman no longer married to a Nine, faced a similar situation. His central complaint to his wife was that she was forgetful about commitments and often withdrew too much. Looking back now, he recognizes that "The relationship was too important to me. I found my value and worth in another's love of me." Gradually, he said, "I differentiated more and more, being more truthful about who I am and what I value." Eventually Manuel and Gloria parted ways. His advice to a younger Two is, "Be centered on life in some way other than the person who is your significant other. Be self-accepting and practice self-care." Important advice for a Giver – but certainly not easy to do.

The Giver "helps," the Mediator resists

When the Giver's relationship with a Mediator is not going well, the Giver is likely to mistakenly believe that he or she always knows what is best. This comes from a Giver's fundamental pride. Because Mediators aren't forthcoming about their needs and desires, the Giver may be quick to jump in and try to take the lead, feeling he knows what direction the relationship — and even his partner— needs to go. But unfortunately, implementing the plan might not be done gently or lovingly. Michelle a Two, explained it this way, "I have difficulties in accepting situations as they are, I push too much, and I am controlling." Some Givers can be very Eightish, quite intrusive, basically telling people, "That doesn't look good on you. Change it, and you'll do better in the world." Others manipulate in a more subtle introverted way,

As we stated earlier in this chapter, Twos can be committed to helping Nines achieve their potential – even if they don't want to. So when the Nine procrastinates or gets distracted or doesn't go along with the plan, the Two can become very frustrated and reacts by nagging, complaining and getting angry. This may consist of using guilt, or it can be explosive (thereby accessing their Eight connection). According to Sandra, a Giver, her Mediator husband's complaint to her is, "You always nag – you never understand how I feel about watching my favorite TV shows. You always think you're right. You always want things your way. You never understand my point of view."

Underneath it all, though, Twos want to be successful in their helping. If they think someone acts against what is best in a given situation, the prideful Giver can become resentful. Their complaint most likely will be, "How dare you not accept my help? Just wait until you really do need my help and then see what happens!" When resentful, Givers can turn withholding into a work of art.

The Mediator's response to this intrusive helping has nothing to do with mediation. Instead, imagine him or her sitting in your living room having somehow become a large immovable boulder. The Nine's motto at this moment is probably, "I may not know who the hell I am, but I'll be damned if I let you tell me!" They are now in a power struggle, each stubbornly stuck. They are still enmeshed, but the relationship is no longer sweet. The situation is not hopeless, however. If the Two and Nine use this time as an opportunity for personal and spiritual growth, they can finally come home to themselves and connect with each other as whole individuals.

Nines have difficulty talking about the thorny issues, which can build up and destroy the relationship. They won't talk about their true needs and desires, but instead, will store up one resentment after another. One day he will unexpectedly announce to his incredulous partner that he is finished with the relationship.

Twos' demands

Diana, a Mediator with a Self-preservation subtype wrote about her difficulties with her long-term husband, a Giver with a Sexual subtype:

My husband has been going through dismay at realizing that his meeting ours needs has not gotten him what he thought it would -- 'his needs met'. He always over-did for others, feeling it was money in the bank - of IOU's. Others rarely have enough energy and interest to pay back in measure all that he gave out. I on the other hand have been dealing with feeling the sacrifices I've made in not getting my needs met from other people in order to get the approval I desperately wanted. I've come to realize the approval I need to cultivate is my own.

It's ironic that Twos, who are famous for insisting that they have no needs, can, through their overdoing for others, project an expectation of being rewarded that can be overwhelming. Diana described this as an IOU that she just didn't have the energy and interest to pay back. The result can be that both partners feel resentment – the Two for not being appreciated for all he's done, and the Nine for feeling that she's expected to repay giving that she didn't want in the first place. Helen Palmer writes about this outcome in her book, *The Enneagram in Love and Work*:

A crisis will emerge if the Two becomes indispensable and the Nine feels controlled. The Nine will suspect that he is filling Two's unrecognized needs and will stubbornly refuse to cooperate. Nines hold back their own potential as a way of getting even. Twos get bored if Nines fail to achieve their potential and furious if attention is withdrawn. Twos will resent feeling forced to take the rudder in the relationship when they prefer to be inspired and led. Feeling abandoned by Nine's lack of initiative, Two may become complaining. (p. 196)

When Nines feel controlled and get angry, rather than expressing their feelings directly they withdraw into other activities. They may give the Two the silent treatment, which for a Giver constitutes severe punishment.

Sex, intimacy, and conflict

A Giver wrote about a recurrent conflict in her 12-year marriage to a Mediator:

Because of my desire to please – to give my all in a relationship – my Nine husband has consistently disappointed me. I've addressed the desire to my husband to have a closer and more physical and emotionally intimate relationship, and his excuse is that because I'm not prudent with money, he is angry – deep down -- and can't respond to me in a more physical way. We finally had a major fight and he admitted that his lack of desire was just that – He wasn't interested in sex, and money matters were not the factors in a sexless marriage – he just doesn't think of sex at all.

Many long-term relationships exist in which the Nine basically has given up on sex. It was just too much trouble, too much effort. Usually, the Nine prefers to focus on creature comforts and social activities, while physical affection and emotional intimacy disappear along with the sex. For partners who crave intimacy – Givers, Romantics and others with a Sexual subtype – this can be a big disappointment and source of distress.

Typically, Nines won't state their feelings directly. Instead, they may hit upon something that the partner may have done, even years ago, and they use it as an excuse to avoid the real issue, to do the work of the relationship. It's hard to say what's the real truth is. For example one Nine told his partner, "It's the crumbs you leave on the kitchen table – I feel you don't care." A Giver related, "Early in our relationship, when we had an issue, she avoided the conflict. I confronted it, in love and truth – and that persuaded her to do the same. Heretofore, she had never known a man to care enough to stay with and move through an issue."

Exercises for the Giver-Mediator couple

The following exercises highlight the classic issues that challenge the Two-Nine pairing:

The Giver-Mediator combination is usually thought of as a very sweet pairing – maybe even overly sweet. The Two comes from this romantic, heart centered place, while the Nine comes from an unconditional love and acceptance approach. Neither of them handle conflict well, which causes them to avoid issues that they could most likely defuse early on instead of allowing them to fester until they are now relationship-ending material. In the minds of Twos and Nines, conflict just does not fit into their love theme. Givers and Mediators need to learn that by being so conflict avoidant they may damage or destroy their relationship to a point of no return. So what should they do? Try doing the exercises below and confront the conflict head on – look at it as a tough love approach.

- For both of you: Together, discuss what scares you about conflict or at least what blocks you from tackling it head on. Brainstorm the benefits that might result from constructive conflict. And finally, make sure that the unspoken issues get discussed -- that they are given a voice that will balance out each partner's wants and needs in the relationship.

- For the Two: Examine the specific characteristics of your Type that block conflict, such as pride, image, giving/withholding, love, etc.

- For the Nine: Examine the specific characteristics of your Type that block conflict, such as merging, separation anxiety, anger, love, etc.

- For the Two: From a spiritual perspective, try to convert the lower aspects of personality, which for you is pride, to the higher aspects of personality, which for you is humility. Try to determine what role they play when it comes to conflict in your relationship.

- For the Nine: From a spiritual perspective, try to convert the lower aspects of personality, which for you is sloth, to the higher aspects of personality, which for you is love and right action. Try to determine what role they play when it comes to conflict in your relationship.

Trying to make sure your relationship always looks loving will only damage or destroy it. It is okay to have conflict from time to time and to use that conflict as grist for the mill.

CHAPTER THIRTY-TWO

The Double Achiever (Three-Three) Couple

I was thirty-nine and a single mom for the first time. My four year old had just returned from a month-long visit with his dad. I bustled about, unpacking his things and gathering laundry. I was tense and tired. My son was sitting on a straight-backed chair, quietly watching my every move. After several minutes, I finally stopped and told him that I had missed him very much. He looked at me and asked, 'Do you miss me when I'm here, too?'
-- Meare Demetri from the Sun Magazine

This quote poignantly illustrates how someone can be present physically yet not really be there, missing the moment while thinking about future plans or perhaps multi-tasking, something Threes in particular tend to do. Achievers are image types -- they care so much about how others "see" them that they may seem to be AWOL or preoccupied, basically otherwise involved.

One Achiever told about attending his graduation ceremony. Asked how it felt when they finally handed him the diploma after years of hard work, the Achiever said, "I don't remember getting the diploma at all, because I was so focused on how I appeared to the audience as I walked across the stage."

Being image conscious can really motivate a Type Three. He wants to truly be the achiever in the world, successful in whatever he sets out to accomplish. Certain Threes set a successful relationship goal and succeed at that. But often, their "go-go-go" mindset and potential for workaholism takes its toll on their intimate liaisons. So how do two Threes together manage?

A Double Achiever couple can get along with each other exceedingly well, as they are energetically well matched. They are uncommon as marital partners, however, and no Three-Three pairs responded our survey. In our survey, though, Threes picked the Achiever as the Type they most like. Some comments were: "We have a natural affinity. They are easy to work with and understand." "At this stage of my life [age 39], I know what I want and need and I have little time to waste. I want someone who is committed to peaceful coexistence and meaningful work." "They get things done, have good ideas, are great conversationalists." It makes sense that Achievers would find themselves compatible with their counterparts, especially in the working world. Achievers admire the same qualities in others that they bring to a project -- bright, quick thinkers, able to assess the job and know what it will take to successfully reach the end goal. Probably the desire for a "peaceful coexistence" referred to above is the Three wanting someone on the same wave length about the definition of success and the exclusion of "messiness" (i.e. feelings) that could get in the way and slow down the project.

Threes enjoy sharing activities and are more comfortable *doing* things together than just hanging out. They will bond around attaining common goals, and looking good while doing so. Achievers enjoy socializing with friends who share similar work interests. Since both partners tend to focus on the positives in life, their relationship can be upbeat and positive. And when problems arise, each will work hard to solve them. Neither partner wants to admit failure, so they will not let the relationship fail easily.

Challenges of the Double Achiever pairing

Competition

Achievers are natural competitors. One Achiever relates that he even competes with himself every time he mows the lawn. He sets the timer on his watch and then starts mowing, each time trying to beat his previous record. Threes have to be careful about taking that same competitiveness into the relationship and competing with their partners. They may want to be the better parent or the better partner in the eyes of their children.

Intimate relationships can a great opportunity for Achievers to work on developing partnership skills. This challenges them to be equal both in the relationship and in the eyes of others, something not easy for someone who usually feels that only winners are worthy of love. But if they can do it, they can truly discover more about their heart, their vulnerability, and what it means to connect with another human being — not as a competitor but as a person who has needs and feelings. They can also connect with their own needs and feelings without thinking that they have to compete to get the "goodies." Healthy relationships can help the Achiever open his or her heart in a humbling way that teaches about true partnership and teamwork.

Avoiding feelings

Achievers are uncomfortable expressing their feelings, so their relationship could lack a strong emotional connection. The focus becomes "looking good and successful," whereas inside, one or both might sense that something is missing. Since feelings can be "messy" to Threes, they tend to avoid them and could end up having a shallow and meaningless partnership.

Honesty versus deceit

Two Achievers together need to commit to being totally honest with each other so that that deceit doesn't play a role in the relationship. This will free them from the ongoing striving to be the best in order to win love and will free them from always having to project that image. Threes can struggle with being honest with themselves and others. It makes sense when the lifelong message seems to be, "Be the best" or better yet, "Did you do your best? Did you win?" If you are an Achiever, you might wonder what bad thing is going to happen if you don't succeed. Do you not get the love? If this is the case, it would make sense that the Three may twist the truth at times, both with him- or herself and with others. If the two Achievers don't get caught up in colluding around this issue, each could be the perfect partner for helping the other to heal this childhood wound. Who better to know how important it is to be loved for who you are and not for what you do?

Workaholism

It was probably a healthy Three who came up with the saying "No-one on their death bed states, 'I wish I would have spent more time at the office.'" These were words of an Achiever, who after experiencing all of the losses in his or her life caused by workaholism, finally reached a point where he realized it wasn't worth it. Achievers can be not only competitive, but driven as well.

Someone once asked a rich man how he would know when he had enough riches — in other words, "How much is enough?" The rich man replied, "Just a little bit more." This is how can be for Achievers -- they need just a few more successes, a few more dollars in the bank, a few more material things, before they finally will have enough and can turn their attention toward a partner or family. Of course, that day rarely comes. Very few enneagram panels are sadder than the ones where Achievers talk openly about lost relationships, about people who were important to them but whom they let slip away while trying to be successful. Older and wiser Threes will tell the younger ones to make sure they have their priorities in order, to take care of those they love and who love them before they find themselves in that "death bed" scenario.

Because Achievers tend to be workaholics, it is a challenge for a Double Achiever couple to avoid getting over-involved in outside projects at the expense of the relationship. They may put all their energy into work and come home stressed and exhausted. It's all too easy for the couple to go on for days, if not months, without really connecting with one another, becoming like two ships passing in the night. They will need to specifically schedule time together.

Wings and subtypes

As with other same-type pairings, it helps when the two Achievers have different wings and/or subtypes. This usually creates more balance and a little less collusion, allowing them to positively challenge each other. The more we believe that we have the "right way" with regard to how the world should work and how it should look, the more entrenched we stay in our personality type. Achievers who bring different wings to the relationship can teach each other different approaches to life and relationships. For example, a Three with a Two wing could bring a caring about other people and their needs, while a Four wing could bring more caring about feelings and the importance of relationships. This is a time in relationship where differences may be more beneficial than similarities.

Exercises for the Double Achiever couple

Long-lasting Three-Three couples are uncommon. All too often Achievers get over-involved in their work to the detriment of the relationship. Additionally, the reluctance of Achievers to express their feelings, or even to examine their feelings, means that the Three-Three pairing may lack a deep emotional connection. Rather than an intimate loving relationship, they may look more like a working partnership, collaborating to succeed in various projects such as career or parenting. Threes who are willing to undertake the work of personal growth have usually bottomed out with their personality issues and are ready to tackle the higher aspects of personality and/or the spiritual aspects of their Type.

The following exercises highlight the classic issues that challenge the Three-Three pairing:

- Two Threes together need to commit to one another to keep each other on track. If they "fall off the wagon" they need to support each other in getting back on track. No one knows them like they know each other – so what better person to keep an eye on the other and to catch each other when they fall.

- The Achiever's main work is to move from the "human doing" to the "human being." Accessing the being aspect of oneself involves feeling one's feelings, staying put when one wants to go, go, go, turning the applause sign off, and become willing to be authentic with themselves and their partner rather than being satisfied with "looking good."

- Finally, do the spiritual work. Instead of placing one's hope in oneself, trust the universe – place your hope in the universe. Be honest with yourself and others – don't be deceptive. Let people love you for who you are – not for what you do.

Commit to doing the work together – calling each other on any B.S. Support each other in feeling the feelings – go slow, don't judge. Finally, make amends to those whom you hurt on your way up the ladder. Do the best you can to rebuild damaged relationships.

CHAPTER THIRTY-THREE

The Achiever-Romantic (Three-Four) Couple

When we travel, my organized and responsible Three nature makes reservations early, organizes, and finds our way, while his Four personality helps me take it slowly, relax, and savor the beauty. In family problems I am more proactive and focused on effective communication, while he is more sensitive, accepting, and patient.

-- Leslie, a Three

Both Achievers and Romantics are in the heart (or image) triad or center– very tuned into how other people perceive them. Achievers want to be seen as successful and accomplished, whereas Romantics want to come across as unique or special. Enneagram teacher Helen Palmer refers to this combination as "successful elegance." Threes' inner world is filled with thoughts of their work and how they are perceived outside, whereas the interior of the Four is focused on feelings and inner dramas, which usually have to do with relationships. Threes help Fours connect with reality and the outside world, follow through on their goals and get things done; Fours help Threes get more in touch with feelings and individuality, to stop running and, as the quote above puts it, "take it slowly, relax, savor the beauty." Fours, who are more in touch with the dark side of life, appreciate the Three's optimism and ability to put them in touch with the positives. Besides being from the same (heart or image) center (see p. 31) , each is also a wing of the other (see page 33 for a discussion of wings), which can give them shared values and help each understand the other better.

We heard from an Achiever-Romantic couple married 15 years - an Achiever with a Four wing, whose Romantic partner has a Three wing, both with a Social subtype. This is a very compatible combination. Leslie, the Three, wrote that the way she helped her relationship thrive was, "I supported Ken in exploring his true calling, following his heart's desire." Achievers can be good at championing their partners, helping them with their goals. Leslie apparently made sure that Ken's goal was authentic to her – something very important to Romantics. She also stated that she brought "support for a strong family life." A Three who is focused on her family can help it run efficiently, taking great pride in its accomplishments. Leslie also commented that Ken's contribution was his "sensitive expression of feelings." Romantics will bring an emphasis to the emotional lives of the family members, usually making sure that everyone's feelings are heard. When working together, Threes and Fours can bring a balance of successes and satisfaction to the relationship and to their family.

The Challenges of the Achiever-Romantic relationship

The major challenge for the Achiever-Romantic couple is balancing the former's workaholism with the latter's overemphasis on emotions and relationship. As Helen Palmer writes in *The Enneagram in Love and Work*, Fours overvalue emotional life, whereas Threes undervalue it. The Romantic's complaint list will look something like this: The Achiever spends too much time on work, promises to spend more time with me but then backs out because he's too busy, is too interested in impressing others at the expense of authenticity, avoids feelings and criticizes me for my sensitivity and depression. The Achiever, on the other hand, will defend himself by saying he's working hard for the sake of the family, and that his long hours on the job are a demonstration of his commitment to the relationship.

The Achiever is uncomfortable analyzing feelings and is put off by the Romantic's moods, high drama and depression. It can all seem so senseless and inefficient! The more the Romantic is in pursuit of greater intimacy and an emotional connection with the Achiever, the more likely it is that the quarry will escape by scheduling even more work-related activities, staying even later on the job or getting more involved in this or that project.

The Achiever's workaholism can play into the Romantic's tendency to pursue the even slightly unattainable, which can keep him or her hooked, ever hoping to make the relationship perfectly satisfying and intimate. This scenario also allows the Four to spend time fantasizing about a desired image and downplaying potential rejection or abandonment.

A common difficulty for the Three-Four couple is their differing approach to problems. When Fours describe their troubles to their mate, what they want above all is a listening ear, someone to sit with them, listen empathetically and validate the depth of their grief or pain. What more typically happens, if the Three doesn't withdraw to the den, is that his solution-focused worldview leads him to rapidly assess the problem and offer up a quick solution. Achievers are problem solvers at heart -- fix it and move on. To the Romantic, this looks like their feelings are being discounted. A frequent complaint is, "I just want to feel *heard*," and what's really being said is, "I want my feelings to be heard and acknowledged."

Although Achievers can be attracted to the uniqueness and creativity of the Romantic, they are more concerned about presenting an appropriate public image or one that will lead to some form of success. Sometimes they can be embarrassed by the Four's flamboyant style of dressing or failure to accomplish a goal. Leslie, a Three wrote that her husband's Type-related difficulties in the relationship were, "his tendency to feel different, special — he resists going along with what someone else decides or works out." This has led to their recurrent disagreement:

My need to manage situations for optimal outcome is perceived by Ken as my controlling him. I may get embarrassed by his "poor" performance and try to get him to improve. He gets offended, angry, sulks, tells me to stop controlling, which hurts my feelings and makes me angry. What works for us is to each accept responsibility for our part, apologize for what are truly our own issues.

The above scenario is a good example of how important it is to make sure we don't see our partners as extensions of ourselves whom we can change. When we find ourselves attracted to someone very different, it's important that we work on acceptance and also to realize we are attracted to this person for a reason. Threes are attracted to Fours because of their connection to feelings and valuing of authenticity. Fours are attracted to Threes because of their ability to set goals and because they are not controlled by their feelings. Unfortunately, many times we will try and turn the other into replicas. We do this because they are usually manifesting a part of us that we might be trying to avoid. When our partner has a behavior that is driving us a little nuts, we need to be able to say to ourselves, "My partner drives me crazy at times -- and I love him."

Exercises for the Achiever-Romantic Couple

The following exercises highlight the classic issues that challenge the Achiever-Romantic pairing:

This is one of those cases where opposites attract. When people gravitate toward their opposite in relationships, it's likely because there is something they want to learn. If this true, then the best approach is to see each as a teacher to the other. This means seeing that person as someone who knows about something more than I do. It may mean that they know what I need sometimes more than I do.

- For both of you: Are you each willing to surrender a certain part of yourself to your partner? Are you willing to see your partner as someone who knows about something more than you do – someone who may know what you need more than you do? What do you each need to let go of to be able to do this?

- For the Three: How can you allow the Four to teach you about feelings versus doing, about slowing down versus go, go, go, about savoring the moment before rushing to the next project? About listening and empathizing rather than quickly seeking a solution?

- For the Four: How can you allow the Three to teach you about the glass being half-full rather than half-empty, about always doing versus being, about focusing on the present moment versus the past or future?

- For both of you: Together, commit to doing the higher aspects of the work: attaining true intimacy, image versus authenticity, and being loved for who you truly are.

CHAPTER THIRTY-FOUR

The Achiever-Observer (Three-Five) Couple

Workaholism has __not__ taken a toll on our marriage. I really think that my husband likes me being a workaholic, because it brings in more money that we can have for security. Also, he is a real homebody and loves excuses to be alone in front of the computer or TV. I guess I am lucky in this regard. However, for a happily married couple, we do a lot of things without one another. Is that so bad?

-- Alexis, an Achiever, married to an Observer

This insightful quote allows us to peer into the Achiever-Observer relationship. It was written by a young, high-achieving Type Three lawyer, married to a Type Five engineer, after she read a brief description of her Type. Her comments refer to the workaholic habits of Threes that often cause problems in their primary relationships. But for the most part, according to her Achiever mindset, her workaholism works in her relationship with her Observer husband. She claims it produces more money, which symbolizes success, helping her feel better about herself. It could also satisfy the Observer's need for security, thereby lessening his intrinsic fear of scarcity. Her work-focused lifestyle also appears to mesh with the habits of her homebody spouse, who enjoys his solitude. Her only concern is whether they do too many things without each other. Threes and Fives can find themselves leading parallel but separate lives, which can actually mitigate their fear of intimacy.

According to enneagram teacher Helen Palmer in *The Enneagram in Love and Work*, the Achiever often chooses the Observer for relationship, the stated reason being a balance of opposites (p. 299). The Three-Five couple above illustrates, however, that similarities are important in maintaining their happy marriage: both require a lot of time away from each other, and neither seeks a great deal of emotional intimacy or deep discussions of feelings. Even though Achievers and Observers have very different personalities, their relationship can work very well because they tend to share similar values.

Positive aspects of the Achiever-Observer pairing

Lots of space - Few emotional demands
The Achiever and the Observer both keep busy with their individual activities, and appreciate their partner's willingness to give them the time and space to do this. Each works well independently. Because both Types are more logical than emotional, neither is very emotionally demanding. One of the Achievers, Rita, wrote, of her Observer partner:

Troy gave me a tremendous amount of freedom within the relationship. In fact, four months after we married, I went overland to India – alone -- and was gone for five months. I really valued that he never tried to put any brakes on whatever I wanted to do. I used to jokingly say that I chose him because he "got out of my way," unlike other boyfriends who would try to get me to do what they wanted to do. He completely respected my desire to control my own life.

Threes and Fives together can take on the high-powered couple persona, where one lives on the East Coast and the other on the West Coast. Each may have top-notch positions at their job, and they may commute every weekend to meet. The Three, who has an abundance of energy, will most likely be the one to travel to the Five. It should be noted, though, that there are two different types of Fives, some who are very possessive and controlling, and others, like Troy, who aren't. The controller Five may object to business trips that take the Three away from home. Observers don't attach easily, but once attached, they can become fearful of losing a precious commodity; this leads them to try to hoard their partner. They can appear very Eight-like, although their bullying will be mental rather than physical. Or if they don't get their way, they might sulk. This looks like conflict to the Achiever, which is uncomfortable. To avoid this, Threes may try to cut back on their workload. If, however, it continues, the Three will hide out at work -- which will only exacerbate the situation. This pattern can become a vicious circle. However, since both are problem solvers, this can be rather business-like. Using logic, they can negotiate wants and needs and the amount of time they will spend together. The Observer needs reassurance that the Achiever isn't going to just keep going and going when out in the world.

Observers and Achievers can make a great team

The Five-Three relationship can look much like a business partnership. According to Helen Palmer, the Achiever is usually the couple's social secretary, filtering phone messages and engagements, consulting with the Observer in private, and then conveying their decisions to the world at large. Of course, the Achiever's desire for social contact has to be weighed against the Observer's need for privacy.

Both types value competence. Fives gather information and share it with their partner, as well as supporting him or her in accomplishing goals. Rita, the Three, wrote about her Five partner,

Troy had a vast knowledge of a lot of things I knew nothing about before I met him, which opened up to me many worlds that I didn't know existed. He was also excellent at playing devil's advocate, which forced me to re-assess my beliefs and be analytical about them.

When Fives and Threes collaborate on a project, they can be a dynamite team. The Observer has the knowledge, the objectivity, and the calm approach. The Achiever can provide the ability to take the project out into the world. As Leticia, a Five explained, "What I admire about Jason is that he can make my ideas and dreams become reality."

Challenges of the Achiever-Observer Pairing

In our survey, Achievers listed the Observer as one of the types they most struggle with, which is unexpected, considering how common this pairing is. But in the following quotes and stories, you'll hear the Three's frustrations and the totally opposite approach that the Five brings to the relationship. Achievers wrote about the Observers that: "They are withdrawn, secretive, reluctant to commit." "They don't respond to me emotionally; I believe they always see themselves as intellectually superior, and I don't like it." "I'm not sure what he's all about – he's ambiguous." Achievers are doers in their primary relationship; they don't want to spend a lot of time figuring out what their partner wants and how to get them to move. Threes are very practical and sometimes chafe under the Observer's tendency to talk rather than act. Looking at the other side, an Achiever wrote that her Observer partner's central complaint is; "I feel overwhelmed by the options you present and the intensity of your need for me to make a decision ASAP."

The frustration of the action-oriented Three is evident in the words of Rita, who complained about her Five husband Troy who was easily overwhelmed. "He won't take the initiative to see what needs to be done. He won't act unless he fully understands why." Observers are researchers at heart and are vigilant about gathering plenty of information before making a decision. This can be especially frustrating to the Achiever, who is most likely raring to go. Robin, another Three, admits that one of her challenges is, "I'm future-oriented. 'Where does this lead to?' is part of the experience. Time is short for me." She seems to understand that wanting to move forward quickly keeps her from effective problem-solving. She admits that one of her issues was "not giving the other enough time for him to express what he was struggling with." This is an honest look at the Three's part in the relationship and indicates understanding that the Five given enough time to process things in the relationship would certainly be happier.

Rita provided another bird's-eye view of the Three-Five as she described the progressive difficulties in her relationship with Troy, the Five:

My desire to have a home, career and family -- the "full catastrophe", as Zorba called it -- conflicted with Troy's desire to read, study and think. It wasn't something we really fought about – I just went ahead and did what I wanted, and he kind of came along for the ride. Tom Condon notes that Fives often feel like they "can't say no." That was certainly my experience. He would go along with my program because I wanted it (and because I would take action to make it happen), but then got progressively more passive-aggressive because it wasn't what he really wanted.

Inevitably, I became a nag and would consider him wrong for not being ambitious, not caring about how things looked (e.g. dead plants, laundry in the living room, etc.) He felt I was in control of everything and, in retrospect, I believe he deeply resented that. We did not figure out how to resolve this dilemma. We divorced (rather calmly in the end) after twenty years and two children. I wish I had known about the enneagram early in our relationship. It might have provided some insight to help the relationship work better or at least to get out of it sooner!

The above scenario describes what can happen when the Three pushes and the Five doesn't stick up for what he wants. In this situation, the

Achiever's go-for-it attitude trumped the Observer's passivity and conflict avoidance. It ended badly when the Five eventually spoke up for himself, but in a passive-aggressive, sabotaging way. This scenario confirms the wisdom of Achiever Robin's advice from the preceding story, to be patient with the other's process. Communication is most important in this relationship and yet so difficult for them because of their personality Types: Threes won't want to take the time, while Fives will find it draining.

In the following vignettes, you'll hear again about Rita, a Three who decides to take control and Troy, a Five whose reaction is to withdraw. When the Achiever pushes too hard and the Observer pulls back, a destructive parent-child dynamic can result:

With my husband, there was a lotta talk but little action. Discussions would just go round and round. There was lots of intellectual analysis, talking about what was meant by this word and that, or by this concept and that, but never arriving at any agreement on what action to take. Or, if we agreed about action, he often failed to follow through with it. It was as if he moved more and more into his inner world and could cope less and less with the world outside of his head.

He would not take the initiative to see what needed to be done. I ended up feeling like an employer instead of a spouse. He'd do what I asked him to do (though less and less as time went on), but I was the one who had to notice that the lawn needed cutting or the gutters had to be repaired. It was as if he just didn't see it, and I was left with the responsibility for remembering everything that had to be done.

I made him feel more inadequate and ineffectual by criticizing whatever he did do and pushing him aside to do it myself. That, of course, resulted in his being even less willing to take any action, my getting more frustrated and annoyed, etc. etc. It became a vicious circle that neither of us could find our way out of. He didn't leave physically, but emotionally he totally checked out of the relationship.

Rita's criticisms made Troy feel increasingly incompetent, and as a result, he withdrew further. When the Three has to keep pushing the Five to take action, the Five is likely to withdraw, while the Three becomes more insistent and controlling. A power struggle usually ensues where no one wins.

The Achiever's workaholism – from a negative perspective

Achievers may see their marriage as yet another project. This was expressed clearly by Rita, married for 20 years:

The relationship was incidental to my life, which was about work, accomplishment and having the possessions I felt I should have in order to be considered a success (however one defines that term for him/her self). The relationship can become an object rather than a process. It's sort of like: "Well, now I have a husband, I can check THAT one off my to-do list."

Robin, the younger Achiever whose relationship with an Observer lasted only a few months, wrote, "When I asked Cliff what was going on, complaining that he was acting different and asked what I did wrong, he stonewalled. I felt that my time spent with him and the little efforts I carved out of my busy day were no longer appreciated." Robin had a legitimate complaint about her partner's withdrawing, but inadvertently she clearly expressed her priorities. The message she was giving her partner was, "How I show my love is that I carve time out of my busy schedule, and I want to be appreciated for it." Whereas the Type Two's codependent cry is, "After all I've done for you!" the Three's cry usually goes something like this, "After all the work I've done for us!" Achievers do show their love and commitment by working hard and providing for their families; it is what they know best. But it is a fine line between the workaholic Achiever working for the other person, when the reality is that their most important relationship is with their occupation, and there isn't much time for the partner.

For their part, Fives, whose stonewalling does not lead to effective problem solving, need to learn how to state their needs when they feel that the Three partner spends too much time away from home. Observers who sense that they are peripheral to their partner's life need to drum up the courage for an active challenge. Leticia, an Observer, wrote that a central complaint she had about her Achiever husband was, "You never think of my needs first. You're always on your own time schedule and in your own world when I need your attention." This very legitimate complaint would be a good starting point from which the Three and the Five can start talking about their issues.

Need for social contact versus desire for privacy

Achievers may want lots of action – activities, social contacts, noise. Observers prefer quiet and solitude. In Dr. David Daniel's Touchstone Column in the *Enneagram Monthly* in 2007 an Observer married to an Achiever wrote,

He loves the limelight and is constantly looking for it. I, on the other hand, am exhausted by social demands. Having a calendar full of meetings and social commitments is a very overwhelming thing for me; for him this is the icing on the cake.

Leticia, an Observer, complained, "The noise from his TV was disturbing. I need peace and harmony. I turn the TV down and go into the living room and read. I ignore him." Again, this is an area in which Threes and Fives are opposites. If they allow the other to be a teacher for them, the Observer can teach the Achiever about privacy and silence, and the Achiever can teach the Observer about interacting and having a social life.

Mutual avoidance of feelings - Fear of intimacy

Both Achievers and Observers avoid feelings and have a fear of intimacy. Feelings to Threes are messy and inefficient and only hold them back from being successful. Feelings often scare Fives and often cause them to retreat into their heads when they feel overwhelmed. Observers can feel drained or smothered from intimacy or others' needs, so therefore withdraw. Achievers fear that if you get close enough, you'll see their emotional immaturity or even the emptiness inside caused by their inexperience dealing with their feelings. Achievers have been performers most of their lives, wearing just the right mask to get the accolades. Being that far removed does not build an authentic self. Is it any wonder why these two Types mutually attract and repel?

Rita, the Achiever, writes eloquently about her fears of intimacy:

I tend to hide who I am a lot of the time when I'm in a romantic relationship. I always fear that if I say exactly what I feel or think, the other person will be displeased with me and go away. I don't feel that a man would want me as a partner if I have any flaws or weaknesses. I fear that he will despise me for any weaknesses or failings. My underlying belief has been that my value is in my ability to take care of myself (a form of "success"), and that if I need help (read: failure) then no one will want me. Certainly no man would want to take care of me. At its worst extreme, I have thought that asking for help is being pathetic or needy in the clinging vine sense, and that a man would simply be disgusted by any helplessness at all.

Believing that their place in life is to take care of things, including them-selves, and that to do otherwise is to fail, it's no surprise that Achievers place great value on projecting success and are so hesitant to show their imperfec-tions and vulnerabilities.

Many Observers tend to avoid conflict; withdrawing is easier for them. According to Leticia, the Observer, "I don't delve too deeply when problems arise. I escape into books, music, myself."

The result is that neither the Three nor the Five is willing to ask for their needs to be met by the other. Unwilling to be vulnerable in any way, how will they connect, except on a very superficial level? Their relationship may be very distant, they're each very self-sufficient, and they may look as if they don't need each other.

Even though Achievers and Observers get on each other's nerves, they are attracted to each other because they can collude in avoiding feelings and intimacy. It is safer to live separate, parallel lives than to open yourself up to another. If both partners are able to take an emotional leap, the Three will usually take the lead, and the Five will not resist. An Achiever probably stated it best, when she said, "For Gods sake…just let me in!"

Observers may withhold their feelings. For an Achiever who likes cer-tainty and feedback, this can be very frustrating. Robin, the young Achiev-er whose relationship with an Observer ended after only a few months, explained,

I would try to get some input on what we would do. Cliff would say, "What-ever you decide." Then I would arrange something but I rarely knew if he liked and enjoyed it or he was just being polite. "Whatever makes you happy. . ." is not an answer. I wanted him to be happy too!

Achievers also tend to avoid showing their feelings, weaknesses and vul-nerability. Rita related, "I want everything to look perfect, even where there are serious issues. I'll stuff down my complaints, trying to make nice and get along, make everything look okay, then finally blow up (though I followed this pattern much more in the past than now.)"

Exercises for the Achiever-Observer Couple
The following questions highlight the classic issues that challenge the Three-Five pairing:

During an enneagram meeting, an Achiever reported she was married to an Observer who very much liked the enneagram. When asked why he wasn't at the meeting with her she responded, "Why do you think? Anyway, he's waiting for me to bring the information back to him." During the course of the meeting, there was a discussion about how the Types handle feelings. The Achiever was lovingly poked a little about how she balked at the prospect of connecting to her feelings. At a certain point, she stated with a snicker, "Oh you would think I'm the most feeling person going if you could see my Five husband." She was then asked how that affected their relationship. She thought about it for a bit, and then said, "Why do you think I married him?"

- The preceding story is about a Three and a Five living separate yet parallel lives. How can you live a life where you deal with intimacy, vulnerability, and conflict in a way that bonds you as a couple and serves to build authenticity with your individual selves?

- Since neither Threes nor Fives like feelings, how can you risk feeling the feelings in order to deepen the level of intimacy in your relationship? What would the overall payoff be for you as a couple and as individuals?

- Seeing yourselves as teachers to one another, how can the Three teach the Five about social and personal interactions while the Five can teach the Three about slowing down and being more mindful?

CHAPTER THIRTY-FIVE

The Achiever-Detective (Three-Six) Couple

My Three husband can be very confident and positive. When I'm feeling afraid or negative, he tries to get me to "think positive," which I usually appreciate, although I have to admit that at times I feel like he's negating my particular view of things, and I question whether always looking at the positive side of things is a good thing. How can you trust in the positive if you don't look at the negative?

-- A Detective

The Achiever and Detective are an uncommon combination that might lead you to ask, "What in the world are they doing together? What could possibly attract them to each other when they are such opposites?" It's a bit similar to a Perfectionist-Leader (One–Eight) combination, where you just know they are going to kill each other before it's all over. The partners in the Three–Six pairing most likely aren't going that far, but if they don't quickly work out some of the important differences in the relationship, mutual insanity might ensue.

Detectives criticize Achievers mainly because of the deceit that their radar picks up. Detectives look for someone they can trust, and they don't usually give the other person many chances for redemption if he or she appears untrustworthy. They are also usually more attracted to the underdog or someone who is oppressed in their eyes – characteristics that Achievers just don't possess. Conversely, Achievers talk about being attracted to Detectives, yet complain that the constant skepticism and questioning is beyond frustrating. "They always think I'm trying to put something over on them - why don't they just trust me?"

Why then would Detectives and Achievers link up? One reason is that they share a connecting line on the Enneagram diagram, which means they can take on characteristics of the other Type. For instance, Threes can assume the Six's humility and loyalty and become more of a team player, and Sixes can acquire the Three's confidence, allowing more risk taking and enjoyment of successes that result from extending themselves. Ron (co-author of this book) was once friends with an Achiever who had a fruit and vegetable juicer that he and his Detective wife wanted to sell him. Ron tells the following story about his experience:

Bob, the Achiever, had just bought the latest and fanciest juicer on the market and he wanted to sell their old one. They invited me over for breakfast one morning and Jane, the Detective, served me wonderful mixed fruit crepes and fresh orange juice straight from their brand new juicer with all its bells and whistles. At the end of breakfast, they brought out their old juicer and Bob proceeded to give me one of the best salesman's spiels I've ever heard. By the time he was done, I was convinced that their used juicer was the greatest invention since the potato peeler.

I was getting out my money to purchase it when I caught Jane out of the corner of my eye staring down Bob as if she couldn't believe what she had just heard. I then turned to Jane and asked her, "What do you think about the juicer?" Jane, stood at attention in front of me and, like a small school girl who is being asked to tattle-tell on her best friend, she seemed to be repeating to herself under her breath, "I can't tell a lie...I can't tell a lie." She then admitted to me that one of the blades had broken off recently and that it had been in the shop for a week getting repaired. She demanded that Bob tell me the rest of the truth. With his head down he reluctantly told me about a couple more mishaps the juicer had had during the time they had owned it.

I decided to buy the juicer anyway and while Bob was getting some of the attachments for it in another room, I asked Jane, "So, what do you think about Bob, now that you've been together for awhile?" Expecting to hear the worst about him given the bit of dishonesty he just demonstrated, she instead gave me the biggest smile and said, "Bob won't let me say anything negative about myself. When I get down on myself, he'll encourage me to look at the positive side of things. I've always had a tendency to expect the worst and to see the glass as half-empty and now I not only am able to see it as half-full, even full at times. I've never felt so good about myself!"

Detectives, with their doubt and questioning, can undermine their own self- esteem. Many of us believe that an examined life is better, but there is a fine line between a healthy examination and over-questioning. Achievers bring a balance to the relationship with their lack of questioning, instead focusing on the positive side of life and how to get to the goal. Because of this tendency, Achievers can champion Detectives, encouraging them to "just do it" and to look at their past successes as reminders that good things can happen.

A commonly recommended empowerment exercise is for them to keep a box of their "wins" and go through this when they are feeling down. Achievers can serve the same purpose for Detectives as the "win box," reminding them what good things they have going. On the other side, Detectives can help Achievers tell the truth.

Achievers grow up with the childhood message that only winners are entitled to love, whereas people who come in second don't get the "cookies." All of this motivates them to do whatever it takes to be winners, even if it means distorting the truth so that they end up looking good. Remember though, that the Six's questioning and the Three's needing to be seen in a positive light are coping strategies which, as with all the personality Types, are put in place at an early age to help someone feel safe. Well-practiced coping strategies can be the gifts we bring to the world and relationships, but they can also become overused, permeating relationships at all levels and threatening their well-being. In the case of the Three–Six pairing, their coping strategies are truly "opposites attracting," and if they don't get on each other's nerves too much, they can be great at challenging each other to move to their opposite, a spiritual conversion that can benefit both of them.

Both Types share values – both are competent, conscientious and organized, and value their work. Both can have a good sense of humor. Achievers appreciate Detectives' loyalty. Detectives appreciate Achievers for who they really are, not just for what they do. Threes see the glass as half-full, whereas Sixes worry that the glass is going to break. Threes and Sixes have very different views of how to reach their goals: Achievers believe in going full-speed ahead, focusing on the potential accomplishments, whereas Detectives hesitate as they work out all the possible downsides. The Three can remind the Six of past successes and encourage the Six partner to try new activities and go for their goals.

Challenges of the Achiever-Detective relationship:
The Three-Six relationship has many challenges. Each partner comes with a set of wants, needs and expectations that form a contract, one that is usually unspoken. This can cause partners to fight about things without recognizing why because they don't know what is vital and crucial to the other. Each member hopes that his or her personally important values and needs are compatible with others' and that mutual support is possible. These relationships tend to break down if their divergent values and approach to life can't find an accommodation and interface.

Success is highly important to the Achiever, whereas for a Detective it can be anxiety provoking, making him or her feel more vulnerable. If the Three encourages the Six to move ahead, the latter may doubt the former's motivation and may feel threatened.

Detectives not only have radar for dishonesty, but also are put off by the Achiever's image-focus and self-deceit. Sixes become reassured by identifying potential adverse outcomes before proceeding, tending to downplay the negatives. Sixes' anxiety and pessimism can burn out Threes, who quickly get tired of trying to reassure and refocus. Threes want to take action, and soon, and may feel held back by the Six's doubts. They tend to reframe negative situations and outcomes into a positive light and will complain about their partner's worries and anxiety.

When Sixes get anxious, they want to stop and talk about it. As a head type, they like to analyze, assess and discuss, to get to the bottom of things to make sure there isn't something there that can hurt them. They can also become accusatory in their questioning without recognizing it -- which will scare the other. When the Detective feels that important issues aren't being discussed, his anxiety increases. Threes have the opposite approach – when they feel anxious, they want to speed up and take action; they are uncomfortable analyzing emotions or feeling anything. A Six may complain that the Three doesn't take his fears and concerns seriously enough, or suspect that the other must be hiding something if he or she isn't willing to talk about it. On the other hand, Threes can feel frustrated and exhausted by the Six's need to question everything to death.

Threes are sensitive to criticism, but quickly reframe it and move on, while Sixes tend to pick up even the smallest slight and run with it, responding defensively or aggressively. They are good at reframing everything into a criticism and can make Threes feel they have to walk on eggshells. Healthy relationships find a balance between letting things go and talking about what truly needs to be discussed. Sixes can have a hard time letting go of the "small stuff"; Threes with their avoidance of conflict can let too many things slide.

Achievers are often much more focused on their work than on their family, many times wearing the workaholic label as a badge of honor. A frequent complaint by the Six is that the achievement-oriented Three doesn't give enough time and energy to the relationship. The Detective will most likely want more sit-down time, so that they can process their thoughts and emotions, something that the Achiever finds uncomfortable.

Grace, a Detective, brought her Achiever boyfriend in for pre-marital counseling and to make sure that George was the right person for her. Grace had detected some instances of deceit, and wanted him to change. George had said he was going to do something but didn't follow through. Many times he stated that he hadn't done what he said he was going to do because he felt it benefited them more if he did it differently. This was clearly a case of deceit in her mind. In his, it was simply being able to change at the drop of a hat so as to be efficient – something Threes can be good at.

Grace's other complaint was that George didn't think he needed therapy. She complained, "I don't think he really wants to be here." She felt he was just doing what it took to satisfy her whereas deep down he thought *she* was the one who had the problem. She found it hard to believe that he truly loved her or that he was really invested in the relationship.

George, on his side, agreed that he didn't want to be in therapy, but he wanted Grace to give him credit for at least doing what she wanted him to do. His complaints were that she tried to make him have feelings that he didn't have. When they talked about their problems in session, he had a hard time as a Three drumming up patience for sitting and listening to her, especially with all the conflict that was being stirred up.

In individual therapy George was taught what is called the "drive-through" listening technique, something that might especially speak to an Achiever. This technique is taken from when someone orders food at a fast food drive-through. Research had shown that fast food restaurants lost a lot of money in their early days because they were constantly getting what people ordered wrong, especially in the drive-through. They became successful when they started repeating back a person's order to make sure they got it right.

George seemed to take to this business/listening idea and began to use it in therapy with Grace, the Six. He started listening more carefully and then reflected back what she said, asking her if he got it right. Unfortunately he didn't express much emotion with his drive-through listening technique. This concerned Grace, who complained, "Did you hear that? I don't think he's in touch with his feelings! I don't think he really cares about what I feel strongly about!" She was looking for reassurance in his tone of voice, thinking that if he was able to express the same emotions she had just expressed, she would have proof that he really understood and cared about her. In the end, this was a case where the Detective needed to make sure that her fears didn't make her expect too much too soon. On his side, the Achiever needed to continue to work on his feelings, realizing that emotional intelligence is an important component of all healthy relationships.

Achievers and Detectives make for a rather odd pairing. But as in all relationships where opposites attract, it is really up to the partners as to whether they are going to use it as a positive or whether they are going to let it sabotage their relationship.

Exercises for the Achiever-Detective couple

You could refer to the Achiever-Detective combination as an opposites-attract pairing, but in other ways they round each other out. Paired together, the Six becomes the Three's external conscience, while the Three represents the Six's personal life coach. In certain ways these two types are drawn together like peanut butter and jelly, yet in other ways these two Types are determined to drive each other to distraction. In our television world of sit-coms, these two Types could probably have a hilarious hit titled, "The Coach and The Conscience".

The following exercises highlight the classic issues that challenge the Achiever-Mediator pairing. They will probably not make it if they don't take a particular approach to their relationship. Detectives cannot take everything as life or death and Achievers do need to take things more as life and death – at least the things that the Detective points out to them. For example:

- At the height of the Three's non-stop going– the Six's "conscience" is going to step in to discuss feelings, especially feelings that question where they are going.
- At the height of the Six's feelings of doubt – the Three "coach" is going to try to reassure the Six with positivity.

- At the height of success and accomplishment – the Six's "conscience" will doubt the success, seeing it as a kind of boasting on the part of the Three and will also have a form of amnesia with regard to success in general.

The Achiever and the Detective must find a way to deal with this "coach" and "conscience" dynamic. If they do, they will have found a way to resolve core issues regarding their personalities and their spiritual path.

CHAPTER THIRTY-SIX

The Achiever-Adventurer (Three-Seven) Couple

Tina and Tom met in their freshman year in college. Even now, many years later, they enthusiastically recall the many activities and trips they shared, the high energy they each brought to any project, and their positive approach to life. They really enjoyed each other's company, and eventually married. Tom, an Adventurer, was very disorganized. In retrospect, he might have been diagnosed with Attention Deficit Disorder. Tina, an Achiever, was the opposite -- very focused and with no trouble setting goals and then working nonstop to achieve them. Tom recalls,

Tina asked me, 'What do you want to do with your life?' I told her I had a lofty dream, to be an airline pilot, but I didn't think I'd be able to do it; I didn't think I had the follow-through even to apply to flight school, much less do the work. Tina said she'd help me with the steps, and she did. She walked me through every bit of it. It was a six-year epic struggle, but I did it. Now I'm a pilot with a major airline. I love my work. I get to travel a lot, see new places, meet new people – and I couldn't have done it without Tina.

When Tina spoke about this time in their life, she didn't consider what she had done to be a big deal. She said, "That's just how my mind works – here are the steps you take, and that's how you get to your goal. It was so familiar to me."

The Achiever-Adventurer couple has many positive attributes. The Three, who perceives the glass to be half full and can see the potential in people, champions the Seven. In our survey, Achievers chose Adventurers as one of the types with which they feel most compatible. Their reasons emphasized the Seven's fun-loving nature: "They appreciate lightness, are fun-loving and have high energy." "They help me have fun, feel free, less responsible." "They like to do things, and are often willing to go along with any fun plan I come up with. So I get to be in control of the agenda and also have an enthusiastic companion."

As is evident from these comments, Threes appreciate the Seven's high energy, creativity, optimistic nature, quick mind, and wide ranging interests. Both Types are energetic, positive, adventurous, and enjoy being with other people; neither puts a high priority on feelings or introspection. Achievers tend to be low-maintenance partners, as their careers take a high priority, which creates a sense of independence and keeps them from making many emotional demands. This gives the Adventurer freedom to pursue his or her own interests. Similarly, a Seven's multiple activities keep him busy while the Three is immersed in her goal-oriented tasks. When it comes to accomplishing a goal, the Achiever and Adventurer make a great team.

Sevens can help Threes stop working for other people's approval and instead satisfy some of their own pleasures and needs. This can be huge for the Achiever, whose life has basically been about gaining others' approval. At the end of the day when the Achiever talks about how her day went, the Adventurer will be amazed at how much she depends on what other people think about her. The Adventurer's perspective is, "Why don't you just do your own thing . . . why don't you just have fun?" If the Achiever can internalize this message, it can be truly liberating. On the other hand, Achievers can model for Adventurers how to work with a steadiness of purpose and the pleasure that producing something can bring. This can be life changing for the Adventurer. Threes can provide a vital part in the Sevens' machinery that somehow went missing early on. If the Adventurer can absorb the Achiever's discipline and singular focus, he or she can accomplish goals and still have fun.

Sevens' focus is on the future rather on the past, the positive rather than the negative, and this allows them to forgive and forget, to think positively and move forward. This is an approach in life that the Three also values. Christine, a Seven, described her gifts to the relationship: "I'm able to rationalize difficult situations and accept them. I find it easy to forgive and go on to the next thing." Sevens don't want to destroy the positive possibilities for the day — their attitude is, yesterday is yesterday, let's not let it interfere with our happiness today. The Three finds this particularly gratifying. Focus on the positives and don't rehash emotional issues, as that can feel uncomfortable.

Cynthia, an Adventurer, has been married over 30 years to Rex, an Achiever. Cynthia wrote approvingly, "Nothing stops Rex. He is a very focused person. When we had marital problems a couple of years ago, he concentrated on our relationship, and it changed everything." Achievers are born problem solvers; when a relationship gets into trouble, they can put the same approaches toward their relationships that they use in the workplace. Like an athlete who hits the game winning shot at the last second, Achievers can succeed even when others might think all hope is lost.

Our survey asked the respondents to describe something that they and their partner have done well together. Christine, a Seven, wrote, "Raising children to be proactive and goal-oriented." Both Types live in the future to a great extent. Sevens avoid pain through their ideas and planning, while Threes avoid failure through goal setting and hard work. Another Adventurer, Julie, said that what worked for her relationship with Abe, an Achiever, was "his ability to start his business – his zest for success and accomplishment; my (Adventurer) willingness to accept risk." Accepting risks can be a strength when someone needs to move forward in the face of uncertainty. Even though Achievers can be very successful in their own right, their tried-and-true approach can be even further enhanced by the Adventurers' go-for-it attitude.

Unfortunately, Achievers can become impatient, and if the goal isn't reached fairly quickly, they may choose to give up. For the Achiever, waiting for a plan to develop or a problem to get solved allows feelings to surface, which makes him very uncomfortable. Similarly, if the Adventurer feels held back and limited for too long, he or she may also quit, believing that the grass is likely to be greener on the other side. Because neither handles emotions well, both have difficulty staying the course if there are long-term problems.

Threes and Sevens are at their best when working toward an identifiable shared end. For example, Cynthia, the Seven, related,

We do best when we have a common goal – something that we both want to achieve. We like to work in the garden together. We have a lot of energy to get things done. For instance, one of our daughters got married in our garden last year. We worked very hard for many months to make the yard and house really nice. We didn't fight too much – But it is better when we work at different jobs, rather than on the same one at the same time.

Cynthia sums it up well. She mentions the high energy both have and gives an example of how they can put it to good use, creating a common goal and then accomplishing it. She does acknowledge that they do better when they don't work closely with each other. Both are leaders in their own way, and each is quite independent. Closeness will usually bring about a mutual deepening of emotions, but those intimate feelings can result in a degree of anxiety because of their shared discomfort with emotional expression.

Enneagram teacher and author David Daniels characterizes the Adventurer with four "Ps": They "plan for positive, pleasant possibilities." The Adventurer's optimism can be especially helpful in times of crisis. Shirley, an Achiever, stated it beautifully in one sentence: "When I was diagnosed with breast cancer, Michael stood by my side and saw the bright side of life." Adventurers can shine for those who are oppressed or feeling down.

Challenges of the Achiever-Adventurer relationship

All couples eventually face the age-old relationship question – how close are we going to get, and how much time are we going to spend together? This question seems especially important for the Three-Seven pairing. Several of the nine enneagram personalities (especially the Achiever, Observer, Adventurer, and Leader) are more comfortable with activities than feelings. Couples comprised of any of these types risk becoming like two ships passing in the night. The Three-Seven pair, with its high energy level and focus on work or multiple other activities, can become so involved with outside concerns that unless the partners make it a point to spend quiet time together, they may wind up giving each other weekly news updates.

Reframing negatives into positives, avoiding problem solving

When different personality types pair up, they can collude in behaviors that help them both feel safe yet not challenge them to grow. For example, Achievers and Adventurers are both optimistic souls who want to focus on the positive. Both excel at reframing negative situations into something positive. Both want to avoid conflict and negativity. This is good in specific situations, as in dealing with a serious illness in the family, but can prevent them from working on their relationship. Thomas, a Seven, acknowledged that one of his difficulties was "not dealing with problems head on." It may be more comfortable for both to maintain a superficial emotional level in the relationship rather than dig deeper. Closeness that involves feelings and intimacy tends to be anxiety provoking for the Three, who may react by working harder. For Sevens, a deepening emotional commitment can feel as if their options are disappearing. The co-illusion for the Achiever-Adventurer pairing has both of them seeing the world and relationships as upbeat and positive, not taking into consideration issues and problems that need to be dealt with in the relationship and therefore which accumulate over time, finally breaking up the couple. Cynthia, a Seven, had this to say about her Three husband:

Rex doesn't like to talk about problems – actually he feels there are no problems, so why talk about something that doesn't exist. He is so positive it seems like he is living on some other planet – he makes me, a positive person, look like a negative person. He forces me to be the one to deal with anything negative in our relationship. This ticks me off because I look like the "bad guy" in this respect.

Shirley, an Achiever, said about her Adventurer husband Michael, "He doesn't want to look at problems. He has a hard time making and keeping commitments. He doesn't always see trouble before it hits, plus he has ADD [attention deficit disorder]."

Aside from the ADD comment, either an Adventurer or an Achiever could have written both of these quotations. They illustrate how in this pairing, both partners tend to reframe negatives into positives and avoid dealing with problems. Commitment is another shared difficulty. When the Seven is of the Sexual subtype, the lack of commitment can manifest in extramarital affairs. Threes have their own way of avoiding commitment and intimacy, getting so caught up in their work and goals that they forget about their partners.

The Achiever-Adventurer pairing is a great example of what happens when look-alikes come together. In such a pairing, each can be initially attracted to the other because both seem to feel the same way about many things. This is collusion, or better put, co-illusion. The subliminal message is, "Oh you feel that way? I feel that way too." With the Three -Seven pairing, the message goes something like this . . . "Oh you don't like to focus on problems, neither do I." As the relationship advances and difficulties arise, that subliminal message changes to something like…"You never want to focus on our problems!" and the response will usually be . . . "You're not so hot at that either!" The final message that will most likely be heard from the Seven will be; "She never wanted to deal with our issues, and it caused me too much pain." Or from the Three . . . "He never wanted to deal with our issues, and it caused us to fail." Both Types like a lot of attention in the relationship, although neither is big on intimacy. Each likes to be at the center of things, including their partner's life. From our survey, we heard about this regarding the Adventurer in particular.

Avoiding intimacy

Cynthia, a Sexual Seven woman, describes how powerful the idea of goals is to her Three husband Rex (whose subtype was Self-Preservation), leaving her feeling ignored:

He seems so focused on his goals that he doesn't notice anybody. My response to this after many years of being ignored was to find someone else who would listen to me. That has changed in the past three years – we went to counseling. He now realizes that if he wants me to stay, he has to pay attention to me (at least some of the time).

Another Adventurer, Julie, had a similar complaint about her long-term Achiever spouse, "I wish Abe was more romantically and personally attentive. 'I love you' is an empty phrase for him." Apparently, Threes and Sevens are look-alikes in this area as well. We could have easily heard a similar complaint from the Three. Sexual subtype Achievers feel ignored when their Adventurer partner places the spotlight on someone or something outside the relationship. Both partners need to make sure they recognize each other in this regard.

Fear of criticism

Relationships consist of three primary aspects: Nurturing and Love, Challenging and Criticizing, and Transforming and Healing. Healthy relationships need to be built on a foundation of love and nurturing. Then we can mirror our partners in a challenging way to help them grow, plus heal or even transform ourselves. If we are not challenged, we lose the opportunity for growth. Unfortunately, neither Achievers nor Adventurers handle criticism well. Shirley, the Achiever, says that her Adventurer partner's fear of conflict hindered effective problem-solving. Julie, the Adventurer, says of her Achiever husband: "Michael is self-protective and out of touch with his emotions. He's over-sensitive to suggestions, labeling them 'criticisms.' Fear of criticism limits honest communication between us." Both types struggle when challenged and seek to avoid conflict. In turn, the partners cannot learn about themselves and therefore do not grow personally or allow the relationship to blossom.

Follow-through, or lack thereof.
One final area in which Threes and Sevens can differ significantly is their attitude toward work and responsibility. Threes are very focused, goal oriented, and naturally stick with projects. They can be very frustrated with the Seven's lack of accountability, inconsistent follow-through, tendency to be irresponsible, frequent change of plans and tendency to get sidetracked. When a Three and a Seven begin a project together, both may be quite enthusiastic about it. They are likely to have a great start. But if the Seven then loses interest, the Three is likely to get annoyed and unhappy.

Exercises for the Achiever-Adventurer Couple

The following questions highlight the classic issues that challenge the Three-Seven pairing:

Both Types are high-energy personalities with plenty of interests or goals. If they are not careful, they'll find their relationship being like two ships passing in the night, meaning that they are not spending much time together, nor do they share common interests. Both can fall into treating the relationship as if were a hobby. They'll highlight the positives they get out of it and minimize the negatives. Both are happy to keep the relationship on a rather superficial level; neither wants to admit or discuss if they are having difficulties or with the relationship. If they are going to have a relationship with substance they must get serious about it. Ideally, they should share a common purpose. Try discussing and committing to the following ideas:

- For both of you: What goal or common purpose could you both commit to that would give your relationship purpose and meaning?
- For both of you: You need to treat the relationship as you would a major work project. This means not to minimize or rationalize the everyday kinds of stressors, and also to follow through even if the situation has become routine or ordinary – which, of course, is typical of family and long-term relationships. More specifically, Sevens vow to discuss with their partner issues of any boredom or limitations, while Threes need to address openly with their partner when they feel they are not being sufficiently appreciated or admired.
- **For both of you:** Vow to deepen the love between each other by dealing with the anxiety that will naturally surface when work is lessened, commitments are agreed upon, and feelings arise.
- **For those on the spiritual path:** Threes commit to incorporating more honesty and humility into their lives, placing their hope in the

universe instead of in themselves. Sevens commit to staying instead of leaving, limiting one's options, and realizing that sometimes some of our greatest growth comes from pain.

CHAPTER THIRTY-SEVEN

The Achiever-Leader (Three-Eight) Couple

The Achiever-Leader couple can be a high-powered team that works well together to accomplish common goals. A powerful example of this is the story of Joel, an Achiever in a six-year relationship with Tim, a Leader. He described their participation in AIDS Lifecycle, a bike ride from San Francisco to Los Angeles: "I signed us up, researched and purchased equipment. Tim built the donor web sites, pushed me to train, and cut through obstacles to complete the event." In that description, you can hear a combination of finesse and power. Joel, the Achiever, wrote that he brought "structure, momentum, optimism, and decision-making," and his Leader partner Tim brought "loyalty, concept of family, and a deeper sense of love."

Threes and Eights are considered look-alike enneagram Types -- capable, confident, hard working, energetic, and successful -- and each appreciates these traits in the other. Eight's loyalty and generosity and Three's optimism help them get through crises and setbacks. Martha, an Achiever, formerly a member of an Achiever-Leader couple, substantiated this by saying: "We dealt with crises well. We were good at helping the other get through visits with difficult people." Eights can help Threes feel loved for who they are rather than for what they accomplish, and to focus on themselves rather than on what others think of them. Leaders can model for Achievers a direct and straightforward style and can encourage the other to be honest. Martha, the Achiever, related, "I brought creativity, passion, tools (i.e. fair fighting techniques, negotiation). I wanted the best for both of us."

Nonetheless, the Achiever-Leader pairing is distinctly uncommon. Often they do better in a business partnership than in an intimate relationship. Neither personality type is comfortable with feelings or being emotionally vulnerable. Enneagram teacher Helen Palmer states in her book *The Ennea-gram in Love and Work,* "Personal power is accentuated in both profiles, but neither partner is experienced with the power of emotional surrender." Their high energy and focus on adventure and goals may result in a relationship that exemplifies two ships passing in the night, similar to other pairs like Three-Three or One-Three. In fact, Type Three seems to be generally at risk for this syndrome — activity galore, but insufficient attention paid to feelings and intimacy. Leaders need to learn how to surrender to their own vulner-ability, whereas Achievers need to learn how to be loved for who they are, not for what they do. Both types fear rejection. Together they can positively collude, supporting each other's fears by moving slowly until they are more comfortable. Unfortunately, their fear may be so great that feelings happen only when the Leader is driven to his knees by something outside himself more powerful than he is, while the Achiever may need to experience a sub-stantial failure that opens him up.

Challenges of the Achiever-Leader relationship

With both types accustomed to being in charge, this couple may get into power struggles over decision-making. Control and competition can be ma-jor challenges. Additionally, Achievers are very image-conscious and may be embarrassed in public by the Leader's earthy, tell-it-like-it-is style and pos-sible lack of attention to appearance. Achievers work hard at pleasing people and protecting their image, and may feel uncomfortable and upset at the way Leaders can sometimes mistreat and offend others. On the other hand, Leaders can be bothered by Achievers who are more interested in trying to impress others than being authentic – and may also dislike the Achiever's chameleon-like ability to reinvent themselves to please others.

Joel, an Achiever, complained about his Leader partner Tim's "mood swings and anger issues, abrasiveness and inability to get along with oth-ers." When Eights hone in on some injustice or something that needs to be changed, they tend to tune out other people's feelings in a single-minded effort to get their way. Martha's complaint about her Eight partner Lisa re-flected this when she stated, "You think everything is about you." She added, "Lisa was a tyrant when she didn't get exactly what she wanted."

Leaders want to know what the truth is in any given situation and may tire of the Achiever's desire to match up to what other people are asking for. The Leader is soon going to question, "Who are you really? And can I trust you?" Martha described the "classic fight" between her partner and herself this way: "As a Three, I experienced Lisa's direct confrontation as an invalidation of my competence. She saw my Three nature and adaptability as weak or wishy-washy."

Achievers don't like conflict and tend to withdraw, which can really irritate Eights, who want direct discussion and an open expression of anger. Martha wrote that Lisa's central complaint about her was: "You always withdraw or avoid conflict." It was hard for Martha to be the object of anger and criticism. "I needed Lisa's respect and to value my work; and I was hurt and angry at perceived or actual criticism. I sometimes played the role of a partner instead of being real. (Whatever the hell that is!)"

As image types, Achievers want to be recognized for their successes and can be sensitive to conflict and the Leader's criticism, and they may also be on the lookout for what their partner's requirements are. Achievers will then make themselves into that image and perform accordingly. Image and authenticity can become so linked that Achievers themselves don't know where reality ends and performance begins.

Conflict resolution can be difficult for the Three-Eight couple. Eights' approach to conflict can be summed up in the following statements: "A belief that she was always right" and always, "angry and defiant." Additionally, Martha, the Achiever says, "I have a hard time knowing how I feel or what I want or need." Another Achiever related, "I've learned to be much more direct with him rather than being nice when setting boundaries." The Eight can teach the Three to show up, challenge and set boundaries, a very important lesson for the Three, who has to learn to be more direct. In fact, Eights welcome direct expression of anger by their partner.

Because both Achievers and Leaders tend to overdo it when making a mark in the world, this pairing is uncommon — they simply don't make time for each other. Even when they do, Eights can be very possessive of their partners. The Three can be so driven that he or she barely finds time for the relationship. Tim's chief complaint, according to his partner, was, "You never stop 'going.'" And even though both Threes and Eights can be overachievers at work, Leaders can be just as excessive in their relationship life, Achievers less so.

Almost all couples need to answer the questions – Who is going to control the relationship? And how close are we going to get? These two questions are especially important to Threes and Eights given their personalities. With regard to decision- making, they need to commit to a "no power struggle" relationship and instead work toward having an equal partnership. How close they get to each other will likely be determined by their courage and willingness – on the Achiever's part to take off the mask, and on the Leader's part to allow vulnerability.

Exercises for the Achiever-Leader couple

The following questions highlight the classic issues that challenge the Three-Eight pairing:

The Achiever-Leader couple often act more like business partners than romantic partners. In a business setting, neither has to figure out how to emotionally surrender to the other. Instead, what you'll usually see is the Three finessing an extremely difficult or complicated deal so that the deal finally is negotiated and that the Eight is seemingly brought in from out of nowhere to drive the hard bargain right into the Three's back pocket. The Eight is then generously compensated and an arrangement has been agreed on that ensures that there is no questioning the long-term loyalty of the Three to the Eight.

How, then, can a pairing like this one work in the romantic setting? The bond between them was often forged during a time of failure when adversity caused them to lean on each other and to truly trust one another. At the time, a deal-breaker was spelled out very clearly: That neither of them will lie or try and take advantage of the other. The bond they share is a commitment to having each other's back. No ifs, ands, or buts.

- For both of you: Was the bond between the two of you created in a way that allows you to truly trust one another and that to commit to having each other's back? Do you both agree that this is a deal breaker between the two of you?

- For both of you: Do you both agree that you cannot lie or try to take advantage of the other? Do you both agree that this is a deal breaker between the two of you?

- For those on a spiritual path: For the Three: Be honest. Allow feelings to surface without running off to work. Allow your partner to love you for who you are – not for what you do. For the Eight: Allow feelings of vulnerability to surface. Trust your partner so that you can emotionally surrender.

CHAPTER THIRTY-EIGHT

The Achiever-Mediator (Three-Nine) Couple

My Nine husband is a very loyal, accepting, supportive father. I'm more de-manding with higher expectations, but combined it's a nice balance, and our (now adult) children all seem happy, focused, hard working and self-aware.
-- Janet, an Achiever, married 33 years to Philip, a Mediator

Mediators, who tend to procrastinate, have difficulty making decisions and easily lose their focus, find the high-energy Achievers very appealing and are helped when someone else motivates them to take action. Mediators tend to merge with their partner's goals and will support Achievers in their accomplishments. Together, they can form a team in which the Achiever provides the structure and goals and keeps things moving at a fast pace, while the Mediator can assist and provide damage control if necessary, resolving conflicts and soothing hurt feelings. As the vignette above illustrates, this partnership can work very well within the family, especially when raising children. Phillip provided acceptance and support, while Janet could be rather demanding, having high expectations.

A highly regarded Nine physician for many years worked in several large organizations as an executive coach of sorts, assisting troubled professionals to find their footing again. His Mediator skills served him extremely well in his counseling of defensive physicians and clergy. He was able to get them to trust him and to open up to him, which allowed him to formulate an effective treatment plan for them. His dream was to start his own treatment program, but the logistics seemed overwhelming. He needed someone else to make it happen. After some years, he married an Achiever who had excellent managerial skills. He told her about his dream, providing the big picture, and she set about fulfilling it. She created the organizational structure, arranged financing, found a building, hired other professionals for the agency, planned the marketing effort, and brought the plan to fruition. The Mediator physician, by now well known for his positive "Nineish" style, was the drawing card for the counseling program, which thereby attracted many patients. She was the business head. Together they formed a very effective and successful partnership.

The Achiever-Mediator pairing is especially prone to function much like a business or even in reality as a business. It can be beneficial for certain couples like this one to focus on other projects rather than each other, such as a cause or business where they each have an assigned role that helps them feel recognized in their own special way. Because of the Nine's non-recognition issues, this can be especially important.

When asked how she helped their relationship thrive. Janet, an Achiever, had this to say about what she had brought to her long-term marriage with a Mediator:

I accomplish a lot and my income has given us a lifestyle he likes (and maybe even needs). I've improved his status in life. I'm high energy. I like to do things and we enjoy our free time. I'm game for socializing, travel, the arts – and Phillip likes that too. I'm intellectually his equal and we're good in front of people together.

In the quote above, you'll notice that feelings do not play much of role in the Achiever's relationship life. The Achiever's gifts are energy, accomplishments, activities, and the status he or she can provide. Janet gave her husband exactly what Nines value in Threes: She was high-energy, set goals and got to them, arranged activities they enjoyed doing, and had interesting conversations with him.

Nines admire Threes' energy and productivity, because it's something they usually struggle with. The Three's inherent vanity takes great pride in the Nine's admiration. Mediators are accepting, nonjudgmental people, which is also very appealing to Achievers. Achievers work very hard to project a successful, popular image, but remember, Three children usually believe they have to win love, that people who come in second don't get the cookies. Janet, the Achiever, wrote that some of her Type-related traits were "terror about not having 'enough' money, always wanting to 'look good' and be admired, extremely jealous feelings over 'popular, beautiful' people, social insecurities."

The unconditional love and tolerance that Mediators bring to a relationship is very appealing to Achievers, who deep down fear being judged and then possibly losing the desired love. But with a Mediator partner, the Achiever can finally relax, be him- or herself, engage in "non-productive" activities without feeling guilty, dream about what he or she really wants to do, and not have to make an impression, and --if really lucky – have a feeling or two.

Challenges of the Achiever-Mediator relationship

The very qualities that first attracted a couple to each other can cause the biggest problems later on. A power struggle that may appear insoluble can be the result. For a Three, the Nine's procrastination and indecisiveness can eventually become aggravating, while the Nine may tire of being pushed and prodded and rebel by "going to sleep," tuning out or digging in his heels, and passive-aggressively resisting. Nines can also numb out by becoming over-involved with their own work or social relationships to the detriment of the marriage. Janet complained of Phillip's "procrastinating, getting into mind-numbing" activities that waste time. He doesn't make enough money, and is unaware of 'image' and why it's important." She continued, "I get frustrated with everything from socializing to money management to chores around the house. I like to make quick decisions, get to it, and do it! He likes to think about it, mull it over, procrastinate, and put it off." Threes are fast-paced, thrive on efficiency, and can get frustrated when Nines can't make a choice or are not certain what they want — even in small matters. Threes can be persuasive in getting the other moving in a particular direction; but if he or she wakes up and discovers that wherever they are is not where they wanted to go, the Achiever gets blamed for the unhappiness.

When faced with criticism or conflict, the Mediator may withdraw rather than engage in problem solving. Janet related about Philip, "He shuts down in the face of anger or conflict. He's afraid to excel and is willing to accept intolerable situations."

Nines may find it difficult to live with Threes, who rarely just relax and enjoy the moment. Janet wrote that Philip would tell her, "You are a workaholic, too judgmental, too quick to jump to conclusions, never satisfied, impatient, demanding." The Mediator, who is usually self-effacing, may also be put off by the Achiever's tendency to boast.

Another aspect of the Three-Nine pairing is that they tend not to make many mutual emotional demands. Neither is comfortable connecting with their feelings, so they in turn do not ask their partner to reciprocate.

Unfortunately, the consequence of this collusion is that it may be difficult for the couple to ever talk about feelings or build emotional intimacy. Personality Types like Threes and Nines, who struggle with their feelings, are like automobiles without temperature gauges or directional compasses. If the temperature gauge needle in the car moves toward hot, most people pull the car over, lift up the hood, and take a look at the engine to see what is going on. Feelings work similarly. If your internal feeling gauge is starting to move away from normal, it is time to open the "hood" and take a look at what is going on inside you. Once your feelings are located, you can then use them like a compass. Your personal feelings can point out what you need to look at in your life or they can point you in an authentic direction. Achievers and Mediators need to embrace their feelings so as to deepen emotional intimacy. There is nothing worse than for a Three or a Nine than to wake up down the road and find out that they've arrived at an unwelcome destination.

Exercises for the Achiever-Mediator Couple
The following questions highlight the classic issues that challenge the Three-Nine pairing:

In some ways, Threes and Nines lost their original personal agenda and life goals in a similar way. Nines merged with others at an early age, losing their wants, needs, and goals. Threes sacrificed their *being* for *doing* at an early age to gain the love of others. Some even point to a grooming that took place at an early age much like what happened with champion golfer Tiger Woods who is most likely a Three. Both the Three and the Nine look for their personal agenda in their own unique way. The more common dynamic appears to consist of the Nine struggling to find themselves, while the Three is more than willing to coach them so they can bloom even if late. The Achiever needs to be careful in encouraging the Mediator in the right direction. Mediators are known for "waking up" somewhere down the road, now dissatisfied with where their life path has taken them. When this happens, a common result is a power struggle, with the Three pushing the Nine, who resists with passive-aggressive behavior and procrastination.
- For the Three: How do you help your Nine partner who may be struggling with their own goals without putting them on the wrong path?
- For the Nine: How willing are you to allow your Three partner to help you find your personal agenda? How can the Three best help

you without a power struggle developing over the direction your life should take?

The partnership between the Three and Nine can take several twists and turns. Feelings and intimacy can push the Achiever even more into their workaholism. Fortunately, the Mediator is usually non-threatening. The main problem with feelings is that Threes and Nines are much like the blind leading the blind; neither Type is experienced with recognizing and expressing feelings.

- For the Three: How do you stay put when it comes to intimacy and your feelings with your Nine partner?
- For the Nine: When it comes to love and intimacy, how are you able to be there for your partner and yet not lose yourself?

For those on a spiritual path, it takes almost a reversal in how you regularly lead your life. Threes become spiritual by staying in place instead of going. Nines become spiritual by self-remembering instead of self-forgetting.

- For the Three: How can you let your partner love you for who you are instead of for what you do? How can you place your hope in the universe instead of in yourself?
- For the Nine: How can you self-remember and take love and right action toward those things that renew your and your partner's spirit?

CHAPTER THIRTY-NINE

The Double Romantic (Four-Four) Couple

My partner is very good at helping me process and think through interpersonal problems; we tend to meet the challenges of other people by thinking through the issues together. Otherwise our strengths and weaknesses are so similar that I can't think of an instance of accomplishing a goal with Type strengths that we couldn't have done on our own.

In day-to-day life we're so ridiculously compatible. We only have one fight (a big and perpetual one), and it's always about the fact that Kyle has trouble fully "committing" to the relationship. On the other hand, because of his lack of commitment, we both get the freedom we need. I guess his fear of commitment (and need for freedom) mirrors mine, so I can adjust to it more easily, and for a longer period of time, than other people would. But we both work on the relationship a lot, too.

-- Sarah, 39-year old Romantic, married 3 years

Both of us being Fours, we were immensely interested in emotional honesty. So when I told my girlfriend that I was interested in other men, she actually appreciated my honesty and helped me (immensely) with coming to terms with my homosexuality. Sylvia was selfless in this regard."

-- Saul, a Romantic

The shared focus on feelings and other similar personality traits of the Double Romantic couple can be a real asset to their relationship. This can be true even when the relationship is short-lived, as suggested by Saul. On the other hand, the shared moodiness and emotionality can make for a volatile relationship. Saul continued:

Because of the Four's penchant for drama, each of us often interpreted the slightest disagreement or emotional disconnection as "the relationship is over." By simply acknowledging this feeling we could see how silly it was, and we'd often be better after a day apart.

Double Four couples responding to our survey were scarce, and the ones who did respond reported that their relationships were short-lived, lasting from several months to three years. Romantics can initially find other Romantics very attractive. They'll think, "Wow, finally here's someone who understands me, who comes from the same place I do, who's always been misunderstood like me." As with the Double Perfectionist couple, two Romantics together can initially react as if they have found their soul mate, someone who shares their unique worldview and values and is attracted to intensity, authenticity, melancholy and intuition. They seek to connect deeply on an emotional level, and respond with empathy to the other's depression or sadness. Both are likely to be interested in some creative endeavor and to be sensitive to the beauty of their environment.

When asked about their gifts, Romantics replied, "I'm not afraid of problems and communicating with my partner about them." "I have a large capacity to listen to my sweetie when she is very emotional and intense, and not react." "My intensity – my Four partner prefers me to be emotionally 'real' and hates it when I try to be even or less emotional (this is not always a good thing, as I'd like to be more even)." Notice that each one of the writers focuses on emotions and communication/connection. Whereas other Types may be put off when the Romantic gets into high drama and deep feelings, concerns and emotional intensity, their Four partner is not. Finding someone who understands and accepts their moods, emotional intensity, and struggle to be real is a powerfully attractive force between them. On the other hand, as Saul related, their shared tendency to overreact emotionally can sabotage an opportunity to create a sense of balance and equanimity within themselves.

Romantics tend to confuse intensity with intimacy. In reality, intimacy is about making oneself vulnerable, not about drama or high intensity. Romantics can sometimes think of abandonment and the loss of the beloved as a kind of death, and believe that the antidote to this -- feeling alive and connected to the other -- must take the form of intensity. Again, this is the conflating of intensity with intimacy.

Fours confuse feelings and emotions. If we use the ocean as an analogy, emotions are like the waves on the surface of the water: they rise and fall sometimes with great fanfare, but in the bigger scheme of things, they really don't amount to much. Feelings can be associated with the powerful currents near the bottom of the ocean floor. These can literally shift the sand and affect the tides. Relating this to the feelings that we all have, if we can connect with our feelings instead of our emotions, we can effect powerful changes deep within and we can feel bonded to something larger than ourselves.

Romantics reported that they appreciate their partners' "hunger for truth and emotional inquiry." Others valued: "His creative ability to express himself via the written word as a means of connecting intimately"; "His Intelligence, introspection, love of animals and nature, deep need to connect and communicate, gregariousness/volubility, spontaneity, adaptability, love of cuddling and touch"; "Her ability to express love through caretaking, the ability to let anger go quickly, love of learning, physical beauty, love of the natural world, intimate sexuality, intelligence, athleticism, the ability to procure and cook healthful foods, and much more." Not surprisingly Romantics chose the Romantic as one of the three most compatible enneagram types. (The others were the Observer and the Mediator).

Challenges of the Romantic-Romantic relationship:

Four-Four pairings generally last for only a short time. One reason, (see Chapter Seven) is that Romantics tend to find themselves in push-pull situations; difficulty with commitment is a recurrent complaint about them. When both are Fours, the relationship may lack a stabilizing influence. They can get involved in endless pursuit-withdrawal-looking elsewhere. Sarah, a Four still in relationship with another Four for more than three years, complained,

Kyle has never been never willing to commit to me; I've never been given so much love, nor had so much love taken away. If I come in his direction he has to fight himself not to back off (and I too do that when he comes too far in my direction).

Saul, a young Romantic, wrote:

Sylvia complains, "You're not available for a committed relationship." I long for other partners sexually, even when I feel deep love for the one I'm with. Sylvia would like me to be available for sharing our lives together, instead of

getting frightened when we seem to be getting too serious. I wish she would allow me to be fickle and sporadic with the relationship.

Marlo, a 37-year old Four in relationship for less than one year with Shawn (also a Four) wrote that her motto on a T-shirt would be, "Love: can't live with it, can't live without it." She believes that Shawn's motto would be, "Why have a relationship in the present when you can safely relive in reverie the lost loves of the past?"

Romantics are one of the most relationship-focused of all enneagram Types, but they struggle with a fear of commitment and intimacy. They search for the beloved, long for the ideal relationship, yet tend to run away if it stares them in the face. Being connected to someone is one of the primary core needs for the Four, but their fear of abandonment -- one of their deepest wounds – drives them away.

One of the ways that the Four personality tries to compensate for its fear of abandonment and intimacy is by gravitating toward partners who also struggle with commitment. That's why a Romantic may link up, for example, with a Mediator, a common pairing. Romantics may sense the "safety" that the Mediator's emotional unavailability brings and also the abandonment that comes with the Nine's occasional "checking out." It not only affirms the Four's life theme that people get abandoned, but also means they don't have to put themselves on the line and let people see them for who they really are – that's what intimacy is all about, to get naked not only physically but also mentally, emotionally and spiritually.

Being special and unique is a common characteristic for Fours. Two Romantics together may have so much in common that they begin to wonder, "How do I become unique in this relationship?" and compete with each other to be special. This is seen as an overcompensation for feeling "defective," which is perceived as the reason they were initially abandoned. The Romantic needs to move toward being ordinary, where feelings of loss can be uncovered and help heal abandonment issues.

Fours, with their tendency for self-absorption, withdraw into their own world, where they "forget" that they're in a relationship with a partner who needs attention. Sarah explained how the Four's self-absorption can make her husband can feel slighted: "Kyle says that I'm not curious to 'see him for who he is,' but rather I impose my emotional agenda (when discussing the relationship); and that I don't ask enough questions about 'where he is' in the relationship."

One chief problem for Romantics is envy. They long for what they don't have and see the flaws in what they do. They can at times be critical of those they love and blame partners for not measuring up to their image. They find themselves saying, "If you were enough, then I'd feel different, so you must be the source of my pain." The result is that a relationship between two Romantics is likely to be volatile, full of drama and wide swings of emotions.

Romantics can live through feelings and imagination to the point where they can miss the realities and practicalities of life. Oliver, a Romantic, wrote about his partner, "Ella had a childhood with an alcoholic father and an unloving mother. She fantasizes about 'how compatible we are' and ignores the realities of problems." Sarah wrote about Kyle, "He tends to see only his emotional experience of things . . . or sees only the emotional side, so we get bogged down in that and not practicalities." The endless analyzing and discussing of feelings and of the relationship can replace enjoying each other or solving practical problems. Fours often are advised to expend more energy on the outside world and less on taking their own temperature or the temperature of the relationship. As a Seven friend might tell them, "You need to lighten up and have fun."

Solutions

When asked what advice they would give another Romantic in relationship, Sarah wrote:

Try to have a sense of humor about your emotions and not take them too seriously; try not to create stories without checking in with your partner; be aware of your tendency to "not want to belong to any club that would have you as a member," and do not push your partner away when s/he comes toward you.

Exercises for the Double-Romantic Couple

The following questions highlight the classic issues that challenge the Four-Four pairing:

The Double-Romantic pairing is rare. Understandably, this combination works better as a friendship than as a marriage or committed relationship. Because the Romantic wants to be unique in relationship, it is not satisfying to him or her to have a very similar person staring back. Also, the negative aspects of the Four are doubled in the Double Romantic pairing. In this volatile relationship, the couple may get caught in a negative loop with endless analyzing and criticism of the relationship and of each other. Enneagram authority Helen Palmer puts it this way in her book, *The Enneagram in Love & Work*:

> Needless to say, the blame factor is compounded in a double Four relationship. At a low point each suffers and sees the other as the source of suffering, each wants a perfect lover, and each feels flawed. Each criticizes the other for being imperfect, and each wants to bail out as his or her own flaws are unearthed. (p. 323)

As is evident in Palmer's words of wisdom, this pairing is similar to looking into not only a mirror but also a magnifying glass. The Four has a connection to type One (the Perfectionist) on the enneagram diagram -- which can just heighten their tendency to criticize. This pairing could use affirmations to stay away from shaming and criticism.

- For both of you: On a regular basis, say to one another: "You are perfect just the way you are...nothing is missing."
- For both of you: Before going to sleep every night, turn to your partner and tell them one positive thing that you appreciate about them.
- For both of you: For those on a spiritual path, you must have balance in the relationship. Teach each other how to handle your mood swings. What to do...what not to do. Commit to doing these things with one another and promise to not try to trip each other up for the sake of drama.

CHAPTER FORTY

The Romantic-Observer (Four-Five) Couple

We worked together as composer (him) and librettist (me) in close collabo-
ration. Working side by side, coming from our own strength, we both re-
spected and admired each other enormously. We worked together through
difficult challenges but were there for each other. We listened to each other,
moved back and forth in an exquisite dance. This is my great life partner
and soul mate. He has a strong Four wing, and we share an artistic spirit
and being a little out of step with societal norms. I value his work, and I feel
we bring out the best in each other and balance each other.
-- Penny, a Romantic, in relationship 7 years with Russell, an Observer

Logically, it would seem that Romantics and Observers, a diehard feeling Type versus a thinking Type, would be so different that it would be hard
for them to find common ground. After all, Romantics focus on the heart
and emotions, whereas Observers approach the world from an intellectual
and mental stance. Yet this pairing is common and for good reason. First is
the classic attraction of opposites, which gives each the opportunity to balance the other. Fours and Fives are neighbors on the enneagram diagram,
although from different centers or triads -- the heart (Four) and the head
(Five). But because they are adjacent, it is not a stretch for them to understand each other. This is even truer if the Five has a strong Four wing (as does
Russell) and vice versa.

Also, because each brings a very different approach to life and relationships, they can teach each other about their specific ways of being in
the world. Observers will bring thinking, detachment, and objectivity to

Romantics, balancing the latter's tendency to be overly emotional, and in turn, Romantics help Observers access their feelings. Both can have an introverted, contemplative approach to life. Fives need solitude and privacy, which Fours, especially those with a Five wing, can certainly understand. Fours, also, are private people who like their space and spend a great deal of time in their imagination. Both have a rich inner world (although the Five's tends to be intellectual and the Four's emotional).

Both Types are likely to feel safe around each other. Observers, (like Nines, the Mediators) are unlikely to impulsively leave; they thus bring stability to the relationship, alleviating the other's fear of being abandoned. Observers, who sometimes feel as if they don't fit in, can feel safe with Romantics, who understand feeling different and probably won't judge. Fours and Fives both favor the nonconformist and unconventional and can appreciate each other's eccentricities. They tend to have many interests in common, including travel, art and music. Fours range far and wide in the world and brings their experiences back home to share, which the Five appreciates.

In our survey, Romantics chose Observers as one of the most compatible Types. They wrote, "I too like a lot of autonomy and privacy." and "They are fellow introverts." Other Romantics said, "I'm intrigued by their mental processes, depth of intelligence." and "We can talk about interesting, meaningful things." Romantics can fall in love with an Observer's mind, multiple talents, and ability to discuss life's deeper issues. Fours described Fives with such adjectives as "steady, calm, slow, sensual, and sensitive," things that either turned them on or made them feel safe. Other Four descriptions were, "I like the objectivity, their non-judgmental nature . . . they respect confidences and boundaries." Romantics can be sensitive to criticism and feel misunderstood at times, so they appreciate the Observer's nonjudgmental nature.

With regard to the gifts they felt they brought to the relationship, Penny (who has a Three wing) wrote, "I have been independent with a lot of interests and friends. Feeling secure in our love helped me give Russell the emotional space he needed. When I didn't expect him to fulfill all my emotional needs, it went better." This seemingly nonchalant statement is actually powerful, with much wisdom, practical advice and insight for Fours. Fives can give the Four partner, who often has abandonment issues, a feeling of security. Observers don't commit easily, but when they do, they are usually there for the duration. Even with this kind of commitment, though, Romantics may unfortunately be tempted to test the Observer with their push-pull scenario, shifting moods and drama.

The Observer may say to the Romantic, "I am here for the duration, but what you have now is all you are going to get – so deal with it." This kind of statement will likely imply to the Four that "something is missing." The next likely step will be a power struggle. The Five will contract to keep from getting overwhelmed and to protect his energy, while the Four will be in pursuit to get more. In the above quote, Penny somehow found the "enough" in the relationship and took responsibility for any other needs or attention from the other intimates in her life. Ideally, both types will try to meet each other half way.

Observers need to learn more about attachment, while Romantics need to experience more detachment. Observers need to open their hearts more, be more generous in spirit and experience their feelings, but also hold on to themselves. The Romantic needs to integrate head with heart and find that interior primary connection.

Romantics listed the following strengths they brought to the relationship: "My empathy and sensitivity." "My keen intuition, warmth, and ability to be deeply intimate. I am a good listener." An Observer, Miriam, wrote of her Romantic husband: "He's outward going, generous, and demonstrative." As heart Types, Fours can be empathic as well as intuitive. Because Fours have usually traversed their own inner world and explored the human condition in depth, they can more easily know and accept others.

As for her gifts to the relationship, Observer Miriam said, "I am very grounded and more discerning than he is." This statement addresses the practical nature of the Observer. Penny (a Four) described Russell, her Five partner: "He has great sensitivity and ability to listen. Incredible capacity to love, and total unconditional acceptance of me." Another Romantic, Francine, wrote that her Observer husband Nick has: "Intelligence, interest in human behavior, large areas of total compatibility" And Les, a Romantic, wrote about his Observer partner: "He has objectivity, intense feelings, loyalty, trust, humor, lightness, introversion, warmth, emotions." Briefly, Observers can be grounded, which is especially useful with strongly emotional partners. They also can be objective and bring their own kind of unconditional love and acceptance.

Fours and Fives can both be deep thinkers, with similar intellectual interests. Miriam, the Five, reports: "We work together in an institute and problem solve together. We share the same interests, sense of humor and do a lot together." Joining their strengths in head and heart can make the Romantic/Observer couple an effective team: Maria, a Romantic, related: "When my husband's father was dying of cancer, I was able to help him stay present for his father. He was able to help me manage our home on my own for several weeks (via phone calls) as the situation took place several thousand miles away." This is a great example of opposites attracting and using that for equal good.

Challenges of the Romantic-Observer pairing

Space versus togetherness
Two of the most primary questions that all couples have to answer are, "How close are we going to get?" and "How much time are we going to spend together?" The biggest problem in the Romantic-Observer pairing is likely to reflect their differing needs for space and togetherness. Penny, a Four, describes herself as "empathetic, willing to work on building the relationship, and I either want all your attention or I want you to leave me alone." Although Romantics are often thought to be endlessly in search of the missing connection, in fact they typically want a great deal of alone time. Romantics have a connection to the Giver (Two); if they go to the low side of type Two, they can become rather codependent, but when they're firmly planted in their Four space, they might prefer to focus inward on their rich world of emotions and fantasies alone; it's easy for them to become self-absorbed. At different times, they may experience one extreme or the other. Penny writes, "My biggest difficulty is that my fear of being abandoned makes me either cut and run first or get emotionally demanding. Secondarily, jealousy. I think my reactivity is most damaging." Miriam, an Observer, described her central complaint about her Romantic husband Jerry: "It is always about Jerry and his emotions, so that sometimes there's no room for anyone else."

Observers are notorious for their own need for privacy and solitude. Like Romantics, they tend to send their partner mixed messages about how close they want to be. They are easily overwhelmed by the Four's emotions and desire for attention, and at such times may distance themselves and act unfeeling and critical. Miriam, the Five, stated that Jerry's central complaint about her was, "I am too quick to be negative and judgmental."

When the Five withdraws, the Four is likely to feel abandoned and may intensify her pursuit or alternatively, withdraw into melancholy. A worst-case scenario is a Five holed up in a shell, while the Four tries to either break through with drama or falls into a depression and feels abandoned. The need for some kind of mediation and compromise is necessary if they are to keep from drifting into an intense power struggle.

Heart versus head

Another source of difficulty for this couple is their differing focus on emotions versus cognition. Romantics react instinctively with their emotions, whereas Observers pride themselves on their logic and objectivity. Les, the Romantic, admits, "I'm quick to judge and a bit swept away by negative emotions before I can be objective." Maria, also a Four, relates that what prevents her at times from effective problem-solving is "my 'emotionality.' It's hard for me to stay as logical, un-removed, as Jose. I get overwhelmed with more and more and more information." In contrast, the Observer, Miriam, wrote, "I am very grounded and more discerning than Jerry is. I'm a good problem solver, but I can be too direct and stubborn." Fours in relationship deplore the Five's reluctance to focus on feelings, as the following report from Maria shows:

Jose always is "going away" -- emotionally more than physically, but physically as well. He just tunes out and seems to only "come back" if I protest. He also wants to talk about logical facts instead of feelings.

Penny complained about her partner's "tendency to hole up in an emotional castle and his ability to shut off feelings." On the other hand, she recognizes that, "I get lost in a feeling and can't see my way out of or beyond that feeling."

For their part, Observers can lose patience with the Romantic's mood swings, drama, and endless processing of feelings. When Maria, a Romantic, was asked what might cause her Five husband Jose to leave the relationship, she wrote, "Be loudly and angrily explosive. I can do this (easily), but I control it out of compassion for Jose – it scares him."

Maria describes how she and Jose were wearing each other out -- because of his emphasis on processing information and her focus on emotions. They have apparently found a solution for their differing attention to logic versus feelings, though. She wrote,

Probably one of the ongoing disagreements is his need for more and more information (logical) and my getting overwhelmed with it. The ways we have worked on resolving this is to only talk about "more information" for a discrete period time (say, 15 minutes), and then make a decision. Or if it's more concrete (e.g. buying a new shed for the home) I ask him to research it to his heart's content and then narrow it down to 2 choices, and then present it to me and I'll decide on one or the other.

Whereas Fours tend to process feelings endlessly and often want their partner involved, Fives are more likely to leave their partner in the dark until they have reached a conclusion. For example, Les, the Four, wrote about his Five partner: "Ralph has an ability to not deal with issues until he has figured them out, and what appears to be a 'final product' is what he shares with me." This can be especially troublesome to the emotionally oriented Four. Observers take introversion to a whole other level. They are likely to go about their business very independently and internally, and don't make their partner privy to any of it. Sometimes the Observer decides to leave and announces it as though it's a spur-of-the-moment decision. But usually, he's been thinking about it for a long time.

The Fours' and Fives' differing attitudes about feeling versus thinking can be a deal breaker: When asked what she thought would make her partner leave, Penny wrote, "If I made too many emotional demands on him." Miriam echoed this: if her Romantic partner, Jerry, were to "put too much pressure on me to go against my inner nature." We assume what she meant by "inner nature" was the side that struggles with strong emotions and feels more comfortable with the introverted thinking process.

Solitude versus socializing

A recurrent source of difficulty for many people (of all types) in relationship with an Observer is the discomfort and awkwardness that many have in social situations. They tend to prefer to spend time at home, alone or with their spouse, not wanting to go out much. Observers can also be possessive about their partners. Miriam, who has a self-preservation subtype that amplifies her Type Five traits, related:

I tend to be antisocial, while Jerry, a Social Four, is very people oriented. He has people in his life I don't enjoy, and it annoys me at times when they make demands on him that impinge on our time together. He is too generous with people at times and sets no boundaries.

Les describes how he and his Self-Preservation Five partner Ralph solved their differences in this area. He writes, "We never really want to be social at the same time with others. We agree that if commitments (social) are made in advance, the agreement is honored, and you show up." This agreement respects Ralph's need for knowing beforehand what is going to be expected of him, so that he can prepare himself. It also satisfies his Four partner in that he knows that Les is going to participate in at least the social events that have been agreed upon beforehand.

The Observer's compartmentalizing, versus the Romantic's quest for "authenticity"

Francine explains how she and her Observer husband of 45 years differ with regard to his being able to compartmentalize and her valuing the authenticity of situations:

As a Social Five, my husband Nick enjoys singing in a choir and feels that this is important enough that he will attend a church whose pastor and ambiance we both agree are totally lacking in spiritual content. I don't see how Nick can do this. Just walking through the door offends my Four aesthetic and spiritual sensibilities. Nick feels I should be willing to go there on special occasions to listen to him sing as I would attend my child's kindergarten play, and I absolutely can't do it.

While I'm generally easy going, there are some areas that are absolutes for me and I become unbending when anyone tries to get me to move or accommodate on them – aesthetics, spirituality, anything that touches what I perceive as my integrity. I refuse to put myself in a position where I must interact with people whom I dislike.

Fives are good at compartmentalizing – keeping different parts of their life separate and focusing on one part of it at a time. For this Observer, his interest in singing is separate from his opinion about the church. His Romantic wife, on the other hand, sees the whole picture, and her dislike of the church prevents her from appreciating any of its activities. The Romantic's strong attachment to feelings will probably not allow her to change her thinking about this situation as readily as her Observer husband might.

Helen Palmer, in *The Enneagram in Love and Work,* nicely summarizes the process that the Four-Five pair needs to work through in order to have a successful long-term relationship:

Each will have to adjust his or her style of relating to accommodate the other: Observers have to stay with their feelings, and Romantics have to throttle back. The saving grace of balancing the most contracted and the most emotionally dramatic Enneagram type is that they really have something admirable to teach each other. (P. 326)

As you see, the Romantic-Observer pairing is rich and complex in many ways. If they are able to meet in the middle and become teachers to each other, their relationship can hold numerous gifts for each of them.

Exercises for the Romantic-Observer Couple

The following questions highlight the classic issues that challenge the Four-Five pairing:

The differing inner worlds of the Four and Five

The Romantic-Observer is a relationship where opposites attract-- Five is a hardcore thinking Type, whereas Four is a deeply feeling emotional Type. They resemble each other in that both can be introverted, living their lives deep inside themselves. Of course, the interior world of Romantics is primarily about their emotions and mood, whereas that of Observers revolves around their intellectual pursuits and mental problem solving. As in most relationships of opposites, couples can become teachers to one another, turning the other onto the very thing that they themselves experience little of.

- For both of you: How do you make sure your partner is privy to your inner world? Is there a teaching moment for both of you by discussing your feelings and thoughts?

This couple needs to make an effort to come outside themselves and connect with each another on a regular basis.

- For both of you: How do you make sure that you are spending enough time together, instead of just hanging out in your own inner world? How much is enough for each of you and how do you negotiate any differences?

Push-pull and boundary setting

Observers are notorious for their difficulty in expressing emotions. When Fives withdraw into their own space, Fours' fears of abandonment can lead them to intensify their emotional pursuit of the Five. This may result in further withdrawal by the Five, who now feels invaded. You may remember the comment of Miriam, an Observer, about her Romantic husband: "It's always about Jerry and his emotions, so that sometimes there's no room for anyone else." It's all too easy for each partner to blame the other for the problems they're experiencing (e.g. he doesn't think logically, she's overly emotional, etc). In order for the relationship to succeed, each needs to modify their preferred to reach a balance. They need to set boundaries that allow each of them to get their needs met while respecting the other's needs (for example, for solitude versus time together, for emotional distance versus closeness)

- For both of you: To make sure you are not focusing on each other's inadequacies, how do you make sure that healthy boundaries are in place and respect is there for one another?

- For the Four: Discuss with the Five how you can get your need met for emotional connection with your partner when the Five tends to be so detached.

- For the Five: Discuss with the Four what you are willing to do to maintain some emotional and physical connection with him or her.

- For the Five: Discuss with the Four how you can get your need for solitude and detachment met when the Four tends to be so focused on emotions.

CHAPTER FORTY-ONE

The Romantic-Detective (Four-Six) Couple

Four and Six share the need for intensity in relationship. Finally I set aside my doubts and thought to myself, "I don't know how she feels about me, but I know how I feel about her. I am going to show her how much I care about her." That is when our relationship changed for the better. Even though we had been married over 30 years, we had always had a push-pull relationship. Until I decided to set aside my fears, she would express doubt regularly as to why she was staying with me. This only worsened my Six fears and led to a tenuous relationship. My change in attitude and corresponding behavior change brought stability into our relationship. We started to build on a base of certainty that we both craved.

-- George, a Detective, married to Shoshana for 44 years

On the surface, Fours and Sixes can be look-alikes, for example, with commitment a huge issue for both. If asked to specify what about commitment is so difficult, the Romantic would probably say, "You want me to open myself up to being abandoned? Are you crazy!?!" The Detective would probably respond, "You want me to open myself up to getting hurt? Are you crazy!?!" In the above quote, you can see that this couple didn't really commit until 30 years into the marriage. Until then, their relationship was likely based on an unspoken, yet somehow agreed-upon, safe distance between them. George and Shoshana are like dancers whose rhythmic movements are intense, a fierce pushing away from each other at times, as well as a childlike holding on and pulling the other toward them. Angst and suffering fill the air, and intensity is confused with intimacy.

For George, a Detective, taking the first step in moving toward intimacy must have demanded an amazing amount of courage, a huge leap of faith, and a stepping off into what surely feels like the abyss. The core issue for the Detective is fear; when they act with courage, they transform fear into its opposite. Look again at George's words in the opening paragraph: "Finally I set aside my doubts and thought to myself, 'I don't know how she feels about me, but I know how I feel about her. I am going to show her how much I care about her. That is when our relationship changed for the better." This is a great example of a Six moving into the heart space, making himself vulnerable and ultimately reaping the benefits that love and commitment provide.

One of the reasons both Romantics and Detectives struggle with commitment is that the latter have trouble accessing their heart space, whereas Romantics feel wounded. How, then, do Romantics achieve a similar level of commitment and intimacy? They have to push beyond their fear, although in their case, it has to do with their fear of abandonment, allowing someone to see them warts and all. They also have to let go of their problematic coping strategies such as the push/pull, focusing on what's missing and the accompanying drama.

Another look-alike characteristic that draws Romantics and Detectives to each other is the shared quest for the truth or what is "real." Fours use the word "authenticity," which to them means an honest, in-depth connection that cannot be easily broken. Sixes may use the word "truth," looking under the surface for any hidden intentions that may point to dishonesty or possibly betrayal. Both are looking for a sense of safety in their connection with others, an attachment that hopefully excludes betrayal and abandonment. Neither wants to be hurt, and neither wants to hurt the other. This can create a mutual loyalty, but both still need to take that leap of faith (demonstrated in the quote at the beginning of this chapter), announcing their love without a guarantee that they are loved or knowing for sure whether the other will stay. This opens the vulnerable heart and creates a relationship that comes from love instead of fear.

Another quality these types share is their angst about life. For the Romantic, the pain comes from loss, of being abandoned or a fear of abandonment, of losing the beloved or not finding one's soul mate; for the Detective, the pain comes from a fear of being all alone in an untrustworthy, frightening and oppressive world. So when the Romantic talks about how terrible the world is, how you can't really trust people because they abandon you, the Detective will most likely chime in about issues of betrayal and oppression.

They believe they have been mistreated by the world, and they can connect around their perception of universal suffering.

The challenges of the Romantic-Detective relationship:
Having described the attraction and similarities of the Four/Six pairing, some of the challenges of this partnership – in other words, how they can step on each other's toes or collude and keep each other stuck – are as follows.

Romantics like to seem unique; they often give a lot of energy to their image, the way they present themselves to others. A Four really cares about how others feel about him or her, even almost scripting out their life's future events. Some of this reflects abandonment issues: they feel if they can make themselves special enough, then others won't leave them. But Detectives, who ferret out and distrust anything that appears not to be the "real thing," may question the Four's image and whether they are being sold a bill of goods. This is usually an issue at the very beginning of the relationship; eventually, the Six can see that the Four is only trying self-protection, something perfectly understandable.

Additionally, Detectives (especially men) may struggle with the intensity of a Romantic's feelings and often respond with problem solving. The Detective will try to fix the Romantic, who then gets annoyed. Throughout their lifetime, most Fours have been told to deal in healthy way with their strong emotions, and someone trying to repair them will not be appreciated. Of course, many Sixes also experience strong emotions and do not appreciate someone else trying to control their feelings. As a result, both Fours and Sixes can become quite reactive. George described his volatile relationship with Shoshana and their reactive style this way: "When we get into stressful circumstances, I need to watch out for intense responses. It is too easy for me to respond in kind and amplify the situation. Until we learned to watch for this problem, it was easy for a situation to escalate into an intense problem."

Relationship expert John Gottman calls this kind of behavior a "harsh start-up" (See page 129). In this interaction, one or both will be easily triggered by what the other says, and they blow up. Gottman claims that discussions between couples that begin thus are almost always unsuccessful. Romantics and Detectives need to be careful that harsh start-ups do not become a part of their relationship.

Besides harsh start-ups, both types tend to be mutually critical and prone to blaming each other, which can lead to stormy arguments. The Romantic hears in the criticism that she is deficient or defective. This causes her to become defensive and possibly volatile. Criticism toward the Detective will cause him to feel that he isn't measuring up, which leads him to also become defensive and volatile.

With regard to criticism and reactivity, Roxanne, a Romantic, stated this about herself and her Detective husband of almost four decades:

One of us reacts negatively to something and the other flares up (we're both reactive types), and a big fight gets going. After learning about our Enneagram types and using the idea of being "present" to each other's pain, we rarely flare up like that any more. I, the Four, am more likely to let things go (not be so sensitive), and Gerald, the Six, is more likely to laugh or be friendly and funny instead of being critical. We have transformed a pretty difficult marriage into a great relationship in the past three years.

With both persons aware of their tendency to be reactive and sensitive to criticism, now knowing the Enneagram, they are able to go beyond the surface aspect and truly be present to the pain and fear embedded in each type. What a great gift to give that ends up transforming the relationship.

The Detective may see the Romantic as having a chip on his or her shoulder, which will irritate (read: scare) him or her. Some Sixes see cockiness as something that may cause problems in the relationship. If you get overconfident, you might not see things that you should be aware of, or you might consider yourself a target. Detectives usually feel that being humble or keeping your head down is the safer way. A Four stated that when he told his Six wife he was invited to speak on a panel about spirituality, she was quick to say, "You be sure and tell them about your non-spiritual side as well!" The Six's statement may sound a little cold, but she is actually just trying to keep something bad from happening.

Romantics may be mired in emotions, but Detectives, who are in the 'Mental' triad, are often more comfortable thinking than feeling. Sixes may complain of Four's focus on their feelings, but Fours decry the Six's avoidance of emotions. One Four, Irene, complained, "As a phobic Six, Vince preferred to ignore emotional problems rather than face them. His denial helped him deal with pain, but didn't help with effective problem solving. Anything technical, mechanical, he'd fix right away."

Push-pull vs. testing

Because of their fear of intimacy and commitment, Romantics will usually resort to a push-pull approach, whereas Detectives will test. If the Romantic is uncertain of the Detective's love, she will want to push him away before she gets abandoned. Because Fours tend to substitute intensity for intimacy, they can send mixed messages – loving sometimes, but withdrawing and rejecting at other times. The Six needs frequent reassurance, so that the push/pull of the Four just serves to increase the Six's fear. Joyce, a Detective, explained that her spouse Brian "needed to stimulate me periodically to the same emotional intensity he carried in himself. Push/pull – he loves me/ he loves me not." It is important for the Romantic to practice staying put and being present. This creates a balance.

On the Six's side, the Detective who feels insecure or uncertain of his partner's love will usually test and question. To see where his partner stands, he may make broad statements such as, "Maybe we should just get a divorce." or "I'm not sure you still love me." He wants to know if his partner is going to fight for him. Testing can be exhausting and confusing for the partner, who does not understand why the Detective is saying these things. Romantics in particular may feel as if they are going to be abandoned; this can throw them into the previously mentioned push/pull mode. Both types need to take responsibility for their own defense mechanisms in order to stop the on again/ off again cycle.

The glass is half empty, or the glass is glass and it could break

Both Fours and Sixes can fall into the trap of seeing the glass (or the relationship) as half empty. Romantics see things as hopeless, whereas Detectives focus on worst-case scenarios. Both need to be careful not to collude around the negative aspects of life and relationships. Fours can fall into the trap of always seeing what is missing. They become depressed or melancholic as they focus on lacking what others seem to have. Sixes can fall into the trap of going to worst-case scenarios, and their fear can cast a dark cloud over everything. Both can spoil what could be good times in the relationship if they are not careful. Romantics need to stay present, appreciating the good things in the relationship. Detectives need to spend at least as much time in best-case scenario thinking as they do in worst-case scenario thinking.

Some Sixes, for their part, feel criticized for their lack of intensity. Joyce (a Six) reported hearing from her Four spouse: "You always seem aloof. You're concerned with the everyday stuff. You're not romantic." Fours are continually in quest of intensity and romance. Guy (a Romantic) wrote that a problem in his relationship is, "My emotionality, sometimes I see patterns and problems that aren't really there, because I've been running scenarios in my head based on incomplete information."

Romantics have a tendency for self-absorption. They may be more involved in taking their own emotional temperature than in paying attention to the needs of their partner. Alyssa, a recently married Detective, wrote of her new husband, "Dale can be self-oriented when it comes to sharing my activities. He wants me to share his, but he doesn't always reciprocate."

The Romantic's sense of loss can result in significant depression, which may interfere with the relationship. Anger and hostility are often seen in Romantics of the Sexual subtype. They may look like Leaders (Eights) — caustic, angry, intense and aggressive. Roxanne, a Romantic of the Sexual subtype, related, "I can be very angry and hostile; moody; suffer from depression." Irene, the now-widowed Romantic, recalled, "At times I felt emotionally abandoned and misunderstood, which led to feelings of unworthiness and depression, at times. Also, I had crying jags and angry outbursts."

Four's focus on what's missing, on the potential for an elusive, perfect relationship, can be another real problem, especially for a Six, who will find it almost impossible to trust her partner. Guy reported that he had difficulty "staying in the present moment, not wanting something that's missing or longing for the past." Joyce lamented her Four husband's "belief that the 'right person' was out there waiting for him."

Fear and doubt

Sixes' tendency to challenge what their partner says, question their words and actions, and voice mistrust of their partner and others can diminish others' self-confidence. Fours may lose patience with the Six's worrying, their negativity, and tendency to revisit decisions. Sixes are constantly questioning the relationship, giving in to their fear, doubting and mistrust. Every little thing can cause them to doubt. This can be very difficult to live with and can erode the relationship. Because of the Six's fear, their first response to suggested actions is often "no." But when they are given time to reflect, they sometimes change their mind.

Detectives place a high premium on honesty, and on knowing what's happening beneath the surface. As Alyssa, a Detective, wrote when asked what might make her leave her husband, "If he lied to me, I would not trust him and it would fall apart."

Some Detectives, especially Counterphobics, become aggressive when they feel fear. Joyce, a Detective, admitted, "I have self-doubt. I attack as a way to get reassurance of my desirability." George found himself going on the attack: "When we get into stressful circumstances, I need to watch out for intense responses. It is too easy for me to respond in kind and amplify the situation. Until we learned to watch for this problem, it was easy for a situation to escalate into an intense problem." Four looks for authenticity and Six looks for what's under the surface. It probably looks like the same thing to them.

Romantics and Detectives both value constant connection, although they seek it in different ways. Romantics want emotional reassurance – expressions of love, cards, an affectionate touch, and roses. Detectives don't necessarily want the petting, but they do want the ongoing mental contact. They'll say, "I need talk." Because of the Romantic's fear of abandonment, they particularly appreciate the Detective's loyalty. They also value their ability to organize and structure things. Sixes like the Four's emotional depth, creativity, and ability to stimulate feelings. Both types tend to question authority.

Exercises for the Romantic-Detective Couple
The following questions highlight the classic issues that challenge the Four-Six pairing:

Romantics and Detectives are considered look-a-like Types. Not only do they have similar behaviors, they actually do approach the world in a similar philosophical manner. These related approaches can cause them to think and feel alike, strengthening the overall relationship.
- For both of you: In what areas do you feel you have a similar take on the world? How do you believe these similarities strengthen your relationship?

The Four/Six pair's similarities can also cause them to become trapped in the quicksand of life, where neither makes an effort to move away from certain aspects of negative thinking.
- For both of you: In what situations do you feel your similarities work against you as a couple – where neither of you are able to bring a fresh approach to a negative situation?

Reactivity and harsh start-ups
Both Romantics and Detectives are sensitive to criticism and tend to react with defensiveness. Unfortunately, both can be mutually critical and prone to blaming each other. Their arguments can be stormy, often beginning with a "harsh startup," in which the partner who identifies a problem describes it in a negative and accusatory manner. Often they do not even

realize how their approach pushes away the partner, and tends to escalate the conflict rather than works to resolve it.

- For both of you: If you have trouble understanding your partner's unhappiness with you when you disagree, try flipping on a tape recorder the next time you have an axe to grind and approach your partner. Later, listen to your words and tone of voice, and that of your partner as you attempt to discuss the issue. It might be a real eye-opener for you!
- For both of you: Practice healthier conflict resolution. It might be helpful to read John Gottman's books which describe how to avoid harsh startups and teach effective problem solving. See the Appendix for titles.

Suffering

Fours and Sixes can identify with the suffering and sadness in the world, but have very different approaches to this suffering. Romantics suffer because of their long-standing fear of abandonment and believe that no one can really understand them, whereas Detectives, a fear-based Type, are always scanning for the potential negative outcomes. Sharing the higher aspects of Type with regard to this suffering can benefit each of them greatly. The higher aspects of the Four are equanimity and balance, and those of the Six are courage and faith.

* For those on a spiritual path: Where can you share the higher aspects of your type with your partner as they relate to a specific type of suffering in the world (In other words, collude with your partner not only around the negative aspects of life that you can both relate to – but make sure you also cooperate around the higher aspects of your Types, especially when it comes to the suffering you both can understand.)

CHAPTER FORTY-TWO

The Romantic-Adventurer (Four-Seven) Couple

These vignettes from the film "Out of Africa" are an excellent introduction to the Romantic-Adventurer dynamic. Denys, an Adventurer in Type and spirit, has returned from yet another trip to spend time with the long-suffering Karen, a Romantic:

Karen: When you go away on safari, are you ever with someone else?
Denys: I would be with you if I wanted to be with someone.
Karen: Ever get lonely?
Denys: Sometimes.
Karen: Ever wonder if I'm lonely?
Denys: No, I don't.
Karen: Do you think about me at all?
Denys: Often.
Karen: But not enough to come back.
Denys: I do come back.
(A discussion about marriage takes place.)
Karen: I just thought we might do that (get married) someday.
Denys: (Laughs) How would a wedding change things?
Karen: I would have someone of my own.
Denys: No you wouldn't.
Karen: There are some animals who mate for life.
Denys: I would mate for life – one day at a time.
***
Karen: When you go away, you don't always go on safari do you?
Denys: No.

Karen: (You) just want to be away?

Denys: It's not meant to hurt you.

Karen: It does.

Denys: I'm with you because I choose to be with you. I don't want to live someone else's idea of how to live. Don't ask me to do that. I don't want to find out one day that I'm at the end of someone else's life. I'm willing to pay for mine. To be lonely sometimes. To die alone if I have to - I think that's fair.

Karen: Not quite. You want me to pay for it as well.

Denys: No you have a choice. And you're not willing to do the same for me. I won't love you more because of a piece of paper.

Karen: Why is your freedom more important than mine?

Denys: It isn't. And I've never interfered with your freedom.

Karen: No – and I'm not allowed to need you, or rely on you, or expect anything from you – I'm free to leave. But I do need you.

Denys: You don't need me! If I die, will you die? You don't need me, you confuse...mix up...need with want. You always have.

Karen: My God! In the world you would make, there would be no love at all.

Denys: Or the best kind – the kind we wouldn't have to prove.

Karen: You would be living on the moon then.

Denys: Why!?! Because I won't do it your way!?! Are we assuming there is one proper was to do all of this!

(There is talk of another woman.)

Karen: But if she is not important, why won't you give her up? I have learned a thing that you haven't. There are some things worth having. But they come at a price and I want to be one of them. I won't allow it.

Denys: You have no idea the effect that language has on me!

Karen: I used to think there was nothing that you really wanted. But that's not it, is it? You want to have it all!

The Romantic-Adventurer combination is uncommon. But when they do connect, it is definitely an attraction of opposites. On one hand, Adventurers, upbeat and considered the optimists of the enneagram, always find a way to turn lemons into lemonade; on the other side are the Romantics, who experience melancholy as a kind of sweet sadness that lets them know that something is always_missing. When one Adventurer talked about his Romantic sister, he scrunched up his face and divulged that he can't stand to be around her for very long, as she brings him down. He admitted he had to "swear off of her" for several years at one point in his life. He said it as though he was describing a bad habit he had acquired. And then there are the Romantics who describe Adventurers usually with one word (although they will repeat it several times) "superficial, superficial, superficial."

Given that they can have such a strong negative reaction toward each other, what might bring this combination together? The Four is attracted to the Seven's ability to lighten things up, but in an ongoing relationship, this might end up as an annoyance because of the "superficial" issue. Sevens gravitate toward Fours because they might see a helpful role model for going inside and deeper, something the Seven finds difficult. But eventually, the Adventurer may get very tired of the ever present pain and misery and will want to shake him and say, "Snap out of it!" or "Get a life."

If Romantics and Adventurers can remain receptive, they will probably discover that each holds what is good for the other – something that will help balance them, something that is missing. Sevens tend to focus outwardly and overlook what is going on inside, whereas Fours may focus excessively on inner life and depth of relationships. Fours tend to see what is lacking and not enjoy what is actually there; Sevens see life as a smorgasbord just waiting to be enjoyed.

Because of these tendencies, Romantics and Adventurers gravitate to friendships, and some say that they make better friends than lovers. Their opposing traits may work in a friendship but create difficulties when it comes to being soul mates. According to Laurie, an Adventurer:

I mostly have Fours and Ones as friends. I cheer up the Fours, and they make me really look at my emotions. Also, they're great to have around when I do get into my pain and have to deal with it. They're very supportive, because they've been there.

When it comes to romantic relationships, Fours may become attracted to a Seven's charm and initial intense interest. Especially during the beginning stages, they may be fascinated by another's personal stories about their life and travels. Sevens can make that person feel as though a spotlight is trained on him or her. This intense attention can make a Four feel special and unique. In the movie, "Out of Africa," actress Meryl Streep, who plays Karen Blixen, a Four, and actor Robert Redford, who plays Denys Finch Hatton, a Seven, express this very dynamic. Karen says:

We lived disconnected and apart from things. I had been making up stories while he was away. In the evenings, he made himself comfortable in front of the fire and with me sitting cross-legged like Scheherazade herself, he would listen clear-eyed to a long tale from when it began until it ended.

One of the challenges that Romantics and Adventurers must address in their relationship is fear of commitment. Romantics have abandonment issues and fear rejection, reasons for them to not give their heart away easily. Adventurers fear limitations, something they may see as going hand-in-hand with the responsibilities and restrictions that come with a committed relationship. Sevens may resort to on-again-off-again relationships or multiple partners. Fours may become critical where things aren't good enough or something is missing, eventually pushing the partner away. A collusion of sorts with regard to their various fears can occur between the two Types. Commitment-phobic Fours may be attracted to an unavailable Seven, and the Seven might use the Four's push-pull dynamic as a form of on-again/off-again, something Sevens use to maintain a sense of newness in the relationship so as to ward off boredom.

The Romantic's fear of abandonment can be triggered when the Adventurer's impulsivity, avoidance of unpleasantness, and tendency to speak before thinking leads them to broadcast their transient feelings. For example, Jake, the Adventurer, reported, "I get frustrated and threaten to leave, which decreases my partner's trust and openness."

Fours often indulge in excessive dissection and discussion of their emotions, whereas Sevens hesitate to review the past or even to discuss negative events in the past. Darlene, the Four, wrote that her Seven husband tended to "hide his upset and conflicting emotions, and to avoid confrontation." The Four may end up pushing the Seven to emote; the Seven then feels caged and wants to escape.

Ryan, an Adventurer, was quite enamored of Julie. He seemed to want to have every imaginable experience with her and the sooner the better. The night they met, with rain falling "in buckets," Ryan held Julie's hand and encouraged her to jump up and down in the puddles with him. She was charmed by his childlike sense of fun and spontaneity and ability to create charged moments.

As their relationship evolved, though, Julie complained that Ryan was always on the go. On Sunday mornings, for instance, she wanted him to linger in bed, having breakfast, reading the Sunday paper and cuddling. But to Ryan this sounded boring. It began to seem that Julie was always dwelling on what was supposedly missing in their relationship and wanting more. For her part, she felt that he couldn't handle criticism, pain, or anything negative. He'd leave and stay away until everything blew over.

All these are common issues in the Four–Seven pairing. Sevens prefer a fun and light relationship, yet what they really need to experience are depth and moments of pain and growth, something Fours can help with. Enneagram teacher Helen Palmer states in her book *The Enneagram in Love and Work*, "Sevens grow by staying instead of leaving. They grow by dealing with pain." Staying put is good advice for Sevens who feel a need to escape during times of pain and negative emotions. Fours need to learn how to stay in the present moment also. Romantics have a tendency to escape into their fantasies, imagining either the past or the future as a way to avoid predictable relationship ordinariness.

Dr. David Daniels, writing in his advice column for the Enneagram Monthly, gives the following suggestions about self-absorption to a Romantic-Adventurer couple who are considering having a child:

On the down side, Fours can get stuck in moodiness and . . . dwell on what is missing (plenty of opportunity for both of these in parenting). And Sevens can get stuck, yes get stuck, in trying to escape negative feelings and limitation (also plenty of opportunity for both of these in parenting). Since both types have a strong self-referencing tendency, they can get self-absorbed and, at worst, spiral into hurt, anger and withdrawal, none of which are good for the relationship or the parenting process. You both need to stay aware of your tendencies and use this awareness to support each other and ultimately your child if you choose to bring one or more into the world. Healthy attachment for children depends on receptivity and mindfulness.

Adventurers can also be somewhat narcissistic. Darlene, a Romantic, complained about her Adventurer husband: "He always thinks of himself first." Jake, an Adventurer, agreed: "I tend to be insensitive at times." Since Romantics also have a strong self-referencing tendency, the pair can get into a cycle of self-absorption, hurt, anger and withdrawal. Adventurers like constant activity and consider sitting and listening or talking about feelings to be a wasted opportunity. Jake admitted that the chief complaint he heard from his Romantic partner was, "You never listen to me. You don't let me finish talking. You always have to be 'doing, doing, doing.'"

Sevens, in turn, complain about Fours. Jake wrote, "You often take things too seriously, take things too personally and sometimes you court adversity. You expect too much." And, "You never communicate your feelings or thoughts openly. You are always moody." Jake continued, "He has difficulty opening up to true feelings under the drama. Difficulty with being 'okay,' with how things are. He needs to exaggerate, emotionalize or dramatize simple, daily events." Jake clearly has a great deal of insight about his partner. Sometimes Fours seem to wallow in pain, endlessly dissecting their feelings. Sevens, on the other hand, do their best to avoid pain and often don't have much patience for Fours' moodiness.

This mutual self-absorption can cause the couple to behave like two ships passing in the night. The Romantic may be involved in many solitary activities (often mental); the Adventurer may be endlessly busy. It is important that both types stay in touch with their hearts and with their love for each other. According to the enneagram diagram, they both have a connecting line to Type One, the Perfectionist. This means that they could meet there and take on a healthy dose of compassion for some of the injustices and unfairness in the world, thereby moving away from their self-centered focus and allowing them to do noble and compassionate work. This ideally could spill over into their personal relationship. However, if they become critical and judgmental as they actualize this meeting, they end up looking very similar to unhealthy Ones.

As we mentioned earlier, Romantics can provide the emotional depth and Adventurers the spiritual. For the most part, both are "idea people". Fours see what's missing in a situation, while Sevens see what is possible. Together, they have the potential to create something unique that synthesizes several ideas. Enneagram teacher Dr. David Daniels, writing in the *Enneagram Monthly*, put it this way:

> Both Fours and Sevens share a number of important positive attributes: idealism, a passion for possibilities, intensity, and love of adventure to name just a few. And these types can complement each other. Fours bring depth of feeling, acceptance of suffering, focus on relationships, and interest in the inner world while Sevens bring optimism, playfulness, resilience, and a penchant to keep life up (October 2005, page 4).

This is a powerful description of the highest level of relationship that Romantics and Adventurers have the potential to create. Each will have to allow their partner to affect them. Because of their fears, they will have to build and maintain trust and respect in the relationship. They will need to fully commit to each other and stay in the present moment.

Exercises for the Romantic-Adventurer Couple

The following questions highlight the classic issues that challenge the Four-Seven pairing:

The Romantic-Adventurer pairing is unique in that it can fit into both the opposites attract category and the look-a-like category. They are opposites in that Romantics approach the world through their feelings and through allowing pain into their life whereas Adventurers look through the lens of their thoughts and want only to plan for pleasurable activities. Yet they are similar in that they both perceive life as an intense adventure. These two categories are depicted authentically in the movie "Out Of Africa," where, as we described at the beginning of this chapter, Robert Redford plays a high-flying, unavailable Seven while Meryl Streep plays an abandoned Romantic who longs for the unavailable Adventurer. Moviegoers can feel the juice and the intensity in their relationship and surely most want the couple to work it out somehow.

- For both of you: What in your partner initially attracted you to a Type that has both look-a-like qualities and opposites attract characteristics? Do you feel you can make it work long term? In "Out of Africa," it appeared that for the couple to stay together, certain sacrifices would have had to be made. What do you believe you will have to sacrifice in order for *your* relationship to work?
- For the Seven: Do you feel it is possible for you to see the Four's depth of feelings as either interesting or stimulating –a reason for you to stay together?
- For the Four: Is it possible for you to be attracted to being lifted out of your depression by the Seven's ability to uplift others – a reason for you to stay together?
- For both of you: For those on a spiritual path – Opposites attract: The very thing that attracted you to one another in the first place, the thing that is missing in yourself that the other holds, can both energize you and help you to grow spiritually. Think about what your partner can teach you, something that if you adopted it, would

balance you out and make you feel more whole. Just for fun: What did Robert Redford need to learn from Meryl Streep and vice versa?

Dissecting emotions versus living in the moment

As demonstrated so clearly in the scenes from the film "Out of Africa" quoted in this chapter, Fours want extensive discussion of the relationship, of their feelings, and of their concerns about problems, whereas Sevens want to focus on the positives of the present and on future plans. In their quest to avoid pain, they want to avoid rehashing the past, and instead enjoy the moment. Discussions about the relationship feel like a waste of time for the Adventurer. These differences can be a recurrent problem in the relationship.

- For both of you: Given these very divergent approaches to the relationship, try to figure out some middle ground where the Four can express his or her feelings and concerns without the Seven feeling cornered and uncomfortable.

Fear of commitment

Both Fours and Sevens have difficulty with commitment. Fours, in their fear of rejection and focus on what's missing, tend to intermittently push away their existing partners, while Sevens' mantra is "Don't fence me in."

- For both of you: Brainstorm some ways of building some stability into your relationship.

CHAPTER FORTY-THREE

The Romantic-Leader (Four-Eight) Relationship

We met through an online dating site. As soon as I read her profile I knew she was the one for me. The first time I spoke to her I told her she might as well stop resisting, as we were meant to be together forever. We lived a thousand miles apart and yet within a month I had moved in with her. Upon moving in, I brought six cars that I was either fixing or restoring, a motor home, four dogs, and a criminal record. She seemed to like the excess and danger initially, but I guess we just burned out eventually.
-- David a Leader, in relationship with a Romantic

Romantics and Leaders are both attracted to intensity, and their high-energy relationship is likely to be one of drama, lust, fights and a charged emotional climate. If things ever calm down and get boring, one or both will do something to ramp up the energy. Fours interpret Eights' bluntness and lack of pretentiousness as authenticity, which they strongly value in a partner. They also appreciate Eights' exuberance, helping to lift recurrent depressions. When Fours slip into their push-pull behaviors, pursuing and then withdrawing, Eights will stay the course, avoiding enmeshment in the drama. Eights can enjoy the Fours' intensity, gain an appreciation for their emotional depth and share their willingness to stand up for their beliefs.

The positives of the Romantic-Leader pairing
When you think of the Romantic-Leader relationship, some similarities with the Double- Eight pairing come to mind – they both make you wonder, how in the world would they survive? This couple (depending on their level of health, of course) can be good for each other if they play their cards right.

Both Romantics and Leaders feel as if the way to ward off abandonment and also have a real, in-depth connection with the beloved is to be authentic. In order for them to let their guard down and display their vulnerability, they need truth and honesty in the relationship. If Fours and Eights make sure they don't confuse intensity for intimacy, they have a good chance of mutual reassurance with their honesty. Therefore they might be able to create a relationship where both can experience vulnerability and intimacy.

When Romantics try their push-pull maneuver or fall into their pit of despair, the Leader plays dumb, and this lack of response can cause the other to give up this behavior when they see it isn't having an effect. Alternatively, the Romantic may become so angry that this in itself can cause him to shift away from his typical pattern, and a heart-to-heart talk can take place instead. If the Romantic's behavior does persist, it is not unusual for Leaders to get tired or bored and leave. Perhaps if the air can be cleared during these episodes, the Four and Eight might understand each other on a wholly different honest and authentic level. It is at this moment that the Leader will probably ask the Romantic, "What do you want!?!" This cuts to the chase and causes the Romantic to truly identify their wants and needs and allows the partner to get to know them better.

Eights can benefit from the Four's complex interior life and valuing of feelings. They have a tendency to see things in black and white. They are truly "what you see is what you get" kind of people. If the Eight opens up to the Four's world of complex feelings and insight about the human condition, they can be powerful in a more holistic way. Partners of Eights sometimes describe how with great strength and tenacity, he or she seemed to provide the vehicle that transported the person out of the stuck place and onto the other side while the partner did the personal work. The Leader can thus find his or her own deeper feelings, eventually unearthing a richer, more complex person hidden inside.

Together, Romantics and Leaders can make great partners in the external world of projects and accomplishments. If the Four is truly the "artist" or idea person yet is too afraid to be assertive, the Eight can champion the Four, helping him or her to find the courage to self-promote. This trust and cooperative spirit can also extend into the intimate aspect of the relationship, and their intense focus can get diffused in a healthy way, transformed into a deeper level of intimacy. The Romantic is now willing to drop his or her guard first, and the Leader will follow suit, resulting in them truly trusting each other.

Challenges of the Romantic-Leader relationship

The shared intensity of the Four-Eight couple means that their challenges, just like their shared positive traits, can loom very large. It's not surprising that in our survey, both Romantics and Leaders considered the other's Type as among the personalities they struggle with the most. Yet Romantics who love a Leader and Leaders who are drawn to a Romantic do exist.

With time, Fours may perceive Eights as dominating, insensitive, bull-in-the-china-shop controllers. Some of the negative statements that Fours made about Eights were: "They want to control and domineer." "They are too controlling of the partner and at the same time often don't pay adequate attention to them. They seem to be the least sensitive of the types." "Their 'big energy' takes over and I don't feel seen." These are very strong statements. Romantics are not easily controlled unless they are unhealthy. Leaders want to control things that are important to them, even possess them — including partners. Both types can be powerful in their own way, and the power struggles can be intense. Leaders need to make sure Romantics feel understood, while Romantics need to make sure that Leaders feel respected.

Fours, who are image types, place great value on their appearance and presentation and may complain about the Eight's lack of interest in style. Fours might flip-flop, wanting their Eight partner to "show well," but also feeling a sense of freedom in watching them break societal rules. In her book *The Enneagram in Love and Work,* author Helen Palmer states, "Both are likely to think of themselves as above the rules…(Fours) are special enough to be above the law, or Eights, who feel stronger than the law." (P. 338)

Romantics want their partner to open up and reveal innermost feelings, and they feel frustrated when that doesn't happen. Pedro, a Romantic, complained to his partner Mary, a Leader, "You always want to fight. You can't allow your vulnerability to show." In truth, though Fours are just as good at hiding their intimate side as Eights, Romantics are afraid that you'll see their "flaws" and then leave. Neither Type is good at putting themselves out there. However, with the strong emotions they express, Fours appear more ready and willing. In actuality, both are probably waiting for the other to open up so that they can feel safe enough also to be vulnerable.

With time, Leaders often perceive their Romantic partner as a self-absorbed "drama queen" who is emotionally demanding. Some of the negative statements Leaders made about Romantics were: "The drama was just too much for me and I fantasize about telling them to get a life. Get real." "Roller coaster rides and emotional turmoil." As you can see, Leaders struggle with the drama and strong emotions of Romantics. These behaviors just don't fit into the Eight's approach to the world, especially their image of being "real." Eights tend not to believe that the Four's drama serves any useful purpose.

One Leader saw Romantics as a "bottomless pit of neediness," and struggled with their "self pity." Again, neediness and self-pity do not fit into the overall worldview of the Leader. Eights want to make sure they are perceived as strong and powerful, yet, the very thing they need is to get in touch with their own vulnerability. As in most relationships, we usually attract people who push our buttons and put us in touch with our shadow side and the lessons that we most need to learn.

Bernard, a Leader in our survey, considered it a problem that his Romantic wife, Rachel, "longed for what others have." Bernard's perspective was "I wanted more of what *we* have." Envy and longing are particular to Romantics as they focus on what is missing in the moment and then wonder why they don't have it. Leaders focus on the present. Longing is a foreign term for them as they usually go directly for what they want. No wonder they confuse and frustrate each other at times. Yet with the Enneagram, both types have an opportunity to understand the other's coping strategies that help them feel safe in the world. It is through this knowledge that we can have both understanding and compassion, support each other in our work with our very different personality styles.

Exercise for the Romantic-Leader Couple

The following questions highlight the classic issues that challenge the Four-Eight pairing:

The Romantic-Leader pairing in a word is about intensity. Neither Type can handle boredom or repetition and both will intensify their environment -- Fours by drama and suffering and Eights by fighting. Fours appreciate Eights' ability to stay put during the Romantic's dramatic push-pulls. Leaders respect partners who can handle conflict. Neither Fours nor Eights are big fans of intimacy or vulnerability.

- For both of you: What purpose does the intensity or conflict serve in your relationship? Do you think you confuse intimacy with intensity?

The Romantic-Leader combination works fairly well with the Four's push-pull and tendency for depression and with the Eight's wanting to fight.

- For the Four: How do you think your Eight partner handles the push-pull in the relationship and your tendency toward depression?

- For the Eight: How do you think your Four partner handles conflict?
- For both of you: What balance or stability do you think your combination provides overall?

Power struggles

Romantics and Leaders are each powerful in their way, and their power struggles can be intense.

- For both of you: How can you resolve your power struggles in a constructive way?

Emotions, feelings, and drama

Romantics are known for their focus on emotions and feelings, whereas Leaders seem to translate every negative feeling they may have into anger. Eights want action and not an endless discussion of feelings. They are loathe to expose their inner core and vulnerability and prefer to project an image of strength. They have no patience for the Four's drama.

- For the Four: Given your partner's aversion to explore their own feelings or to discuss yours, how can you meet your need to feel close to the Eight and to be able to express yourself?
- For the Eight: Given your aversion to drama and to the Four's attention to feelings, how can you and your partner incorporate these needs of the Four into your relationship?

For those on a spiritual path: Fours look for truth and authenticity while Eights look for truth and vulnerability.

- For both of you: How do you think you support your partner in accessing the higher aspects of their type? How do you think you support your partner in general on their spiritual path?

CHAPTER FORTY-FOUR

The Romantic-Mediator (Four-Nine) Relationship

He is sweet and accommodating and absolutely hates conflict or chaos in his life-- we were probably a mismatch, since drama and communication and confronting issues head-on are all things that I gravitate towards (all things that he avoids at all cost)! After being threatened by his ultra-Christian mom that she would virtually disown him if he continued dating me, he stopped answering his phone calls for a couple weeks, and the next thing I knew, he was breaking up with me to appease her. So it has been a strange month--he is really a sweet and interesting person, so it's come as quite a disappointment. On the other hand, I'm not sure that I can be with someone who's terrified of communication and confrontation. It was a challenge already.

-- 25-year-old Romantic woman, about a Mediator

My need to have some processing time especially with regard to relationship issues clashes with my Four partner's need to immediately confront any issue she may perceive as a problem, and her need to work it until there is some resolution. Gayle finds it very frustrating when I can't offer my thought or feeling at that immediate moment and I seem to "check out." I find it frustrating when Gayle continues to press me for that thought or feeling which is really not accessible to me at that moment.

We both recognize these type differences. To make these differences easier to work with, I acknowledge to her that I'm not blowing her off. I ask for some time to process, and we agree on a time to revisit the issue. I actually could blow it off, but Gayle doesn't allow me to do so, and holds me to the time frame agreed on for my revisiting it. I in turn honor that commitment.

OK, if life was that easy. There are still many times we get lost in holding and defending our own type and not look at the big picture of recognizing we often come from different "type"-related places and needs. It's always a work in progress.
-- Norman, a Mediator and teacher, in a 1-year relationship with a Romantic

I want Jerry to open up, to want to talk, to want to listen, and to want affection and time together. He stays closed and quiet to keep himself safe. He wants honesty but not about our relationship. His Nine behavior of avoiding intimacy works against my Four's desire to bathe in intimacy. His "laziness" lies mostly in refusing to discuss issues, so it's not really laziness, but rather strong determination.
We haven't solved the dilemma. I've once again lapsed into resignation that nothing will change, and I opt to remain married because I have nothing to move to, and also the kids so strongly want the family united. I try to focus on enjoying my life by fulfilling my other pursuits: counseling and creativity. Jerry tends to his many social groups, and we're cool.
-- Maria, a Romantic, writing about her "classic fight" with her husband

Jerry, a Mediator married to Maria for more than 50 years, replied, avoiding facing the issue in classic Mediator style:

Boy this is complex – and I have a six-day trip scheduled (fortunately for me?!). I'm going to use avoidance – and excuse it by hoping you need these back in some reasonable time. And I doubt that another six days would give me that series of acute Ahas which I think I would need to penetrate myself and answer.

Romantic-Mediator is a common pairing. Romantics, who fear loss and abandonment, are attracted to the accepting, non-judgmental Mediator who is unlikely to leave them. In turn, Mediators bask in the energy and vitality of Romantics. Differences in these personalities, however, result in both having unfulfilled needs: The Four wants ongoing romance and attentiveness, real engagement and in-depth discussions of feelings from the Nine, who tends to tune out. The Nine prefers comfort to confusion and confrontation and wants reciprocal unconditional acceptance. Romantics tend to focus on what's missing and try to change the Mediator.

The two Types process information differently: Fours want to discuss things immediately, whereas Nines, who see all sides of an issue, need time to sort it out. Many Nines are wonderful public speakers who, though fluent in front of a microphone or with friends, may be tongue-tied in therapy or in a one-on-one discussion. They need time even when motivated, and their avoidance of conflict delays thinking about it. In Jerry and Maria's 50-year marriage the recurrent issue was engagement in the relationship. Maria describes a decades-long effort to get Jerry involved on the deep emotional level she seeks, and his avoidance. She focuses on what's missing in the marriage; he feels criticized and he tunes out.

Positive aspects of the Romantic-Mediator relationship

Like most other types, Romantics react very positively to Mediators. In our survey, Romantics chose the Mediator as one of the most compatible personality Types. Their reasons included: "I can help Nines get in touch with their own needs." "We share conflict avoidance." "I love their mellowness." "Nonjudgmental and kind, calming." " My Nine friends are kind and understanding, comfortable companions who listen well." "Their ability to see the whole picture and to empathize with others."

Fours like Nines (according to Baron & Wagele) because they are nonjudgmental and treat them gently, have a spiritual and empathetic sense and listen even if they don't completely understand what is being said. Nines like Fours because they can feel important and be listened to. Fours can also help the Nines get more in touch with their feelings.

Romantics see themselves in relationship as "Generous, adoring, needy." "High maintenance, expressive, caring." In apparent reference to his authenticity, one man wrote, "I've been using my love of truth to explore my own emotional depth and sensitivity." Several Four women wrote, "I share my thoughts and feelings as much as he'll let me." "Communicate, communicate, communicate (the good, the bad, and the ugly)."

One Romantic described her Mediator partner as "easygoing, content, communicates on a surface level." Other characteristics ascribed to Mediators were, "His accepting behavior. I never felt out of place with him." "She is a peacemaker and is able to love unconditionally." Listing gifts to the relationship, a Mediator wrote, "My sense of humor and compassion." "I am supportive to my partner as an individual and with personal issues (issues outside the relationship). I encourage him to feel good about himself." Damaris, a Four, wrote,

When I left the corporate world, I wanted to make a life with more meaning and fulfillment. My husband was very supportive, made no demands, and was very happy to be the stable, secure person who is able to meet my needs. I

am more competitive, risky, and accomplishment-driven (Three wing), and his nature allowed me to do this.

In summary, Fours appreciate the Nine's accepting nature, which can counteract their fear of abandonment and frequent low self-esteem. For their part, Fours can help Nines get in touch with their feelings, and the Four's energy and drama counteracts the Nine's tendency to tune out.

Challenges of the Romantic-Mediator relationship

Romantics and Mediators approach life very differently. Romantics' tendency to melancholy and self-absorption plus their focus on what is missing is the opposite of the Mediator's optimistic, trusting, and outgoing nature. A push-pull relationship can ensue. Romantics want intensity and drama; Mediators want peace. Romantics pursue, Mediators disengage. Fours feel abandoned; Nines feel pressured. Fours are all too clear about their desires and what is missing in the relationship; Nines have difficulty directly communicating what they want or need. Fours can see Nines as boring; Nines can see Fours as overdramatic. Here are some particular issues:

Romantics want authenticity, Mediators seek comfort and avoid confrontation.

In their quest for peace and comfort, Mediators will accept conditions that are far from ideal, ignoring their own wants. Marlon, a Four in a long-term marriage, wrote disapprovingly of his Nine wife, "She puts her own needs after everyone else's." When asked what slogan they thought their Nine partners would put on a T-shirt, one Four wrote, "Don't rock the boat. Peace at any cost. Make nice, and don't make waves." Another Four wrote that her Nine husband would have a T-shirt saying, "It's better than nothing." Clearly, neither of these Romantics approved of this approach to life. A Mediator recognized that, "I'm too laid back. Too peaceful – too easily relaxed – too conflict avoiding – too passive." A Romantic wrote, "He's a couch potato, into comfort and stability (this is both positive and negative)." Tanya, a Sexual-subtype Romantic who split up with a Mediator after several years, related:

Oren didn't want to make the effort to make his own friends when he moved back to the area after living 200 miles away for ten years. So he just "adopted" his old friends' group of new friends. They hosted gatherings, dinners, parties, and engaged in small talk. It met his Nine need for socializing without having to put out much effort. The Four in me craved authentic connection with people – not cocktail party talk about who makes the best red wine. I was not into the enneagram at the time we were dating; rather, I was into my "extreme emotions" and would just deplore his friends' gatherings.

Were that to happen today, I might have less intense emotions about it, but I still like to be able to talk to people about meaningful things. We never resolved that issue and are no longer together. It was a mutual decision to split up.

Romantics want intensity and deep connection, but Mediators aren't present

Norman, a Mediator, quoted his wife Gayle voicing one of the most common complaints Romantics have about Mediators: "You never share your feelings unless I ask you! I don't know what's going on in your life because you don't share much about your daily stuff. And when I ask, it's like pulling teeth." Mediators in their reticence may think, "Even if I say things, she won't care. It doesn't really matter." Or, "I don't want to burden you, it's no big deal." This is part of the 'forgetting themselves' that is often attributed to Mediators. Romantics wrote: "He hides from interaction of a personal nature, preferring the safety of groups and crowds." "He's not connected to his feelings or needs. He's not passionate about anything in life (except baseball). He's passive-aggressive. He watches TV a lot!" "He is unwilling to discuss problems. He fears 'getting in trouble.' He stays closed and quiet to keep himself safe. He wants honesty but not about our relationship." Conversely, Norman wrote,

Gayle is always analyzing our relationship in order to keep it on a constant high. She is very self-judgmental. She is critical (mostly self-directed). She always needs the relationship to have a spark or even be on fire, which leaves little room for the uneventful stuff which is also a part of relationships. Fours have a hard time dealing with the ordinariness of life.

The Mediator may wonder in exasperation, "Do you have to make everything extraordinary?"

Status quo vs. what's missing

With their fixation on what's missing, Romantics are always aware of how they would like their partner to be different – more attentive, more involved, more open, more romantic. Mediators seek comfort and consensus. They settle into a pattern and are content with it. The extra energy they initially put into their primary relationship settles down to a calmer, more serene level. Their attention may go elsewhere – work, friends, or nature. Jerry, a Nine, reports that Maria complains, "You are gone too much. You do things outside the house. You don't pay enough attention to me. You don't talk to me enough." Maria recognizes her contribution to the relationship problems: "I have a constant focus on what's missing. I'm more self-referenced and don't put enough focus on Jerry."

Marlon acknowledges having trouble "dealing with my longing for something that is missing in my life and projecting this onto my mate as her responsibility to be or become what I am creating in my imagination."

Romantics can project all their fantasy desires onto their partners, and conclude that the Mediator can never be enough, can never measure up. They may try relentlessly to change him or her and can come across as being very critical. Maria, a Romantic, writes that Jerry complains, "You're trying to control me. I can't make you happy." Indeed, Jerry writes that he keeps telling Maria, "You criticize me too much. You're like my father. I'm never good enough to suit you." He continues, "Nothing's good enough over the long haul. Maria's attitude is, 'I want what I don't have. Four envy!'" This is echoed by Marlon, who relates, "Brittany [his Nine wife]'s biggest complaint has been that I correct or criticize how she does things."

Nines may thus feel they are living with a bottomless pit of needs. The Nine will react to the Four's efforts to change them with passive-aggressive behavior or withdrawal.

Commitment

Fours and Nines both have an uneasy relationship with commitment. Many Romantics, after spending time in one failed relationship after another, finally recognize their problem with commitment. Ever aware of what is missing in their relationship, the possibility of abandonment always looms. They recognize that the more they love, the more they risk being hurt if their partner leaves. Because Mediators are so accepting of others' flaws, so nonjudgmental, and so loyal, the initial attraction may be strong. However, although Mediators may be physically present, they can also be emotionally unavailable. This is one of the major complaints about Nines by partners of any personality type. The Mediators stick around but mentally and emotionally bail out. This behavior affirms the Romantic's life theme that people get abandoned, but it also means that they themselves don't have to show up, put themselves on the line, and have people see them for who they really are. To be emotionally and spiritually naked to another person defines intimacy, so the Romantic-Mediator relationship, after the initial spark, may ultimately lack intimacy. Couples who are willing to discuss the problems can reach a solution, even if it's not easy and doesn't easily happen. Norman, a Mediator, wrote about Gayle, the Romantic:

Gayle and I had developed a close friendship over a year. Feelings shifted toward a relationship of intimacy. She wanted but was reluctant to take it to this level for fear of it not working out and then losing this close friendship. I reassured her that I was not the type to abandon relationships and if anything, I hold on to them too long. I assured her that if our attempt at being intimates should fail, we would always have our friendship, as it is important for me that we stay connected. As we chose to look at "us" in a different way, I suggested that we "check in" with each other periodically to sense how we are both doing. My commitment to keeping a connection and my suggestion that we check in helped my partner feel more comfortable taking our friendship to another level.

I would usually not follow through on the "checking in" part. More often I put my energy into avoiding relationship conversation for fear of confrontation. But Gayle, being the Four she is, makes sure we check in periodically (sometimes too often!) to keep us focused on this transformation in an authentic way. And, she does not let me get away with diverting the conversation to something else. Between my honest commitment to not abandon a wonderful friendship and Gayle's desire to always check in on this transition of ours (which I know is important but have trouble doing on my own), we have supported (some of) our concerns and needs in relationship.

Norman's perspective describes his attempts to counter key elements of his personality that might undermine an intimate relationship. Mediators tend to begin well, but then the juice drains out. They lose their focus and then shift their attention elsewhere. Norman is being called on that, and his willingness to look at his part reflects a Mediator's ability to see the other person's viewpoint. Nines can be very supportive of their partners.

Advice from Romantic- Mediator couples

Nines suggest
- To the Four: Balance being a couple in relationship with being independent in relationship. Give me both space (independence) and recognition of my importance as a person and in the relationship. Don't criticize too much.

- To the Nine: Allow yourself to be vulnerable, fully engaged, and present. Nothing you can do will make it perfect. Don't take criticism too personally.

Fours suggest
- To the Nine: Share your thoughts and feelings, be open, make physical intimacy follow naturally. Make me laugh – bring out the kid in me. Share your feelings. Be able to connect with me spiritually.
- To the Four: Focus on what is here (the good things), vs. what's missing. Study the enneagram thoroughly so you can be aware of your "stuff," and be aware/sympathetic to your partner's challenges. Find peace within yourself. Accept total responsibility for your own happiness. Find someone you adore and then become worthy of that person's love.

Exercises for the Romantic-Mediator couple
The following questions highlight the classic issues that challenge the Four-Nine pairing:

Many enneagram enthusiasts think that the Four-Nine pairing is the most prevalent of all the combinations. Initially there may be a powerful connection between the two. This is because the Four-Nine couple exhibits such strong charm. The Romantic seems to have found someone who won't abandon them and who accepts them flaws and all. Eventually though, the Mediator reverts to some of his or her old behaviors, such as zoning out, and the Romantic feels abandoned once again.
- For both of you: Discuss the difference between the initial infatuation stage and the stage where the Four feels abandoned because the Nine is emotionally unavailable, not really present.

During this next stage a power struggle can occur. Fours initiate drama when feeling abandoned, while Nines feel blamed although they don't recognize that they have not been engaged with their partner and would say that they have no intention of exiting the relationship.
- For both of you: Discuss how each person's behavior feels for the other. Be open to discuss your perceptions so that misperceptions can be corrected.

The next stage could be referred to as, "the push-pull" versus the "it doesn't matter anyway" stage. In response to the Nine's merging and zoning out behaviors, the Four will take on a push-pull dynamic in which they both adore and reject the Nine. Because the Nines probably felt overlooked in childhood and now senses alternately love and rejection from the partner for no obvious reason, Nines will read this as "it doesn't matter" and then finally, "I don't matter."

- For the Four: Discuss your push/pull behavior with your Nine partner.

- For the Nine: Discuss with your Four partner the connection between feeling overlooked as a child and at present feeling alternately loved and rejected. Express what it's like for you to believe that you just don't matter.

- For both of you: For those on a spiritual path, how will the Four transform drama to balance and the Nine transform sloth to right action?

CHAPTER FORTY-FIVE

The Double-Observer (Five-Five) Relationship

Because Ben and I are the same type, we are able to gently and lovingly point out blind spots, often with a great deal of humor. We know the usual defenses so well – the tendency to withdraw when things get tough – that we pick up the signs and language early on, before the mind grabs a tight hold.
-- Ruth, an Observer, in relationship for one year with another Five

Observers are people who live in their heads. They like to gather information and analyze it thoroughly before drawing conclusions. They need private time and space, and they respect other people's needs for space, alone time, and time to process their feelings. It's easy for Fives to feel invaded by others. Not surprisingly, then, in our survey, Observers indicated their own type frequently as people with whom they feel most comfortable.

The Positives in the Double-Observer relationship:
Because Observers feel comfortable being alone and detached, they often don't connect with each other. A good analogy is with desert tortoises. How do they find one another and pair up? Certainly there are no singles bars for tortoises, not that they would ever attend them if there were, as they don't seem to be sufficiently sociable. Tortoises have a hard shell covering their most vulnerable parts, wear a poker face, exist on very little, and never make a sound. Nonetheless, a walk through the desert often shows tortoises paired up with one another. It's interesting to wonder how this happened and whether they are truly happy that they had found someone so similar and so unique as them.

What does a Five-Five pairing look like? The following Observer statements as to why Fives like being with other Fives will give you a flavor for the relationship: "I like people who think and feel. I like people who are reclusive like me. They understand the value and reason for reclusiveness and don't judge it as something bad." "With another Observer, we can have quiet time together and read without being bothered and do separate quiet activities in one room." "This is the best ever! I feel understood, I don't have to work so hard to explain."

Many people appreciate those who are similar, but Observers especially like this because they feel different or unique when it comes to relationships or socializing. Fives together understand each other's desire for solitude and can also share each other's desire to conserve time, energy and space. Being aware of a sense of emptiness, Observers pair up, but they also fear being smothered in relationship. What better partner than a fellow Observer who will respect boundaries and essential privacy! In the Five's private moments, they often replay previous interactions in their mind's eye and then attach feelings to them. Accordingly they recognize that they are deeply embedded in their Five partner's mind and feelings.

Helen Palmer, in *The Enneagram in Love and Work,* deftly describes such a couple's life as follows:

> A double Five lifestyle is often focused on short, meaningful interactions followed by emotional rest. Time apart allows each to review the feelings that are suspended during face-to-face encounters, and the conclusions that emerge in solitude may be especially poignant because they fill the inner emptiness.

When asked about the gifts her partner Ben brought to the relationship, Ruth replied, "Humor, integrity, devotion to truth, genuine compassion and love."

Challenges of the Double-Observer pairing

The Observer-Observer couple faces challenges to the relationship that are primarily related to their fears and anxieties, need for space, tendency to intellectualize feelings, and propensity for withdrawing. Ruth, a Five, acknowledged, "Because of my experience with complications in my past relationships, I tend to withdraw when problems appear, feeling that it's not worth working on things." She reports that her partner Ben's chief complaint about her is that she tends to believe her own insecurities. Her advice to a young Observer in relationship is "Expose the truth, but don't take it so seriously!"

Fives withdraw, physically and emotionally, especially if they feel that there is too much closeness or intensity. It is sometimes much easier for a Five to say, "I can do without this." Healthy levels of intimacy require partners to stay put during difficult times. If we tend to withdraw when strong emotions surface, both of us are doing the relationship a disservice. Observers enter into a relationship because they have become aware of emotional emptiness, but that emptiness can serve as a saving grace, an anchor, keeping you in place if there is an urge to flee. Baron and Wagele have a Type Eight (Leader) quotation in their book that says, "Don't go to bed mad, stay up and fight!" Observers need to memorize this saying. When they are able to stand and fight with their partners, it is usually a sign of a deep connection.

For an Observer to allow strong feelings to arise in the presence of another person is quite a compliment. In those moments though, Observers should be careful of their razor-sharp tongues and their need to "tell it as it is" or, as our quote says, "expose the truth." Observers tend to either say nothing or everything. They think that truth is the most important thing, so they won't pull any punches. They may say, "If it's the truth, how can it be wrong to tell him?" But this tendency not to temper their comments can be hurtful. Tact and diplomacy are skills that Fives need to learn. For Ruth and Ben, because they apparently are able to mitigate the naked truth with caring, it seems to work. Ruth reports: "He's so good, so ruthlessly honest, so willing to expose what is required that our 'problems' get resolved readily."

Fives strongly value competence. Having thoroughly researched an issue, they may believe they have "the truth" and therefore can seem arrogant, a dark side of their commitment to honesty. Ruth wrote that what keeps her from effective problem solving in her relationship is, "believing I am 'right' and he is not." This is where Observers can look a lot like Perfectionists (Ones). Therapists often find themselves asking a One the question, "Do you want to be right or do you want to be happy?" The more relevant question to pose to Observers might be, "Would you rather be 'all-knowing' or truly know another?" All knowing comes from the head, knowing another comes from the heart.

Both partners share a fear-based personality, tending to anxiety and worries about the future of the relationship; one or both might decide it's easier to give up than to work things out. Ruth wrote about this very problem:

For each of us, our biggest fear is not that the relationship will sour and end, but rather that things will continue to go undeniably well! What we keep coming back to is that the more we surrender to the unknown and trust its unfolding through us, the better and more relaxed we are. To allow the natural flow of love to have its way instead of thinking we are somehow in charge and can control it has been the single most important thing we can do.

As you see, Ruth beautifully describes how Observers struggle with control versus letting go in the relationship. As with all head types, Fives try to control situations with their minds instead of accessing their heart space – where the "natural flow of love," as she eloquently puts it, exists.

Exercises for the Double-Observer Couple

The following exercises highlight the classic issues that challenge the Five-Five pairing:

My friends tell me I have an intimacy problem. But they don't really know me.
-- Gary Shandling

Because Observers seek solitude and tend to be out of touch with their emotions, many people don't understand why a Five would even seek a relationship. Fives can begin to dread the emotional emptiness they may experience after years of detachment. The Double-Observer pairing is not as rare as one would guess. This couple truly understands each another and has little difficulty respecting the boundaries of the relationship.

- For both of you: Discuss what initially attracted you to each other. Talk about the possible emotional emptiness of being alone and the bonus of having someone in your life. Share with each other any fears you had about being in a relationship and how pairing with another Five may have made it easier.

The Fives' environment may consist of something like a little house behind a house – sometimes referred to as a mother-in-law house. Each chooses one of the houses (or part of their home) as their separate space and then both usually reside together in one of the homes on the weekends. At some point they may question whether they are "cheating" since they are not doing relationship in a traditional manner.

- For both of you: Because you have the option of withdrawing, do you ever feel like you "cheat" or cut intimacy short by checking out during difficult moments? Do either one of you close down before a conversation is finished – frustrating the other one at times – much as you frustrate other people who want information from you?

For those on a spiritual path: To paraphrase from the movie "A Beautiful Mind," "Perhaps it is a great gift to have a beautiful mind, but even greater is to have a beautiful heart." Unifying head and heart helps the Observer develop.

- For both of you: How can you balance your head and heart? Discuss with each other the difficulties and benefits of allowing your feelings to emerge in the moment, in face-to-face to encounters with each other as opposed to allowing your feelings to emerge only in private?

CHAPTER FORTY-SIX

The Observer-Detective (Five-Six) Relationship

I've been married for seven months to a great man. I'm 43, had never been married and was very happy being single. I enjoy my solitude and autonomy and didn't think I was cut out for marriage, which was fine by me. Then this man came into my life ... totally loving, accepting of my idiosyncrasies, a great partner in every way. I didn't exactly feel fireworks, but I'm mistrustful of fireworks anyway. With him it was a more gradual awareness of the quality of person he was, the way that he loved me and how lucky I was to have someone like him in my life. I approached the relationship with openness and made a very thoughtful decision to share my life with him. So, I moved out of my little home in an inner-city neighborhood, which I loved, and we got a house together. But if I'm honest with myself I'm not happy sharing a home with anyone. I don't want out of the relationship or marriage. I just want to go back to living by myself ... seeing each other several times a week as we did before. I want to be able to come home from work and have the house to myself sometimes, not have him always be there.

We do have separate bedrooms, which has helped some. And if I wanted to do more things with my friends or independently he'd have no problem with that. But my gut is telling me that's not the issue and that I'm just not cut out to live with anyone; that I'm always going to need to have my own place to be deep-down-in-the-core happy. (Dec. 8, 2005, Salon.com)

This letter appeared in an advice column by Cary Tennis. The writer was probably an Observer (Five). In the letter, you hear the frustration and the dilemma of living alone versus living with someone the writer appreciates and loves very much. Traditional and fairy tale marriages are about falling in love and living happily ever after – together. They don't take into account that a person might find it difficult to live with someone else because, although he or she might be totally in love, there's the problem of feeling intruded upon.

An Observer-Detective (Five-Six) couple, Larry and Linda, experienced similar issues. They had been together for over fifteen years, doing all the things that married couples do, except that they didn't live together. They had made several failed attempts, in fact. Linda, the Six, loved and respected Larry, but she really wanted a wedding and a traditional marriage in which they went to bed together every night and woke up together every morning. Larry, the Five, had earlier tried to live with Linda because he loved her dearly, and he truly wanted her to be happy. But with each attempt, his reaction seemed almost phobic or as if he was allergic to such a living arrangement.

In counseling sessions, Larry worked on scarcity and depletion, typical Observer fears. Specifically, he feared that Linda might become ill one day, and he would be depleted by having to take care of her. With his fear acknowledged and worked through, he eventually became more abundance-minded and began to trust that they could solve these problems. Eventually, he became more "generous" in spirit. Linda, who had lost her father during a critical juncture in childhood, addressed her own fear, which embodied needing a protective figure in her life. She eventually was able to find her own sense of strength and individuality as well as respecting Larry's need for space. Together, they were ultimately able to live "happily ever after" under one roof.

Positive aspects of the Observer-Detective relationship

The Observer-Detective couples share many characteristics. Both are in the head center (Five, Six, and Seven), meaning that they are most comfortable relating mentally rather than through emotions. The Five and Six are each other's wings, so the Five can understand the Six's fear, while the Six is empathetic to the Five's need for solitude and often shares this need. In our survey, Detectives listed the Observer as one of the types they get along with best. "With my strong Five wing, I tend to fit right in with them and even am mistaken for a Five." They understood the need for space: "I know you respect my privacy." And then finally, their minds: "I admire their intellectual bent." "I can have a rational discussion with them."

Their conversations can be animated and wide-ranging, while at the same time both are content to sit in the same room for hours and read without interrupting each other. Helen Palmer wrote in her book *The Enneagram in Love and Work,*

Both types are known for long-term relationships because permanent commitment and the feeling of "forever" cut through detachment and doubt. They are also low-maintenance people, able to pull together against adversity and to endure long periods of worldly frustration. Once committed, they relate through shared ideas as much as through romantic involvement. . . Sixes are unusually susceptible to affection. . . In Five-Six relationships, a single tender moment can become a cornerstone of commitment when it is cemented in the mind forever. (P. 348)

Another Detective, Cheryl, explained that she helped her relationship thrive by planning well. Martin, a Five, wrote that his Six wife Olive's gifts were "loyalty, caring, and the ability to foresee problems." Martin's own gift to the relationship was, "I can understand/see patterns (problems) develop and can bring them out in the open early for discussion." When asked about challenges they met successfully, Cheryl replied,

We've remodeled an older home together – resolved the issues about what was wrong and needed fixing and created a really nice house. We are good at working together to create something. We are good at researching things. We have a comfortable relationship but there is no fire.

You can feel the camaraderie, the gifts each brings to the relationship. With regard to the lack of fire, also mentioned in the advice column, the Five writer says, "I didn't exactly feel fireworks, but I'm mistrustful of fireworks anyway." Fear types may distrust fireworks but do need to make sure that the heart center plays some role in their relationship.

Martin, the Observer, described his contribution to the relationship: "Raising children – I could ease her doubt about the safety of things to do – She would be able to have us better prepared for possible problems." Observers bring the strength of knowledge, and Detectives bring the strength of preparedness. Other than Nines (Mediators), healthy Observers can feel unconditional love better than anyone. They put the beloved on a pedestal and are totally committed

Another Five-Six couple included Ashley, a Detective whose mood would swing from manic to depressed; perhaps she was bipolar. Sometimes she would just stay in bed. After she'd been in her bedroom for a few hours, her Observer husband Gene would come in, undress her, carry her into the shower, bathe her gently, and hold her until her depression began to lift. Gene was totally there for her in these ways. He loved Ashley, and nothing shook him.

Challenges of the Observer-Detective relationship

Observers need time and space to sort through events and issues and to recognize their feelings about what happened. This can be problematic in any relationship, but the Detective's fears can exaggerate it. The Detective can interpret the Observer's desire for solitude as emotional withdrawal and lack of caring or else as being punitive or quietly hostile. His fears get projected onto the Five and worst-case scenarios are imagined. Sixes need reassurance about their partner's love and resolution of relationship uncertainties, but an insecure Six's repeated requests for signs and words of affection can make the Five feel invaded. The response might be further withdrawal. In this way, the Six will have brought about a self-fulfilling prophecy.

Complaints, challenges, and type-related difficulties for the Observer

Martin, an older, Self-Preservation Observer, recognizes that "I am liable to get too concentrated in what I am doing and as a result not pay attention to the other. I often do not communicate what is on my mind, then think that I did." He reports hearing from Olive, his Detective wife: You don't see me!" "I don't talk enough, and she needs me to read her mind/know what she wants." This Observer advises younger Fives in relationship, "Be more open more to feelings, both expressing and feeling them."

Cheryl, a Detective wrote exactly the same thing about her Observer spouse: "You don't communicate. Why can't you tell me how you are feeling, am I boring you, would you rather be somewhere else?" Notice that the Six personalizes the Five's actions, concluding that he might be bored, not wanting to be with her.

Fives have a tendency to detach and provide a minimum of information about themselves. This is very unsettling for Sixes, who need to know how things stand in order to feel safe. Helen Palmer, a Six herself, continues,

> Observers may not realize how punishing their detachment can be. By saying nothing, they appear to be aloof and un-caring, and that silence broadcasts as an admission of guilt to Six. . . Fives respect people who can contain their feelings. It helps immensely if the Six can back off, agree to a time for discussions, and assume an attitude of neutrality. . . Observers

can help by revealing their own thinking. A Five's honest 'I don't know' is infinitely more reassuring than saying nothing. . . An Observer holds enormous power in this relationship because a Six's fears are activated by lack of presence. (*The Enneagram in Love and Work*, p. 347).

Palmer explains perfectly the typical dance of the Five-Six pairing. Sixes need to avoid personalizing the Five's need for privacy. Fives must make an effort to communicate what appear to be the simplest bits of information, perceived as valuable nuggets, to keep the Six partner reassured.

Complaints, challenges, and type-related difficulties for the Detective

Sixes' fears, when triggered by a Five's withdrawal, can escalate into paranoia. Cheryl, a Detective, described her tendency toward "worst-case thinking. Silence on his part equals rejection. It must be my fault if. . ." Recognizing this about herself, Cheryl advised other Detectives in relationship "Remember that not everything that is bad will necessarily happen. It's not always about you."

Cheryl has heard complaints from Rob, her Observer husband, that, "You always think the worst, overdramatize, overreact, beat yourself up. You take on too much. You are too self-critical." In their tendency to overanalyze, be too self-critical, and work very hard, Sixes and Ones are look-alikes. The difference is that the Six is doing this out of fear, whereas the One is driven by perfectionism and anger. As Helen Palmer puts it, "Sixes need to spend as much time in best-case scenario thinking as they do in worst-case scenario thinking."

Another challenge for Detectives is their difficulty in making decisions. Martin, an Observer described a central complaint about his Six wife of 40 years: "Olive never makes up her mind." Fives, ever researching facts and logic with a "not enough data" mentality, may struggle with coming up with a final analysis when pressed to make a decision, but they can have an easier time when it comes to emotional issues.

The relationship between an Observer and a Detective may lack juice because many Fives would rather withdraw than argue, and phobic Sixes may fear confrontation — even counterphobic Sixes, who have no difficulty aggressively challenging workplace peers. Fives and Sixes are both good problem solvers, but may have difficulty engaging emotionally. Cheryl, the Detective married to an Observer, wrote, "Actually we are very good at solving problems except for intimacy or emotional issues." When asked to describe a "classic fight" they repeatedly have in their five-year relationship, she wrote,

Rob's distance emotionally, even though I like it at times, has driven me away. We don't connect emotionally or intimately as a couple. His looking to me to be the planner, the provider, the drive behind the relationship, has worn me out. I'm tired of making all the decisions. I feel I have helped him come out of his isolation and find new challenges – and I know he is grateful – but I feel it's been at the expense of me. I feel supported and loved – but I don't feel passion.

Some Fives have difficulty moving from observer to true participant in life. As children, their coping strategy was to watch the action from the sidelines. To feel safe, their strategic defense was to withdraw, to not get involved. To show up, as the Six wants the Five to do in the prior example, can be challenging for them.

Take George, an 82-year old Observer and his 61-year old Detective wife, Celeste. When George developed multiple medical problems, Celeste complained to a friend that George had stopped taking his medications, was in a lot of pain, slept very poorly, and seemed to have given up on life. But each time George saw his doctor (who was also Celeste's physician), he acted gracious and in control and denied any significant problem. In the past, Celeste's friend had suggested that Celeste speak with the doctor and explain what's really going on, but when Celeste had asked George for permission, he said no. This time Celeste's friend suggested speaking with the doctor without first asking George's permission. George seemed depressed, and surely his doctor would want to know this.

Celeste, however, insisted that there was no way she would speak to George's doctor without his permission, even though she understood that his medical care might be improved if she did. "It would be treating him like a child, rather than with the respect that my husband deserves," she explained. "I can't do that to him. It would be disrespectful. It would be different if it were an emergency, but this isn't."

In this example, you hear the Six's tremendous loyalty to her husband –loyalty to a fault. Deep down, she might be afraid that he would leave her if she "disobeys" him. She is determined to treat him with the same respect she would want for herself. The projection of the Six might involve her own worst fear, which would be to lose her sense of independence and be dominated by someone else. And finally, she may have recognized how important George's sense of self-sufficiency is to him and did not want to take that away.

Exercises for the Observer-Detective Couple

The following questions highlight the classic issues that challenge the Five-Six pairing:

The Five/Six pairing is a fairly common, if not romantically then at least as good friends. When two head Types such as the Observer and Detective link up, the primary bond is likely to be mental and they just might fall in love with each other's mind. They'll respect each other for how smart they are or just how they think in general. Complete the incomplete sentences below to get more in touch with this issue. Be sure that each of you answers the following questions several times.

- I love how your mind works in this particular way. . .(Remember to go back and forth with each of you answering these questions several times.)
- I love the way you think about the following. . .

Getting to the Observer's core

Overall the Six trusts the Five and seems to enjoy him or her as one enjoys a complicated puzzle. Sixes like to figure Fives out. ? Once they feel they have found the right combination and have seen the Observer at his core, Sixes feel they can trust Fives even more. Given the need for privacy that Observers have, how do you get to the core of who they really are?

- For the Five: How does it feel to allow someone else to figure out your combination and then approach your own inner sanctum? Because it's a Six, does this make it a little easier for you to let your guard down? Do you fear being engulfed or smothered as you let your guard down?
- For the Six: Talk about how you go about working your way into the inner sanctum of the Five after the initial attraction. How do you keep the Five from feeling smothered and how can you respect the Five's space? How does it feel to take the lead in the relationship, when in most other cases you are usually the authority?

Communicate with your partner by finishing the following sentences:

- For the Five: I know I need to be more open about. . .
- For the Five: What I would like to tell you that I haven't yet shared with you is. . .
- For the Five: Please tell me one area that I could show up better and be a more active participant and truly help us in our relationship.

"Trouble in River City."

If the Observer, for whatever reason, doesn't feel comfortable moving forward in the relationship, he or she will meet the Detective with a strong withdrawal or in computer terms an impenetrable firewall and a blank screen. The Five will withhold information and possibly even sex – as sex is usually seen as a way to trade information.

- For the Five: Are there any other ways that you would protect yourself if you felt uncomfortable in the relationship with the Six?
- For the Six: If the Five withdrew as stated above – what response do you think you would have? If the Five were interested in working things out, how would you recommend they approach you?

Fear

For those on a spiritual path: Fives and Sixes are both fear types. Both will response with some fear-based action if they experience a problem in the relationship – stinginess of some type for the Five, fight or flight for the Six. At the same time, fear can also be wisdom. For example, it makes us look both ways before crossing the street.

- For both of you: Tell each other how fear shows up in your life in general
- For both of you: How do you handle fear?
- For both of you: What roles do trust and faith play to help you with your fear?
- For both of you: How can you support each other when fear arises for each of you?
- For the Six: When I become accusatory and untrusting toward you, what is really scaring me is. . .
- For the Six: What I would like to request from you connected to my fear is. . .
- For the Six: With regard to my fear, I promise to take more responsibility for . . . .
- For the Five: Fives on a spiritual path needs to question the three S's: Secrecy, Superiority, and Separateness.
- For the Six: Sixes on a spiritual path need to remember that the antidote for fear is faith.

CHAPTER FORTY-SEVEN

The Observer-Adventurer (Five-Seven) Relationship

When we would give lectures on addiction together, she was the advance person. She would get in front of an audience and they would get quiet and pay attention. Just like that. She introduced the topic and I did an hour and then questions. She was always a package of goodwill in support of what I was doing. There is no way that this Five could have reached that pinnacle of success out of the sunshine – we often got standing audiences at the conclusion.

-- Oren, an Observer married to an Adventurer

The Observer and Adventurer pairing can work well. On the enneagram diagram, a line connects them. This means they see part of themselves in the other, that at different times in their lives they will have each traveled down that line to the other point, taking on in their own way some of the other's characteristics. As with Oren and Jeanette, the high energy and enthusiasm of the Adventurer can propel the Observer into more professional and social interactions with other people. Observers feel more comfortable thinking than doing, and they appreciate the Adventurer's ability to get them going. Another Observer, Jason, once told us, "I was so analytical that I could live alongside a problem and wanted to parse it instead of fix it. I hope and think that this has changed."

In the vignette at the start of this chapter, Oren, an octogenarian Observer, recalls his shared professional experiences with his Adventurer wife Jeanette and explains clearly the roles that they each assumed as they lectured together. They balanced each other: Oren as an Observer provided the content, while his Adventurer wife was a "package of goodwill" with her introductions. And then finally, he felt like he reached a "pinnacle of success," which he couldn't have done without the "sunshine" the Adventurer provided.

Sevens enjoy bringing Fives out of themselves to introduce them to novel pursuits. Both types like independence and escape, although the way they play it out differs: The Observer prefers solitary intellectual pursuits, while the Adventurer will be out in the world, planning and executing an endless variety of activities. Each appreciates the lack of pressure to spend more time together.

The Five cuts the Seven slack. In fact, some say that the Five gives the Seven just "enough rope" – or at least the opportunity if the inclination is there. An Adventurer can go see the world, and when he comes back, the Observer is usually there waiting. The Adventurer also shares his experiences, and the other is not only interested in new knowledge, but especially appreciates not having to exert herself to gain that knowledge. All of this can make the Adventurer feel energized and important, while the Observer is stimulated yet has conserved his energy.

Sevens give Fives a lot of time in which to pursue their intellectual interests; Fives make few emotional demands on Sevens and appreciate their many creative ideas and activities. Both are in the thinking or head center, so they are more comfortable with ideas than emotions. Both Types are fear-based, although their approach to handling their fears differs: Observers seek information whereas Adventurers divert their attention from fear to mental and physical activities. They also share an attitude of analysis and unconventionality rather than acceptance of dogma. They appreciate each other's ability to draw independent conclusions.

Observers can model for Adventurers how to concentrate and follow through on a project, something the latter, with their wandering minds, can struggle with. On the other hand, Sevens can bring out playfulness in the all too serious Fives. Oren summed it up succinctly when he stated, "I was incapable of feeling that free before my Seven showed me how." Adventurers convince people to give themselves permission to do things they have never done before.

Challenges of the Observer-Adventurer pairing

Although the Observer and Adventurer's contrasting approaches to life have a unique compatibility about them, their sometimes-glaring differences can pose a challenge for the relationship. One common compromise area involves social interaction. Observers may feel pressured by Adventurers to socialize, finding the Seven's high energy and desire to mingle overwhelming and exhausting. When the Seven wants to entertain in the home, the Five may feel like hiding out. An Observer-Adventurer couple, Jim and Misty, humorously described what they initially went through. Jim, the Observer, related,

She, the energized and ever-ready bunny that never runs down, with dozens of friends (she can make friends with a statue), bouncing from one place to another like a pinball, had a rather difficult time understanding why her husband (me) was such a stick-in-the-mud and unsociable character. She once told me, "If all the men in the world were like you, it would stop and all social life would be cancelled due to lack of interest!" I, on the other hand, couldn't understand why we had to be on the go all the time. Why all the people, why all the activity? In response to her negative observation, I patiently explained that if all the women in the world were like her, half of them would probably be institutionalized for "too-muchness."

Jim's account demonstrates how important a sense of humor is in a relationship where there are significant differences. His description of those differences is not only funny, but provides clarity when he describes his "lack of interest" and Misty's "too-muchness" when it comes to socializing. In contrast, Misty speaks about Jim's "lack of interest":

I so badly wanted to give love and compassion; I knew Jim had been living like a hermit – perhaps he could die from the deprivation of human contact. I knew I had to help him. I lined up lots of friends and colleagues who shared his interests in computers, music, science, etc., and I even found some who didn't always need to talk about their "feelings" and personal dramas. Confident that he would be grateful for all my efforts, I arranged these gatherings to fill his void for love and friendship. Backfire! Jim resented me for "invading" his space and for my assumption that he was eager to share anything about himself with anyone!

And who said that Adventurers don't look like Givers (Twos)? You have to give Misty credit as well for her humor and her valiant attempt to help her husband. Her drive to help Jim have "more" reflected the Seven's fears rather than Five's needs and created resentment. Janet, a Seven, in relationship with a Five for three years, explained the extroversion versus the introversion problem this way:

Vito's need for privacy definitely clashed at times with my need to commu-nicate and connect. I would carry him socially a lot as he'd never say much to people. He'd like to be left alone to work that out himself. In retrospect, I prob-ably pushed too much."

Oren, the Observer whose relationship eventually ended, told us what it was like to experience the other side of the relationship equation:

I wonder how many ways I was wanting in Jeanette's eyes. She wanted to dance, and I had had my fill of that decades ago. She wanted to see the world because she had led a sheltered life, but I had seen enough of it. I enjoyed taking this little girl to new places, but she was always ready for more when I had had enough.

Observers can be grateful to others who help them learn the social skills they've never been able to develop on their own. But they don't necessarily want to be turned into extroverts. We live in such an extroverted world that it is easy (especially for an Adventurer) to see the Observer's basic approach to life as wrong or unhealthy. This can be a lesson for all of us, that even though we have things to learn, we also need to accept each other's unique-ness -- parents with their children and we with our partners. Don't forget, the enneagram is primarily about understanding and compassion. When we actively set out to change someone, we are going down the wrong path. This doesn't mean we shouldn't challenge our partners, but challenging takes on a different quality that says, "This is how I see you showing up in the world – is that how you want to be?" Or we may bring our wants and needs to our partners and respectfully request that they help us meet them. This is a far cry from trying to change someone.

Another potential problem in the Observer-Adventurer pairing con-cerns spending money. As Misty recalls,

On one shopping trip, I bought Jim seven sport shirts. They were all great shirts—high quality, great design, and only half-price. I could tell he liked all the shirts, but after considerable agonizing he said, "I'll take this one." Was this a joke? "No, Sweetheart," I said. "We're keeping all seven shirts. Jim calmly explained how such extreme purchases were not "normal." I wanted to laugh at such absurdity (over a few shirts on sale) and to cry because of his inability to enjoy life's abundance and richness. The shirts, I suspected, were only the tip of the iceberg. This smacked of pathological self-denial.

This scenario is a great example of another classic challenge of this pairing, with the Five being a minimalist and the Seven, expansive. Jim certainly demonstrates a more conservative approach to spending and the accumulation of material things. And, in fact, he sees Misty's buying habits as extreme and "not normal." On the other hand, when her Five husband chooses only one shirt out of seven, the Seven sees him as having an "inability to enjoy life's abundance and richness" possibly to the point of "pathological self-denial." Despite their different perspectives, both are considered fear types, and in a situation like this, you might say that both have a fear of running out of things. Observers handle their fear by either not getting too attached to things or through conservation, whereas Adventurers handle it by believing that you should get while the getting is good.

Imagine both types stranded in the desert, dying of thirst, when a lush, water-filled oasis pops up. Not knowing when the next oasis will come along, Observers would want to conserve the water, while the Adventurer would undoubtedly want to drink and be merry. Two very different approaches, yet at the core, both fear running out of water. When this dilemma appears in the relationship, Fives can help Sevens with their excess and immediate gratification issues and Sevens can help Fives shift from their scarcity mindset to one of spontaneity and abundance.

We could say that it is about "more" for both the Observer and the Adventurer. This is less apparent with Observers, because their connection to "more" primarily consists of conserving things in order to assure an adequate supply, whereas Adventurers create "more" by simply creating more. In another Observer-Adventurer coupleship, the Adventurer creates more through her work. As a teacher, she stays late, sacrificing herself, helping the other teachers in planning and setting up their classrooms. She sits on committees and organizes student activities. In her mind, she is sacrificing in the now so as to gain more in the future. It is similar to investing. All of her hard work represents dividends that will one day pay off, when the community she is working so hard to build will turn into more for everyone.

What, then, helps the Five-Seven pairing thrive? When opposites attract, each must respect the other's differences and be willing to learn from the other in areas that seem both foreign and familiar to them. They also must make sure they don't become like two ships passing in the night with their different interests and activities, where one contracts and the other expands in the world. They must work hard to stay on the same wavelength, stimulating each other with their thoughts and plans. Because they are not comfortable with their emotions, they must find an emotional and mental depth that satisfies both of them – committing to "more" in the relationship where each of them has a tendency to bring less.

Exercises for the Observer-Adventurer Couple
The following questions highlight the classic issues that challenge the Five-Seven pairing:

The Five-Seven pairing is common. Although they differ in many ways, there is an innate cooperative spirit between them. The Adventurer goes out into the world to explore, bringing stimulating material and experiences back to the Observer. The Five then seems to decide what would most benefit the couple in the long run. Both Types are independent and do not make excessive time demands of one another. However, both need to make sure that they spend enough time together, that they don't become like two ships passing in the night.

- For the Seven: Because of your independent lifestyle, and especially with your penchant for exploring the world, how do you assure that you and your partner are including each other sufficiently in your life?
- For the Five: Because of your introverted nature, how do you assure that you and your partner are spending enough time connecting and communicating with one another?

At an enneagram workshop, an Adventurer was asked about the dynamic between her and her Observer partner. She replied with a chuckle, "He gives me just enough rope to hang myself with." With a little more seriousness, she went on to say that they are both very aware that there is some slack in the metaphorical rope that represents their relationship, and that there is also a certain amount of slack in their actual relationship. She stated she had abused that "slack" in the rope before and had almost hanged herself with it -- and that she had nearly taken the relationship down too.

- For the Seven: Given that the relationship has just enough rope to hang yourself with, how do you make sure that you remain conscious, not hang yourself, and not destroy the relationship as well?

The Five can become enthralled with whatever the Seven brings back to them to explore – this is the part of the Five's rope that they can possibly hang themselves with.

- For the Five: How do you make sure that you don't get lost in the material that appears so inviting? How do you stay present and connected to your partner so that you and your partner do not drift apart, but instead, you and your partner and the relationship as well stays intact?

Minimalism versus expansiveness

Earlier in this chapter we described what happened when Misty, a Seven, bought 7 sport shirts for her Five husband Jim. Jim's reaction was that "such extreme purchases were not normal." Misty's take on Jim's response was that he was that he was demonstrating "his inability to enjoy life's abundance," representing "pathological self-denial." This example illustrates how Observers and Adventurers are at opposite poles when it comes to an attitude of scarcity (the Observer) versus abundance (the Seven). Fives want to conserve what they perceive as scarce resources, whereas Sevens want variety, excess, and immediate gratification. In a related fashion, Fives want solitude, whereas Sevens want to surround themselves with people. These very different perspectives can be a source of conflict in the relationship.

- For the Five: When my partner wants "more" in his or her life I feel . . . because I'm afraid of/that. . . .
- For the Seven: When my partner wants "less" in his or her life I feel . . . because I'm afraid of/that. . .
- For both of you: Brainstorm ways in which you can get your needs met while respecting your partner's need for. . .

Intimacy versus escape

The Observer-Adventurer pairing usually does not involve intimacy or real discussion of feelings. Both Types are in the head or thinking triad or center, meaning that that's where they live most of the time. Fives follow their intellectual pursuits, while Sevens fill their heads with variety, options, and plans. Neither type is really connected to their feelings. Fives avoid talking about feelings, and Sevens prefer activities to wasting time talking about feelings.

CHAPTER FORTY-EIGHT

The Observer-Leader (Five-Eight) Relationship

We were married in our mid 40s. Roberto (a Five) was a creature of habit and only dreamed of travel and adventure until I came along. He always thanks me for leading him to his own courage. He encourages my own courage. We have faith in each other and ourselves.

--Diana, a Leader, married 7 years to an Observer:

The Observer-Leader pairing, a common one, is an attraction of opposites, at least on the surface. Fives are known for their ability to get along with little, whereas Eight's chief passion, lust (as in lust for life), speaks to their desire to get more of everything. In a group, Fives are likely to be on the outskirts, not drawing attention to themselves, whereas Eights are a very visible and audible presence. In emotionally charged situations, Fives tend to withdraw and Eights may amp things up even more.

The brief vignette above illustrates why each finds the other so attractive. The Leader helps the Observer climb out of his shell, and the Observer trusts the Leader to tell him the truth. Leaders fear being dominated; Roberto, the Five in the vignette above believed in the Eight and "encouraged her courage." On the enneagram diagram, Five and Eight share a connecting line, seeing a part of themselves in the other, so that they have a mutually intuitive understanding. Because they are at opposite ends of the same connecting line, each also has much to learn from the other.

In our survey, Leaders chose the Adventurer as one of their most compatible types. Their reasons included: "I like them in a social situation – their minds and thinking process." "They help bring down my energy level. They stay calm rather than withdraw or match me." "They allow me my space; they make space for my energy." "They are quiet, not intrusive, and have good boundaries." "I like the balance." Probably "balance" is the key to the comments given by Eights on the survey. When Leaders and Observers pair up, they have an opportunity to balance each other.

Both Leaders and Observers value their independence, are self-reliant, and appreciate this quality in the other. They don't have to worry about entertaining the other, as they each have an agenda of their own. In fact, they are a couple who typically sees relationship as one those life goals they can now check off their list -- they can go about their business accomplishing other goals. But it's easy for them to take the relationship for granted and become like roommates.

Eights can teach Fives to be more direct and assertive. Fives especially value the "juice" of the Eight, which can inspire moving from thought to action. Neither Type lets their guard down easily to experience intimacy; therefore Leaders will appreciate the Observer's trustworthiness and tendency to guard received knowledge. This makes the Eight more willing to be vulnerable with the Five and to disclose personal information. On the other hand, Eights demand truth and honesty in a relationship, which the Five values as well, and this can make the Five feel safer overall. The Observer's natural tendency to withdraw and experience feelings after the fact can be jolted into the present moment by the Leader's emotional bluntness, which can release the Observer's usual self-control.

Leaders, who have a tendency to speak first and think about it second, value Observers' logical thinking and store of information, as well as their willingness to defend the correctness of their conclusions. Both types tend to distrust authority figures and will stand up for themselves.

Eights can help Fives access and express their anger, and Fives can teach Eights to tone down their tendency to pick a fight or to attack with a take-no-hostages approach. Eights can learn from Fives to respond more thoughtfully, slowly, and moderately. In many long-term relationships, partners will often take on similar characteristics, making them look alike in many ways. Fives learn to become more assertive, whereas Eights develop calmness and self-control.

Jonathan, a Leader, wrote, "My wife does the thinking and I the doing. When a situation needs to be thought out, she is the best and when the situation is spontaneous, I take the lead." Anita, an Observer, related, "In dealing with crises with our children, my Fivish qualities of being calm, measured, thoughtful, and to not overreact become important. At the same time, Pete's instinct, intuition, and quickness to react have been valuable. We have balanced each other out."

These are great examples of people who recognize that their partner has strengths in certain areas that they may not. Realizing this, they allow the other to take the lead in those particular situations.

Regarding the positive attributes they bring to their relationship. Connie, an Observer, replied, "My independence, my dependability and my calmness." Diana, a Leader, valued her Observer partner's "Slow, deliberate communication," and she appreciated that "he is willing to hear me out and act as quickly as he can." Rita not only values Roberto's communication skills and his ability to hear her completely, but she also seems to understand that it takes some time for her Observer spouse to take action after hearing about the situation. Rita seems to understand some very important principles of a healthy relationship. She not only appreciates the unique gifts that Roberto brings, but she also accepts the personal characteristics that could just as easily get on her nerves. In addition, she seems to do what we talked about earlier -- she trades or exchanges her Eight-like behaviors with Five-like behaviors – she gains patience and is able to respect her Five partner's pace and overall approach to life.

When Eights talked about their own contributions and the gifts they bring to their Five partners in particular, Diana stated, "I encouraged him to have confidence." This clarifies what Diana said in the vignette at beginning of this chapter where she "led him to his own courage." Not being meek, Marcie, a Leader, described her contribution as "I ask for what I want." And when problems do surface, Jonathan, an Eight, explained, "I like to get issues on the table and resolve them before theybecome a bigger problem," exhibiting the Eight's typical emotional bluntness. If the Leader doesn't overwhelm the Observer, the intense emotions may jolt he Five into their feelings before they have a chance to do their typical withdrawal.

Anita, an Observer, described what it was like to live with her Leader husband, Pete: "excessive love, commitment, sensitive heart." Observers have a way of making Leaders feel safe, and her description of him suggests that she has been able to access her husband's vulnerability and that she welcomes it. It is nice to see that she describes Pete's excessive nature as having to do with love instead of power or control. Leaders need keep their priorities are in order – the power of love vs. the love of power. We can only guess what it is like for the sometimes self-negating, minimalist Observer to experience "excessive love."

Challenges of the Observer-Leader relationship

Not surprisingly, the typical problems of the Observer-Leader relationship revolve around the Observer's discomfort with the Leader's direct, overwhelming approach to life, their earthiness and argumentativeness, and their black-and-white thinking. For example, Anita, an Observer, stated very succinctly that the challenges her Leader husband Pete brings to the relationship include "anger, being right, and steamrolling over me."

On their side, Eights can get very frustrated with the Five's strategy of withdrawing rather than engaging, their tendency to replace actions with words, their lack of "juice" and low energy, and their intransigence once they have done their research and reached a conclusion. Anita recognized that one of her problems was "not communicating my feelings," and added that Pete would complain to her, "You don't communicate – you emotionally leave." Additionally, each can get upset with the other's judgmentalism, and neither may be willing to compromise. Because both types fear being controlled, this pairing can get into big power struggles. Helen Palmer, in *The Enneagram in Love and War*, states this delightfully: "Eights…take control" while "Fives… exercise remote control."(P. 357) The Eight wants to engage aggressively and hammer out problems; the Five is more comfortable withdrawing. This can cause problems for both. Marcie complained, "He couldn't express conflict or disagreements." The other Eight woman, Diana, expresses below, how she has been able to help resolve this typical dynamic in the Five–Eight pairing.

My direct confrontational style made my husband feel continually challenged and helpless. This would lead Roberto to go very silent, which would be my cue to relax my "attack." Until that time, I didn't realize that my behavior had an "attack" effect.

This is a great example of a Leader becoming more conscious of her particular style and its effect on her partner. The Leader's behaviors can be compounded by the Observer's sensitivity to being intruded upon. Couples can learn to recognize childhood wounds and to share that information with a partner they can trust. The partner's responsibility is then to make a real effort not to re-wound their partner. In the example above, Diana, an Eight, is aware of her partner's sensitivity to intrusiveness and how her behavior may feel to him like an attack. Below, Jonathan (an Eight) expresses his perspective when the Five withdraws:

I hate it when Lydia withdraws. It's as if I do not exist. I cannot get a response from her. She needs her privacy, but so do I on occasion. She always asks me "why" questions as if I really thought about something I did, which I do not. When Lydia withdraws, we cannot have a discussion about the issues. After two or three days, she re-emerges and is ready to discuss the issue after thoughtfully examining it in minute detail. By this time, I have forgotten it.

In this scenario, we hear how Lydia's withdrawing makes Jonathan feel as if he doesn't exist. The Eight's fear of domination is sometimes linked to their life force and the fear that it will be drained away. This can be a childhood wound for the Eight that the Five needs to be aware of and to work to avoid repeating. The Observer will benefit as well by matching the Leader's emotional force. By enlivening themselves, they counteract their tendency to withdraw and are then better able to stay in the present moment with their feelings.

Finally, neither type is comfortable with expressing feelings (this is particularly true for Fives with a strong Six wing), and they often have difficulty even recognizing them, so that emotional intimacy may be largely absent from the relationship. Both types need to make a conscious effort to access the heart space. Eights have a connecting line to Type Two (the Giver), and when they are in love, they can enter the heart realm if they trust their partner. Feelings that surface for Fives can be scary, but they can be an indicator that the Five truly cares about someone. Both types also have a hard time trusting the other when it comes to love, which in a sense makes them a good fit. Observers can have great respect for how the Leader appears, while the latter's demand for the truth can help the former to trust. Both need to be careful that they don't fall into a power struggle, which says, "I can easily live without you – I don't really need you."

Observers with a strong Romantic (Four) wing are more in touch with their feelings and may feel a hole in the relationship where emotions should be. Connie, an Observer with a Four wing, formerly in relationship with a Leader, wrote: "My need for intimacy (to talk things over, spend time together, work out problems together, etc.) conflicted with Duane's need to be controlling and not let me know his private self. We never resolved it." The challenges her partner brought to the relationship were "his inability to be intimate . . . He wasn't able to see human needs and did not have empathy."

Diana, a Leader, acknowledged that she "struggled to trust," while another Leader, Marcie, said, "I'm afraid to trust, and I have too long a memory about forgiveness." She added, "My partner expected me to trust him long before I was ready." Yet Leaders may want lots of attention and intensity from their partners. Anita, an Observer, believed that Pete, her Leader husband, would leave "If I didn't give him the emotional intensity, one-on one attention he likes/needs."

Exercises for the Observer-Leader Couple

The following exercises highlight the classic issues that challenge the Five-Eight pairing:

The Five-Eight pairing is a rather common one and there are probably a number of reasons why it is. Because this is a relationship of opposites, Fives and Eights can be teachers to one another. Fives look up to Eights, envious of the Leader's physical power. At the same time, Eights respect Fives for their mental power. Both respect each other for their overall autonomy in the world.

- For the Five: How can taking on some of the Eight's physical aggressiveness or assertiveness benefit you in your life? How could your partner turn you on to their approach more easily with less resistance on your part?

- For the Eight: How can taking on some of the Five's mental acuteness benefit you in your life? How could your partner turn you on to their approach more easily with less resistance on your part?

- For the Five: What if you became more of an initiator than an observer, felt your feelings in the moment, stated your needs, fought for your needs, and spoke off the cuff?

- For the Eight: What if you tamed some of your aggressiveness, learned to wait, go inside rather than outside yourself, thought more logically and systematically, and became more moderate and less excessive in your consumption and acquisition?

Feelings

Neither Observers nor Leaders let their guard down, and both hide their feelings. Fives not only have trouble expressing feelings, they often don't seem to know what they're feeling. Eights have no trouble feeling or expressing anger, but anger is often their only outward expression of fear and other negative emotions. Finding emotional intimacy in such a relationship can be a real challenge.

- For both of you: Take turns telling each other about childhood events that influenced your lifelong tendency to hide your vulnerability. The Five: Describe to your partner why it felt safer to build a wall around yourself. The Eight: Describe to your partner why you concluded that the world was a dangerous place and you had to protect yourself, be strong, and not let anyone in.

- For both of you: Describe to your partner one highly emotional experience you've had, either in childhood or as an adult.
- For both of you: Tell each other what initially attracted you to your partner.

Unfortunately, most people in a relationship don't take the time to tell our partners how much we appreciate them. There is a couples exercise in which every night, just before going to sleep, you and your partner tell each other something you truly appreciate about them. If you were to stick with this exercise over several years, just imagine the quantity of positive strokes you would be putting in each other's emotional bank account!

- For both of you: commit to giving positive strokes to one another at an agreed on time on a regular basis. Be sure to challenge yourselves!

CHAPTER FORTY-NINE

The Observer-Mediator
(Five-Nine) Relationship

Patricia, a Mediator (with a Social subtype) has been married for many years to James, an Observer, who until his retirement worked as a ship's captain and was gone from the home for much of the time. Both are introverts, and she raised their child largely alone:

People have always wondered how in the world I managed. My need for space and privacy may explain why my marriage to a sea captain worked so well. Now that we are together all the time, it is working too, but there are times I crave being alone in the house. On the other hand, James does not demand too much of me when we are here together. We sit down to meals together, but in between, he leaves me generally alone and does not talk my ear off as some husbands I know. He is in his own world, reading mostly, and working in the garden.

I think what saves our marriage from a humdrum existence is his affection for me. I talk him into doing things he normally would not do, such as taking a walk or going to certain movies he certainly would not consider, or to see a play. It takes some engineering and scheming, but in the end it works. The only thing is that sloth is on both sides, and we (I) have to constantly fight to overcome that "deadly sin."

As I write this I am thinking that if I could have more time to myself, I could better recharge and have more energy. I covet the time I can be alone, if only for a couple of hours. I feel that part of my sloth comes from us being on top of each other so much without enough personal breathing space for me. The ideal situation for me was when James had a post-retirement part-time job. He enjoyed it and I found that by being out of the house part of the day, he afforded me the best of both worlds. I didn't have to work too hard at recharging, which came from having built-in quiet time for myself. And I loved the routine of knowing when he would be in and when he would be out.

I have lots of friends from when I was working, and I love to entertain without necessarily including their husbands. This remains an issue. How to do it without throwing him off balance? I know that one way is to meet them outside in a restaurant, but sometimes, I would like to have them, whether in a group of one or two, here in my home, but it makes him uncomfortable.

Last year I wanted to go to Europe to visit our son and James's cousins and do some touring. I absolutely couldn't get him to go with me, and I ended up planning a trip without him. He gets fearful in amorphous situations; things have to be somewhat clear in his mind as to what he's getting in for. This has gotten worse as he's gotten older. More recently, a friend offered her cottage in France for a month, and I really wanted to go, but James wouldn't budge. I told my friend that at least for now, it is not meant to be! I am still dealing with my disappointment. Another person may think that it is not fair of James not to give the cottage a try. But I'm okay with it. Not only do I think there will be another chance, but I also understand where he's coming from.

Both James and I like each other's companionship. We do not converse much, but when we do, we like talking with each other. It's no effort for me to be with him, but outside of the house I have to consider the situation beforehand. Our affection and love are mutual. I don't think the marriage would work otherwise. Ultimately, the affection allows for compromise. And, as for myself, I'm given enough free space to decide what to do with that space.

This story reveals much about the dynamics of the Observer-Mediator relationship. Although Observers are known to crave solitude, the fact that many Mediators want to have alone time too is often unappreciated. They therefore give each other necessary space, and are comfortable being in the same house while each does his or her own thing. Neither feels pressured to have constant interaction.

The downside is that they may live like roommates, with little connection and minimal emotional intensity. Additionally, they may have difficulty making decisions and taking action. This could be a very low-energy relationship, with neither partner taking the leader in initiating activities.

We also should point out that James' Self-preservation subtype (see Chapter Three) accentuated his need for solitude and conflicted with Patricia's need to be with friends. Another Observer husband (also a Social subtype) very much enjoyed having his wife's friends over at his home. After a long day's solitary work at his lab, socializing with friends was a way for him to relax. Subtype issues can increase or decrease particular aspects of each personality type.

Patricia illustrates the Mediator's reluctance to stand up for herself. Seeing all sides of every issue, she can understand her husband's position and is reluctant to push for herself. The Mediator focuses on her spouse and rationalizes her disappointment by consoling herself that other opportunities will come along in the future. In reality, Observers are uncomfortable with a partner's emotional dependency and tend to withdraw if it seems that their spouse has "excessive" expectations.

Helen Palmer in *The Enneagram in Love and Work* writes beautifully about the Five-Nine pairing

> Both types have delayed emotional reactions. A Mediator's position emerges slowly over time, and Fives commonly suspend their feelings during an interaction. This is a couple that gives each other plenty of space. Both dislike feeling pressured to take action. Nines dig in and go stubborn when they're expected to make a decision, and Fives withdraw from other people's expectations. A no-conflict agreement can develop that allows each to become absorbed in a private world, effectively leaving the other alone. A Mediator's spread of activities probably won't disturb an Observer unless the home routine is affected, and an oblivious Nine will not question the Five's compartmentalized life. A no-conflict agreement can also deaden a relationship. Fives habitually detach from their feelings and Nines go on auto-pilot by numbing out through obsessive routines. (p.358)

Positives aspects of the Observer-Mediator relationship

The Observer's intellectual, objective approach can be a big asset to the Observer-Mediator relationship. Nina, an Observer related, "As a Five, I have enriched our relationship with information and many activities, educational and personal." Patricia, the Nine, credits James's clear-headed thinking in making decisions about their son:

> *My husband was often a counterweight to my "softness" in bringing up our son. Sometimes he was too harsh, but often he made solid, wise decisions in*

guiding him. One such decision was sending our son to boarding school when he wasn't doing well in public school. Alone I would not have thought of that.

It is important to note that a couple's roles in the family are influenced not only by their Type, but also by their life experiences. For example, in another Observer-Mediator pair, Ken (the Five) had lost his previous wife to cancer. Partly in response to her death, he was overly indulgent to his son. Andrea (the Nine), a psychotherapist, believed it was important to set appropriate limits for children, so she took on the role of disciplinarian in the family.

The Observer-Mediator couple's mutual need for space can make them very compatible. Andrea, the Nine, reported,

Ken spends most of his time working in a lab alone and isn't home a lot, including evenings and weekends. This leaves me alone much of the time. Actually, I like it. Because I'm easily distracted, it takes me more time to get things done. By having all this alone time, I actually have time to be quiet and do things I want to get done. My previous husband was very controlling and was constantly telling me what to do. I am much more comfortable in my current situation.

Wanting to be alone can work very well for both partners, who equally need space and autonomy as well as peace and quiet. Observers know their tendency to merge can drain them. They get tired of all the noise and need quiet time to unwind. At times, Mediators want to hibernate. The Five-Nine pairing can work very well in a commuter marriage.

Mediators in our survey reported that their gifts to the relationship include, "Being able to see all sides of an issue and consequently, adapt to circumstances." Two Observers wrote about the gifts of their Mediator partner: "His sense of humor and caring nature." "Her understanding, patience, and commitment."

In our survey, Mediators were one of the three personality types that Observers said they most liked. Their reasons included: "They don't make any demands on me." "They are willing to fit into my agenda. Good listeners. Open to discussion." "It's easy to connect with Nines, and they help me relax my mind and get into my body."" They are flexible and easygoing." Interestingly enough, Fives also chose Nines as among the types they most struggle with. The Fives wrote, "I never know what they're thinking." "They don't do enough to truly help themselves and don't get things done (at first) the way

I think they should and could be." "I need them to be more decisive." "Won't stand up to me – instead aligns too closely." "Not knowing what they want drives me crazy."

Challenges of the Observer-Mediator relationship:
Observers tend to keep their own counsel and not to express their feelings. They need time to process their emotions and often do so alone, after the immediate situation has passed. The Mediator partner may feel that the Observer is a mystery. Carol (an Observer) wrote of her tendency "not to able to fully express my thoughts and feelings in a timely manner. Instead of telling him directly, I assume he knows what I'm thinking." She said her husband's central complaint about her is that "I always come to conclusions in a different way than he does."

Observers are cerebral; they think with their heads rather than their hearts. (Mediators, too, spend a lot of time in their head and tend to get into obsessive thinking). Dina (an Observer) wrote that Christopher, her Mediator husband, complained that she "is too quick with an answer or analysis of him and of others, that she's too ready to make changes and that she really likes new experiences." Christopher prefers the comforts of the known. She wrote about him:

He likes to keep things as they are; he's not open to new ideas and is resistant to change. He has tunnel or one-way vision. He's not creative in the problem-solving department, and he also dislikes suggestions for how it could be better. He is willing to live in a state of constant clutter.

Some Nines who live surrounded by clutter explain that they would prefer more order, but that they find it overwhelming to try to get out of the mess.

In their desire to avoid conflict, Nines often prefer to withdraw rather than engage. They can be wonderful conversationalists and supportive friends, but for them to get involved in discussion of conflicts or difficult subjects can be a problem. Nines' tendency to withdraw compromises their relationships with a partner of any type. We heard again and again, from partners who have various enneagram styles, what Carol, the Five wrote of her husband Bill, a Nine: "He's not present. He doesn't listen." Another Mediator woman explained it this way, "I have a strong desire to engage with others, but because of my fear of conflict and other dire consequences, I withdraw instead, especially about issues that I feel would reflect badly about me." Nines are great mediators – as long as it doesn't involve them directly; if it does, they may prefer to withdraw.

Mediators are almost always willing to give to others. They do this as a way of engaging with the other. In contrast, because of their scarcity thinking, Observers may want to hoard their resources, including their time and attention. Patricia (the Mediator) complained about James (the Observer): "He's reluctant to extend himself to certain people and circumstances. He is socially awkward and disinterested." A Social subtype for the Observer can mitigate this tendency, making it more likely that the Mediator will engage with other people.

The core issue of the Nine has been termed sloth. It's difficult for them to meet deadlines, and they are often overextended. One Five complained about the Nine's "lack of focus and lack of discipline." Nina (a Five) complained about, "his lazy stubborn side. He dislikes reminders about what needs to be done." Like Nina, frustrated partners of Nines might think the Mediator is lazy, but in fact, their difficulty taking action is more likely based on their fear of the task because it seems too immense to complete. The Nine's laziness is a form of self-forgetting: they neglect themselves and others. "It doesn't matter" can easily become "I don't matter."

Andrea (the Mediator) explained that she too dislikes reminders about what needs to be done, because this increases her level of anxiety. Observer Nina's solution was to urge Christopher, her Mediator husband, to make lists. "When he makes a list for himself, things go much smoother. Lists are a must for all Nines as far as I am concerned. Lists are neutral and impersonal, and the Nine can then have control of the time element to do something."

This is basically good advice, except that Nines tend to take care of the least essential things on the list first and the most important last. They therefore may need help prioritizing their list. If you are a therapist or a coach working with a Nine, be sure to ask if he or she has made a list of items to discuss during the session.

Many Mediators gravitate toward high-energy partners such as Perfectionist (One), Achiever (Three) or Leader (Eight). When a Mediator hooks up with an Observer, the downside may be a low-energy relationship with minimal engagement. The relationship could lose energy or life and lack juice. Even a sexual relationship might be just too much trouble. The Nine who merges with the Five will probably operate out of his or her head space, with a lot of thinking about things and not much feeling. Sex can be an important positive component in this partnership, putting both into the gut or belly center, which can make them feel alive. This couple needs to be careful that the relationship doesn't take on a deadening quality that can lead to affairs or divorce because each needed a fresh breath of life. This pair needs to embrace occasional explosions in their relationship, which can energize it. Also, relationships demand from us that we fully show up, that we connect with our partners and stimulate them and that we make sure to regularly include novel, interesting experiences.

Another challenge for partners of Observers, no matter what their Type, is their need for solitude. In the Five-Nine pairing, both partners may end up lonely and resentful. When the Observer is a Self-preservation subtype, and the Mediator spouse is a Social subtype, this problem is exacerbated. Here's how Patricia, in typical Mediator fashion, dealt with this issue:

I have finally given in to James's need for privacy. It has been very difficult for me because I love to entertain, especially if I can be of some use. For instance, my nephew from out of state was at a local university for four years, and I felt useful having him come out for a visit to vary his routine. I enjoyed equally entertaining my son's friends and my own friends. But because of the privacy factor, I saw that I had to curtail such activities, especially after James retired. One way I solved the problem was meeting my guests elsewhere, such as at restaurants. It has been a viable solution. As a compromise, James allows me to invite guests here, especially close friends and family, but only on an occasional basis and as long as he doesn't feel overwhelmed.

Observers are very task-oriented and are very good at focusing on the project and getting it done. They have little tolerance for mistakes. In this, they tend to resemble Perfectionists (Ones), with whom they are sometimes confused. Mediators, of course, have difficulty with procrastination. Unless they are on a strict deadline, they tend to put off decisions. Their comfort level may require getting lots of opinions, looking at all sides of the issue. At times, it's easier for them to live with the status quo rather than to take action.

Driving together can bring out the different perspectives of the Observer and the Mediator. Nina wrote,

As a Five, I want to take the quickest, most direct route. We have had many disagreements over this in the past. To get to Highway 15, we have a choice of two routes, a crowded business street or a wide industrial road. Christopher told me he avoids the industrial road because it has too many lights, is bumpy in places, and is hilly. I prefer the industrial route because it seems faster, smoother, and more direct. The hills were very small. When we checked it out, there is almost the same number of lights. What I learned is that for him driving is about hills, lights, narrow streets, potholes etc -- all physical things. For me getting some place is about the most direct quick route.

The above observation could serve as a metaphor of sorts. Observers and Mediators have different priorities – the Nine is usually more physical and has great awareness of the environment. Because Nines are usually into comfort, it's logical that he would pick out the more comfortable road. The Five's focus is on conserving and therefore it would make sense that she would prefer the more direct route.

Exercises for the Observer-Mediator (Five-Nine) Couple
The following exercises highlight the classic issues that challenge the Five-Nine pairing:

Reclaiming the warmth and energy
Fives are classically out of touch with their feelings (especially Fives who have a Six [Detective] wing rather than a Four [Romantic] wing), and Nines tune out their feelings with their fixed routines and their focus on comfort. Both Types ardently desire to avoid conflict, so problems are swept under the rug rather than discussed. The warmth and passion of the early days tend to gradually fade into a relationship of low energy, minimal emotional intensity, an absence of real engagement, and with neither partner initiating activities. The challenge of this pairing is to re-light the fire, reconnect with each other and incorporate some new and interesting shared experiences. This requires both partners to "show up" in the relationship and actually discuss things. If you are both interested in improving your coupleship, here is a suggestion:

- If you haven't talked with each other for a long time about things deeper than what's for dinner, pick a time to sit down for a real conversation. Put it on your calendar. When the time comes, begin by recalling and telling your partner all the things that attracted you to her or him in the first place, and reminisce about some positive joint experiences in your past. Next, comparing it with the present, take turns telling each other one thing that you would like to have different in the relationship. Finally, plan some joint activity of a type you really enjoyed in the past but haven't done recently, or else some activity you've wanted to do but haven't thus far. Schedule it, put it on your calendar, and commit to doing it. If you get through this conversation, take a moment to praise yourself and your partner for having done this exercise. It takes courage to begin a conversation like this because both partners are afraid.

- Agree to spend one evening per week with each other for a date. No housework, no work project, just being together. See a movie together, go to a concert, or have dinner out. Pick the evening that will regularly work for you and commit to spending that evening together each week. Put it on your calendar. The only exception is if you find some activity you'd both like to attend that falls on another evening that week.

- Take a daily walk together. It's much easier to talk while you're walking because both Fives and Nines are anxious, and the physical activity while walking will calm you down.

At home

Observers are private people. They prefer solitude to having guests in their home, especially Observers of the Self-preservation subtype. This can be a problem for their partners of any Type, but especially for the conflict-avoiding Mediator, who tends to ignore their own needs and just goes along with the Five's wishes. Nines are well-liked people who usually have many friends, and Nines often enjoy getting together with friends and relatives.

- Brainstorm ways in which you can each have your needs met. Each of you will have to stretch a little. For example, the Nine agrees to get together with friends primarily outside the home. Discuss what to do about meetings that are particularly important for the Nine to have the Five present – will you (the Five) join them at the restaurant at these times? The Five agrees that when it comes to special occasions the Nine can invite people to the home, and the couple negotiate about whether the Five will join them or not. In other words, the Five needs to consider this as a logical, problem-solving enterprise; the Nine needs to give herself permission to state what is important to him or her.

CHAPTER FIFTY

The Double-Detective (Six-Six) Relationship

Of all the nine same-type pairs, two Detectives probably have the easiest time. Detectives are complex enough – for example, the phobic versus the counterphobic varieties -- that two Sixes are likely to have many differences. And when it comes to the underlying fear, nobody understands that as well as another Detective. They share the same worldview, see each other as being oppressed, and can champion each other, even if their position is unpopular or controversial. When one partner is stuck in worst-case scenario thinking, the other can help him or her see the brighter side of things. When both are anxious about the same event, they can validate each other's fear and reassure each other about their concerns. Detectives can be at their best in a time of crisis, tremendously helpful to each other.

Sixes constantly question everything, so that two Detectives can have stimulating and invigorating discussions. Both enjoy questioning things and ferreting out the nuances of any situation. Their sense of humor helps them get through difficulties. Their loyalty will result in a mutual commitment. In contrast to two Romantics, two Detectives have no difficulty staying in the relationship.

A Six with a Five wing (often phobic) tends to be more contracted, more shut down emotionally, than the Six with a Seven wing. The latter, often counterphobic, is more out there, more ready to do things. He or she may feel frustrated over their phobic Six partner's low energy level and difficulty taking action.

In our survey we received only one reply from a Double-Detective couple – two young women, together for two years. As expected, one was phobic (Andrea) and other counterphobic (Mary Anne), and they also differed in subtype and wing. Phobic Andrea had a Five wing whereas Mary Anne was more outgoing and had a Seven wing. Mary Anne wrote that she likes more excitement than Andrea, and that what helped her relationship with Andrea was "predicting problems and talking about internal experiences." Mary Anne, who wrote that she tends to get carried away in confronting others and being aggressive, appreciated Andrea's calm demeanor, but at the same time complained about her lack of energy and conflict avoidance. She advised younger Sixes in relationship of "the need to identify when fear is triggered and develop a way of relating and holding it."

Challenges of the Double Detective relationship

Despite the compatibility of the Six-Six pairing, this combination is uncommon. Baron and Wagele, in their book, *Are You My Type, Am I Yours?* suggest that this is because they tend to reinforce each other's negative and suspicious nature. Both turn everything into a catastrophe, they doubt almost everything, are both unpredictable yet crave predictability, and may have trouble making up their minds. This couple can get caught in a spiral of doubt and false beliefs and can reinforce each other's catastrophic thinking.

This couple can become cynical or skeptical about each other, and that can lead to a downhill slide in which they become less understanding. In addition, they tend to be centered in their heads, not their hearts. For example, counterphobic Mary Anne wrote that a problem she brought to her relationship was her own "lack of emotion," but she also complained about phobic Andrea's "lack of connection to her emotions." Two such partners will have a head-centered relationship and intellectualize everything. They may burn themselves out, with constant thinking, talking, and analyzing every facet of their relationship and their lives. In some situations, they may get so caught up in arguments and counter-activity that neither will take action.

Exercises for the Double-Detective Couple

The following exercises highlight the classic issues that challenge the Six-Six pairing:

Most people enjoy being with others of their same personality type – they often have similar priorities and can really understand each other. Two Detectives, for example, can join in worthy causes, see each other as being oppressed, can support and reassure each other, and both enjoy questioning things. The loyalty of the Six means that they can remain very committed to each other. Yet committed relationships consisting of two people of the same Type are unusual. Here are some of the issues that face this combination.

Detectives are very sensitive to the potentially negative consequences of every situation. Two Detectives can reinforce each other's suspicions and negative thinking, turning minor setbacks into catastrophes.

- Sixes often live in their head while fearing the worst. Learning to connect to all emotions will help the Six become mindful of all their feelings and not just fear. Our core emotions of joy, pain, fear, loneliness, anger, guilt, and shame are experienced knowingly or unknowingly, in different parts of our bodies. For example, we tend to feel shame in our head and neck (flushed face and neck when embarrassed for example), fear in our chest (quickening of heart due to fight or flight response) and joy in our hearts (sensation of well-being). In order to learn how to identify your feelings sit in a quiet place and notice what thoughts you are having? Ask yourself, "About this thought, what am I feeling and where *in my body* do I feel this emotion?" Learn to practice this ritual 3 or 4 times a day and begin to connect your thoughts with your emotions. By experiencing and feeling all of your emotions you will become less reactive to other people's fear, especially that of your partner.

Sixes are known for their detailed and prolonged analysee. A Six couple can find themselves analyzing and rehashing every aspect of their relationship, to the point that they can wear themselves out.

- Plan with each other some activities that will counteract the potential of the constant analyzing to bring down your relationship. For example, think back to what attracted you to each other in the first place. Make it a habit to frequently tell your partner the things you appreciate about him or her. Plan enjoyable activities together and carry them out on a regular basis. Combat the Six's fears about the partner's feelings by regularly checking in with each other, keeping up to date about your relationship.

CHAPTER FIFTY-ONE

The Detective-Adventurer (Six- Seven) Relationship

We work very well together in training situations. Our styles complement each other. Generally I am more process oriented. She has "up" energy that I sometimes lack.

-- Stuart, a Detective

We work together in a psychiatric practice. It is great to work together. I can provide a lot of groundedness, and he can provide ideas and energy.

-- Liana, a Detective

When asked for an example of a situation where the Detective-Adventurer couple together accomplished something better than either would have done alone, two Detectives quoted above gave remarkably similar answers, providing insight into the strengths of the Six-Seven pairing.

It is tempting to assume that the natural pessimism (or skepticism) of the Detectives and the optimism of Adventurers would deter them from forming a partnership. However, in our survey, Detectives chose Adventurers as one of the types with which they feel most compatible. Their reasons included: "I have fun with them." "They can let go and move on." "[They are] my wing. I like adventure." "Keeps my calendar full of interesting activities – enthusiastic." Detectives may instinctively recognize that Adventurers can be the natural antidote to anxiety and negative expectations. A Seven can add zest to a Six's life, encouraging him or her to be adventurous and try new things. Detectives and Adventurers are both in the head or mental triad or center, meaning they both approach the world primarily through their thinking function. Both enjoy spending a great deal of time on fascinating discussions and can stimulate each other with their thoughts and ideas. Head types can truly fall in love with each other's minds.

Both Six and Seven are fear-based personality Types who cope with their underlying fear in different ways. Sevens defuse feelings of fear by filling their minds with multiple options, plans, and interests and stay focused on best-case scenarios. Sixes are more in touch with fear and anxiety, focusing on worst-case scenarios. Counterphobic Sixes actively face their fears because actions seem less frightening than imagined consequences. The two Types share a desire to feel safe, making each empathetic to the other's concerns. Adventurers' idealism and expectations of the best outcomes can provide a healthy rebuttal to the Detective's doubting mind.

In turn, Adventurers can learn useful lessons from Detectives, who provide a balance and grounding for their skewed enthusiasm and flights of fancy. Eileen, an Adventurer, explained that she particularly likes Detectives because of "the balance to my optimism, their pessimism. Their concern with safety, their loyalty, and their groundedness." Adventurers typically try to avoid pain, but when illness, loss or other difficulties inevitably arise, the Detective's boundless loyalty and support can be very comforting to the Adventurer. Sixes' work ethic, ability to bring tasks to completion and sense of duty counterbalance the Seven's impulsivity with getting into new projects, often before the current task is completed. Sevens, with their "monkey minds," particularly enjoy the Six's curiosity, endless questions and active engagement in intellectual discussions. Both types have a good sense of humor and enjoy laughing with each other. Having fun together, especially when being active, can reassure the Six more effectively than endless talk and little action.

According to Eileen, an Adventurer married for 30 years to a Detective, "Sam's gifts to our relationship are his honesty and integrity, his willingness to persevere, his awareness of physical safety, his willingness to question the universe and our place in it, his devotion." Sam provided a solid foundation to their relationship. Liana, a Detective married 35 years, related: "I am incredibly loyal – a giver – a nurturer of others. I work very hard and support others, sometimes to my detriment." She also described Brendan, her Adventurer husband, as "upbeat, lover of life, good-natured, optimistic, charismatic, a good father and lover." Stuart, a Six, characterized his Seven wife as "cheerful, willing to let go and move on." Sixes tend to hold on to their problems and anxieties, discussing them endlessly, considering all options. The Seven has little patience with this approach and quickly moves on, which can be helpful for the stuck Six.

To the question, "what key things do you feel you do to help the relationship thrive?" Eileen (an Adventurer) replied: "Independence. I do not expect my partner to meet all of my needs. I have friends and family to support me as well." This quality of the Adventurer can take the pressure off a Detective. Partners who bring many wants and needs to a relationship can actually scare the Detective. Adventurers too are likely feel tied down if they have to depend on just one person to meet their needs.

Challenges of the Detective-Adventurer relationship.
In many ways, the Six-Seven pairing is one of attraction of opposites. Unfortunately, as is so often true of relationships between very different people, the very characteristics that attract them can be the source of problems. For example, the Seven's impulsivity and enthusiasm can clash with the Six's need to process and consider the potential outcomes of actions. As Eileen, the Seven, wrote,

I tend always to see the positive side of everything – Sam does not. I have great ideas and am interested in many different things and I sometimes have trouble completing a task before I become interested in a new one.

On the other hand, according to Liana, a Detective,

I need a certain amount of time to adjust to change and new things and to feel like I am being heard. I have trust issues, wanting to slow down and look at all possible outcomes before moving through on something. Brendan tends to rush into things or get excited about things and I have to realize he is just excited—he's not necessarily going to take action just because he's talking about it.

Detectives will question the Adventurer's tendency to act without giving adequate notice. Detectives like to be consulted and prepared for things and may interpret the Adventurer's impulsivity as untrustworthiness. Partners of Adventurers need to understand that part of the fun is the planning even if it's not always translated into action. The Seven wants to start doing whatever he or she gets excited about at the moment, which can be very scary for the Six partner. Liana adds,

He will sign up for something new without talking to me first, or he will say he's going to do something and stay for the excitement, then move on, leaving

me to the dirty details. He's always looking for something new or someone new to be excited by.

The Six's natural conservatism can frustrate a Seven who perceives the other as confining, even imprisoning. Sixes see limits as comforting and reassuring. Liana reports that Brendan's central complaint about her is, "you find the negative first, and you try to slow me down." Detectives, much of the time, will push aside the positives in a situation and naturally look for what can jump up and bite you in the end. Adventurers just want to focus on the positives. Liana relates:

The skeptical side of me does get in the way, but less than it used to because I can realize what is happening. As I've grown personally I have developed more confidence in myself and my abilities.

Janna, another Detective, writes of her Adventurer partner,

Sometimes my doubting mind, manifested as lack of sureness, lack of trust in myself and in others' abilities is very frustrating for her. Sometimes she goes to One and can be sharp and judgmental of me, which jars me."

Because of their sensitivity, Sixes perceive criticism even when it is not intended as such; if they are predominantly counterphobic, they are likely to respond defensively with an attack. Sixes want guarantees before they commit to anything, whereas Sevens hate to be pinned down.

The Detective can be like a little dog nipping at the Adventurer's heel, trying to get the latter to stay in line. The Adventurer is likely to be impatient with the Detective's nipping and may respond critically. He or she might try to manipulate the situation, thus making the Detective more distrustful. Sixes shouldn't keep trying to control their partner. Sevens need to avoid adding to their partner's fears and insecurities by distorting the truth.

The Seven's reluctance to discuss negative issues contrasts with the Six's need to regularly process matters in depth. Liana listed her central complaint about Brendan as "Lack of talking about <u>hard</u> things, not wanting to hear the bad stuff." Stuart wrote that what keeps his Seven wife from effective problem-solving in their relationship is "Janna's lack of ability to look deeply at her own 'stuff.'" What may be helpful in these situations is for the Detective not to take things so seriously, trying to make sure she is also focusing on the positives, while the Adventurer needs to maintain awareness of the problems.

When an Adventurer makes a mistake, the Detective looks for an apology as proof that it won't happen again. Adventurers, on the other hand, usually hesitate to apologize; instead, they are more likely to make a joke about the situation or minimize its possible severity.

Detectives sometimes complain that their Adventurer partner is too busy with activities to pay sufficient attention to the relationship. Eileen said: "My number one challenge, I think, is that I have a tendency to take on too much and end up exhausted by my schedule." Sixes can get resentful when Sevens go places and meet people without them, seeing this as a lack of commitment. They can easily imagine a worst-case scenario such as that their Seven partner has been unfaithful.

Both Adventurers and Detectives are fear-based types who have security needs, and also vivid imaginations. Usually, Adventurers imagine best-case scenarios whereas Detectives imagine the worst case. Sharing a propensity to live in their imaginations, each can feel very frustrated at what they perceive as their partner's unrealistic assessment of the future. Sixes can criticize the Seven for being too hedonistic and self-indulgent, while Sevens may find themselves frustrated with the Six's negativity. This same trait can be a positive at times: Because Detectives can more easily state their fears, the Adventurer can learn to get more in touch with their own fears or be able to process them through their Detective partner.

Exercises for the Detective-Adventurer Pairing

Sixes and Sevens are both part of the fear or thinking center of the enneagram but have different strategies for coping with their fear. Sixes focus on identifying potential worst-case scenarios and avoiding or pre-emptively defusing them, whereas Sevens distract themselves by filling their minds with endless options and plans. They are definitely optimists, in contrast to the Sixes' pessimism. These two Types can balance each other in their approaches to feeling safe. They are also each other's wings (adjacent types on the enneagram diagram [P. 11], so they understand and empathize with each other's concerns. The following questions highlight the classic issues that challenge the Detective-Adventurer couple.

Reaching a decision

When making decisions, Adventurers are impulsive and quick to act. Because planning is half the fun and a decision can be limiting, Sevens may leap to new options rather than carrying through with the original choice. Sixes also have difficulty with decisions, but thi is because they need to carefully explore every option to be sure there are no significant negative consequences. Sixes can become very anxious at Seven's impulsivity and enthusiasm, whereas Sevens can get very impatient with Six's endless rumination before becoming comfortable with a decision.

- Discuss with each other how you can make your decision-making more comfortable for both of you.
- Take a moment to learn what concerns and struggles exist for your partner. Learn to understand what the world looks and feels like from your partner's perspective.

The agony of processing negative issues

For Sixes to feel safe, they want to process issues at length, reviewing what has happened, what might happen, how to make it likely that a good outcome will ensue, etc. This includes lengthy discussions about the relationship. This can be agony for the Seven, who prefers to leave the past behind and focus on the possibilities for the present and future. Sevens don't want to look deeply at their stuff, and in fact do their best to reframe anything negative into its opposite, which can increase the Six's anxiety. Sixes are reassured when the Seven apologizes and takes responsibility for some hurt he caused the Six in the past, but Sevens are loathe to revisit painful times and express remorse.

- For the Adventurer: In order for your relationship to have intimacy, you need to be willing to sit with the pain, open yourself up to your Six partner, listen to her fears and concerns, reflect her words to her, and own up to what you could have done better.
- For the Detective: Understand the Seven's reluctance to process negative issues, and realize that you can't unload in large chunks; prioritize your concerns, ask for a short time in which to discuss one of them. This is important to do while also setting a time frame for making a decision and settling the issue. Avoid harsh start-ups (see pages 158 and 167), and give your partner a chance to respond.
- For the Adventurer: Commit to following through on what you agree to do to improve your relationship, and make it a point to actually follow through by giving yourself a time frame in which to do so. Setting specific goals instead of vague outcomes will allow for more specific actions to be taken and solutions to be reached. This is particularly true if procrastination is an issue for you.

- For both: Use any means to hold yourself accountable for time and for goal-oriented solutions. This can include setting clocks, reminders on your smartphone, and rewards for reaching your goals.

CHAPTER FIFTY-TWO

The Detective-Leader (Six-Eight) Relationship

When I have an idea, I tend to barrel down the road. Maggie (a Six) makes me ponder and ask questions. We tend to build on our strengths. She is detail-oriented, so she checks the emails' grammar, spelling, all of the fine details. I tend to keep us in motion, building our company and meeting the challenges. She keeps me sane, and vice versa.

-- Dina, an Eight (Leader)

Above is a great description of the Detective-Leader pairing, demonstrating the combination of action and thinking. This couple makes their relationship sound like a so-called muscle car equipped with the latest electronic technology that acts as the automobile's brains. Relationships are like vehicles -- they can take us on a wild ride or a smooth one, or they can break down on the side of the road leaving both partners stranded. Powerful motors can explode, and fancy electronic technology can go haywire. This chapter is about the vehicle and the kind of ride the Six-Eight pair experiences.

Leaders have a great deal of enthusiasm and optimism and may act impulsively, whereas Detectives want to thoughtfully weigh the pros and cons. Together they can make an effective team. Helen Palmer writes in *The Enneagram in Love and Work*,

> An excellent interaction shows the bigger-than-life Eight relying on the advice of the more mental and strategic Six. Sixes can wait rather than rushing in to take charge, they can observe complicated motivations, and they are far more

political about potential repercussions. Equipped with good counsel, Eights can move mountains. [p.371]

The Detective-Leader pairing is common. Detectives are attracted to Leaders' confidence and ability to make decisions and take charge, their loyalty, and fierce defense of those they love. Sixes look for someone to champion and protect them, and Eights can fill that role. Eights value Sixes' loyalty and trustworthiness, thoughtful opinions and attention to detail. Sixes and Eights do well together in times of adversity: The former's awareness of potential negative outcomes can rein in the latter's expansiveness and action-orientation. Detectives often have a good sense of humor, which Leaders value. Leaders also appreciate being admired for their courage and support. Both types value honesty and loyalty. Sixes look for hidden intentions that some people bring to an interaction. But Eights are so straightforward, they're not hard to figure out, and sometimes, Sixes will set about trying to find something that most likely is not there.

Leaders have a "what you see is what you get" approach to life that can help the Detective to relax a little and trust that the sense of safety in the relationship is real. On the other side, Eights can sense the Sixes' undying loyalty to their partners, which can help them let their guard down and be vulnerable – something not easy for the Eight to do. Neither type will allow others into their inner circle easily, but when they do, it's for good.

Leaders tend not to respect people who are wishy-washy or won't stand up for themselves. Given that the Eight needs to respect his partner, how does this work with a phobic Six who seems too diffident to make the slightest decision? The likely answer is that the Leader sees his Detective partner as vulnerable and an underdog, so he will champion him or her. But in other situations, the Six needs to be willing to stand her ground. It is a fine line. Sixes are capable of this if they feel physically safe.

Eights, especially when stressed, can be controlling when they feel their loved ones are in danger — even to the point of accidentally hurting the other. When we asked what strengths our respondents felt they brought to their relationship, two Sixes replied, "I choose to trust rather than indulge the fears" and "I am extremely loyal." One Leader cited his "ability to make decisions and not worry what others think." Detectives listed their partners' gifts as "decisiveness, lust for life, and fun" and as "solid character; he's protective of me and the relationship." The Six-Eight pairing fits nicely into the original themes and scripts that each of these Types brings into a relationship. The Detective's theme is to find a protective figure, be loyal to that person, and then the Six will be safe. The Leader's theme is to be strong and to protect the innocent from injustices and unfairness.

Challenges of the Detective-Leader relationship

Leaders are forceful people who make quick decisions, and who can become impatient with someone's need to question and reconsider. They might perceive Detectives to be wet blankets or indecisive. In our survey, the Leader was one of the types with which Detectives most struggled: "I fear their assertiveness." "They come across as sullen." "They can be judgmental." "I can't bear the confrontational, angry expression." "They threaten my sense of control." Even though an Eight can be a Six's protector, they can also bring out the latter's worst fears.

Security vs. Risk-taking

The combination of the Leader's impulsivity and the Detective's tendency to focus on potential bad outcomes (especially true of phobic Sixes) can cause clashes. As Helen Palmer reports, "The Eight partner, when pushing for the truth, or when seeking to revitalize the relationship, may become punitive and say the worst. Dealing with what now looks like an overbearing and possibly dangerous mate, Six's imagination ignites and moves to the divorce court." (P. 371)

Another issue that can be problematic is finances. Here's how James, an Eight, described how he and his partner, Keith, solved the problem of their differing comfort levels with fiscal risk: "I take more risks financially. Keith does not. Even after 23 years, most of our assets are kept separate with 'payable on death' benefits and Power of Attorneys. This arrangement solved this issue."

Power struggles

Sixes look for protection and security, but they also tend to rebel against authority and question everything. Detectives seem to say one thing one day, and something different the next day, and this can drive a Leader crazy. Eights like to be the authority. The Six wants an authority to trust, but then rebels against it. This can be very confusing to the Eight, who wants directness and consistency. On the other hand, the Eight may also give the Six a mixed message. James, an Eight, wrote that he would leave his Six partner Keith "if he didn't stand up to my strength." The Leader wants the relationship to be on his terms, but he also doesn't want to be with a wimp. It has been said that there is nothing worse than a bored Eight. They also like to know where people stand. They believe that the truth comes out in a fight, and therefore if you stand and fight with them, they now know not only where you stand but also whether they can trust you.

The couple can get into power struggles about "truth." The Six's question is, "How do you know it is the truth?" or "What proof do you have?" The Eight's response is simply, "Because I know so." Sixes of the Sexual subtype are more often counterphobic than phobic, and they can have explosive arguments with an Eight partner. Palmer writes, "The Eight can't surrender control until a mate looks strong and trustworthy, and the Six can't commit fully until the Eight looks less dangerous." [P. 371]. If they can work it out – and it may take a lot of work – especially around respecting and accepting each other, then the relationship can work very well.

When a Detective feels dominated, he or she may respond with passive-aggressive behavior, say, "I'm going to do something," and then not do it, or else do it differently. When the Detective has difficulty making a decision, the Leader hastens to act. The Detective then perceives the Leader to be acting unilaterally and complains, "It always has to be on your terms." From the Eight's perspective, he has the truth, knows what's best, so why not take action? Additionally, he may be so fearful of being dominated that if the Detective tries to balance out the power, the Leader may immediately conclude, "My partner is trying to control me."

Challenges for the Detective:

Stacy, a Detective, wrote that her challenges include being "Somewhat passive, depressed, maybe paranoid and, of course, very afraid." Debra, also a Detective, reported "I look for answers outside of myself; I test the relationship; I have contradictions in many areas." Dina, an Eight, feels that her Six partner "doubts himself and at times, me. He also has difficulty believing or remembering how wonderful he truly is." Another Leader, Rebecca, concurred: "My husband is reliable, fearful, and holds a grudge," and that he "is too fearful and paranoid, which makes him unpredictable about problem-solving. I usually have to handle his fears before I can get him to focus on any other issue I'd like to talk about."

Most of us are aware of the core issue of fear with which Detectives struggle.. They sometimes test partners to see if they can be trusted. Detectives will test again and again, until finally they may end up pushing the partner away. The conclusion? "See, I told you I couldn't trust him." Detectives use questioning to get at any possible hidden agendas. But this is also the cause of their contradictory nature. If someone makes a decision and then questions it, there is a good chance that his or her mind will be changed about that decision. The Six's self-esteem can be in jeopardy because of too much questioning.

Challenges for the Leader:

When Leaders and their partners were asked what challenges they brought to the relationship, Rebecca, a Leader, reported, "I'm too strong; it took me a long time to show my vulnerabilities." She added that her Detective husband tells her, "You always act like you know everything." Debra, a Detective, said that her Leader husband, Orville, "can be self-centered; he invades my space and can be overwhelming; he can be intimidating and mis-understand me." Another Detective, Stacy, said of her Leader husband, "It's my way or the highway . . . sad but true. . . All ideas must come from Christian. To get him to accept my ideas, I need to package them as if their his. He's unable to empathize with me. He's very afraid of feelings. He uses alcohol for an anesthetic." Dina, a Leader, described her own challenges as "my need to not be controlled and remain in charge of almost all I'm involved with. My high sexual needs/desire and relational intensity. My drivenness." James, also a Leader, considered his challenges to be his ability to go into denial and that "I don't wait to process issues." Sixes describe Eights as earthy, blunt, con-trolling, and powerful. Eights require someone who is strong in their own right and can stand up to them. Many of us want to be around Eights when we need or want their power, but when we feel they are going overboard, we then want them to change or go away. When we choose partners, we need to make sure that the very foundation of the relationship is built on love and acceptance, or we shouldn't be with them. Sixes have the ability to be loyal and/or to stand up to Eights. They also have the ability to accept them for who they are and to reap the benefits of the immense love and protec-tion, trust and reassurance that come with the "what you see is what you get" personality.

A Leader's Story

Rebecca, a Leader with an Adventurer wing, has been married for 10 years to a Detective who has an Observer wing and a Self-preservation sub-type. Asked to describe the "classic fight" she has with him over the years and how they dealt with it, Rebecca wrote,

He's always had a hard time with my direct confrontation, and I've always had a hard time putting up with his 'dodging' the issues. Soooo... I worked on

a much softer style and I learned to lead with loving and caring before bringing up an issue. He finally learned to trust me whenever I needed to raise issues. I also let him know when I felt vulnerable in discussing things. He felt like he had company in his fears. Today we're much better at all of this and remain loving.

Rebecca advises other Leaders, "Work on your denial! Show your vulnerability, be soft."

Exercises for the Detective-Leader couple

The following exercises highlight the classic issues that challenge the Detective-Leader couple.

The Six-Eight pairing is common, and no wonder – both Types are always on the lookout for dangerous situations. Eights react aggressively, as do counterphobic Sixes; phobic Sixes really appreciate the Eight's willingness to protect them. Sixes appreciate the Eight's directness, while Eights are reassured by the Six's loyalty. This can be a very successful pairing. However, some issues seem inevitable for this couple:

Power struggles: Feeling protected versus feeling controlled

Detectives, a fear-based Type, are attracted to Leaders because Leaders are confident, take-charge people who protect those they care about. Sixes feel safe with Eights watching their backs. At the same time, Sixes tend to rebel against authority and resist being controlled. Power struggles are likely to result.

- Brainstorm with each other ways of breaking an impasse that occurs when each of you is wedded to your own position.

- The Dalai Lama said, "Most of our troubles are due to our passionate desire for and attachment to things that we misapprehend as enduring entities." The fear- based Detective is not willing to allow for uncertainty. Practice letting go of a desired outcome by allowing your partner to decide for the two of you. By doing this, you experiment with loosening your grip on control of outcome and invite a new way of being in the world. First, practice with decisions or situations that have a lower risk or jeopardy, then over time experiment with letting go of other decisions in the relationship.

Quick decision making versus questioning

Leaders tend to make rapid decisions and are comfortable with this style, whereas Detectives need to question, reconsider, and consider all options before they can feel secure. Leaders can become very impatient with what appears to be the Six's indecisiveness, while Sixes can get frightened at what appears to be the Eight's rush to action.

- For both of you: How can each of you increase your comfort level with your partner's style of decision making, and how can each of you reassure the other?

- For both of you: Remind yourself, "I can be right or I can be happy." If you are striving for perfection and being right in your relationship, then the goal of being happy will suffer. Remind yourself, "It doesn't have to be my way or the highway!"

Aggressiveness and disagreements

Counterphobic Sixes and Eights are look-alikes in that both tend to aggressively challenge others – Eights if they feel the other is trying to control them or is disrespectful, Sixes if they perceive danger or feel that the Eight is trying to intimidate them. Harsh startups are common in this relationship (see page 129). Explosive arguments can result. Eights may quickly forget, but Sixes tend to remember and hold a grudge.

- Try to figure out rules for how the two of you can disagree with each other in a respectful and accepting way, being protective around each other's soft spots.

- Allow for outcomes that permit both of you to be happy. "If I'm right then you are wrong" does not allow for compromise and growth. However, easing up on an outcome in favor of growth will make for easier interaction.

CHAPTER FIFTY-THREE

The Detective-Mediator (Six-Nine) Relationship

I went through a serious bout of depression, to the point of having to be hospitalized for a while. My Six wife, being loyal and conscientious, was there with me the whole time. Heather organized financial arrangements with the insurance company and hospital, complained to my therapist if things were not the way she thought they should be, etc. Heather was a real advocate for me and made sure I had quality care. I was open and honest with her throughout the whole ordeal so that she always knew what was going on. It was important to me that she not suffer more than necessary. I knew that keeping her informed of all my thoughts and problems would ease things for her—keep her worries of the worst- case scenarios in check. I was also concerned about Heather's well being throughout the experience. So the Six loyalty and the Nine "keep everybody happy" traits helped us get through that time and grow to appreciate the other even more.

-- Robin, a Mediator describing her relationship with a Detective

In the above vignette, The Detective's loyalty and her willingness to fight for her partner is obvious. Robin's empathic nature is in true form and even though she was hurting, she kept Heather, her Detective partner, informed so that Heather felt she had enough information to be prepared for the worst without needing to go into worst-case-scenario thinking. This is a good example of a relationship in which each partner has taken the time to truly get to know one another, as well as to respect, accept and support each other.

On the enneagram diagram, the Six and Nine share a connecting line. This means they likely have each spent time in the other's space. Nines can look a lot like Sixes, especially when they are under stress, and Sixes can take on Nine-ish characteristics when in love and when they are able to let go of their fear and anxiety. This connection can draw them together and help create positive aspects. But as with almost all couples, they can also get on each other's nerves.

The Positive Characteristics of the Six-Nine Pairing

The Detective-Mediator is a very common pairing. In our survey, the Types that the Mediators reported feeling most compatible with were Detectives and other Mediators. Here were some of the Mediators' reasons for their attraction to Detectives: "(Counterphobic) loyalty, someone to always 'cover my back,' and a way of merging intensities." "I admire the courage, enjoy the loyalty and loving heart." "They are thoroughly nice friendly people – and maybe I don't threaten them. We often share a fight for some cause." "I think I understand the paranoia and for the most part it does not bother me. I think Sixes are clever, relational, and quick to let go of the stuff that doesn't really matter." In these comments, one can detect the influence of the connecting line.

On their side, Detectives admire the Mediator's ability to bring unconditional love and acceptance to the relationship. The Nines' nonjudgmental support and ability to trust the universe appeals to the Six. Detectives, who worry a lot, find the Mediator's calmness and even temper soothing, helping them to relax and trust that everything is going to be okay. A Mediator is willing to listen to a Detective's fears and concerns and can encourage him or her to see the big picture with its positives as well as the negatives. Nines are attracted to the Sixes' loyalty as well as their sense of humor and warmth. Sixes can be wonderfully childlike, which can perk up a Nine. When the Nine does feel anxious or worried, or even depressed, the Six can empathize and be loyal. Nines also appreciate the Six's competence and ability to step in at a time of crisis and take necessary action. In fact, Sixes can be at their best when they are being tested. This was demonstrated by Heather during Robin's depression and also by Lynn, another Six, when her Nine husband Sidney was incarcerated. Sidney wrote,

When I went to prison, I accepted that fact and worked on surviving my circumstances. My Six wife Lynn went to work, studied law, got a paralegal degree, and worked for a law firm to challenge the courts, change the laws and get me out of prison.

The combination of the Detective's loyalty and competence can make her a very effective advocate for the Mediator, who often has difficulty advocating for himself.

When asked about what positive traits they felt their Detective partner brought to the relationship, one Mediator listed the following: "Steadiness, loyalty, attention to detail." Another said, "His loving heart, humor, loyalty." Several Detectives listed loyalty as an important gift they bring to a relationship. They wrote, "I am extremely loyal – probably too much." "Despite my doubts I have been very loyal and have stuck it out through some not so great times." For the most part, the Detective's loyalty is an asset to their relationships, yet like most gifts, they can be overused. This can cause the Detective to be blindly loyal or stay too long when they should have left. Coincidentally, staying too long is also a characteristic of the Mediator, which is why this pairing tends to endure.

Sidney, the Nine who spent years in prison, wrote that what helps his relationship thrive was "My ability to accept reality and do the dishes." He also listed his "ability to live in the moment, to find good in every circumstance and be encouraged by it, to make people laugh and want to play." On the plus side, Nines can have a Zen-like quality mixed with humility. On the minus side, they tend to focus on the non-essentials of life, accepting these as both their "reality" and destiny, denying the gifts they bring to the world. One Mediator stated, "I am easy going, relaxed and calming. I am interested in a wide variety of things and have been the spice of the relationship." The unexpected "spice of the relationship" might be the Mediator's sense of humor toward people who are constantly calling him a couch potato. And finally, one Nine simply stated his gifts as, "patience and tolerance," which are great qualities for a partner to have.

Sixes listed the positive aspects of their Nine partners as: "liveliness," "calmness, gentleness, creativity," "He loved my family, my animals, me. He cooked well. He planned trips well." "Love, tenderness, affection, wisdom, interesting life." "Stability, perseverance, intellectual prowess, loving-kindness." It is not surprising to hear Mediators using the word "love." Partners can feel quite loved by the Mediator, yet love can be something that Nines have a hard time giving to themselves. Stability is another characteristic that Detectives admire. Sixes frequently report experiencing inconsistency and unpredictability in the families they grew up in, and therefore they prize the Nines' ability to help them feel secure.

In the Detective-Mediator relationship, the Six may see the Nine as not having an agenda and therefore not getting things done. The Six, with a strong work ethic, will often jumpstart the Nine, as well as get him or her to ask the hard questions about life. The *Serenity Prayer* by Reinhold Niebuhr states, "God, grant me the serenity to accept the things I cannot change, the courage to change the things I can, and the wisdom to know the difference." Sidney, the Mediator, stated this in his own way when he said life is about "accepting reality and doing the dishes." Mediators are often accepting of their lot and don't question.

When it comes to being in a situation one cannot change, acceptance is generally a good thing. In most circumstances, however, Nines need to learn how to question, especially "Who am I?" and "What am I here to do?" The Six personality Type, which has also been called the Questioner, can lead the Nine to ask who he is and how he can make a difference in the world. Since the Mediator usually has a hard time taking charge in a relationship the Detective has the opportunity to practice being the authority, something they usually avoid.

Detectives struggle in relationships in which their partners try to be the authority. This is rarely a problem in the Six-Nine pairing, because of the Mediator's tendency to avoid the authority role. Nines can appear somewhat oppressed, leading Sixes to champion them as the underdog. Sixes feel they themselves are the underdog; therefore they tend to both empathize and bond with the Nine. The relationship then takes on a non-threatening aspect, something the Six will truly appreciate.

Challenges of the Detective-Mediator relationship

When Sixes were asked about the challenges they felt the Nine brings to a relationship, they mentioned the Nine's tendency to become obstinate or passive-aggressive when angry instead of being direct. Mediators avoid conflict and suppress their anger. Their identity hinges on the connection with loved ones, and they are afraid that a fight will push away that person. Sixes, on the other hand, want things to be out in the open, so the Nine's behavior can be maddening. Detectives want to know exactly where someone stands.

Sixes also complained about the Nine's tendency to "criticize me for taking too many precautions; tune me out at times and leave me feeling insecure and alone." Nines sometimes take pride in not letting things get to them or not worrying. This can make the Six feel put down or laughed at. Robin, a Nine, described her complaint to her Six partner, Heather: "You take too long to make a decision; you have to go over everything with a fine-toothed comb. Let it go, and be a little more intuitive. Trust your gut."

Detectives are usually quite verbal, and Mediators may zone out while Detectives are talking. This can trigger childhood issues for Sixes, who may have heard from their parents that "children should be seen but not heard," and in some situations, not even seen. Finally, Sixes complained that Nines are "not always active enough – I like to keep moving; (Nines) don't take the initiative, so I don't know what they really want." This knowledge is crucial to a Detective.

Nines reported having trouble with Sixes because they "are often bothered by my quietness," "try to get a reaction out of me or control me," "look for hidden meanings behind what I say," "blame me for everything that goes wrong, can be unforgiving, and freak me out with their paranoia," and "turn everything that happens into a big deal." These are descriptions of an unhealthy Six-Nine relationship. Mediators often can be relatively non-verbal, leaving the worry-prone Detective with a blank screen upon which to project worst-case scenarios. When Sixes don't get much reaction, they go digging for trouble. The Nine, who just wants to be left alone, will find this very irritating. Sidney, the Nine, gave us a relevant example "She always checks up on me." His take on this is that his wife is trying to control him. He complains to Lynn, "Why don't you trust me? You are never going to trust me." From her Six perspective, however, Lynn is just trying to get reassurance. Dawn, a Detective, sums up her relationship challenges in just a few words: "Projection, overreacting, vigilance, fear, questioning too much."

The Power Struggle

The Six-Nine couple can get stuck when the Six becomes afraid that something important, at least in his or her mind, is not going to get done, while the Nine procrastinates. When things become heated, the Six will likely complain: "You always say you're going to do something, and then you don't do it. You never do what you say you will." These can be fighting words for the Nine. To the Mediator, the Detective is trying to push or control him. But instead of responding directly, the Nine will likely become passive-aggressive or obstinate, resisting any action. A power struggle results. June, a Six, gives a great example of this dynamic:

We have disagreed on how to get our house renovated and how to start building a new house. I wanted a schedule and deadlines when certain tasks should be completed. Barry didn't want any "pressure" put on him. When I would try to pin him down on what action to take (he is an architect), he would resist.

Our solution was to go to a counselor, who explained that my demands drain Barry of energy. Now I have stopped asking him anything about his actions (or lack of actions) regarding house renovations. I am attempting to suspend my doubts that it will never be completed and to work on my trust. This has been and still is difficult for me since I feel I have no control in the situation. However, since Barry says he will do it if I "get off his back," then I have to try this approach.

We will be seeing the counselor in three months for a check-up and I will then see how much progress we have made. In the meantime I am trying to stay in my own Nine space, completely oblivious to what is happening re our home. My "insurance" is the meeting with the counselor in mid-June where I will have a third party to negotiate.

Although the counselor in this situation was well intended, her advice was probably not the right one for this couple. Yes, June was draining Barry with her demands, but it is not a good idea to leave a Nine to his own "(de) vices." June's effort to stop her doubting and nagging and instead just trust, although possibly good for her spiritual development, will not help her learn how to ask for her own down-to-earth needs to be met in a non-reactive way.

Getting into a power struggle with a Mediator is easy to do – it can happen any time the Detective wants something from the Mediator and he or she resists. The Nine's partner is unlikely to win. To resolve the power struggle, one of the first things to explore is whether the Nine really wants to act. Mediators often give the impression that they agree simply because they can't say no and at all costs want to avoid conflict; in reality, they are not agreeing. If the Nine feels just a hint of control coming from the other person, he may resist in order to preserve his own sense of self, no matter how small that sense of self may be. The Nine's unspoken motto is, "I may not know what I want to do . . . but I'll be damned if I'll let you tell me what to do!"

Finally, it's important to keep in mind that the Mediator's core issue is a form of self-neglect or other-neglect. Even things that are important can feel overwhelming and that they will take too much effort to accomplish. A form of low self-esteem is at the heart of the matter. For the Nine, it always comes back to the idea of love being fractured in some way. Accomplishing things usually requires us to love ourselves, and then be able to fall in love and commit to the project at hand, something Mediators struggle with. This is why for the Six to just get off the Nine's back most likely won't work. It is far more complicated than that. Detectives need to make sure there is a healthy sense of separateness in the relationship and that from the beginning, they take an active role in the relationship and not depend on the Mediator to initiate action. Sixes and their doubting minds can collude with Nines with their difficulty with decision-making so that both can have difficulty moving forward in the relationship.

It is better for each of them to chart their own personal goals and not wait for the other to take the lead. This will cut down on potential power struggles. When Sixes become frustrated or angry in the relationship, they need to make sure that their harsh startups don't cause the Nine to withdraw. Instead, Detectives need to utilize a non-violent communication style. Mediators need to receive the same love they are so good at giving to others, so the combination of Six and Nine provides the perfect opportunity for a Six to access heart space so as to commit without doubt, and to love unconditionally.

Exercises for the Detective-Mediator couple

Communication: Verbal versus Non-Verbal
Mediators can avoid conflict by saying very little while diverting their attention to something else. This trait typically leaves the Detective worried that their issues have not been fully discussed with their partner. Anxious to resolve problems, Detectives may jump into a deep conversation with their Mediator partner and then become angry or withdraw when the Mediator attempts to get a little personal space by bringing up something out of context. Although Mediators want to reassure their partner, they find the inevitable barrage of facts and possible outcomes that the Detective wants to discuss so overwhelming that they begin to tune out while waiting for the end of the story.

- For both of you: In order to better resolve issues with your partner, first establish the level of priority or importance that each of you has assigned to the issue. This does not mean that the other person is insignificant or unimportant. It means that each person gets to understand the level of priority that the outcome holds for the other. This perspective helps calm fears and anger about the decision-making and the outcome for each.

- After recognizing the importance that each person assigns to the decision, allow one or the other to have the final outcome. This compromise will lower the level of distress and hostility. Not all decisions need equal input from both people in the relationship. One person's strengths may make for a better outcome in decision than the other.

- Try adding a physical activity to a discussion of an issue that may need resolution or a decision. For example, take a walk or hike, drive out to a picnic site, or paddle a rowboat or kayak. Planning a physical activity gives the Mediator something to divert part of his attention while giving the Detective a specific timeframe in which to discuss the issue with their partner. The "interruptions" to look at a bird in flight, or pull out the picnic basket, can help the Mediator take a short mental break and then re-focus their attention on the points the Detective feels the need to make.

Power struggles: Certainty versus spontaneity

The Detective, fearing that something important won't get done, tends to demand solid commitments from their Mediator partner. Wanting to be agreeable, but also wanting the flexibility to be spontaneous, the Nine may be vague or procrastinate and resist, feeling that he or she is being controlled. This couple has to find a way to communicate about projects, tasks, deadlines and schedules that meets the Detective's need for a committed plan but leaves room for the Mediator to delay an actual decision if they have agreed to do something at a given time, or to be able to change it while providing a level of certainty for their partner.

- Create a master calendar and plan a time each week to review what has been penciled in. This tool may help the Detective feel more secure and reassures the Detective that the Mediator knows about activities important to them. At the same time, this technique allows the Mediator the opportunity to change plans if something else comes up and gives them a feeling of control over their choices.
- Divide up the decisions to be made so that each partner knows what they are responsible for.
- At some point both need to learn how to let go of the outcome. Learned serenity is a virtue!

Decision-making: Too much versus too little consideration

Both Mediators and Detective struggle with decision making and, when paired together, may have trouble agreeing on actions to take together, or even actions to take individually. When fully expressing their character trait the Nine will jump from one decision to the next, unable to prioritize and unwilling to deeply consider the implications of any given decision. The Six, on the other hand, is unable to move forward, paralyzed by all the possible negative outcomes. As a couple, the Detective tries to hold the Mediator back from trying new things and the Mediator may drag their partner into situations that a little forethought might have prevented. But this couple also has the potential to support each other in making positive, proactive decisions. When the Detective yields to the enthusiasm of the Mediator to do something, and the Mediator yields to the ability of the Detective to reduce possible choices to the ones with the least negative outcomes, this couple can take advantage of the strengths of both of these personality traits.

- Decide together how many choices should be on the table for joint decision-making. When narrowing your options, include potentially positive outcomes as well as potentially negative outcomes. For example, recognize only three outcomes that are acceptable to both individuals so that the process becomes more about the solution than about problem solving. Being solution-focused instead of problem solving allows both partners to work towards an outcome and not against each other and to calm their fears and anger.

CHAPTER FIFTY-FOUR

The Double-Adventurer (Seven-Seven) Relationship

Adventurers enjoy being with like-minded people, high-energy individuals like themselves who are upbeat, want to have a good time, and are up for an adventure. When someone makes a last-minute change of plans, they can find it stimulating. They love to emphasize the positive, especially when it comes to new things, places and people. Adventurers are usually quick-witted and funny, and their focus is on future possibilities rather than past mistakes or unpleasantness. They are interested in those who share their dislike of being trapped or stuck and who agree that boredom is to be actively avoided.

In a nutshell, fun-loving people enjoy being with other fun lovers. This was confirmed in our survey, where Adventurers chose their fellow Adventurer as one of the Types they are most attracted to. Staying true to their Type, they even described their relationship in a lighthearted way when asked what they liked about being with other Sevens: "Need you ask?" "It's party central with two Sevens in the house!" "Best Type – let's be honest." "We are light-hearted, kind, and understand each other." "Similar senses of humor." "Fun, entertaining." "Enjoys life. Knows it's not forever." In an interview with the wife of a Seven comedian, the interviewer asked her if her husband was as funny at home as he was on stage. With some disdain, she answered, "He's funny all the time." What she was saying was that humor can also be used to avoid the serious aspects of life and allows the joker to resist making him- or herself vulnerable. These qualities can create challenges in a relationship.

Challenges of the Adventurer-Adventurer pairing:

Despite all these positives, Sevens tend not to choose other Sevens. Why are long-term relationships between two Adventurers so rare? The answer probably lies in the difference between friendships and committed relationships. As we described in Chapter Ten, Adventurers like to have multiple options. Friendships don't require exclusivity and do not limit one's possibilities for adventure and relationships. We generally don't have to answer to our friends or be responsible to them. Marriage, on the other hand, involves a lasting commitment -- the big "C" word that can frighten Adventurers. The commitment is not only to sexual monogamy, which is especially difficult for the Adventurer of a Sexual subtype, but also to working through difficult times in the relationship and placing limitations on one's activities. As Helen Palmer put it so well in her book *The Enneagram in Love and Work* "Sevens use words like *predictable* and *permanent* as if they meant 'boring' and 'stuck.'" (P. 378)

Most Adventurers like to keep things light, avoiding deep emotions whenever possible. When problems emerge, as they inevitably do in committed relationships, the Seven's tendency is to escape through planning and activity. When the going gets rough, it's tempting to run. Because they want to avoid pain, Adventurers are also sensitive to criticism. When given negative feedback, they tend to make excuses and reject blame. In-depth discussions of what went wrong are difficult. Enneagram teacher Tom Condon states, "When Sevens get caught with their hand in the cookie jar, they'll call you small-minded about the cookies."

When Adventurers pair up and collude around these tendencies, there is no one "at home" to ground the relationship or to present an alternative approach. Healthy relationships consist of three characteristics – love/nurturing, challenging, and the transformation that results from the first two characteristics. But even though Sevens chose another Seven as their favorite person to hang out with, it was not their choice for a committed relationship. Adventurers gravitate either consciously or unconsciously toward partners who will provide the necessary stability, loyalty and depth that balances them. Of course, as with all same type pairings, differences in wings or subtypes may provide the dissimilarity they need.

Sevens can sometimes be self-centered. One Adventurer who dated another gave us a reason it didn't work out: "We both wanted the spotlight too much." When two Sevens are together, one of them may think, "Uh-uh. Here's someone who wants to be noticed as much as I do, and that's not going to work." Also, if an Adventurer's partner is too dissimilar, the latter may set about trying to change the former. Adventurers may believe they have the right way, and the message will be, "If you want to be happy, be more like me . . . and then if you are more like me and happier, I'll be happier."

Adventurers are also notorious for thinking out loud, over-planning and misjudging deadlines and appointment times. You can imagine the nightmare that can ensue when two Sevens in relationship are thinking out loud, over-planning and missing deadlines!

Double-Seven couples who desire a lasting relationship must work out creative ways to have their need for novelty and options met. This could include living apart, having many separate activities, and in some cases, a sexually open marriage. A Double-Adventurer couple who were involved in swingers' group tried this approach. They referred to themselves as "polyamorous" (which stands for "many loves"). They felt it was a perfect fit for their Seven mindset. This is the reverse of the more common monogamous relationship in which we commit to a single partner in order to deepen our love for him or her. Instead, the polyamorous couple believed that through having many lovers, they would deepen their love for each other. Instead of using monogamy to deal with the issues of insecurity, jealousy and possessiveness, they believed that they would deal with these in reverse. By having many partners, they would have to directly confront the issues of control and jealousy.

This idea rationalized their tendency for a gluttonous lifestyle and perhaps rationalized their aversion to limitations. Ironically though, an "open" relationship usually requires more rules and more communication than does a monogamous one. People in various types of non-monogamous but committed relationships (including living in threesomes or groups) are able to stay together for more than a short time only by developing an increasingly complex set of rules about their outside sexual relationships. Whenever one member of the couple inadvertently hurts the other by some action, they typically create yet another rule to avoid repeating this. For example, one rule might be that if the husband had plans to meet an outside sexual partner and the wife had had a hard day at work and felt she needed her husband's support that evening, he would cancel his outside date. In the end, couples who are able to negotiate a long-term polyamorous relationship live a life extremely limited by rules, just the opposite of the freedom and spontaneity that Sevens normally seek.

When two Sevens come together, they need to avoid colluding around their mutual tendencies. For example, "Wouldn't my partner want me to do this if it will make me happy?" This is just a rationalization that allows them to do what they want. If both of them take this approach, it eventually just creates more and more distance between them.

A more traditional approach for enabling the Double Adventurer pairing to endure requires them to develop a singular focus, a commitment from the heart. They will need to talk about their pain, both past and present, and to take responsibility for their actions. This means not only thinking about oneself, but also thinking about a partner's heart and the general health of the relationship.

Exercises for the Double Adventurer couple

The following exercises highlight the classic issues that challenge the Seven-Seven pairing.

Where's the commitment and stability?

Adventurers like novelty, get bored easily, and when the going gets rough, their temptation is to run. When both partners have these characteristics, there is no one to provide stability, loyalty, and depth to ground the relationship. When one or both are of the Sexual subtype, the likelihood of extramarital sex can also destabilize the relationship.

- To remind yourself of why you are in this relationship, think about your early days together, and describe to each other what attracted you to your partner, why you fell in love, and the reasons you decided to spend your life with him or her.

- Think about the things your partner has done to promote your relationship, and what you can do. Here's an exercise for each of you to do: On a piece of paper, make a vertical line down the middle. Label the left side: "Your gifts to me." Review the past week and write a list of caring things your partner has done for you. For example: "Because I was so busy Thursday, you made an extra trip to the post office to mail a package for me." "You agreed to go with me to go to dinner with my friends even though I know you'd rather have stayed at home." Label the other side of the paper, "What I can do better for you," and list the caring things you plan to do for your partner in the coming week. Exchange the lists and discuss them. Commit to doing this once a week, and set aside a specific day and time on your calendar to repeat this exercise.

Problem solving

Because they want to avoid pain, Adventurers are sensitive to criticism; their response will probably be to make excuses and reject blame, and to quickly spin the situation into a more positive light. In the Seven-Seven pairing, it's difficult for the couple to discuss the problems in the relationship and how to improve it.

- Pick a time when neither of you has immediate distractions, sit down together, and discuss with each other strategies for addressing problems when they arise. Practice having a conversation about some problem that one of you may have that affects the relationship; role-play how you can talk about it constructively while the other truly listens.

It's all about me

Adventurers enjoy the spotlight and may find it difficult to focus on their partner's needs. In a relationship of two Adventurers, each may live life meeting his or her own needs and desires without truly considering their partner. In this exercise, complete the following sentences and then discuss them with each other:

- One thing I really wish you would do for me is . . . .
- One thing we haven't done together (recently or ever) that I'd really like us to do is. . . .
- One thing I would really like to change in our relationship is . . .

CHAPTER FIFTY-FIVE

The Adventurer-Leader (Seven-Eight) Relationship

I am . . . (are you ready for this Seven idea?) . . . having a parade for my 60th birthday; you guessed it, I am going to be the queen of the parade and raise money for several of my favorite causes by auctioning off places in the parade. My Eight husband would never make such a spectacle of himself, but he will support my efforts with gusto. I think it will be fun and I have no problem making a fool of myself; plus, of course we will make some money for people who need it!

-- Kimberly, an Adventurer

If you know anything about the Adventurer and Leader, thinking about them pairing up could raise an eyebrow. Sevens are known for their fun and adrenaline highs, while Eights exemplify excess and a larger-than-life approach. Helen Palmer calls this combination "fun hunger." So . . . besides plenty of juice, what really does happen when these two types pair up?

According to the enneagram diagram, the Adventurer and Leader are not strangers. They are wings of each other, meaning they have an innate understanding of their partner. They can also meet at Type Five (the Observer), their connecting point. (See the enneagram diagram on page 11). For the Seven, Five constitutes the security point, a place where they go when feeling good; in contrast, for Eights the Five constitutes the stress point, where they go to hide during difficult times. However, according to Helen Palmer, writing in *The Enneagram in Love and Work*, "the couple's shared Five tendency tempts them to detach rather than to deal with difficulty."

Sevens who have an Eight wing can look quite different from Sevens with a Six wing, so that two Adventurers with opposite wings may appear dissimilar in relationship. For example, Sevens with Eight wings won't be as fearful as those with a Six wing when it comes to the Eight's built-in anger and conflict. The disadvantage is that a combination of Eight with a Seven who has an Eight wing is likely to have even more juice and excess.

Leaders and Adventurers are attracted to each other because of their mutual passion for life. Both like to play hard and can be ambitious in their own way -- Sevens with their abundance of ideas and Eights with their strong work ethic and determination to achieve their ambitious goals. Assuming they can avoid addictions and other forms of unhealthy excess, this couple can be very successful. Kimberly, a Seven, talks about the blending of the different characteristics of the Adventurer and the Leader:

My husband (an Eight) and I are sponsors (founders) of a school, but we don't do anything for it on a daily basis. When I get discouraged as an outsider trying to help the school, but, without the hands-on work that would keep me going with more immediate gratification, he reminds me of the bigger mission of helping kids feel good about themselves as learners so I can keep helping with fund raising (a good task for a Seven) and creating enthusiasm for the new school. When I get frustrated or angry, I want to abandon ship; when he gets frustrate or angry he wants to save the ship, so I think that works well for us. I need more recognition (my narcissism I presume) than he does, so when I complain of being unappreciated, he is very clear that we are helping to create opportunities for kids who need more support than they are getting, not to create positive feedback for ourselves. I am more willing, however, to go directly to people and ask for support and help, while he tries to do more himself.

Positives of the Adventurer-Leader relationship

When we asked what gifts they bring to the relationship, an Adventurer wrote, "I bring the social life to the relationship." "Adventurous spirit, sense of humor, light- hearted, fun, funny, generous." Anybody who has hung out with a Seven knows how much fun they can truly be.

Regarding the gifts and strengths Leaders bring to a relationship, Adventurers wrote, "Good with money, good in career, good provider." "Generosity of heart and spirit, patience with me, big picture grasp of the world, energy, confidence, perspective, loving heart, forgiving spirit."

Challenges of the Adventurer-Leader relationship

Obviously, not all Seven-Eight relationships work well together. In fact, many may actually like the separation this combination can create. Both

Types tend to be guilt-free about their actions, both are self-referencing, and both prefer to answer only to themselves. They admire these qualities in each other and enjoy the independence that this provides them. Paraphrasing Gestalt psychology originator, Fritz Perl, probably an Eight himself, "You do your thing and I'll do mine, and if we happen to meet, groovy." The problem with this kind of relationship is that the partners might feel too separate from each other. An Adventurer responding to our survey stated, "I can't honestly think of anything (we've) done together that accomplished anything. We have pretty separate lives." In Kimberly's statement above, you can hear the distance between them.

Another significant problem with this pairing is that as the relationship matures, they may find themselves drifting apart. This isn't usually a relationship where one leads and the other follows, and it is not one where they depend on or are responsible to each other. Additionally, Sevens may have difficulty with commitment, but an Eight needs a commitment from the Seven before he or she can feel comfortable in an intimate relationship. Because of this, it is important that they make a conscious effort to "remember" the relationship as well as the commitment they have made. When the Adventurer and Leader are able to collaborate, great ideas mixed with great energy may result. Kimberly said, "We just started a non-profit middle school and have done a lot of charity community work because we are both generous, energetic, open minded. We trust and support each other."

In the following statement, an Adventurer describes her tendency to escape and the Leader's perseverance.

I like to escape and quit when things get tough, he hangs in no matter what. And vice versa. I think he hangs in too long on projects that drain him of energy and us of money. He tolerates people that I think are takers. He champions losers until they start dragging him down. We really resolve disagreements by agreeing to disagree and going on. We don't spend much time and energy at odds with each other, and we don't complain about each other much. I think we treasure our time together.

In the preceding comment, we hear about the different characteristics of each of the types and their ability to accept those differences. At the end of the comment, we also hear about their most likely Sevenish approach, easygoing and joyful.

However, Adventurer-Leader couples who maintain separate space and personhood will probably not unite even during difficult personal times. For example, when they have been hurt or burned by the outside world and their energy and high evaporate, they are unlikely to lean on each other, but instead will retreat to their connecting point, Type Five, which serves as a bunker for the Eight and a "crash zone" for the Seven. The result is they withdraw from each other and their problems and do not really try to work things out. On a more positive note, meeting at their Type Five space can provide a period of quiet for both, as well as a truth zone, where both are interested in getting to a solution in a truly thoughtful and pragmatic way.

Probably the biggest risk for this pairing is the lack of self-observation and a sort of amnesia that both take on regarding their actions and behaviors. Neither is likely to question themselves extensively. Sevens dislike criticism and would prefer to see themselves as having it all together. Eights, on the other hand, feel as if they have the truth and don't want to be talked out of it. Neither of these qualities lends itself to being challenged.

The three main aspects of all relationships are: love/nurturing, challenging and transformation. Relationships are built on love and nurturing. With these qualities as a foundation, partners are then able to act as mirrors to their partners, challenging them to question who they are, their behaviors, and their actions. It is as if the partners are saying to each other, "This is how I see you, is this the way you want to be?" If it is done in the right way, it can lead to the next stage, which is change or transformation for each of them, thus transforming the relationship as well. In this pairing, however, Sevens would rather not be challenged (it feels too negative) while Eights may feel that their partner is trying to control them. In their quest to avoid feeling controlled by another, Eights can become quite controlling. A power struggle can develop between the Seven and Eight if the Eight tries to place limits on the Seven. An Adventurer wrote, "The only way things work for us is if it's my husband's idea or at least he thinks it is. He thinks I'm on the go too much, and I find that he wants to do very little. If there's a project to be done (remodeling, etc.), it has to be done his way."

On our survey, we asked the question, "What is your central complaint to your partner?" The Adventurers' comments about Leaders were: "You always undermine what I'm trying to do or say. You second-guess me or take other people's opinion instead of mine." "Too angry. Demand your own way. You always need to be right" And then finally, "You does not take good enough care of himself, eat bad stuff, are overweight, and you've already had a heart attack." The preceding statement seems to speak to the control issues in the relationship and the excess that Eights can fall into.

The central complaint about the Seven was, "You always change your mind." This simple statement speaks to the capriciousness of the Seven, which could irritate an Eight who wants structure and discipline – what you see is what you get.

To the question. "What challenges do you feel you brought to the relationship?" an Adventurer responded, "I'm much more upbeat – I go with the flow, I'm a happier person than my husband. I don't deal well with angry or depressed types. I also want to do everything, which drives my husband crazy." Another Adventurer is quite critical of herself when she says: "I speak before I think, I'm critical, judgmental of others, impulsive, spend too much, unrealistic, shallow, self absorbed, self serving." Yet another Adventurer related, "I'm always looking for a stress-free life, and sometimes I won't do the hard work required of me." We also heard such negative words as: "Scatterbrained, changeable, shallow, self-absorbed."

Helen Palmer says that a "sober" or single-minded Seven still has the pleasant diversions of a complex mind, but can also remain steadfast during the limiting and painful phases of commitment. Adventurers can be helped to deepen their relationships by significant others who note the signs of rationalizing their behavior and avoidance of pain, who bring attention back to the present, and who welcome so-called negative emotions when they are appropriate.

Exercises for the Adventurer-Leader Couple

The following exercises highlight the classic issues that challenge the Seven-Eight pairing.

Separate lives and disconnection

Adventurers hate limitations, while Leaders believe in following their own rules. Each marches to their own tune, entertaining their own personal interests and enjoying their independence. Their tendency to lead separate lives is enhanced by their joint connection point at Five (the Observer), meaning that at times they will retreat to their own space and withdraw from the other rather than trying to work things out together. In addition, the difficulty Sevens often have with commitment will also separate the couple. With time, they may drift apart.

- Given the tendency you both have to disconnect, brainstorm some ways you can reconnect, affirm your commitment to each other, and plan for joint activities.

Lack of self-observation and dislike being challenged

Both Adventurers and Leaders dislike introspection and reflection about how they are feeling; Adventurers reframe the negatives into positives and recast everything into fun, while Leaders appear to transform fear, insecurity, or other negative feelings into anger. Both tend to quickly forget negative events and interactions that happened even recently and avoid rehashing the past. Sevens deflect criticism while Eights tend to react with aggression. Neither Type is very willing to sit down, discuss feelings and problems, and search for solutions. Neither Type likes to be challenged. Intimacy requires a willingness to be open and vulnerable about oneself, not a strong suit for either Type. The result is a lack of real intimacy and communication between the pair.

- Brainstorm with each other how you can increase the intimacy in your relationship. This means taking the time to really talk with each other and being willing to make yourself vulnerable and open yourself up to your partner, and to consider making changes.

Structure and discipline v. desire for change

Adventurers don't want to be caged. They like to have multiple options. They enjoy making plans – and to have the freedom to make multiple plans and to change their minds at the last minute. On the other hand, Leaders like to feel in control, which often includes having structure in their lives and plans that stay in place. The Adventurer's changeability can be maddening to the Leader. One solution may be to lead separate lives, but this is not optimal for the relationship.

- Try to figure out with each other how you can make plans while satisfying your conflicting needs for freedom and multiple options on the one hand, versus structure on the other. For example, you might agree to schedule the dates of a vacation in advance, but maintain open options for where you will go. (This will take some concessions on both sides).

CHAPTER FIFTY-SIX

The Adventurer-Mediator (Seven-Nine) Relationship

Carla, an Adventurer, married Josh, a Mediator, when both were 21 years old and each the youngest in their family of origin. Despite some doubts from various family members, they are still together in a positive relationship 10 years later. They now have two children, stable jobs and a fun-filled life. Carla likes to travel and enjoys making plans for vacations, and Josh goes along with them. The family has moved several times, replaces their cars frequently, and lives at the edge of their incomes. Josh has followed Carla's lead regarding financial decisions. When their home was foreclosed and they went bankrupt, Carla, like a good Seven, reframed the experience as an opportunity to get a new start in a more convenient location. Carla is loyal to her husband and involved with her children. She maintains an upbeat attitude, is always open to new options and the more enjoyable things in life. Josh is grounded and supportive.

One of the reasons Mediators are attracted to Adventurers is that the high energy of the Seven can jumpstart the Nine's internal battery. The Adventurer makes plans for enjoyable activities and the Mediator is happy to go along. Even when not directly participating in the Adventurer's activities, a Mediator can live vicariously, enjoying hearing about the Adventurer's many experiences when they return home.

Adventurers are very sensitive to criticism, so they appreciate their partner's nonjudgmental attitude. The Adventurer is likely to run the show, at least initially, but eventually the couple can get into a power struggle, especially if the Mediator feels that plans are being made without consulting him or her. To a certain extent, Sevens and Nines are considered look-a-likes in that they are both escapists. The Seven escapes through fantasy, the Nine through tuning out. Neither likes conflict, and both want life to be pain-free and pleasant. Also, both have a difficult time making decisions – the Adventurer because everything looks so good and commitment to one thing is hard, whereas with the Mediator, everything looks equal, making it just as hard to choose. Not making a decision can cause a Nine to focus on the non-essential aspects of life. As a couple, both Sevens and Nines need to ask themselves the difficult questions; "What do we really want?" and "What is really important to us?"

In their book, *Are You My Type, Am I Yours*, authors Renee Baron and Elizabeth Wagele, in their somewhat playful way, list the "likes" that these types have. Sevens like Nines because they are easygoing and fun to hang out with; don't like confrontation; are accepting and nonjudgmental; appreciate the Seven's idealism; like to listen to the Adventurer's stories and enjoy the good things in life, and give the Adventurer plenty of attention. They go on to say that Nines like Sevens because they: have a positive outlook; are enthusiastic and make activities lively and fun; have an open and questioning mind; come up with interesting new ideas and things to do, and are idealistic. This is a sweet list of compatibility characteristics, although some people would argue that the relationship can lean toward superficiality, that both of them will struggle when it comes to intimacy and emotions, that they will prefer that it primarily consist of comfort, action and escape instead of anything deep or emotional. The issue of commitment will be at the core of this relationship. Both have difficulty committing – the Mediator has trouble showing up, while the Adventurer doesn't want to be pinned down.

Positives of the Adventurer-Mediator relationship

When asked how they helped the relationship thrive, Adventurers reported: "My exuberance and passion combine with her exactness and groundedness." "I help my Nine husband do everything and go faster." "I bring a fun and upbeat attitude to our relationship." "I'm creative and open to new concepts, I'm committed to making it work, and I'm fun." Mediators wrote: "We share spiritual values." "The good side of not taking myself seriously enough is not taking myself too seriously – something that helps in a relationship. It lets me detach and deal with the issue." In these comments, you hear the fun side of the Adventurer and the humility and self-deprecation of the Mediator.

When we asked Adventurers what they appreciated about their Mediator partner, they stated, "Maturity, being stable, quiet, unassuming." "Her concern for others, her giving nature, her strong interest in spirituality." "She agrees with me." "She wants to please me." "She's steady, easygoing, grounded, she loves me." What Mediators appreciated about their Adventurer spouse included: "his vitality, enthusiasm and excitement," "his interest in many things and people, energy, fun-loving." "His optimism. He has a great sense of fairness, even to his 'enemy' if he has one. He is extremely generous and he is a great problem solver." Obviously, the Seven brings a high level of optimism, excitement, and enthusiasm, qualities that can liven up the Nine's life.

Nines are great at giving others permission to do the things they may be inhibited about, or just aren't comfortable doing. Nines can be hesitant about rocking the boat or trying to accomplish certain goals. They may tell themselves that whatever it is, it will most likely never work out, so whyeven engage? In contrast, Sevens will usually think, why *not* just proceed? They can be great at encouraging Nines to go ahead and take a risk.

Another positive characteristic that Adventurers and Mediators share is their unique view of the world. Adventurers are good at synthesizing. Since they appreciate the many different options and opportunities the world has to offer, they can also see how very different ideas can come together to produce exciting and sometimes futuristic plans. Mediators notice how things link together and see the world in a highly systemic way. Both Adventurers and Mediators can bring together interesting people with diverse points of view, honoring the wonderful differences that will be present.

Sevens and Nines are opposites in certain ways but they balance each other out. Adventurers like the rush of novelty, but they get bored easily with the monotony that lengthy projects entail. Mediators usually have an eye for detail and seem to like the ordinariness and predictability of long-term projects. The Nine's steady pace can also balance out the Seven's stops and starts.

One Adventurer-Mediator couple works at a high level in the education field. Both are extremely intelligent and are able to see the big picture. Anita, the Seven, writes about and synthesizes progressive concepts regarding classroom education. Her Nine husband, Anil, sees the big picture as well, although more in a down-to-earth way where progressive concepts involve actual students and schools. Their home resembles a bed-and-breakfast inn with diverse people coming and going, sharing their complex ideas. Anita is willing to move from one coast to the other at the drop of hat if it means that more of her ideas and plans might come to life. She will jump on a jet or put the top down on her sporty convertible and zoom to a school that will serve as a lab to put her progressive ideas and plans into action. Anil, the Nine, will load up the U-Haul truck with their golden retriever dog in the front seat and casually drive across country, determined to test both of their ideas in a nuts-and-bolts way at an ordinary school where he will work.

Challenges of the Adventurer-Mediator pairing

Some of the very qualities that help this pairing to work well together can also create challenges. Earlier, we talked about the expansive worldview that both partners can bring to the relationship, but this attitude can only go so far. If you are going to be successful, you must take a stand or put a plan into action. This is hard for both Adventurers and Mediators, so that each can remain stuck and the pair may have trouble settling on what they're going to do. They also remain stuck if when the Adventurer proposes her exciting ideas and plans, the Mediator resists, not wanting his or her comfortable routines upset by change. On the other hand, Adventurers have their own resistance when faced with having to narrow down their multiple options. Both may have a terrible time following through: Sevens gripe at the Nine for their turtle-like pace, Nines criticize Sevens for spinning their wheels and getting nowhere.

The very different personalities of this pair can clash in several areas. A Nine woman provided a list of the common disagreements in her marriage:

- *"Going out" fight – he likes to go out; I like to stay at home.*
- *"Sex" fight – he likes sex; I often don't.*
- *"Exposing" fight – he loves to share indiscriminately; I want privacy.*
- *"Talking too much" fight – I think he draws too much attention to himself; I want to remain in the background.*
- *"Keeping me waiting" fight – he wants to be on time: I am very slow to leave the house.*
- *"Christmas Card" fight – he wants to connect with others; I want the card to be perfect before I send it out.*
- *"Details" fight – he doesn't see the importance of details; I do.*

Some of these may have to do with the Nine's introversion and Seven's extroversion, and others reflect subtype --Sexual, Social, or Self-preservation. (Despite what most people think, not all Adventurers are extroverts.) But most of the disagreements on the list relate to their different personality Types. Below we will illustrate some common areas of potential conflict in the Adventurer-Mediator relationship.

Things that are in motion and things that are at rest

Adventurers often feel they repeatedly have to drag the Mediator into activities and may find themselves complaining that their partner is lazy or resists change. (Note: the activity level is usually significantly higher for social Nines.) Overall, though, the Seven is likely to have more energy than the

Nine for social activities, adventures and possibly even sex. At times, the Mediator can dig his heels in and resist, preferring the peace and quiet of home. Nines tend to procrastinate and be indecisive. Sevens may change their mind several times before the final plan crystallizes and may act impulsively.

Commitment and the work of relationship

Adventurers are reluctant to commit, perceiving it as limiting their options. They may seek novelty in their jobs, possessions or relationships. Mediators, on the other hand, like predictability. Although they enjoy travel and adventure, they savor having a stable home base and relationship. They can become unhappy if too many things change.

Although commitment to monogamy is often a problem primarily for the Adventurer of the Sexual subtype, all Sevens find it difficult to commit to the hard work of resolving relationship problems. In their quest to avoid pain, they prefer to gloss over past problems and focus instead on future opportunities. They are reluctant to confront difficult issues and to work seriously at solutions. An Adventurer reported, "My need to be happy all the time can keep me from dealing with conflict and pain." A Mediator said of her Adventurer husband, "He doesn't like to ruin the good mood by bringing up something controversial or unpleasant."

Mediators, too, seek to avoid conflict. A major goal for them is to have peace and harmony, even if this is only on the surface. Therefore Mediators tend to collude with Adventurers in avoiding anything having to do with relationship difficulties. Usually neither is comfortable talking openly about their feelings. Mediators will instead detach into watching TV, hanging out with their social groups or over-involvement with their work, while Adventurers will flee into fantasy, plans and activities. The couple may end up leading parallel lives, with little intimacy and little commitment to making the relationship work. Marcelle, an Adventurer, wrote of her Mediator partner:

Renee twists a conflict so that it ends up being what's bad and wrong about herself. She doesn't deal with the issues. She withdraws. She gets so angry that she can't express herself. She fears conflict. She's afraid of my anger. Sometimes it feels like I have to do all the work. She holds on to past hurts.

When asked to describe a "recurrent fight," Marcelle wrote,

I guess it is the need for peace, but we rarely fight. We seem to go along with the other's wishes, which do not seem to be far apart. Our life is on a pretty even keel. I have my own money, which could really be a sore spot with us. My spending habits are quite different, and our views on money are way off. But just the fact that we both have our own money and keep separate bank accounts except for household expenses has saved us a lot of fighting.

This Seven's statement illustrates how powerful the avoidance of conflict is. This couple has significantly different attitudes regarding expenses, which they have resolved by leading parallel financial lives rather than working as a team. This is one way to avoid having to deal with conflict and risk negative interactions, but intimacy may be one casualty of such an approach.

The chief complaint of another Adventurer, Reggie, about his wife was "You criticize me all the time." Grace, his Mediator wife, had a strong One (Perfectionist) wing. Under stress, Sevens can move to One. In the Seven/Nine pairing, the Nine may have a strong One wing, while the Seven can slide to Type One, causing them to meet at One. This could make the dynamic similar to a rather unhealthy One/One pairing where both partners are extremely critical of each other.

For the One-Seven – and now the Nine-with-a-One-wing/Seven partnership – one challenge was that the more irresponsible or impulsive the Seven becomes, the more critical and judgmental the Nine spouse can be. The Seven may end up seeing his partner as a critical parent. This couple can take on a look-a-like quality with the One-Seven (Perfectionist-Adventurer pairing – See Chapter 21).

Also, Adventurers and Mediators may step on each other's toes because they hold a shadow aspect of each other. Each is saying to the other, "You need to get a life." But they mean different things. The Mediator thinks about the Adventurer, "You're just floating around, taking everything just on the surface. You need to settle down, be serious, get a life." And the Adventurer thinks the same thing about the Mediator; "You need to get a life, quit procrastinating. Just do it! Commit to something." The message is similar, yet the core dynamics of Sevens and Nines are quite different.

Challenges of the Adventurer

Adventurers can have difficulty prioritizing people and activities. Their focus on multiple options and opportunities may result in leaving their partner behind, emotionally if not physically. Anita, an Adventurer, recognized this in herself with the following comment: "I get scared of being stuck, always looking for freedom to explore new things. I'm changeable. I get caught up in new pursuits that distract me from my relationship and then discount my partner's feelings." This is great insight from an Adventurer about her own core issues and how they might hurt her partner.

Grace, a Mediator, wrote about her Social Seven husband Reggie, "I sometimes feel he doesn't know how to do 'we.' He has a full social life, lots of friends who care about each other, but no private life. I sometimes feel that there is very little that is exclusive in our relationship." Angela, another Mediator, wrote, "He flits from one thing to another, like a giant butterfly, always on the go. . . He's too impulsive, jumps to conclusions, and moves too hastily."

Sevens do not understand the importance of exclusivity in a relationship. To the Adventurer, exclusivity and discernment probably sound too limiting. Adventurers also tend to be rather self-referencing. It may appear to them that everything revolves around them. In relationship, they may assume that their partner's decisions always have to do with them. Sevens of the Sexual subtype may resent it if their partner has other interests or wants to spend time with others. A Seven woman advises younger Sevens in relationship, "try to remember that it's not all about you. Think about the other person's needs, too. Find the balance." This is especially important in the Adventurer-Mediator pairing because of the Mediator's tendency to focus on the other person and lose themselves. This can eventually cause conflict. After some time, the Nine may wake up to the fact that he or she is being unrecognized, and with her underlying anger, she may decide to leave and not look back.

Challenges of the Mediator

Angela, a Mediator, says about herself and her sloth (remember: sloth is defined as a neglect of one self and others.): "I'm indecisive, avoidant. This is based on an attitude that it doesn't really matter (I don't really matter), so I don't deal with things that should be dealt with, at least not in a timely way. I seek peace at any price, to a fault." This kind of negative self-talk can keep the Nine stuck. Why do anything if it isn't going to make a difference?

The paradox for Mediators, who tend to be self-effacing and easily merge with others' plans, is that they are very sensitive to being left out, to finding evidence that they are indeed unimportant. Angela tells Harlan, her Adventurer husband:

You always plan without consulting me and not just have a great idea, but go as far as making at least a partial commitment before I even know anything about it. It comes across to me as if I don't matter, my life and what I may have planned doesn't matter, and whether I go along on (the trip, the event, etc) doesn't matter either, or you would have consulted me before everything was carved in stone.

Respect is an important issue for all the members of the gut or belly center (Eights, Nines, and Ones). When the Seven ignores the Nine, the latter perceives this as disrespect as well as confirming that they don't matter. Sevens need to be careful that given their usual focus on themselves, they don't overlook the Nine.

In conclusion:
The Adventurer and Mediator pairing constitute a fascinating relationship. At its lowest level, it might become superficial and the partners may collude to create an absence of pain and conflict, even at their own expense. They'll also find themselves each doing their own thing, completely separate. Both types have difficulty connecting with the feeling center, and both work to avoid feelings of pain and sorrow. But feelings can act as a barometer, telling us what we really want, and this is also where commitment resides. We fall in love with something and commit wholeheartedly. At the highest level, Sevens and Nines integrate both positive and negative aspects of life. They utilize their gift of seeing the big picture and ask themselves, "What do *we* really want?" and "What is most important to *us?*" Then they will make a decision together and commit to it with their head, heart, and gut.

Exercises for the Adventurer-Mediator Couple
The following questions highlight the classic issues that challenge the Adventurer-Mediator pairing.

The focus is on yourself, the focus is on the other
Sevens and Nines are opposites in that Sevens tend to focus on themselves and their desires, as though the world revolves around them, whereas Nines tend to merge with their partners and can easily lose themselves. This may make for a peaceful relationship, but in reality, the Nine may be accumulating anger and resentment at not being "seen" and may eventually decide to leave.

- For the Seven: How can you let your partner know that they are loved and appreciated, and that you are committed to learning about – and fulfilling – their wants and needs?

- For the Nine: Although it may be more comfortable to "just go along," talk with your Seven partner about your underlying need to be recognized, consulted, and appreciated.
- For both: Recognizing that one result of your combination of Types is that the focus in the relationship is likely to be overwhelmingly on the Seven, strategize how you can make the relationship more balanced in terms of taking into account the needs and wants of the Nine.

Who will stabilize the relationship?

Adventurers seek novelty and tend to make impulsive decisions without always considering the consequences. Their Mediator partner is likely to go along rather than risk conflict by arguing against the decisions. The result can be that there is no stabilizing force in the marriage, no one to point out, for example, that the family budget would be strained by the latest proposed vacation.

- Review together some activity you did, or purchase or decision you made, that had some adverse consequences. Think about how the two of you might make decisions in the future that would be better for your relationship.
- For the Nine: How can you increase your willingness to express a different perspective even if it's a "downer" for the Seven?
- For the Seven: How can you make yourself more likely to consider the perspective of your Nine partner before committing to some fun activity, purchase or decision?

Stability versus reluctance to commit

Adventurers are classically reluctant to commit. They love to move on to new things or new people (extramarital affairs are an example of this, especially for a Sexual subtype Adventurer). Mediators, in contrast, like comfort and stability. They don't like change. The novelty-seeking of the Seven can be a positive force in the relationship, introducing Nines to new adventures. However, a classic disagreement between Adventurers and Mediators occurs when the Mediator resists the Adventurer's efforts to involve him or her in the new activities. One result may be that they drift apart, leading separate lives, the Seven participating in new activities while the Nine stays at home watching TV or relaxing.

- Discuss with each other how you can strike a balance between these two opposing needs. For example, the two of you might agree to go out together once a week to an activity the Seven has suggested, even if the Nine would have preferred to sit by the fireplace.

Conflict avoidance. How do we agree to discuss relationship issues?
Although their motivations differ, Sevens and Nines can be look-alikes in that both avoid conflict. Sevens focus on the present and future, and are very uncomfortable discussing past matters, especially if they were painful or negative. They resist learning from the past in order to do things differently in their future relationship. At the same time, Nines avoid conflict and won't stand up for themselves (other than in passive-aggressive ways, which are usually not a solution-focused strategy).

- For the Seven: A real gift you can give your relationship is to become willing to face the pain and to discuss problems. Your willingness to do this – and to follow through on the changes that you may agree to at the end of this discussion -- will go a long way toward convincing your partner that you are indeed committed to the relationship.

- For the Nine: A real gift you can give your relationship is to become willing to experience some conflict and anger by discussing problems. Your willingness to sacrifice your comfort, to stand up for yourself and let your partner know of your dissatisfaction and your needs, will go a long way toward preventing you from accumulating anger and resentment to the point where you might decide to just leave.

CHAPTER FIFTY-SEVEN

The Double Leader (Eight-Eight) Relationship

"So are you a cowardly custard?"
"I'm not frightened."
"Neither am I frightened."
"Well, then, take it."
"Well, then, you take it."

Then rather curiously they both snapped out the same remark:
"Shut up!"
"Shut up!"
-- From: Peter Pan by J.M. Barrie

If one long-term enneagram pairing is particularly hard to find, it's the combination of two Leaders. As Helen Palmer (herself married to an Eight) has written, "There are plenty of double Boss stories on panels, but they're usually history. 'When I dated this Eight' is a common opening line.' Palmer implies that the Double Leader pairing being talked about has usually taken place in the past. Savvy enneagram enthusiasts, hearing that two Leaders have actually been paired up, at least for a while, quickly ask, "Did they both survive?" Their question shows the power and volatility that is inherent in a Double Eight pairing. Because romantic relationships tend to bring out the worst as well as produce an addictive high, people fear that in this case the worst will dominate.

Responding with a deep sigh and with some wistfulness, one Leader said, "It was quite the roller coaster ride." She recalled that they were young and that both wondered at times whether they would survive. But as with most double pairings, no matter what the Type, she reported that she learned a lot about herself. Being with your own enneagram Type gives you the opportunity to intimately see yourself.

Two Eights together can respect and appreciate each other, and according to our survey, Eights were at the top of the list of the personality Type with which they are most comfortable. They wrote, "We know clearly where we are with each other. I love the lusty, high energy." "I enjoy their honesty. They tell it like it is." "They know what they want." "My own type – understandable and straight." Eights value each other's energy, intensity, sexuality, and commitment to truth and justice. They appreciate not having to hold back, and they enjoy being with someone else who wants to get all the juice and passion out of life. Leaders believe that a good fight reveals the truth about another person, and they enjoy being with someone who doesn't withdraw from arguments and confrontation. For the Leader, an argument can be life affirming and a good way to discharge energy; and usually when the fight is over, they have forgiven and forgotten. Also with fellow Eights they don't have to worry about being told that they are too much and would they please go away. Bosses (Leaders) worry about being "dissed" by others, but less so when they are with their own type.

When both Eights are healthy and mature, the relationship can work. They usually respect each other and agree on how to be in the world or at least to enjoy debating life's major issues. But if they're not mature, it can be deadly. First, Leaders can easily believe that they have the truth about all things. Author Helen Palmer tells a story about getting into a big disagreement with her Eight husband. The petite woman describes herself climbing up the stairs in their home until she gets eye level with her 6' 4" mate and then emphatically stating, "I heard what you said, I just don't agree with it." She claims that the look that came over his face was remarkable – it showed amazement that someone could actually hear what he said and not agree with it. This is a great story about the "truth" of Eights.

Same-Type partners have a tendency to collude. Remember that collusion is defined as the co-illusion held by both partners. Leaders together can powerfully reinforce their ideas about the world – and not necessarily positively – but in a way that keeps them both stuck. Two Leaders can also argue excessively and sometimes even physically fight. They can hurt each other emotionally to the point where revenge takes precedence over the relationship. With each partner seeking control and trying to avoid vulnerability, the pair can find it hard to solve problems or to be truly intimate. Instead, each may deny their own role in the difficulties and blame the other for their problems. Eights find it difficult to take responsibility for their actions and to apologize, mainly because they tend to have a form of amnesia with regard to their actions. They can have a hard time seeing themselves and understanding the impact of their behavior.

When a Leader is in relationship with almost any other Type, the partner may often take on the job of damage control, smoothing over excesses and bringing a dose of reality to his or her action. The partner can often calm the Leader down or make the necessary explanations or reparations. But with the Eight-Eight pairing, no one takes on this role and tempers the aggression.

As with most double pairings, the relationship may provide an opportunity for one of the partners to access and act out their wing or connecting point. It is almost as if they are saying to each other, "You've got the Eight point covered, I think I'll broaden my horizons and try coming from my wing or connecting point." When Two Leaders manage to stay in relationship for a while, it's usually because only one of them fully acts out the aggressive Eight personality type, while the other tends to live at either the Five (Observer) or Two (Giver) connecting point. The Two point can soften the relationship overall, while the Five connecting point can add a little more observation. In addition, partners in a Leader-Leader pairing may also have different wings, bringing more variety to the relationship: a Seven (Adventurer) wing can make the Eight charming and charismatic, although a focus on excess and enjoyment may also be present, whereas the partner with the Nine (Mediator) wing is usually described as having an iron fist in a velvet glove and will probably be more accommodating and giving.

Partners in all relationships need to answer the question - Who is going to control the relationship? How will the relationship be controlled? This question can loom large when two Leaders pair up. Because of the Eight's fear of vulnerability, power struggles can quickly escalate. The Eight's original wounding usually involves feeling dominated and recalling a childhood vow to never let that happen again. Since both partners are probably operating with similar childhood messages, it is important that healthy boundaries are intact for each and that they can then work on supporting each other. When Leaders fight, it's important they not lose sight of the actual issue. Eights can quickly turn an argument into a matter of disrespect.

So . . . two Leaders together . . . will they survive? Or are they only meant to be together for the short term? As with all gut types, respect is crucial. They must respect each other in both words and actions, assuring that they don't allow the relationship to disintegrate through abuse or neglect. How the relationship is going to be controlled and who is going to be in charge needs to be discussed from the beginning. Intimacy and vulnerability are sensitive areas for Leaders, yet these are the primary ways for an Eight to personally and spiritually grow. Eights need to protect each other's soft spots. Collusion, especially regarding any form of excess, needs to be addressed through healthy input from trusted confidants. As much of a cliché as it sounds, the love of power needs to be transformed into the power of love.

Exercises for the Double Leader Couple

The following exercises highlight the classic issues that challenge the Eight-Eight pairing.

Same type, different subtypes and wings

Double-Leader couples who are able to stay together for the long term frequently differ in the strength of their wings or connecting points. The result is that one member may be an obvious in-your-face Eight, whereas the other seems to live in the cerebral Five position or that of the warm, pleasing Giver.

- Before addressing the challenges of this pairing, review the wings and subtypes of the Eight as described in Chapter Three and discuss how the differing wings, subtypes, and strength of the connecting points that each of you has have contributed to the success of your relationship.

Dealing with conflict in the relationship

Eights are comfortable with anger and with conflict, enjoy arguing, and tend to quickly forget what happened and get on with the relationship. But when two Eights argue over something personal, the disagreement may escalate to where each is shooting with all guns blazing. They may forget that the recipient is someone they care about, and they may be more focused on revenge than on the relationship. If one partner feels disrespected, the conflict may turn serious. Additionally, Eights have difficulty apologizing; they would rather wait a little while and then act as though nothing happened. Very few Double-Leader relationships last.

- To avoid this outcome, develop some strategies for handling conflict without contributing to the destruction of the relationship.

Power struggles

All couples have to come to terms with who is going to control the relationship. This is especially true for two Eights, who are particularly sensitive to any behavior that feels as if someone is trying to control them. They are likely to react by becoming further entrenched in their original position and will barely listen to the partner's position.

- Think about and let your partner know what triggers your reactions regarding control. Also, what is the best for your partner to approach you with a need or want in a way that will not cause you to revert to your you-can't-control-me mode and the resultant aggressiveness.

CHAPTER FIFTY-EIGHT

The Leader-Mediator (Eight-Nine) Relationship

Most of us would love to have a partner who would bring us coffee in bed every morning – especially those of us who really value comfort and enjoy lounging around. Metaphorically, that's what the Leader brings to the Mediator – a jolt of caffeinated energy! The Nine is enamored with the energy of the Eight. The Mediator usually goes through life with one foot on the accelerator and the other on the brake, whereas the Leader goes full steam ahead. In turn, the Leader, who may feel he's been disparaged most of his life, appreciates the unconditional acceptance of the Mediator. Nines provide damage control, repairing the damage that Eights tend to do with their bull-in-the-china-shop approach to life, and smoothing the rough edges. Marjorie, a Mediator, in a long-term relationship with a Leader, reflected on the way they work well together:

My husband (an Eight) holds a senior executive position in a national firm. Wayne values my input and asks for it regularly. He often uses me as a 'sounding board' to resolve work-related issues. If Wayne is having difficulties with a particular person or issue at work, he will describe the situation to me, as well as his observations about the person or persons involved, and how all this makes him feel. He appreciates my ability to cut through a lot of the irrelevant issues to get to the heart of the matter. He is often surprised at how well I seem to know this person from a short explanation of the situation. I feel Wayne has told me so much information himself, it was he who spelled out the problem. I think my tendency to merge with him and see the situation through his eyes is helpful. I am also able to offer more conciliatory solutions to work-related matters. At the same time, he is much more capable of taking assertive action where it is required.

What comes through clearly in this description is the respect with which the Leader treats the Mediator. The intuitive Mediator can help the Leader soften his black-and-white view of a situation, as well as provide people skills and conflict-resolution ideas.

Eights and Nines, who are opposites in so many ways, are an extremely common pairing. In our survey, we had by far more such couples than any other combination. The Leader-Mediator pair have much to offer each other. Respect and love are in the relationship, and if they can sidestep power struggles, they can overcome their biggest differences. Lillian, married almost 50 years, said:

I still have compulsive angry outbursts, but far less often than I used to, and an apology usually ends it. My husband has worked on his tendency to procrastinate and I've worked on wanting things done yesterday. I'm more patient and he's more apt to get things done.

Eights need to work on patience and control, and Nines need to learn to take more immediate action. The latter are also good at letting go of things, especially after an apology, and they are usually more productive when a partner is patient.

Positives Aspects of the Leader-Mediator Relationship:

Mediators are attracted to the high energy of the Leaders and enjoy their forcefulness and decisiveness as well as their ability to jumpstart Nines, empower them and even "give" them an agenda. Marjorie, the Mediator, wrote, "I really admire their directness and ability to say it how it is without worrying about possible conflict." She added, "As long as Wayne is around, I don't have to think about my personal security." The Eight's strength can make those they love feel safe.

In our surveys, Mediators talked of admiring the Leader's power, energy and ability to inhabit the relationship in a big way. The following quotes express how the Leader is not about to let the relationship coast, become stagnant or sink to its lowest common denominator. "She's not satisfied with status quo; if there is a problem, let's get it out." "A strong willingness to keep working on the relationship." "Honesty, zest, passion, humor." "Action, outreach orientation and creativity, let's-give-it-a-try." "Strength, support, drive, and excitement."

Benita, an Eight whose husband Bryce (a Nine) was ill with cancer, provided a moving example of an Eight empowering a Nine:

When I don't interfere, Bryce tends to vegetate. He likes to be in a comfortable twilight zone, not challenge anything. In his cancer support group, he's been the least physically active person there. For a while, all he did was sleep, eat, and play bridge. I finally had enough! I was feeling like I was tending a rock garden, there was no relationship, he wasn't doing anything for himself; he just wanted to be taken care of. So one day when he didn't get up until 2 PM, I said to him, "This isn't good for you, and it isn't working for me. It's important for you to exercise and keep your bones strong. These are choices you're making, such as not to get up." It had never occurred to him that his disease was stressful to me. The next day, after he had time to assimilate what I'd said, he had a 180- degree turn. Ever since then he's been setting his alarm and getting up at a reasonable time. He said, "It just never occurred to me I had choices." Until then, he just thought of himself as a victim. He's thanked me dozens of times for that conversation.

The Mediator's core issue is sloth. Sloth is defined as a form of self-neglect and/or neglect of others. The dilemma is trying to discern which is sloth and which is illness. For Bryce, the fatigue of his illness took him even deeper into the self-forgetting of the Nine, and what he forgot, according to him, was that he had choices and that his health still required him to engage in regular activity. Self-forgetting is comparable to ignoring one's problems. This makes it difficult for Nines to sort out why they are reluctant to take action. His wife's stimulation and encouragement was extremely helpful, improving the quality of his life and even prolonging it.

Leaders are comfortable with Mediators because they are each other's wings and because they are both from the same center or triad, the gut or belly. Leaders are attracted to the Mediator's gentleness, loving nature and ability to soften rough edges. Deep down, the Leader is looking for unconditional love and the offered acceptance. Eights feel they've often been disrespected; they've been told they're too powerful, too big, or that they are just too much. Many times, people will want Leaders around when they need their power, but then want them to disappear. Mediators have the capacity to accept Leaders just the way they are. In our survey, Eights chose the Nine as the most compatible personality type. Their reasons confirm what we just described above. They stated: "They are easy to be with" and "They are peace-makers, creative, aware and nonjudgmental."

Other Eights also described their appreciation of Nines: "He's calming, reflects on thoughts, and appreciates outdoors, moods, and moments." "She has peacefulness, charity, forgiveness, worth, love, and appreciation." "His acceptance, patience, and affectionate nature. He's a good father to our cat." "He has a grounded, steadiness, common sense and practicality, a well developed feminine aspect, a romantic attitude, an ease of being, a feeling of being a "safe place." Alexis, a Leader, relates,

We can have difficult conversations and still be very strong. We can handle a lot of problems and emotions. My husband Carlos is better on the emotions, I am better on the confrontation part. So the result is better when we do this together. We are a strong couple. When we travel together, Carlos charms everyone, while I get things done everywhere. So it's nice and we both are able to enjoy and be enthusiastic over the same things.

But what about when the Mediator is too passive in the relationship? Leaders value a partner who can meet them on their own ground but not someone who wimps out, someone who can stick up for him- or herself. They believe that through conflict they can figure out where a person stands. When the chips are down, will the other be there? Devonne, a 60-something Nine, evidently understood this issue and took it on as a challenge. Her response to the question, "What do you feel you do to help your relationship thrive?" was, "I practice standing up for myself." This is not easy for a Nine, given her fear of conflict. However, this definitely benefits the relationship and serves as a true growth edge.

Leaders need to lower their guard and allow themselves to experience being vulnerable with their partner. Samantha, the young married Mediator, wrote about the difficulty Eights have exposing that soft side; "I am tender and loving and create a safe environment for Boyd to be vulnerable." This is a great example of a partner who recognizes her mate's childhood wound and is now committed to creating an environment that will help him heal. Mediators can be instrumental in supporting their partner in the healing process, and can commit to avoid re-creating a dynamic that ends up re-wounding the Leader.

Challenges of the Leader-Mediator couple: It's a matter of respect

Respect is a primary issue for all three Enneagram "gut" types– the Leader (Eight), the Mediator (Nine), and the Perfectionist (One). In a pairing where both are gut types, success of the relationship relies on treating each other with respect. Relationships involving gut types can end – not because they have "fallen out of love," but because they have "fallen out of respect." With gut types, respect is synonymous with love.

Mediators connect respect with recognition. However, because of their fear of conflict and the possible resulting separation, they struggle to stand up for themselves when they feel disrespected by their Leader partner. Samantha, a Mediator, described this issue as follows:

I have difficulty sticking with what I say I need. For example, telling Boyd I need him to be nice to my friends even if he doesn't like them, because they are my friends, and out of respect for me, and that he should at least be respectful of my friends. I say that, but then when he is rude to my friends or sister for the second or third time, I don't end it or do something drastic to show him that his actions are not okay with me.

Nines can have difficulty sticking to their guns when they when they want to set boundaries with someone, thus causing the Eight not to take them seriously and even to disrespect them. Many times, our shadows — the very things we don't want people to do to us -- get projected onto others. Even though Eights hate being disrespected themselves, they can contemptuously turn their partners into one-dimensional caricatures and even poke fun at them.

People who know the enneagram realize how powerful a Leader can be, but often don't recognize the power of the Mediator. This pair is actually a combination of an irresistible force and an immovable object. In fact, some enneagram teachers say that the Nine is the most powerful of all the types. Eights need to be careful not to interpret the Nine's easygoing, laid-back approach as a weakness that allows him or her to take control. In this case, the Nine may store up the Eight's behaviors on their list of injuries and resentments; after repeated passive-aggressive approaches, they may explode or simply walk away. The partner of a Mediator needs to be aware that even if the Nine seems likely to "go along to get along" forever, a saturation point does exist. Once this is reached, the Nine will leave the relationship and not look back, no matter how much pleading and begging a partner does.

Consensus versus confrontation

An ongoing challenge in a Leader-Mediator relationship is the problem of confrontation versus consensus. A type Nine clergywoman, Dallas, explained, "My need to have comfort and accept people means I also don't go down the difficult road. It's a challenge for me to be able to be honest, not to fear bringing up things that might be uncomfortable." Isaac, a Mediator married 25 years to a Leader, related,

One of the things we've worked on relates to my desire for consensus versus my wife Kristen's desire for confrontation. Whenever possible, with children or other issues, we delay the decision or response momentarily while we confer. I have to deal with Kristen's confrontation, and she has to deal with my "peacemaker" side. So I guess we both try to honor each other's stuff and modulate our own.

Myra (a Leader) and her partner Dale (a Mediator) make sure that a core level of respect is present in their relationship, and that they also value each other's approach to the world. Myra wrote,

When we're confronted with a person who appears threatening to me and pushes my buttons – my protective instincts kick in. Dale recognizes my alert status and respects it (at least he doesn't want to hassle with it), but he sees the situation differently, 'no problem at all'. Since I trust his input, I relax from my initial position, but I don't relax completely. Through mutual respect and communication, we decide how to deal with this situation. Somewhere between my elevated concern and Dale's lack of concern would be appropriate.

Our biggest challenge is Dale's defense of his children and his desire to avoid dealing with their issues, versus my plainly stating the issues and forcefully making suggestions how to improve our quality of life and help the kids. Dale tells me I need to be more sensitive in order to not make him defensive. He says he will try to be less sensitive and defensive. It is a tough one.

The Mediator's coping strategy from childhood is to focus on others and gain an identity and a sense of self through merging with someone or something. However, this approach can leave them susceptible to a form of low self-esteem. Balancing the merging with others while maintaining a high regard for him- or herself can be difficult. To the Mediator, it's almost as if the two don't compute. They often discount themselves, which makes them particularly sensitive to criticism; they are protective of whatever sense of self they do have, and they cringe at being confronted or criticized, especially in the direct way that is typical of Leaders.

Power Struggles

Almost all couples struggle with answering the unspoken question, "Who is going to control the relationship?" This question is even more important when two powerful types – Leader and Mediator-- interact. The very thing that initially attracts us to a partner is often what will irritate us the most later on. In the Eight-Nine pairing, this is most true in the area of power and control. Initially, Mediators admire the strength and power of the Leader. Yet several Nines in our survey complained about feeling controlled by their Eight partner, that they weren't heard and didn't matter.

Conversely, the Nine's compliance and easygoing ways attract Eights. Part of what they initially appreciate is that Nines appear easygoing, non-threatening, and re not interested in trying to control anyone. Both Helen Palmer and David Daniels, enneagram experts, have described Mediators as the most powerful type on the enneagram diagram. Leaders often do not appreciate the enormous power that Nines' passive-aggressive behavior wields. When Nines feel controlled, they resist by hunkering down and becoming immovable. They may not yell or lash out, but rather simply disengage, withdraw and not accede to the Eight's wishes. A power struggle between an Eight and Nine can be like two bulls locking horns. This is evident in the following quote, by Douglas, a Leader married 27 years to Ramona, a Mediator:

We always end up unable to resolve or even agree on what the issue is. It turns into a massive power struggle. Ramona retreats. I feel rejected. I try to resolve by communicating. She feels dominated and tells me I don't understand. I get angry and she checks out. We are both alone, even if we are together.

A popular enneagram joke about the Eight-Nine pairing compares the Eight to a Sherman tank and describes the Nine as a swamp. The punch line is that we all know that tanks sink in a swamp. Power struggles are tempting, yet are one of the most unproductive behaviors. They usually leave us feeling "alone, even if we are together." It is similar to playing the game tug-of-war, where each person pulls on opposite ends of a rope. The object of the game is to try to control and dominate the other person while not allowing the other person to control and dominate you. When played in relationships, no one really wins, and a resentful stagnation usually results.

Conflict resolution

Because they are at opposite poles regarding expression of anger -- confrontation versus consensus and a direct approach to problems versus avoidance and postponement -- negotiating conflict resolution is crucial to the success of a long-term Eight-Nine relationship.

Gretchen, a Mediator, recommended the following: "What Saul and I have found is that it's all about getting present enough with ourselves to resolve anything. If we argue, we count to five, calm down, and we can then usually hear each other's needs." It is important for both partners to agree when they are going to get back together in order to resolve their differences. Mediators are likely to just drop the issue, which to the Leader can feel as if the Mediator really doesn't care.

Another Eight-Nine couple suggested a high-tech solution: "We sometimes text each other about tricky issues to lessen our verbal impact on each other." Emailing and texting have a built-in delay, giving the writer an opportunity to review his message, and it also removes the aggressive, threatening tone that Leaders can adopt in face-to-face conflict, and which is so off-putting to the peace-seeking Mediator. Marjorie, a Mediator married 30 years to Wayne, described what has worked for her relationship.

From my perspective, one of the recurring problems in our relationship is that Wayne thinks he always knows best – what to do, when to do it, etc. As a stubborn Nine, I am reluctant to listen to his advice, even when it is good. Sometimes I avoid telling him what I am doing because I don't want the aggravation – why are you doing that? Why are you doing it that way? Sometimes I become passive-aggressive. Sometimes I appear to agree and then go ahead and do it my way.

The only way we've been able to deal with this in an adult way is to talk about it when we are not angry. It has become a joke for us that Wayne always knows a better way. Instead of becoming angry, if I am able to make a joke of his interference, he is often quick to own up to his own behavior and admit there may be other solutions. I am often surprised by his softness when I am connecting with him in a way that is not combative.

Humor can be a great tool in relationship, and in this situation it serves as an effective way to soften up the Eight as well as keeping the Nine from becoming passive-aggressive. Relationship expert John Gottman refers to this kind of strategy as "repair attempts." When a couple keeps getting stuck in familiar, frustrating scenarios that end up eventually damaging the relationship, he suggests that they find sweet and endearing ways to lighten up the situation. Power struggles many times come about because we take ourselves or the situation too seriously. The motto to live by is, "Always be sincere – never serious."

About the Leader: Complaints about, challenges for, and type-related difficulties

The Leader's quick-to-anger style is a particular problem for the Mediator, who assiduously avoids anger and conflict. Mediators tend to react by withdrawing, emotionally and/or physically. "Forcefulness shuts me down," wrote a Nine. A Leader conceded, "My anger, when it's explosive, just pushes him farther away – I'm unable to be objective." Several Nines in our survey complained about the Eight's over-the-top anger: "You are too intense, too angry. You never want peace." When the Eight is angry, the Nine can sit very quietly, nodding, and seemingly agreeing – and then say, "I have to go now, but let's get together tomorrow and discuss this further." In actuality, inside they are saying, "There is not a chance in hell that I'm meeting with this person ever again."

Another Leader recognized her "aggressiveness, wanting to fight, anger" and decided to listen to her Mediator husband, who had this to say, "Your aggressive approach shuts me down, but blow in my ear and I'll follow you anywhere." His statement fits into the aforementioned "repair attempts," plus the dose of humor that seems to work with most Eights. When you are in a partnership with a Leader, you want to strive for the image of two people walking side-by-side, both equal and having a united front toward whatever could harm them.

One of the Nines in our survey called her Eight partner on his behaviors by describing them as: "denial and lack of accountability for his feelings, needs, and behavior. Bullying me to get his needs met; power through force." Leaders may not be aware of their power. According to one of them, "I'm not aware of the impact I have on others, either from my intensity or from my speed of speech."

Leaders often don't recognize how controlling and overbearing they can be. Their perception is that they are merely protecting their independence and defending themselves from others' control. But this trait can be very evident to their Mediator partners. One of them wrote "If he changes or compromises because of some of the things I need from him, then he feels 'controlled.'" Another Mediator confirmed, "His desire to control everything from how our family functions to the weather means that he second-guesses almost every decision I or my children make."

Part of Eights' denial about their controlling results from their perception that they have cornered the market on right thinking. One Leader recognized this when she wrote that what hindered her relationship was "thinking 'my truth' was *the* truth." The result is that it seems natural and appropriate to them to insist that things be done their way.

Nines, who are likely to resist attempts to control them, many times feel that their best response is to simply become immobile. Anti-war protesters take this same stance at rallies when they lie down on the ground and become dead weight when the police try to remove them. There is nothing harder to move than someone who is passive and uncooperative.

The Mediator's primary childhood issue is the feeling of not having been recognized. Our partners often serve as a catalyst for bringing up the "splinters" that lie just under an individual's surface and represent the unresolved emotions from his childhood wounds. One of the Eights in our survey seemed to realize how important it is to the Nine to be recognized. She stated it simply: "I have too much energy, focus and directness, and not enough collaboration."

The Leader's difficulty just "being with" their partner is a frequent source of complaints by Mediators, who wrote: "You show disrespect, lack of presence, caring or quality time. You have no interest in my needs, feelings, or ideas." "You never listen. You never are soft with me when I come to you with real concerns. " "You are stubborn! You don't listen!"

Eights fear exposing their vulnerability. One Leader wrote, "Sometimes I see my partner as one of 'them' who I can't be vulnerable with." When they feel vulnerable, they may go on the attack. Myra, an Eight, says: "Once I feel vulnerable, I get angry and I say things I shouldn't. I don't lie but I can be very hurtful in an uncontrolled manner. I've gotten much better at this. I try to explain why I feel vulnerable instead of getting angry." A Nine man says of his Eight wife, "She has difficulty revealing her tender inner self for fear of being taken advantage of." It is important to remember that Leaders most commonly report that they felt dominated as children and that their childhood vow was to never be dominated again. "Revealing their tender inner self" is synonymous with feeling vulnerable -- which in the Eight's mind could lead to being dominated once again.

According to our survey, Nines struggle with the Eight's reluctance to apologize. For many Eights, to apologize is to admit they were wrong, and also to own up to their own vulnerability. Often they are unwilling to do this;

it is much easier for them to continue to defend their words or actions. "He always has to be right. It is difficult for him to admit his difficulties or failures in anything," complained a Mediator. Another concurred, "He never apologizes after fights and is never tender with me afterwards."

For gut types – Eight, Nine, and One -- an apology is a sign of respect. It's a statement that says that the apologizer understands that they hurt the other person in some way and that they are willing to take responsibility for it. Understandably then, Eights like to receive a genuine apology, although it's hard for them give one. Nines, on the other hand, are all too ready to apologize, at times at the drop of a hat, and this can seem phony to the Eight. Some Nines also have difficulty apologizing because in their minds an apology reduces a person a little, takes something away – and if their self-esteem is not high to begin with, it can seem threatening. Apologies in general are a form of surrender and therefore can be difficult for both Leaders and Mediators, especially if they are locked into their classic power struggle. Both are reluctant to give in to the other.

Some Leaders can be quite possessive of how their partner spends his or her time. Dallas, a Nine clergywoman, wrote about her Eight husband, "Keith resents the time I spend at work. If it takes time away from the family (him) he blows. I can't give extra time at work without paying for it." The Leader needs to work on his possessiveness in order to avoid pushing the Mediator away, and she needs to recognize how she's using work to avoid conflict and to make sure she is not going to be controlled.

About the Mediator: Complaints about, challenges for, and type-related difficulties

A Mediator's indirect, passive-aggressive approach to anger can drive the Leader, who prefers direct confrontation and is comfortable with expressions of anger, a little crazy. A Mediator wrote that her Leader husband complained, "You never tell me when you are upset about something. The first I know of it is the pots slamming in the kitchen." Other comments were, "You always get defensive, then act passive-aggressive." "You never want to deal with problems; you hide or run away from life."

Another Mediator, Jerry, recognized that "like a turtle, I withdraw into my shell when attacked, so it is hard for my Eight spouse to understand, know, control, influence, or obtain what she wants." Nines at times tend to almost hibernate, becoming very inaccessible. If the going gets tough, the Nine will just check out.

Mediators' laid-back style in getting things done can be frustrating to the Leader, one of whom complained, "You never get things done as fast as I'd like you to." Another agreed: "It always takes you forever to do anything." An Eight woman wrote about her Nine husband: "I have to arrange things myself almost all the time. He almost never takes responsibility." Differences in pacing are a common problem in relationships, and this is especially true for the Eight-Nine pairing. Couples need to answer questions concerning the "speed" of relationship — such as, "How fast are we going to go? How soon do we want to achieve things? Are we going to be more impulsive or are we going to plan? Are goals going to accomplished at a steady pace or are we going to wait to the last minute?" Leaders and Mediators can balance each other if they pay attention to pacing.

During courtship, Mediators, especially those with an Eight wing, can take the initiative, be assertive and involved; but later they may behave very differently, dropping out and not really being present. It's as though they've run out of gas. They may promise a lot but then do very little. Their lack of follow-through or their failure to show up can cause tremendous frustration and resentment for the bewildered Eight, who feels as if he or she was sold a bill of goods. The Nine undoubtedly had the best of intentions, but wasn't aware of the effort required to stick with his original bargain. Taking "right action" in the relationship is the key to overcoming this issue.

The Mediator's tendency to avoid problems can be another frustration for the action-oriented Leader. Gina, a Leader, explained,

My Eight stance is to problem-solve as directly and assertively as possible. My husband's Nine stance was more "mañana," -- that is, this is not a problem today, so why bring up things now that will create tension and make him feel bad. And so, the problem would continue. My frustration was greatest about his medical problems. Martin ignored them, and they kept getting worse. I was always picking up the pieces. I felt like I was walking through a minefield – one health crisis after another. Martin blamed me for being too controlling. We experienced a great deal of mutual frustration and anger.

At the core of the Nine's issues is a lack of self-love. They need to learn to value themselves, as well as hold onto themselves, and to believe that they have the right to exist and to make a difference in the world.

Leaders can be good at hitting the nail on the head and are almost brutally to the point. Gina said:

In the beginning Martin was afraid to tell me what was wrong. He never said it, just leaned on me for decisions and then if it did not work out well, he'd complain to me. He never took responsibility. I had to teach him that, so now he does. He used to let problems go, did not solve them, and got stuck. Then Martin tried to forget them by sedation. At times I felt so angry over his zoning otu and/withdrawing from relationship, his passive aggressio, his staying on the fence regarding decisions, his oversensitivity and low self-esteem, his taking criticism and suggestions too personally, his inability to establish boundaries to protect his energy, space, and tim, his frequent forays into the Type Six stress point with its pessimism and paranoia, and his dependence on me for social life and stimulation.

It certainly sounds as if Gina is describing a sleeping Nine. She mentions teaching Martin responsibility; we also hope she was able to help him love himself as well.

Leaders and Mediators advise others:
Through our survey, we were able to collect valuable advice for other Leader-Mediator couples. Based on their experience in relationship with a Nine, Eights suggested:

- Beware that your strong energy can be intimidating.
- Recognize the intensity, dial it down, and get in touch with vulnerability (especially when anger flares up).
- Get spiritually centered first (If you want it to last). Use whatever you can to stay related and centered. This will allow you to be more present to your partner, the relationship, and the process.
- Let go of control, learn to TRUST.
- Make enough time, listen well and let the other know that you did listen, even if you still do things your own way. Tell them you understand instead of only thinking it in your head. Don't provide solutions to your partner; let them find their own. They can't cope with your solutions anyway. Understand that your partner is a different person. Try to understand his or her personality as well as you can. Don't give too much advice. Let them do it their own way.

Nines in relationship with Eights advised:

- Learn to set boundaries and tell people when your boundaries are being invaded – do that *before* considering a serious relationship.
- Acknowledge and understand your anger. Don't just settle for things rather than risk conflict.
- Stand your ground and stick with what you say you want and need from other people. Don't let the prospect of conflict allow your feelings, wants, and needs be overlooked.
- Stand up for yourself. Don't compromise on the behavior and action you want from your partner.
- Find and hold onto yourself! Develop a habit of grounding and connecting with the power of love.

Exercises for the Leader-Mediator couple

The following exercises highlight the classic issues that challenge the Eight-Nine pairing:

Action versus sloth

Leaders are usually ready for immediate action, whereas Mediators, having typically overcommitted themselves by their reluctance to say No, have trouble fulfilling commitments. This can drive the Leader – and in fact partners of *any* Type – crazy.

- The next time something needs to be done, sit down and discuss together in detail what the task is, what the timetable is, and how to avoid the usual obstacles that will delay the Nine in accomplishing the agreed-upon tasks. If this approach is to succeed, the Nine needs to make a commitment to himself or herself as well as to the Eight, to follow through on the agreed-upon program, including asking the Eight for help if obstacles appear.

Control versus resistance

Leaders have no trouble expressing overt anger, and in their desire not to be controlled by others, they actually exert a lot of control over other people in their lives. Mediators will neglect their needs rather than risk conflict. Instead of replying directly to another person's demands, Mediators react in a passive-aggressive manner, agreeing to the demands but then not following through. This can simply escalate the Leader's anger and controlling behaviors.

- For the Eight: To avoid this common dysfunctional pattern, recognize how intimidating your power is and try to dial down your intensity when asking for something. Instead of insisting on your solution, ask your partner's opinion and suggestions and actually listen to them.
- For the Nine: To avoid this common dysfunctional pattern, try standing your ground and giving your opinion rather than avoiding being direct and simply agreeing. Recognize that Eights respect those who stand up to them, and value directness. They say, "Just tell it like it is!"

Comfort versus confrontation

A Leader wrote of her Mediator husband, "He valued his own personal comfort over the painful work it would have taken to salvage our relationship." Whereas Leaders encourage confrontation and direct discussion of issues, Mediators assiduously avoid conflict and confrontation; they prefer their comfort and non-involvement.

- For the Eight: Think of an issue you'd like to discuss with your Nine partner and practice bringing this up in a less confrontive way in order not to drive your partner into denial. Instead of "my way or the highway," ask your partner for solutions and listen to what he or she says.
- For the Nine: Practice moving out of your comfort zone and actually talking about your feelings regarding some issue. If you share your feelings, this will encourage your Eight partner to risk being vulnerable and to do the same.
- For both: Brainstorm with each other new strategies for discussing disagreements without a lot of anger or avoidance. This will involve a willingness by both partners to risk sharing your feelings and needs openly with each other.

CHAPTER FIFTY-NINE

The Double-Mediator (Nine-Nine) Relationship

Last summer we spent 5 weeks on the road driving to Alaska through Canada. We just didn't seem to ever disagree about what to do. We always reached a consensus. We have an expression of "keeping the grid balanced." We seem to do this with money as well as deciding what to do. I cook break-fast; she cleans up most of the time.

-- Corey, a Mediator married for 29 years to another Mediator

When asked who they feel most compatible with as either a friend or possible spouse, many people select qualities that are typical of the Mediator: someone who's easy-going and easy to get along with, someone who will do the things they want to do and support them in their goals, and finally some-one who will love and accept them unconditionally. Mediators themselves, according to our survey, choose Type Nine as one of the Types who they get along with best. Their reasons included: "Comfort and understanding." "I accept them easily. They're not making demands for change and attention. They are accepting." "They are mellower than most types." "It's comfortable, easy." "Easy to get along with, but often boring." "Very accommodating – not demanding." "We think alike." Not surprisingly, most Nines have many friends. Yet primary relationships between two Nines are uncommon.

What can two Mediators in relationship expect? Each is likely to be very accepting of the other, loving the other unconditionally without seeking to change the other. Both are likely to be laid back and relaxed. Each values personal comfort. They are willing to go along with the other wants to do, al-though each may have trouble knowing what that is. When one is committed to some project, the other will provide a lot of help and support. And although Mediators have difficulty loving themselves, they can be very good at loving others.

What may be missing from this pairing, however, is passion. Neither partner is likely to provide much "juice", and one or both may eventually become bored. The fire of the sexual relationship could burn very low -- unless they are using sex as a way to narcotize themselves. In the interest of maintaining a sweet and loving connection, neither will confront issues or push to identify and solve problems. Because conflicts are likely to go unaddressed, the focus on peace can be detrimental to the relationship in the long term. Eventually, the marriage can slowly fizzle out and die or one partner may become attracted to someone more exciting and stimulating and leave.

A possible solution would be for one of the pair to operate out of their wing or connecting point in order to introduce some variety. What is sometimes common in same-type pairings is that one partner may "hold" their true type, which then frees up the other partner to try to adapt the characteristics of the wing or connecting point. In this situation for example, one of the Mediators might take on the role of the Leader (Type Eight) a wing, or the Achiever (Type Three), a connecting point.

Describing the positives in his 27-year marriage to Rose, Corey explained that "I accommodate Rose's needs and wants. I give her space to do what she wants." He listed Rose's good qualities as compassion, flexibility, and generosity. Here's how they resolved a conflict:

Rose is Jewish. I'm not. Religion has been a tension point. So we don't follow any organized religious traditions. I accommodate her if she wants to go to a synagogue or shul; she accommodates me if I want to go on a meditation retreat or to a program or workshop based on Eastern wisdom traditions.

Corey's comments above teach us the importance of flexibility. Being able to adapt to and support each other's beliefs is a very positive quality. They are basically answering one of the most important questions in relationship: How can I totally be there for my partner and at the same time hold onto myself?

Joe, a 70-something Mediator, said that what has helped his 2-year relationship with Judy (also a Mediator) thrive is "my ability to know what she is feeling or thinking. She always says that I can read her mind." Regarding their communication, he relates,

We understand the Nine's tendency to ignore problems until they explode. Consequently we make a great effort to keep the lines of communication open and we talk about everything, including feelings. I presume we could have problems if we had the normal Nine practice of sweeping disagreements under the rug or refusing to confront the other person when we do disagree. Our biggest issue is in the political arena—conservative versus liberal—but we talk about this and so far have agreed to disagree.

This elderly man, in a relatively new relationship, wrote in several places about the political disagreements about politics he and his partner have, in contrast to their agreement in other areas. It appears that this couple has found a way to disagree about politics that allows them to let off steam and may serve as a buffer so that they don't have to disagree on other issues. When asked what might make Judy leave, Joe wrote, "I suppose if our political arguments ever got too personal." This suggests he may be aware that their political disagreements are "safe" precisely because they don't address personal issues.

Nines avoid confronting issues in relationship. Neither wants to initiate unpleasant discussions. At the heart of Mediators' fear of conflict is their fear of separation. Joe and Judy have made a conscious decision to "make a great effort to keep the lines of communication open" which is just the right approach for a Nine-Nine pairing. The key word here is "effort." Nines tend to see these activities as requiring a tremendous effort. They need to push through their resistance to seeing things as an effort and "just do it" in order that their relationship continue to thrive. Joe and Judy's political differences may actually serve the purpose of maintaining their own sense of identity instead of totally merging with each other.

Double-Mediator couples tend to communicate in what we can term "Ninespeak", which is usually not a lot of speaking. They merge so much that they'll complete each other's sentences or they may hardly talk at all. Mediators are in the "gut" or "belly" center, in which they intuit or have a "felt" sense of knowing. Two Nines together can use this sense to communicate deeply with one another without words. In fact, some Mediators state that too many words can confuse them. When two Nines in a committed relationship are separated for a while for some reason, they often express that they still feel very connected.

Challenges of the Double-Mediator pairing

Mediators tend to adopt their sense of identity and agenda from their partners. Two Mediators together may be stuck in inaction, each waiting for the other to make the first move. Adding to the problem that both tend to procrastinate; it's easier for them to attend to trivial pursuits than to make decisions or to complete tasks. Yet another problem is that their mutual desire for a conflict-avoidant harmonious relationship can lead to the accumulation of resentments. This situation might result in a nasty ongoing passive-aggressive relationship or finally end in an explosion.

Corey, for example, wrote that a major challenge for him in his long-term marriage with Rose has been "my sloth – laziness – not knowing what I want." He adds, "I am too averse to conflict – too accommodating – too willing to sweep big issues under the rug." As for Rose, "She is conflict-avoidant. She won't raise big issues." A 58-year old Mediator, Samantha, married to Saul for 18 years, related, "I'm conflict avoidant. I make myself tell my husband when he has irritated me, but it's always difficult to begin those discussions." She advises other Mediators, "Make sure you voice areas of conflict. You can do this in a way that enhances rather than damages the bond between you."

When asked to describe a complaint her husband Saul has repeatedly told her, Samantha wrote, "My lack of attention to details, particularly around cleanliness or housekeeping (leaving lights on, leaving lint balls on the dryer, not putting dishes away.) He's usually reluctant to express those complaints." Cory voiced a similar complaint about Rose, "She never focuses on cleaning up clutter and she doesn't require the kids to do anything to help around the house. She's too permissive with our children. She wants to please and accommodate them to the extreme." Mediators often have problems setting boundaries, which may result in permissive parenting. Children feel safer when they know that there are limits and someone is in charge. Nines need to give themselves permission to be the authority, to state what is right and wrong and where the limits are. They need to make sure that they and their children are not extensions of one another, but instead are separate individuals.

Joe, in a relatively new relationship, says, "We know we are similar so we don't bring up the fact that we are sloppy housekeepers and procrastinators. We are not living together but if we were, I believe the fact that both of us are disorganized housekeepers could cause a problem. We both tend to live in a mess."

Some Mediators take great pride in their home environment, creating a beautiful space that reflects peace and comfortableness. Others, perhaps because of their procrastination or lack of pride, do live in a mess, and may be embarrassed and ashamed. Nines with the Self-preservation subtype can be obsessive, collecting clutter as a form of sloth.

People who are struggling with their tendency to hoard things sometimes find it helpful to use a decision-making process that entails determining whether the item has either a bona fide "use" or whether it has some kind of "value" to the person. If neither is true of the item, then they discarded it or give it away. The process involves sorting through the clutter, and discerning if things hold use or value. Because of their personality, Nines may want to invite a friend or "coach" to help them in the decision-making process. Nines tend to hold onto things in general and to see all things as equal.

A recurrent complaint about Mediators from partners of any type is the Nine's tendency to be "absent" from the relationship. In addition to withdrawing when conflict appears, Mediators seem to have less energy with time for their primary relationship than for other activities. The failure of many Nines to "show up" in their primary relationship can be a problem for their partners of any type, including another Nine. This is especially likely to be upsetting to a partner of the Sexual or One-on-One subtype. Samantha (a Sexual subtype), married 18 years to Saul (a Self-preservation subtype), wrote,

I really want to be "seen" and have someone help me explore the inner landscapes. Saul is happy on the surface; he's bright and sensitive, but not inclined toward psychological exploration, and he loves it when things are comfortable. I sometimes feel bored and lonely when we've had an experience and don't dive as deeply into our reactions and feelings as I'd like. When this sense of disconnection builds up in me, I usually tell him. If I don't, I know the resentment and disconnection grows. I don't know if our differing needs in this area can change.

"Sometimes it feels like I have a roommate," Corey wrote, describing his 29-year relationship with Rose. Joe, in relationship with Judy for only two years, adds, "I fear the Nine-Nine relationship is just too dull for most folks' taste. But we have fun and enjoy each other." Some Nines describe their relationship as a little boring, yet also say that they don't really mind this. They like the ordinariness, the daily routines that they have, and the knowing what to expect. They don't like drama or the roller coaster ride of emotions that some relationships have. They describe their relationship as a kind of "sweet enmeshment." But even Nines need some excitement and stimulation; healthy Double Mediator pairings schedule some adventure from time to time. Each needs to continue to grow in order to remain interesting to each other. They need to take some calculated risks and continue to re-invent themselves. Most of all, they need to make sure they don't go to sleep and that they continue to make an effort to show up.

Exercises for the Double Mediator couple

The following exercises speak to the core issues of the Nine-Nine couple.

Keeping it together – staying together

Nines have a capacity to express great love for another person. Some people describe it as the closest to unconditional love and acceptance that you can receive from another human being. Let your partner know how much you love them by completing the following incomplete sentences, supplying a different reason for each one:

- A reason I love you is. . .
- A reason I love you is. . .
- A reason I love you is. . .

Even though love for others usually comes easily to Nines, they generally have a difficult time loving and accepting themselves. Take turns with your partner answering the unfinished sentences below:

- When it comes to loving myself, what comes up for me is…
- One of the things I have learned to love and accept about myself is…
- One of the things I love and accept about myself now is…
- One of the things I still need to work on with regard to loving myself is…

One of the pitfalls in the Nine-Nine pairing is the tendency for each of them to "go to sleep" in the relationship. See if you can find out where each of you have difficulty showing up at times.

- I know I used to express my love for you by. . .
- I know I don't express enough effort when I. . .
- I commit to expressing my love to you by. . .

The Nine's fear of conflict can cause them to not discuss things that really need to be explored. Addressing conflict in a more straightforward manner helps to get things out in the open and brings to the surface issues that need to be talked about.

- The way I define conflict in relationship is. . .

- The thing that scares me about conflict in our relationship is. . .
- Something that would help me handle conflict better is. . .

Closely connected to the issue of conflict for the Nine is not fully or openly expressing what is going on inside them. Complete the incomplete sentences below in order to gain some clarity.

- The reason it is difficult for me to talk about certain issues is. . .
- Sometimes my inside answer does not match my outside answer because. . .
- I especially don't feel heard about. . .
- I know I sometimes forget myself when I. . .
- When I think about my own agenda and goals, I think about. . .
- My level of anger and resentment over not being seen and heard is...

Two Nines in relationship need to make sure they are stimulating the relationship through fun and adventure.

- What I would like to do next as an adventure is. . .
- If I were going to rock the boat it would be with regard to. . .
- If I had the courage, I would re-invent myself in the following way. . .

Almost all couples have a "classic fight" scenario that they fall into from time to time. It has a here-we-go again feel about it and it leaves both partners feeling exhausted and angry. Working together, answer the questions below:

- Together, write the script of your classic fight. Agree on how it starts, its middle, and how it usually ends. Agree, without criticizing or blaming one another, what each of your roles are during the fight.
- Discuss how the characteristics of your Type are expressed during your classic fight.
- Working with your partner, re-write the script of your classic fight so that it turns out differently, more positively, and so that each of you change your behaviors and how you react to one another. Think of your classic fight as if it were a dance. You and your partner have a dance that you do over and over again with each of you having your own unique dance steps. In this exercise you and your partner are together going to create a new dance with different dance steps that change the pattern of your classic fight.

APPENDIX: RECOMMENDED READING

Baron, R. and Wagele, E. *The Enneagram Made Easy.* San Francisco: Harper San Francisco, 1994.

Baron, R. and Wagele, E. *Are You My Type, Am I Yours? Relationships Made Easy Through the Enneagram.* New York: HarperCollins, 1995.

Coates, M and Searle, J. *Sex, Love, and your Personality: The Nine Faces of Intimacy.* Santa Monica, CA: Therapy Options Press, 2011

Condon, T. *The Enneagram Movie & Video Guide.* Second Edition. Portland, Oregon: Metamorphous Press, 1999.

Daniels, D. and Price,V. *The Essential Enneagram: The Definitive Personality Test and Guide to Self-Discovery.* (Revised) New York: HarperCollins, 2009.

Goldberg, M. *The 9 Ways of Working.* New York: Marlowe & Company, 1999.

Gottman, J. *The Relationship Cure: A Five-Step Guide to Strengthening Your Marriage, Family, and Friendships.* 2002

Gottman, J. *Why Marriages Succeed or Fail: and How You Can Make Yours Last.* New York: Simon & Schuster, 2012.

Palmer, H. *The Enneagram: Understanding Yourself and Others in Your Life.* San Francisco: Harper San Francisco, 1988.

Palmer, H. *The Enneagram in Love and Work: Understanding your Intimate and Business Relationships.* San Francisco: Harper San Francisco, 1995.

Riso, D and Hudson R. *Understanding the Enneagram: The Practical Guide to Personality Types.* (Revised Edition) San Francisco, 2000.

Riso, D and Hudson R. *Personality Types: Using the Enneagram for Self-Discovery.* New York: Houghton Mifflin, 1996.